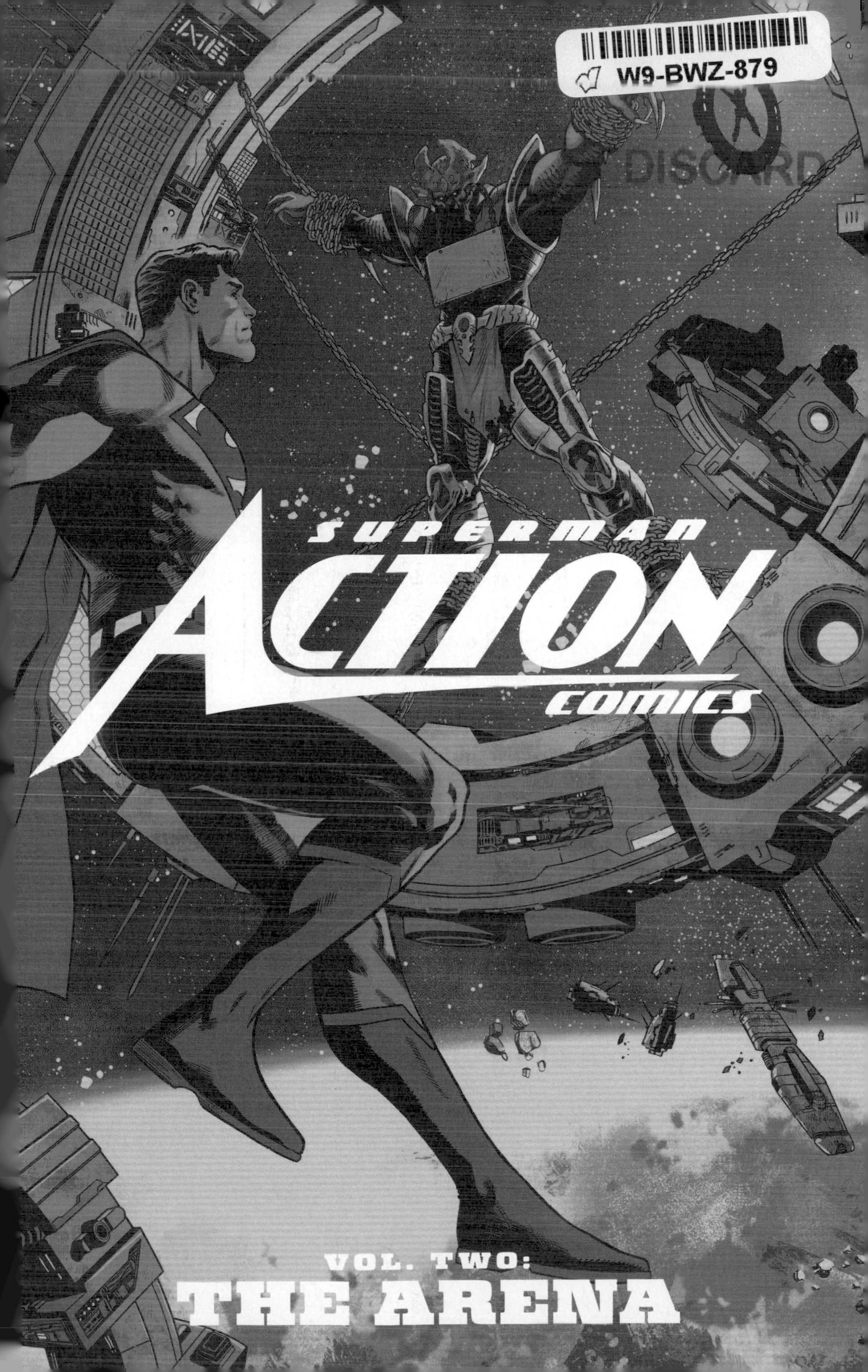
SUPERMAN
ACTION
COMICS
VOL. TWO:
THE ARENA

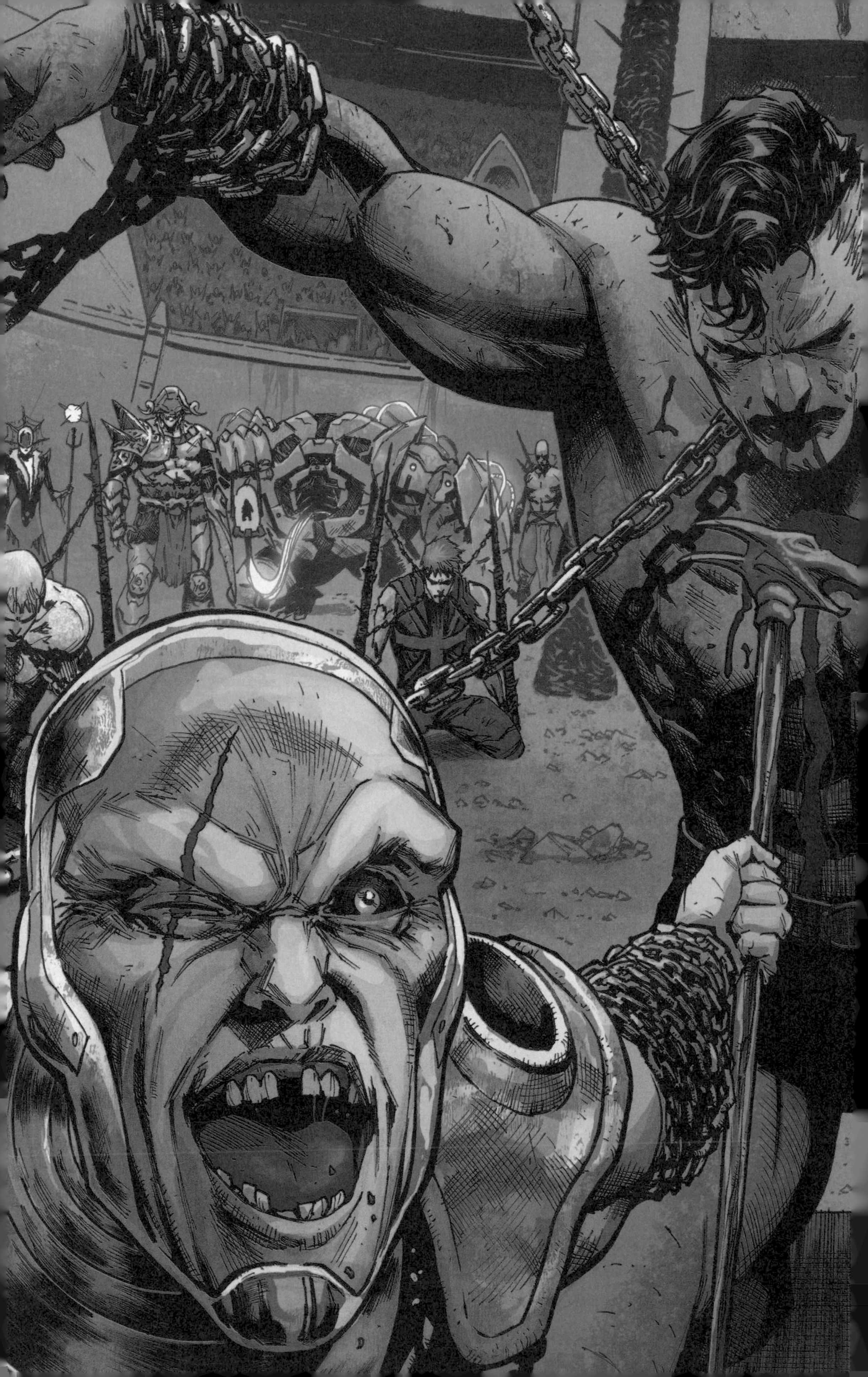

SUPERMAN ACTION COMICS

VOLUME TWO
THE ARENA

PHILLIP KENNEDY JOHNSON
writer

**RICCARDO FEDERICI, MIGUEL MENDONÇA,
DANIEL SAMPERE, DALE EAGLESHAM, WILL CONRAD**
artists

LEE LOUGHRIDGE, ADRIANO LUCAS
colorists

DAVE SHARPE
letterer

DANIEL SAMPERE and **ALEJANDRO SÁNCHEZ**
collection cover artists

Superman created by **JERRY SIEGEL** and **JOE SHUSTER**.
By special arrangement with the **JERRY SIEGEL** family.

TALES OF
METROPOLIS

SEAN LEWIS
writer

SAMI BASRI
artist

HI-FI
colorist

DAVE SHARPE
letterer

MARTIAN MANHUNTER:
A FACE IN THE CROWD

SHAWN ALDRIDGE
writer

ADRIANA MELO
artist

HI-FI
colorist

DAVE SHARPE
letterer

Paul Kaminski Editors – Original Series
Mike Cotton
Diego Lopez Associate Editor – Original Series
Jillian Grant Assistant Editor – Original Series & Editor – Collected Edition
Rob Tokar Editor – Collected Edition
Steve Cook Design Director – Books
Damian Ryland Publication Design
Erin Vanover Publication Production

Marie Javins Editor-in-Chief, DC Comics

Anne DePies Senior VP – General Manager
Jim Lee Publisher & Chief Creative Officer
Don Falletti VP – Manufacturing Operations & Workflow Management
Lawrence Ganem VP – Talent Services
Alison Gill Senior VP – Manufacturing & Operations
Jeffrey Kaufman VP – Editorial Strategy & Programming
Nick J. Napolitano VP – Manufacturing Administration & Design
Nancy Spears VP – Revenue

SUPERMAN: ACTION COMICS VOL. 2: THE ARENA

DC Comics, 2900 West Alameda Ave., Burbank, CA 91505
Printed by LSC Communications, Owensville, MO, USA. 7/22/22. First Printing.
ISBN: 978-1-77951-717-3

Library of Congress Cataloging-in-Publication Data is available.

PEFC Certified

This product is from
sustainably managed
forests and controlled
sources

PEFC/29-31-337 www.pefc.org

WHO'S WHO

SUPERMAN

Orphaned as an infant by the destruction of his home planet, Krypton, Kal-El was adopted and raised on Earth by Martha and Jonathan Kent. Earth's yellow sun supercharges Clark Kent's Kryptonian physiology with greatly enhanced strength, speed, senses, and durability and even gives him abilities that include flight and heat vision. However, some would argue that Superman's greatest strength is the compassion and caring he learned from the Kents, who steadfastly believed in the power of truth and justice.

ENCHANTRESS

June Moone is the formidable sorceress known as the Enchantress. Her powers cover a wide range of magical abilities including energy projection, flight, and telekinesis.

O.M.A.C.

A highly skilled combatant and ferocious in battle, O.M.A.C. wears an armored suit that gives him enhanced physical abilities. O.M.A.C. is in a relationship with Lightray.

LIGHTRAY

Lia Nelson is a super-speedster with energy absorption, manipulation, and projection abilities. She is in a relationship with O.M.A.C.

MANCHESTER BLACK

A 10th-level psychic, Black's powers include telepathy, illusion casting, telekinesis, and mind control. His chronic bad attitude can be a blessing or a curse, depending on the circumstance.

STEEL

Natasha Irons, niece of John Henry Irons, has taken up the Steel identity and improved upon her uncle's technology. Steel's armor grants her enhanced strength and durability, flight, scanners, and more. Steel's primary weapon is her kinetic hammer, which has the ability to increase its power the farther it's thrown.

APOLLO

Living up to his name (inspired by the sun god Apollo), this solar-powered warrior's abilities include flight and enhanced strength, speed, stamina, senses, and durability, along with energy projection and accelerated healing. He is in a relationship with Midnighter.

MIDNIGHTER

Clad in carbon-fiber combat armor and gifted with enhanced speed, strength, vision, and durability, Midnighter also possesses an accelerated healing ability and a "battle precognition" that enables him to foresee and counter almost any possible combat scenario. He is in a relationship with Apollo.

MONGUL

A spectacularly strong and highly skilled physical combatant, Mongul has succeeded his father to become the brutal and ruthless new ruler of Warworld. This violent sphere is the cruel prison of enslaved beings from all over the galaxy who are forced to participate in endless gladiatorial battles to survive.

***Action Comics* #1036**
main cover art by DANIEL SAMPERE and ALEX SINCLAIR

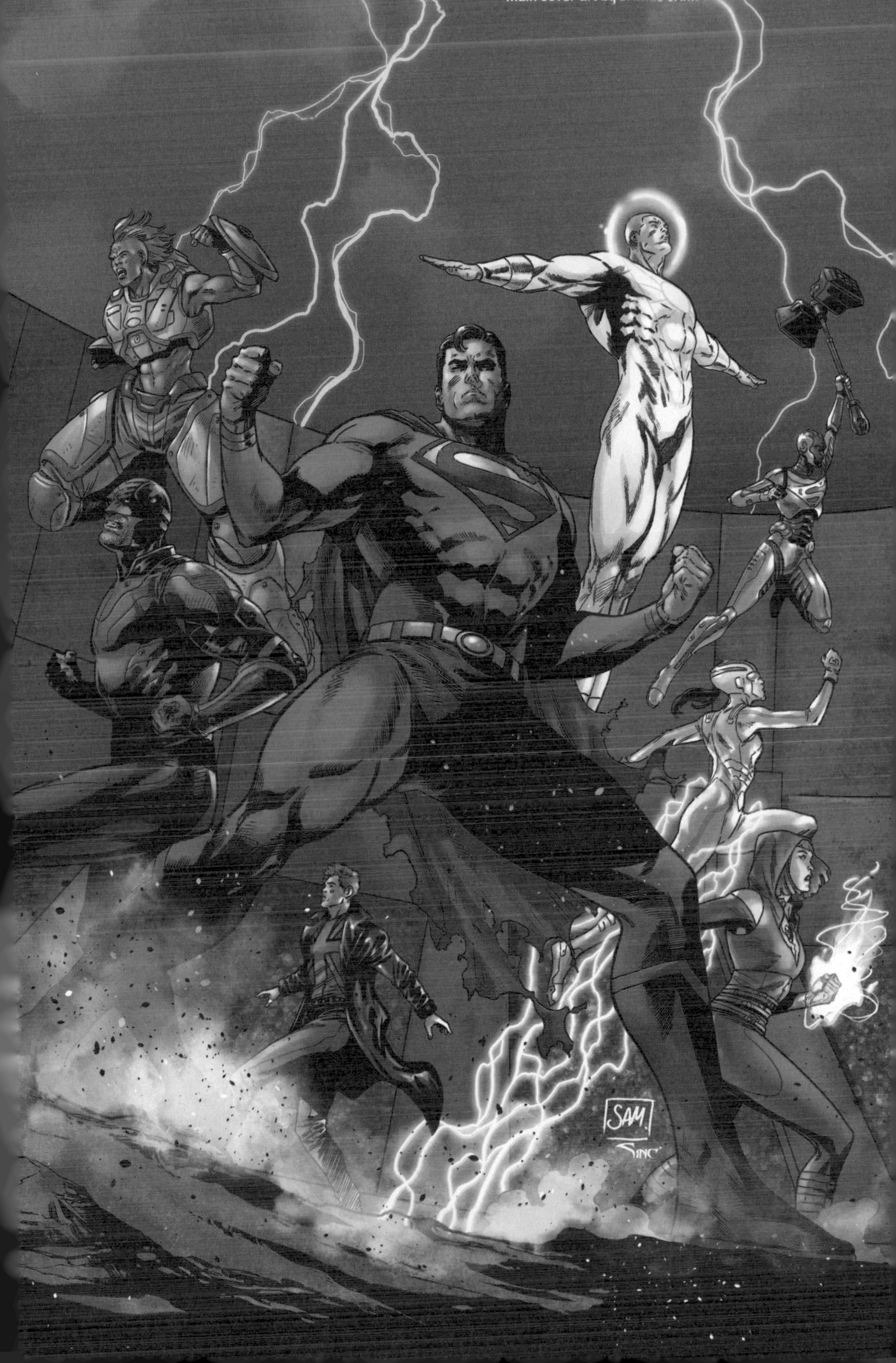
SAM
SINC

***Action Comics* #1036**
variant cover by JULIAN TOTINO TEDESCO

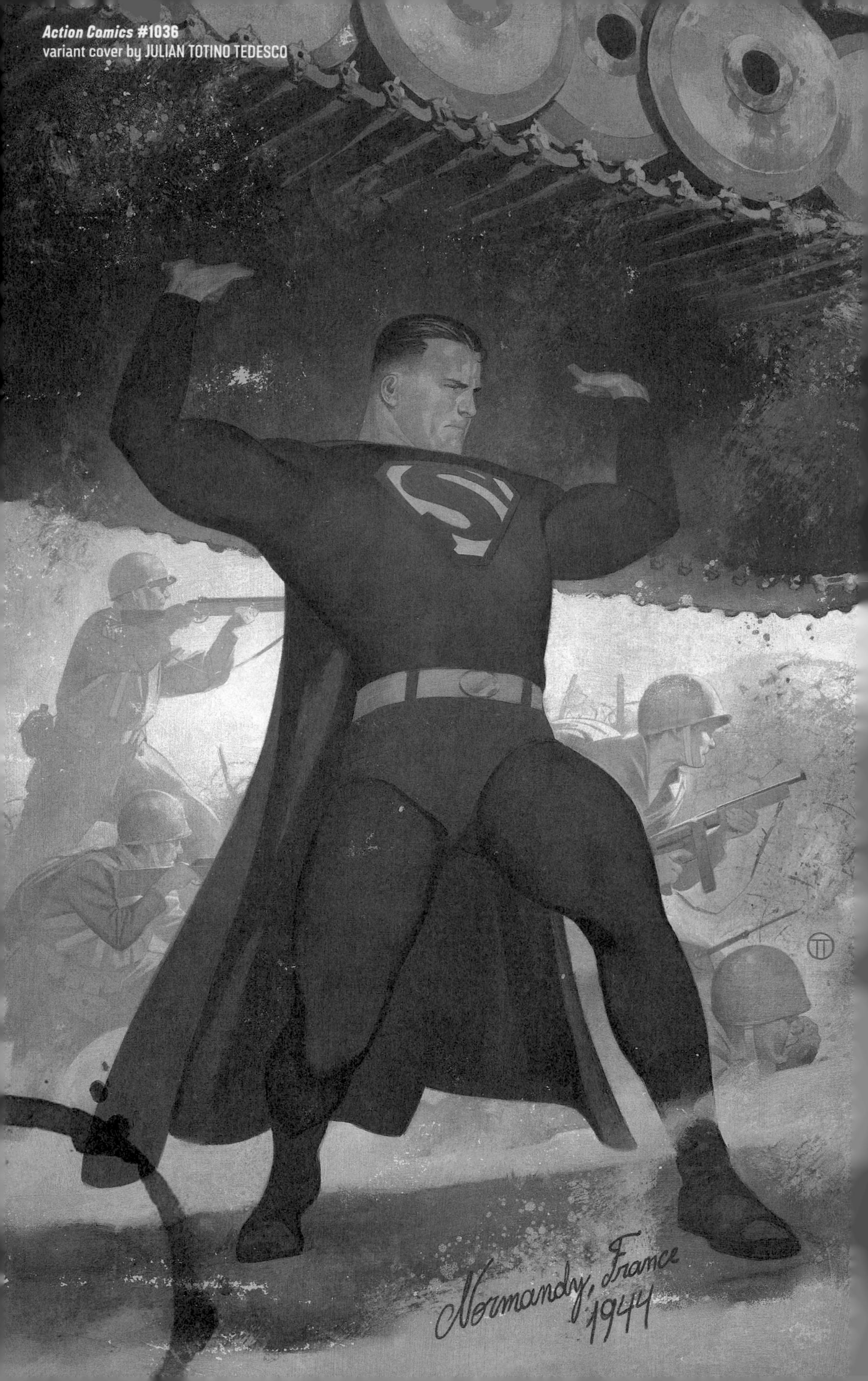
Normandy, France
1944

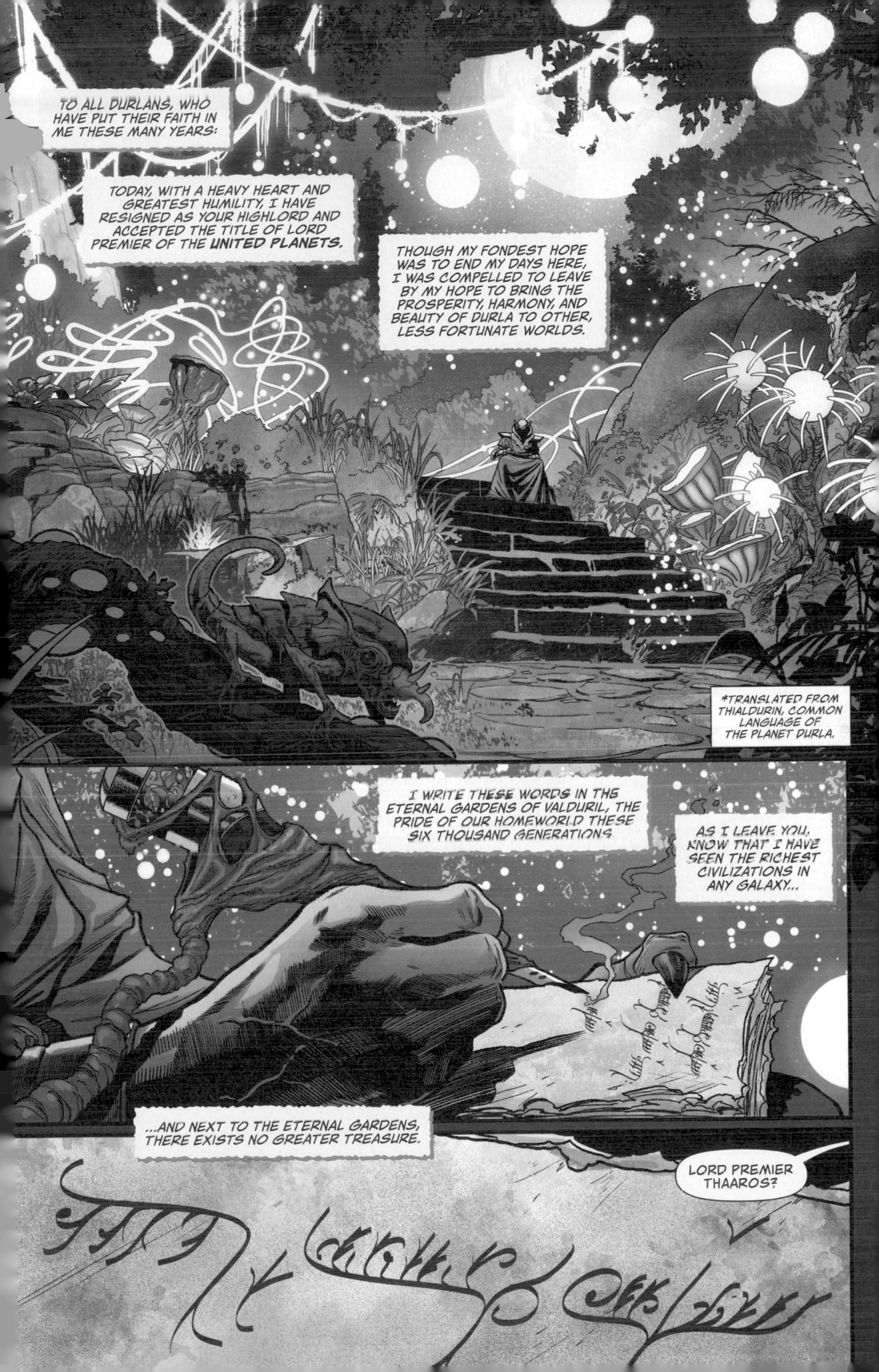
TO ALL DURLANS, WHO HAVE PUT THEIR FAITH IN ME THESE MANY YEARS:
TODAY, WITH A HEAVY HEART AND GREATEST HUMILITY, I HAVE RESIGNED AS YOUR HIGHLORD AND ACCEPTED THE TITLE OF LORD PREMIER OF THE UNITED PLANETS.
THOUGH MY FONDEST HOPE WAS TO END MY DAYS HERE, I WAS COMPELLED TO LEAVE BY MY HOPE TO BRING THE PROSPERITY, HARMONY, AND BEAUTY OF DURLA TO OTHER, LESS FORTUNATE WORLDS.
*TRANSLATED FROM THIALDURIN, COMMON LANGUAGE OF THE PLANET DURLA.
I WRITE THESE WORDS IN THE ETERNAL GARDENS OF VALDURIL, THE PRIDE OF OUR HOMEWORLD THESE SIX THOUSAND GENERATIONS.
AS I LEAVE YOU, KNOW THAT I HAVE SEEN THE RICHEST CIVILIZATIONS IN ANY GALAXY...
...AND NEXT TO THE ETERNAL GARDENS, THERE EXISTS NO GREATER TREASURE.
LORD PREMIER THAAROS?

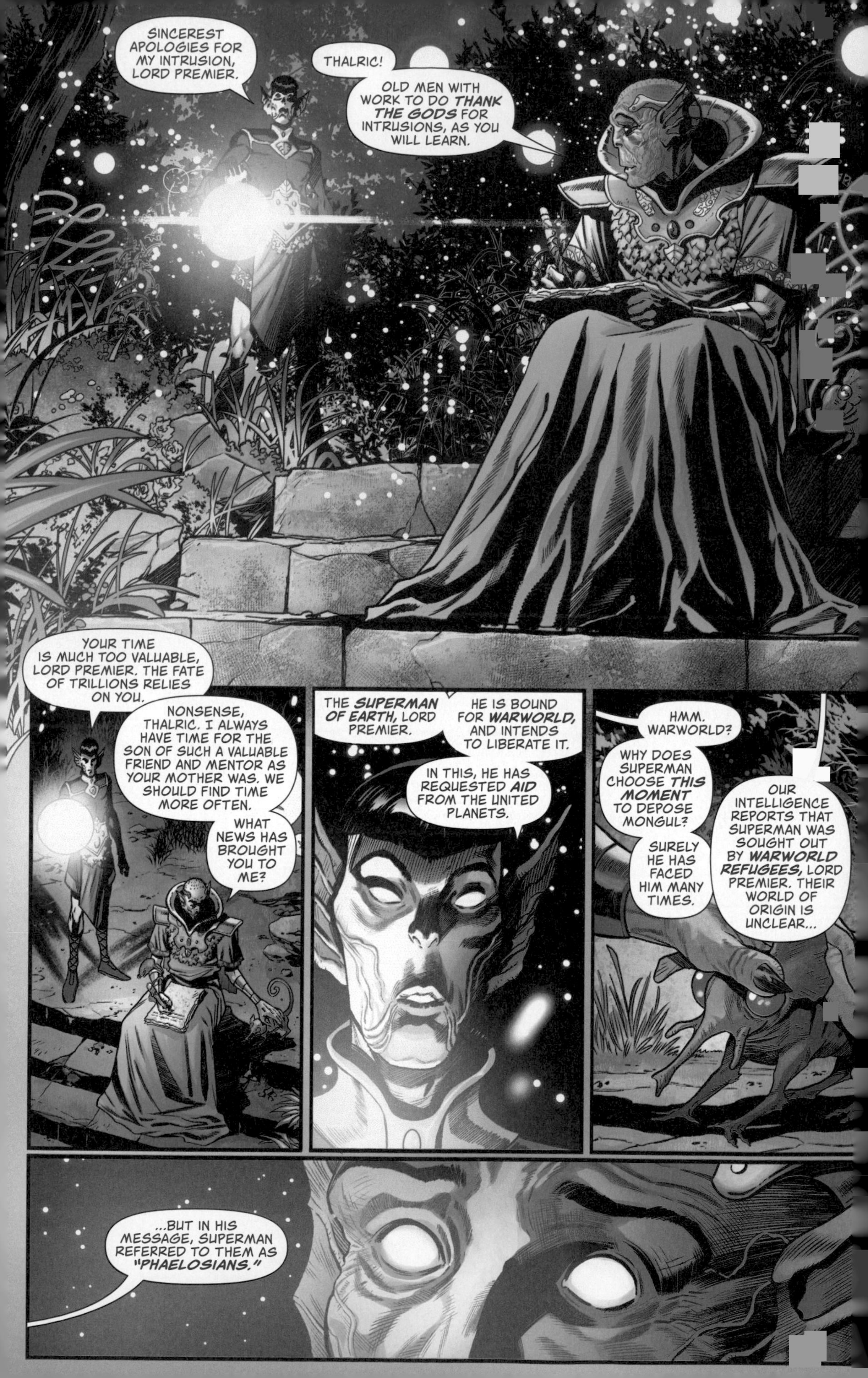
SINCEREST APOLOGIES FOR MY INTRUSION, LORD PREMIER.
THALRIC!
OLD MEN WITH WORK TO DO THANK THE GODS FOR INTRUSIONS, AS YOU WILL LEARN.
YOUR TIME IS MUCH TOO VALUABLE, LORD PREMIER. THE FATE OF TRILLIONS RELIES ON YOU.
NONSENSE, THALRIC. I ALWAYS HAVE TIME FOR THE SON OF SUCH A VALUABLE FRIEND AND MENTOR AS YOUR MOTHER WAS. WE SHOULD FIND TIME MORE OFTEN.
WHAT NEWS HAS BROUGHT YOU TO ME?
THE SUPERMAN OF EARTH, LORD PREMIER.
HE IS BOUND FOR WARWORLD, AND INTENDS TO LIBERATE IT.
IN THIS, HE HAS REQUESTED AID FROM THE UNITED PLANETS.
HMM. WARWORLD?
WHY DOES SUPERMAN CHOOSE THIS MOMENT TO DEPOSE MONGUL?
SURELY HE HAS FACED HIM MANY TIMES.
OUR INTELLIGENCE REPORTS THAT SUPERMAN WAS SOUGHT OUT BY WARWORLD REFUGEES, LORD PREMIER. THEIR WORLD OF ORIGIN IS UNCLEAR...
...BUT IN HIS MESSAGE, SUPERMAN REFERRED TO THEM AS "PHAELOSIANS."

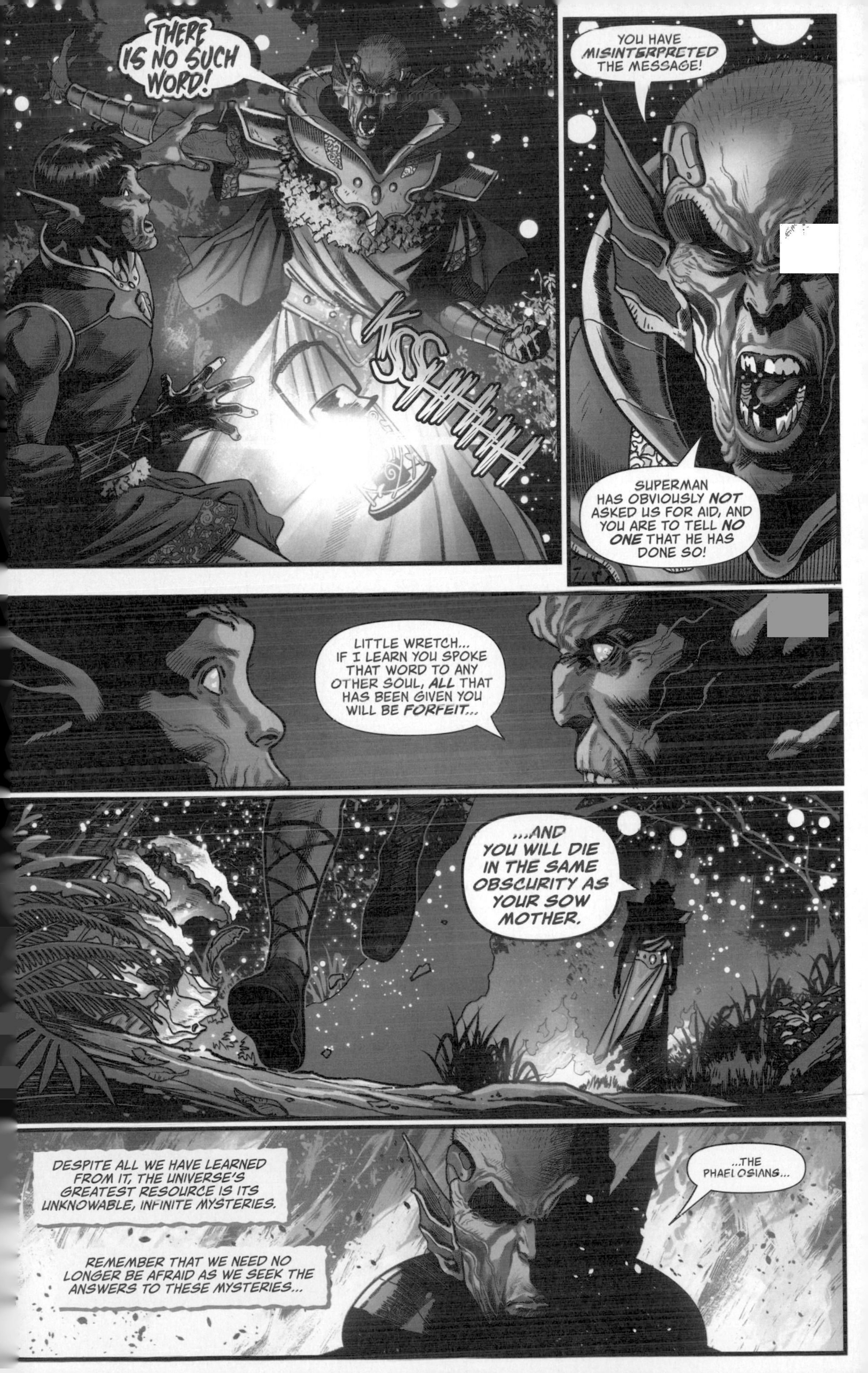
THERE IS NO SUCH WORD!
KSSHHHHHH
YOU HAVE MISINTERPRETED THE MESSAGE!
SUPERMAN HAS OBVIOUSLY NOT ASKED US FOR AID, AND YOU ARE TO TELL NO ONE THAT HE HAS DONE SO!
LITTLE WRETCH... IF I LEARN YOU SPOKE THAT WORD TO ANY OTHER SOUL, ALL THAT HAS BEEN GIVEN YOU WILL BE FORFEIT...
...AND YOU WILL DIE IN THE SAME OBSCURITY AS YOUR SOW MOTHER.
DESPITE ALL WE HAVE LEARNED FROM IT, THE UNIVERSE'S GREATEST RESOURCE IS ITS UNKNOWABLE, INFINITE MYSTERIES.
REMEMBER THAT WE NEED NO LONGER BE AFRAID AS WE SEEK THE ANSWERS TO THESE MYSTERIES...
...THE PHAELOSIANS...

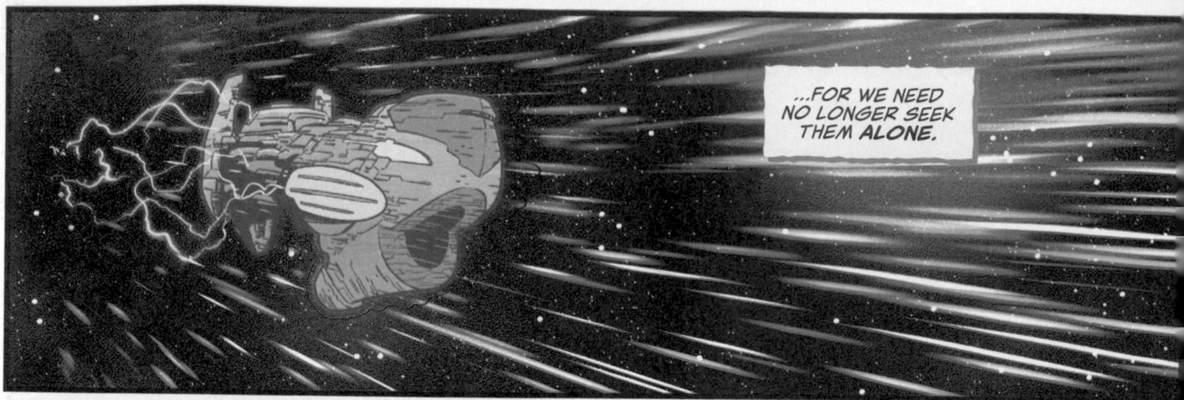
...FOR WE NEED NO LONGER SEEK THEM ALONE.

WARWORLD SAGA PART 1

PHILLIP KENNEDY JOHNSON WRITER DANIEL SAMPERE ARTIST
ADRIANO LUCAS COLORIST DAVE SHARPE LETTERER
DANIEL SAMPERE & ALEX SINCLAIR COVER
JULIAN TOTINO TEDESCO VARIANT COVER DIEGO LOPEZ
ASSOCIATE EDITOR MIKE COTTON EDITOR

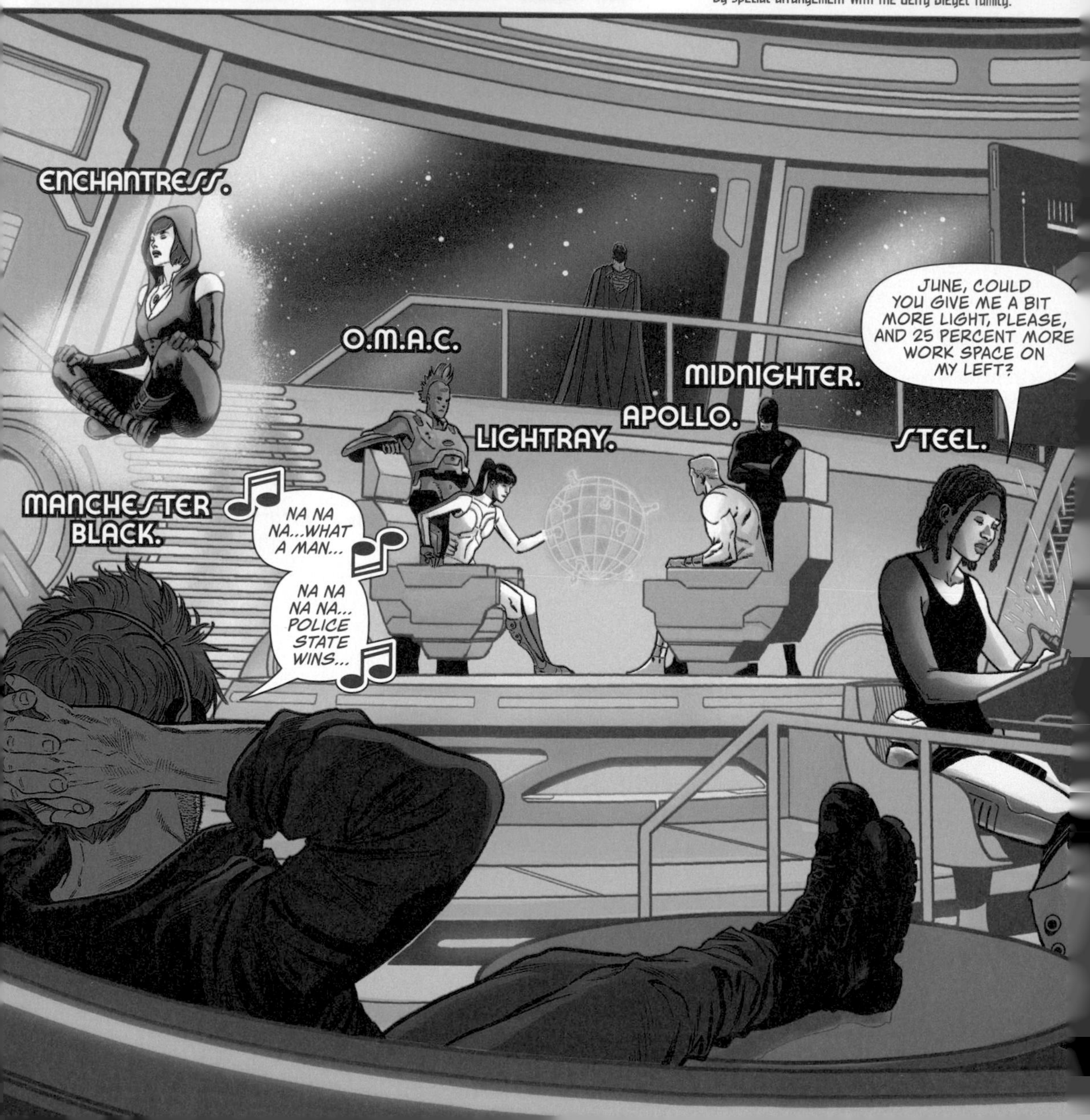
ENCHANTRESS.
O.M.A.C.
LIGHTRAY.
APOLLO.
MIDNIGHTER.
JUNE, COULD YOU GIVE ME A BIT MORE LIGHT, PLEASE, AND 25 PERCENT MORE WORK SPACE ON MY LEFT?
STEEL.
MANCHESTER BLACK.
NA NA NA...WHAT A MAN...
NA NA NA NA... POLICE STATE WINS...

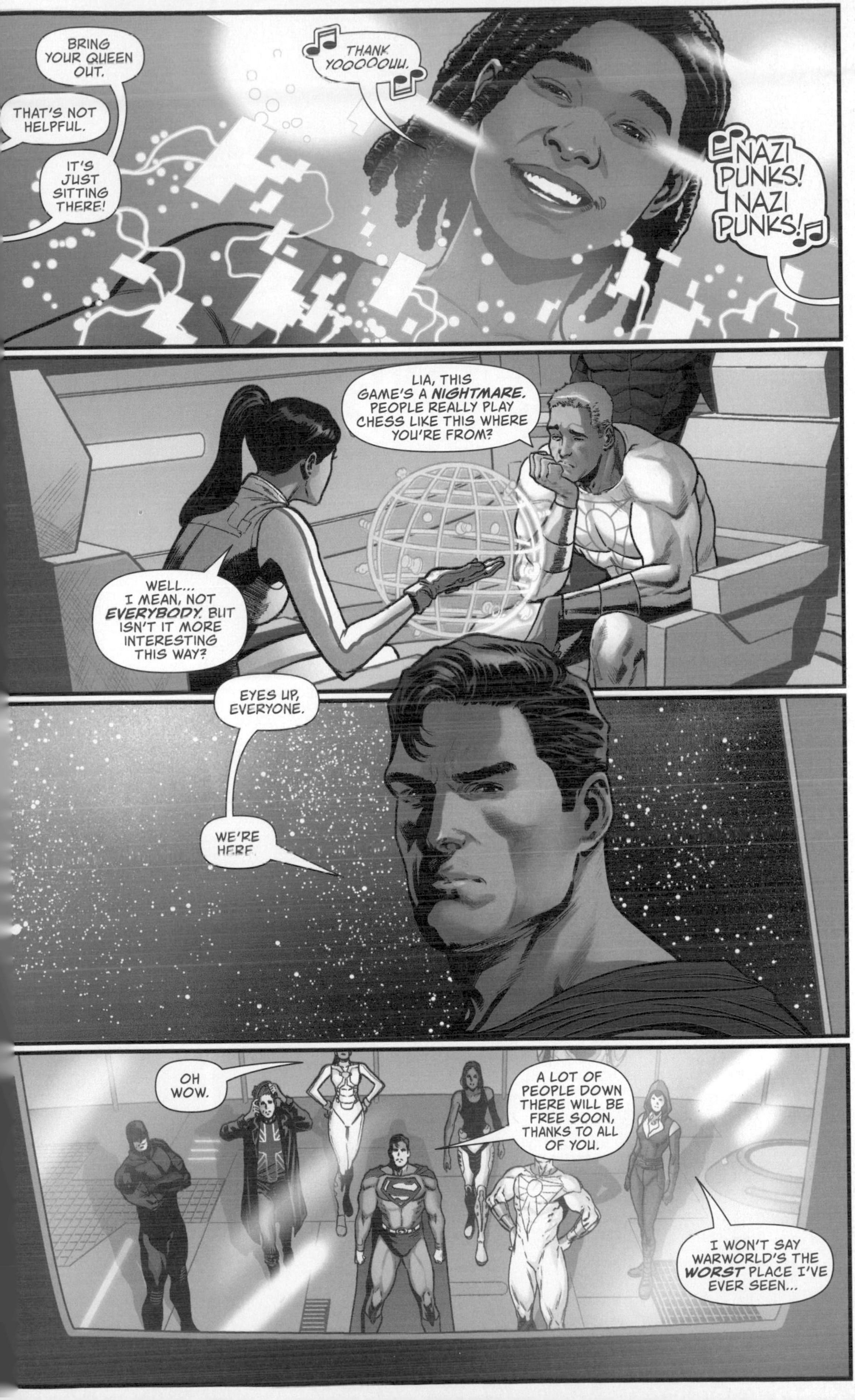
BRING YOUR QUEEN OUT.
THAT'S NOT HELPFUL.
IT'S JUST SITTING THERE!
THANK YOOOOOUU.
NAZI PUNKS! NAZI PUNKS!
LIA, THIS GAME'S A NIGHTMARE. PEOPLE REALLY PLAY CHESS LIKE THIS WHERE YOU'RE FROM?
WELL... I MEAN, NOT EVERYBODY. BUT ISN'T IT MORE INTERESTING THIS WAY?
EYES UP, EVERYONE.
WE'RE HERE.
OH WOW.
A LOT OF PEOPLE DOWN THERE WILL BE FREE SOON, THANKS TO ALL OF YOU.
I WON'T SAY WARWORLD'S THE WORST PLACE I'VE EVER SEEN...

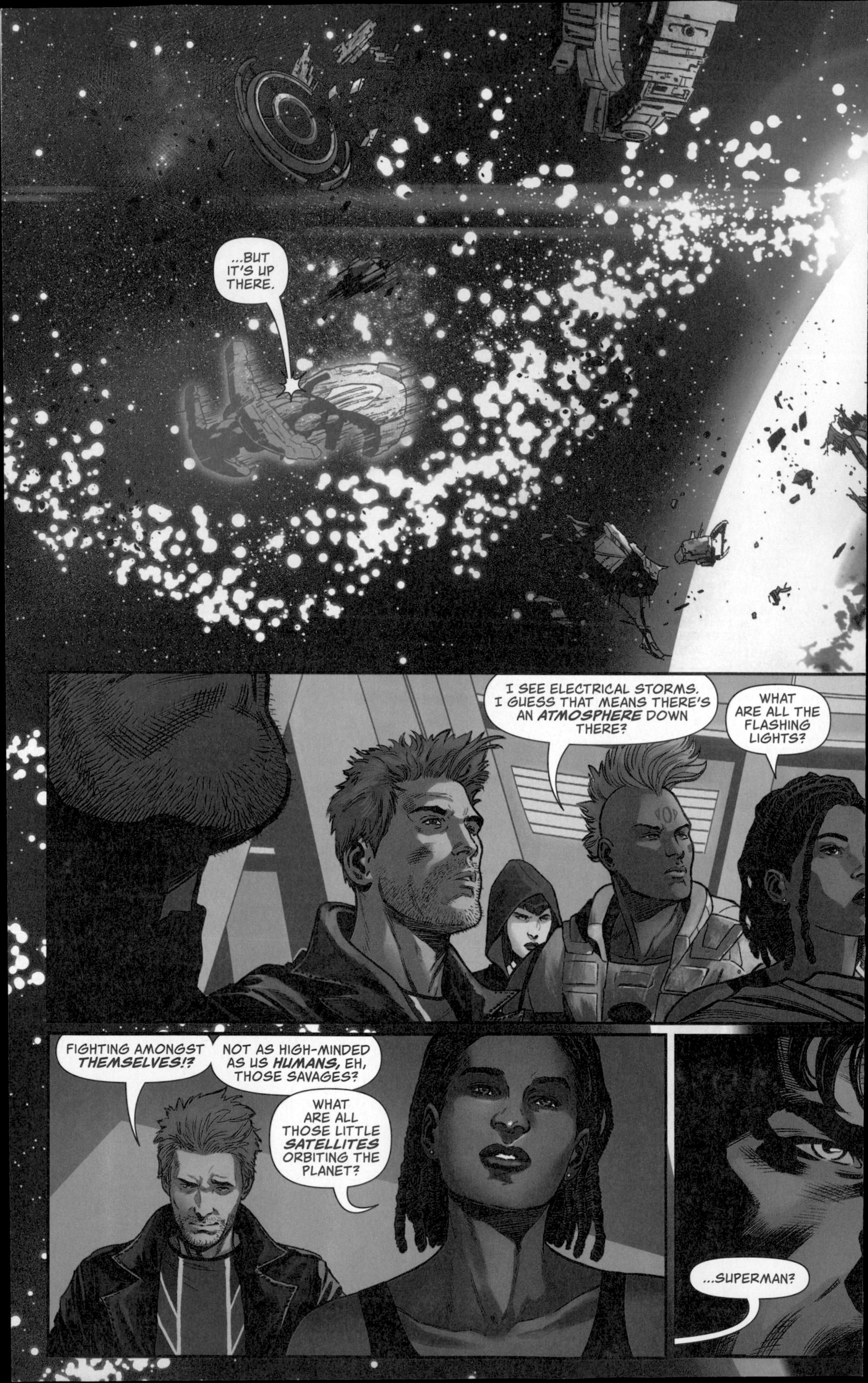

...BUT IT'S UP THERE.
I SEE ELECTRICAL STORMS. I GUESS THAT MEANS THERE'S AN ATMOSPHERE DOWN THERE?
WHAT ARE ALL THE FLASHING LIGHTS?
FIGHTING AMONGST THEMSELVES!?
NOT AS HIGH-MINDED AS US HUMANS, EH, THOSE SAVAGES?
WHAT ARE ALL THOSE LITTLE SATELLITES ORBITING THE PLANET?
...SUPERMAN?

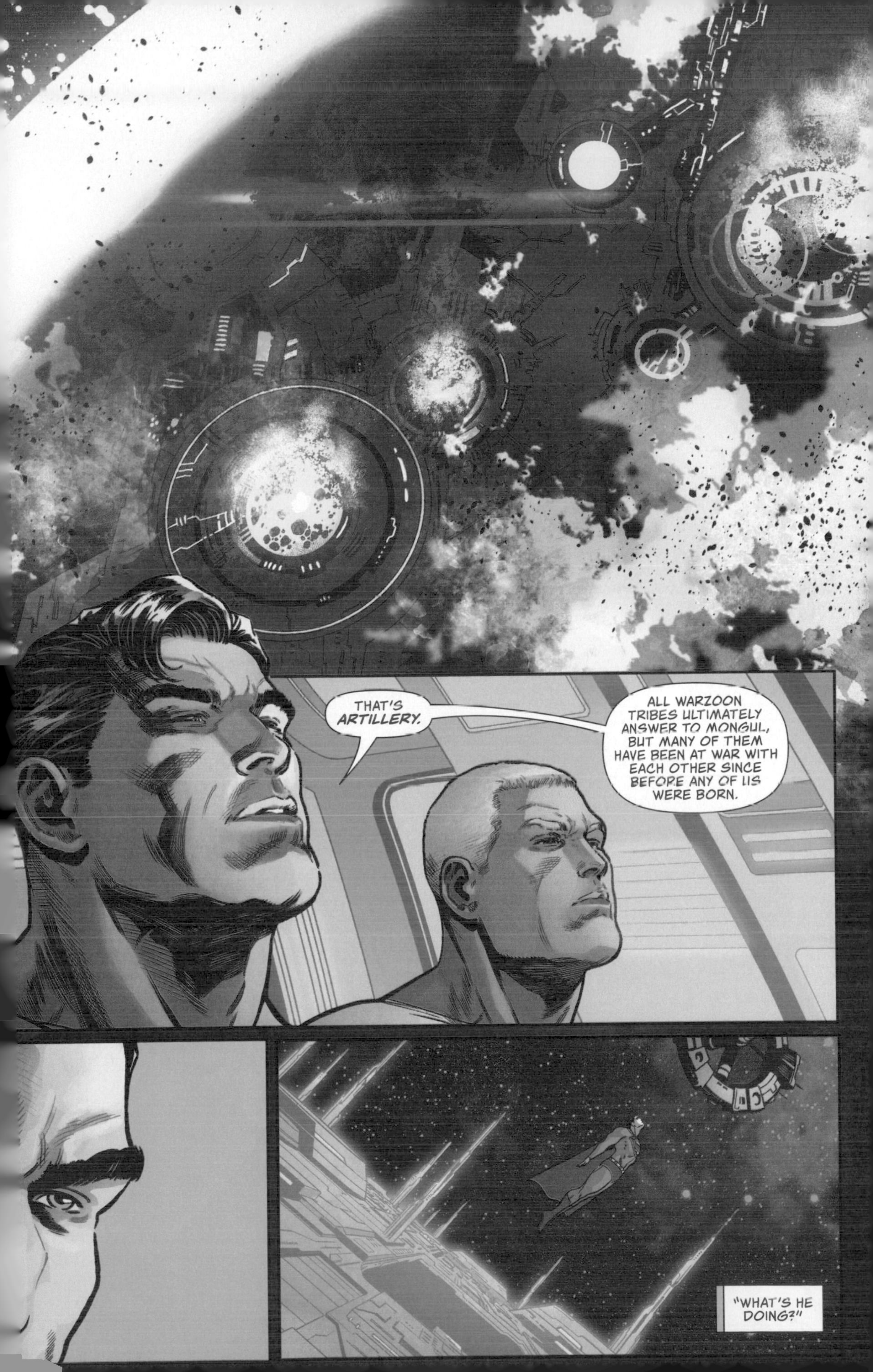

THAT'S ARTILLERY.
ALL WARZOON TRIBES ULTIMATELY ANSWER TO MONGUL, BUT MANY OF THEM HAVE BEEN AT WAR WITH EACH OTHER SINCE BEFORE ANY OF US WERE BORN.
"WHAT'S HE DOING?"

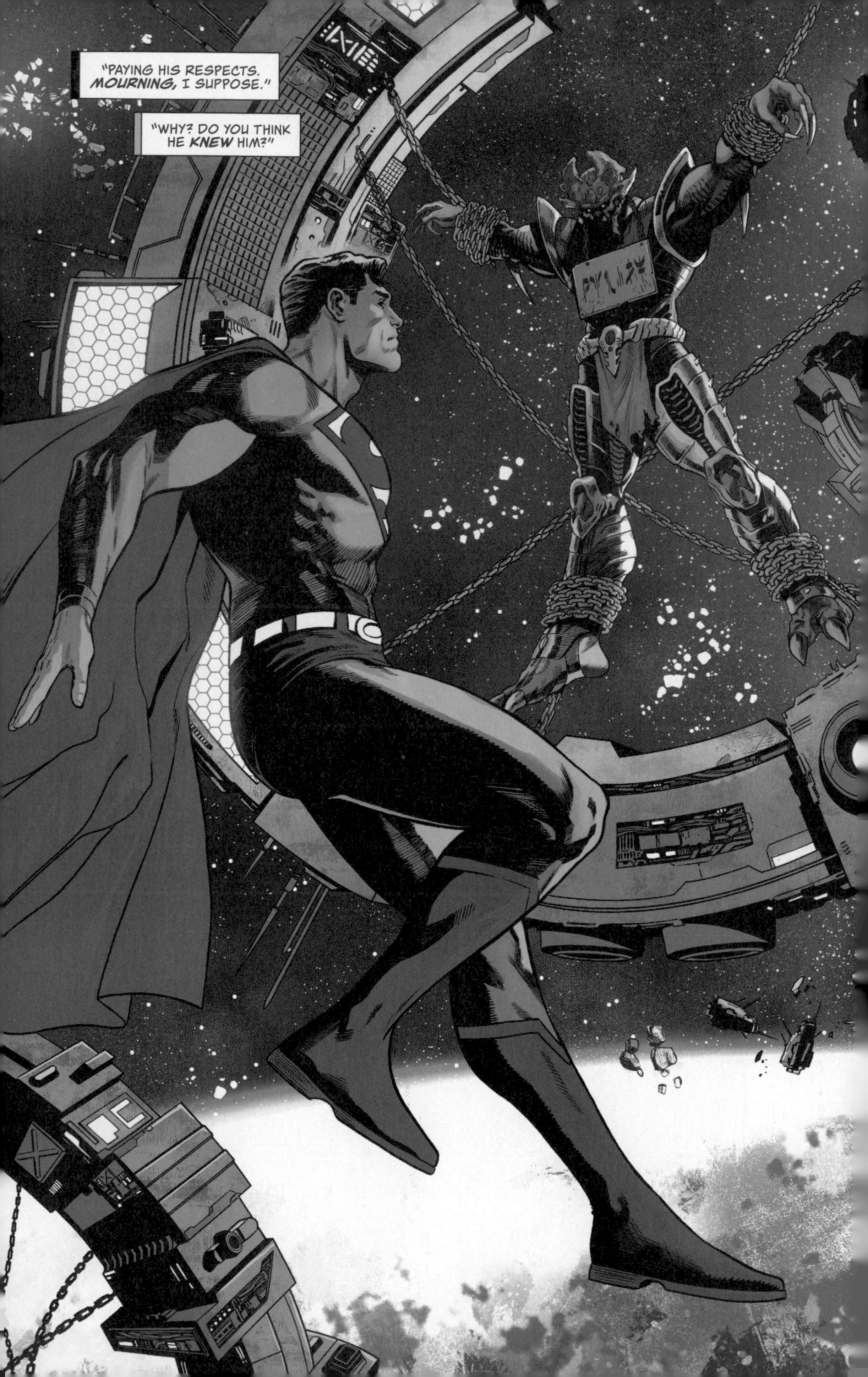
"PAYING HIS RESPECTS. MOURNING, I SUPPOSE."
"WHY? DO YOU THINK HE KNEW HIM?"

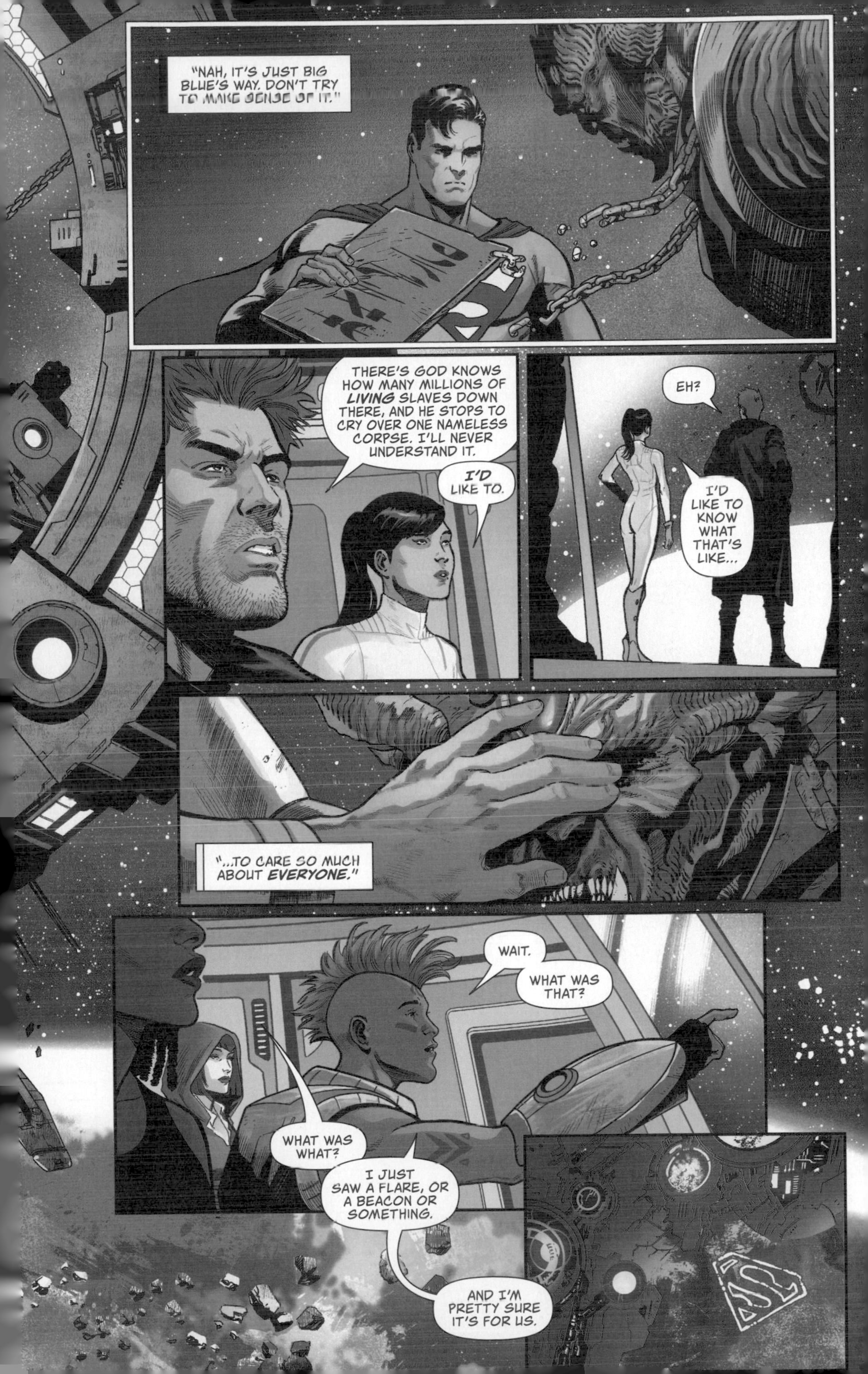
"NAH, IT'S JUST BIG BLUE'S WAY. DON'T TRY TO MAKE SENSE OF IT."
THERE'S GOD KNOWS HOW MANY MILLIONS OF *LIVING* SLAVES DOWN THERE, AND HE STOPS TO CRY OVER ONE NAMELESS CORPSE. I'LL NEVER UNDERSTAND IT.
I'D LIKE TO.
EH?
I'D LIKE TO KNOW WHAT THAT'S LIKE...
"...TO CARE SO MUCH ABOUT *EVERYONE.*"
WAIT.
WHAT WAS THAT?
WHAT WAS WHAT?
I JUST SAW A FLARE, OR A BEACON OR SOMETHING.
AND I'M PRETTY SURE IT'S FOR US.

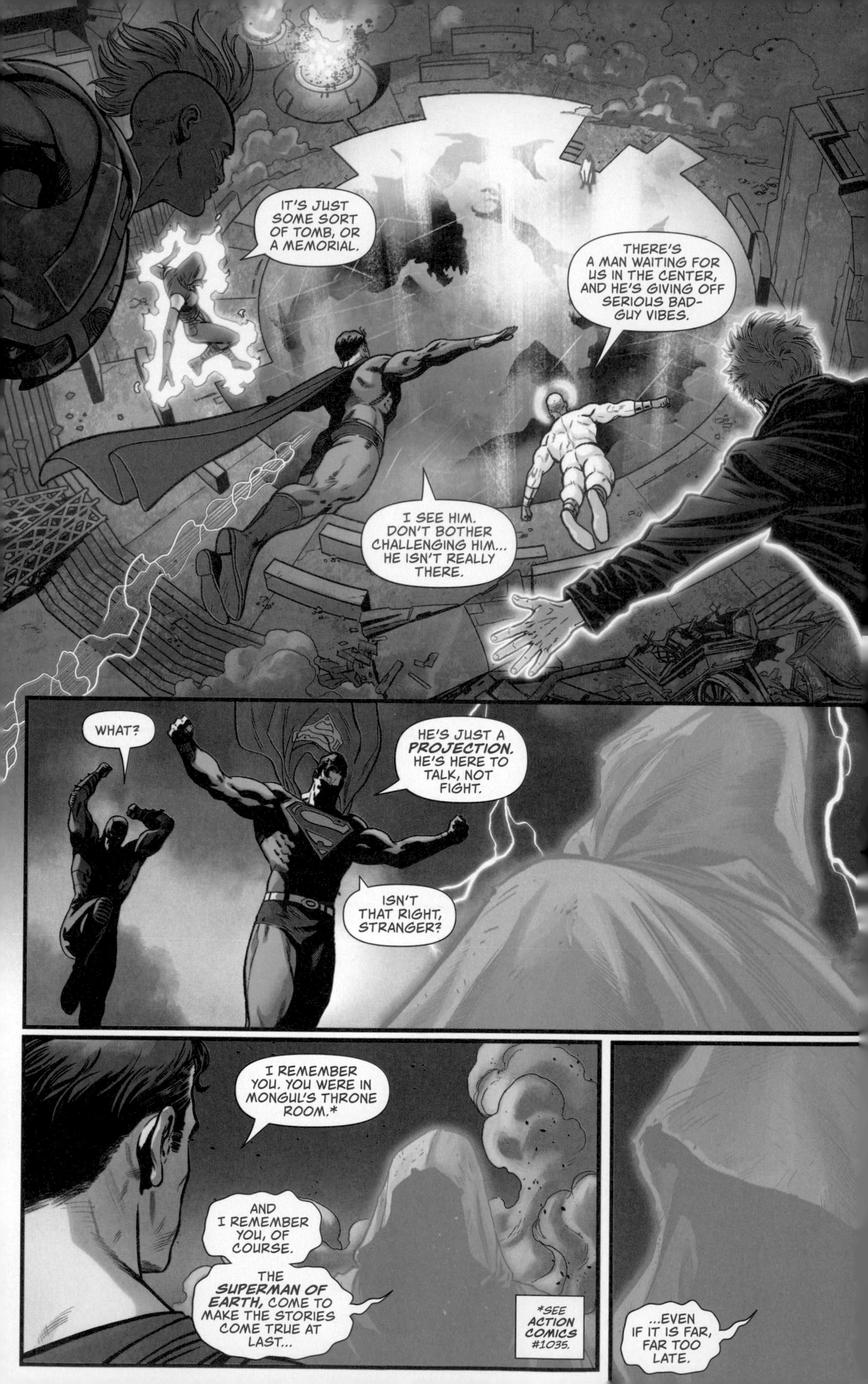
IT'S JUST SOME SORT OF TOMB, OR A MEMORIAL.
THERE'S A MAN WAITING FOR US IN THE CENTER, AND HE'S GIVING OFF SERIOUS BAD-GUY VIBES.
I SEE HIM. DON'T BOTHER CHALLENGING HIM... HE ISN'T REALLY THERE.
WHAT?
HE'S JUST A **PROJECTION.** HE'S HERE TO TALK, NOT FIGHT.
ISN'T THAT RIGHT, STRANGER?
I REMEMBER YOU. YOU WERE IN MONGUL'S THRONE ROOM.*
AND I REMEMBER YOU, OF COURSE.
THE **SUPERMAN OF EARTH,** COME TO MAKE THE STORIES COME TRUE AT LAST...
*SEE **ACTION COMICS** #1035.
...EVEN IF IT IS FAR, FAR TOO LATE.

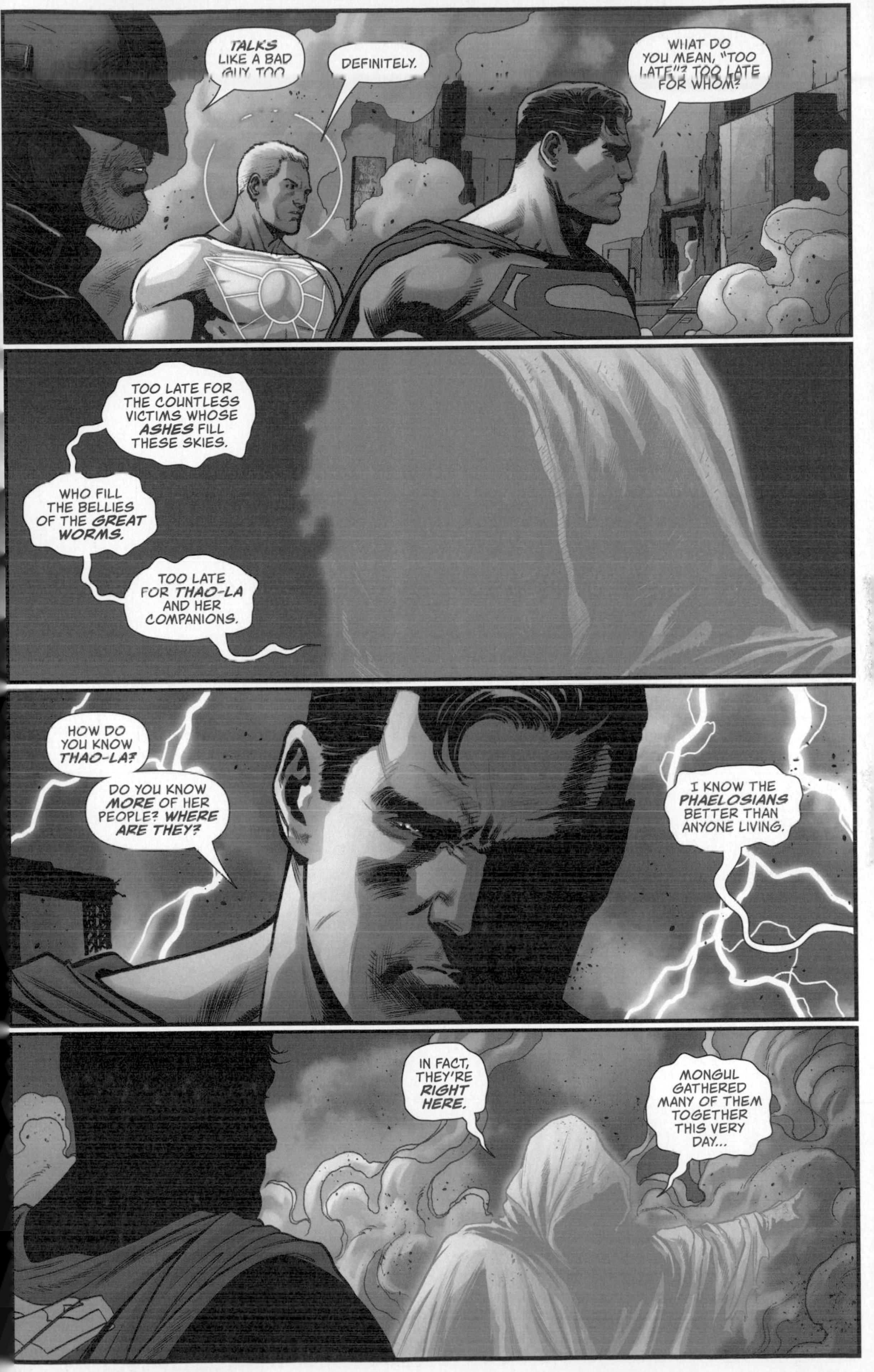
TALKS LIKE A BAD GUY, TOO.
DEFINITELY.
WHAT DO YOU MEAN, "TOO LATE"? TOO LATE FOR WHOM?
TOO LATE FOR THE COUNTLESS VICTIMS WHOSE ASHES FILL THESE SKIES.
WHO FILL THE BELLIES OF THE GREAT WORMS.
TOO LATE FOR THAO-LA AND HER COMPANIONS.
HOW DO YOU KNOW THAO-LA?
DO YOU KNOW MORE OF HER PEOPLE? WHERE ARE THEY?
I KNOW THE PHAELOSIANS BETTER THAN ANYONE LIVING.
IN FACT, THEY'RE RIGHT HERE.
MONGUL GATHERED MANY OF THEM TOGETHER THIS VERY DAY...

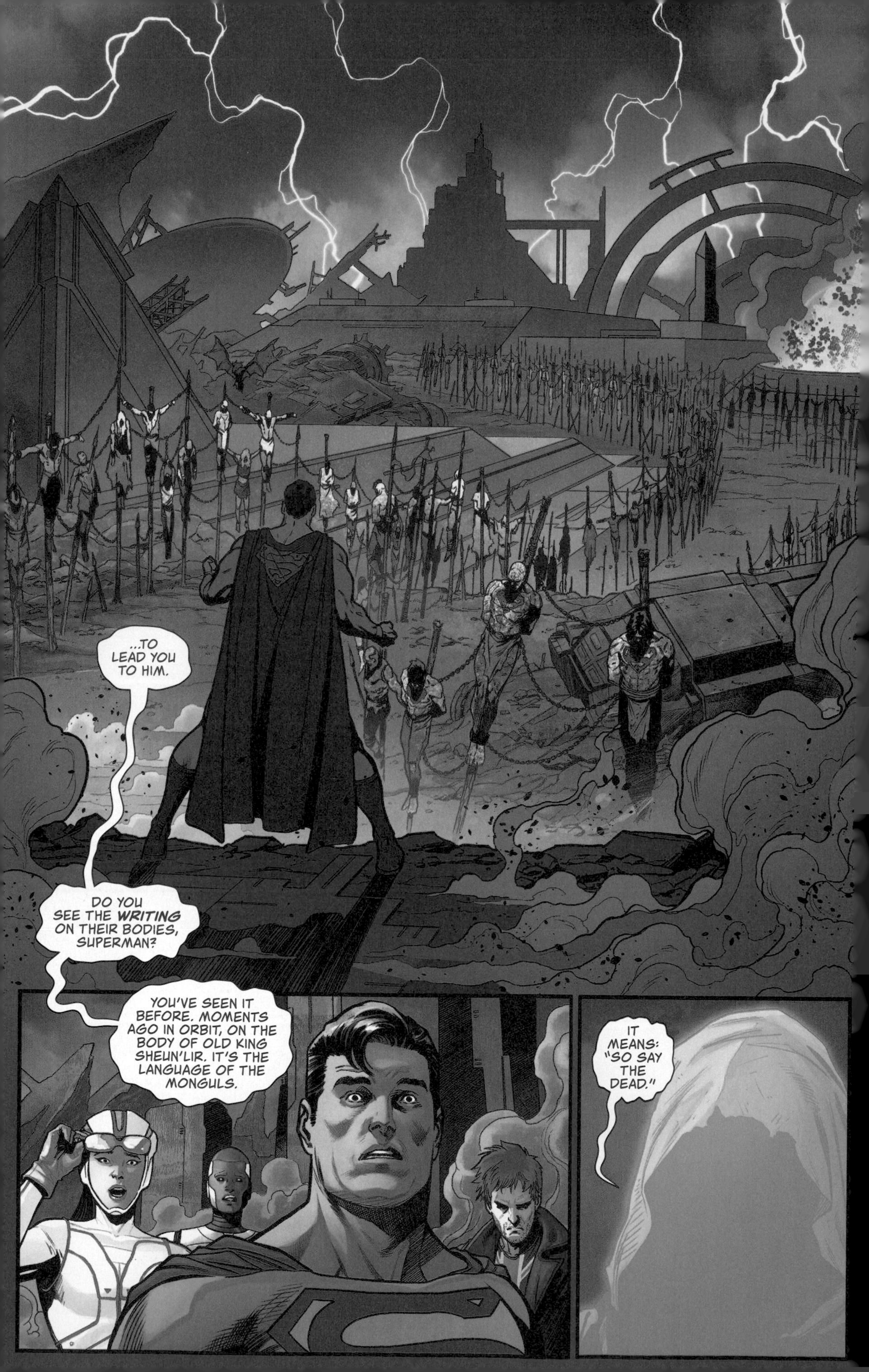
...TO LEAD YOU TO HIM.
DO YOU SEE THE WRITING ON THEIR BODIES, SUPERMAN?
YOU'VE SEEN IT BEFORE. MOMENTS AGO IN ORBIT, ON THE BODY OF OLD KING SHEUN'LIR. IT'S THE LANGUAGE OF THE MONGULS.
IT MEANS: "SO SAY THE DEAD."

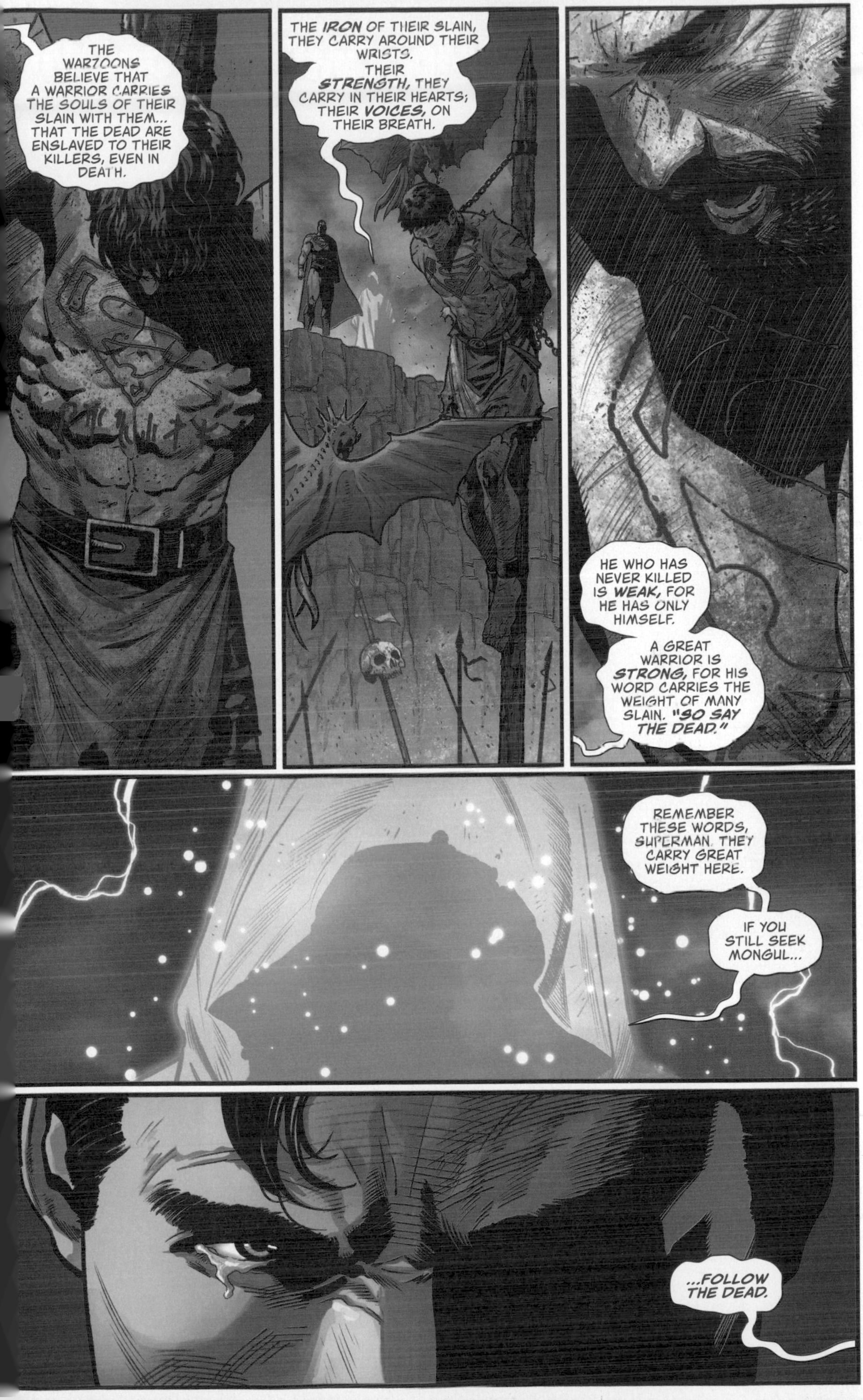
THE WARZOONS BELIEVE THAT A WARRIOR CARRIES THE SOULS OF THEIR SLAIN WITH THEM... THAT THE DEAD ARE ENSLAVED TO THEIR KILLERS, EVEN IN DEATH.
THE IRON OF THEIR SLAIN, THEY CARRY AROUND THEIR WRISTS. THEIR STRENGTH, THEY CARRY IN THEIR HEARTS; THEIR VOICES, ON THEIR BREATH.
HE WHO HAS NEVER KILLED IS WEAK, FOR HE HAS ONLY HIMSELF.
A GREAT WARRIOR IS STRONG, FOR HIS WORD CARRIES THE WEIGHT OF MANY SLAIN. "SO SAY THE DEAD."
REMEMBER THESE WORDS, SUPERMAN. THEY CARRY GREAT WEIGHT HERE.
IF YOU STILL SEEK MONGUL...
...FOLLOW THE DEAD.

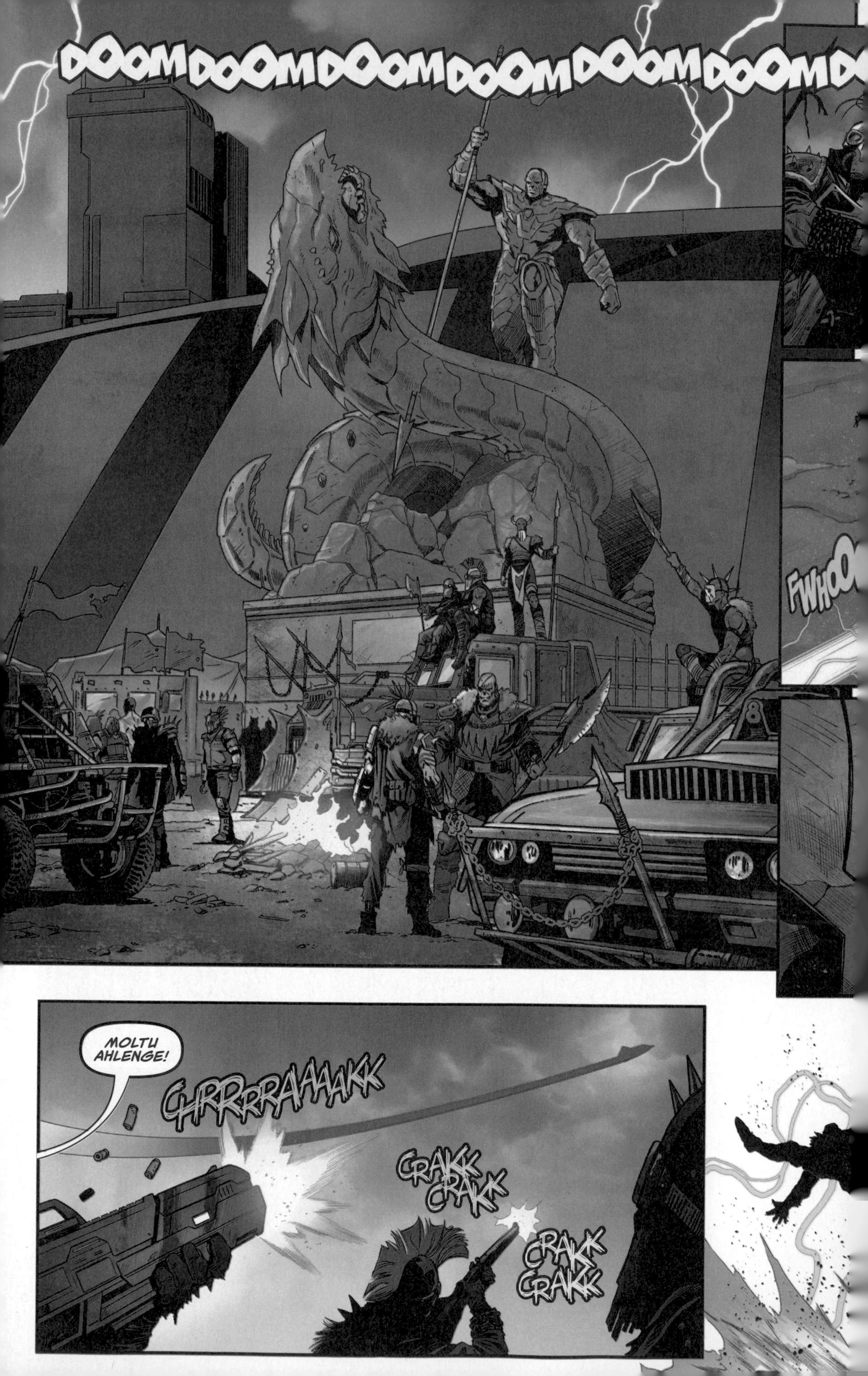
DOOMDOOMDOOMDOOMDOOMDOOMD
FWHOO
MOLTU AHLENGE!
CHRRRRAAAAKK
CRAKK CRAKK
CRAKK CRAKK

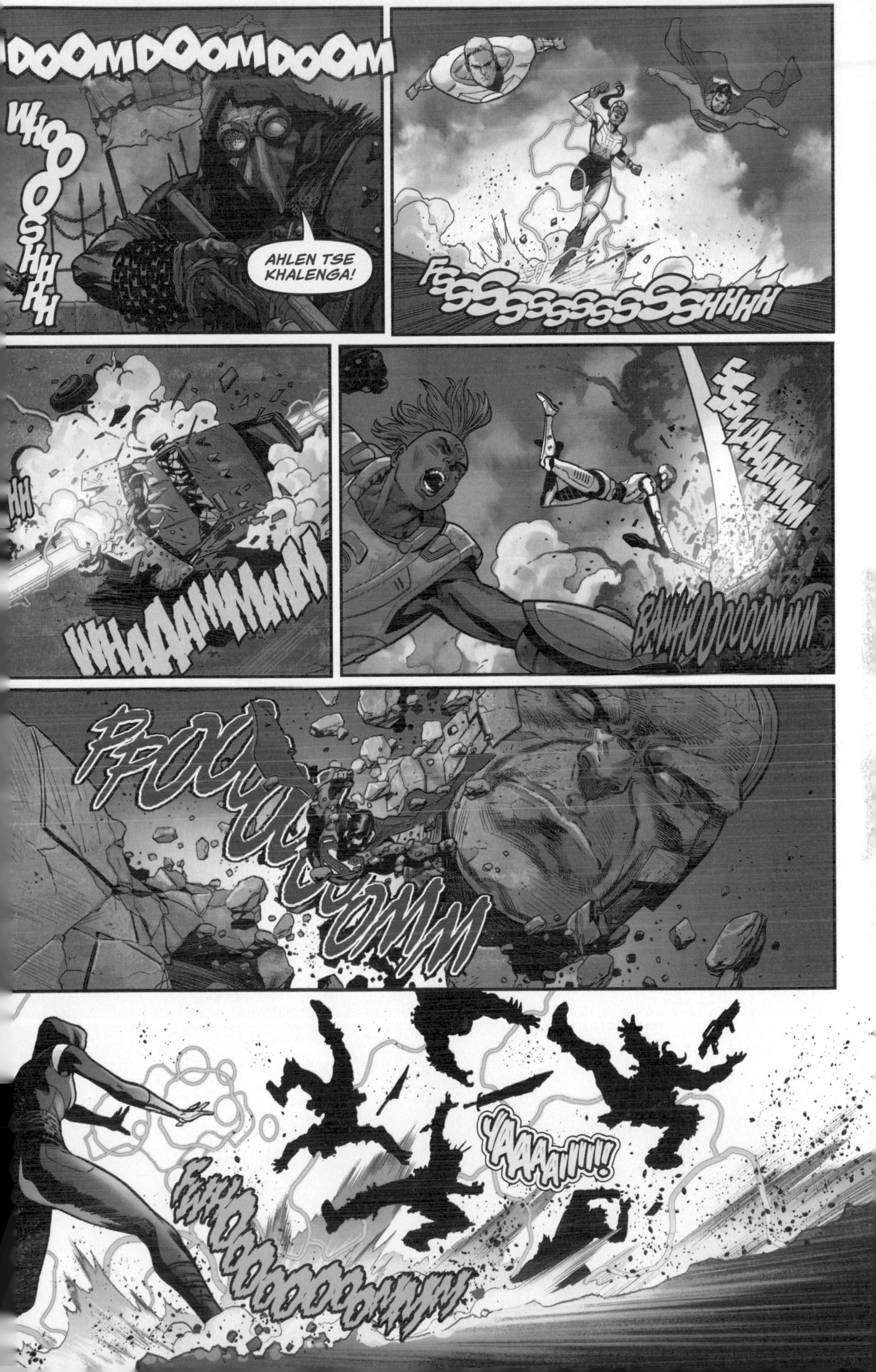
DOOMDOOMDOOM
WHOOOOSHHHHH
AHLEN TSE KHALENGA!
FSSSSSSSSSSSSSHHHH
WHAAAMMMMM
SSLAAAMMM
BAHHOOOOOOMMM
PFOOUUOOMM
YAAAAAIIIII!!
FWHOOOOOOOOOOOOMMMM

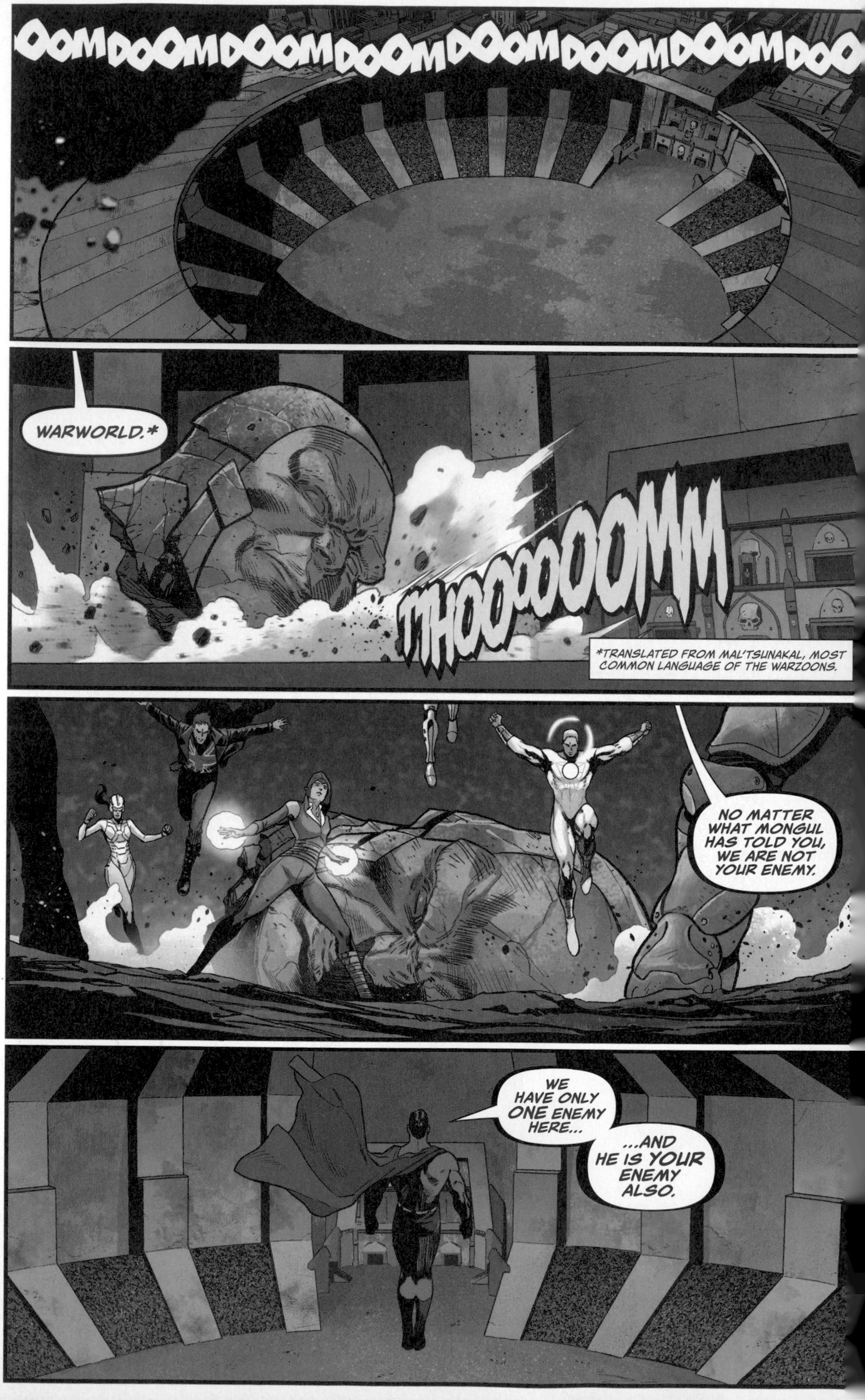
OOMDOOMDOOMDOOMDOOMDOOMDOOMDOO
WARWORLD.*
THOOOOOOMM
*TRANSLATED FROM MAL'TSUNAKAL, MOST COMMON LANGUAGE OF THE WARZOONS.
NO MATTER WHAT MONGUL HAS TOLD YOU, WE ARE NOT YOUR ENEMY.
WE HAVE ONLY ONE ENEMY HERE...
...AND HE IS YOUR ENEMY ALSO.

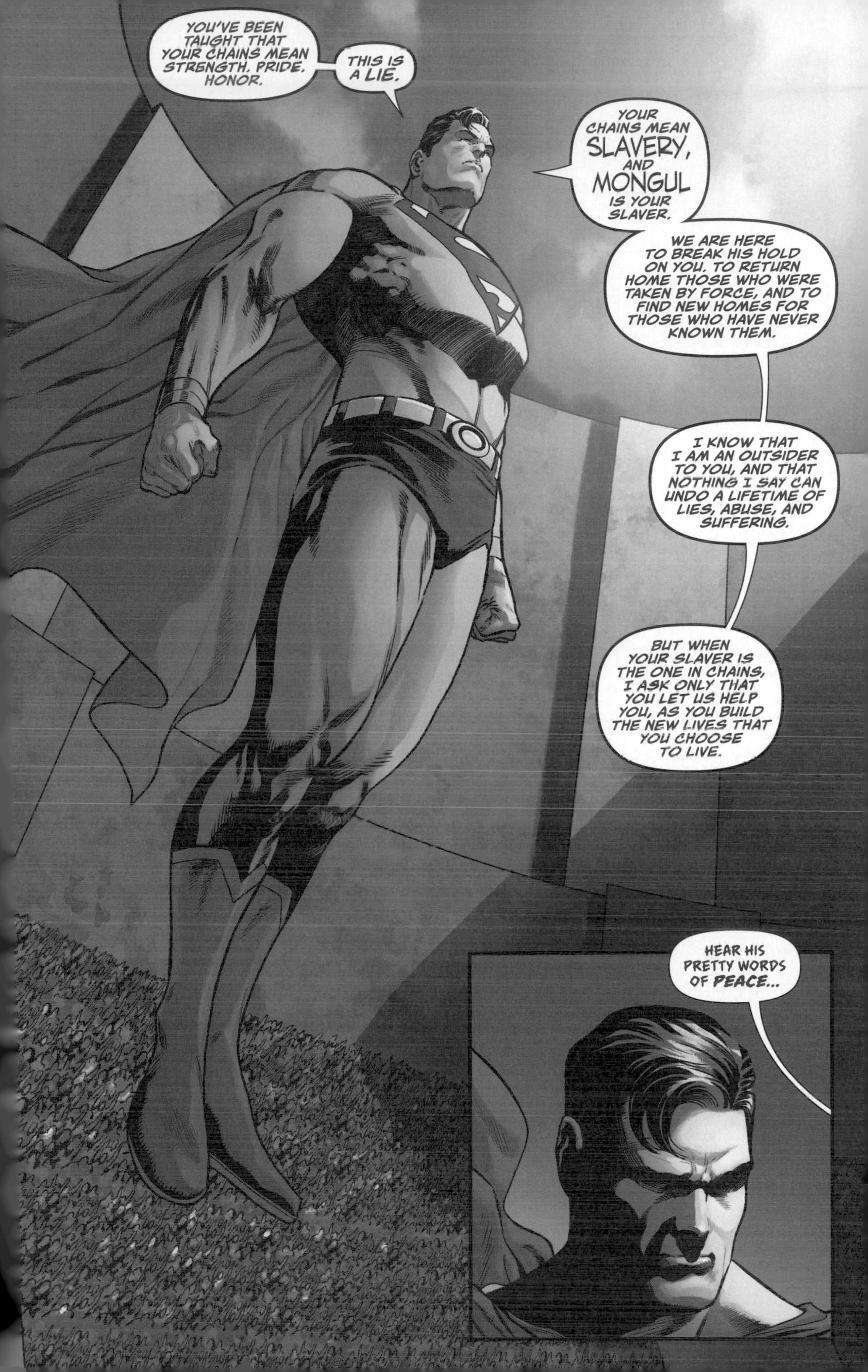
YOU'VE BEEN TAUGHT THAT YOUR CHAINS MEAN STRENGTH. PRIDE. HONOR.
THIS IS A LIE.
YOUR CHAINS MEAN SLAVERY, AND MONGUL IS YOUR SLAVER.
WE ARE HERE TO BREAK HIS HOLD ON YOU. TO RETURN HOME THOSE WHO WERE TAKEN BY FORCE, AND TO FIND NEW HOMES FOR THOSE WHO HAVE NEVER KNOWN THEM.
I KNOW THAT I AM AN OUTSIDER TO YOU, AND THAT NOTHING I SAY CAN UNDO A LIFETIME OF LIES, ABUSE, AND SUFFERING.
BUT WHEN YOUR SLAVER IS THE ONE IN CHAINS, I ASK ONLY THAT YOU LET US HELP YOU, AS YOU BUILD THE NEW LIVES THAT YOU CHOOSE TO LIVE.
HEAR HIS PRETTY WORDS OF PEACE...

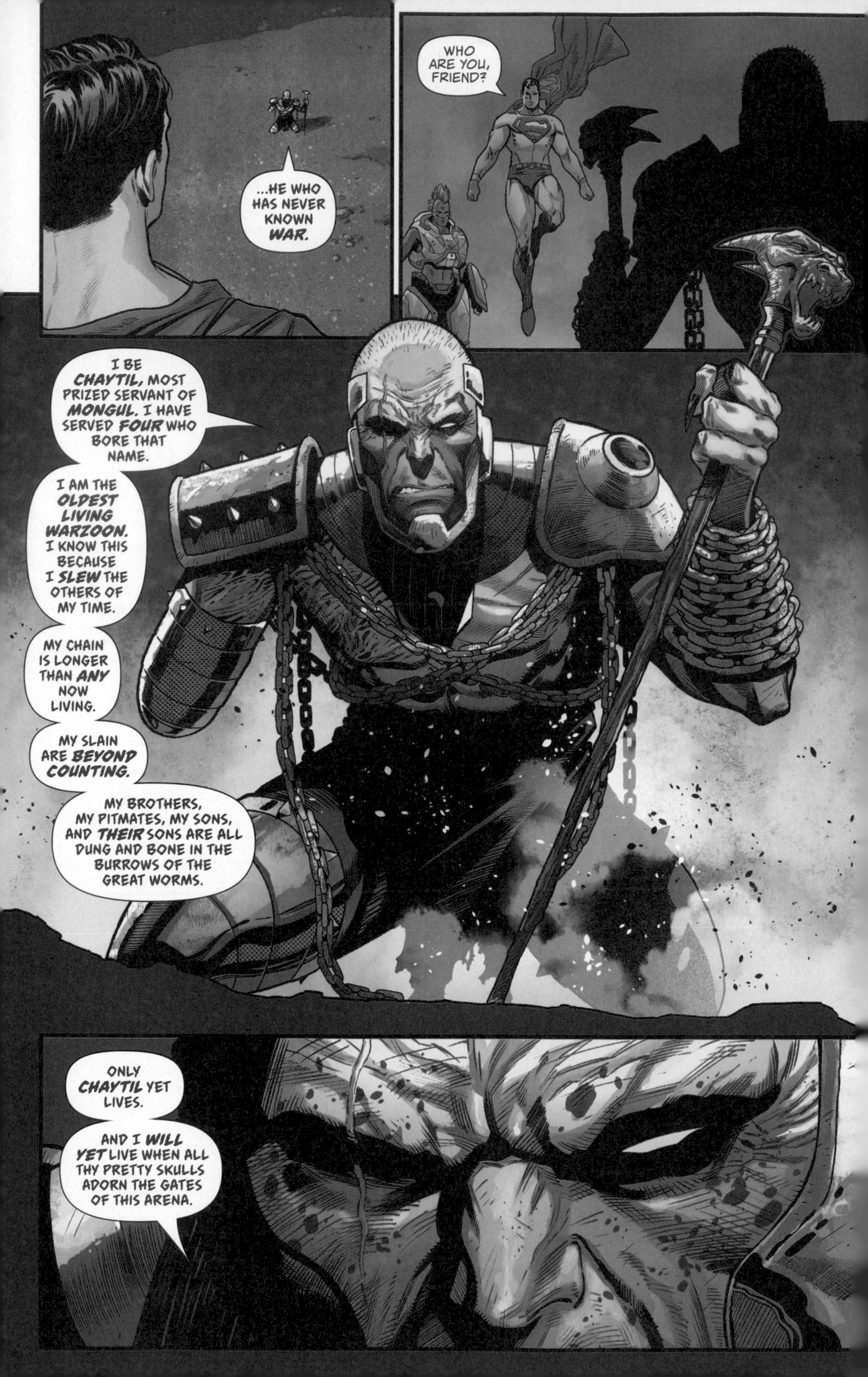
...HE WHO HAS NEVER KNOWN WAR.
WHO ARE YOU, FRIEND?
I BE CHAYTIL, MOST PRIZED SERVANT OF MONGUL. I HAVE SERVED FOUR WHO BORE THAT NAME.
I AM THE OLDEST LIVING WARZOON. I KNOW THIS BECAUSE I SLEW THE OTHERS OF MY TIME.
MY CHAIN IS LONGER THAN ANY NOW LIVING.
MY SLAIN ARE BEYOND COUNTING.
MY BROTHERS, MY PITMATES, MY SONS, AND THEIR SONS ARE ALL DUNG AND BONE IN THE BURROWS OF THE GREAT WORMS.
ONLY CHAYTIL YET LIVES.
AND I WILL YET LIVE WHEN ALL THY PRETTY SKULLS ADORN THE GATES OF THIS ARENA.

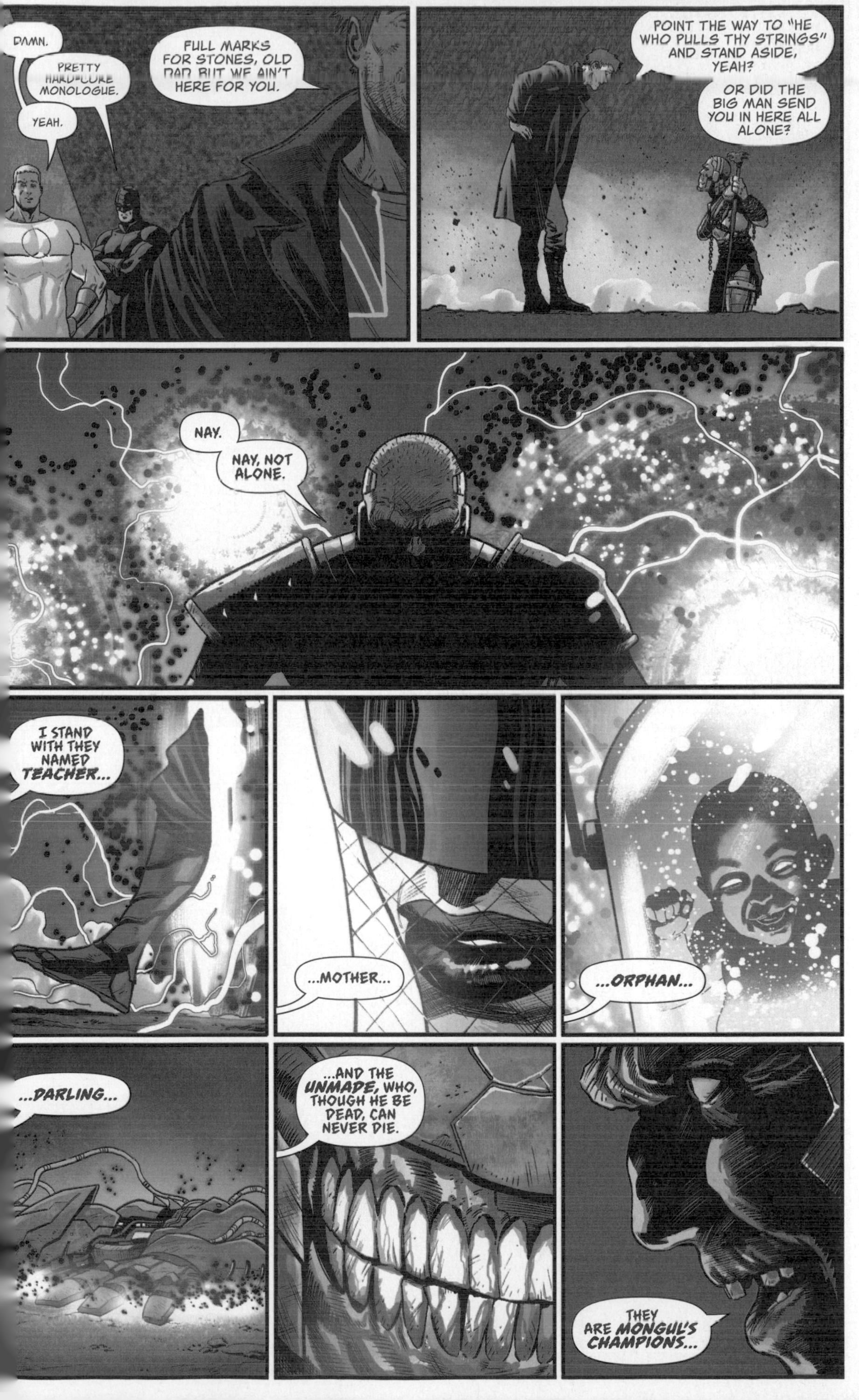
DAMN.
PRETTY HARD-CORE MONOLOGUE.
YEAH.
FULL MARKS FOR STONES, OLD DAD BUT WE AIN'T HERE FOR YOU.
POINT THE WAY TO "HE WHO PULLS THY STRINGS" AND STAND ASIDE, YEAH?
OR DID THE BIG MAN SEND YOU IN HERE ALL ALONE?
NAY.
NAY, NOT ALONE.
I STAND WITH THEY NAMED TEACHER...
...MOTHER...
...ORPHAN...
...DARLING...
...AND THE UNMADE, WHO, THOUGH HE BE DEAD, CAN NEVER DIE.
THEY ARE MONGUL'S CHAMPIONS...

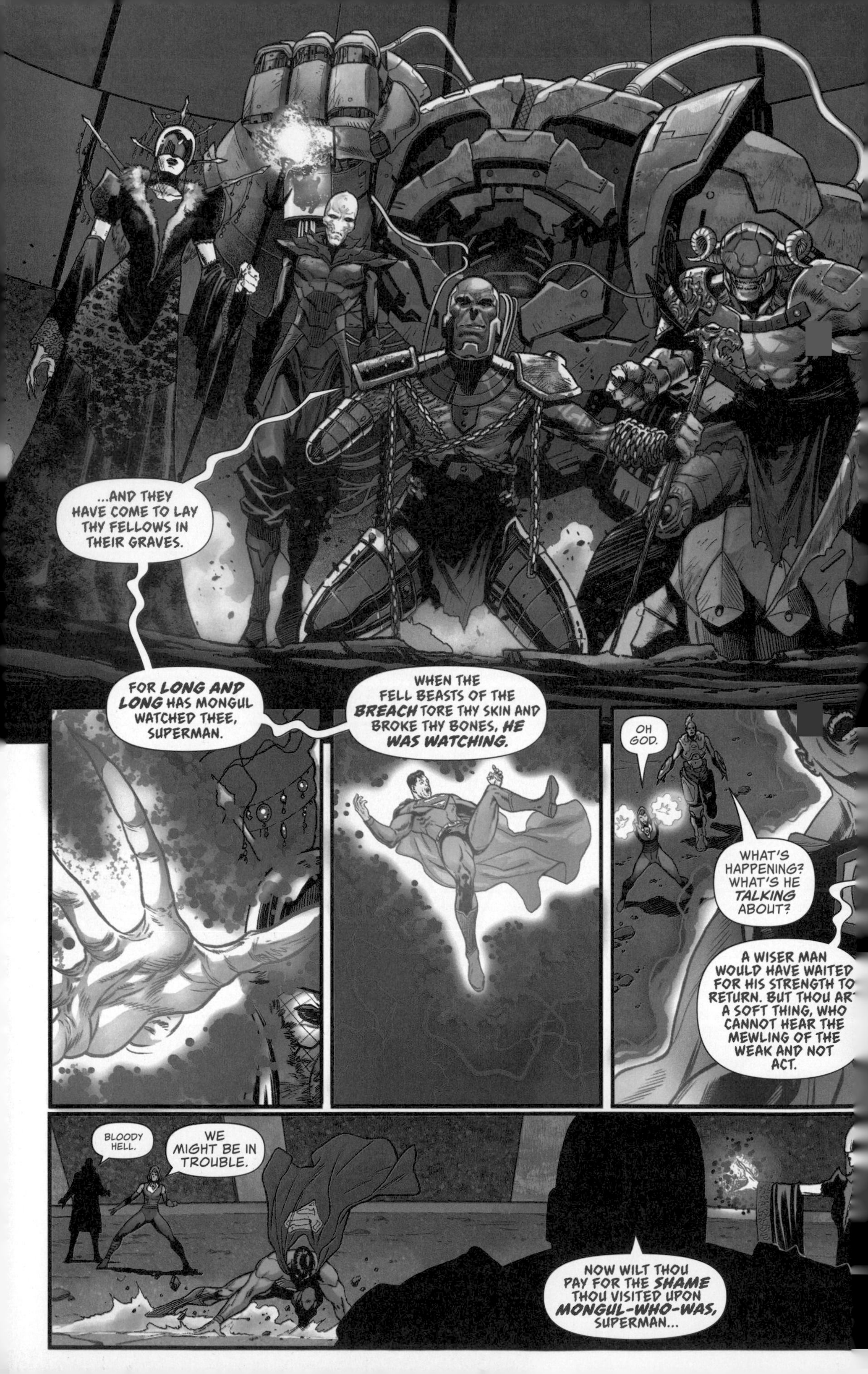
...AND THEY HAVE COME TO LAY THY FELLOWS IN THEIR GRAVES.
FOR LONG AND LONG HAS MONGUL WATCHED THEE, SUPERMAN.
WHEN THE FELL BEASTS OF THE BREACH TORE THY SKIN AND BROKE THY BONES, HE WAS WATCHING.
OH GOD.
WHAT'S HAPPENING? WHAT'S HE TALKING ABOUT?
A WISER MAN WOULD HAVE WAITED FOR HIS STRENGTH TO RETURN. BUT THOU ART A SOFT THING, WHO CANNOT HEAR THE MEWLING OF THE WEAK AND NOT ACT.
BLOODY HELL.
WE MIGHT BE IN TROUBLE.
NOW WILT THOU PAY FOR THE SHAME THOU VISITED UPON MONGUL-WHO-WAS, SUPERMAN...

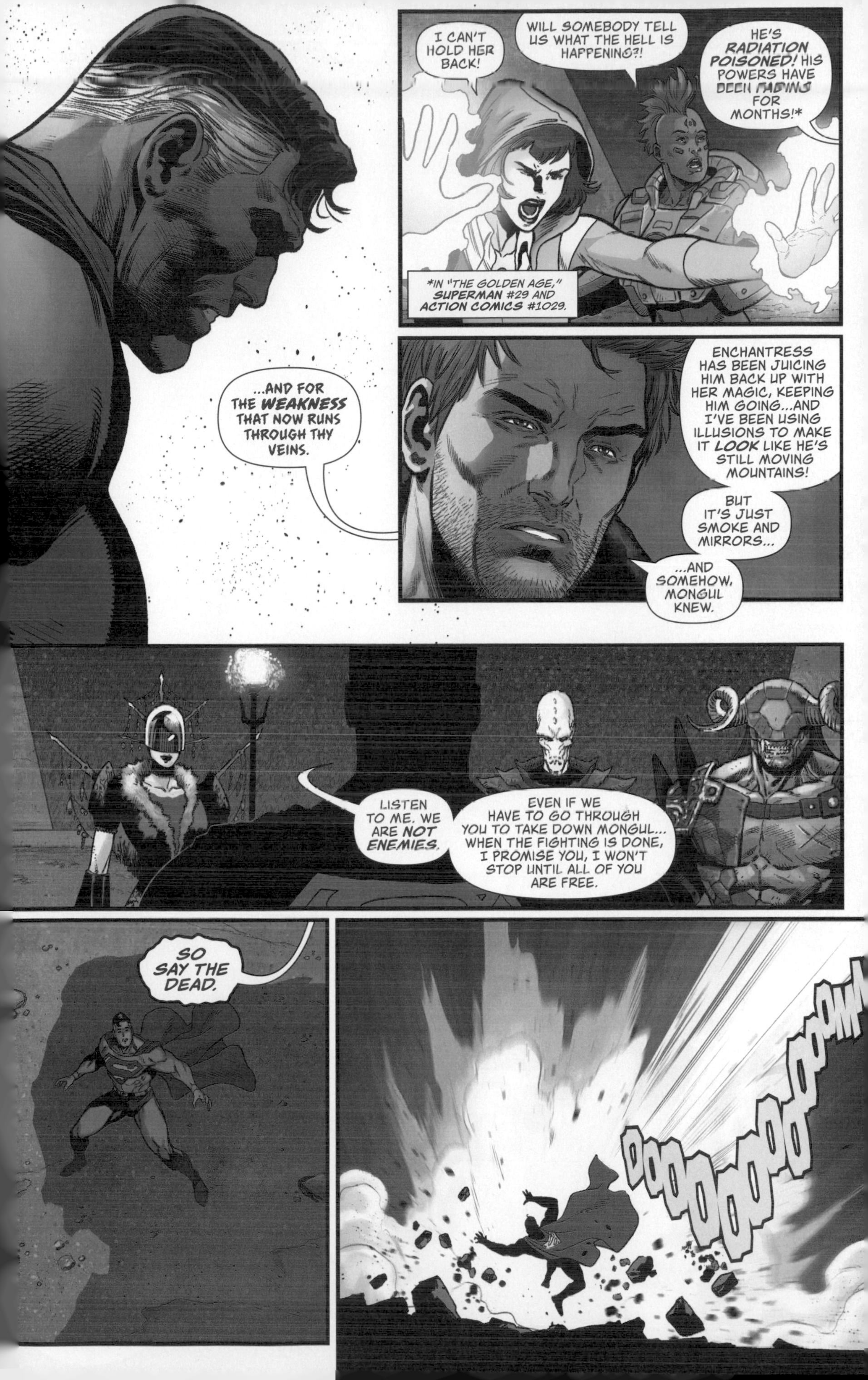
I CAN'T HOLD HER BACK!
WILL SOMEBODY TELL US WHAT THE HELL IS HAPPENING?!
HE'S RADIATION POISONED! HIS POWERS HAVE BEEN FADING FOR MONTHS!*
*IN "THE GOLDEN AGE," SUPERMAN #29 AND ACTION COMICS #1029.
...AND FOR THE WEAKNESS THAT NOW RUNS THROUGH THY VEINS.
ENCHANTRESS HAS BEEN JUICING HIM BACK UP WITH HER MAGIC, KEEPING HIM GOING...AND I'VE BEEN USING ILLUSIONS TO MAKE IT LOOK LIKE HE'S STILL MOVING MOUNTAINS!
BUT IT'S JUST SMOKE AND MIRRORS...
...AND SOMEHOW, MONGUL KNEW.
LISTEN TO ME. WE ARE NOT ENEMIES.
EVEN IF WE HAVE TO GO THROUGH YOU TO TAKE DOWN MONGUL... WHEN THE FIGHTING IS DONE, I PROMISE YOU, I WON'T STOP UNTIL ALL OF YOU ARE FREE.
SO SAY THE DEAD.
DOOOOOOOOOOOOOOMM

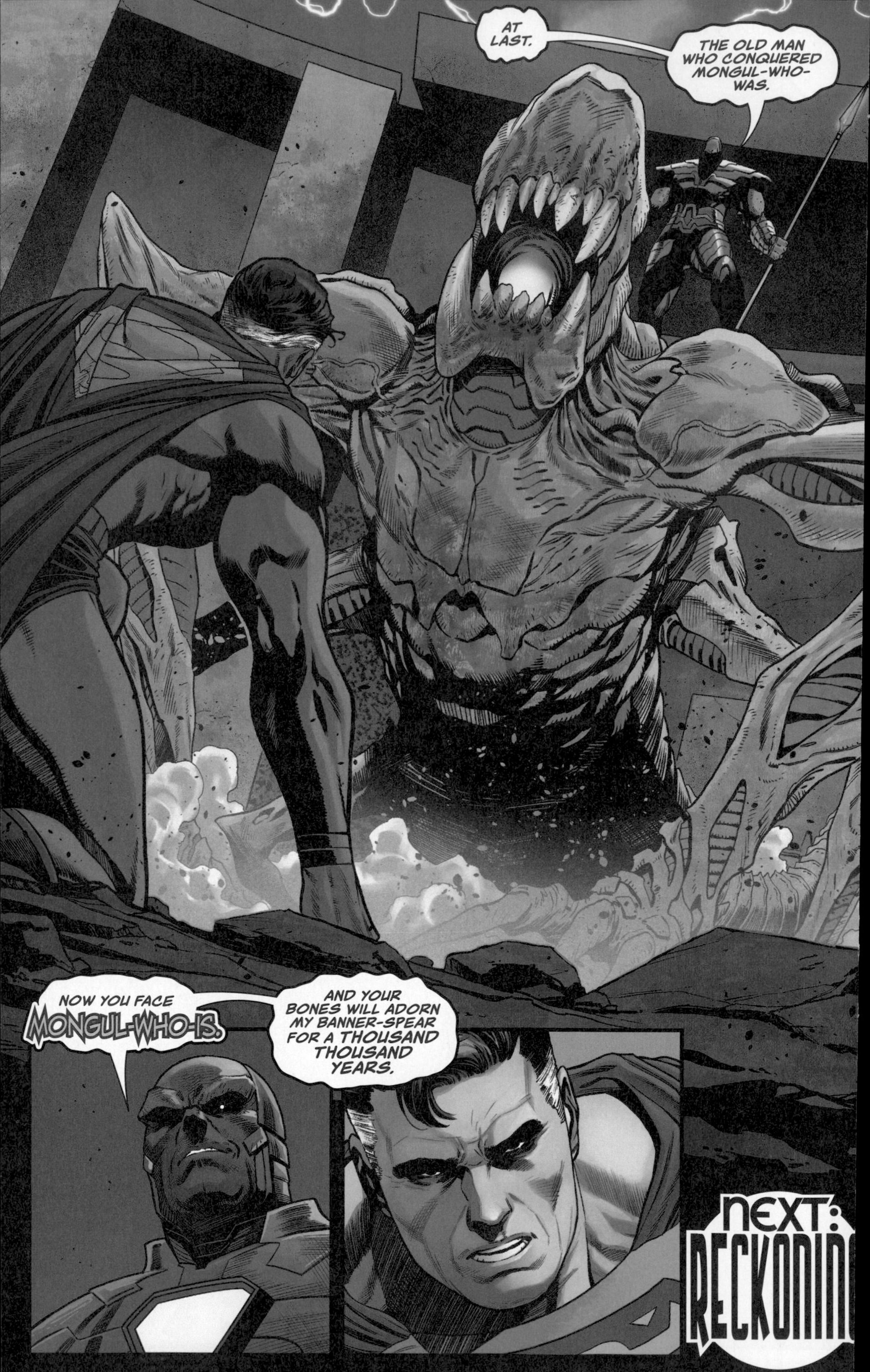
AT LAST.
THE OLD MAN WHO CONQUERED MONGUL-WHO-WAS.
NOW YOU FACE MONGUL-WHO-IS.
AND YOUR BONES WILL ADORN MY BANNER-SPEAR FOR A THOUSAND THOUSAND YEARS.
NEXT: RECKONIN

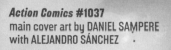

Action Comics #1037
main cover art by DANIEL SAMPERE
with ALEJANDRO SÁNCHEZ

***Action Comics* #1037** variant cover by JULIAN TOTINO TEDESCO

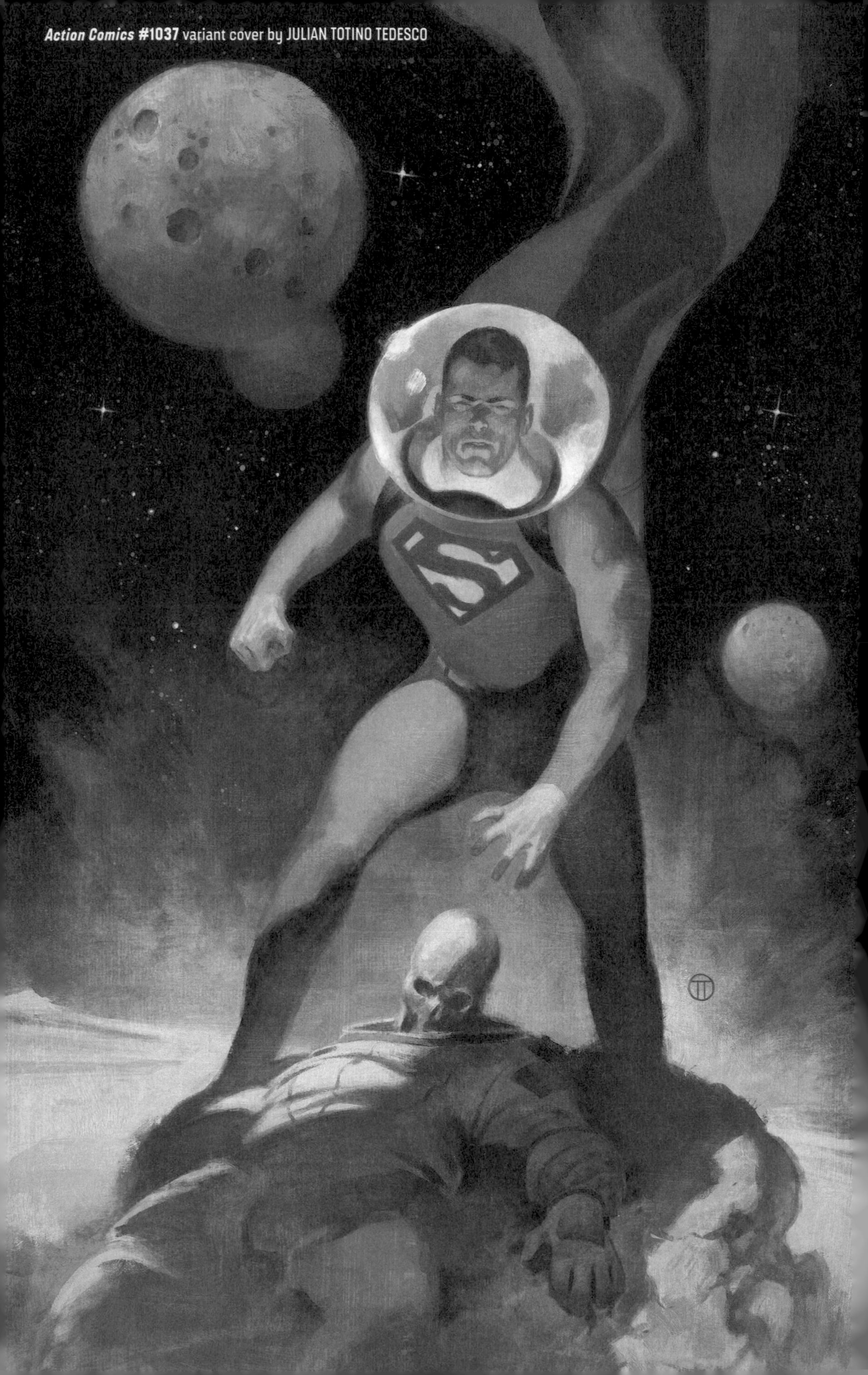

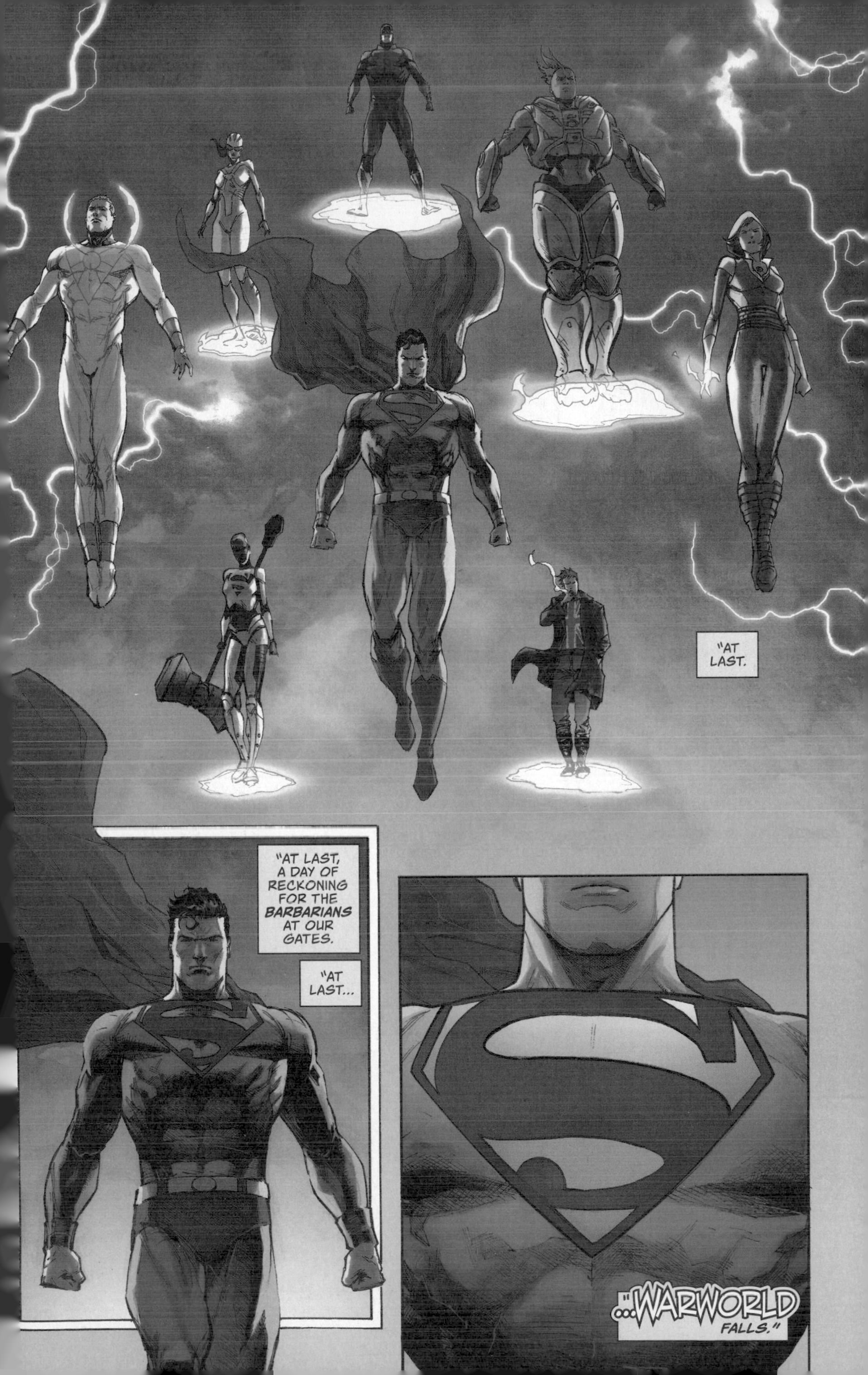
"AT LAST.
"AT LAST, A DAY OF RECKONING FOR THE BARBARIANS AT OUR GATES.
"AT LAST...
"...WARWORLD FALLS."

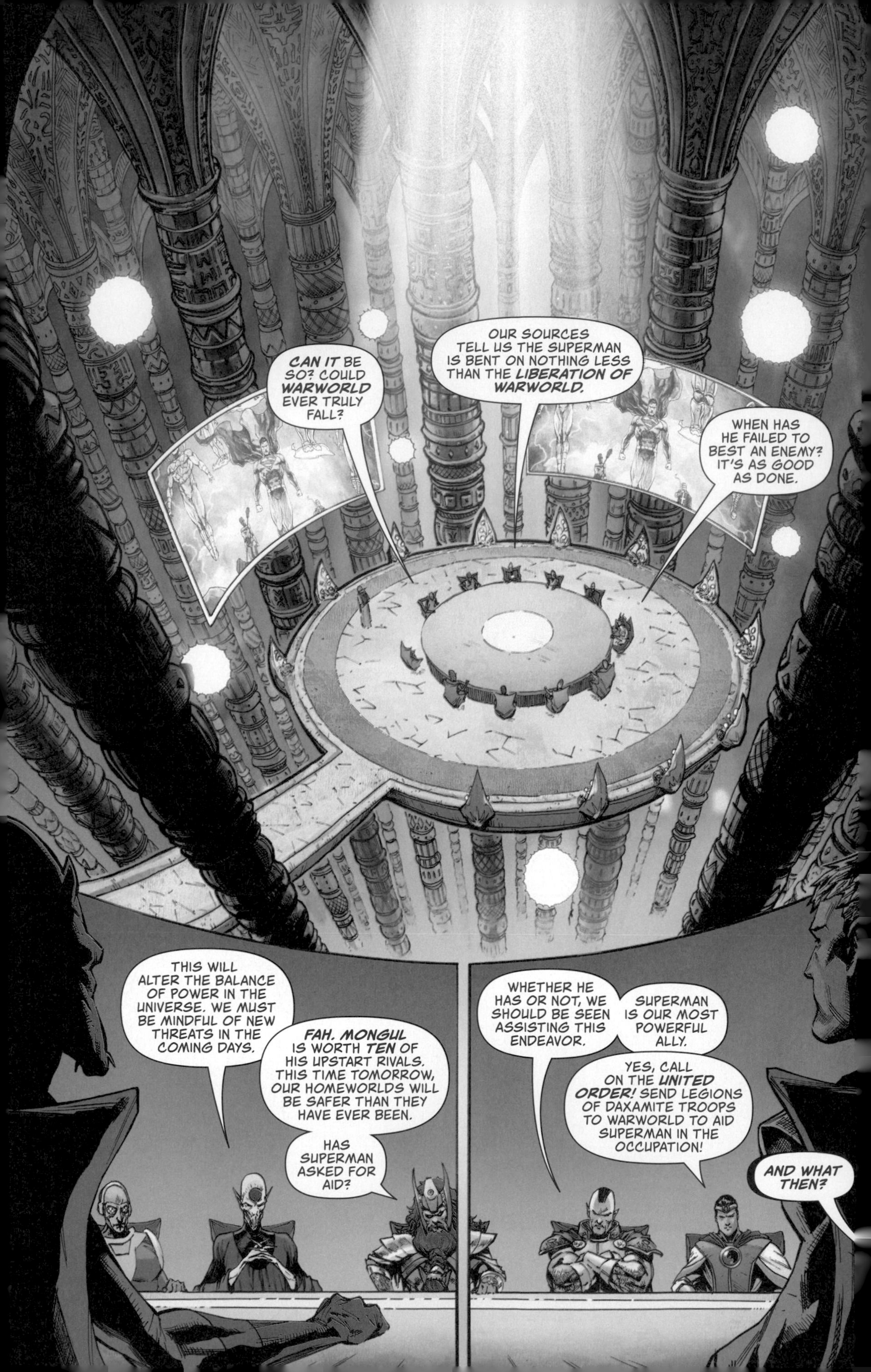
CAN IT BE SO? COULD WARWORLD EVER TRULY FALL?
OUR SOURCES TELL US THE SUPERMAN IS BENT ON NOTHING LESS THAN THE LIBERATION OF WARWORLD.
WHEN HAS HE FAILED TO BEST AN ENEMY? IT'S AS GOOD AS DONE.
THIS WILL ALTER THE BALANCE OF POWER IN THE UNIVERSE. WE MUST BE MINDFUL OF NEW THREATS IN THE COMING DAYS.
FAH. MONGUL IS WORTH TEN OF HIS UPSTART RIVALS. THIS TIME TOMORROW, OUR HOMEWORLDS WILL BE SAFER THAN THEY HAVE EVER BEEN.
HAS SUPERMAN ASKED FOR AID?
WHETHER HE HAS OR NOT, WE SHOULD BE SEEN ASSISTING THIS ENDEAVOR.
SUPERMAN IS OUR MOST POWERFUL ALLY.
YES, CALL ON THE UNITED ORDER! SEND LEGIONS OF DAXAMITE TROOPS TO WARWORLD TO AID SUPERMAN IN THE OCCUPATION!
AND WHAT THEN?

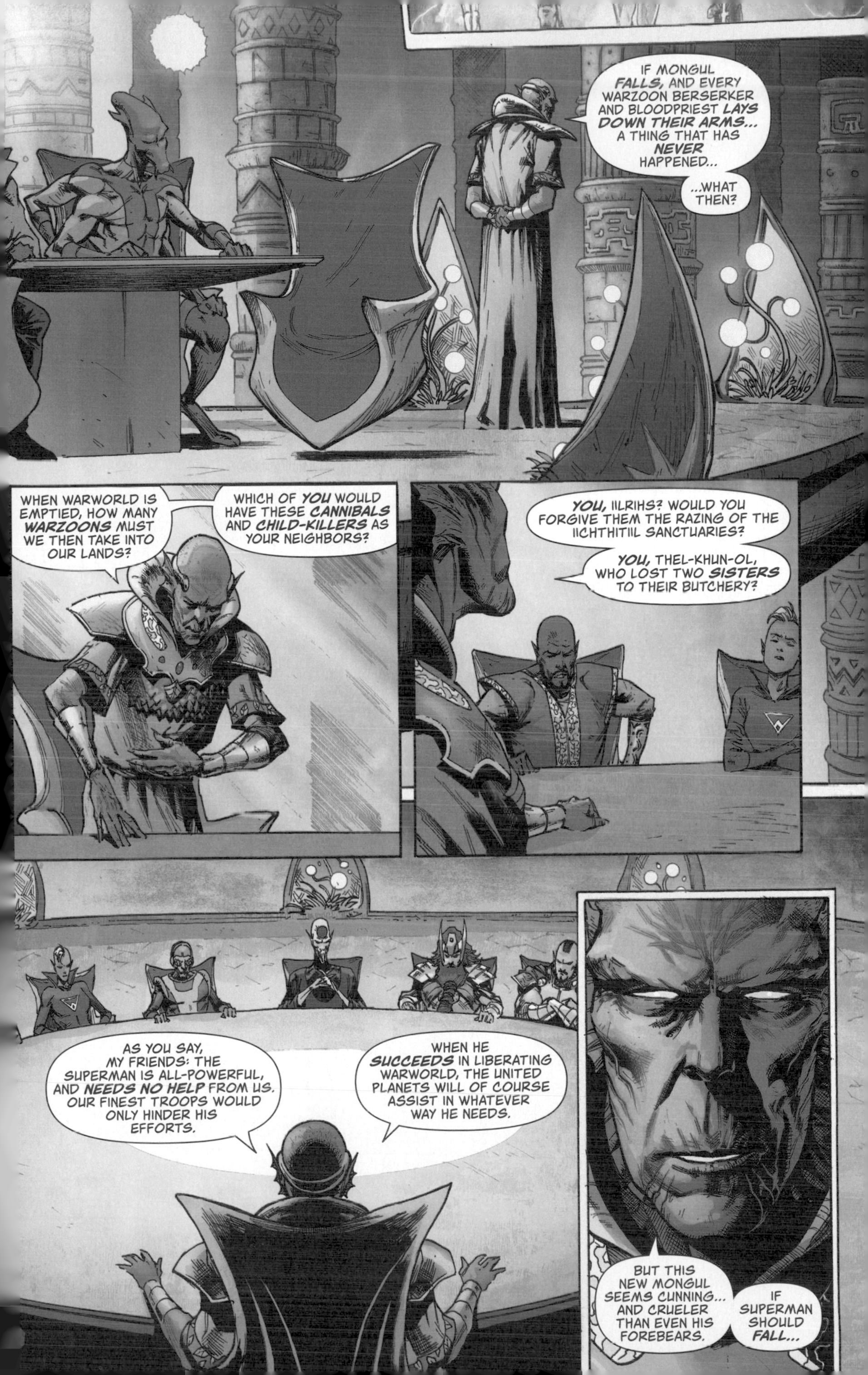
IF MONGUL FALLS, AND EVERY WARZOON BERSERKER AND BLOODPRIEST LAYS DOWN THEIR ARMS... A THING THAT HAS NEVER HAPPENED...
...WHAT THEN?
WHEN WARWORLD IS EMPTIED, HOW MANY WARZOONS MUST WE THEN TAKE INTO OUR LANDS?
WHICH OF YOU WOULD HAVE THESE CANNIBALS AND CHILD-KILLERS AS YOUR NEIGHBORS?
YOU, IILRIHS? WOULD YOU FORGIVE THEM THE RAZING OF THE IICHTHITIIL SANCTUARIES?
YOU, THEL-KHUN-OL, WHO LOST TWO SISTERS TO THEIR BUTCHERY?
AS YOU SAY, MY FRIENDS: THE SUPERMAN IS ALL-POWERFUL, AND NEEDS NO HELP FROM US. OUR FINEST TROOPS WOULD ONLY HINDER HIS EFFORTS.
WHEN HE SUCCEEDS IN LIBERATING WARWORLD, THE UNITED PLANETS WILL OF COURSE ASSIST IN WHATEVER WAY HE NEEDS.
BUT THIS NEW MONGUL SEEMS CUNNING... AND CRUELER THAN EVEN HIS FOREBEARS.
IF SUPERMAN SHOULD FALL...

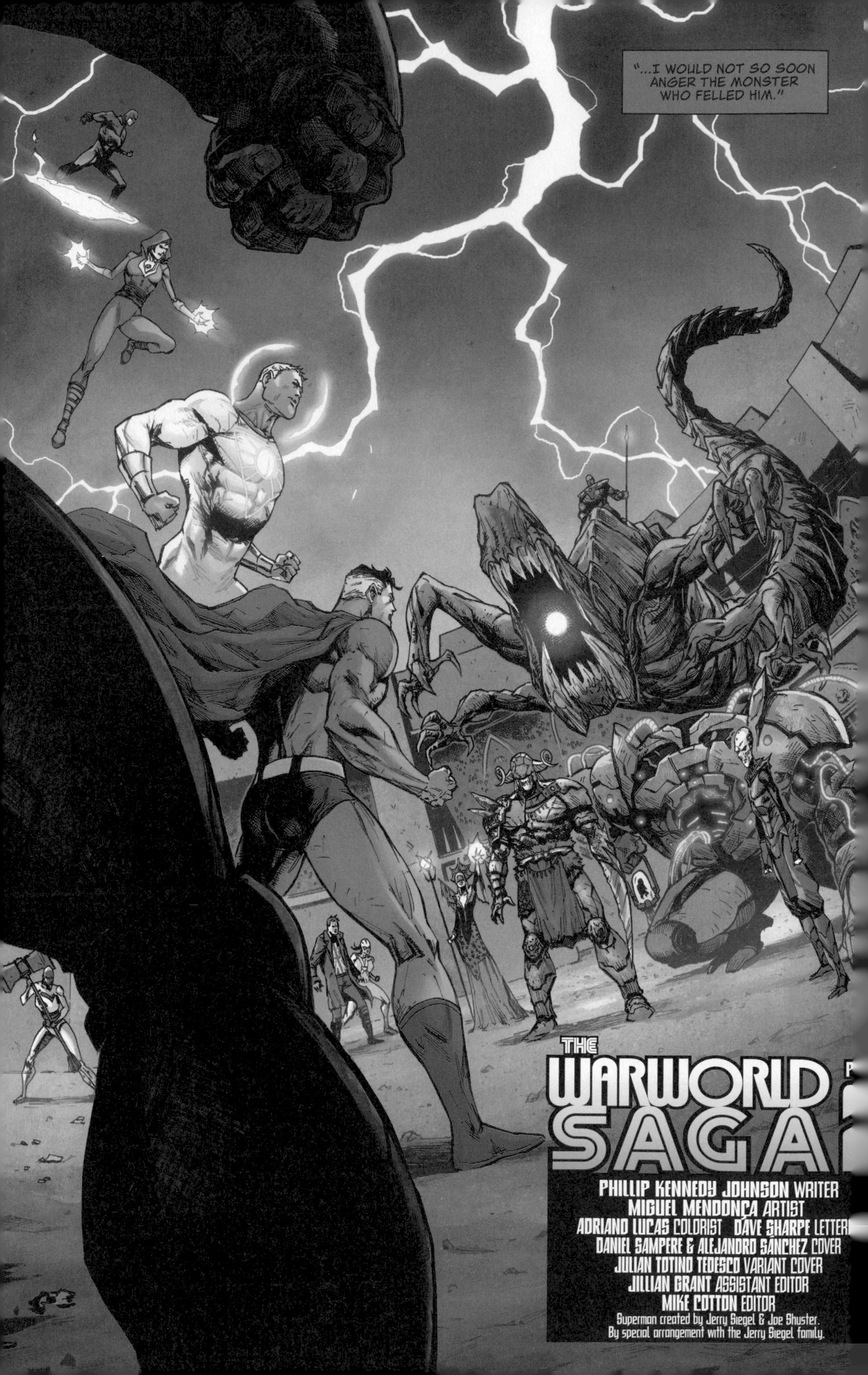
"...I WOULD NOT SO SOON ANGER THE MONSTER WHO FELLED HIM."
THE WARWORLD SAGA
PHILLIP KENNEDY JOHNSON WRITER
MIGUEL MENDONÇA ARTIST
ADRIANO LUCAS COLORIST DAVE SHARPE LETTER
DANIEL SAMPERE & ALEJANDRO SÁNCHEZ COVER
JULIAN TOTINO TEDESCO VARIANT COVER
JILLIAN GRANT ASSISTANT EDITOR
MIKE COTTON EDITOR
Superman created by Jerry Siegel & Joe Shuster.
By special arrangement with the Jerry Siegel family.

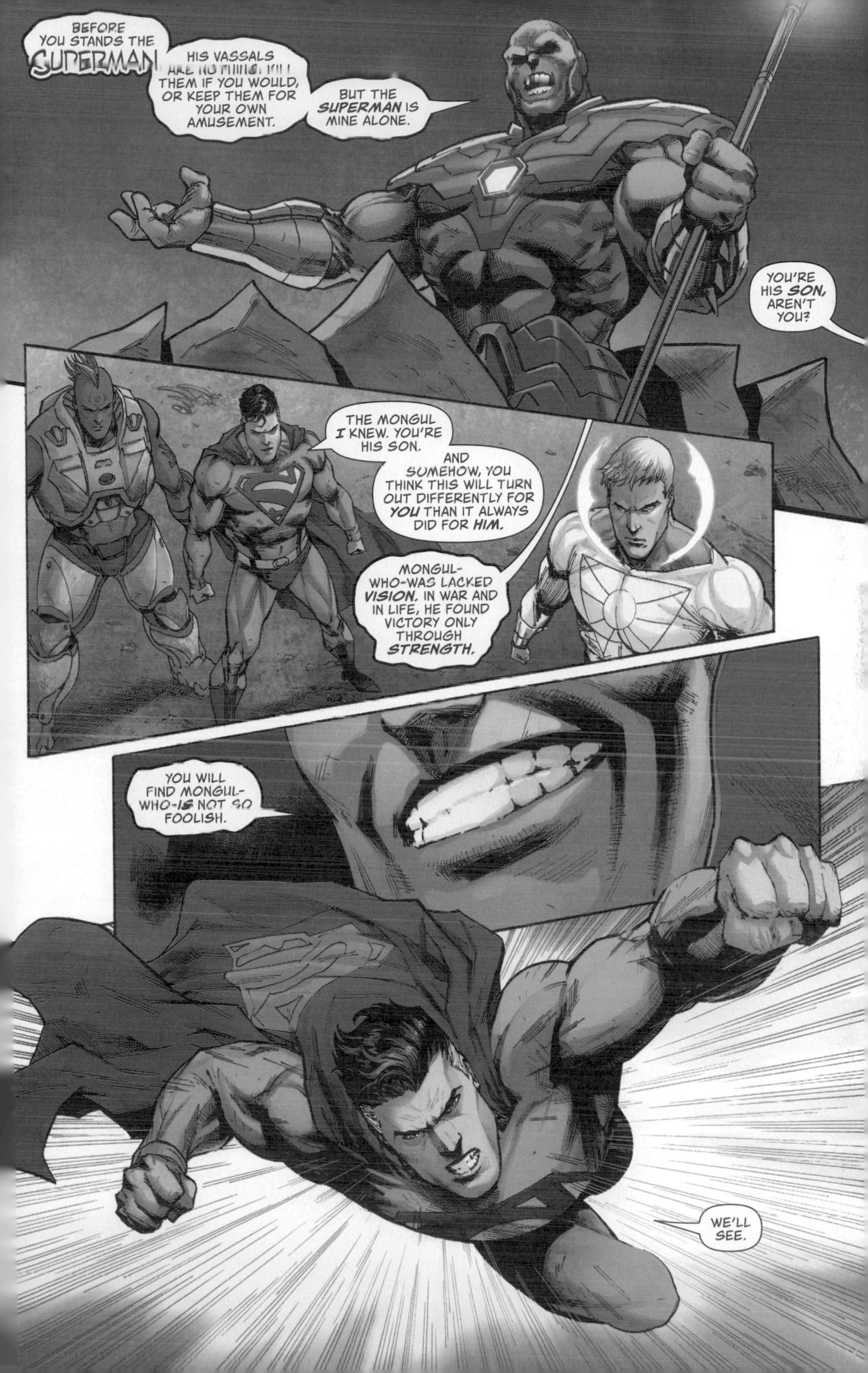

BEFORE YOU STANDS THE SUPERMAN.
HIS VASSALS ARE NOTHING. KILL THEM IF YOU WOULD, OR KEEP THEM FOR YOUR OWN AMUSEMENT.
BUT THE SUPERMAN IS MINE ALONE.
YOU'RE HIS SON, AREN'T YOU?
THE MONGUL I KNEW. YOU'RE HIS SON.
AND SOMEHOW, YOU THINK THIS WILL TURN OUT DIFFERENTLY FOR YOU THAN IT ALWAYS DID FOR HIM.
MONGUL-WHO-WAS LACKED VISION. IN WAR AND IN LIFE, HE FOUND VICTORY ONLY THROUGH STRENGTH.
YOU WILL FIND MONGUL-WHO-IS NOT SO FOOLISH.
WE'LL SEE.

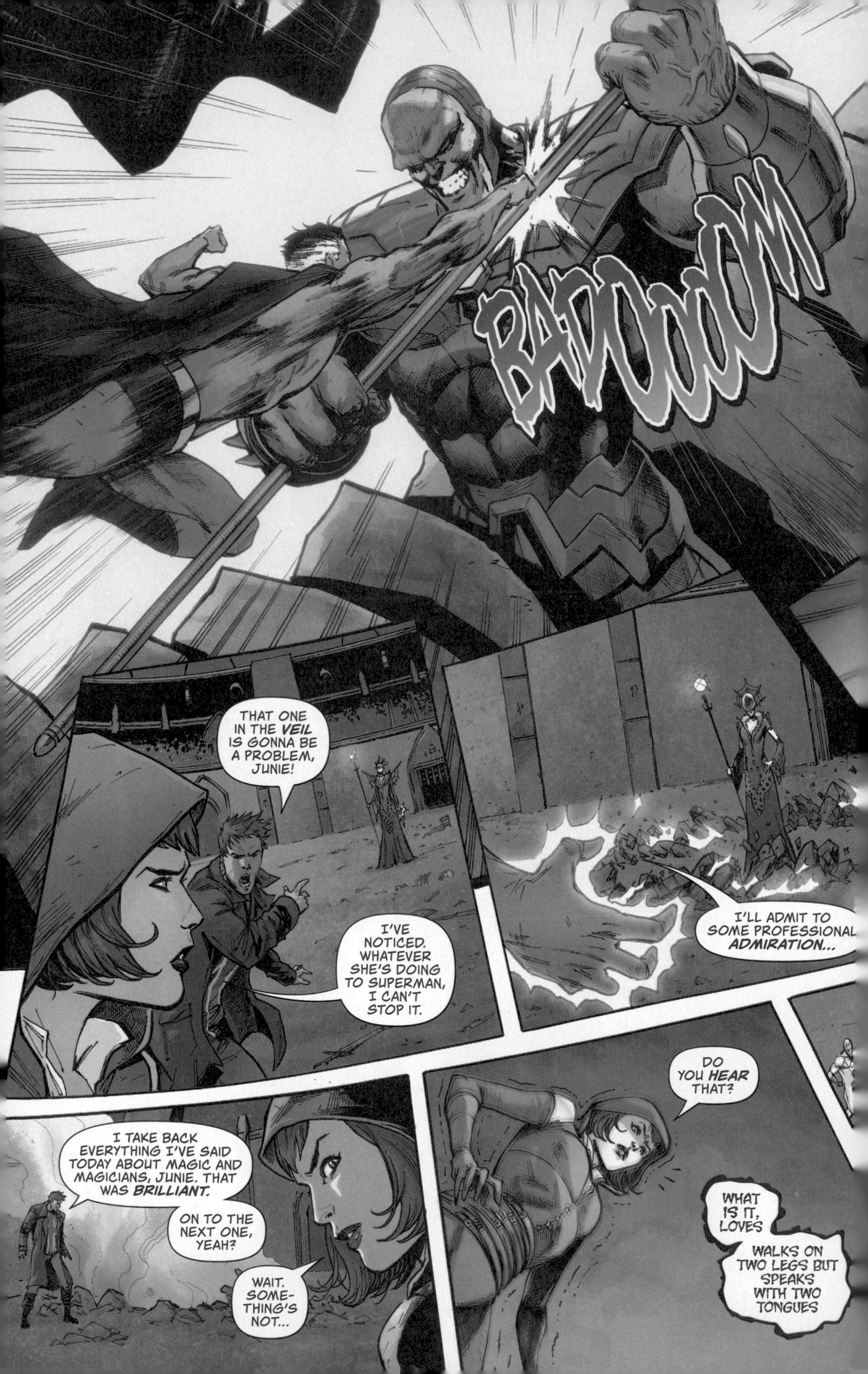
BADOOOM
THAT ONE IN THE VEIL IS GONNA BE A PROBLEM, JUNIE!
I'VE NOTICED. WHATEVER SHE'S DOING TO SUPERMAN, I CAN'T STOP IT.
I'LL ADMIT TO SOME PROFESSIONAL ADMIRATION...
I TAKE BACK EVERYTHING I'VE SAID TODAY ABOUT MAGIC AND MAGICIANS, JUNIE. THAT WAS BRILLIANT.
ON TO THE NEXT ONE, YEAH?
WAIT. SOME-THING'S NOT...
DO YOU HEAR THAT?
WHAT IS IT, LOVES
WALKS ON TWO LEGS BUT SPEAKS WITH TWO TONGUES

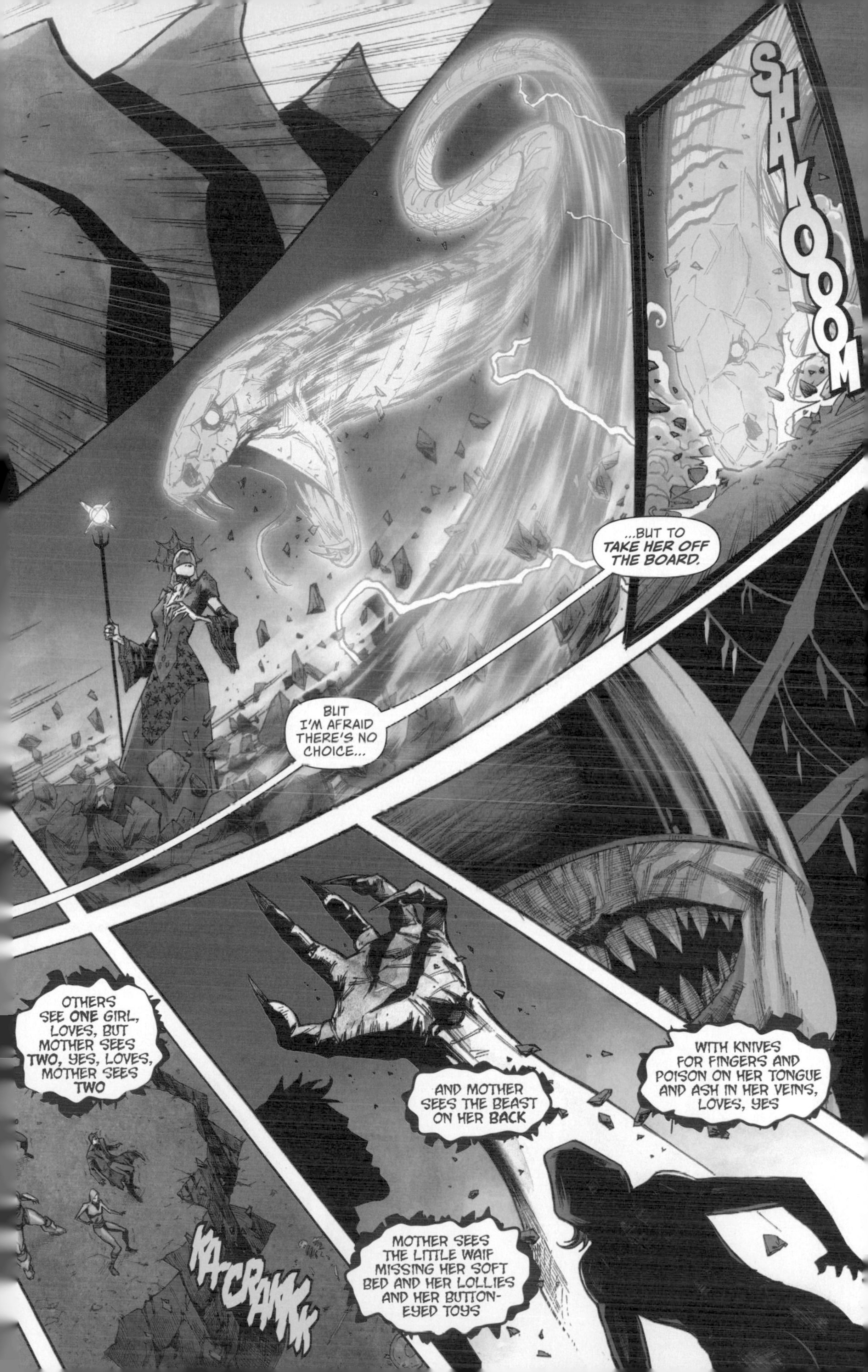
SHAKOOOOM
...BUT TO TAKE HER OFF THE BOARD.
BUT I'M AFRAID THERE'S NO CHOICE...
OTHERS SEE ONE GIRL, LOVES, BUT MOTHER SEES TWO, YES, LOVES, MOTHER SEES TWO
AND MOTHER SEES THE BEAST ON HER BACK
WITH KNIVES FOR FINGERS AND POISON ON HER TONGUE AND ASH IN HER VEINS, LOVES, YES
KA-CRANKK
MOTHER SEES THE LITTLE WAIF MISSING HER SOFT BED AND HER LOLLIES AND HER BUTTON-EYED TOYS

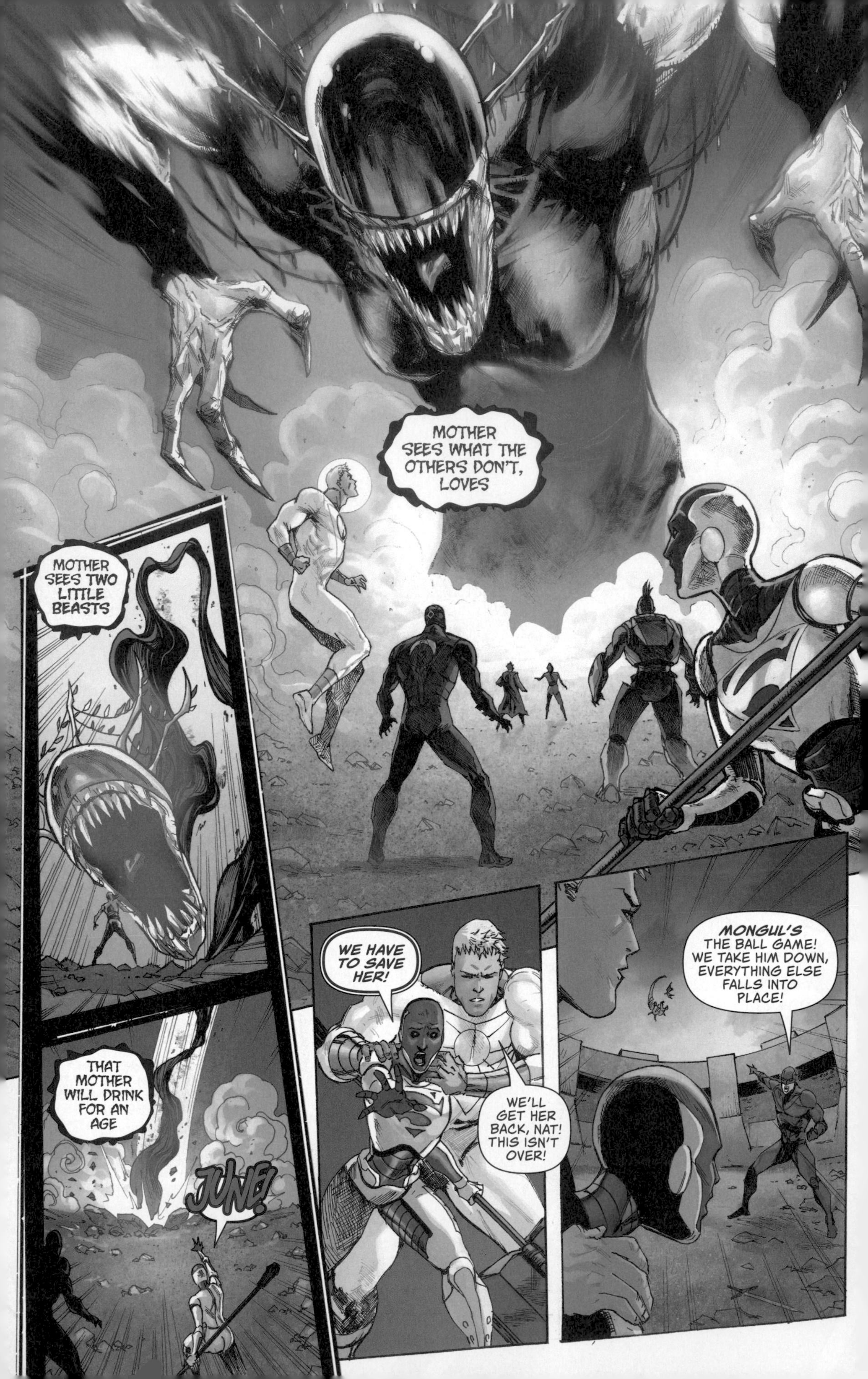
MOTHER SEES WHAT THE OTHERS DON'T, LOVES
MOTHER SEES TWO LITTLE BEASTS
THAT MOTHER WILL DRINK FOR AN AGE
JUNE!
WE HAVE TO SAVE HER!
WE'LL GET HER BACK, NAT! THIS ISN'T OVER!
MONGUL'S THE BALL GAME! WE TAKE HIM DOWN, EVERYTHING ELSE FALLS INTO PLACE!

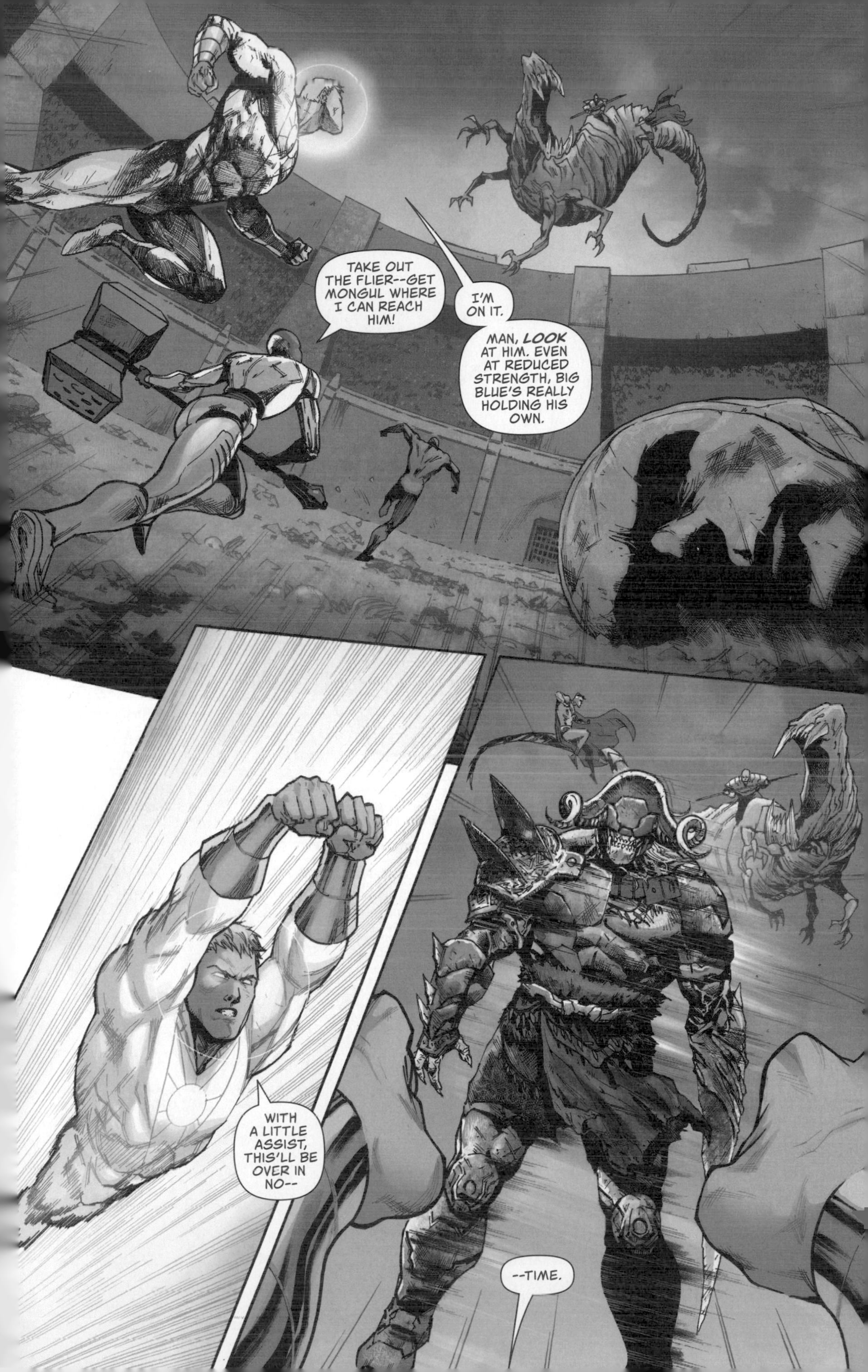
TAKE OUT THE FLIER--GET MONGUL WHERE I CAN REACH HIM!
I'M ON IT.
MAN, LOOK AT HIM. EVEN AT REDUCED STRENGTH, BIG BLUE'S REALLY HOLDING HIS OWN.
WITH A LITTLE ASSIST, THIS'LL BE OVER IN NO--
--TIME.

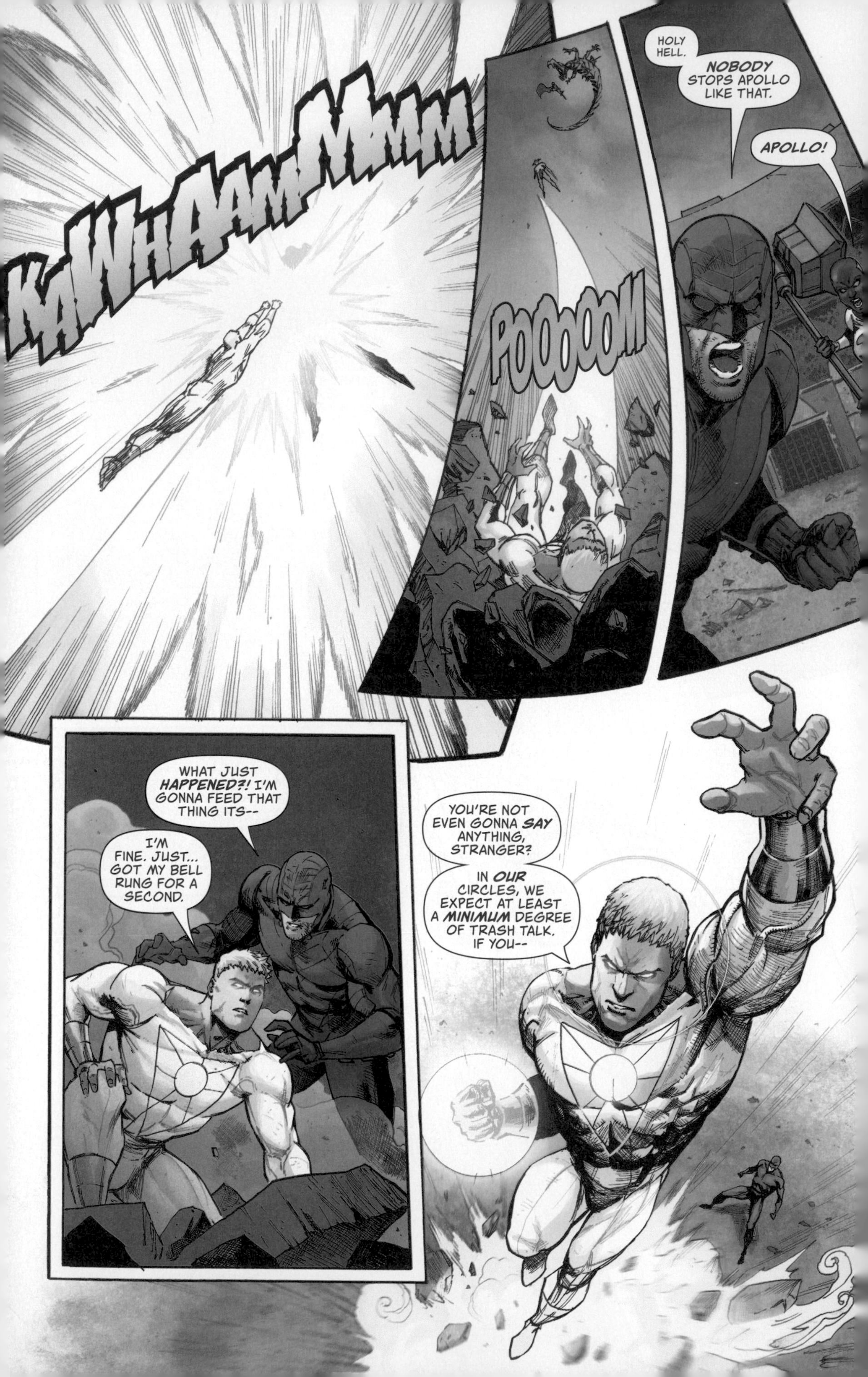
KAWHAAMMMM
POOOOOM
HOLY HELL. NOBODY STOPS APOLLO LIKE THAT.
APOLLO!
WHAT JUST HAPPENED?! I'M GONNA FEED THAT THING ITS--
I'M FINE. JUST... GOT MY BELL RUNG FOR A SECOND.
YOU'RE NOT EVEN GONNA SAY ANYTHING, STRANGER?
IN OUR CIRCLES, WE EXPECT AT LEAST A MINIMUM DEGREE OF TRASH TALK. IF YOU--

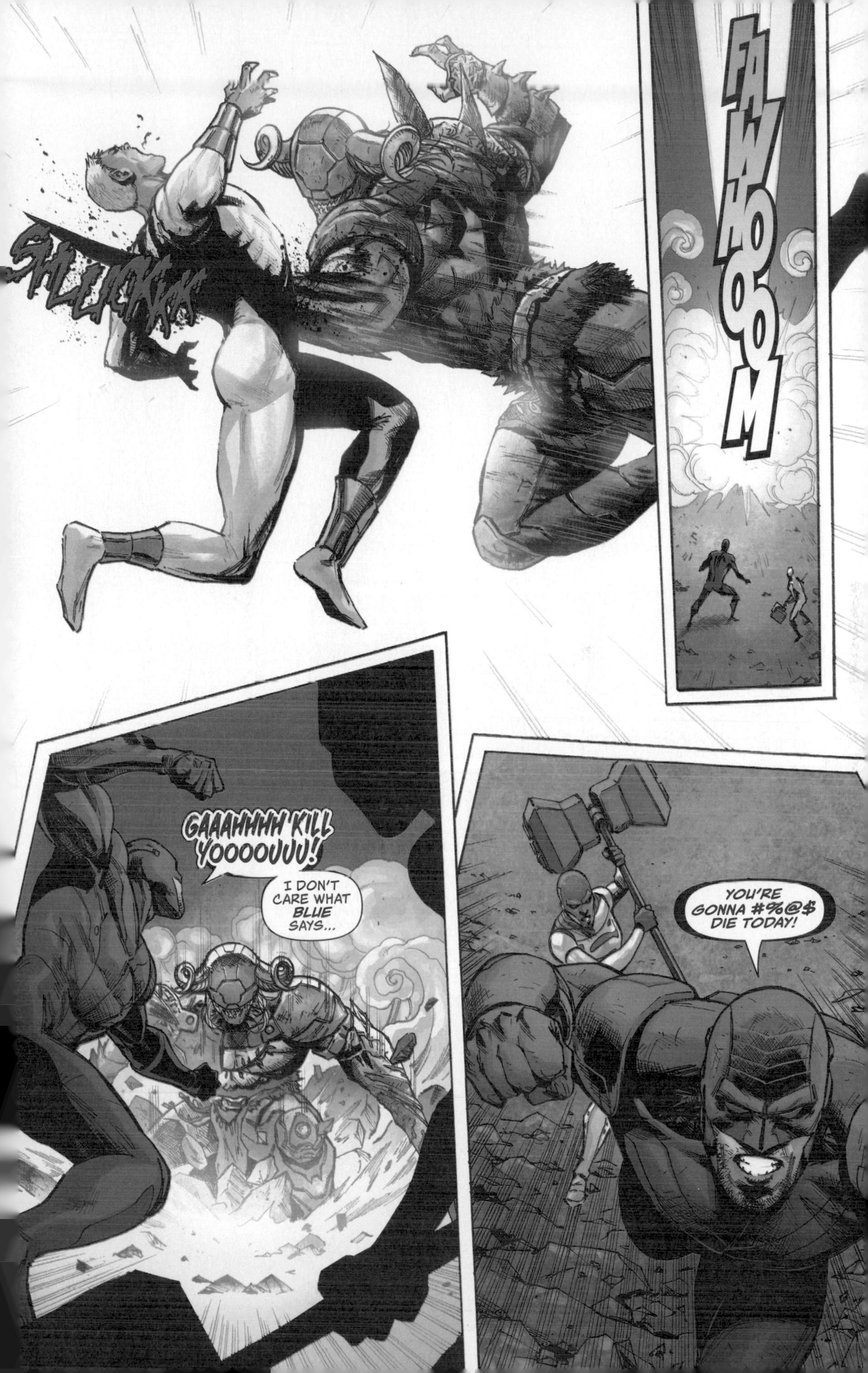
SHLUCKKK
FAWHOOOOM
GAAAHHHH KILL YOOOOUUU!
I DON'T CARE WHAT BLUE SAYS...
YOU'RE GONNA #%@$ DIE TODAY!

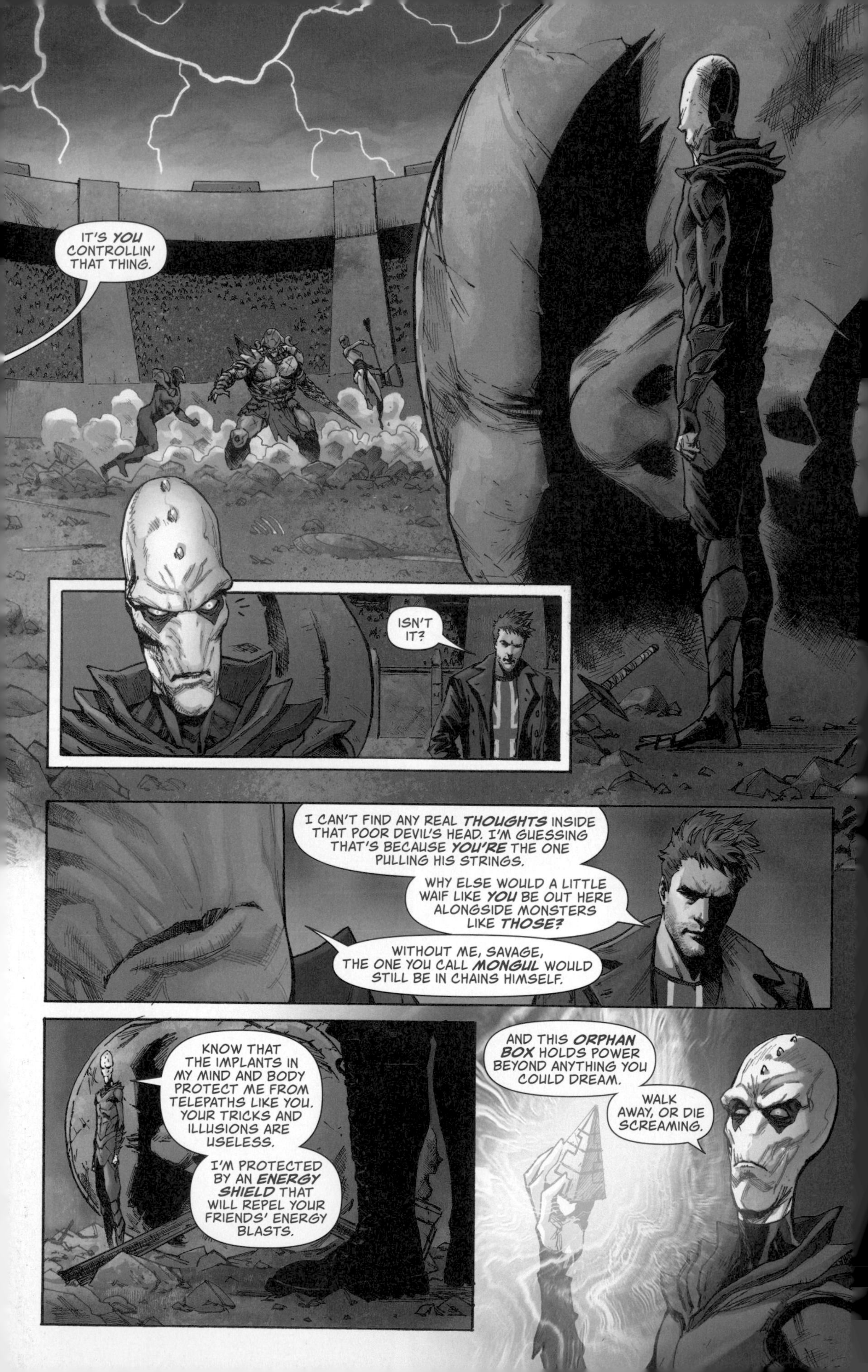
IT'S YOU CONTROLLIN' THAT THING.
ISN'T IT?
I CAN'T FIND ANY REAL THOUGHTS INSIDE THAT POOR DEVIL'S HEAD. I'M GUESSING THAT'S BECAUSE YOU'RE THE ONE PULLING HIS STRINGS.
WHY ELSE WOULD A LITTLE WAIF LIKE YOU BE OUT HERE ALONGSIDE MONSTERS LIKE THOSE?
WITHOUT ME, SAVAGE, THE ONE YOU CALL MONGUL WOULD STILL BE IN CHAINS HIMSELF.
KNOW THAT THE IMPLANTS IN MY MIND AND BODY PROTECT ME FROM TELEPATHS LIKE YOU. YOUR TRICKS AND ILLUSIONS ARE USELESS.
I'M PROTECTED BY AN ENERGY SHIELD THAT WILL REPEL YOUR FRIENDS' ENERGY BLASTS.
AND THIS ORPHAN BOX HOLDS POWER BEYOND ANYTHING YOU COULD DREAM.
WALK AWAY, OR DIE SCREAMING.

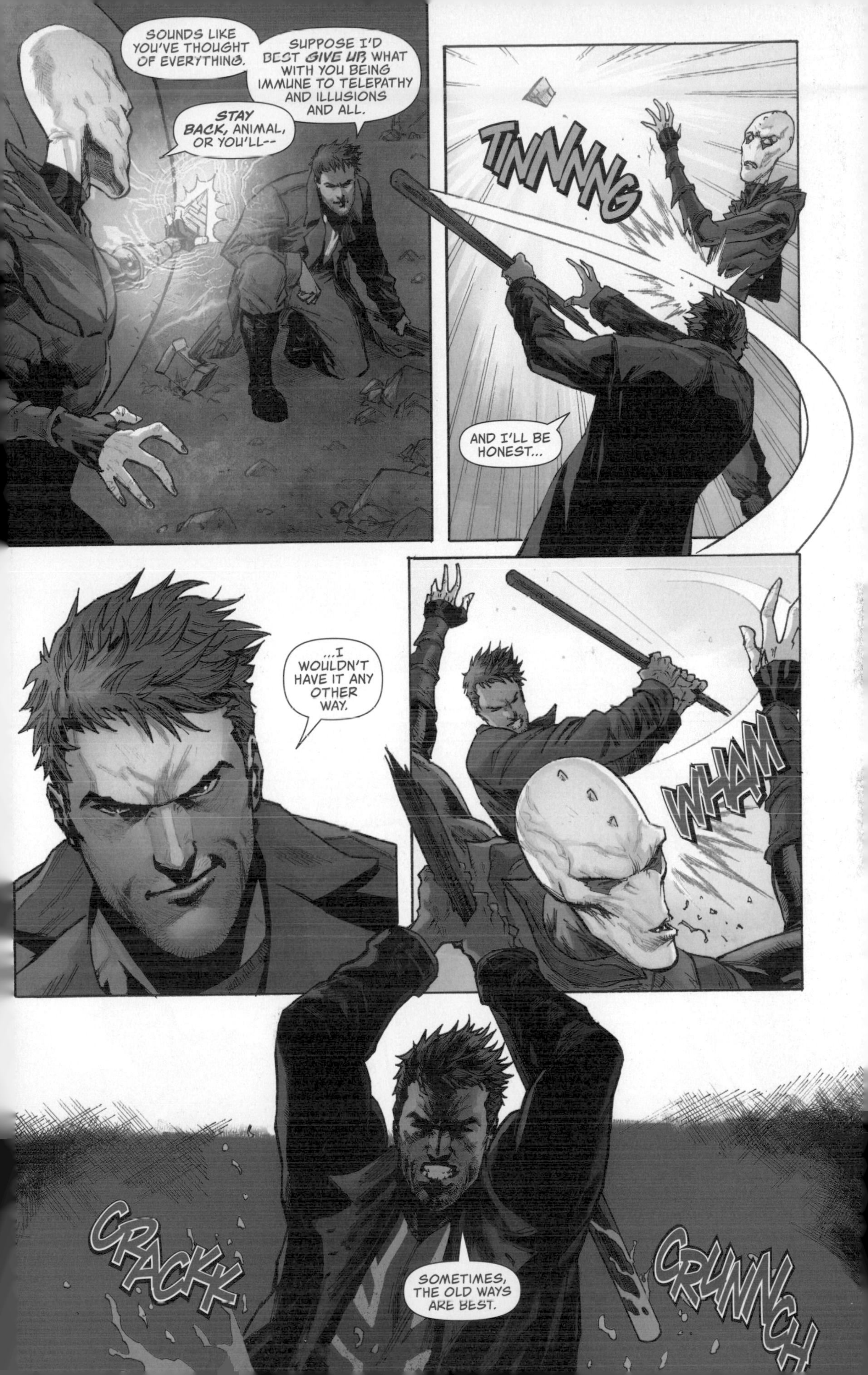

SOUNDS LIKE YOU'VE THOUGHT OF EVERYTHING.
SUPPOSE I'D BEST GIVE UP, WHAT WITH YOU BEING IMMUNE TO TELEPATHY AND ILLUSIONS AND ALL.
STAY BACK, ANIMAL, OR YOU'LL--
TINNNNG
AND I'LL BE HONEST...
...I WOULDN'T HAVE IT ANY OTHER WAY.
WHAM
CRACKK
CRUNNCH
SOMETIMES, THE OLD WAYS ARE BEST.

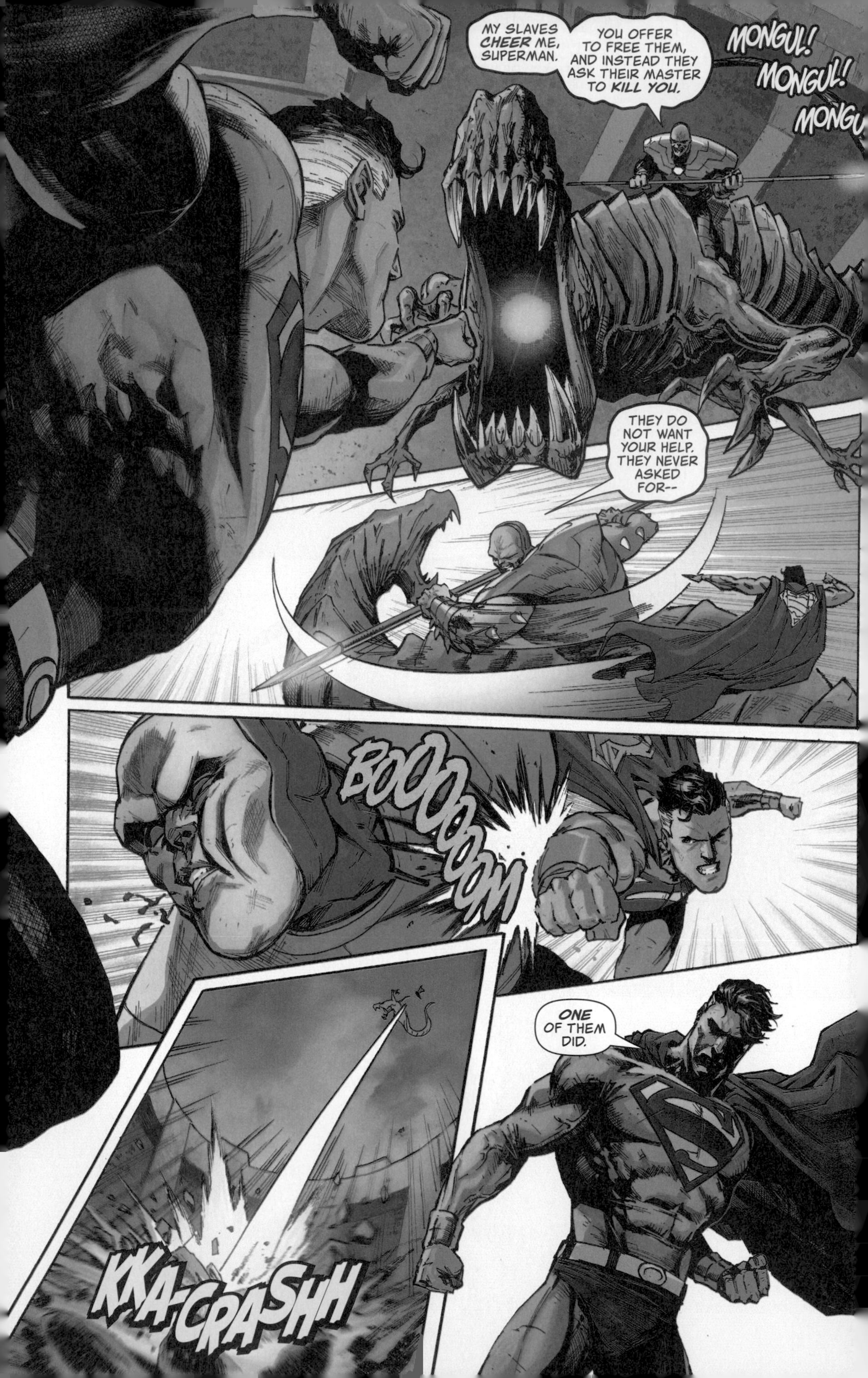
MY SLAVES CHEER ME, SUPERMAN.
YOU OFFER TO FREE THEM, AND INSTEAD THEY ASK THEIR MASTER TO KILL YOU.
MONGUL! MONGUL! MONGU
THEY DO NOT WANT YOUR HELP. THEY NEVER ASKED FOR--
BOOOOOOOM
ONE OF THEM DID.
KKA-CRASHH

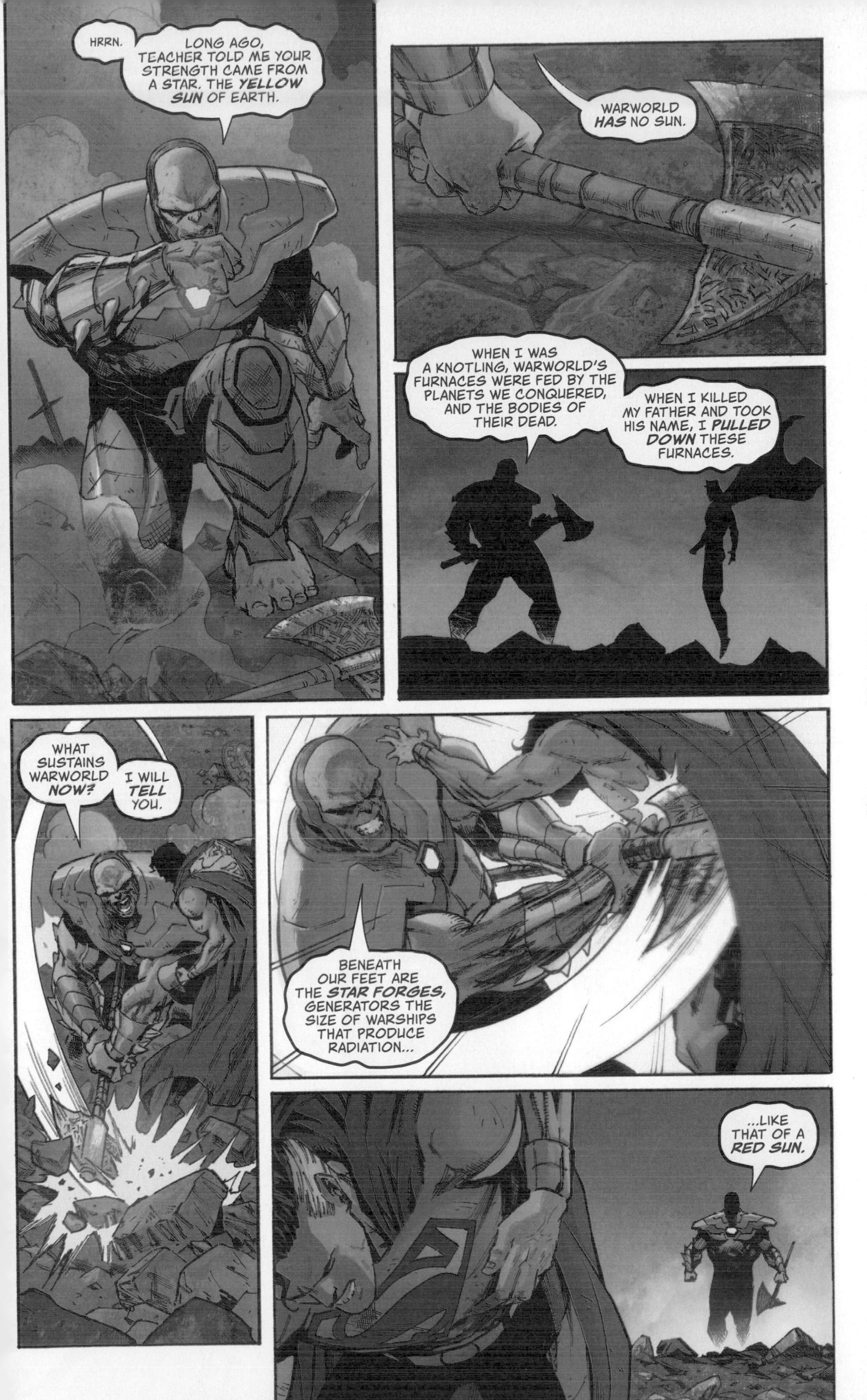
HRRN.
LONG AGO, TEACHER TOLD ME YOUR STRENGTH CAME FROM A STAR. THE YELLOW SUN OF EARTH.
WARWORLD HAS NO SUN.
WHEN I WAS A KNOTLING, WARWORLD'S FURNACES WERE FED BY THE PLANETS WE CONQUERED, AND THE BODIES OF THEIR DEAD.
WHEN I KILLED MY FATHER AND TOOK HIS NAME, I PULLED DOWN THESE FURNACES.
WHAT SUSTAINS WARWORLD NOW?
I WILL TELL YOU.
BENEATH OUR FEET ARE THE STAR FORGES, GENERATORS THE SIZE OF WARSHIPS THAT PRODUCE RADIATION...
...LIKE THAT OF A RED SUN.

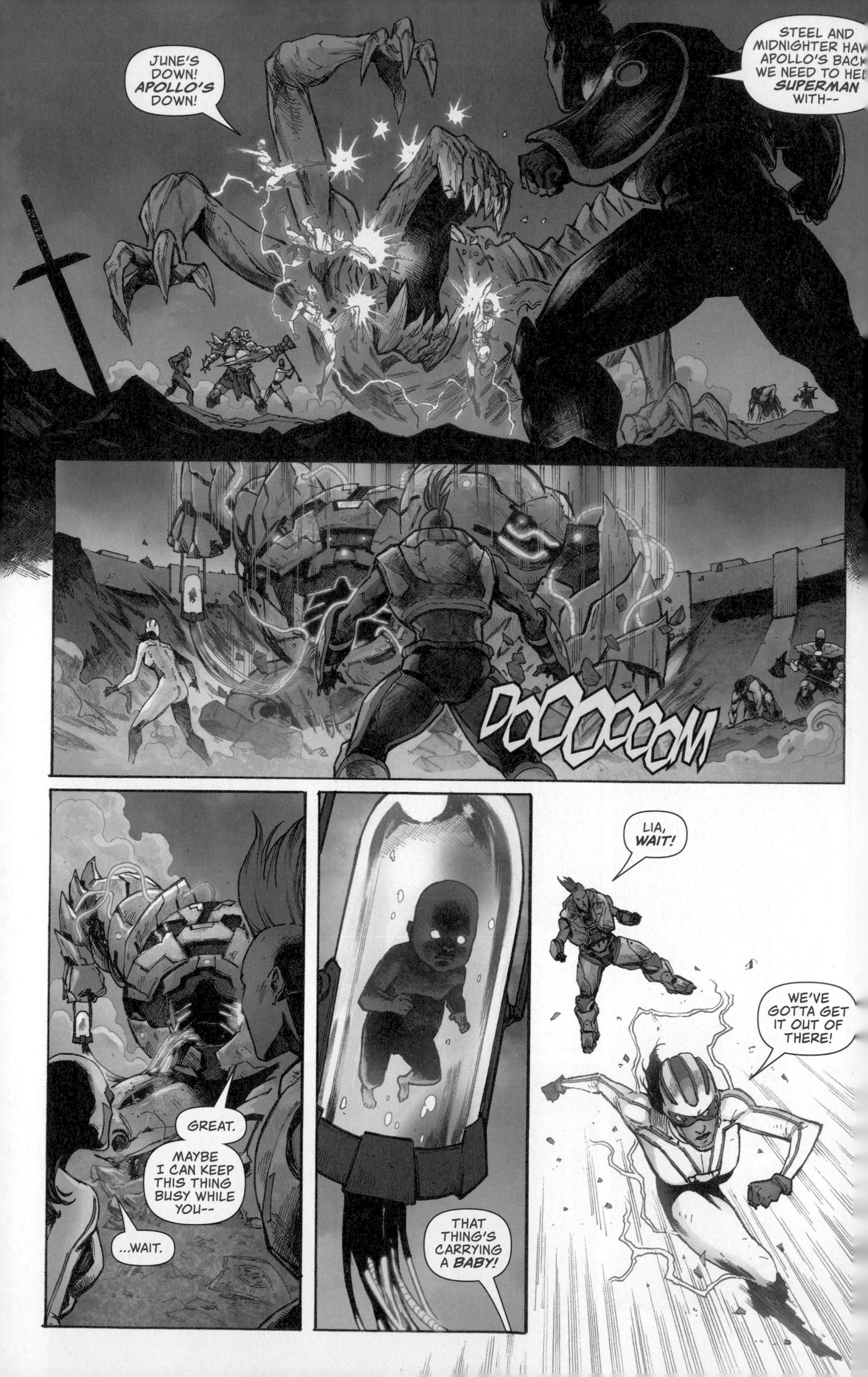
JUNE'S DOWN! APOLLO'S DOWN!
STEEL AND MIDNIGHTER HAVE APOLLO'S BACK. WE NEED TO HELP SUPERMAN WITH--
DOOOOOOOM
GREAT.
MAYBE I CAN KEEP THIS THING BUSY WHILE YOU--
...WAIT.
THAT THING'S CARRYING A BABY!
LIA, WAIT!
WE'VE GOTTA GET IT OUT OF THERE!

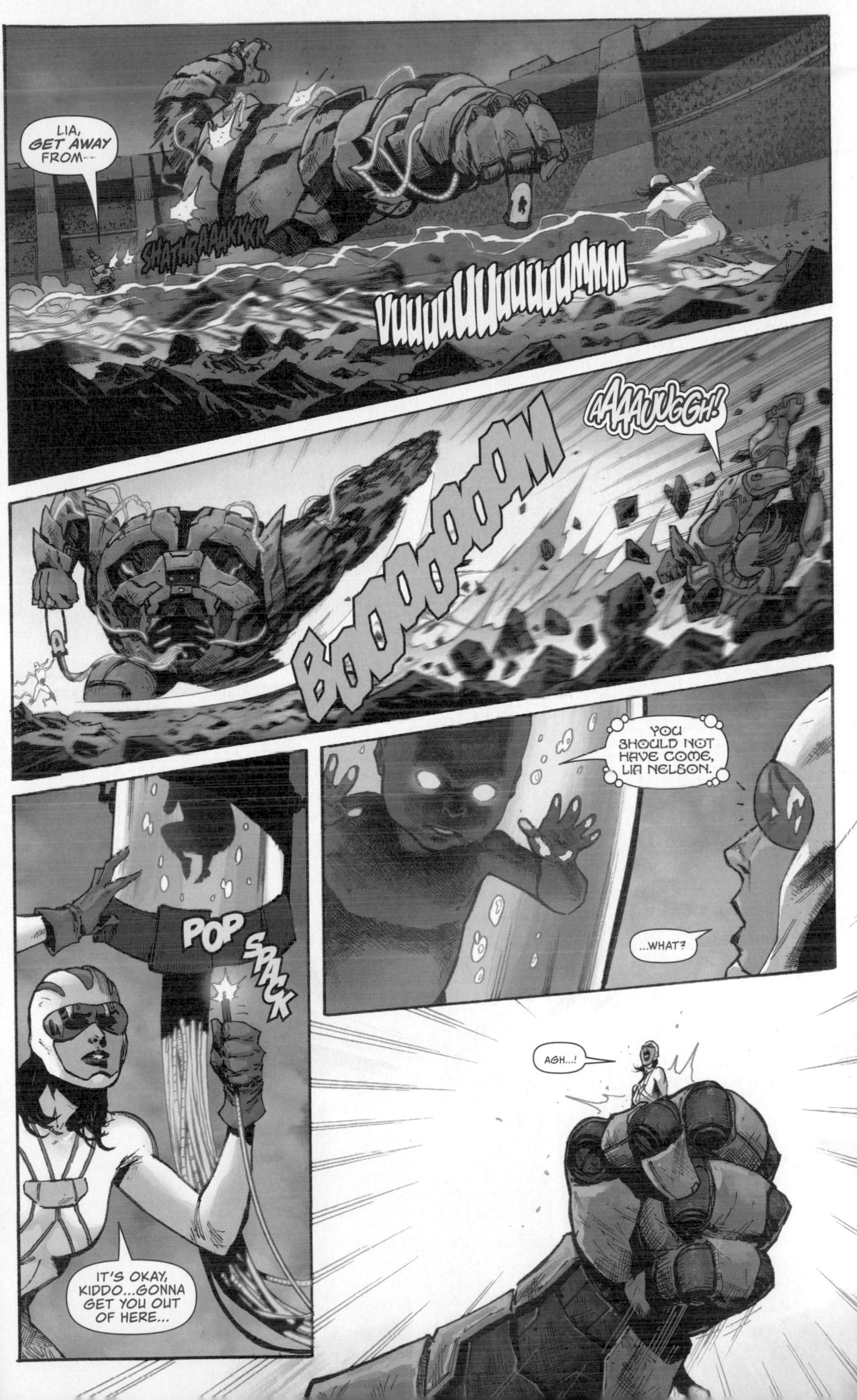
LIA, GET AWAY FROM--
SHATHRAAAKKKK
VUUUUUUUUUUUMMM
AAAAUUGGH!
BOOOOOOOM
YOU SHOULD NOT HAVE COME, LIA NELSON.
...WHAT?
POP
SPACK
IT'S OKAY, KIDDO...GONNA GET YOU OUT OF HERE...
AGH...!

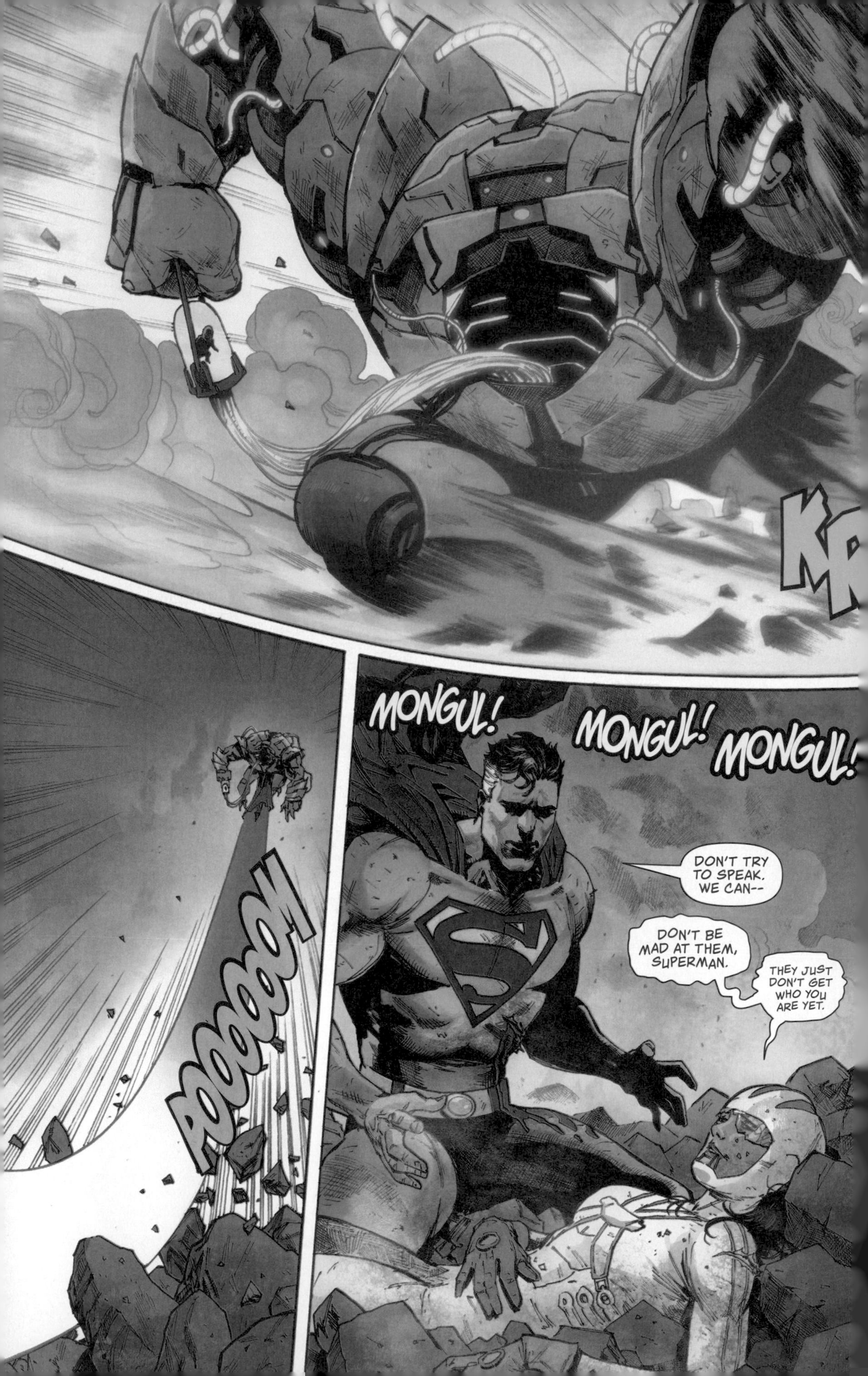
KR
POOOOOOM
MONGUL!
MONGUL!
MONGUL!
DON'T TRY TO SPEAK. WE CAN--
DON'T BE MAD AT THEM, SUPERMAN.
THEY JUST DON'T GET WHO YOU ARE YET.

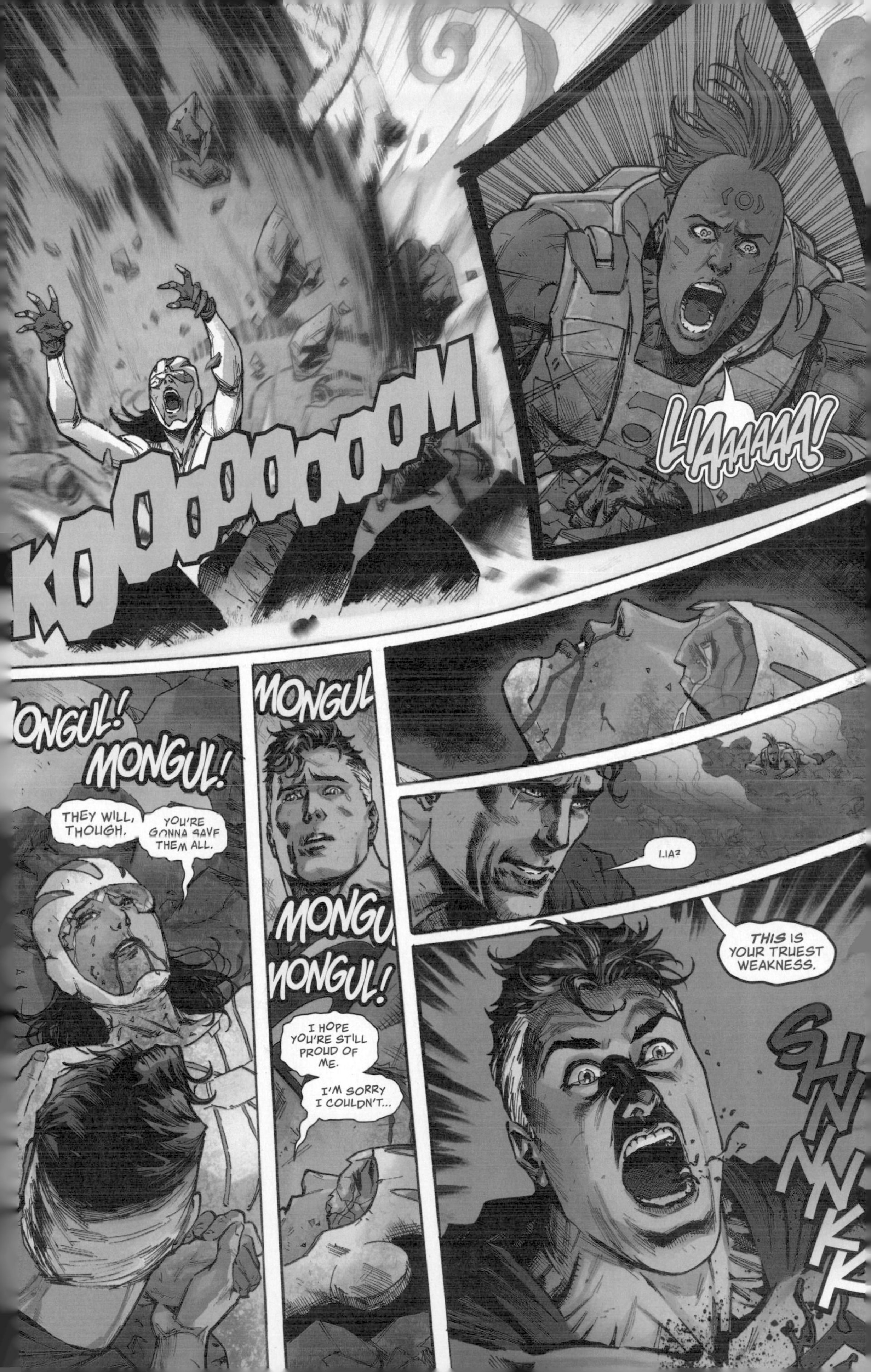
KOOOOOOOOOM
LIAAAAAA!
ONGUL!
MONGUL!
THEY WILL, THOUGH.
YOU'RE GONNA SAVE THEM ALL.
MONGUL
MONGU
NONGUL!
I HOPE YOU'RE STILL PROUD OF ME.
I'M SORRY I COULDN'T...
LIA?
THIS IS YOUR TRUEST WEAKNESS.
SHNNNK

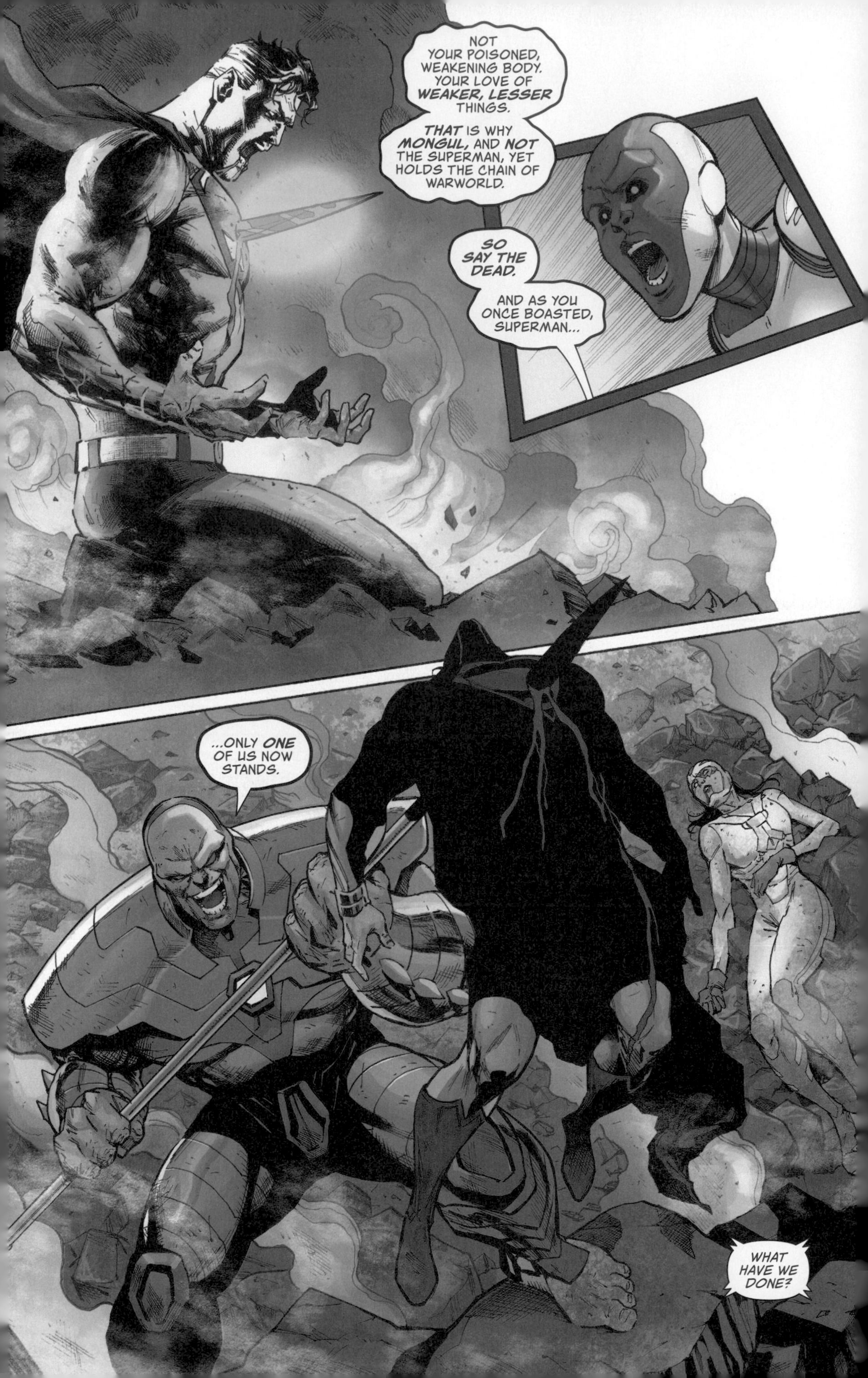
NOT YOUR POISONED, WEAKENING BODY. YOUR LOVE OF WEAKER, LESSER THINGS.
THAT IS WHY MONGUL, AND NOT THE SUPERMAN, YET HOLDS THE CHAIN OF WARWORLD.
SO SAY THE DEAD.
AND AS YOU ONCE BOASTED, SUPERMAN...
...ONLY ONE OF US NOW STANDS.
WHAT HAVE WE DONE?

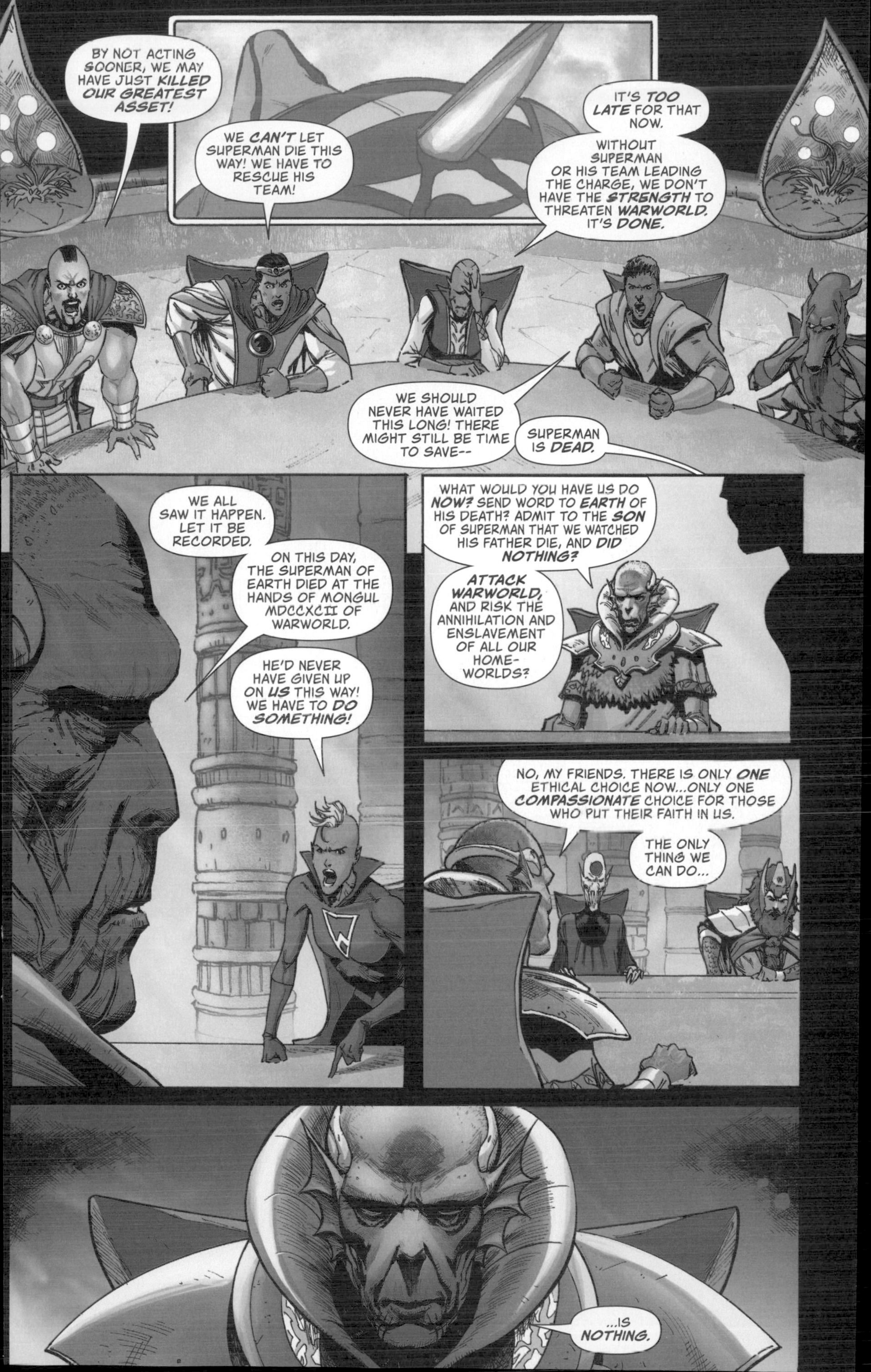

BY NOT ACTING SOONER, WE MAY HAVE JUST KILLED OUR GREATEST ASSET!
WE CAN'T LET SUPERMAN DIE THIS WAY! WE HAVE TO RESCUE HIS TEAM!
IT'S TOO LATE FOR THAT NOW.
WITHOUT SUPERMAN OR HIS TEAM LEADING THE CHARGE, WE DON'T HAVE THE STRENGTH TO THREATEN WARWORLD. IT'S DONE.
WE SHOULD NEVER HAVE WAITED THIS LONG! THERE MIGHT STILL BE TIME TO SAVE--
SUPERMAN IS DEAD.
WE ALL SAW IT HAPPEN. LET IT BE RECORDED.
ON THIS DAY, THE SUPERMAN OF EARTH DIED AT THE HANDS OF MONGUL MDCCXCII OF WARWORLD.
HE'D NEVER HAVE GIVEN UP ON US THIS WAY! WE HAVE TO DO SOMETHING!
WHAT WOULD YOU HAVE US DO NOW? SEND WORD TO EARTH OF HIS DEATH? ADMIT TO THE SON OF SUPERMAN THAT WE WATCHED HIS FATHER DIE, AND DID NOTHING?
ATTACK WARWORLD, AND RISK THE ANNIHILATION AND ENSLAVEMENT OF ALL OUR HOME-WORLDS?
NO, MY FRIENDS. THERE IS ONLY ONE ETHICAL CHOICE NOW...ONLY ONE COMPASSIONATE CHOICE FOR THOSE WHO PUT THEIR FAITH IN US.
THE ONLY THING WE CAN DO...
...IS NOTHING.

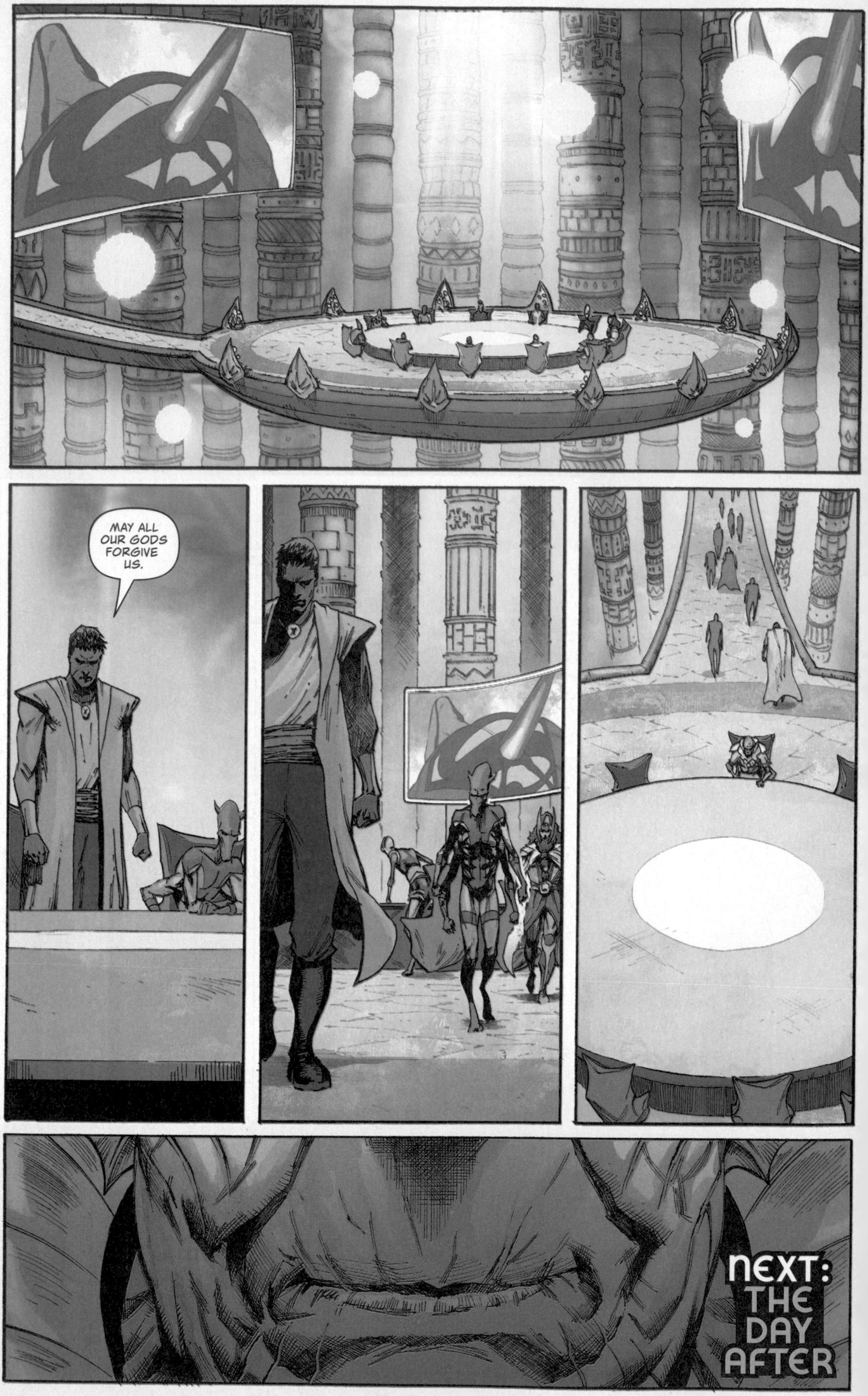
MAY ALL OUR GODS FORGIVE US.
NEXT: THE DAY AFTER

Action Comics #1038
main cover by DANIEL SAMPERE and ALEJANDRO SÁNCHEZ

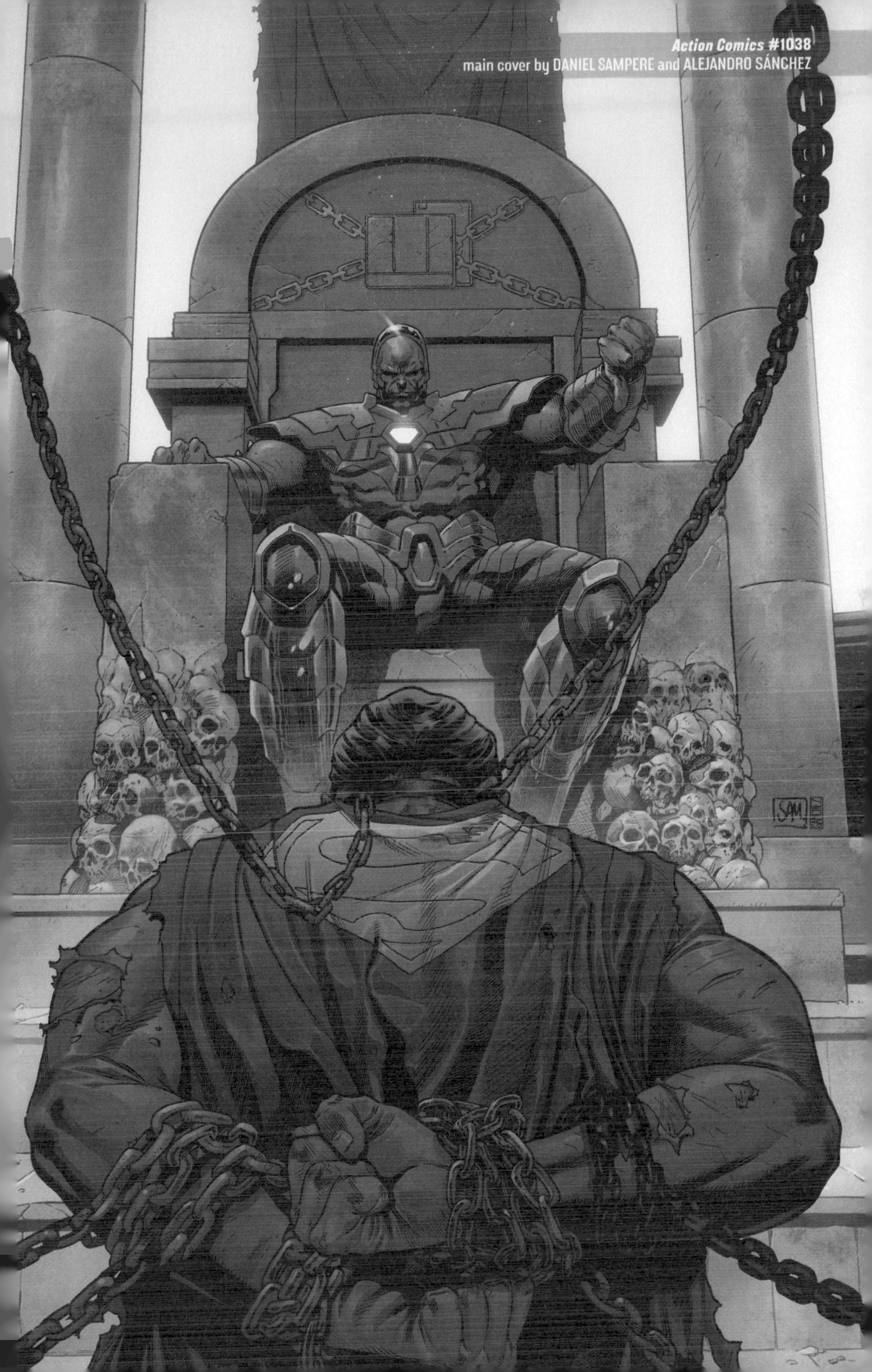

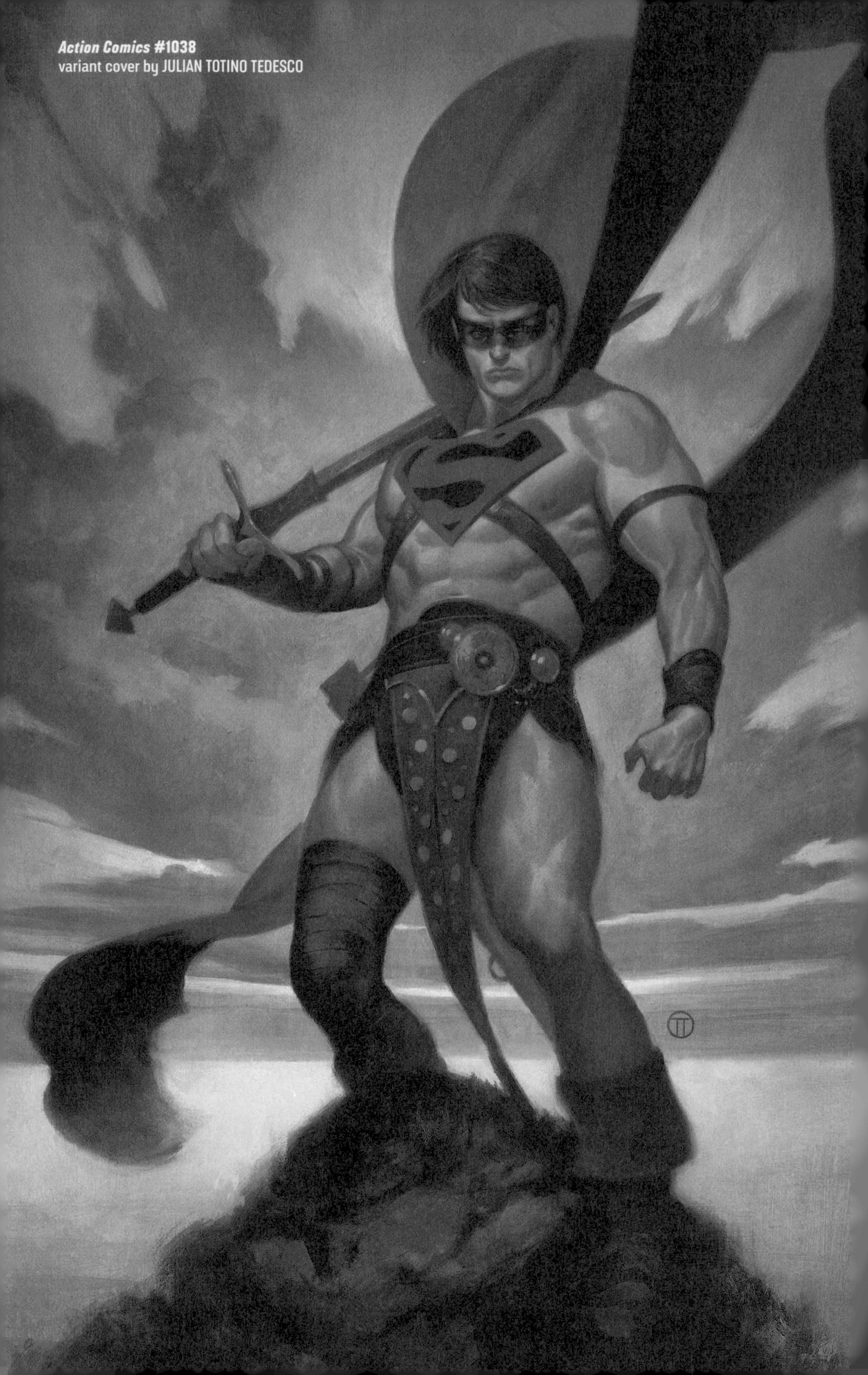

***Action Comics* #1038**
variant cover by JULIAN TOTINO TEDESCO

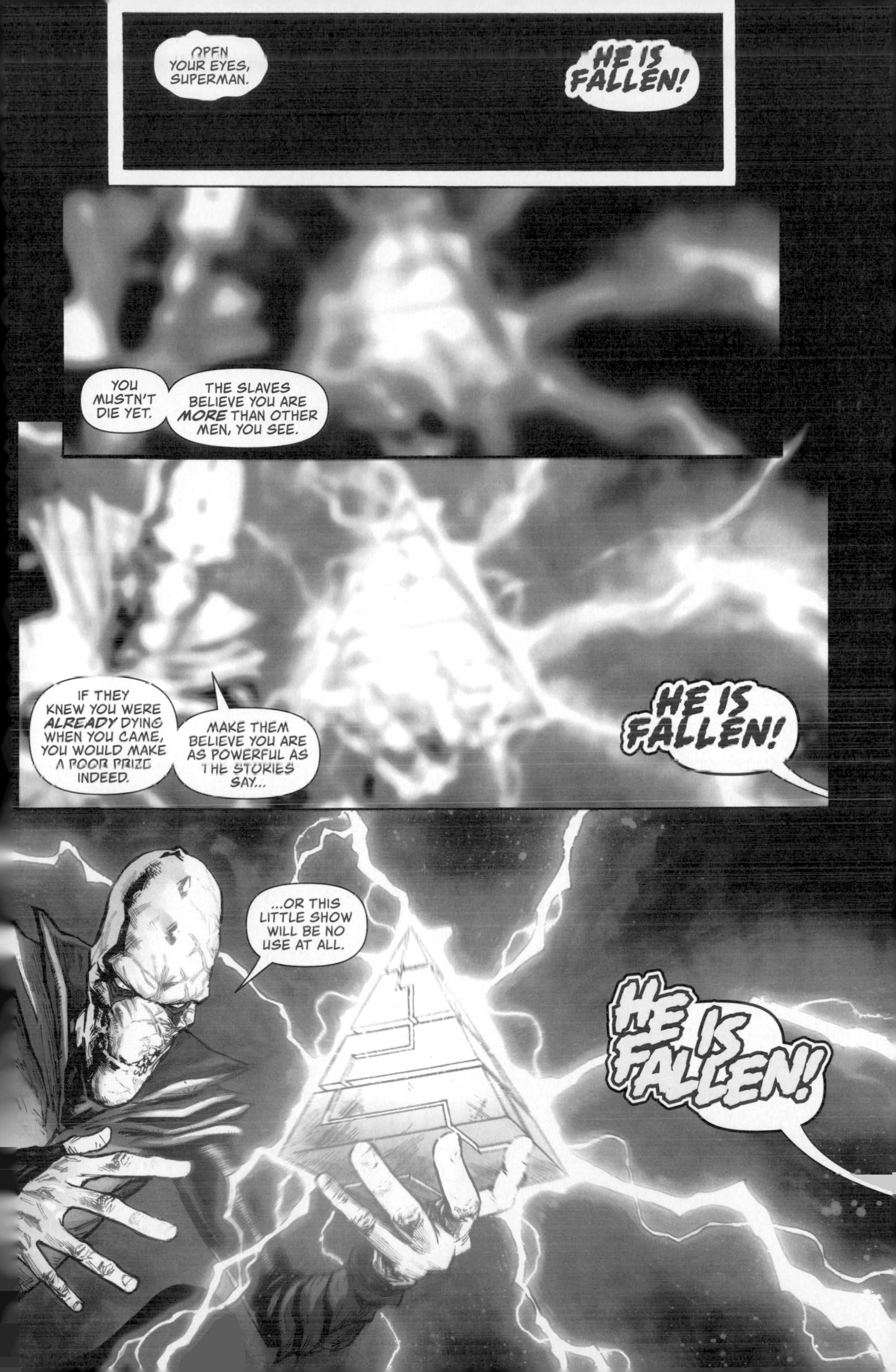
OPEN YOUR EYES, SUPERMAN.
HE IS FALLEN!
YOU MUSTN'T DIE YET.
THE SLAVES BELIEVE YOU ARE MORE THAN OTHER MEN, YOU SEE.
IF THEY KNEW YOU WERE ALREADY DYING WHEN YOU CAME, YOU WOULD MAKE A POOR PRIZE INDEED.
MAKE THEM BELIEVE YOU ARE AS POWERFUL AS THE STORIES SAY...
HE IS FALLEN!
...OR THIS LITTLE SHOW WILL BE NO USE AT ALL.
HE IS FALLEN!

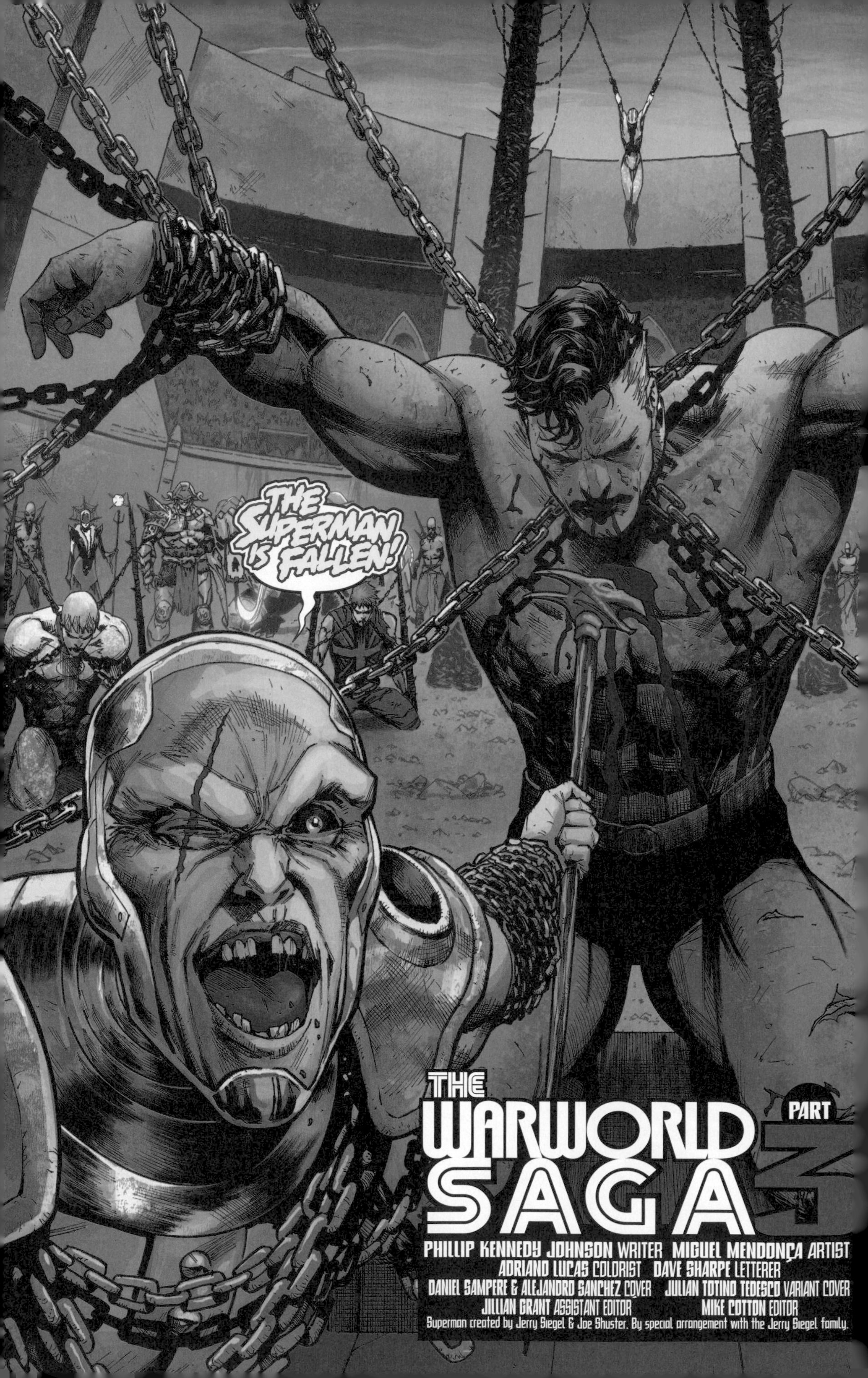
THE SUPERMAN IS FALLEN!
THE WARWORLD SAGA PART 3

PHILLIP KENNEDY JOHNSON WRITER MIGUEL MENDONÇA ARTIST
ADRIANO LUCAS COLORIST DAVE SHARPE LETTERER
DANIEL SAMPERE & ALEJANDRO SANCHEZ COVER JULIAN TOTINO TEDESCO VARIANT COVER
JILLIAN GRANT ASSISTANT EDITOR MIKE COTTON EDITOR
Superman created by Jerry Siegel & Joe Shuster. By special arrangement with the Jerry Siegel family.

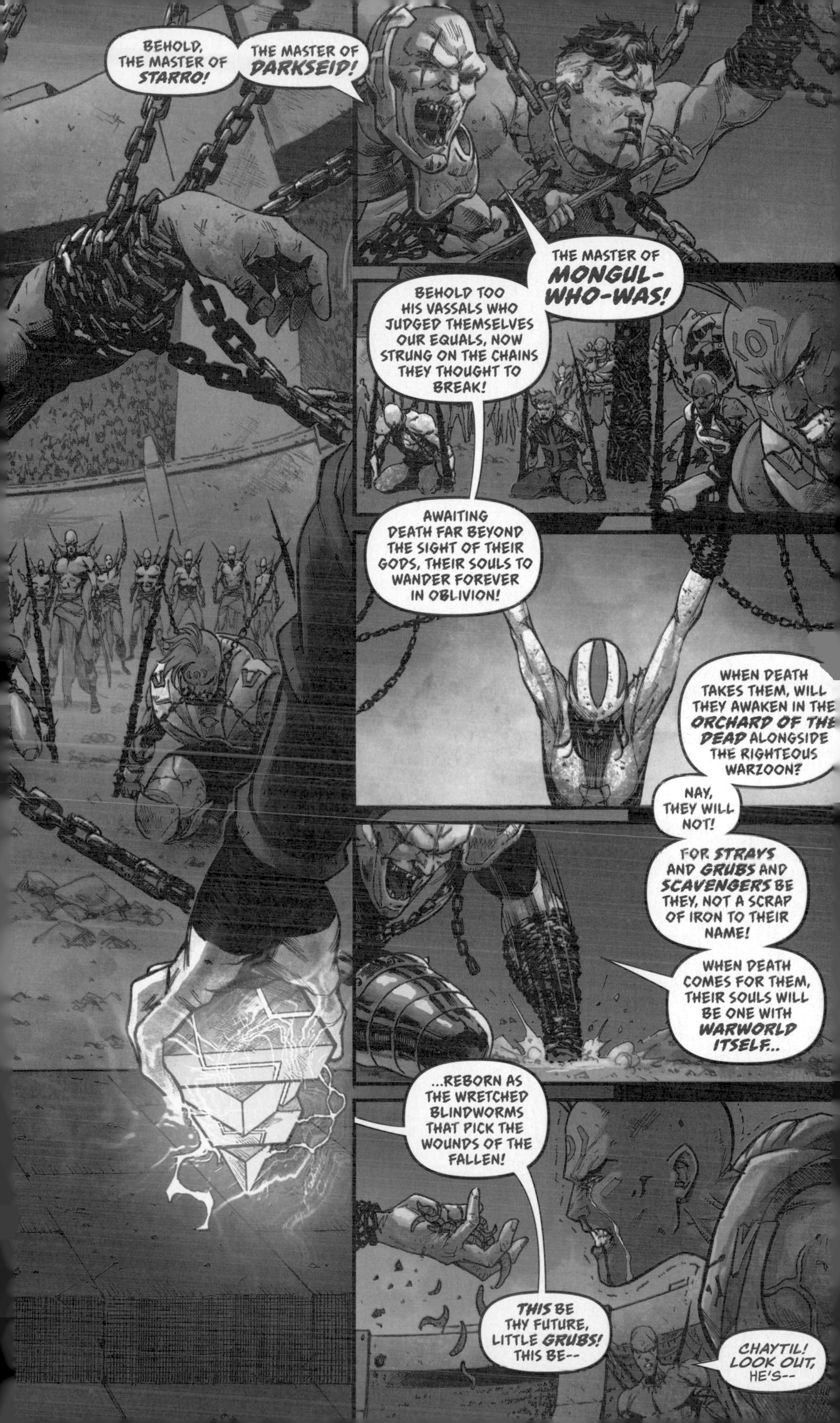
BEHOLD, THE MASTER OF STARRO!
THE MASTER OF DARKSEID!
THE MASTER OF MONGUL-WHO-WAS!
BEHOLD TOO HIS VASSALS WHO JUDGED THEMSELVES OUR EQUALS, NOW STRUNG ON THE CHAINS THEY THOUGHT TO BREAK!
AWAITING DEATH FAR BEYOND THE SIGHT OF THEIR GODS, THEIR SOULS TO WANDER FOREVER IN OBLIVION!
WHEN DEATH TAKES THEM, WILL THEY AWAKEN IN THE ORCHARD OF THE DEAD ALONGSIDE THE RIGHTEOUS WARZOON?
NAY, THEY WILL NOT!
FOR STRAYS AND GRUBS AND SCAVENGERS BE THEY, NOT A SCRAP OF IRON TO THEIR NAME!
WHEN DEATH COMES FOR THEM, THEIR SOULS WILL BE ONE WITH WARWORLD ITSELF...
...REBORN AS THE WRETCHED BLINDWORMS THAT PICK THE WOUNDS OF THE FALLEN!
THIS BE THY FUTURE, LITTLE GRUBS! THIS BE--
CHAYTIL! LOOK OUT, HE'S--

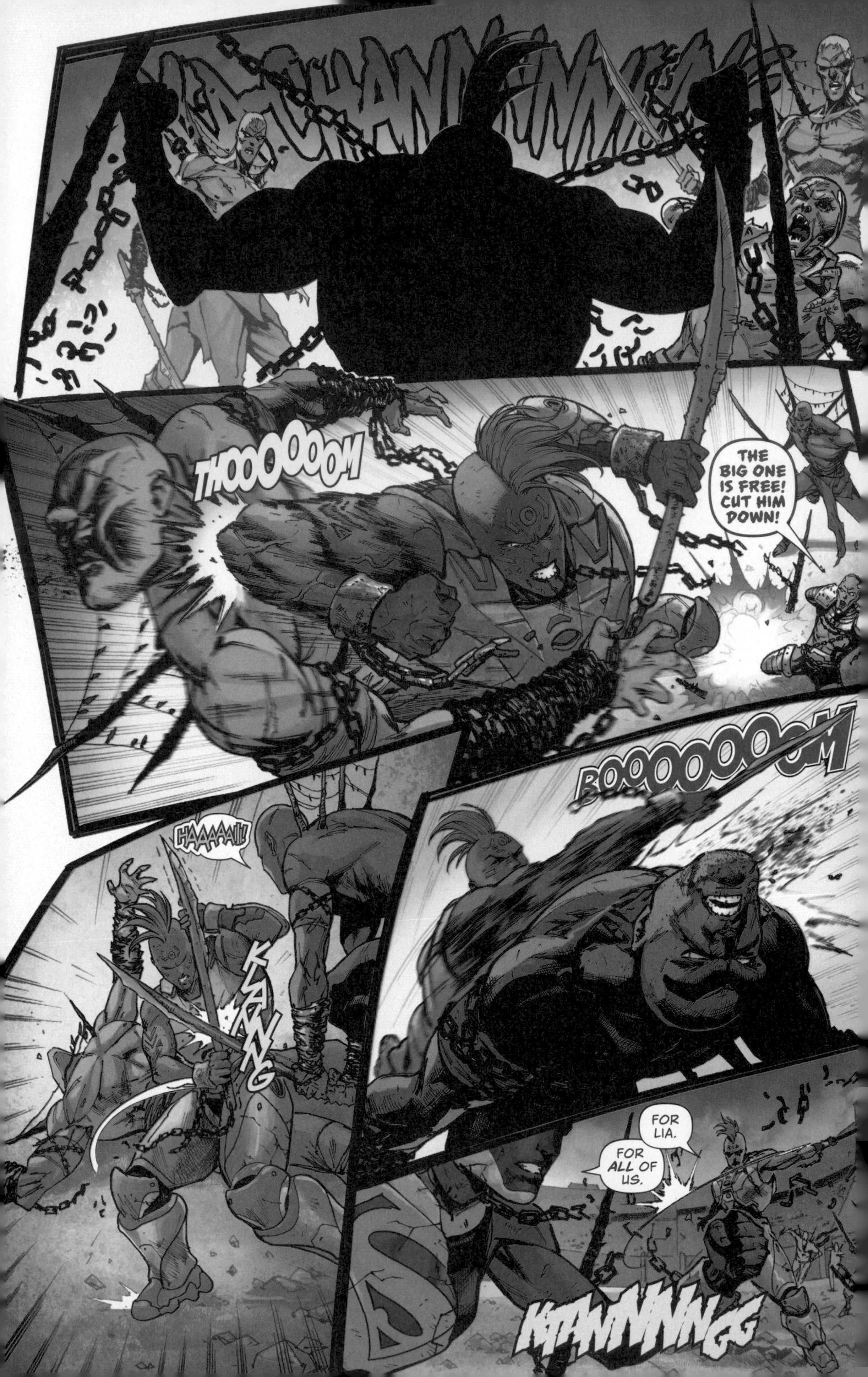
THOOOOOOM
THE BIG ONE IS FREE! CUT HIM DOWN!
BOOOOOOOOOM
HAAAAAII!
KLANNG
FOR LIA.
FOR ALL OF US.
KRANNNNGG

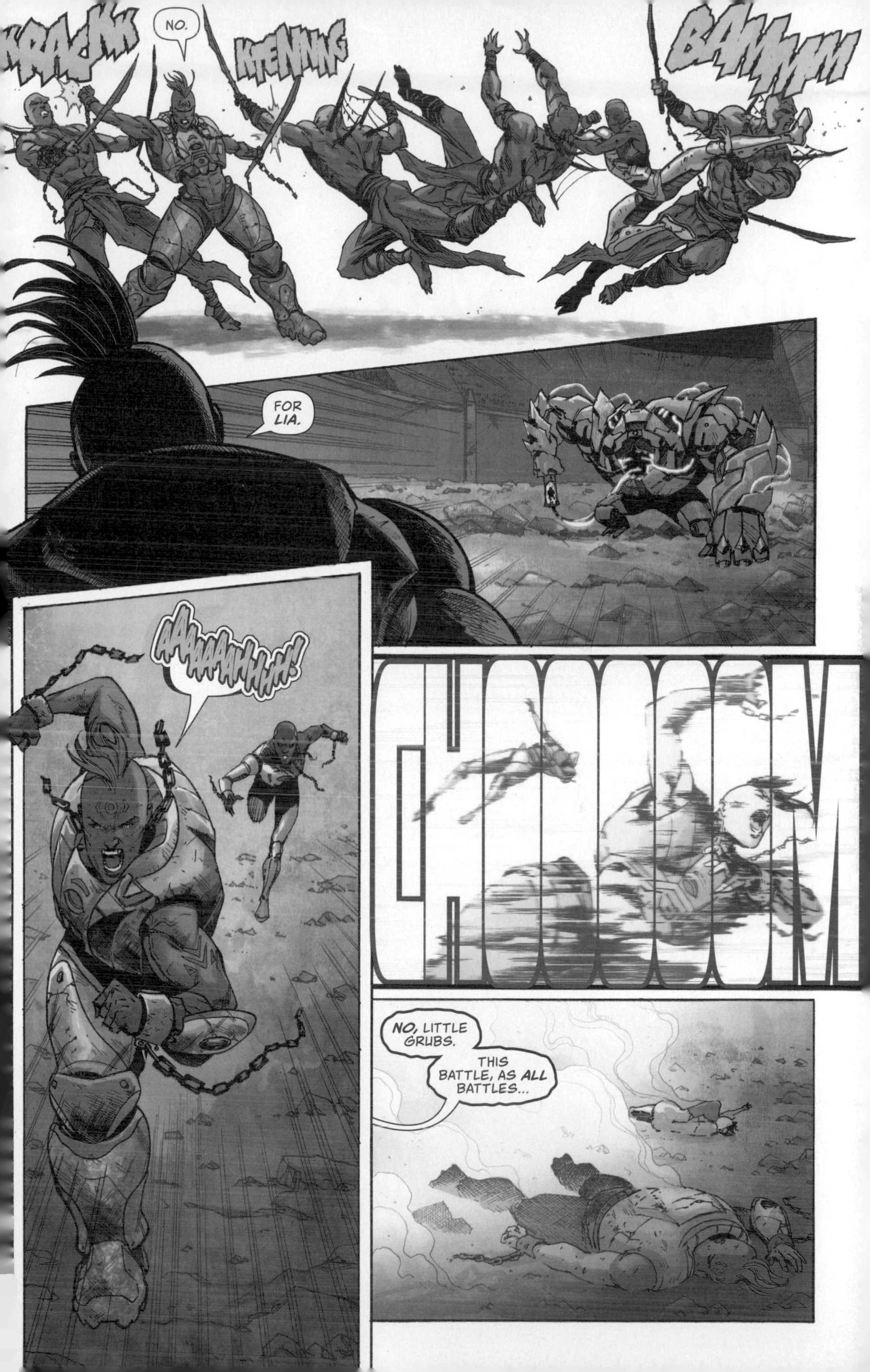

KRACKK
NO.
KTENNNG
BAMMM
FOR LIA.
AAAAAAAHHHH!
CHOOOOOM
NO, LITTLE GRUBS.
THIS BATTLE, AS ALL BATTLES...

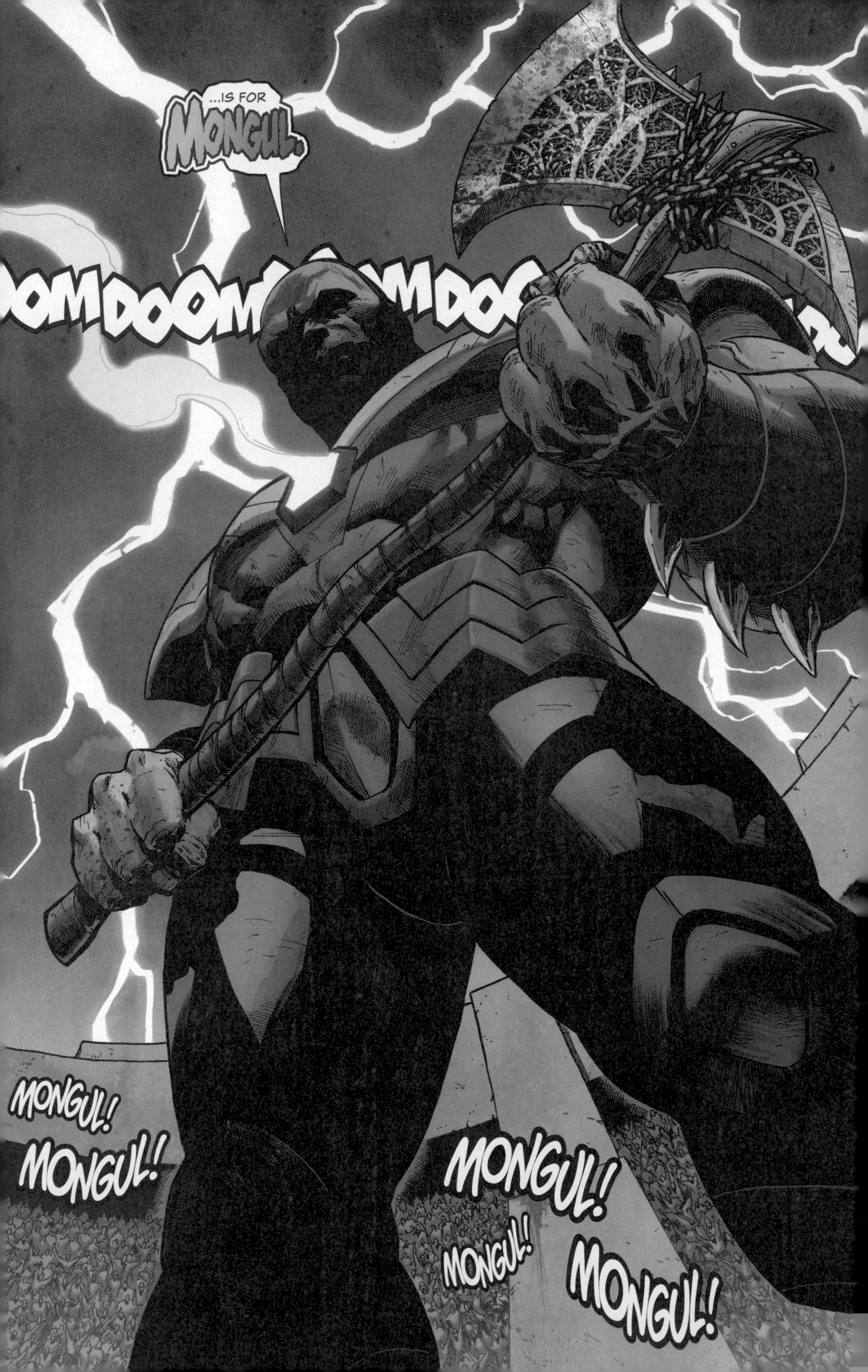

...IS FOR MONGUL.
DOOM DOOM DOOM DOOM
MONGUL!
MONGUL!
MONGUL!
MONGUL!
MONGUL!

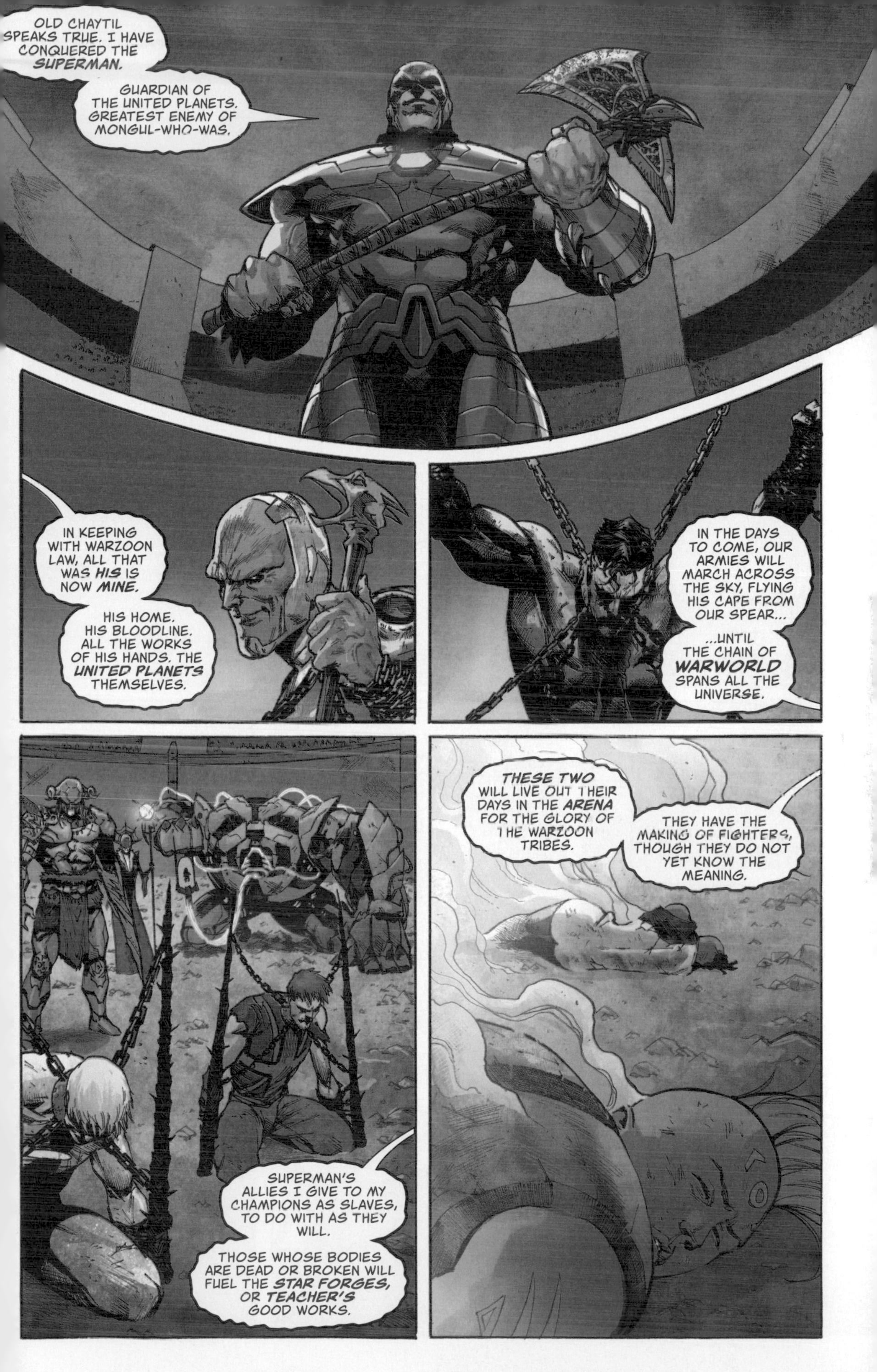

OLD CHAYTIL SPEAKS TRUE. I HAVE CONQUERED THE SUPERMAN.
GUARDIAN OF THE UNITED PLANETS. GREATEST ENEMY OF MONGUL-WHO-WAS.
IN KEEPING WITH WARZOON LAW, ALL THAT WAS HIS IS NOW MINE.
HIS HOME. HIS BLOODLINE. ALL THE WORKS OF HIS HANDS. THE UNITED PLANETS THEMSELVES.
IN THE DAYS TO COME, OUR ARMIES WILL MARCH ACROSS THE SKY, FLYING HIS CAPE FROM OUR SPEAR...
...UNTIL THE CHAIN OF WARWORLD SPANS ALL THE UNIVERSE.
SUPERMAN'S ALLIES I GIVE TO MY CHAMPIONS AS SLAVES, TO DO WITH AS THEY WILL.
THOSE WHOSE BODIES ARE DEAD OR BROKEN WILL FUEL THE STAR FORGES, OR TEACHER'S GOOD WORKS.
THESE TWO WILL LIVE OUT THEIR DAYS IN THE ARENA FOR THE GLORY OF THE WARZOON TRIBES.
THEY HAVE THE MAKING OF FIGHTERS, THOUGH THEY DO NOT YET KNOW THE MEANING.

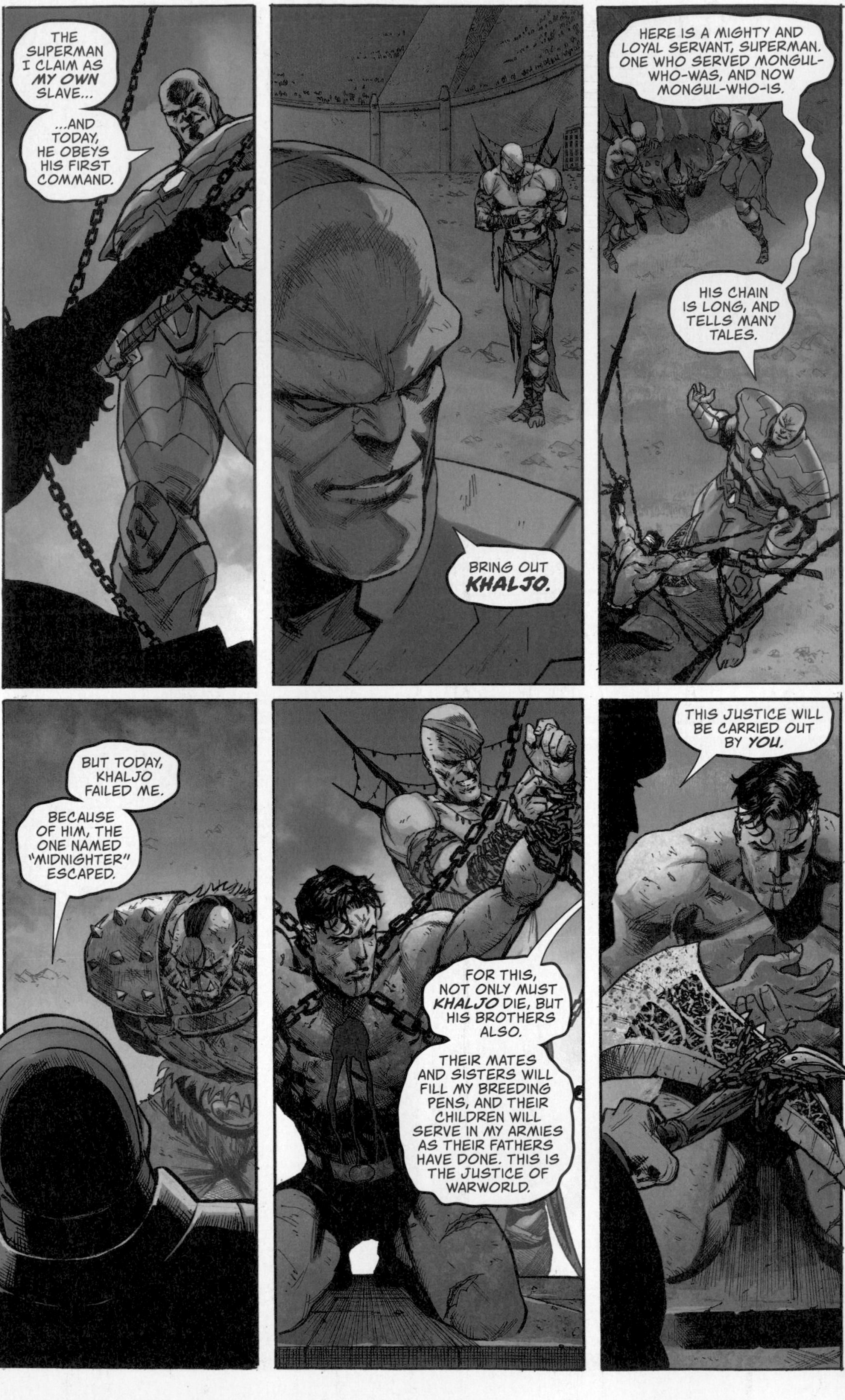
THE SUPERMAN I CLAIM AS MY OWN SLAVE...
...AND TODAY, HE OBEYS HIS FIRST COMMAND.
BRING OUT KHALJO.
HERE IS A MIGHTY AND LOYAL SERVANT, SUPERMAN. ONE WHO SERVED MONGUL-WHO-WAS, AND NOW MONGUL-WHO-IS.
HIS CHAIN IS LONG, AND TELLS MANY TALES.
BUT TODAY, KHALJO FAILED ME.
BECAUSE OF HIM, THE ONE NAMED "MIDNIGHTER" ESCAPED.
FOR THIS, NOT ONLY MUST KHALJO DIE, BUT HIS BROTHERS ALSO.
THEIR MATES AND SISTERS WILL FILL MY BREEDING PENS, AND THEIR CHILDREN WILL SERVE IN MY ARMIES AS THEIR FATHERS HAVE DONE. THIS IS THE JUSTICE OF WARWORLD.
THIS JUSTICE WILL BE CARRIED OUT BY YOU.

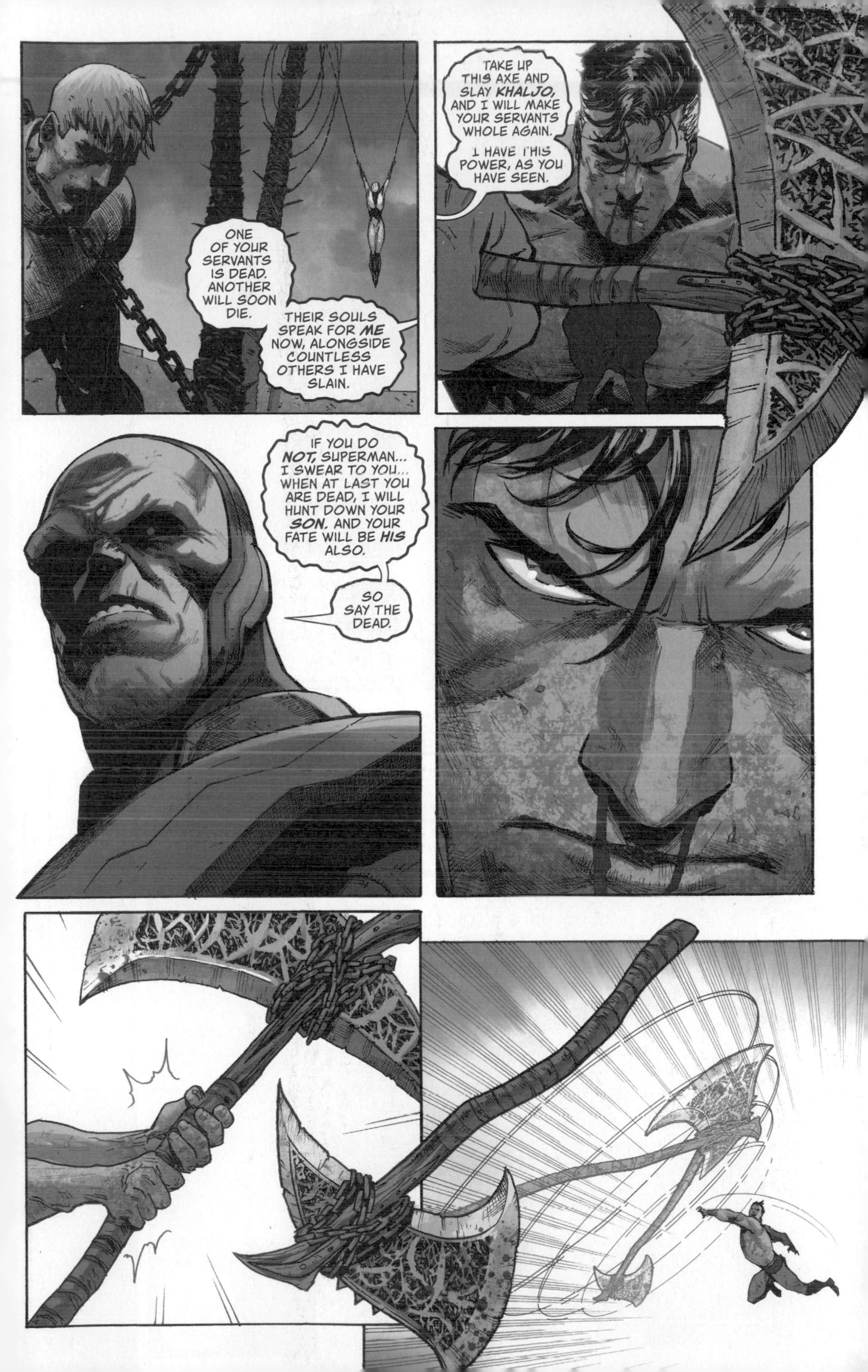
ONE OF YOUR SERVANTS IS DEAD. ANOTHER WILL SOON DIE.
THEIR SOULS SPEAK FOR *ME* NOW, ALONGSIDE COUNTLESS OTHERS I HAVE SLAIN.
TAKE UP THIS AXE AND SLAY *KHALJO,* AND I WILL MAKE YOUR SERVANTS WHOLE AGAIN.
I HAVE THIS POWER, AS YOU HAVE SEEN.
IF YOU DO *NOT,* SUPERMAN... I SWEAR TO YOU... WHEN AT LAST YOU ARE DEAD, I WILL HUNT DOWN YOUR *SON.* AND YOUR FATE WILL BE *HIS* ALSO.
SO SAY THE DEAD.

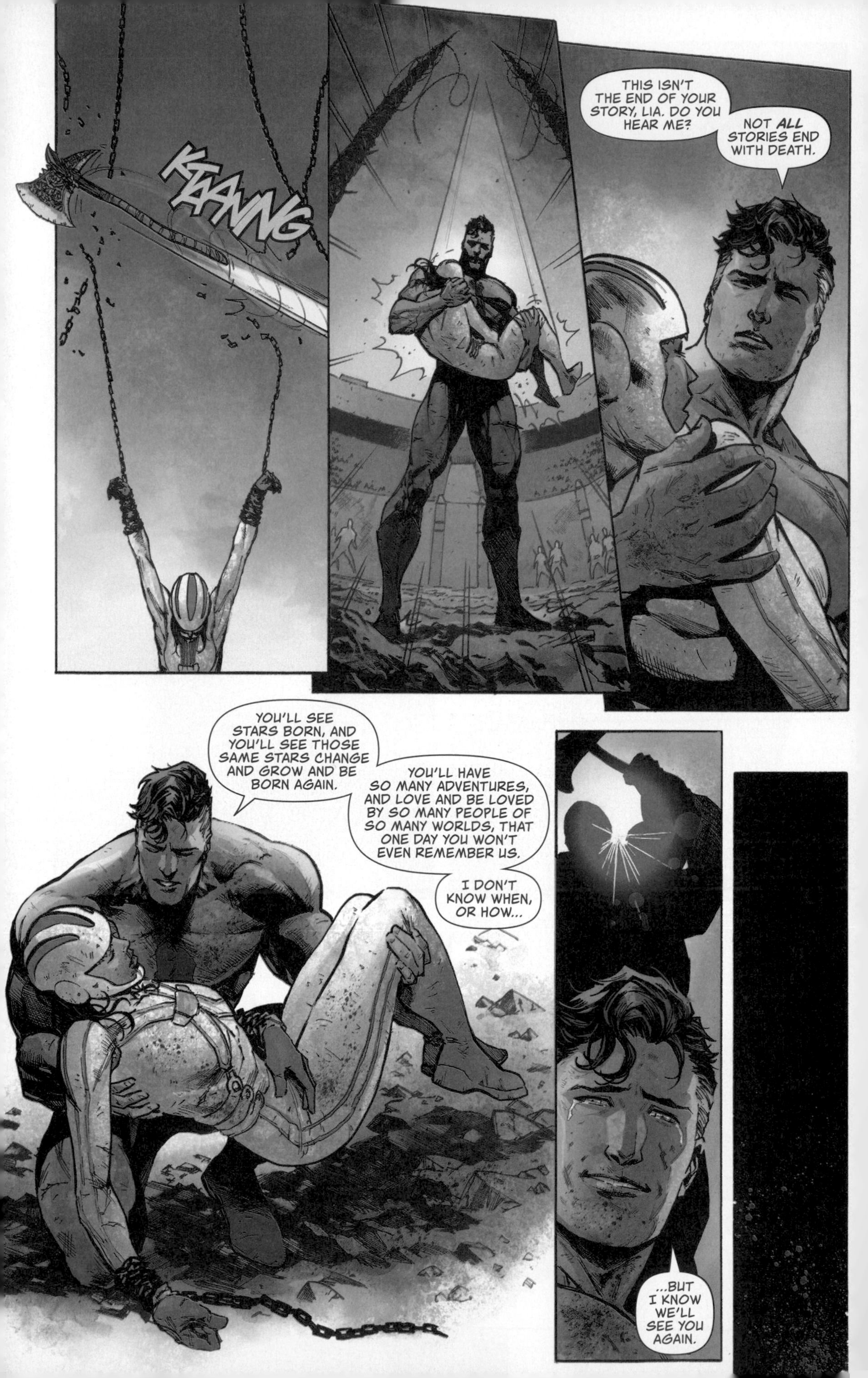
KTAANNG
THIS ISN'T THE END OF YOUR STORY, LIA. DO YOU HEAR ME?
NOT ALL STORIES END WITH DEATH.
YOU'LL SEE STARS BORN, AND YOU'LL SEE THOSE SAME STARS CHANGE AND GROW AND BE BORN AGAIN.
YOU'LL HAVE SO MANY ADVENTURES, AND LOVE AND BE LOVED BY SO MANY PEOPLE OF SO MANY WORLDS, THAT ONE DAY YOU WON'T EVEN REMEMBER US.
I DON'T KNOW WHEN, OR HOW...
...BUT I KNOW WE'LL SEE YOU AGAIN.

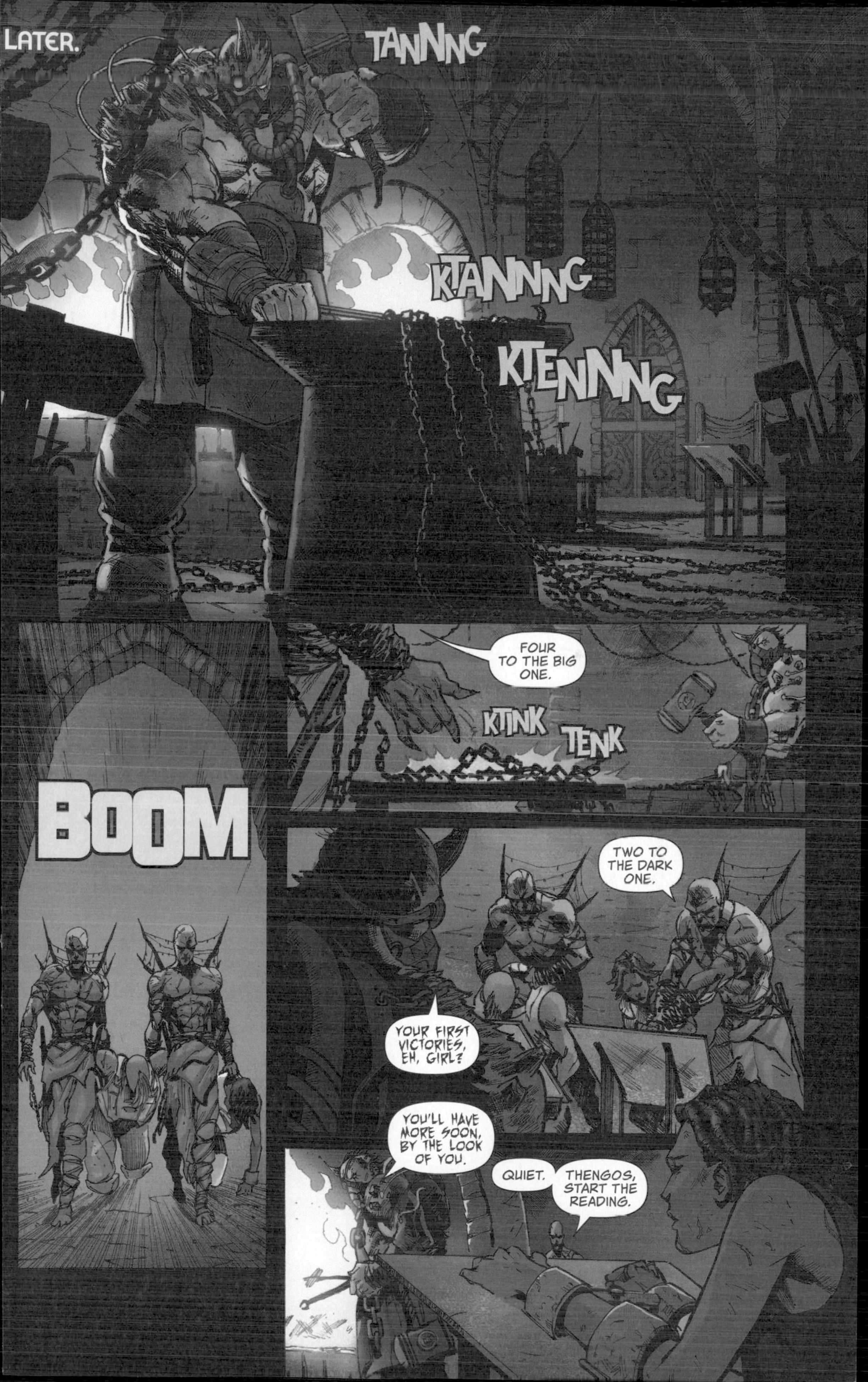
LATER.
TANNNG
KTANNNG
KTENNNG
FOUR TO THE BIG ONE.
KTINK
TENK
BOOM
TWO TO THE DARK ONE.
YOUR FIRST VICTORIES, EH, GIRL?
YOU'LL HAVE MORE SOON, BY THE LOOK OF YOU.
QUIET.
THENGOS, START THE READING.

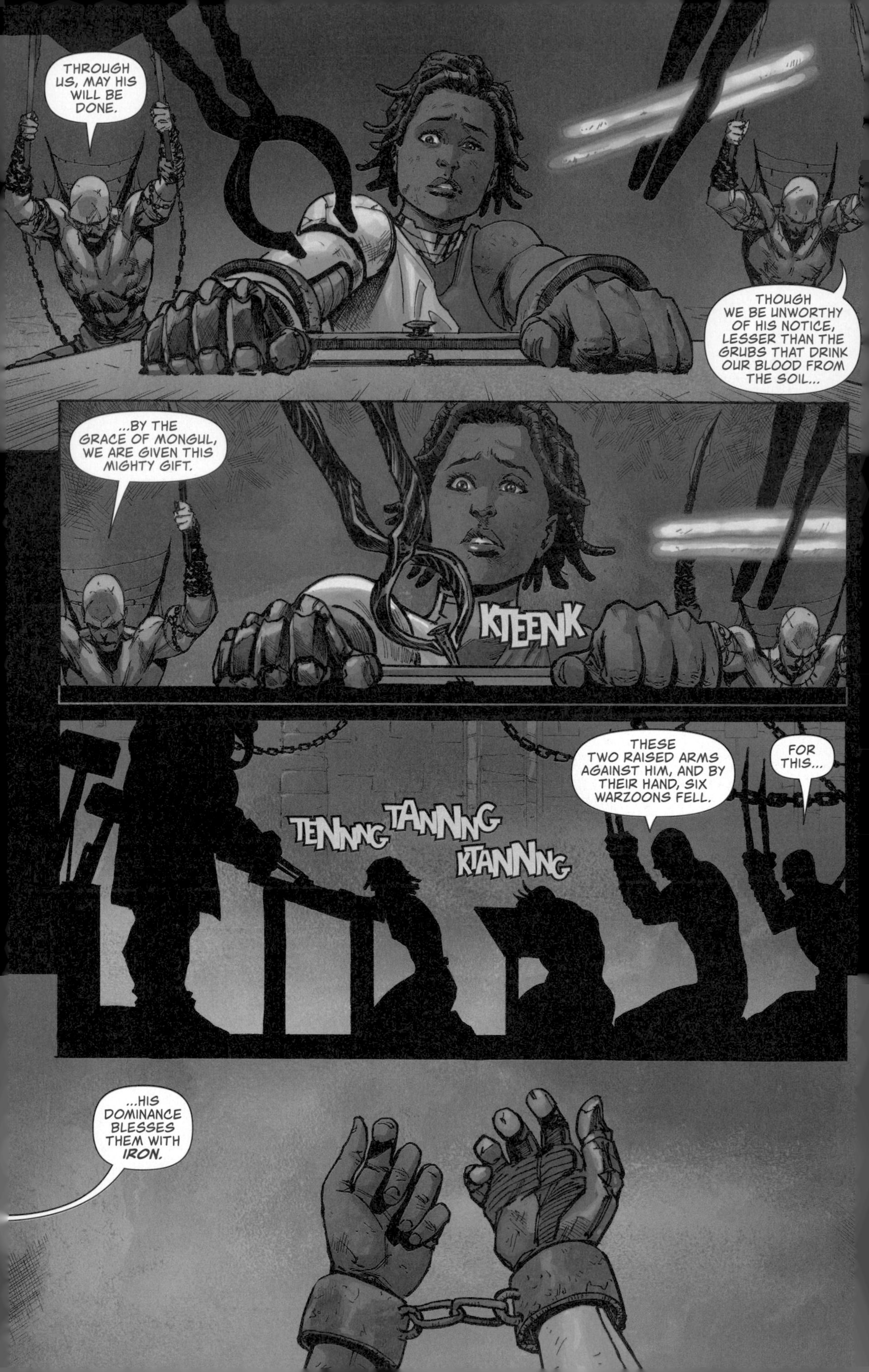
THROUGH US, MAY HIS WILL BE DONE.
THOUGH WE BE UNWORTHY OF HIS NOTICE, LESSER THAN THE GRUBS THAT DRINK OUR BLOOD FROM THE SOIL...
...BY THE GRACE OF MONGUL, WE ARE GIVEN THIS MIGHTY GIFT.
KTEENK
TENNNG TANNNG KTANNNG
THESE TWO RAISED ARMS AGAINST HIM, AND BY THEIR HAND, SIX WARZOONS FELL.
FOR THIS...
...HIS DOMINANCE BLESSES THEM WITH IRON.

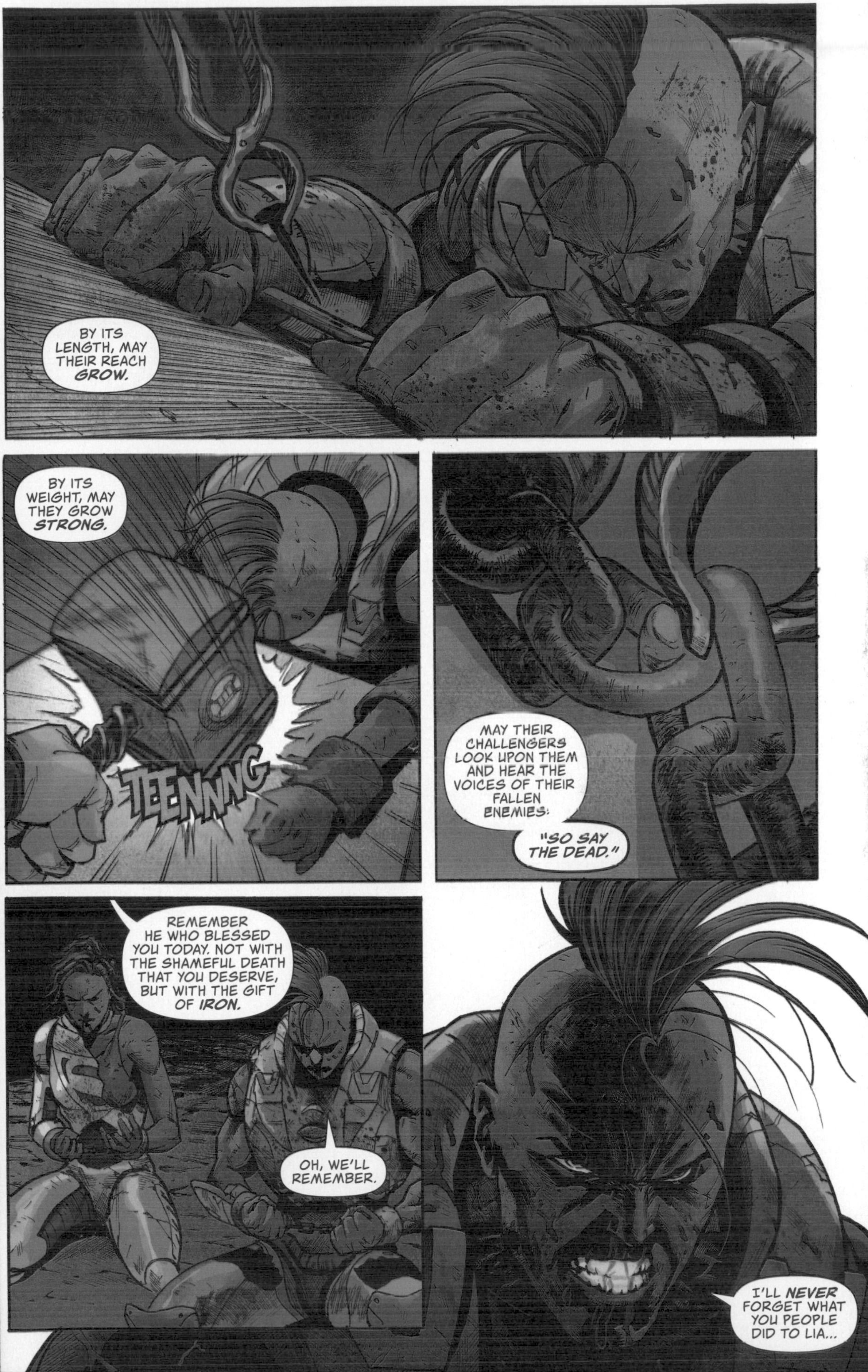
BY ITS LENGTH, MAY THEIR REACH GROW.
BY ITS WEIGHT, MAY THEY GROW STRONG.
TEENNNG
MAY THEIR CHALLENGERS LOOK UPON THEM AND HEAR THE VOICES OF THEIR FALLEN ENEMIES:
"SO SAY THE DEAD."
REMEMBER HE WHO BLESSED YOU TODAY. NOT WITH THE SHAMEFUL DEATH THAT YOU DESERVE, BUT WITH THE GIFT OF IRON.
OH, WE'LL REMEMBER.
I'LL NEVER FORGET WHAT YOU PEOPLE DID TO LIA...

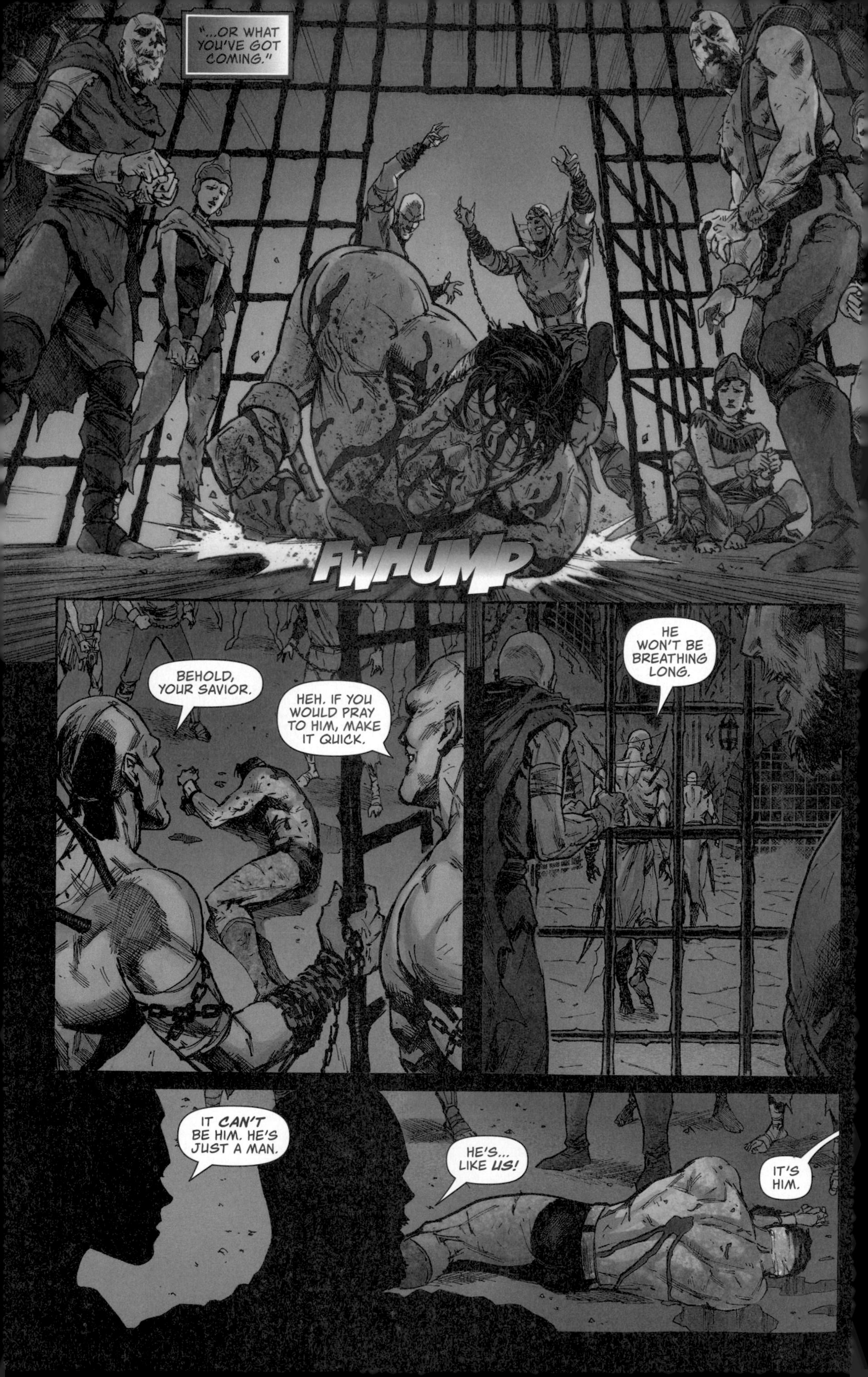
"...OR WHAT YOU'VE GOT COMING."
FWHUMP
BEHOLD, YOUR SAVIOR.
HEH. IF YOU WOULD PRAY TO HIM, MAKE IT QUICK.
HE WON'T BE BREATHING LONG.
IT *CAN'T* BE HIM. HE'S JUST A MAN.
HE'S... LIKE *US!*
IT'S HIM.

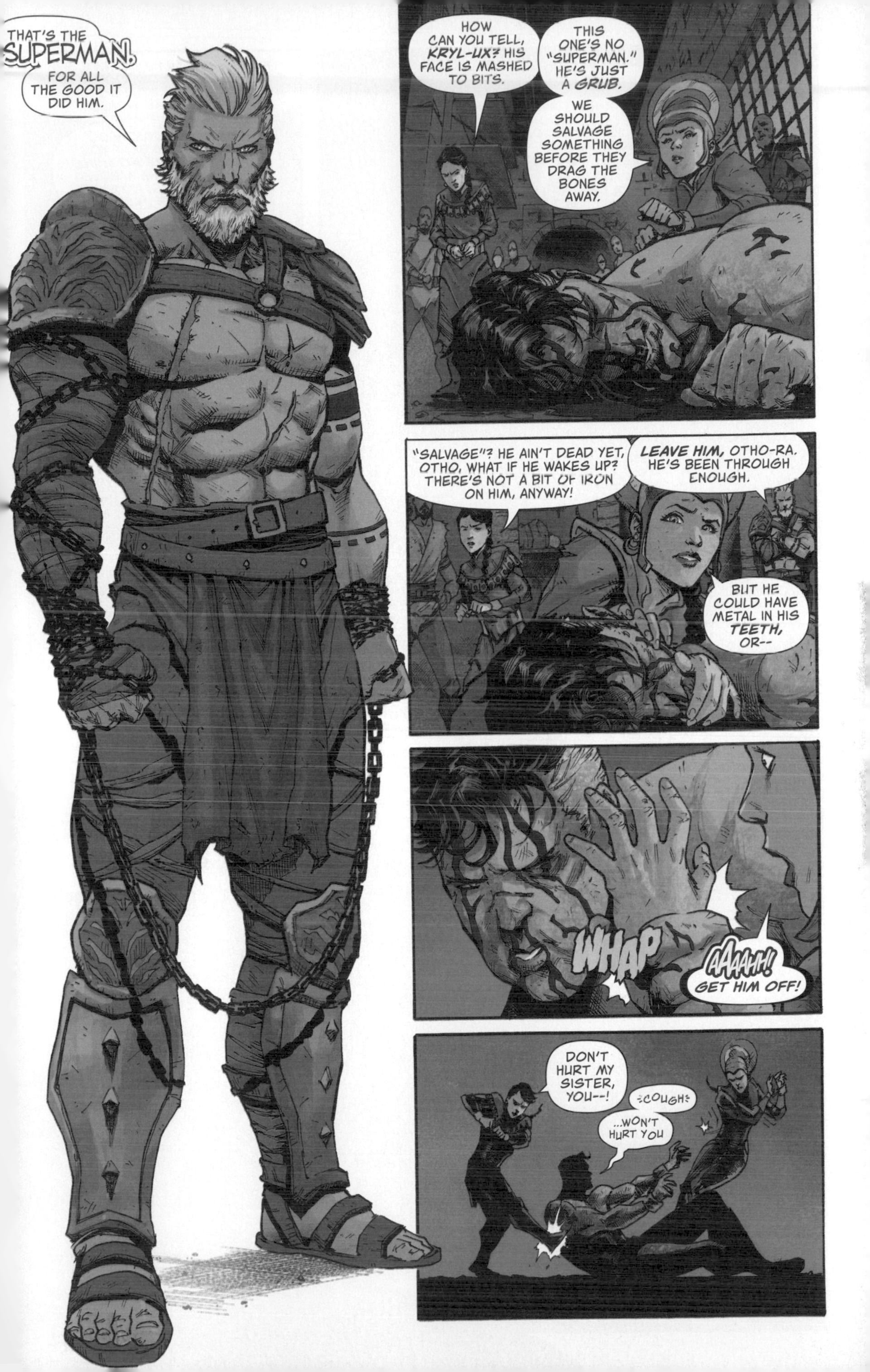
THAT'S THE SUPERMAN. FOR ALL THE GOOD IT DID HIM.
HOW CAN YOU TELL, KRYL-UX? HIS FACE IS MASHED TO BITS.
THIS ONE'S NO "SUPERMAN." HE'S JUST A GRUB.
WE SHOULD SALVAGE SOMETHING BEFORE THEY DRAG THE BONES AWAY.
"SALVAGE"? HE AIN'T DEAD YET, OTHO. WHAT IF HE WAKES UP? THERE'S NOT A BIT OF IRON ON HIM, ANYWAY!
LEAVE HIM, OTHO-RA. HE'S BEEN THROUGH ENOUGH.
BUT HE COULD HAVE METAL IN HIS TEETH, OR--
WHAP
AAAAHH! GET HIM OFF!
DON'T HURT MY SISTER, YOU--!
COUGH
...WON'T HURT YOU

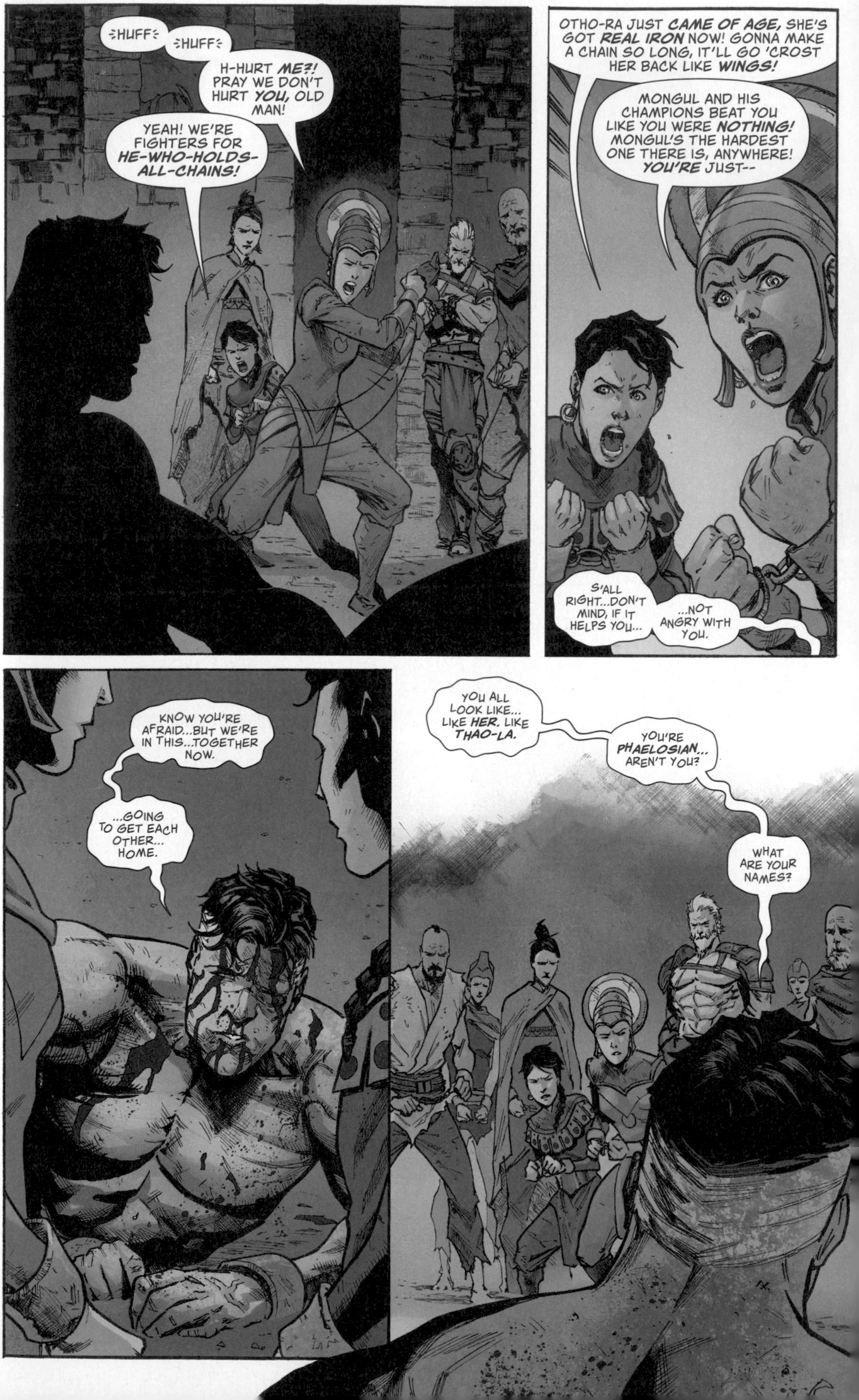
HUFF
HUFF
H-HURT ME?! PRAY WE DON'T HURT YOU, OLD MAN!
YEAH! WE'RE FIGHTERS FOR HE-WHO-HOLDS-ALL-CHAINS!
OTHO-RA JUST CAME OF AGE, SHE'S GOT REAL IRON NOW! GONNA MAKE A CHAIN SO LONG, IT'LL GO 'CROST HER BACK LIKE WINGS!
MONGUL AND HIS CHAMPIONS BEAT YOU LIKE YOU WERE NOTHING! MONGUL'S THE HARDEST ONE THERE IS, ANYWHERE! YOU'RE JUST--
S'ALL RIGHT...DON'T MIND, IF IT HELPS YOU...
...NOT ANGRY WITH YOU.
KNOW YOU'RE AFRAID...BUT WE'RE IN THIS...TOGETHER NOW.
...GOING TO GET EACH OTHER... HOME.
YOU ALL LOOK LIKE... LIKE HER. LIKE THAO-LA.
YOU'RE PHAELOSIAN... AREN'T YOU?
WHAT ARE YOUR NAMES?

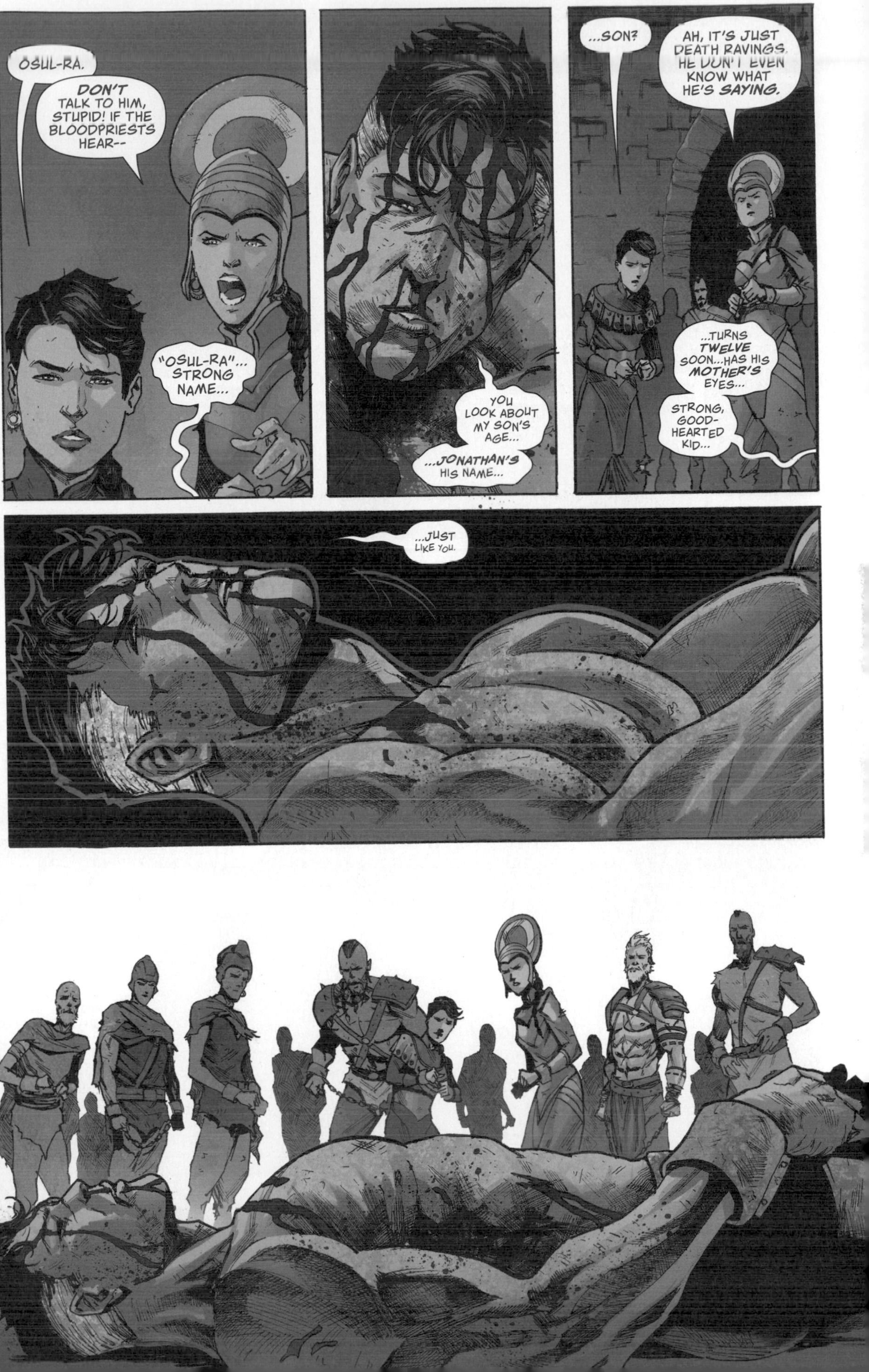
OSUL-RA.
DON'T TALK TO HIM, STUPID! IF THE BLOODPRIESTS HEAR--
"OSUL-RA"... STRONG NAME...
YOU LOOK ABOUT MY SON'S AGE...
...JONATHAN'S HIS NAME...
...SON?
AH, IT'S JUST DEATH RAVINGS. HE DON'T EVEN KNOW WHAT HE'S SAYING.
...TURNS TWELVE SOON...HAS HIS MOTHER'S EYES...
STRONG, GOOD-HEARTED KID...
...JUST LIKE YOU.

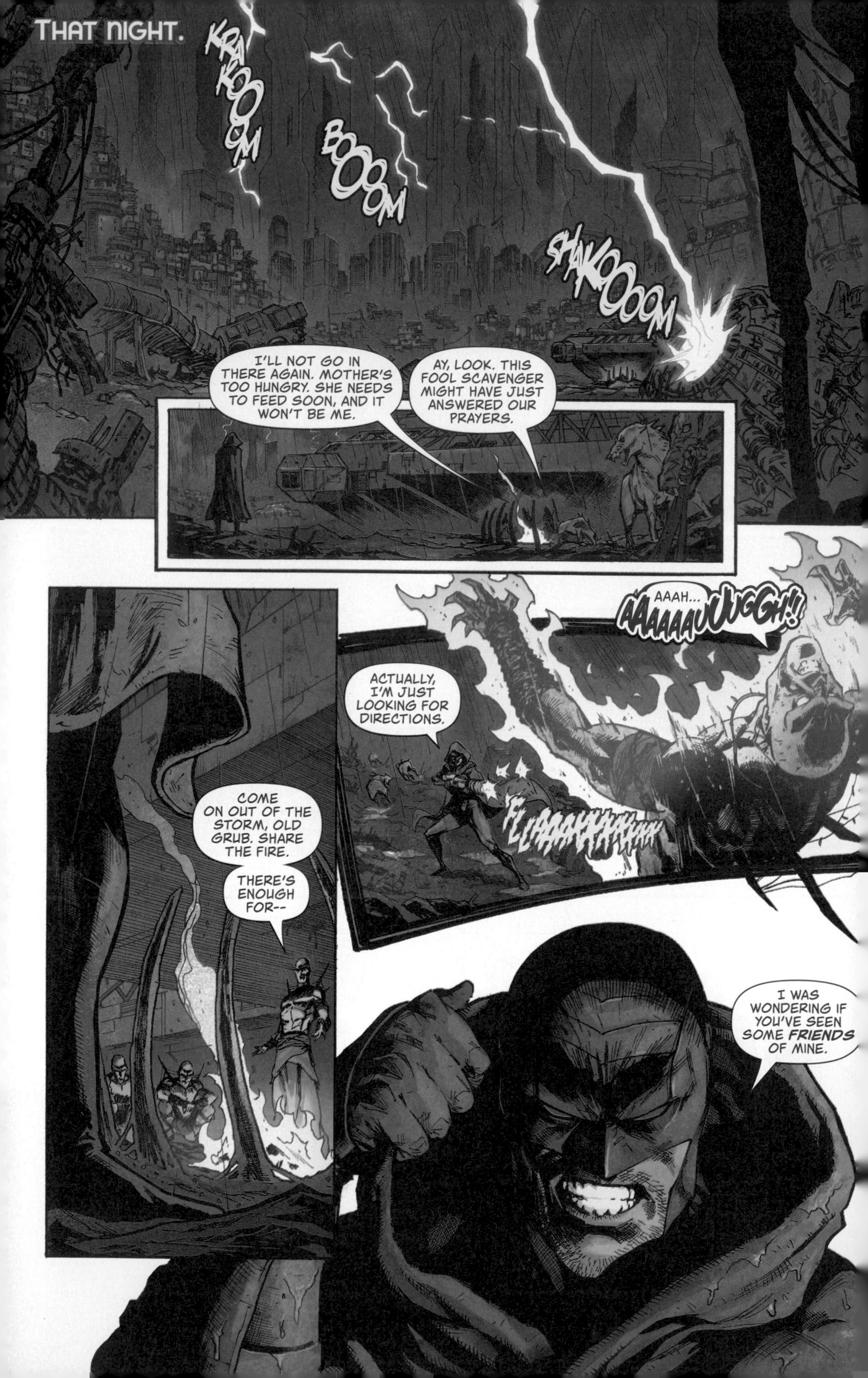
THAT NIGHT.
KRAKOOOOM
BOOOOM
SHAKOOOOM
I'LL NOT GO IN THERE AGAIN. MOTHER'S TOO HUNGRY. SHE NEEDS TO FEED SOON, AND IT WON'T BE ME.
AY, LOOK. THIS FOOL SCAVENGER MIGHT HAVE JUST ANSWERED OUR PRAYERS.
COME ON OUT OF THE STORM, OLD GRUB. SHARE THE FIRE.
THERE'S ENOUGH FOR--
ACTUALLY, I'M JUST LOOKING FOR DIRECTIONS.
AAAH... AAAAAAUUGGH!!
I WAS WONDERING IF YOU'VE SEEN SOME FRIENDS OF MINE.

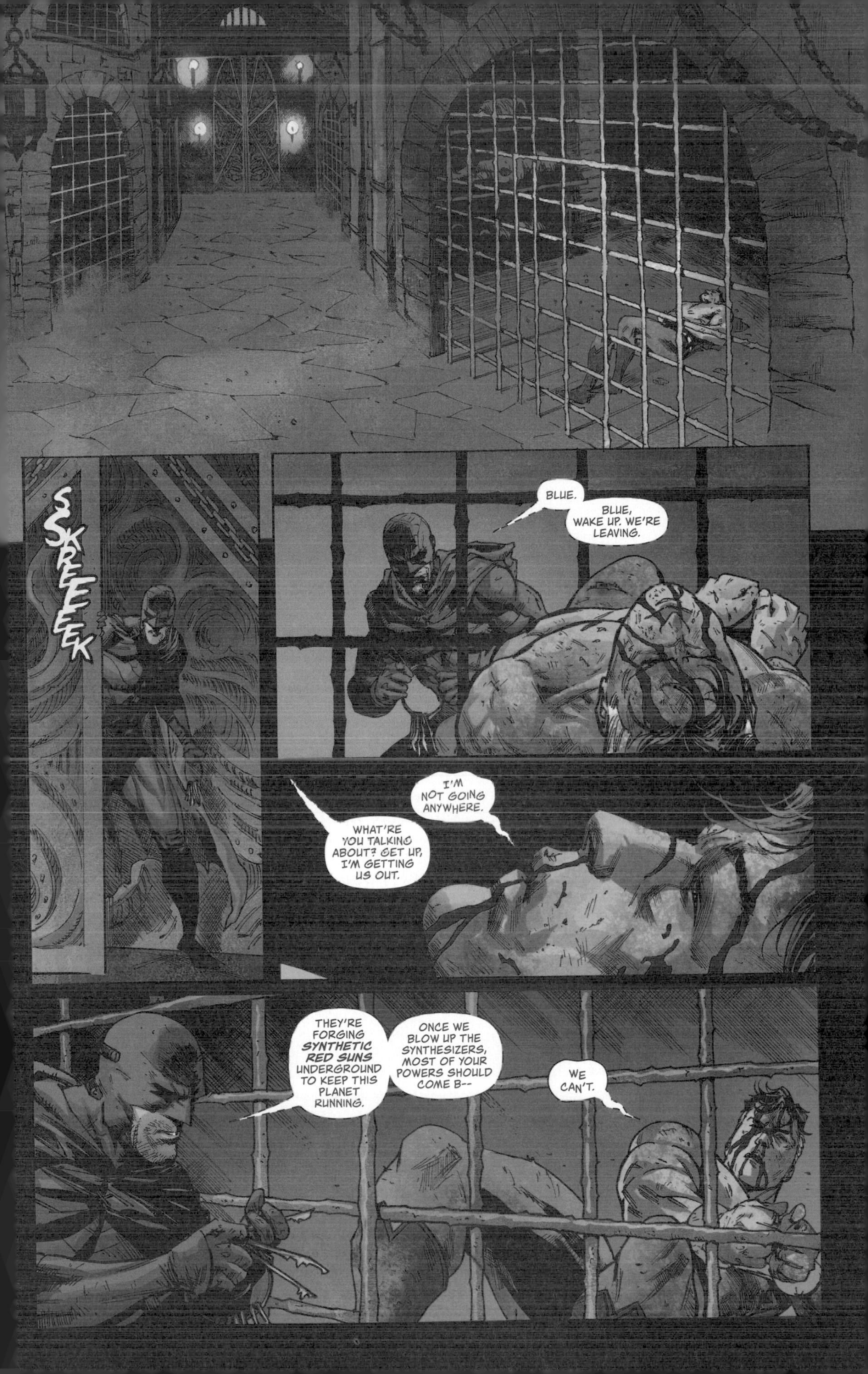
SKREEEEK
BLUE.
BLUE, WAKE UP. WE'RE LEAVING.
I'M NOT GOING ANYWHERE.
WHAT'RE YOU TALKING ABOUT? GET UP, I'M GETTING US OUT.
THEY'RE FORGING SYNTHETIC RED SUNS UNDERGROUND TO KEEP THIS PLANET RUNNING.
ONCE WE BLOW UP THE SYNTHESIZERS, MOST OF YOUR POWERS SHOULD COME B--
WE CAN'T.

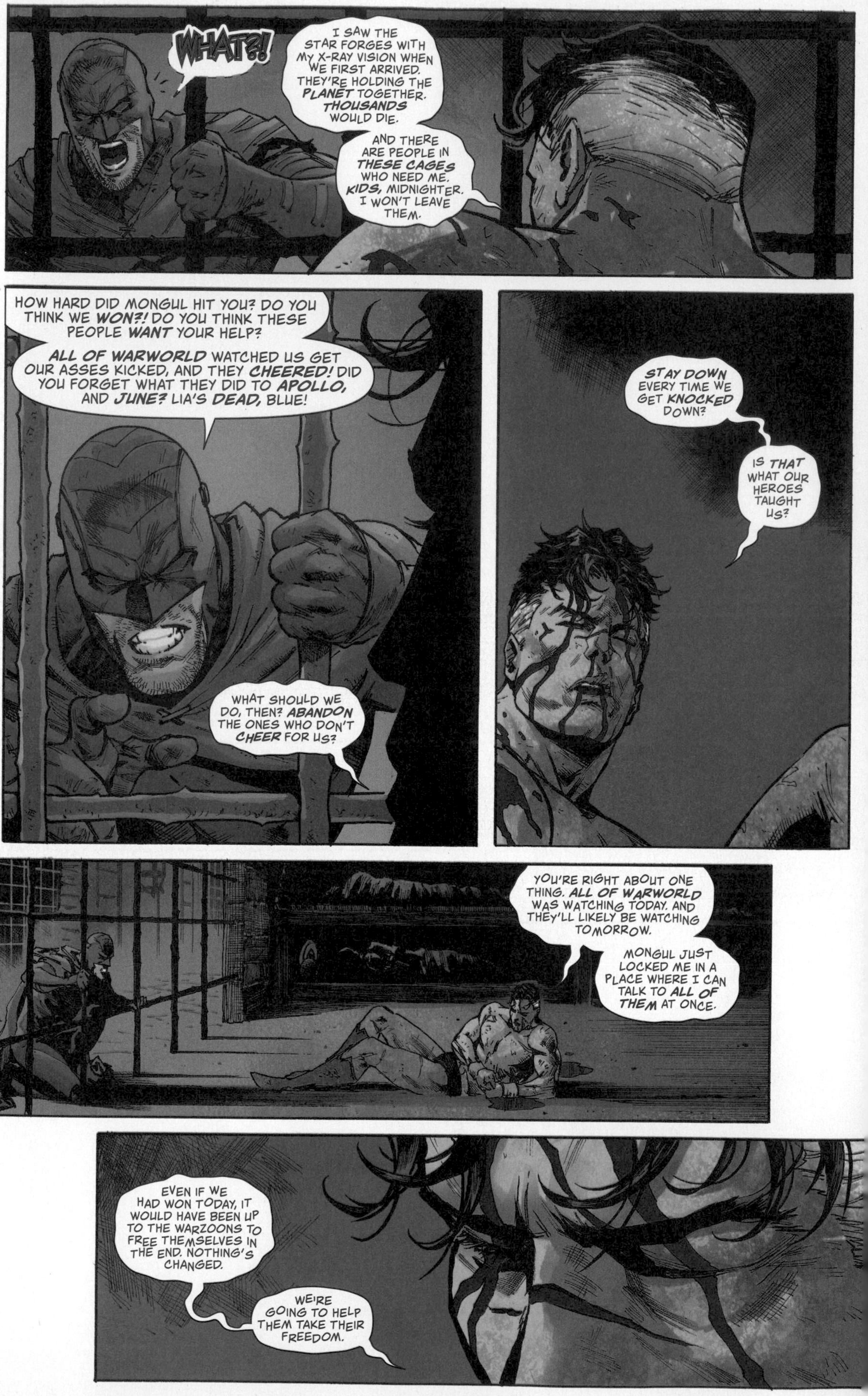
WHAT?!
I SAW THE STAR FORGES WITH MY X-RAY VISION WHEN WE FIRST ARRIVED. THEY'RE HOLDING THE PLANET TOGETHER. THOUSANDS WOULD DIE.
AND THERE ARE PEOPLE IN THESE CAGES WHO NEED ME. KIDS, MIDNIGHTER. I WON'T LEAVE THEM.
HOW HARD DID MONGUL HIT YOU? DO YOU THINK WE WON?! DO YOU THINK THESE PEOPLE WANT YOUR HELP?
ALL OF WARWORLD WATCHED US GET OUR ASSES KICKED, AND THEY CHEERED! DID YOU FORGET WHAT THEY DID TO APOLLO, AND JUNE? LIA'S DEAD, BLUE!
WHAT SHOULD WE DO, THEN? ABANDON THE ONES WHO DON'T CHEER FOR US?
STAY DOWN EVERY TIME WE GET KNOCKED DOWN?
IS THAT WHAT OUR HEROES TAUGHT US?
YOU'RE RIGHT ABOUT ONE THING. ALL OF WARWORLD WAS WATCHING TODAY. AND THEY'LL LIKELY BE WATCHING TOMORROW.
MONGUL JUST LOCKED ME IN A PLACE WHERE I CAN TALK TO ALL OF THEM AT ONCE.
EVEN IF WE HAD WON TODAY, IT WOULD HAVE BEEN UP TO THE WARZOONS TO FREE THEMSELVES IN THE END. NOTHING'S CHANGED.
WE'RE GOING TO HELP THEM TAKE THEIR FREEDOM.

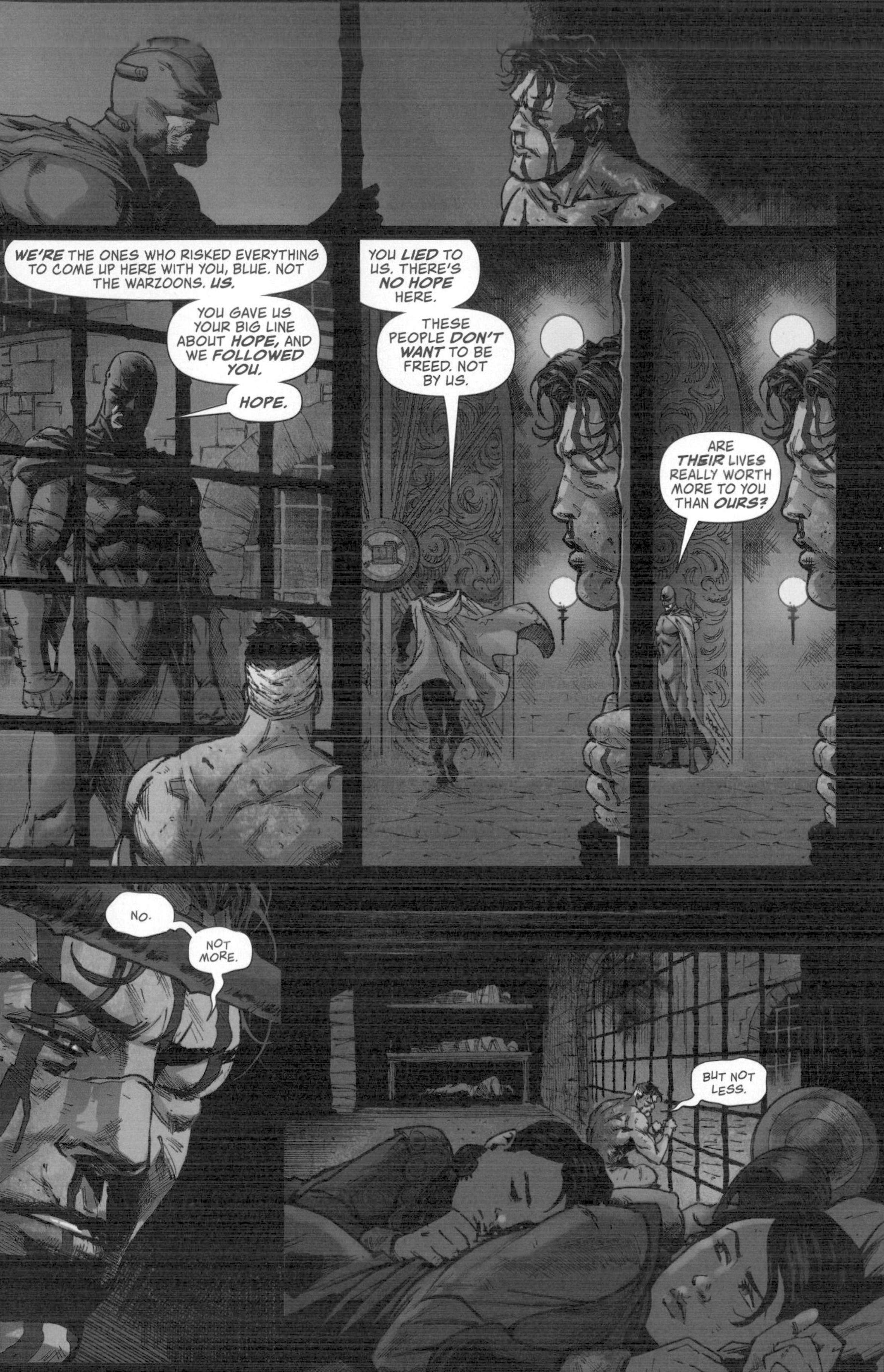
WE'RE THE ONES WHO RISKED EVERYTHING TO COME UP HERE WITH YOU, BLUE. NOT THE WARZOONS. US.
YOU GAVE US YOUR BIG LINE ABOUT HOPE, AND WE FOLLOWED YOU.
HOPE.
YOU LIED TO US. THERE'S NO HOPE HERE.
THESE PEOPLE DON'T WANT TO BE FREED. NOT BY US.
ARE THEIR LIVES REALLY WORTH MORE TO YOU THAN OURS?
NO.
NOT MORE.
BUT NOT LESS.

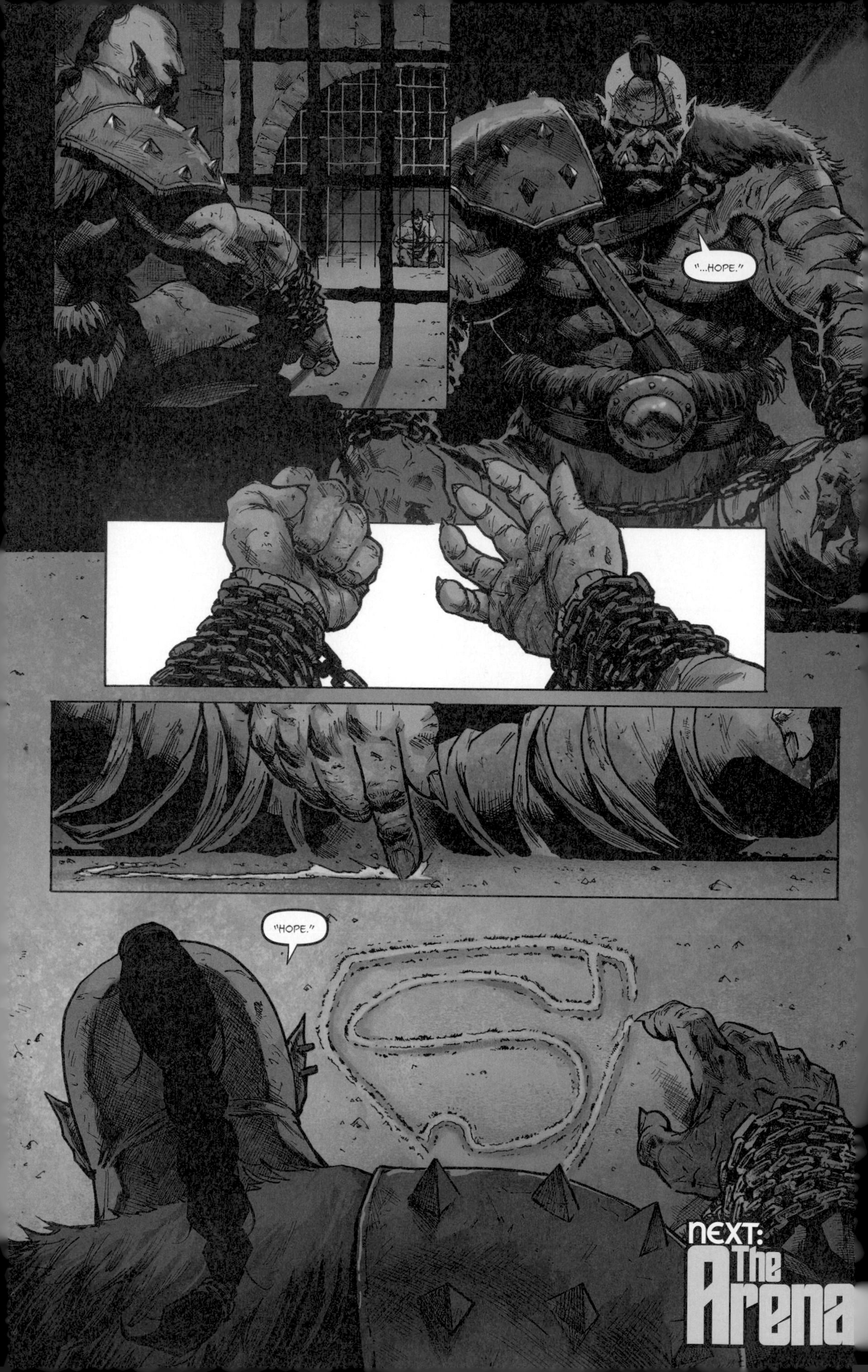
"...HOPE."
"HOPE."
NEXT:
The Arena

Action Comics #1039
main cover by DANIEL SAMPERE and ALEJANDRO SÁNCHEZ

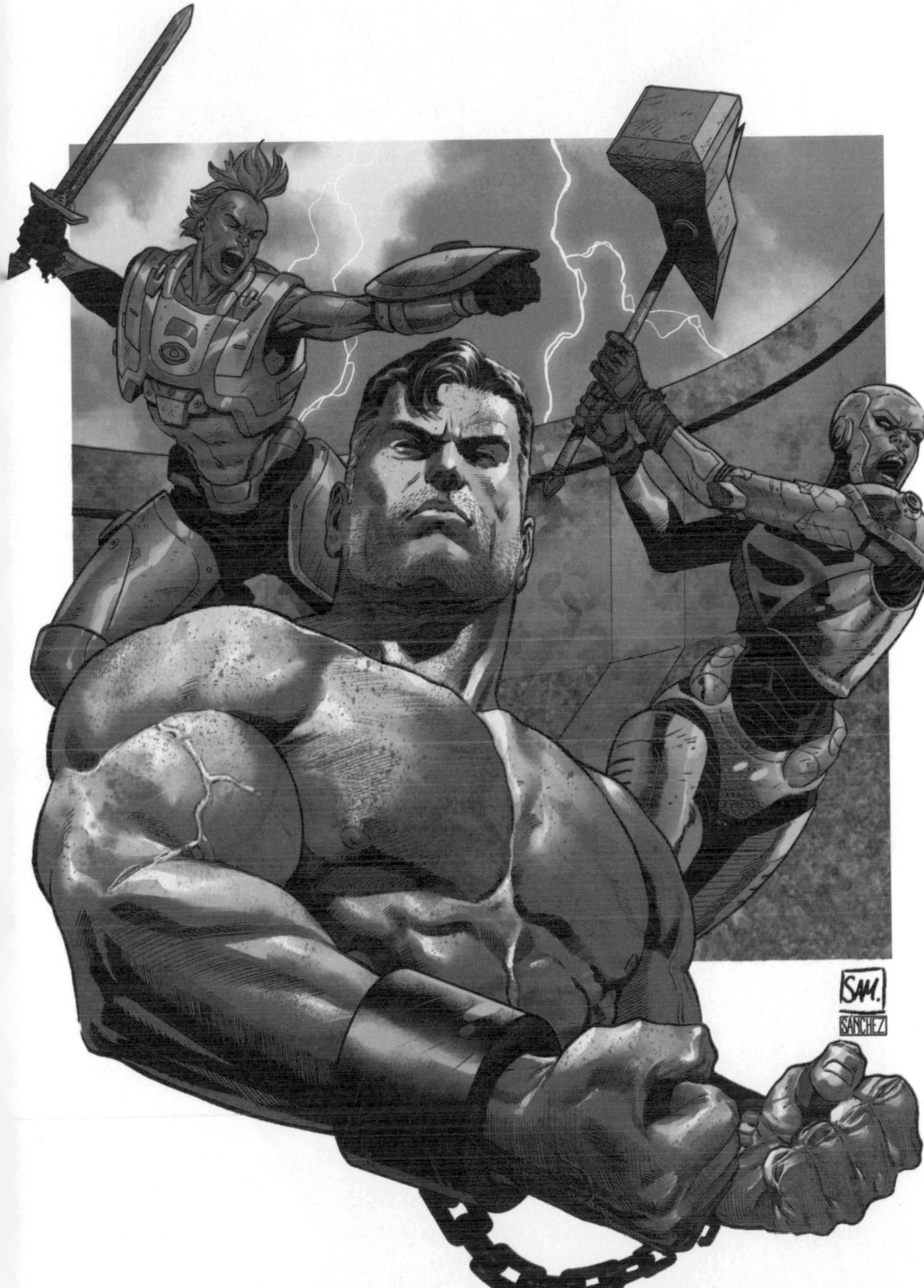
SAM.
SÁNCHEZ

Action Comics **#1039**
variant cover by JULIAN TOTINO TEDESCO

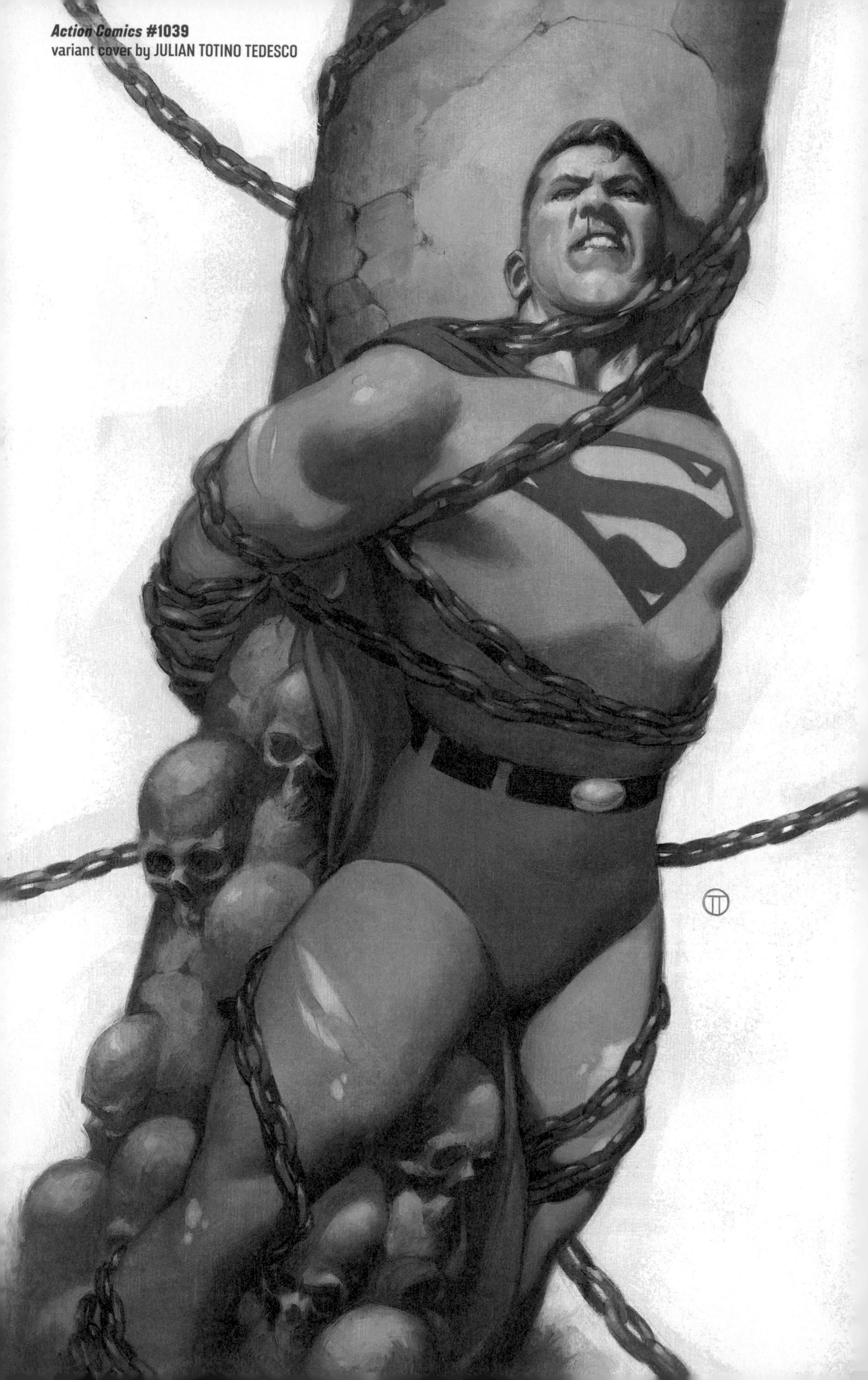

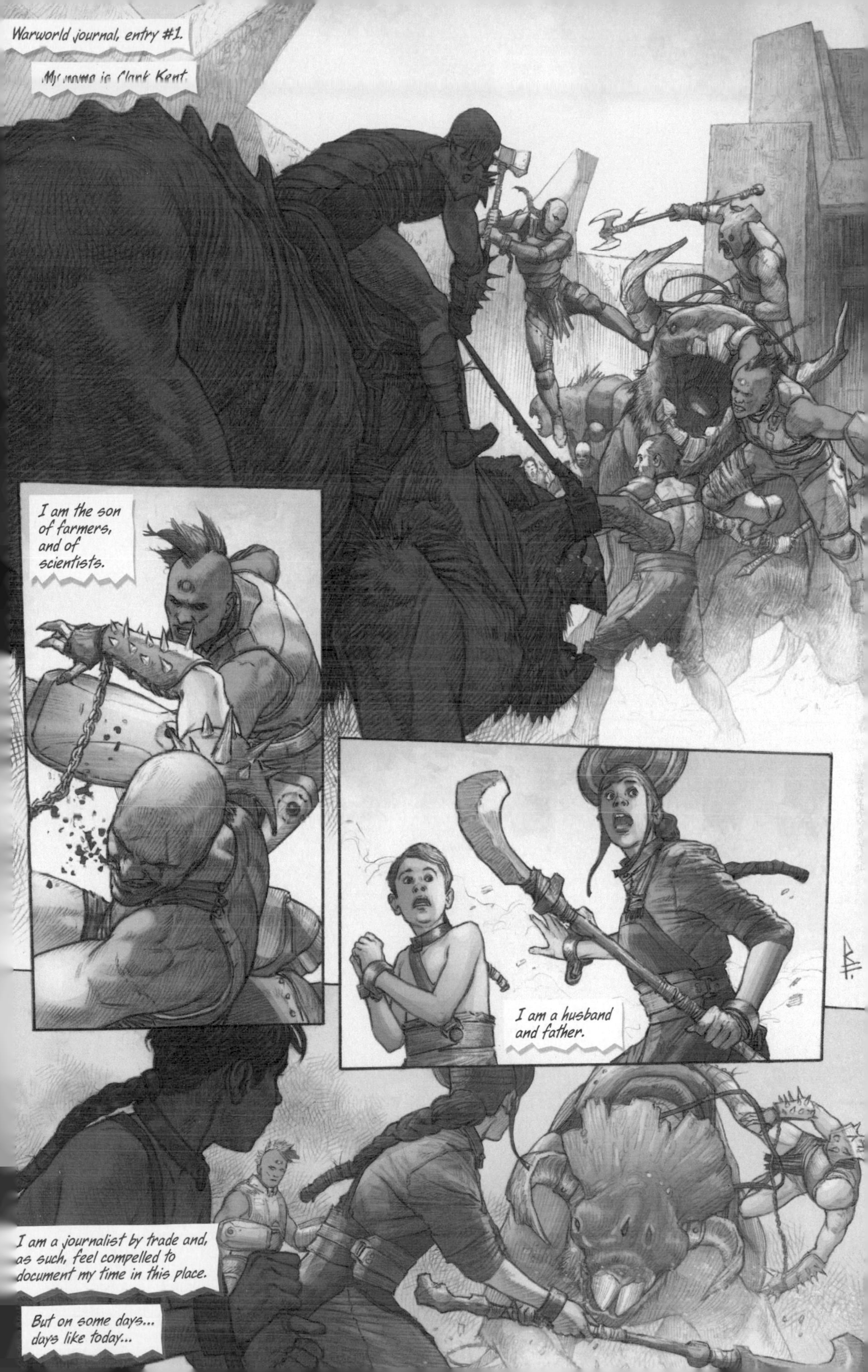

Warworld journal, entry #1.
My name is Clark Kent.
I am the son of farmers, and of scientists.
I am a husband and father.
I am a journalist by trade and, as such, feel compelled to document my time in this place.
But on some days... days like today...

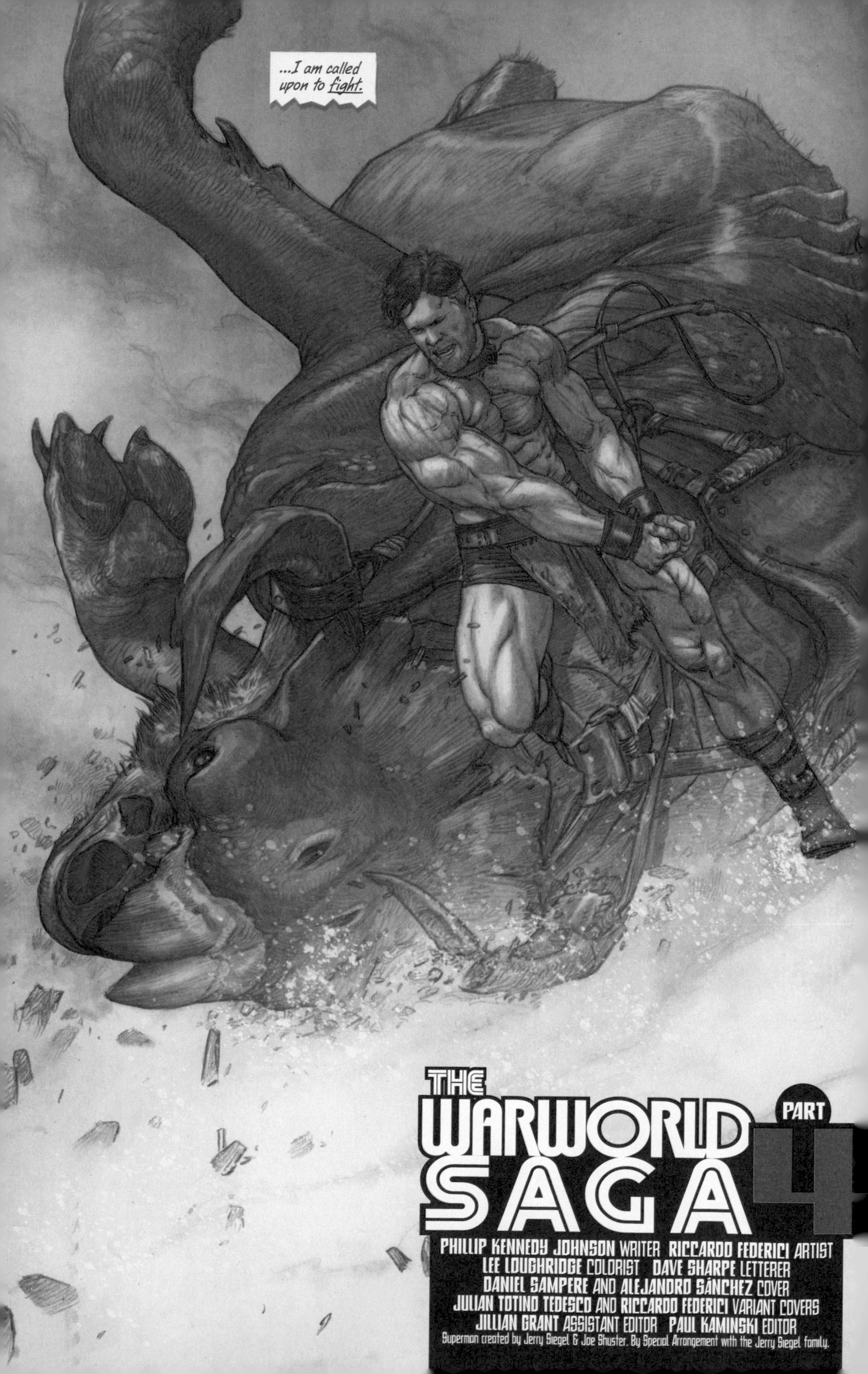

...I am called upon to fight.
THE WARWORLD SAGA PART 4
PHILLIP KENNEDY JOHNSON WRITER RICCARDO FEDERICI ARTIST
LEE LOUGHRIDGE COLORIST DAVE SHARPE LETTERER
DANIEL SAMPERE AND ALEJANDRO SÁNCHEZ COVER
JULIAN TOTINO TEDESCO AND RICCARDO FEDERICI VARIANT COVERS
JILLIAN GRANT ASSISTANT EDITOR PAUL KAMINSKI EDITOR
Superman created by Jerry Siegel & Joe Shuster. By Special Arrangement with the Jerry Siegel family.

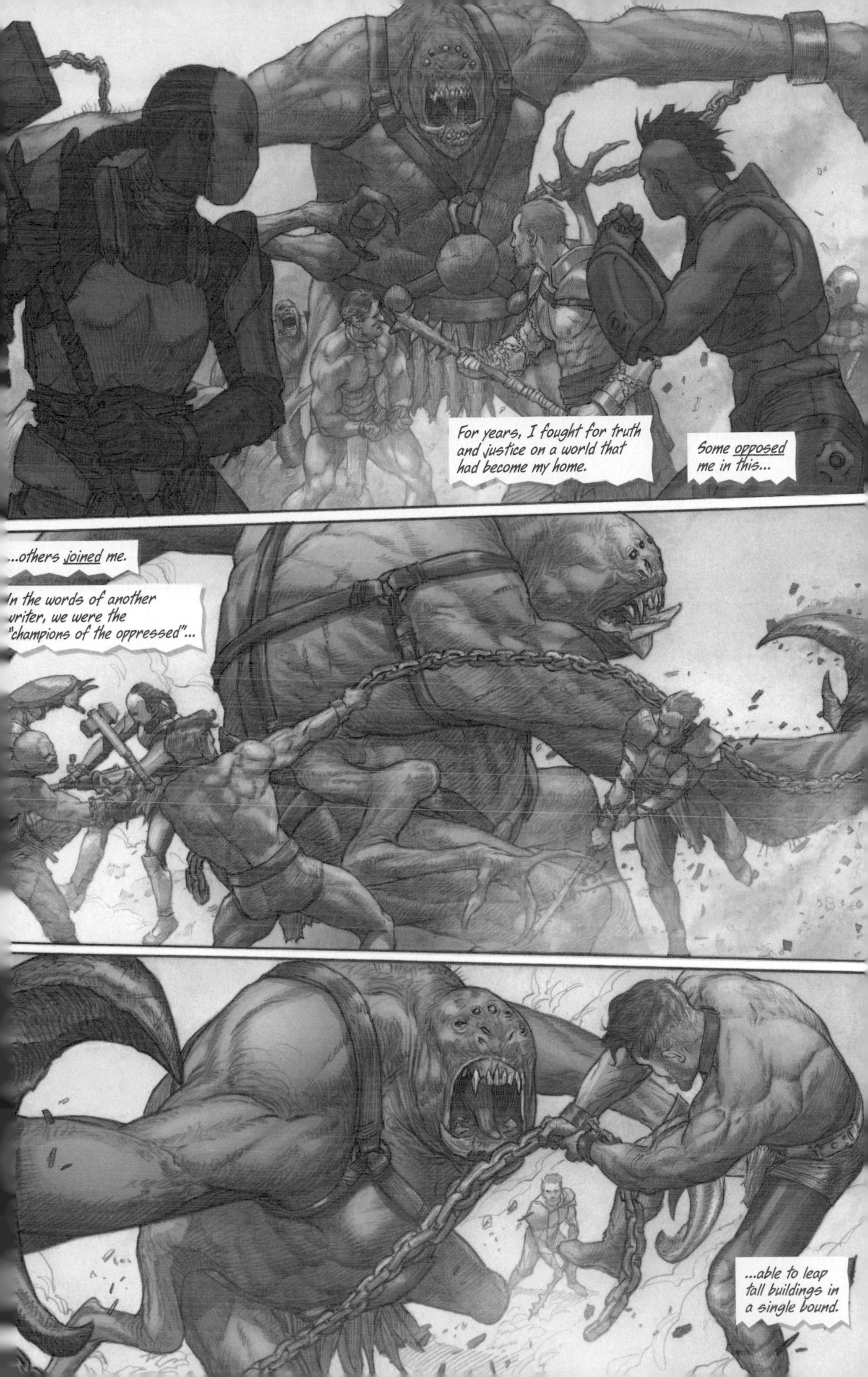
For years, I fought for truth and justice on a world that had become my home.
Some opposed me in this...
...others joined me.
In the words of another writer, we were the "champions of the oppressed"...
...able to leap tall buildings in a single bound.

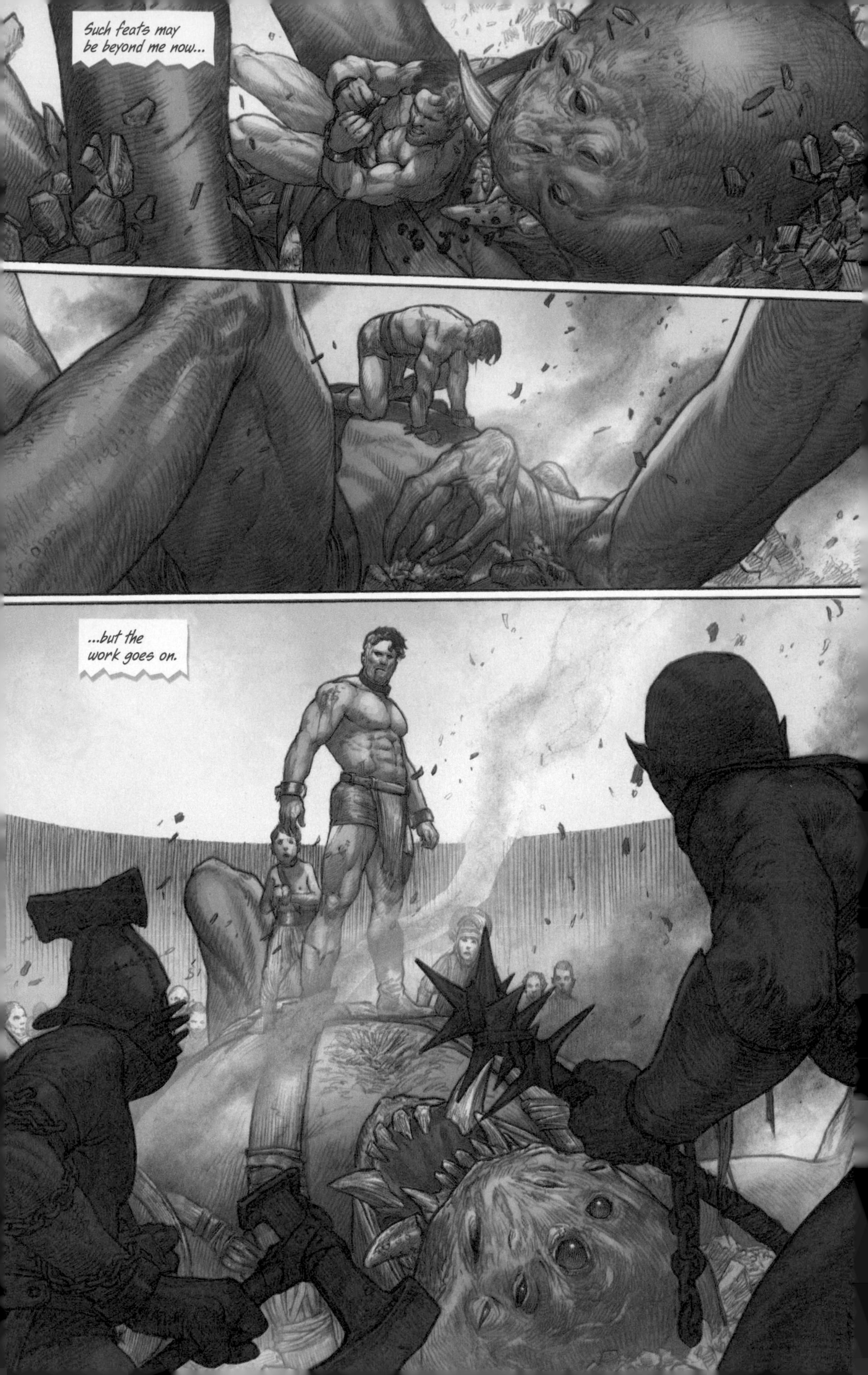
Such feats may be beyond me now...
...but the work goes on.

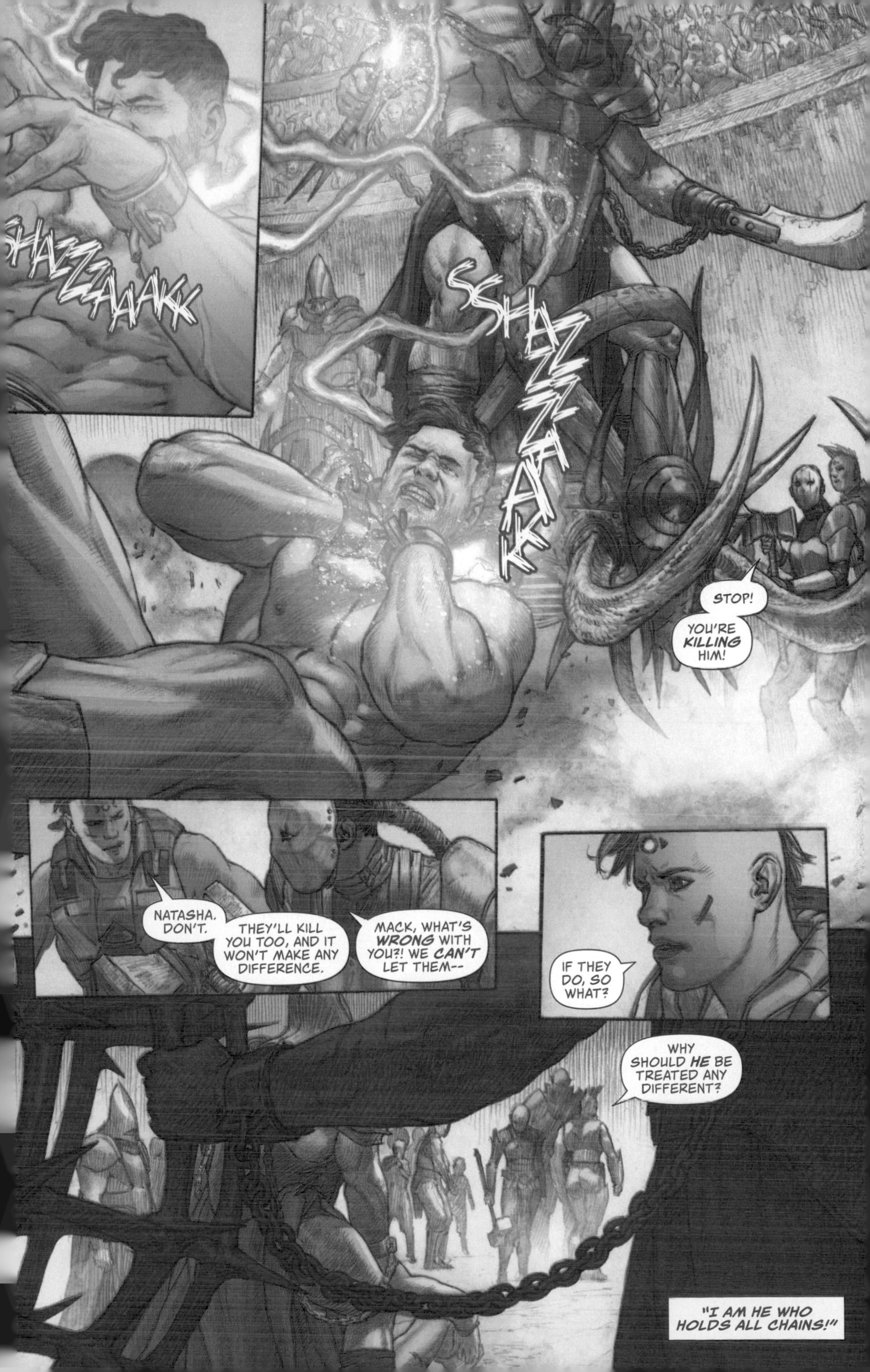
SHAZZAAAKK
SSHAZZZAKK
STOP!
YOU'RE KILLING HIM!
NATASHA. DON'T.
THEY'LL KILL YOU TOO, AND IT WON'T MAKE ANY DIFFERENCE.
MACK, WHAT'S WRONG WITH YOU?! WE CAN'T LET THEM--
IF THEY DO, SO WHAT?
WHY SHOULD HE BE TREATED ANY DIFFERENT?
"I AM HE WHO HOLDS ALL CHAINS!"

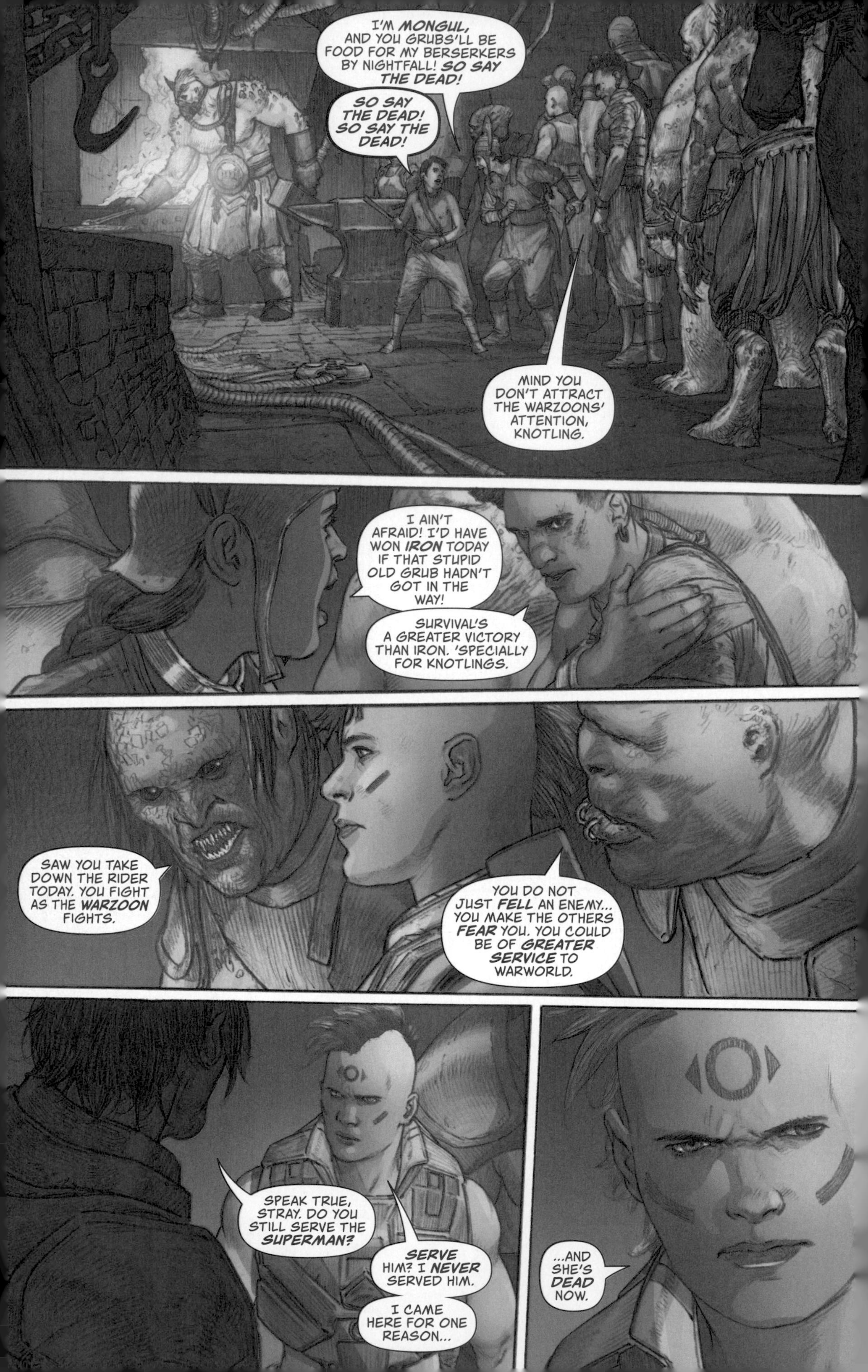
I'M MONGUL, AND YOU GRUBS'LL BE FOOD FOR MY BERSERKERS BY NIGHTFALL! SO SAY THE DEAD!
SO SAY THE DEAD! SO SAY THE DEAD!
MIND YOU DON'T ATTRACT THE WARZOONS' ATTENTION, KNOTLING.
I AIN'T AFRAID! I'D HAVE WON IRON TODAY IF THAT STUPID OLD GRUB HADN'T GOT IN THE WAY!
SURVIVAL'S A GREATER VICTORY THAN IRON. 'SPECIALLY FOR KNOTLINGS.
SAW YOU TAKE DOWN THE RIDER TODAY. YOU FIGHT AS THE WARZOON FIGHTS.
YOU DO NOT JUST FELL AN ENEMY... YOU MAKE THE OTHERS FEAR YOU. YOU COULD BE OF GREATER SERVICE TO WARWORLD.
SPEAK TRUE, STRAY. DO YOU STILL SERVE THE SUPERMAN?
SERVE HIM? I NEVER SERVED HIM.
I CAME HERE FOR ONE REASON...
...AND SHE'S DEAD NOW.

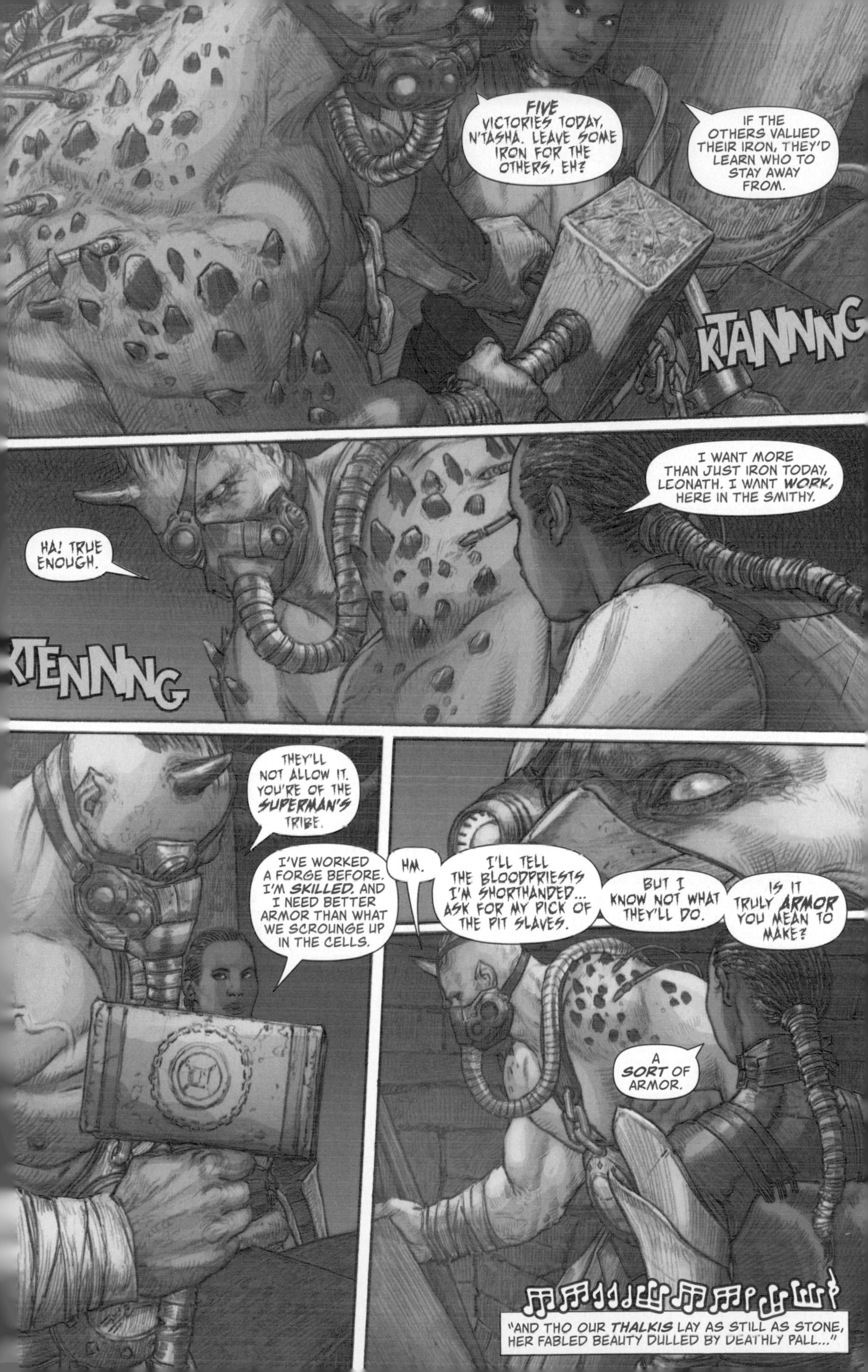
FIVE VICTORIES TODAY, N'TASHA. LEAVE SOME IRON FOR THE OTHERS, EH?
IF THE OTHERS VALUED THEIR IRON, THEY'D LEARN WHO TO STAY AWAY FROM.
KTANNNG
I WANT MORE THAN JUST IRON TODAY, LEONATH. I WANT WORK, HERE IN THE SMITHY.
HA! TRUE ENOUGH.
KTENNNG
THEY'LL NOT ALLOW IT. YOU'RE OF THE SUPERMAN'S TRIBE.
I'VE WORKED A FORGE BEFORE. I'M SKILLED. AND I NEED BETTER ARMOR THAN WHAT WE SCROUNGE UP IN THE CELLS.
HM.
I'LL TELL THE BLOODPRIESTS I'M SHORTHANDED... ASK FOR MY PICK OF THE PIT SLAVES.
BUT I KNOW NOT WHAT THEY'LL DO.
IS IT TRULY ARMOR YOU MEAN TO MAKE?
A SORT OF ARMOR.
"AND THO OUR THALKIS LAY AS STILL AS STONE, HER FABLED BEAUTY DULLED BY DEATHLY PALL..."

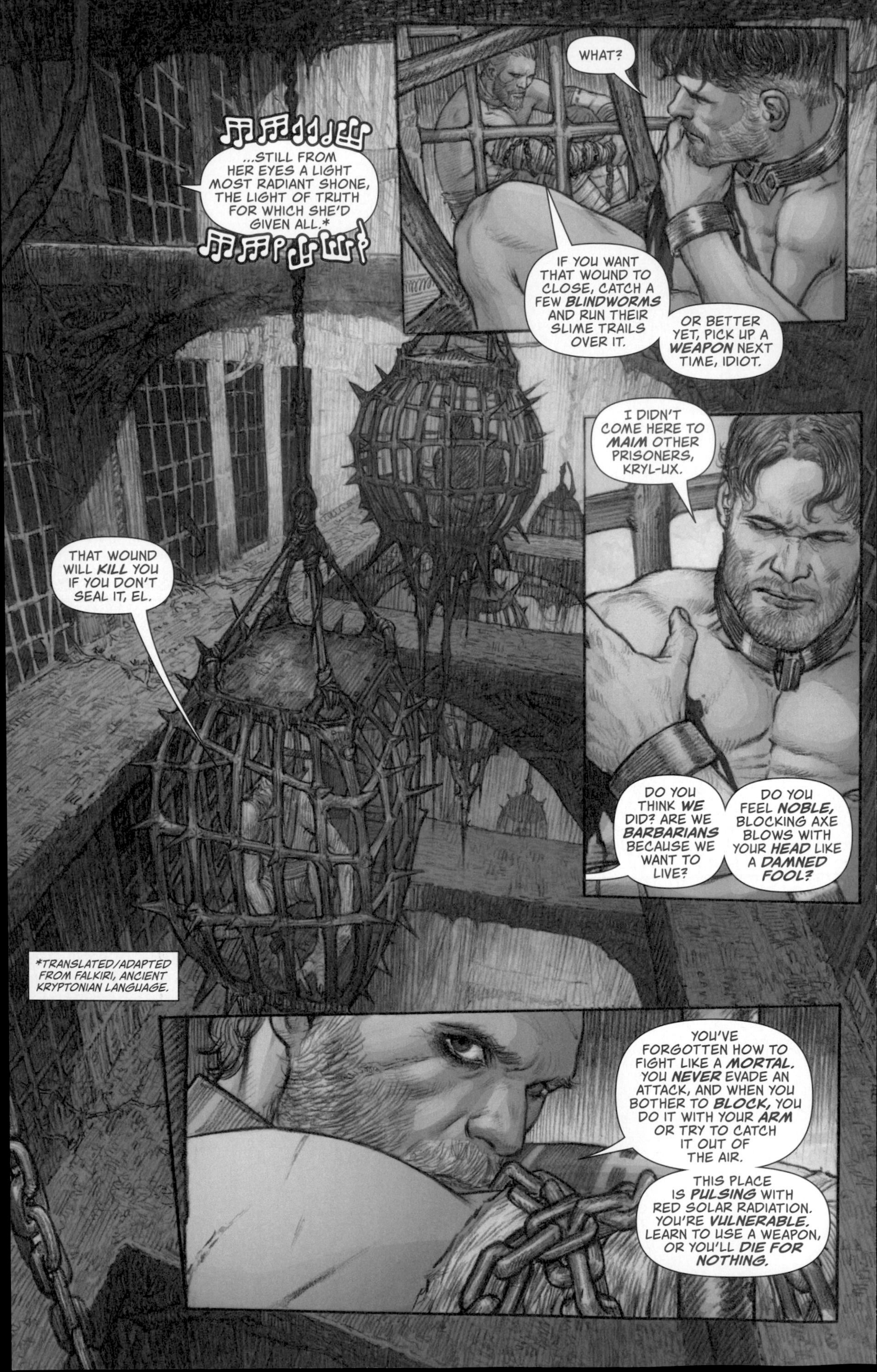
...STILL FROM HER EYES A LIGHT MOST RADIANT SHONE, THE LIGHT OF TRUTH FOR WHICH SHE'D GIVEN ALL.*
WHAT?
IF YOU WANT THAT WOUND TO CLOSE, CATCH A FEW BLINDWORMS AND RUN THEIR SLIME TRAILS OVER IT.
OR BETTER YET, PICK UP A WEAPON NEXT TIME, IDIOT.
THAT WOUND WILL KILL YOU IF YOU DON'T SEAL IT, EL.
I DIDN'T COME HERE TO MAIM OTHER PRISONERS, KRYL-UX.
DO YOU THINK WE DID? ARE WE BARBARIANS BECAUSE WE WANT TO LIVE?
DO YOU FEEL NOBLE, BLOCKING AXE BLOWS WITH YOUR HEAD LIKE A DAMNED FOOL?
*TRANSLATED/ADAPTED FROM FALKIRI, ANCIENT KRYPTONIAN LANGUAGE.
YOU'VE FORGOTTEN HOW TO FIGHT LIKE A MORTAL. YOU NEVER EVADE AN ATTACK, AND WHEN YOU BOTHER TO BLOCK, YOU DO IT WITH YOUR ARM OR TRY TO CATCH IT OUT OF THE AIR.
THIS PLACE IS PULSING WITH RED SOLAR RADIATION. YOU'RE VULNERABLE. LEARN TO USE A WEAPON, OR YOU'LL DIE FOR NOTHING.

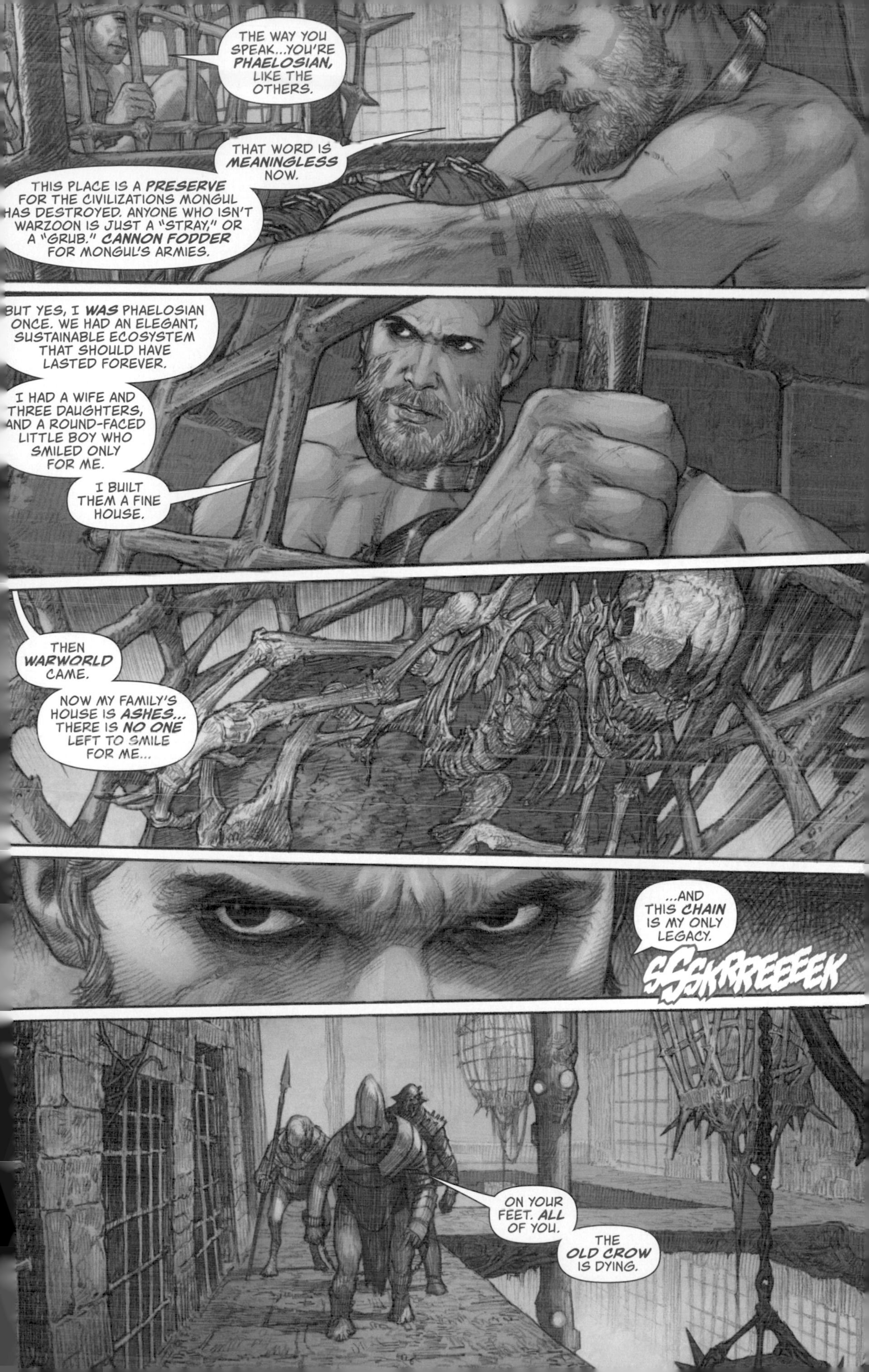
THE WAY YOU SPEAK...YOU'RE PHAELOSIAN, LIKE THE OTHERS.
THAT WORD IS MEANINGLESS NOW.
THIS PLACE IS A PRESERVE FOR THE CIVILIZATIONS MONGUL HAS DESTROYED. ANYONE WHO ISN'T WARZOON IS JUST A "STRAY," OR A "GRUB." CANNON FODDER FOR MONGUL'S ARMIES.
BUT YES, I WAS PHAELOSIAN ONCE. WE HAD AN ELEGANT, SUSTAINABLE ECOSYSTEM THAT SHOULD HAVE LASTED FOREVER.
I HAD A WIFE AND THREE DAUGHTERS, AND A ROUND-FACED LITTLE BOY WHO SMILED ONLY FOR ME.
I BUILT THEM A FINE HOUSE.
THEN WARWORLD CAME.
NOW MY FAMILY'S HOUSE IS ASHES... THERE IS NO ONE LEFT TO SMILE FOR ME...
...AND THIS CHAIN IS MY ONLY LEGACY.
SSSKRREEEEK
ON YOUR FEET. ALL OF YOU.
THE OLD CROW IS DYING.

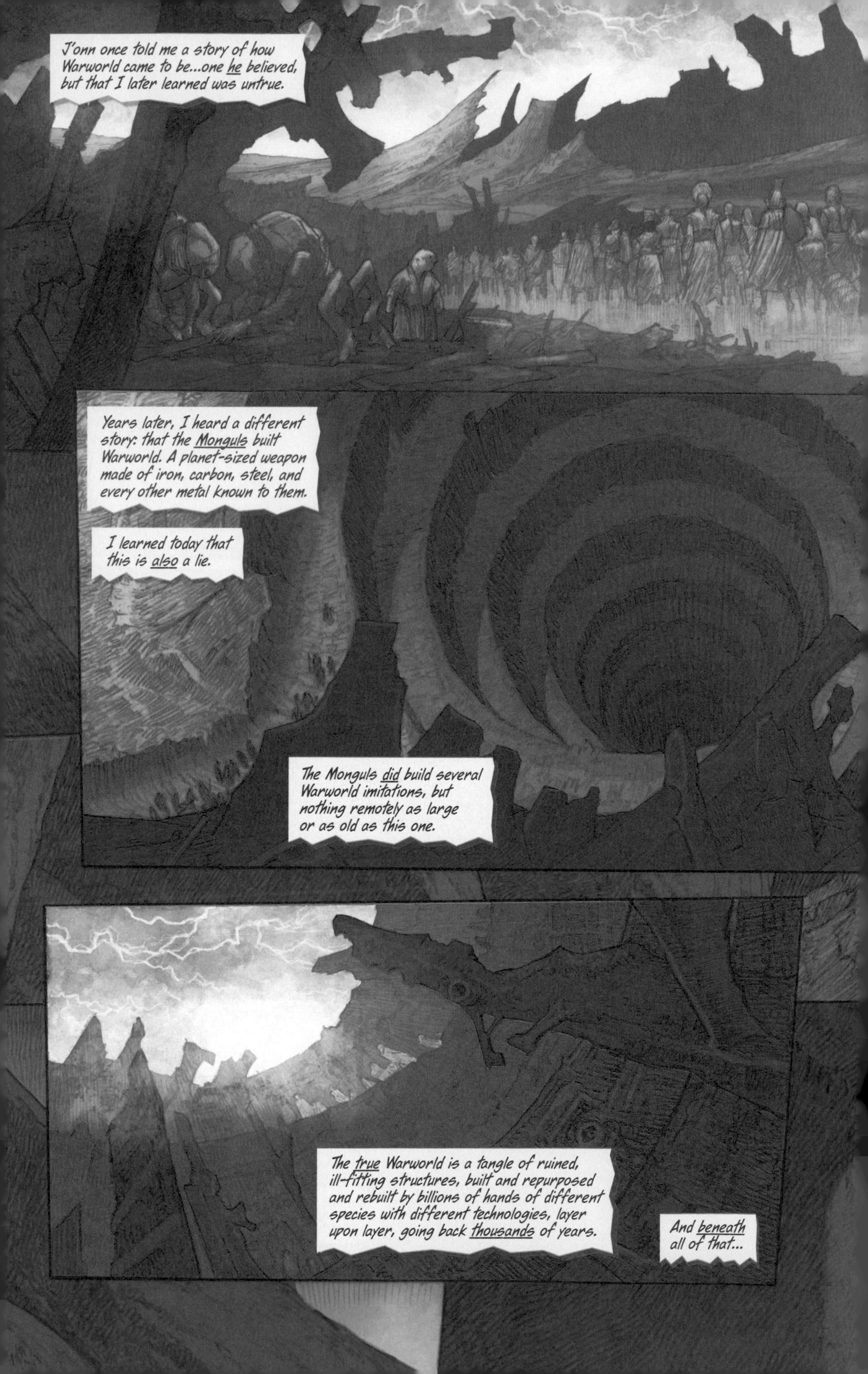
J'onn once told me a story of how Warworld came to be...one he believed, but that I later learned was untrue.
Years later, I heard a different story: that the Monguls built Warworld. A planet-sized weapon made of iron, carbon, steel, and every other metal known to them.
I learned today that this is also a lie.
The Monguls did build several Warworld imitations, but nothing remotely as large or as old as this one.
The true Warworld is a tangle of ruined, ill-fitting structures, built and repurposed and rebuilt by billions of hands of different species with different technologies, layer upon layer, going back thousands of years.
And beneath all of that...

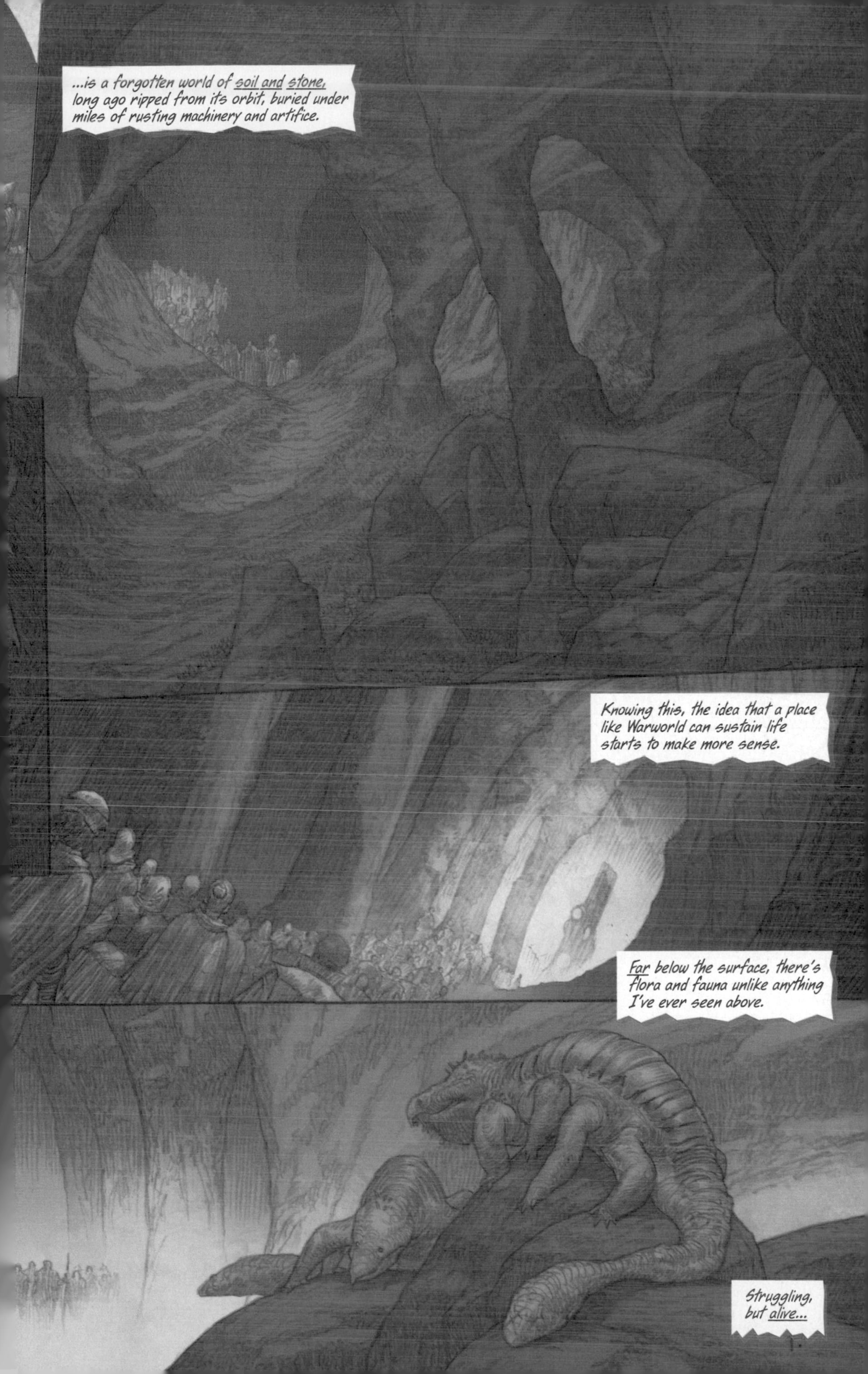
...is a forgotten world of soil and stone, long ago ripped from its orbit, buried under miles of rusting machinery and artifice.
Knowing this, the idea that a place like Warworld can sustain life starts to make more sense.
Far below the surface, there's flora and fauna unlike anything I've ever seen above.
Struggling, but alive...

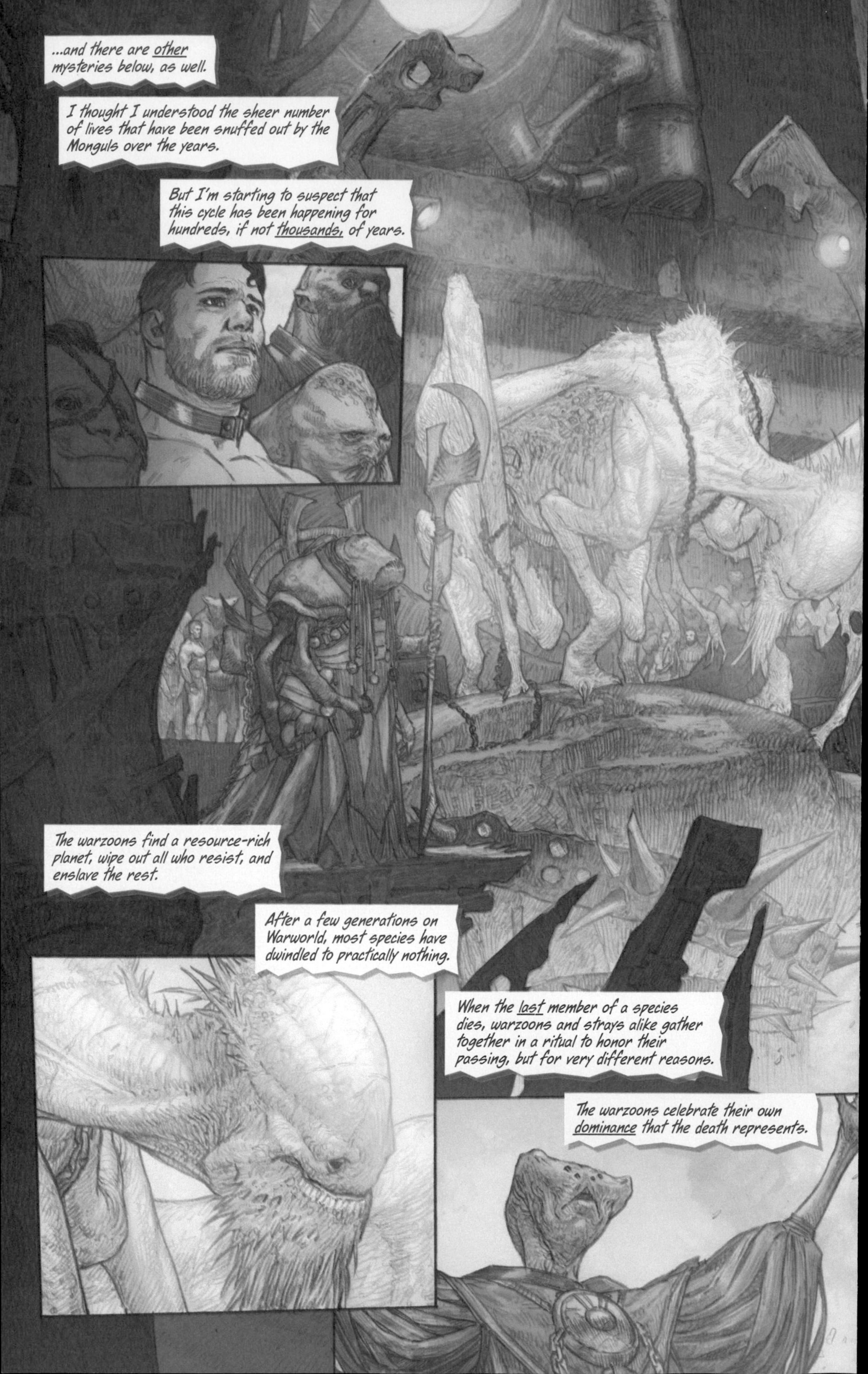

...and there are _other_ mysteries below, as well.

I thought I understood the sheer number of lives that have been snuffed out by the Monguls over the years.

But I'm starting to suspect that this cycle has been happening for hundreds, if not _thousands,_ of years.

The warzoons find a resource-rich planet, wipe out all who resist, and enslave the rest.

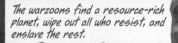

After a few generations on Warworld, most species have dwindled to practically nothing.

When the _last_ member of a species dies, warzoons and strays alike gather together in a ritual to honor their passing, but for very different reasons.

The warzoons celebrate their own _dominance_ that the death represents.

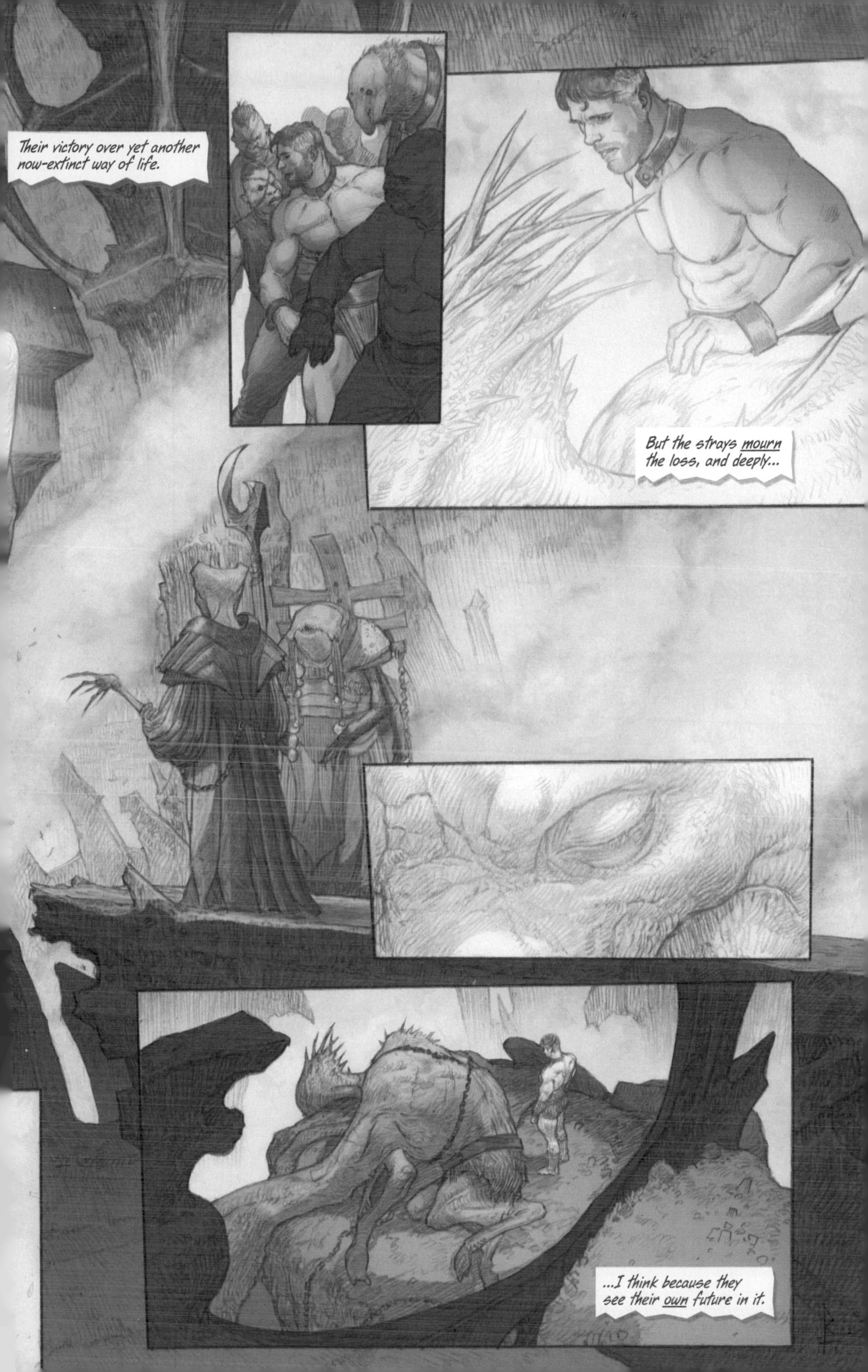
Their victory over yet another now-extinct way of life.
But the strays mourn the loss, and deeply...
...I think because they see their own future in it.

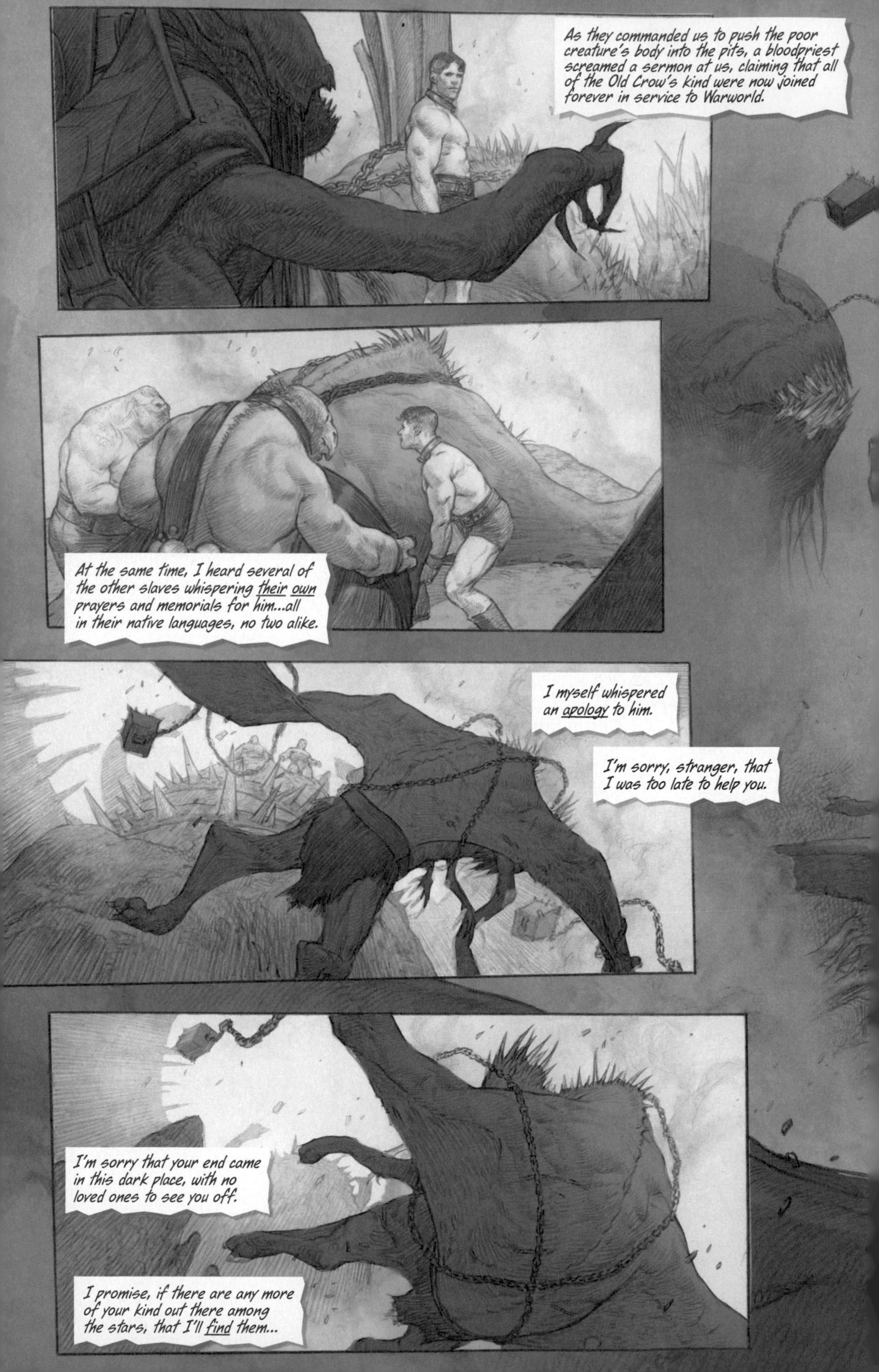
As they commanded us to push the poor creature's body into the pits, a bloodpriest screamed a sermon at us, claiming that all of the Old Crow's kind were now joined forever in service to Warworld.
At the same time, I heard several of the other slaves whispering their own prayers and memorials for him...all in their native languages, no two alike.
I myself whispered an apology to him.
I'm sorry, stranger, that I was too late to help you.
I'm sorry that your end came in this dark place, with no loved ones to see you off.
I promise, if there are any more of your kind out there among the stars, that I'll find them...

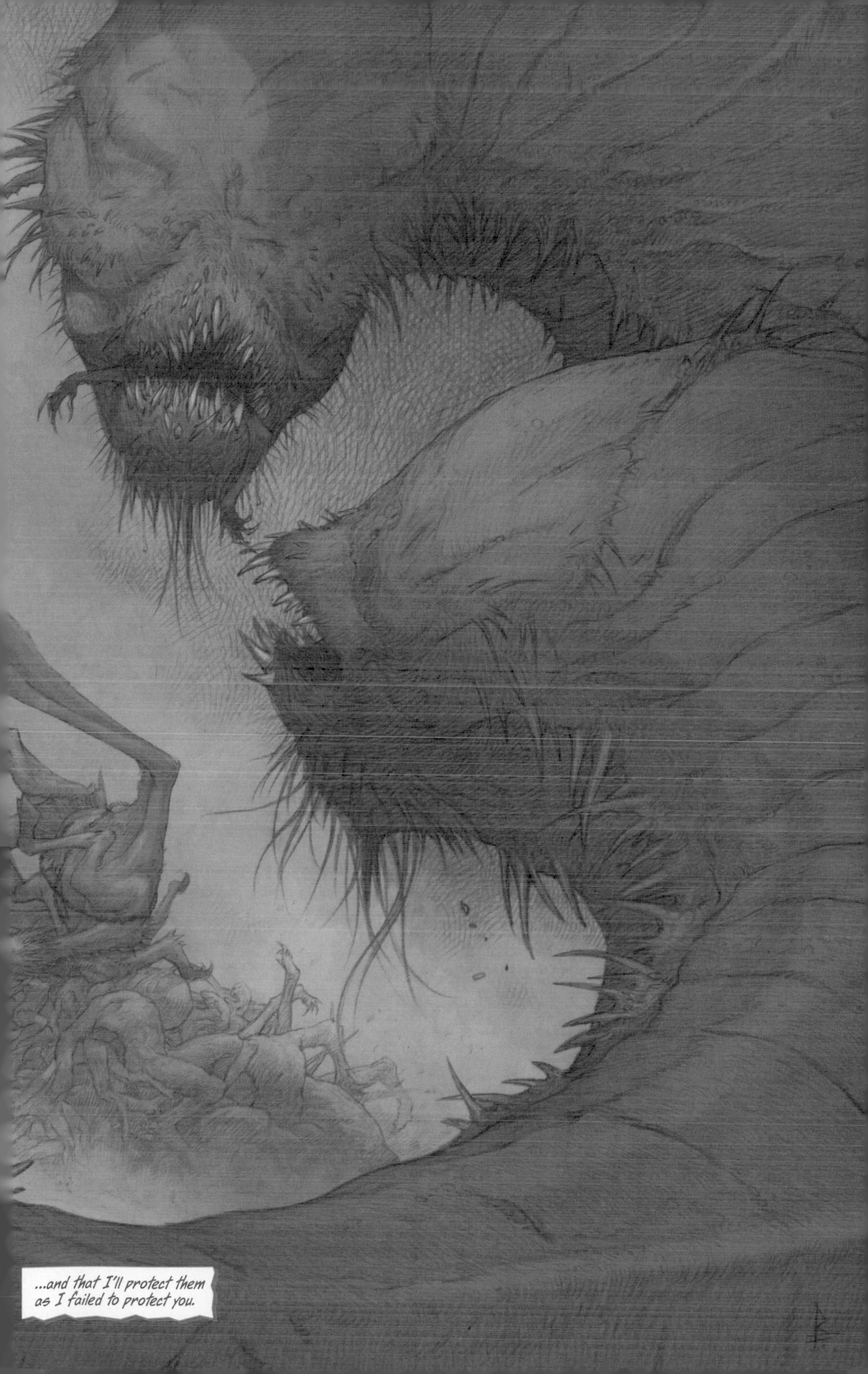
...and that I'll protect them as I failed to protect you.

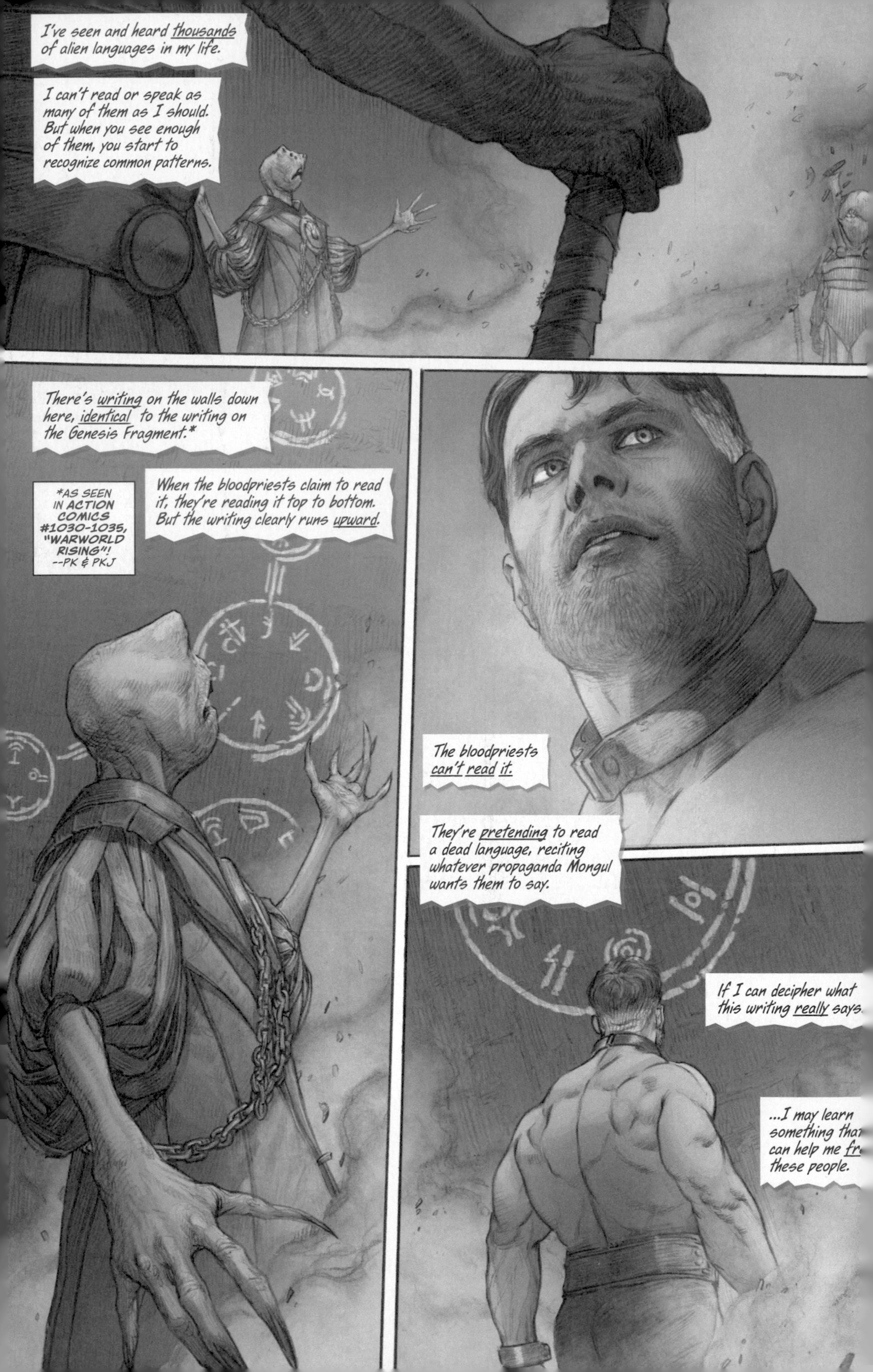
I've seen and heard thousands of alien languages in my life.
I can't read or speak as many of them as I should. But when you see enough of them, you start to recognize common patterns.
There's writing on the walls down here, identical to the writing on the Genesis Fragment.*
*AS SEEN IN ACTION COMICS #1030-1035, "WARWORLD RISING"! --PK & PKJ
When the bloodpriests claim to read it, they're reading it top to bottom. But the writing clearly runs upward.
The bloodpriests can't read it.
They're pretending to read a dead language, reciting whatever propaganda Mongul wants them to say.
If I can decipher what this writing really says.
...I may learn something that can help me free these people.

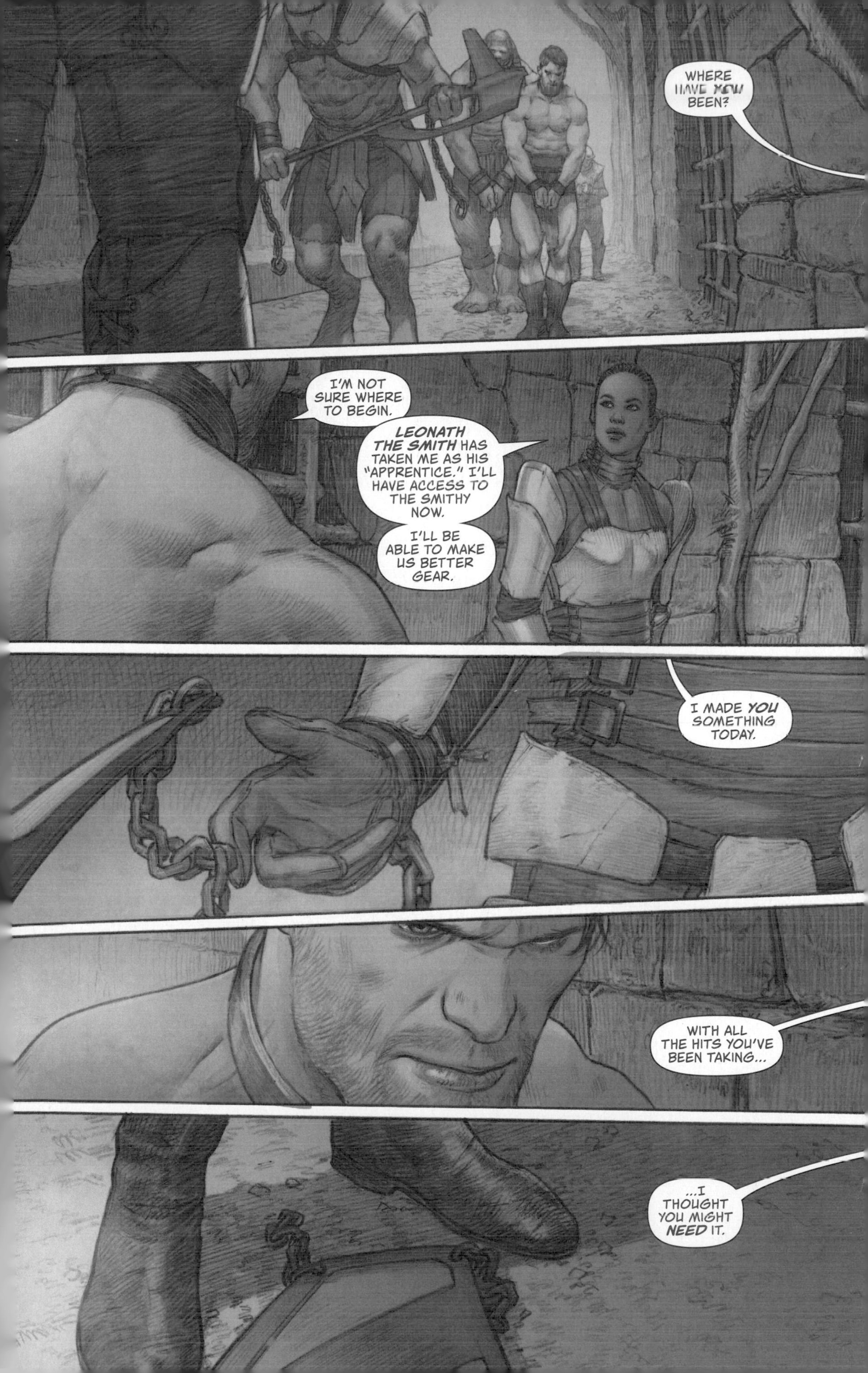
WHERE HAVE YOU BEEN?
I'M NOT SURE WHERE TO BEGIN.
LEONATH THE SMITH HAS TAKEN ME AS HIS "APPRENTICE." I'LL HAVE ACCESS TO THE SMITHY NOW.
I'LL BE ABLE TO MAKE US BETTER GEAR.
I MADE YOU SOMETHING TODAY.
WITH ALL THE HITS YOU'VE BEEN TAKING...
...I THOUGHT YOU MIGHT NEED IT.

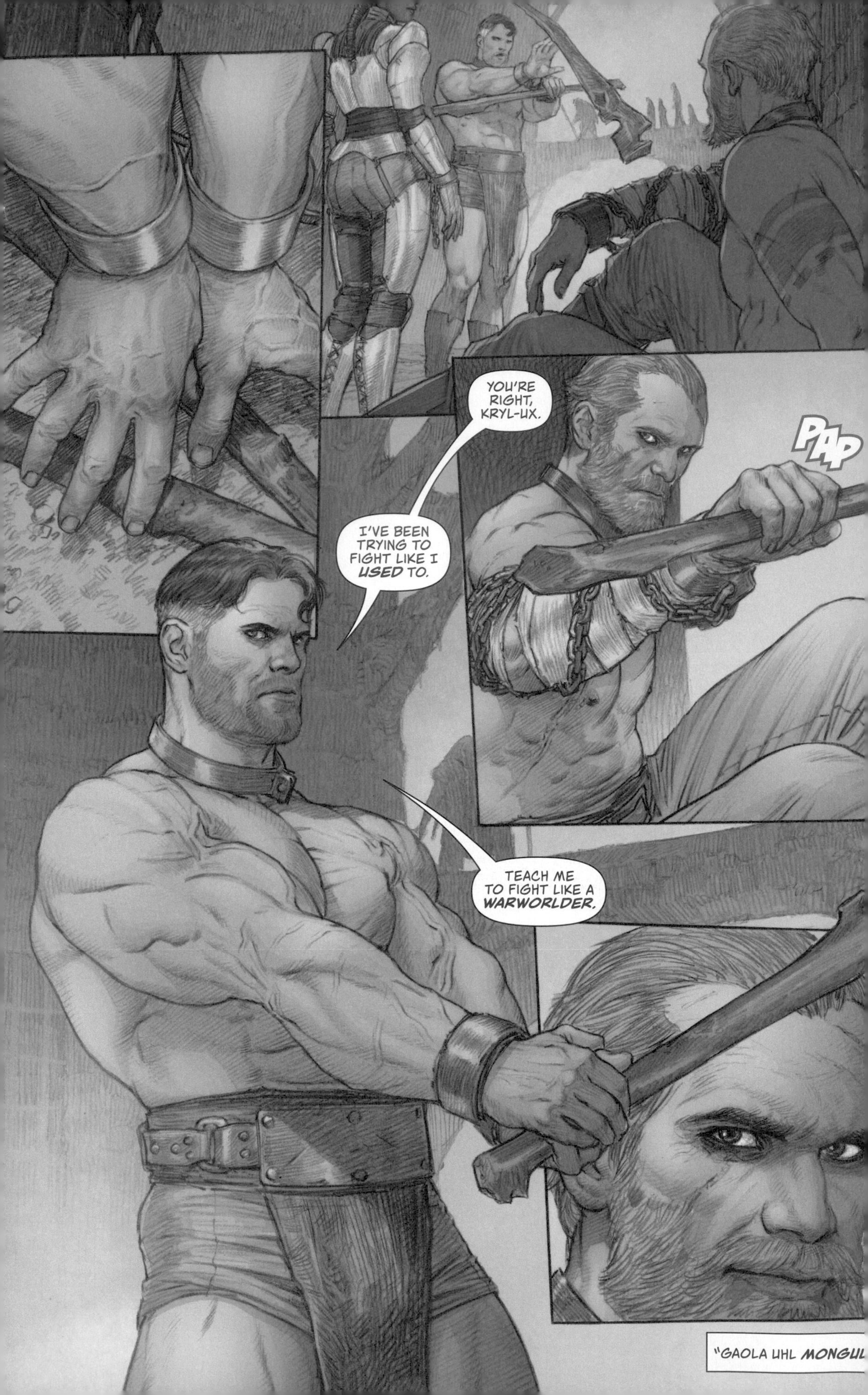
YOU'RE RIGHT, KRYL-UX.
PAP
I'VE BEEN TRYING TO FIGHT LIKE I USED TO.
TEACH ME TO FIGHT LIKE A WARWORLDER.
"GAOLA UHL MONGUL

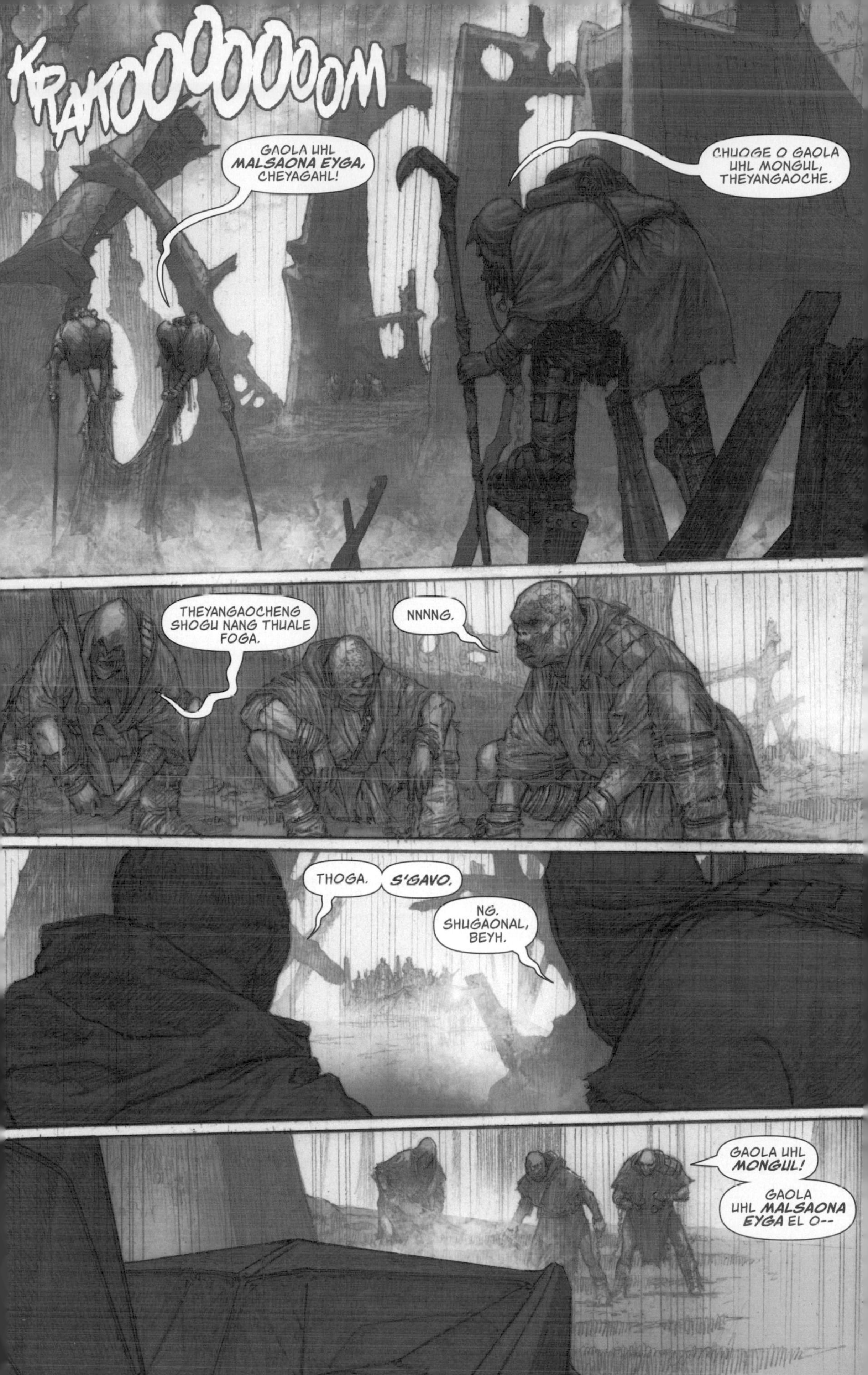
KRAKOOOOOOOOM
GAOLA UHL MALSAONA EYGA, CHEYAGAHL!
CHUOGE O GAOLA UHL MONGUL, THEYANGAOCHE.
THEYANGAOCHENG SHOGU NANG THUALE FOGA.
NNNNG.
THOGA. S'GAVO.
NG. SHUGAONAL, BEYH.
GAOLA UHL MONGUL!
GAOLA UHL MALSAONA EYGA EL O--

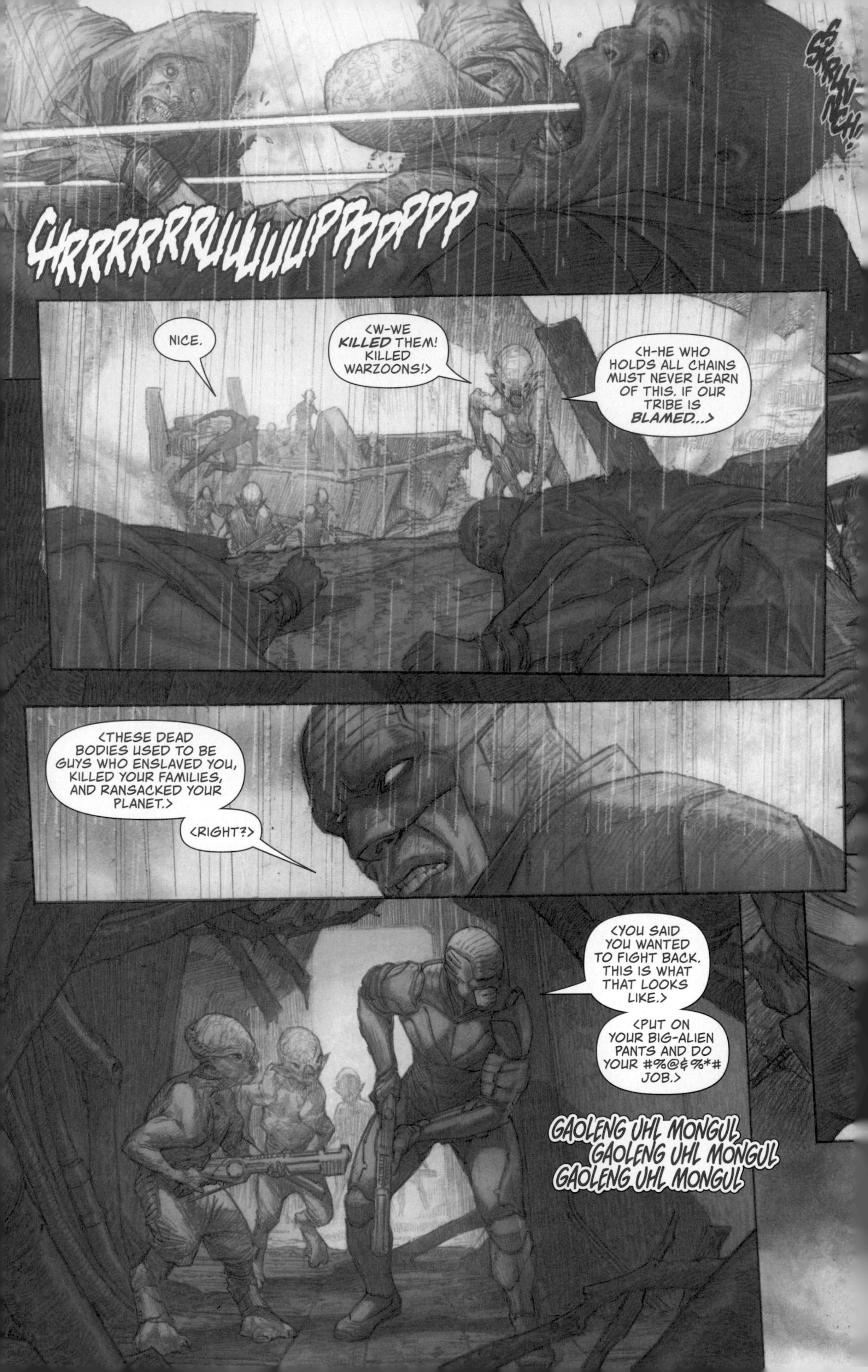
SKRUNCH!
CHRRRRRRUUUUUUPPPPPPP
NICE.
<W-WE KILLED THEM! KILLED WARZOONS!>
<H-HE WHO HOLDS ALL CHAINS MUST NEVER LEARN OF THIS. IF OUR TRIBE IS BLAMED...>
<THESE DEAD BODIES USED TO BE GUYS WHO ENSLAVED YOU, KILLED YOUR FAMILIES, AND RANSACKED YOUR PLANET.>
<RIGHT?>
<YOU SAID YOU WANTED TO FIGHT BACK. THIS IS WHAT THAT LOOKS LIKE.>
<PUT ON YOUR BIG-ALIEN PANTS AND DO YOUR #%@&%*# JOB.>
GAOLENG UHL MONGUL
GAOLENG UHL MONGUL
GAOLENG UHL MONGUL

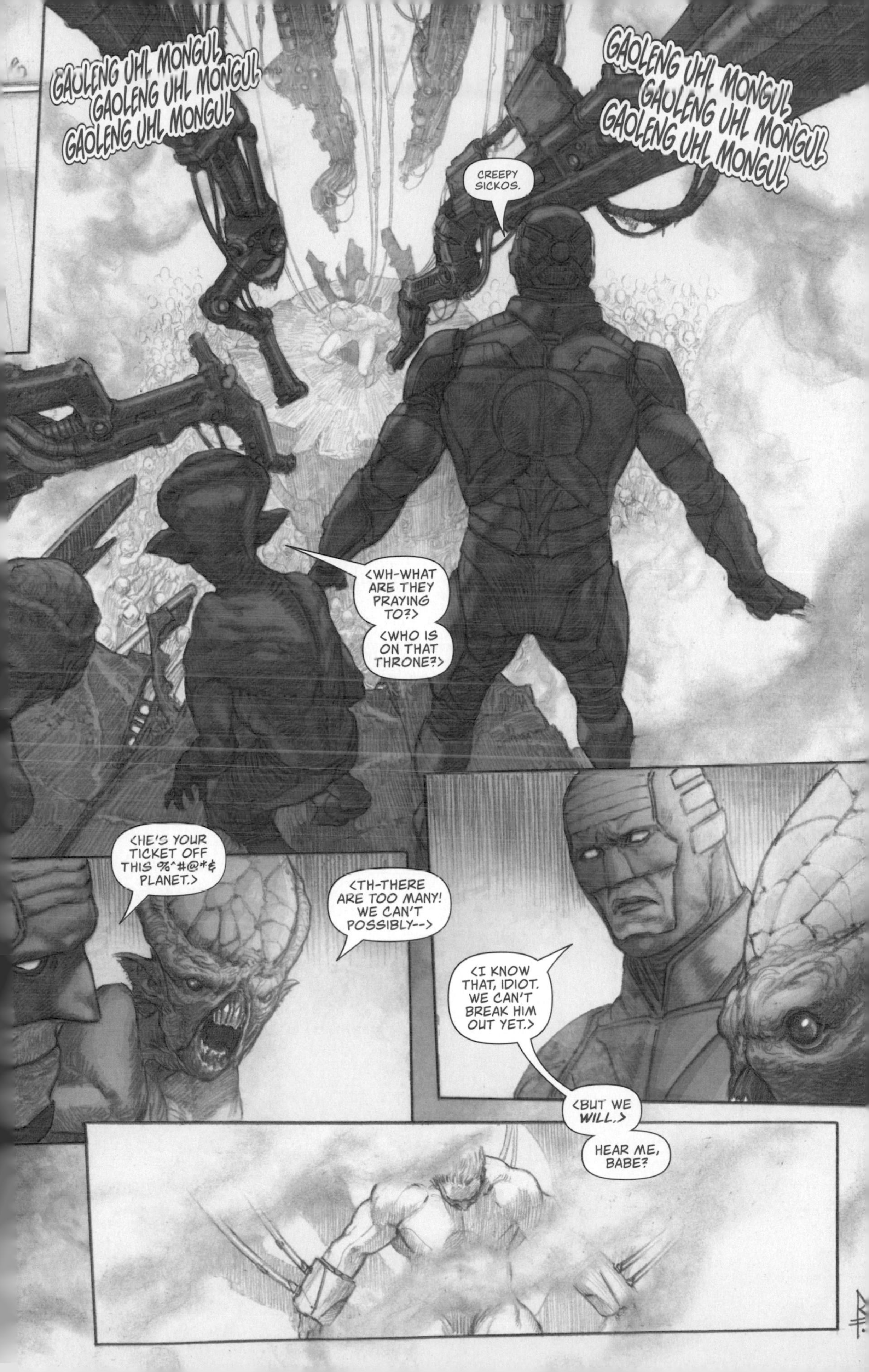
GAOLENG UHL MONGUL
GAOLENG UHL MONGUL
GAOLENG UHL MONGUL
GAOLENG UHL MONGUL
GAOLENG UHL MONGUL
GAOLENG UHL MONGUL
CREEPY SICKOS.
<WH-WHAT ARE THEY PRAYING TO?>
<WHO IS ON THAT THRONE?>
<HE'S YOUR TICKET OFF THIS %^#@*& PLANET.>
<TH-THERE ARE TOO MANY! WE CAN'T POSSIBLY-->
<I KNOW THAT, IDIOT. WE CAN'T BREAK HIM OUT YET.>
<BUT WE WILL.>
HEAR ME, BABE?

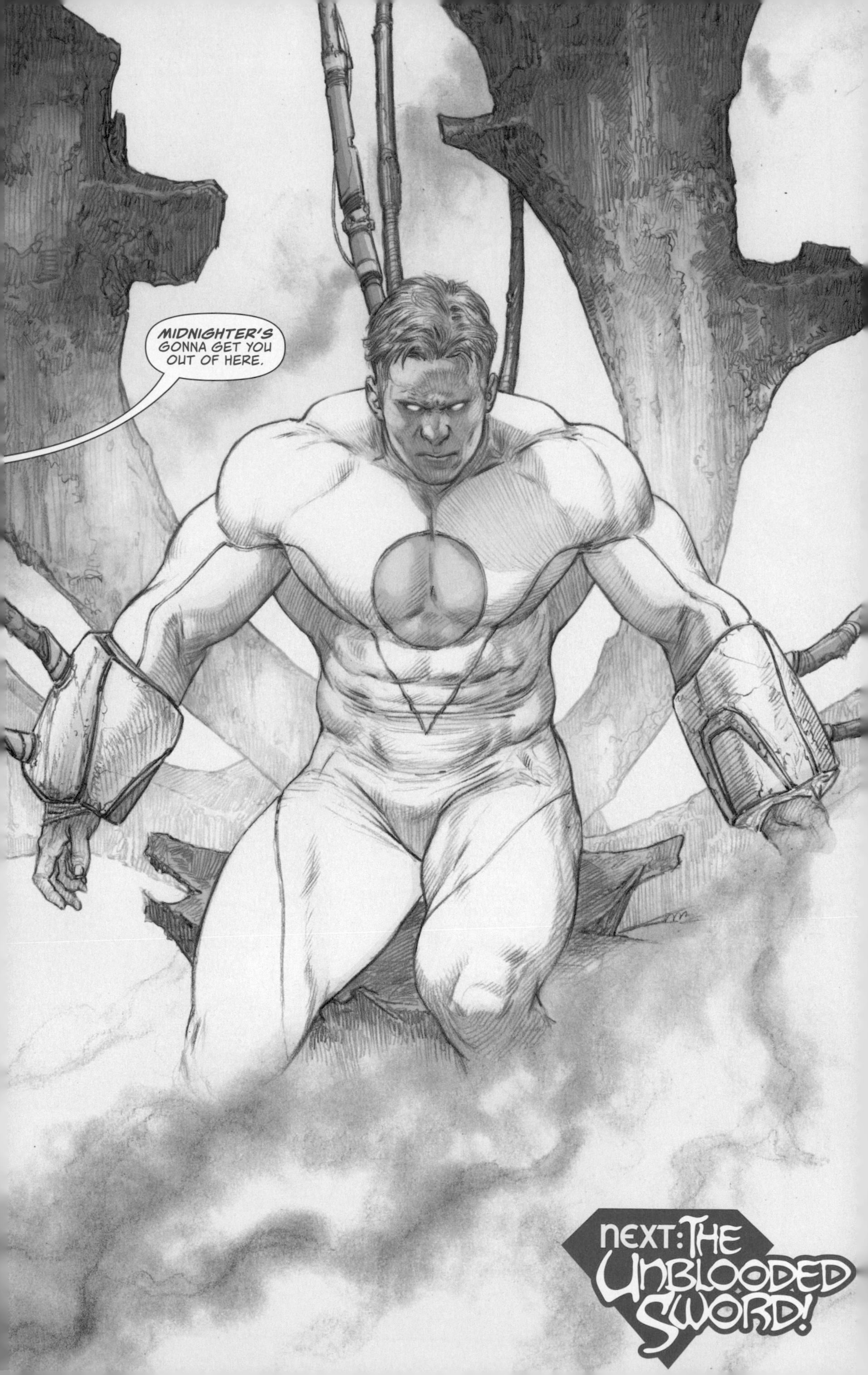
MIDNIGHTER'S GONNA GET YOU OUT OF HERE.
NEXT: THE UNBLOODED SWORD!

Action Comics #1040
main cover by DANIEL SAMPERE
and ALEJANDRO SÁNCHEZ

***Action Comics* #1040**
variant cover by JULIAN TOTINO TEDESCO

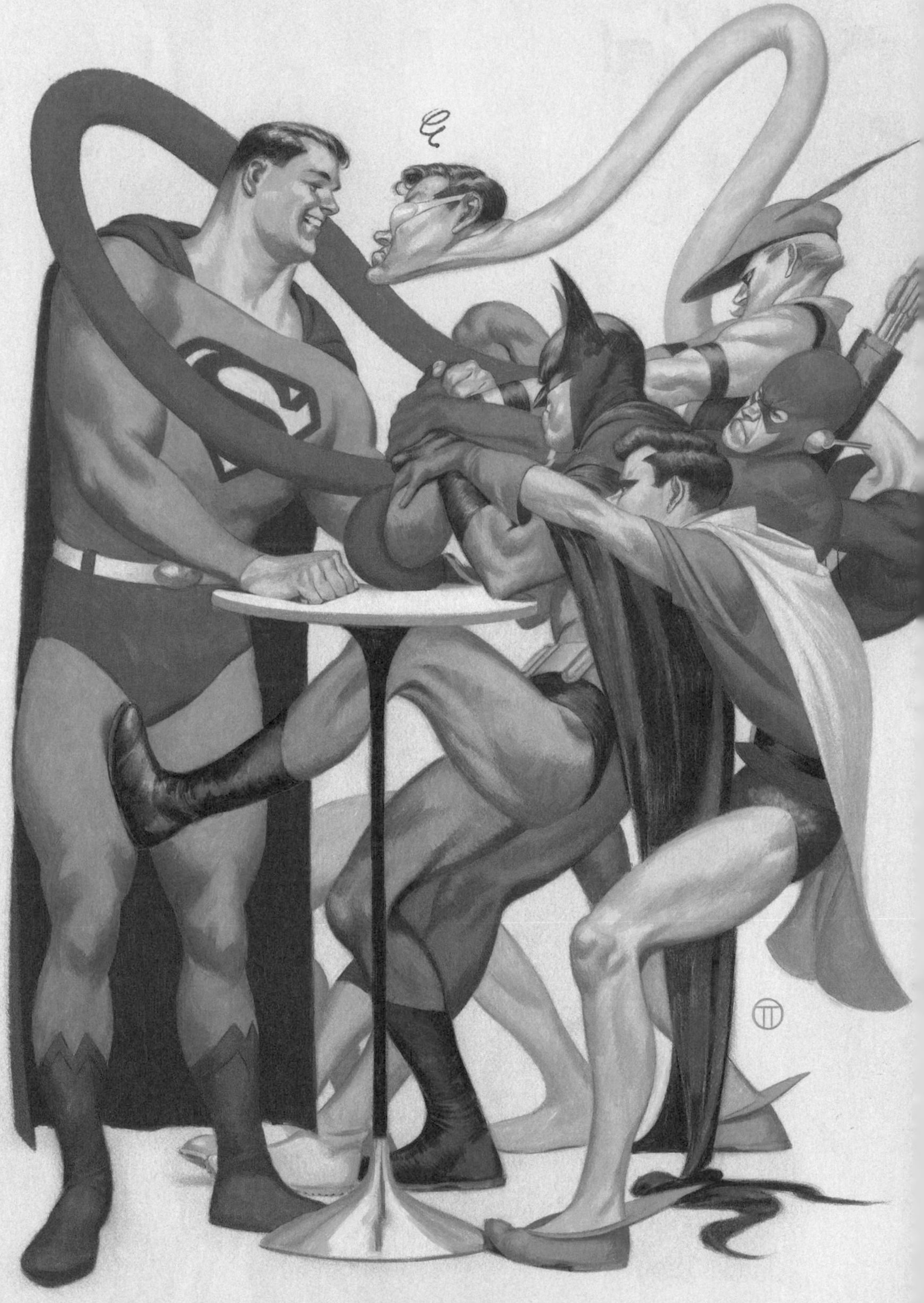

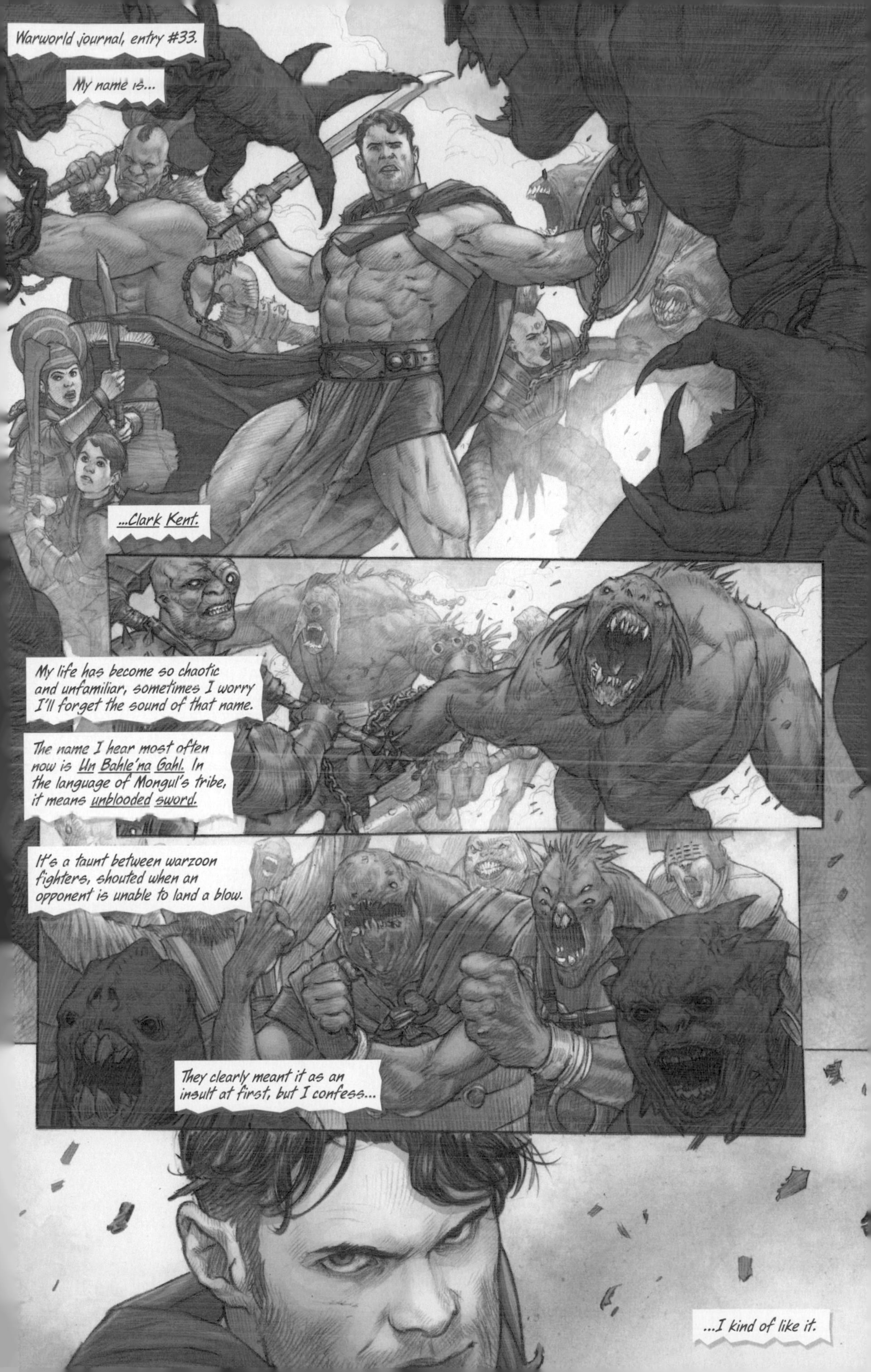
Warworld journal, entry #33.
My name is...
...Clark Kent.
My life has become so chaotic and unfamiliar, sometimes I worry I'll forget the sound of that name.
The name I hear most often now is Un Bahle'na Gahl. In the language of Mongul's tribe, it means unblooded sword.
It's a taunt between warzoon fighters, shouted when an opponent is unable to land a blow.
They clearly meant it as an insult at first, but I confess...
...I kind of like it.

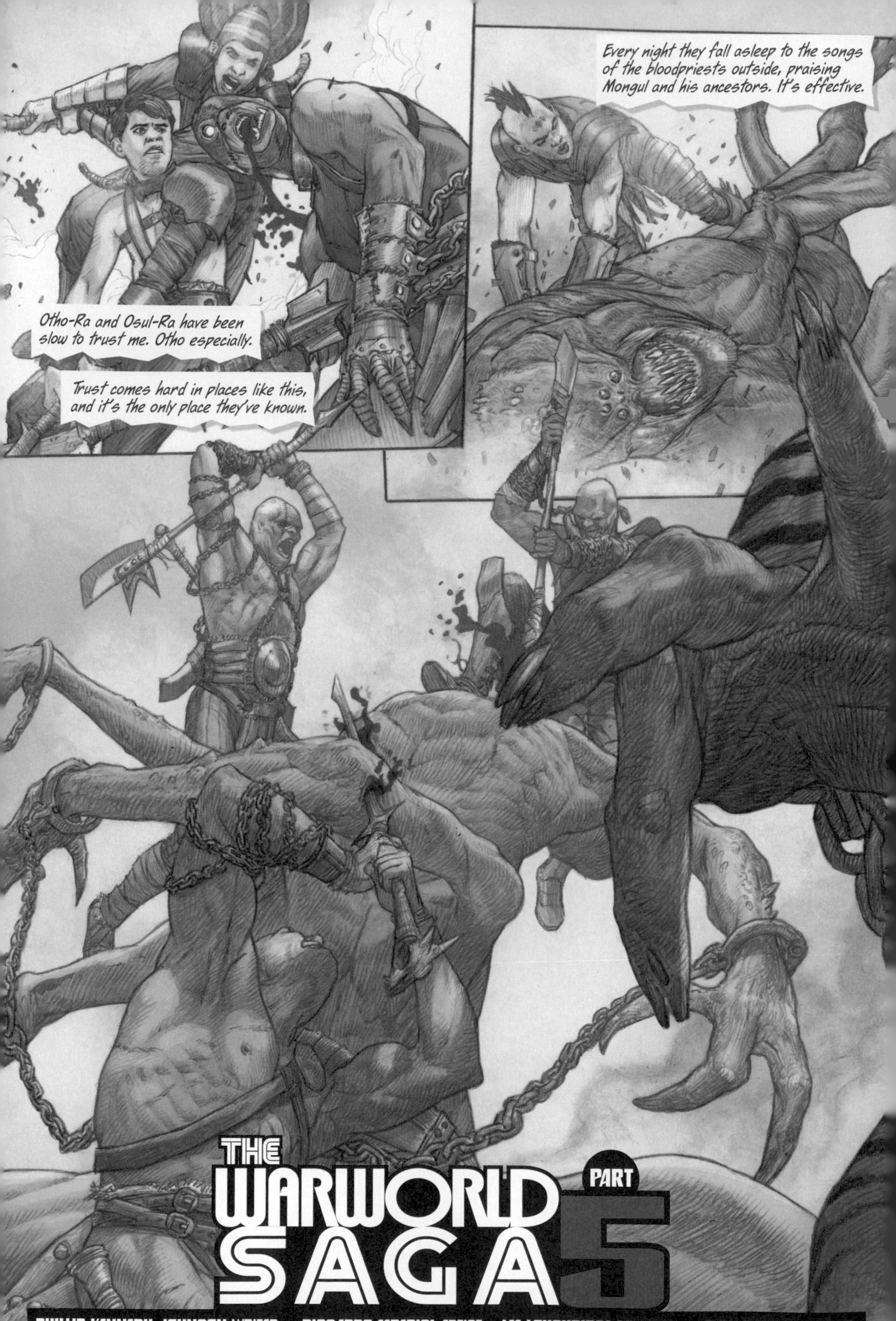
Otho-Ra and Osul-Ra have been slow to trust me. Otho especially.
Trust comes hard in places like this, and it's the only place they've known.
Every night they fall asleep to the songs of the bloodpriests outside, praising Mongul and his ancestors. It's effective.
THE WARWORLD SAGA PART 5

PHILLIP KENNEDY JOHNSON WRITER **RICCARDO FEDERICI** ARTIST **LEE LOUGHRIDGE** COLORIST **DAVE SHARPE** LETTERER
DANIEL SAMPERE AND ALEJANDRO SÁNCHEZ COVER **JULIAN TOTINO TEDESCO** VARIANT COVER **ALEXIS FRANKLIN** BLACK HISTORY MONTH VARIANT COVER
JILLIAN GRANT ASSISTANT EDITOR **PAUL KAMINSKI** EDITOR SUPERMAN CREATED BY JERRY SIEGEL AND JOE SHUSTER. BY SPECIAL ARRANGEMENT WITH THE JERRY SIEGEL FAMILY.

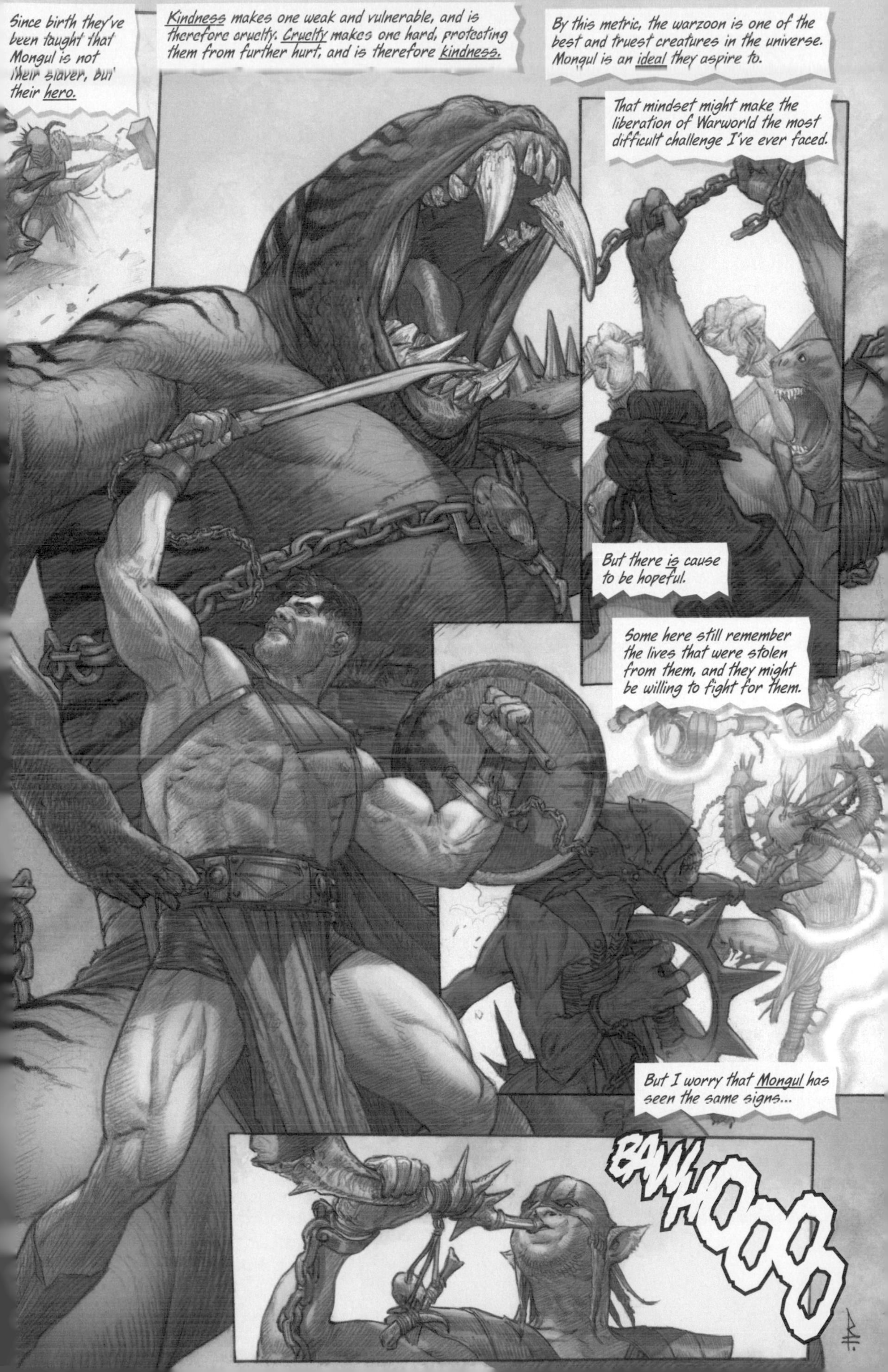
Since birth they've been taught that Mongul is not their slaver, but their hero.
Kindness makes one weak and vulnerable, and is therefore cruelty. Cruelty makes one hard, protecting them from further hurt, and is therefore kindness.
By this metric, the warzoon is one of the best and truest creatures in the universe. Mongul is an ideal they aspire to.
That mindset might make the liberation of Warworld the most difficult challenge I've ever faced.
But there is cause to be hopeful.
Some here still remember the lives that were stolen from them, and they might be willing to fight for them.
But I worry that Mongul has seen the same signs...
BAWHOOOB

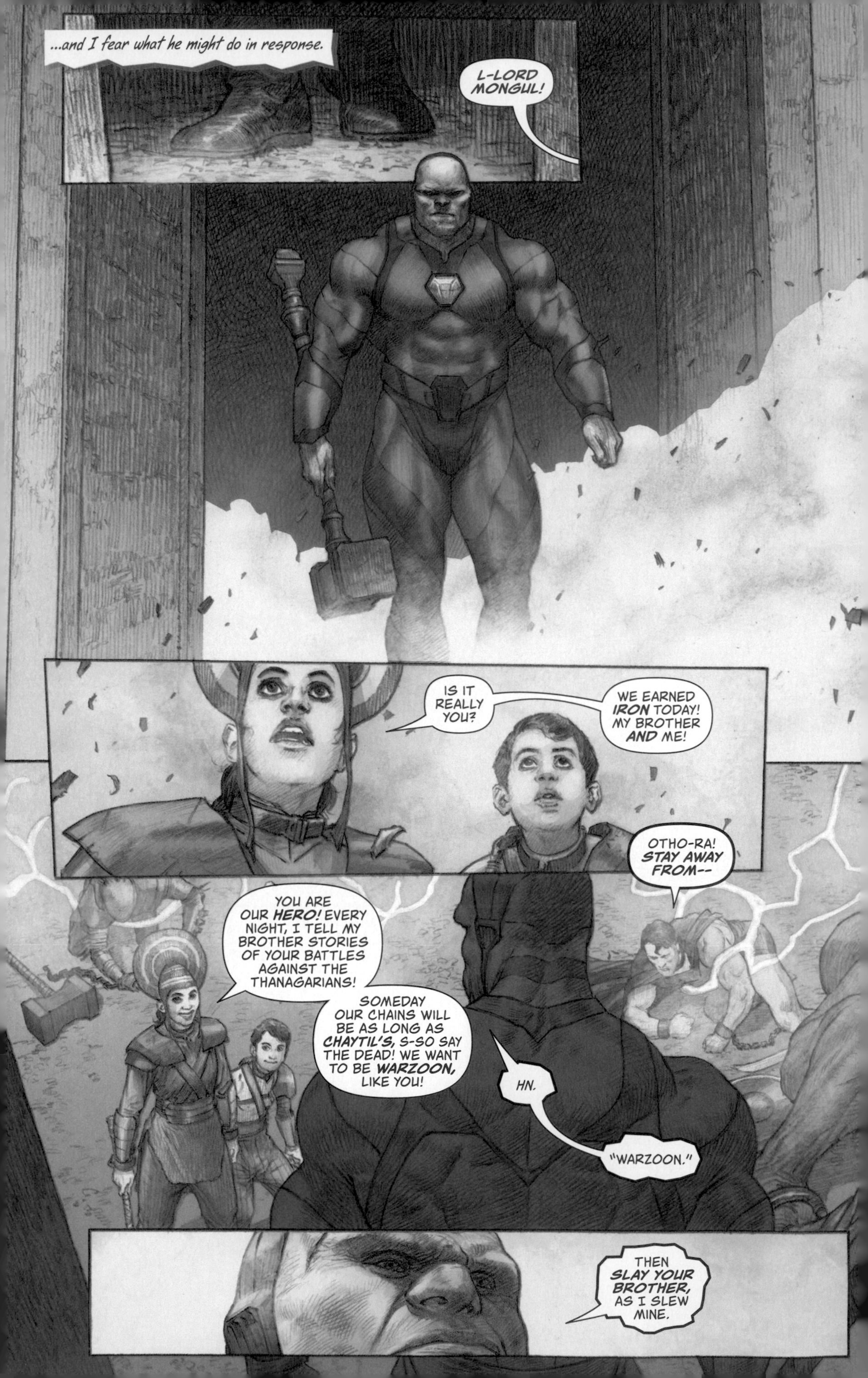
...and I fear what he might do in response.
L-LORD MONGUL!
IS IT REALLY YOU?
WE EARNED IRON TODAY! MY BROTHER AND ME!
OTHO-RA! STAY AWAY FROM--
YOU ARE OUR HERO! EVERY NIGHT, I TELL MY BROTHER STORIES OF YOUR BATTLES AGAINST THE THANAGARIANS!
SOMEDAY OUR CHAINS WILL BE AS LONG AS CHAYTIL'S, S-SO SAY THE DEAD! WE WANT TO BE WARZOON, LIKE YOU!
HN.
"WARZOON."
THEN SLAY YOUR BROTHER, AS I SLEW MINE.

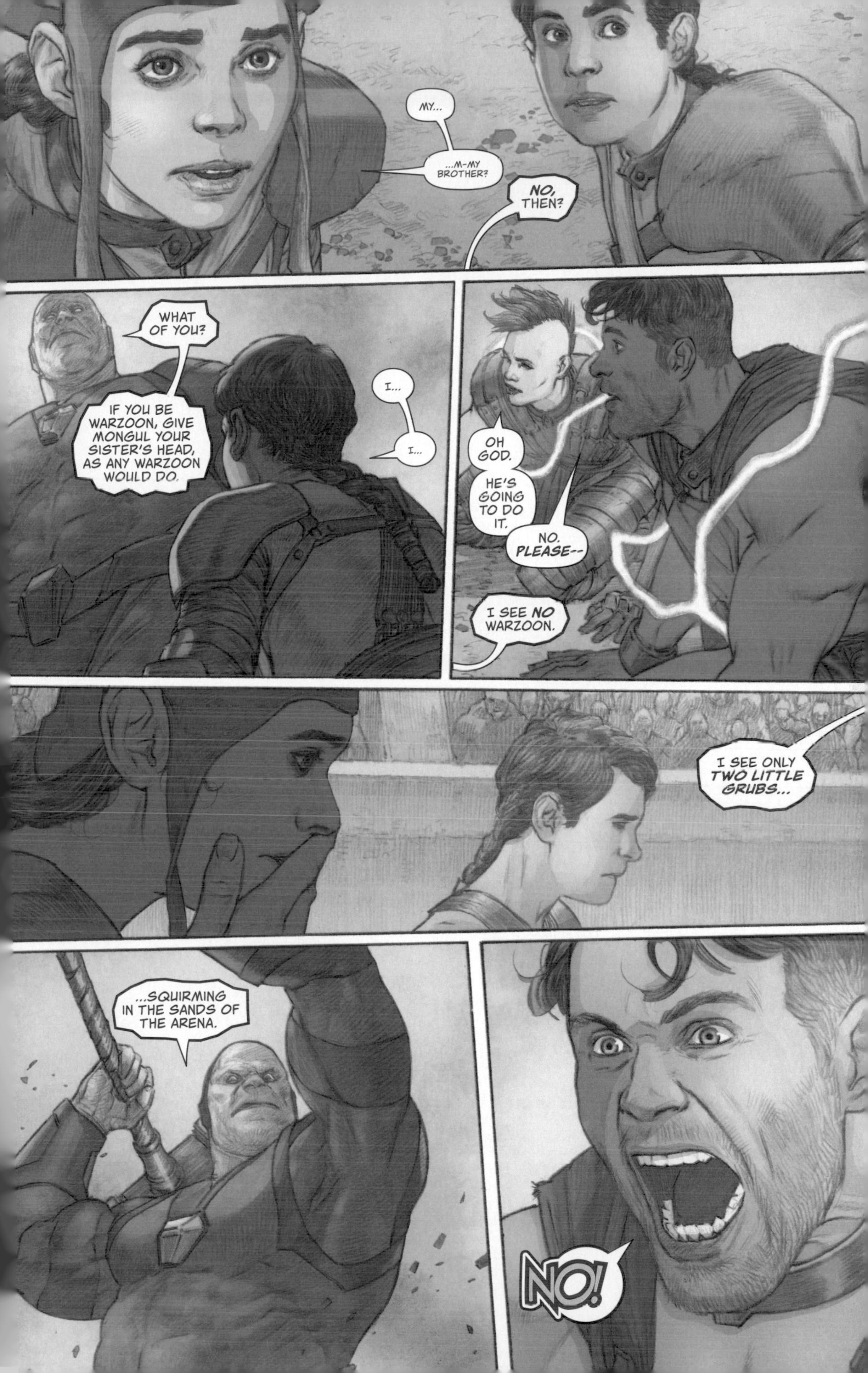

MY...
...M-MY BROTHER?
NO, THEN?
WHAT OF YOU?
IF YOU BE WARZOON, GIVE MONGUL YOUR SISTER'S HEAD, AS ANY WARZOON WOULD DO.
I...
I...
OH GOD.
HE'S GOING TO DO IT.
NO. PLEASE--
I SEE NO WARZOON.
I SEE ONLY TWO LITTLE GRUBS...
...SQUIRMING IN THE SANDS OF THE ARENA.
NO!

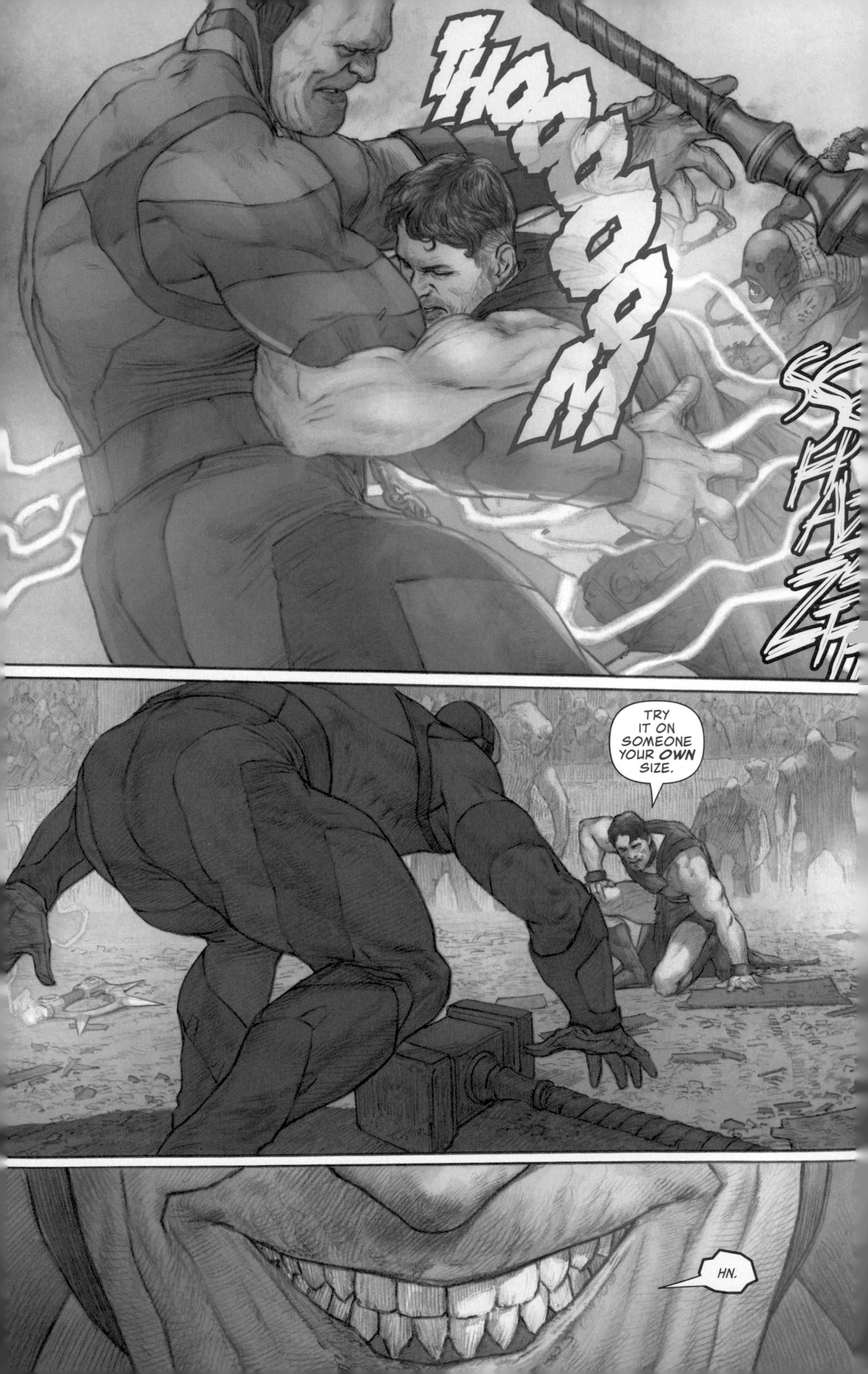
THOOOOM
SHAZZT
TRY IT ON SOMEONE YOUR OWN SIZE.
HN.

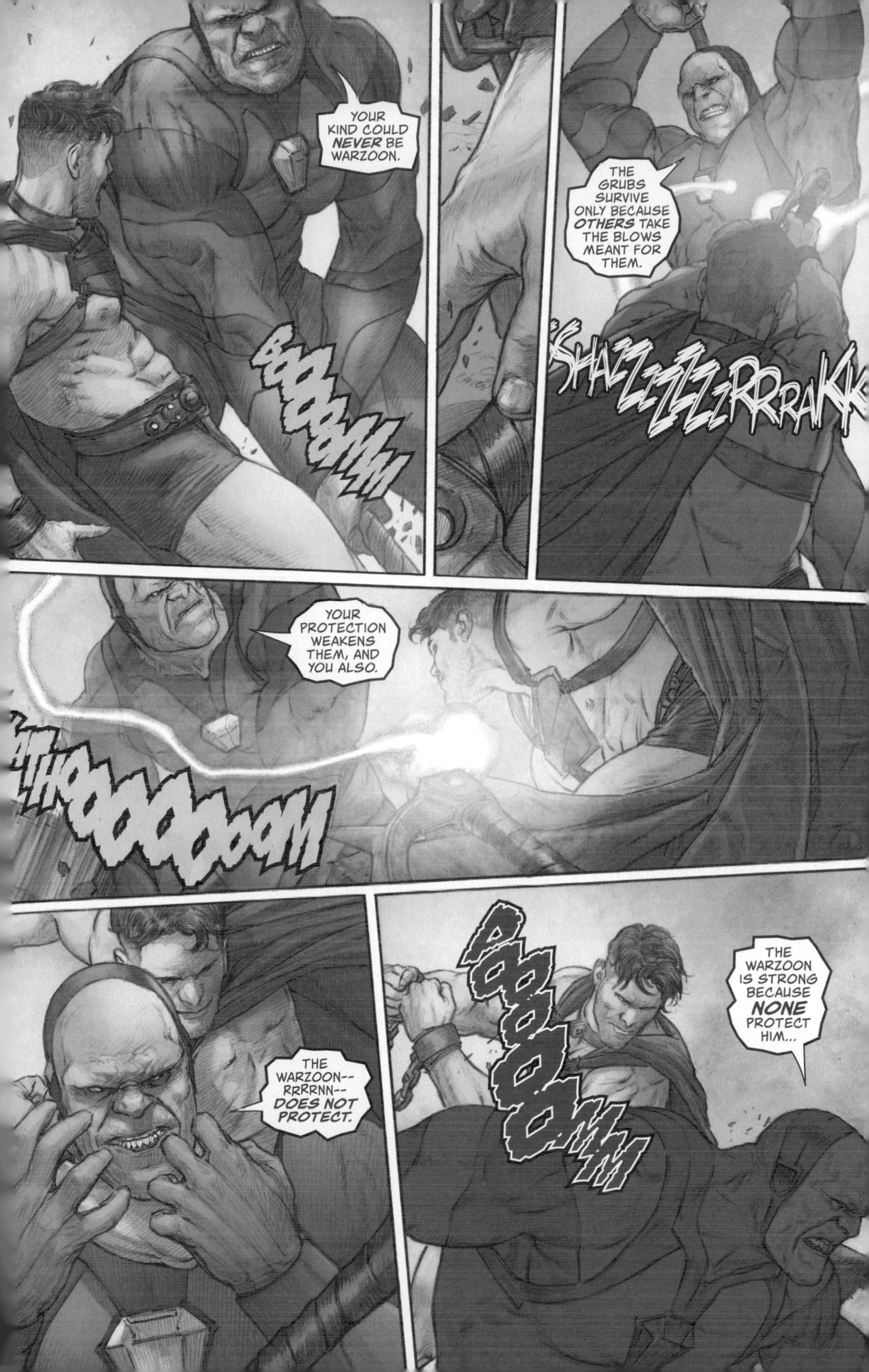
YOUR KIND COULD NEVER BE WARZOON.
BOOOOOOMM
THE GRUBS SURVIVE ONLY BECAUSE OTHERS TAKE THE BLOWS MEANT FOR THEM.
SHAZZZZZZZRRRRAKK
YOUR PROTECTION WEAKENS THEM, AND YOU ALSO.
THOOOOOOOM
THE WARZOON-- RRRRNN-- DOES NOT PROTECT.
BOOOOOMM
THE WARZOON IS STRONG BECAUSE NONE PROTECT HIM...

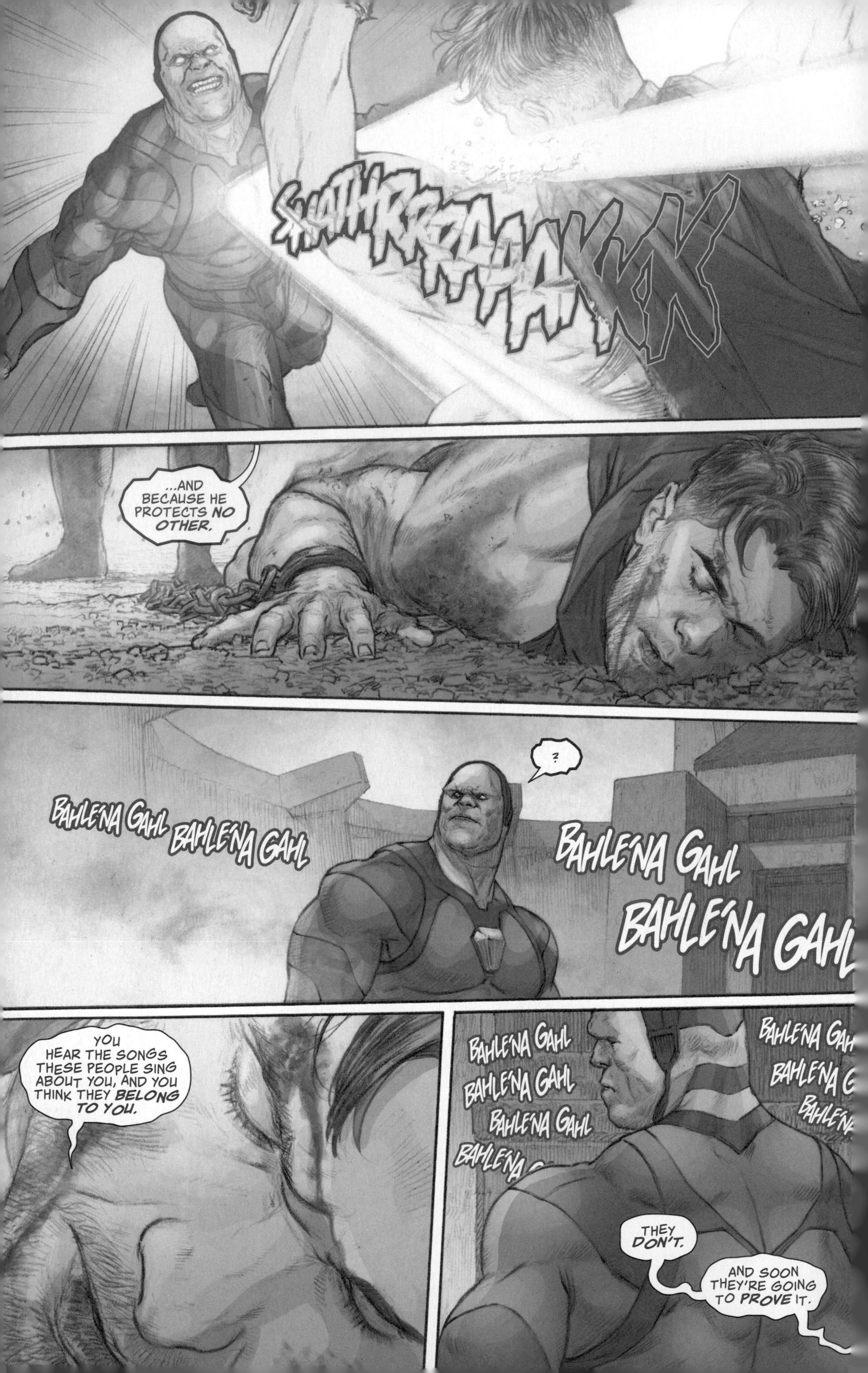
SHATHRRRAAKKX
...AND BECAUSE HE PROTECTS NO OTHER.
?
BAHLE'NA GAHL BAHLE'NA GAHL
BAHLE'NA GAHL
BAHLE'NA GAHL
YOU HEAR THE SONGS THESE PEOPLE SING ABOUT YOU, AND YOU THINK THEY BELONG TO YOU.
BAHLE'NA GAHL
BAHLE'NA GAHL
BAHLE'NA GAHL
THEY DON'T.
AND SOON THEY'RE GOING TO PROVE IT.

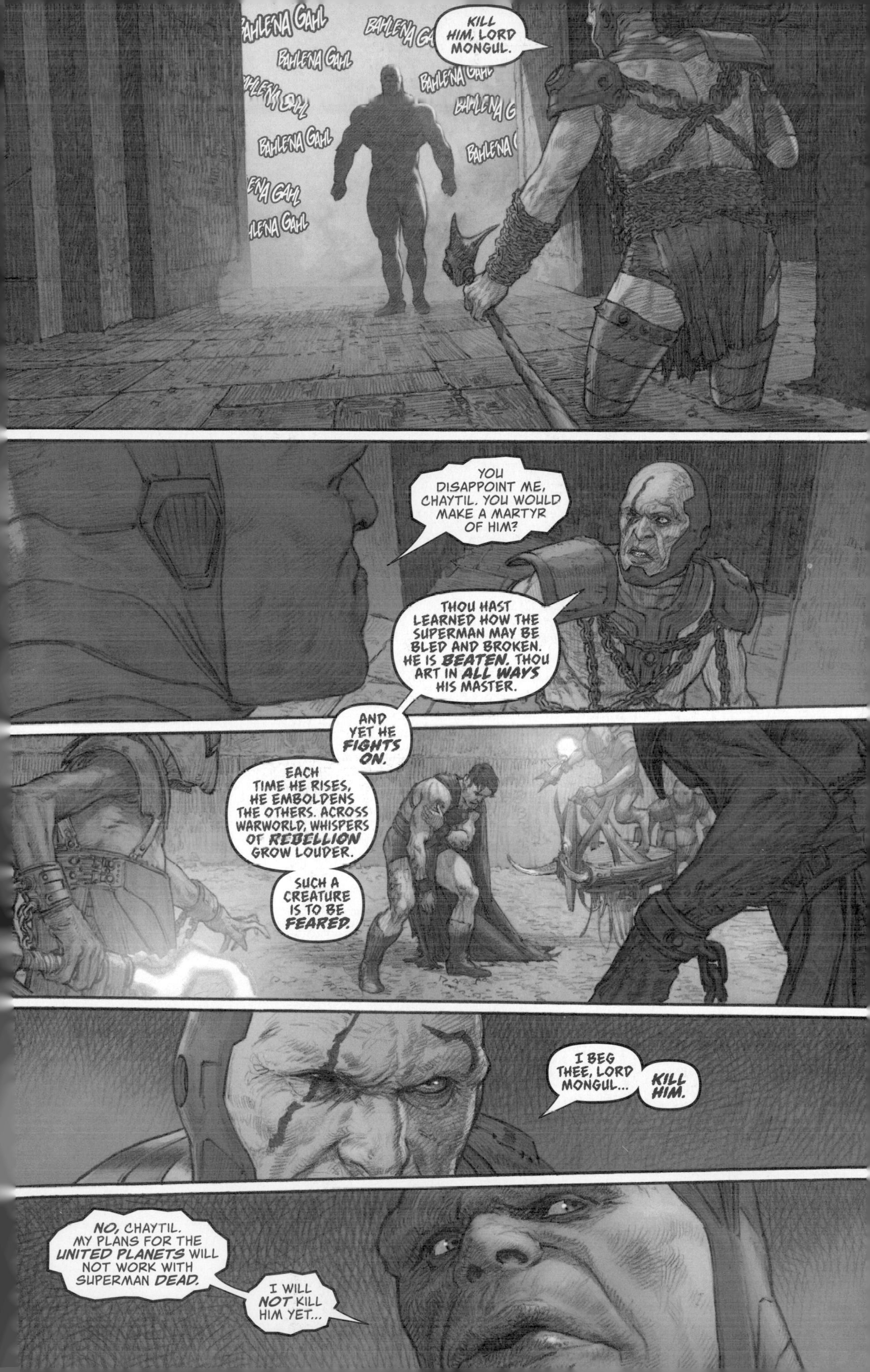
BAHLE'NA GAHL
BAHLE'NA GAHL
BAHLE'NA GAHL
BAHLE'NA GAHL
BAHLE'NA GAHL
BAHLE'NA GAHL
KILL HIM, LORD MONGUL.
YOU DISAPPOINT ME, CHAYTIL. YOU WOULD MAKE A MARTYR OF HIM?
THOU HAST LEARNED HOW THE SUPERMAN MAY BE BLED AND BROKEN. HE IS BEATEN. THOU ART IN ALL WAYS HIS MASTER.
AND YET HE FIGHTS ON.
EACH TIME HE RISES, HE EMBOLDENS THE OTHERS. ACROSS WARWORLD, WHISPERS OF REBELLION GROW LOUDER.
SUCH A CREATURE IS TO BE FEARED.
I BEG THEE, LORD MONGUL... KILL HIM.
NO, CHAYTIL. MY PLANS FOR THE UNITED PLANETS WILL NOT WORK WITH SUPERMAN DEAD.
I WILL NOT KILL HIM YET...

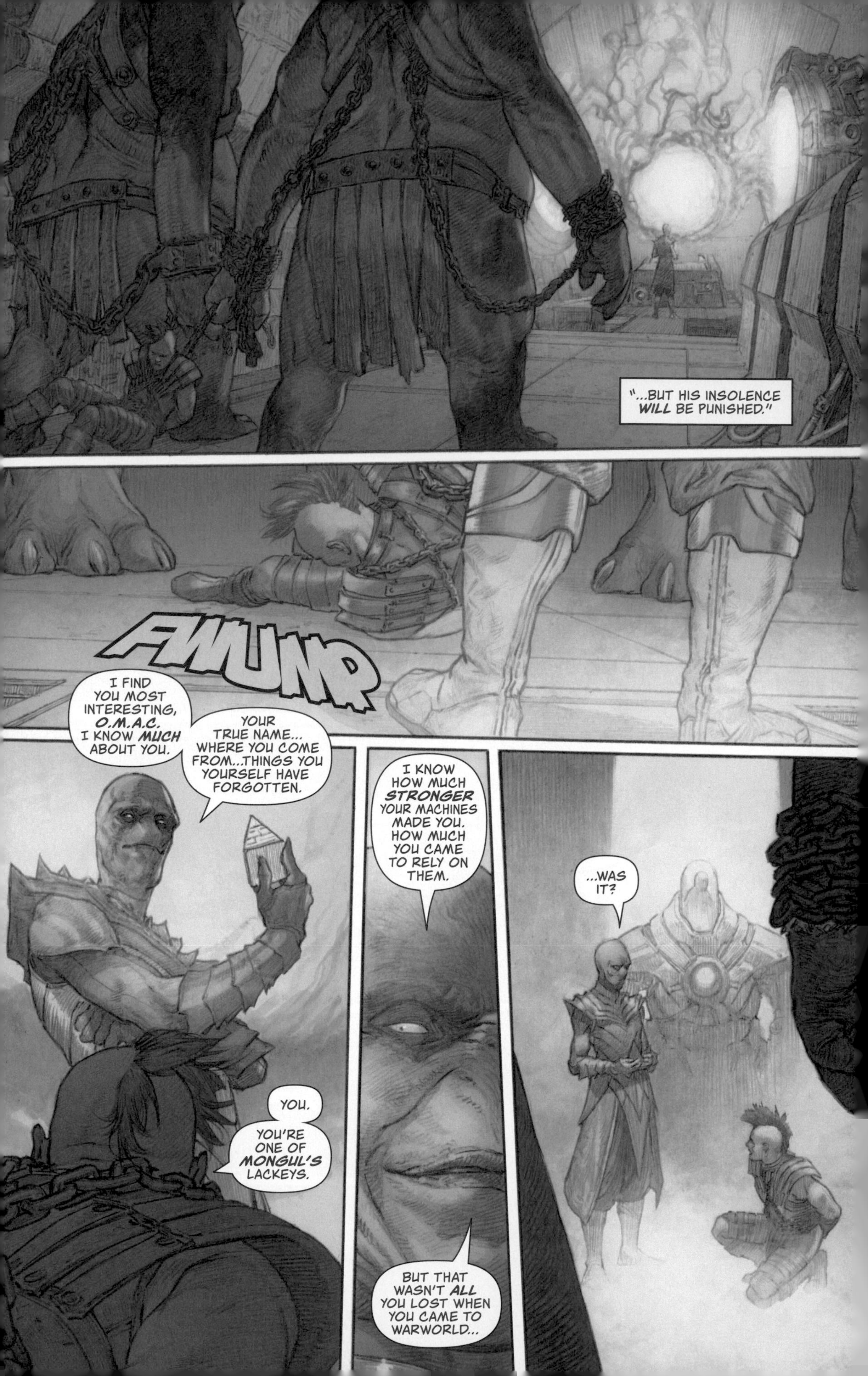
"...BUT HIS INSOLENCE WILL BE PUNISHED."
FWUNR
I FIND YOU MOST INTERESTING, O.M.A.C. I KNOW MUCH ABOUT YOU.
YOUR TRUE NAME... WHERE YOU COME FROM...THINGS YOU YOURSELF HAVE FORGOTTEN.
YOU.
YOU'RE ONE OF MONGUL'S LACKEYS.
I KNOW HOW MUCH STRONGER YOUR MACHINES MADE YOU. HOW MUCH YOU CAME TO RELY ON THEM.
BUT THAT WASN'T ALL YOU LOST WHEN YOU CAME TO WARWORLD...
...WAS IT?

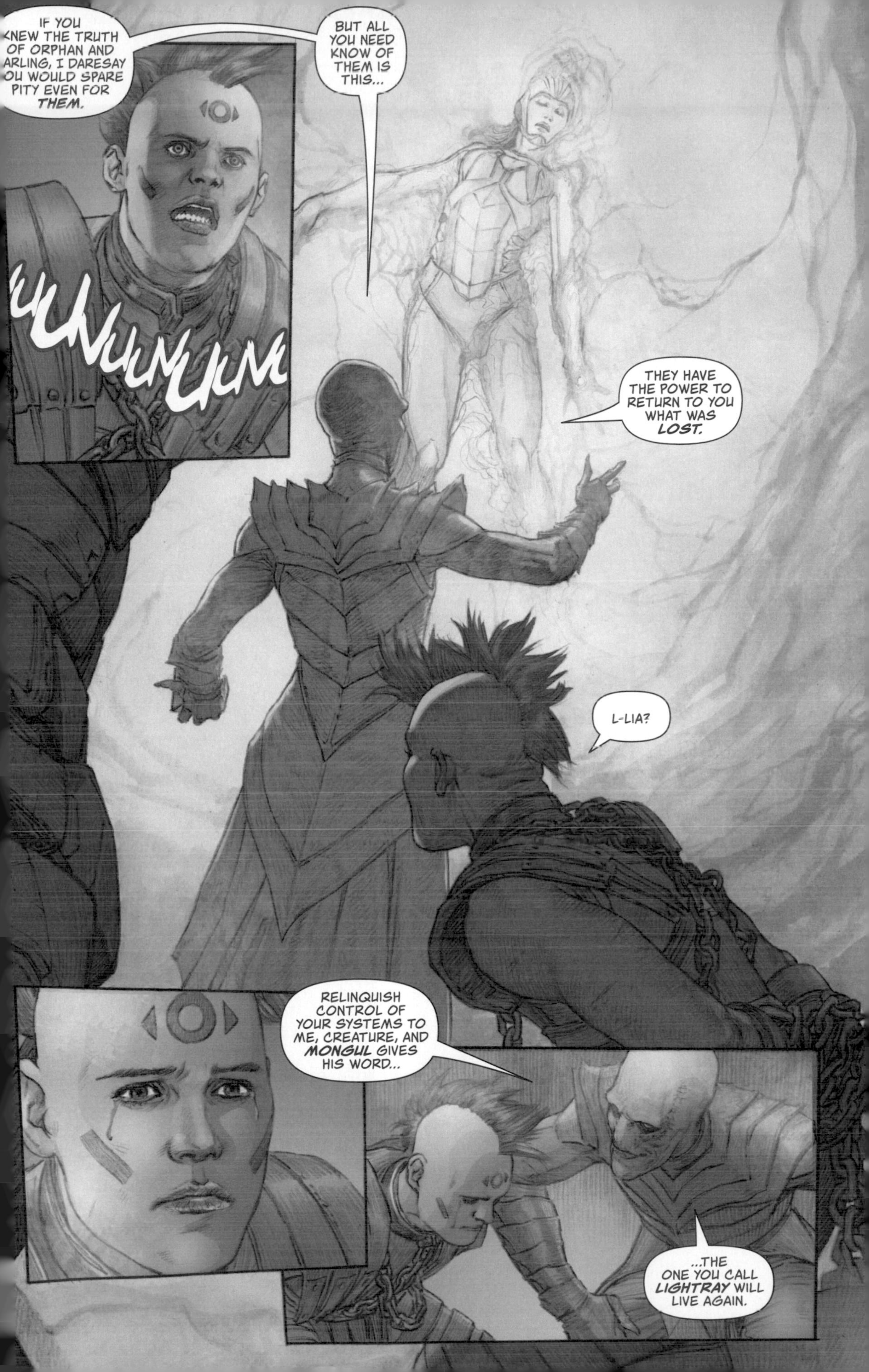
IF YOU KNEW THE TRUTH OF ORPHAN AND ARLING, I DARESAY OU WOULD SPARE PITY EVEN FOR THEM.
BUT ALL YOU NEED KNOW OF THEM IS THIS...
UUNNUUNNUUNN
THEY HAVE THE POWER TO RETURN TO YOU WHAT WAS LOST.
L-LIA?
RELINQUISH CONTROL OF YOUR SYSTEMS TO ME, CREATURE, AND MONGUL GIVES HIS WORD...
...THE ONE YOU CALL LIGHTRAY WILL LIVE AGAIN.

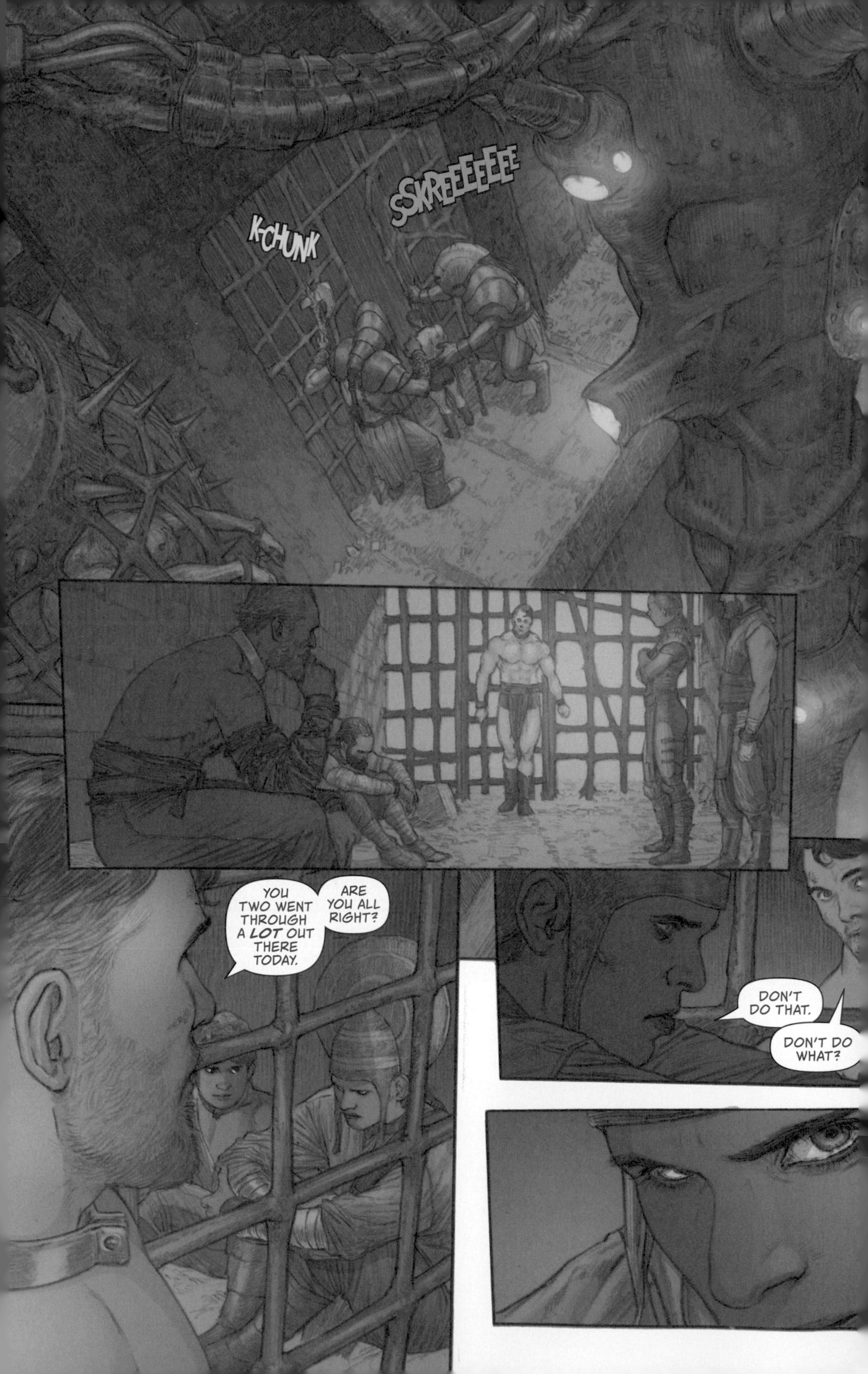
SSKREEEEEEE
K-CHUNK
YOU TWO WENT THROUGH A *LOT* OUT THERE TODAY.
ARE YOU ALL RIGHT?
DON'T DO THAT.
DON'T DO WHAT?

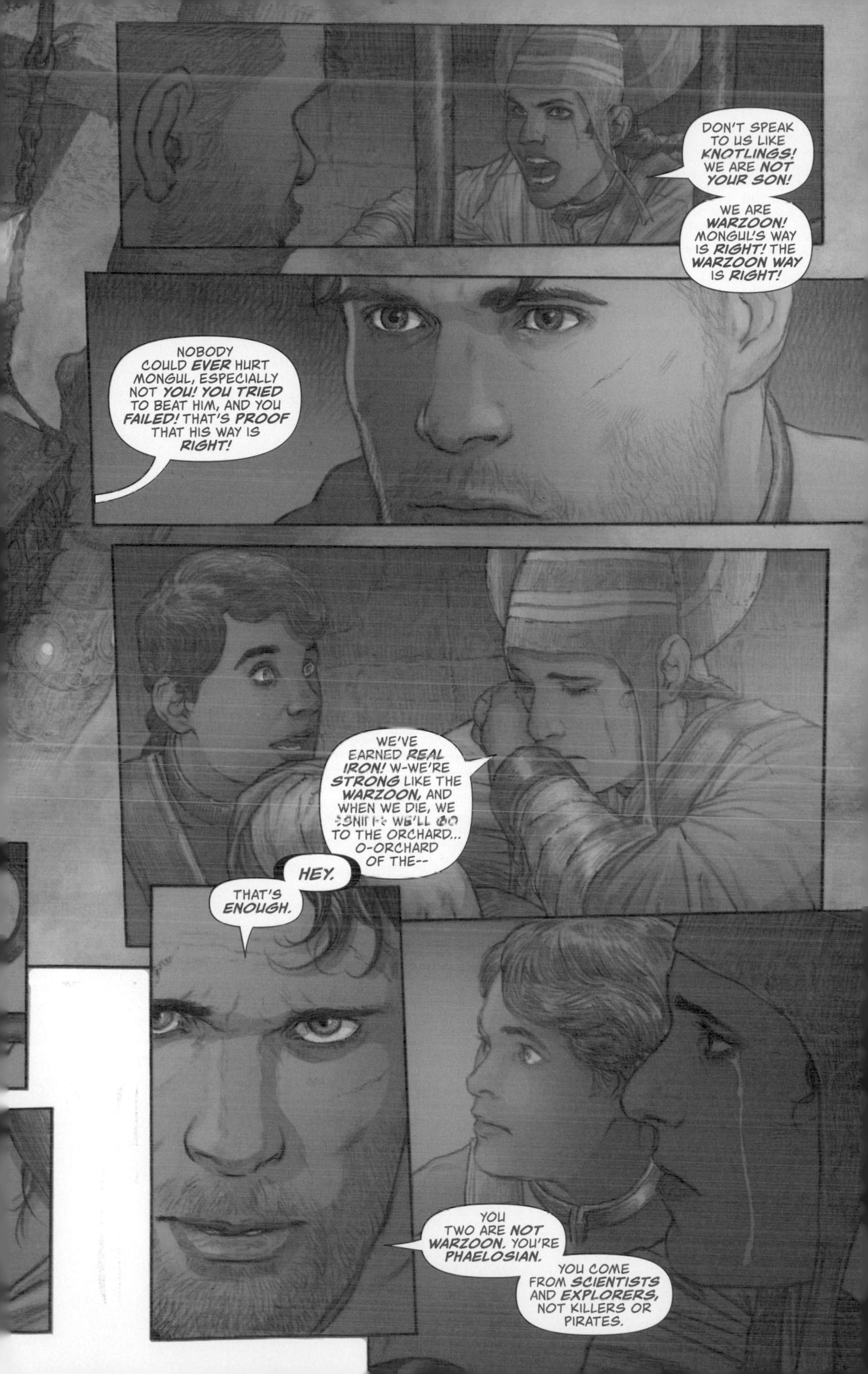
DON'T SPEAK TO US LIKE KNOTLINGS! WE ARE NOT YOUR SON!
WE ARE WARZOON! MONGUL'S WAY IS RIGHT! THE WARZOON WAY IS RIGHT!
NOBODY COULD EVER HURT MONGUL, ESPECIALLY NOT YOU! YOU TRIED TO BEAT HIM, AND YOU FAILED! THAT'S PROOF THAT HIS WAY IS RIGHT!
WE'VE EARNED REAL IRON! W-WE'RE STRONG LIKE THE WARZOON, AND WHEN WE DIE, WE *SNIFF* WE'LL GO TO THE ORCHARD... O-ORCHARD OF THE--
HEY.
THAT'S ENOUGH.
YOU TWO ARE NOT WARZOON. YOU'RE PHAELOSIAN.
YOU COME FROM SCIENTISTS AND EXPLORERS, NOT KILLERS OR PIRATES.

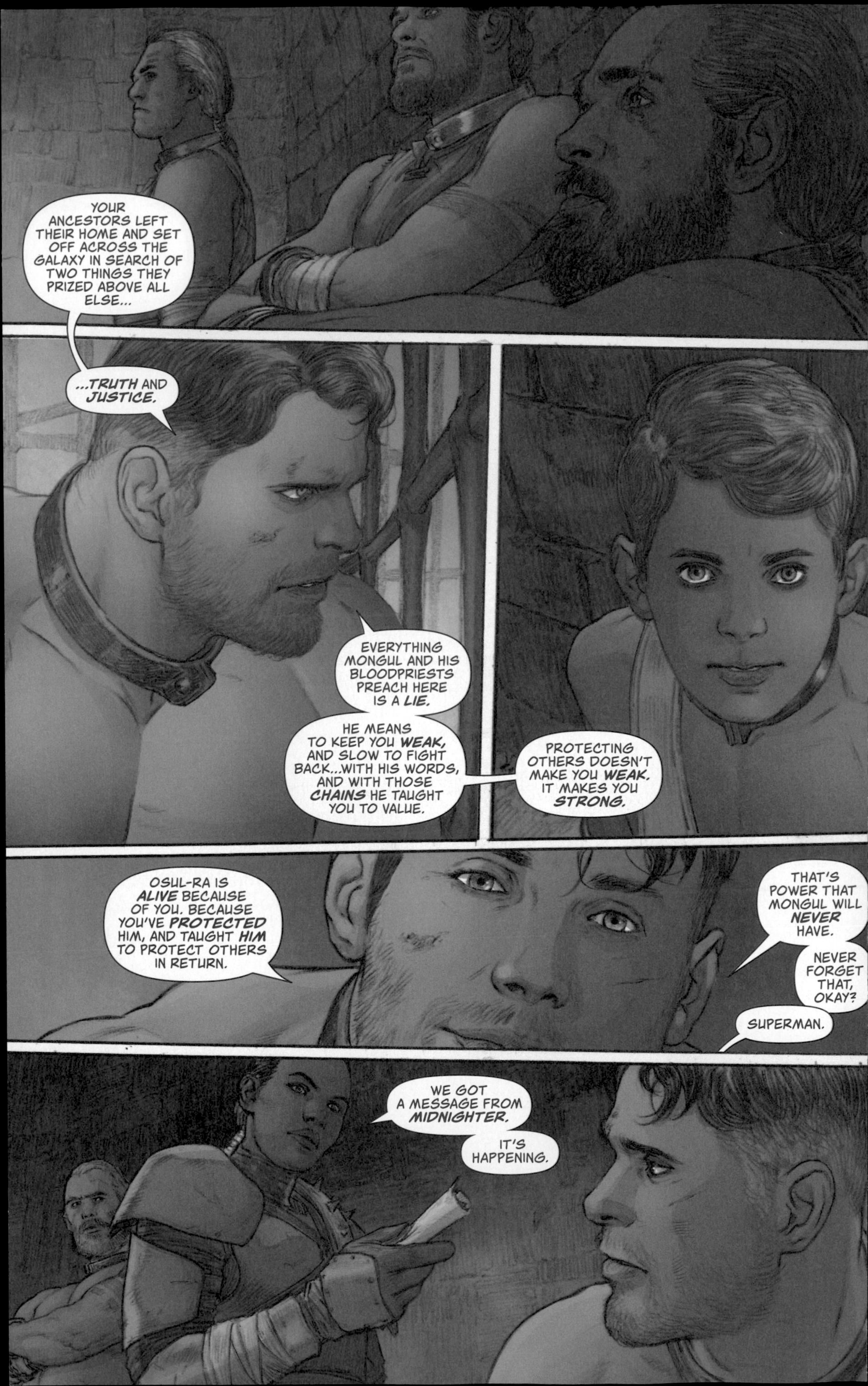
YOUR ANCESTORS LEFT THEIR HOME AND SET OFF ACROSS THE GALAXY IN SEARCH OF TWO THINGS THEY PRIZED ABOVE ALL ELSE...
...TRUTH AND JUSTICE.
EVERYTHING MONGUL AND HIS BLOODPRIESTS PREACH HERE IS A LIE.
HE MEANS TO KEEP YOU WEAK, AND SLOW TO FIGHT BACK...WITH HIS WORDS, AND WITH THOSE CHAINS HE TAUGHT YOU TO VALUE.
PROTECTING OTHERS DOESN'T MAKE YOU WEAK. IT MAKES YOU STRONG.
OSUL-RA IS ALIVE BECAUSE OF YOU. BECAUSE YOU'VE PROTECTED HIM, AND TAUGHT HIM TO PROTECT OTHERS IN RETURN.
THAT'S POWER THAT MONGUL WILL NEVER HAVE.
NEVER FORGET THAT, OKAY?
SUPERMAN.
WE GOT A MESSAGE FROM MIDNIGHTER.
IT'S HAPPENING.

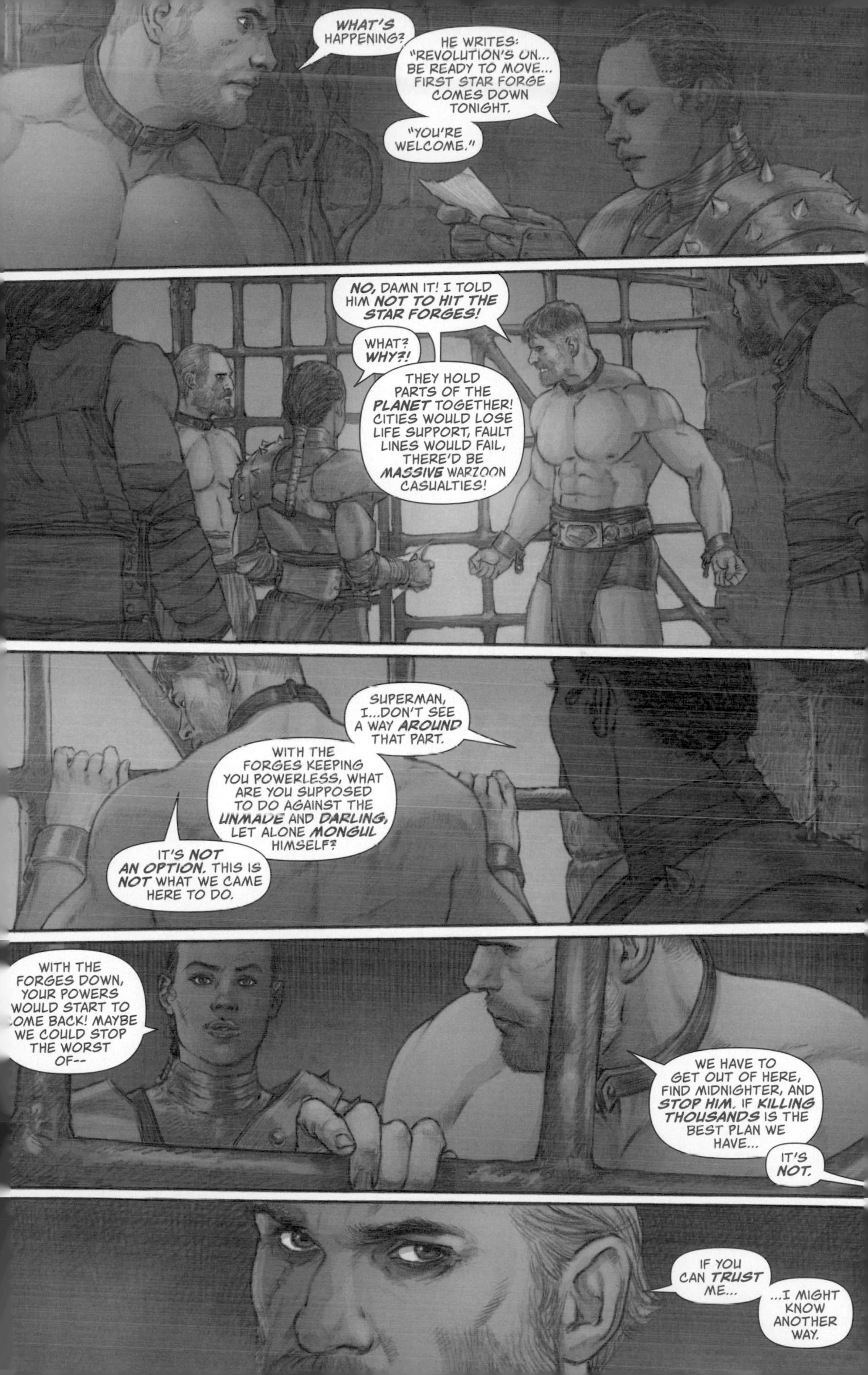
WHAT'S HAPPENING?
HE WRITES: "REVOLUTION'S ON... BE READY TO MOVE... FIRST STAR FORGE COMES DOWN TONIGHT.
"YOU'RE WELCOME."
NO, DAMN IT! I TOLD HIM NOT TO HIT THE STAR FORGES!
WHAT? WHY?!
THEY HOLD PARTS OF THE PLANET TOGETHER! CITIES WOULD LOSE LIFE SUPPORT, FAULT LINES WOULD FAIL, THERE'D BE MASSIVE WARZOON CASUALTIES!
SUPERMAN, I...DON'T SEE A WAY AROUND THAT PART.
WITH THE FORGES KEEPING YOU POWERLESS, WHAT ARE YOU SUPPOSED TO DO AGAINST THE UNMADE AND DARLING, LET ALONE MONGUL HIMSELF?
IT'S NOT AN OPTION. THIS IS NOT WHAT WE CAME HERE TO DO.
WITH THE FORGES DOWN, YOUR POWERS WOULD START TO COME BACK! MAYBE WE COULD STOP THE WORST OF--
WE HAVE TO GET OUT OF HERE, FIND MIDNIGHTER, AND STOP HIM. IF KILLING THOUSANDS IS THE BEST PLAN WE HAVE...
IT'S NOT.
IF YOU CAN TRUST ME...
...I MIGHT KNOW ANOTHER WAY.

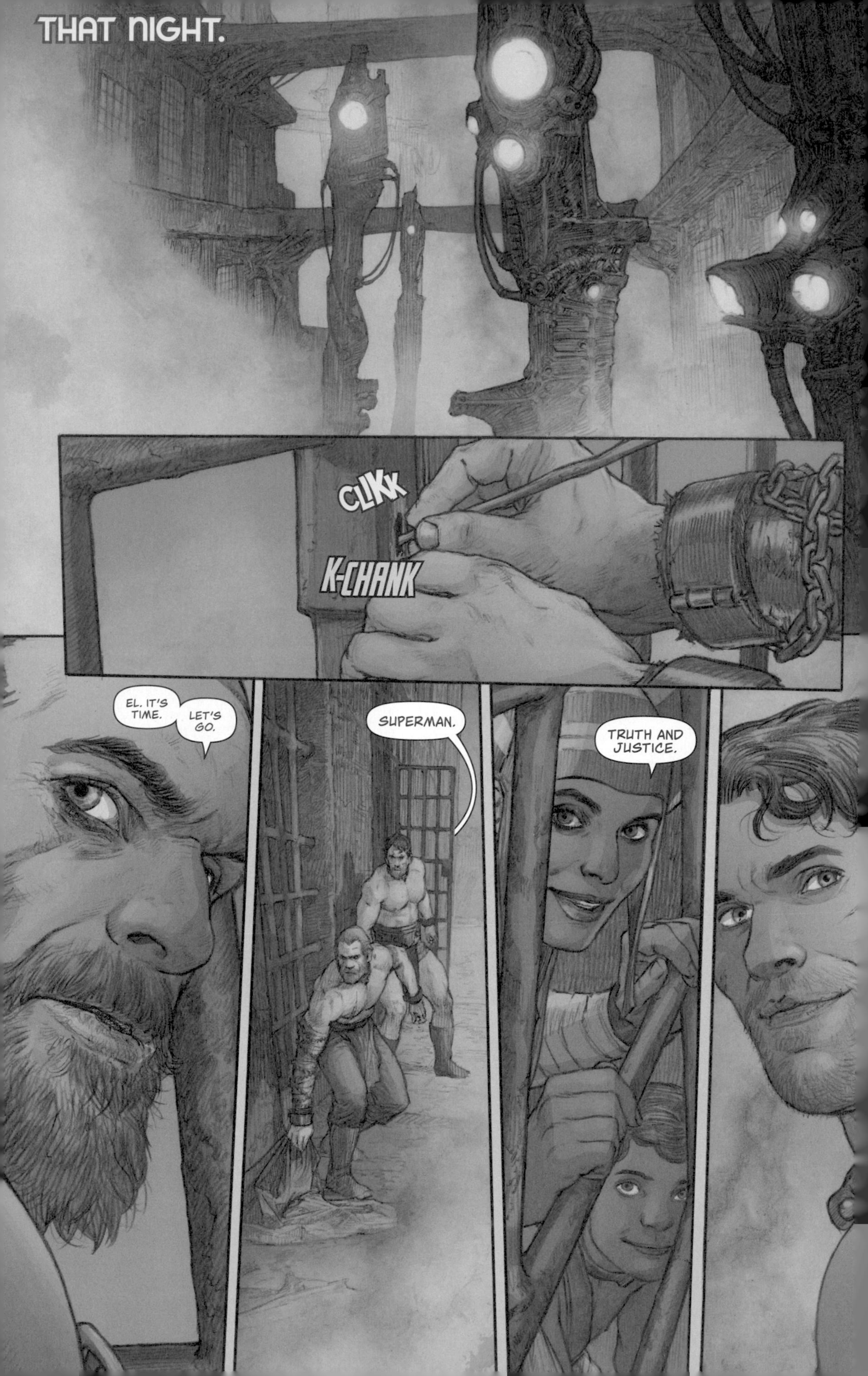
THAT NIGHT.
CLIKK
K-CHANK
EL. IT'S TIME.
LET'S GO.
SUPERMAN.
TRUTH AND JUSTICE.

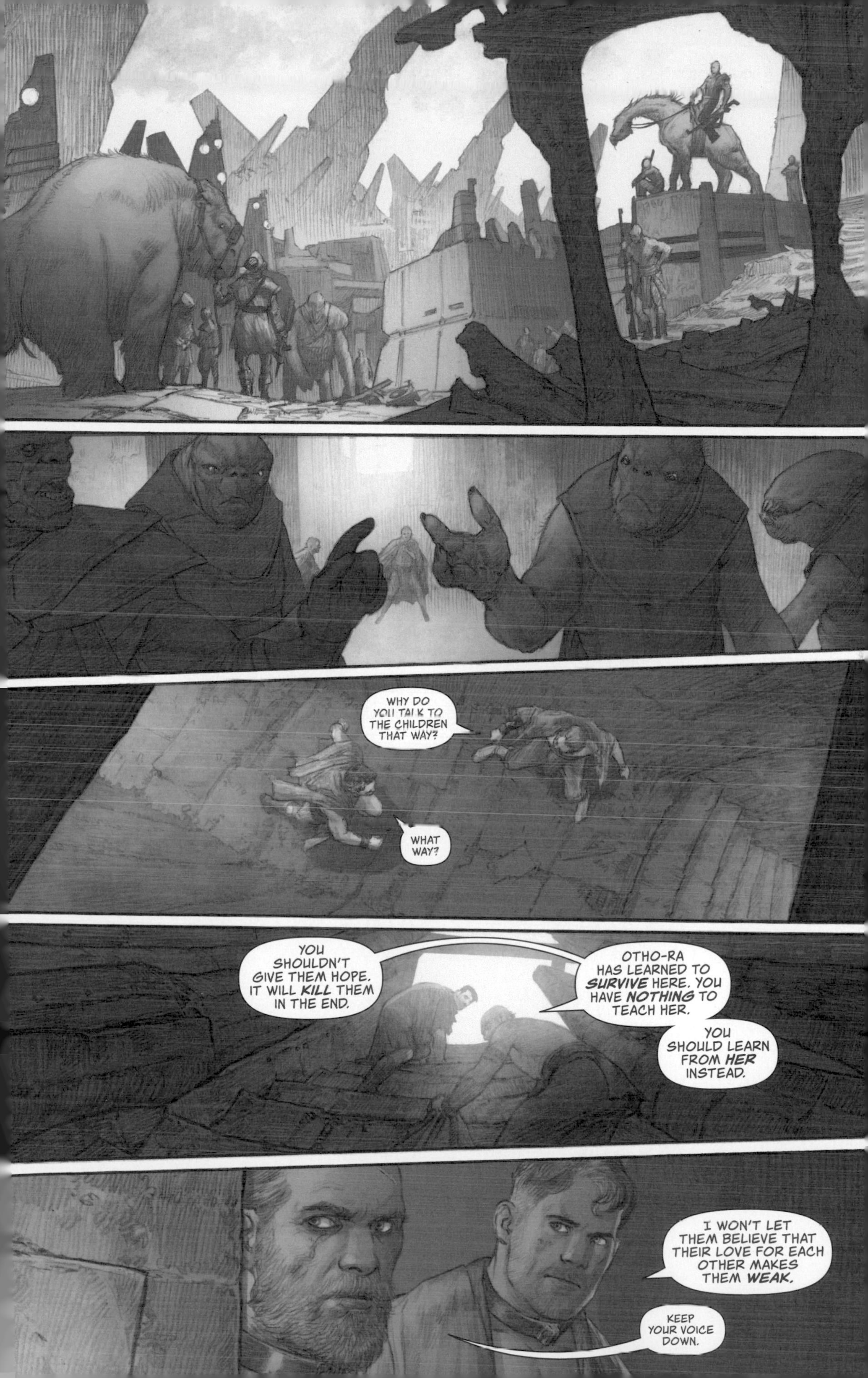

WHY DO YOU TALK TO THE CHILDREN THAT WAY?
WHAT WAY?
YOU SHOULDN'T GIVE THEM HOPE. IT WILL KILL THEM IN THE END.
OTHO-RA HAS LEARNED TO SURVIVE HERE. YOU HAVE NOTHING TO TEACH HER.
YOU SHOULD LEARN FROM HER INSTEAD.
I WON'T LET THEM BELIEVE THAT THEIR LOVE FOR EACH OTHER MAKES THEM WEAK.
KEEP YOUR VOICE DOWN.

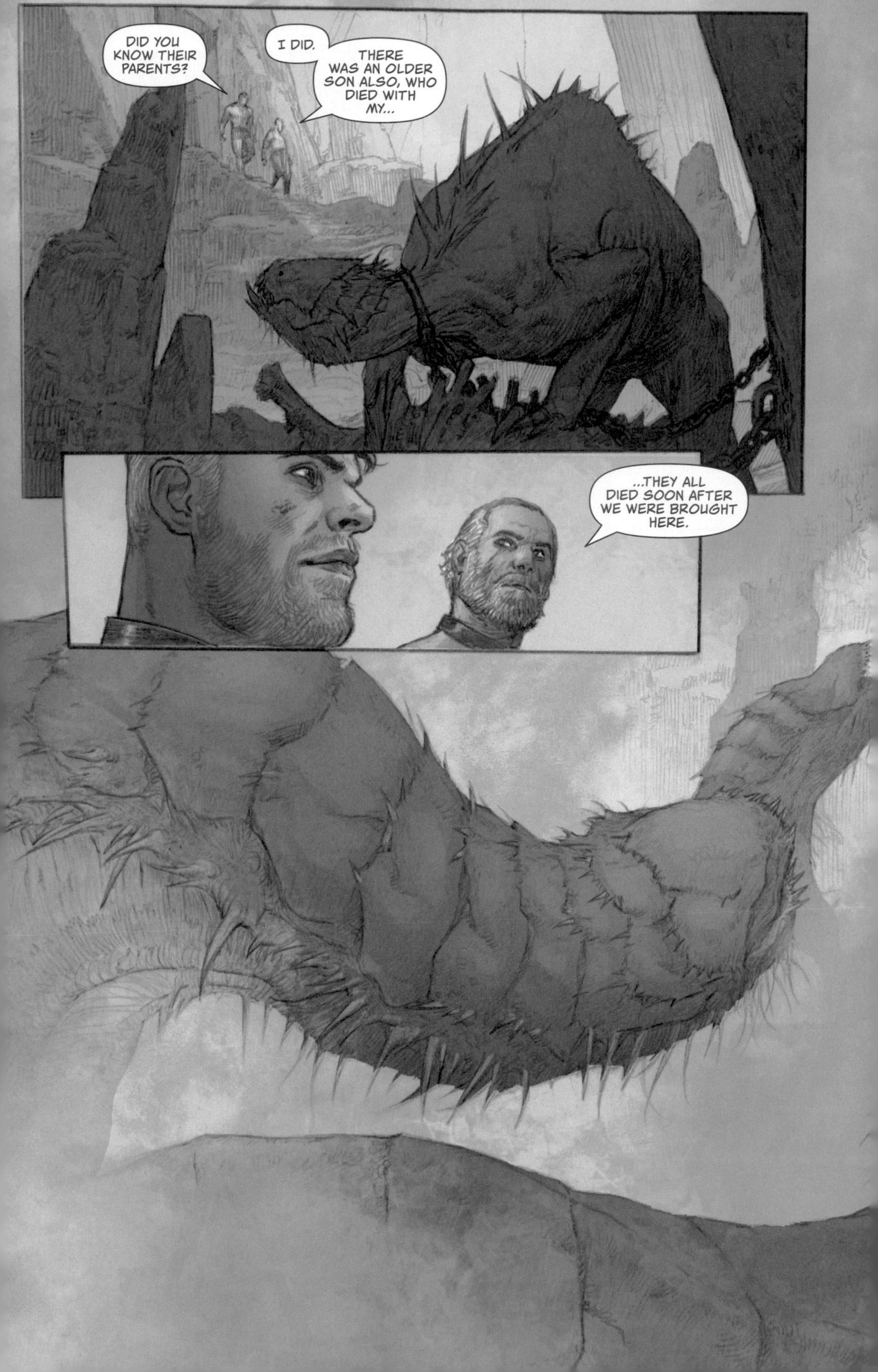
DID YOU KNOW THEIR PARENTS?
I DID.
THERE WAS AN OLDER SON ALSO, WHO DIED WITH MY...
...THEY ALL DIED SOON AFTER WE WERE BROUGHT HERE.

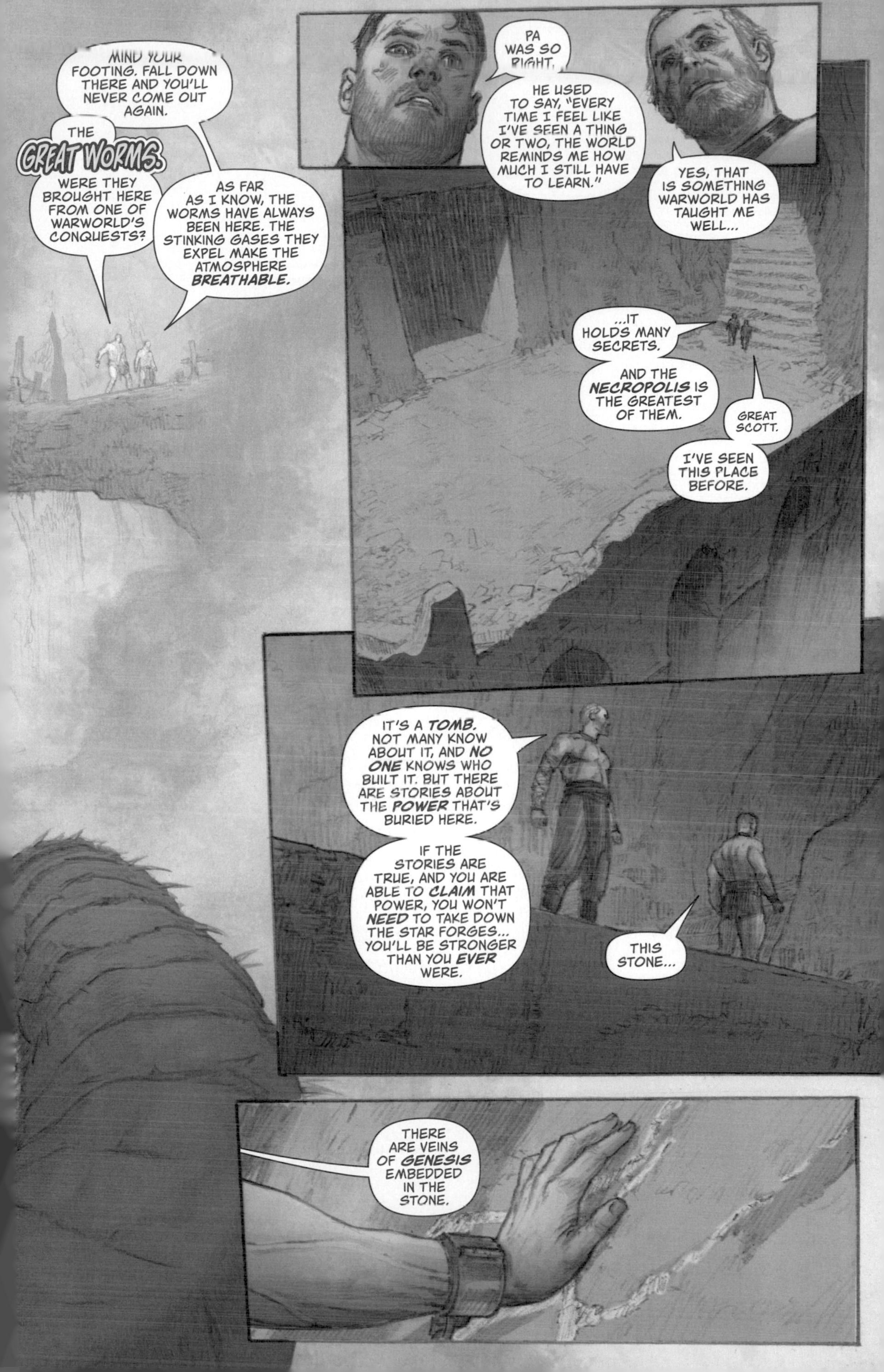
MIND YOUR FOOTING. FALL DOWN THERE AND YOU'LL NEVER COME OUT AGAIN.
THE GREAT WORMS.
WERE THEY BROUGHT HERE FROM ONE OF WARWORLD'S CONQUESTS?
AS FAR AS I KNOW, THE WORMS HAVE ALWAYS BEEN HERE. THE STINKING GASES THEY EXPEL MAKE THE ATMOSPHERE BREATHABLE.
PA WAS SO RIGHT.
HE USED TO SAY, "EVERY TIME I FEEL LIKE I'VE SEEN A THING OR TWO, THE WORLD REMINDS ME HOW MUCH I STILL HAVE TO LEARN."
YES, THAT IS SOMETHING WARWORLD HAS TAUGHT ME WELL...
...IT HOLDS MANY SECRETS.
AND THE NECROPOLIS IS THE GREATEST OF THEM.
GREAT SCOTT.
I'VE SEEN THIS PLACE BEFORE.
IT'S A TOMB. NOT MANY KNOW ABOUT IT, AND NO ONE KNOWS WHO BUILT IT. BUT THERE ARE STORIES ABOUT THE POWER THAT'S BURIED HERE.
IF THE STORIES ARE TRUE, AND YOU ARE ABLE TO CLAIM THAT POWER, YOU WON'T NEED TO TAKE DOWN THE STAR FORGES... YOU'LL BE STRONGER THAN YOU EVER WERE.
THIS STONE...
THERE ARE VEINS OF GENESIS EMBEDDED IN THE STONE.

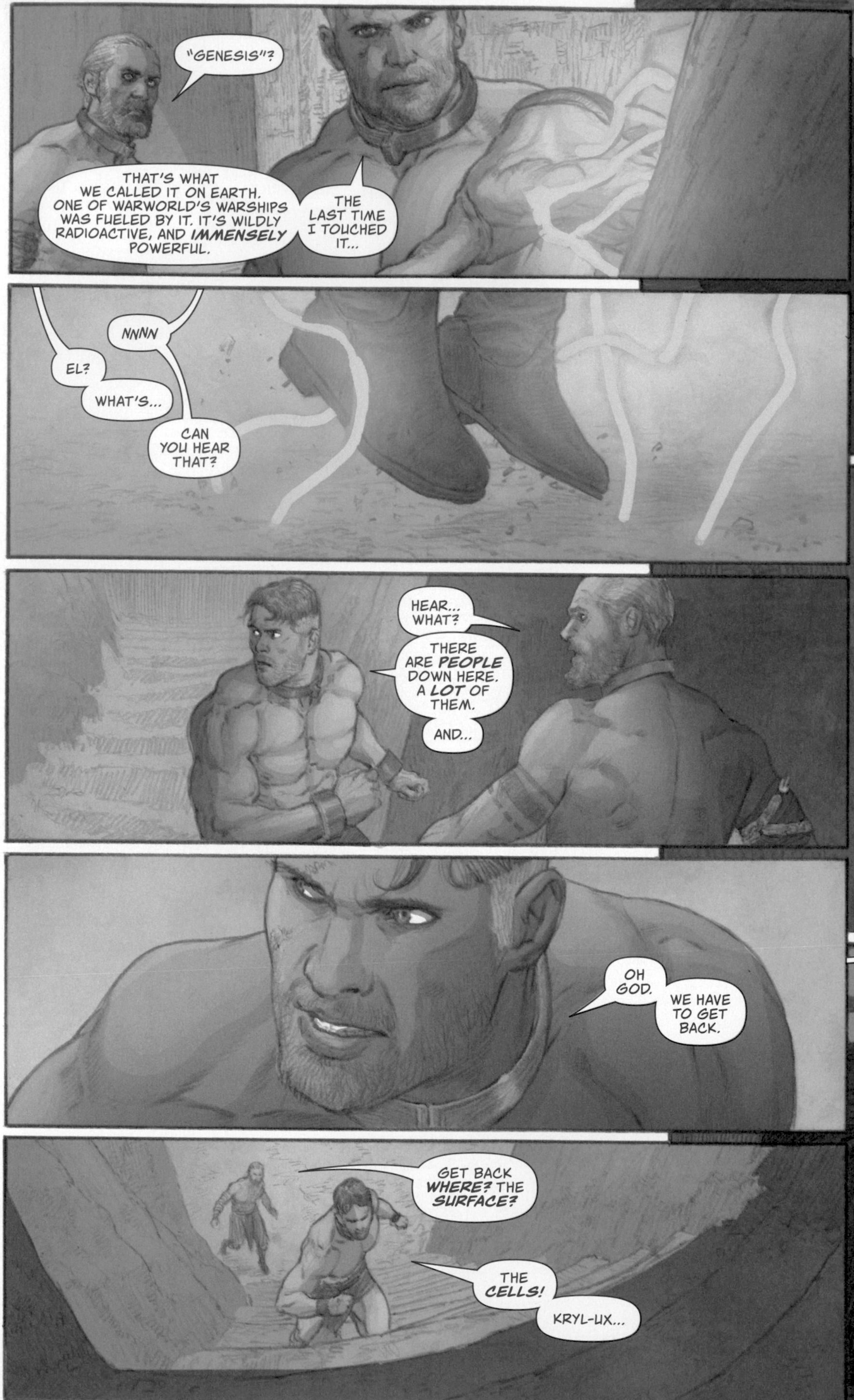
"GENESIS"?
THAT'S WHAT WE CALLED IT ON EARTH. ONE OF WARWORLD'S WARSHIPS WAS FUELED BY IT. IT'S WILDLY RADIOACTIVE, AND IMMENSELY POWERFUL.
THE LAST TIME I TOUCHED IT...
NNNN
EL?
WHAT'S...
CAN YOU HEAR THAT?
HEAR... WHAT?
THERE ARE PEOPLE DOWN HERE. A LOT OF THEM.
AND...
OH GOD.
WE HAVE TO GET BACK.
GET BACK WHERE? THE SURFACE?
THE CELLS!
KRYL-UX...

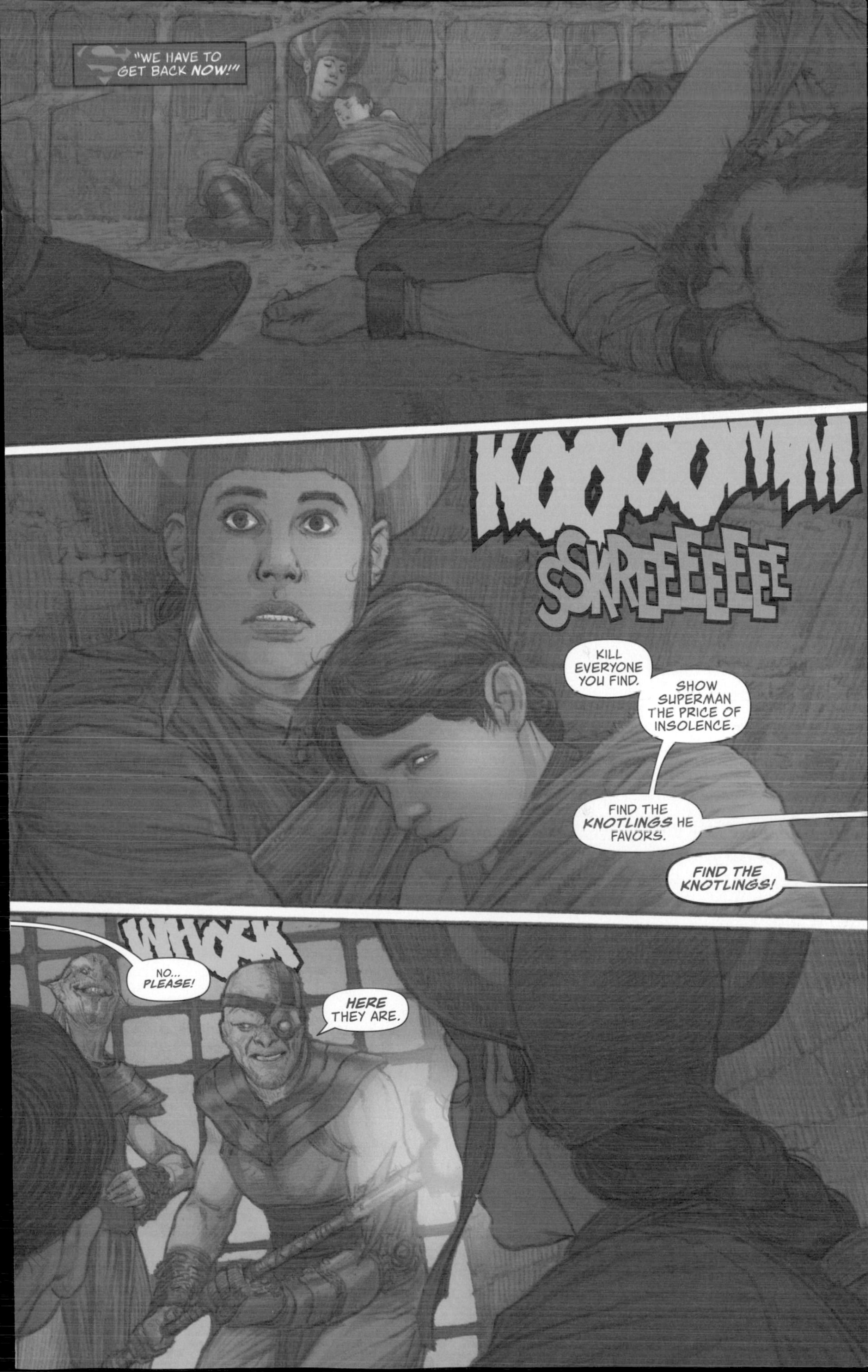
"WE HAVE TO GET BACK NOW!"
KOOOOMM
SSKREEEEEEE
KILL EVERYONE YOU FIND.
SHOW SUPERMAN THE PRICE OF INSOLENCE.
FIND THE KNOTLINGS HE FAVORS.
FIND THE KNOTLINGS!
WHOCK
NO... PLEASE!
HERE THEY ARE.

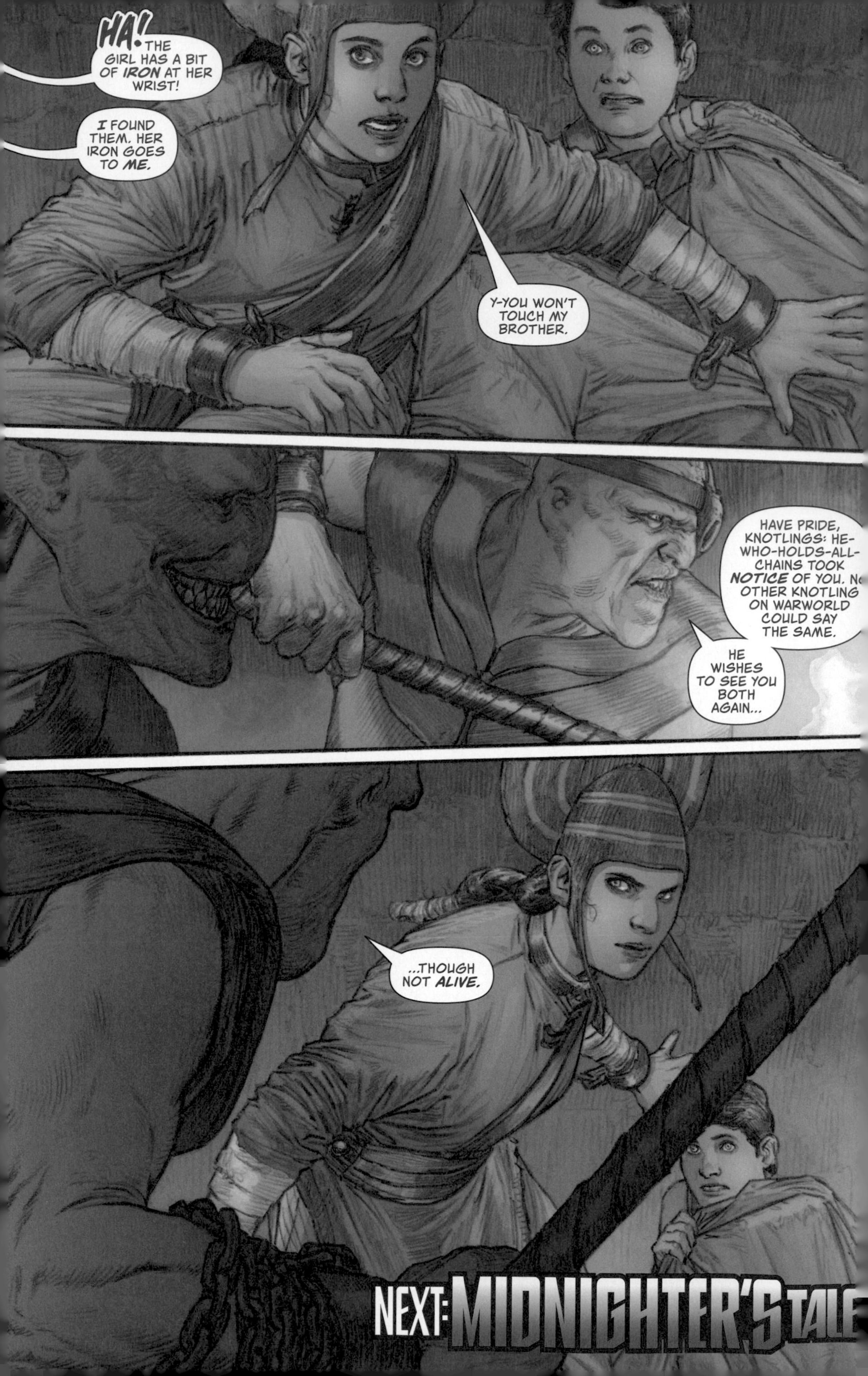
HA! THE GIRL HAS A BIT OF IRON AT HER WRIST!
I FOUND THEM. HER IRON GOES TO ME.
Y-YOU WON'T TOUCH MY BROTHER.
HAVE PRIDE, KNOTLINGS: HE-WHO-HOLDS-ALL-CHAINS TOOK NOTICE OF YOU. No OTHER KNOTLING ON WARWORLD COULD SAY THE SAME.
HE WISHES TO SEE YOU BOTH AGAIN...
...THOUGH NOT ALIVE.
NEXT: MIDNIGHTER'S TALE

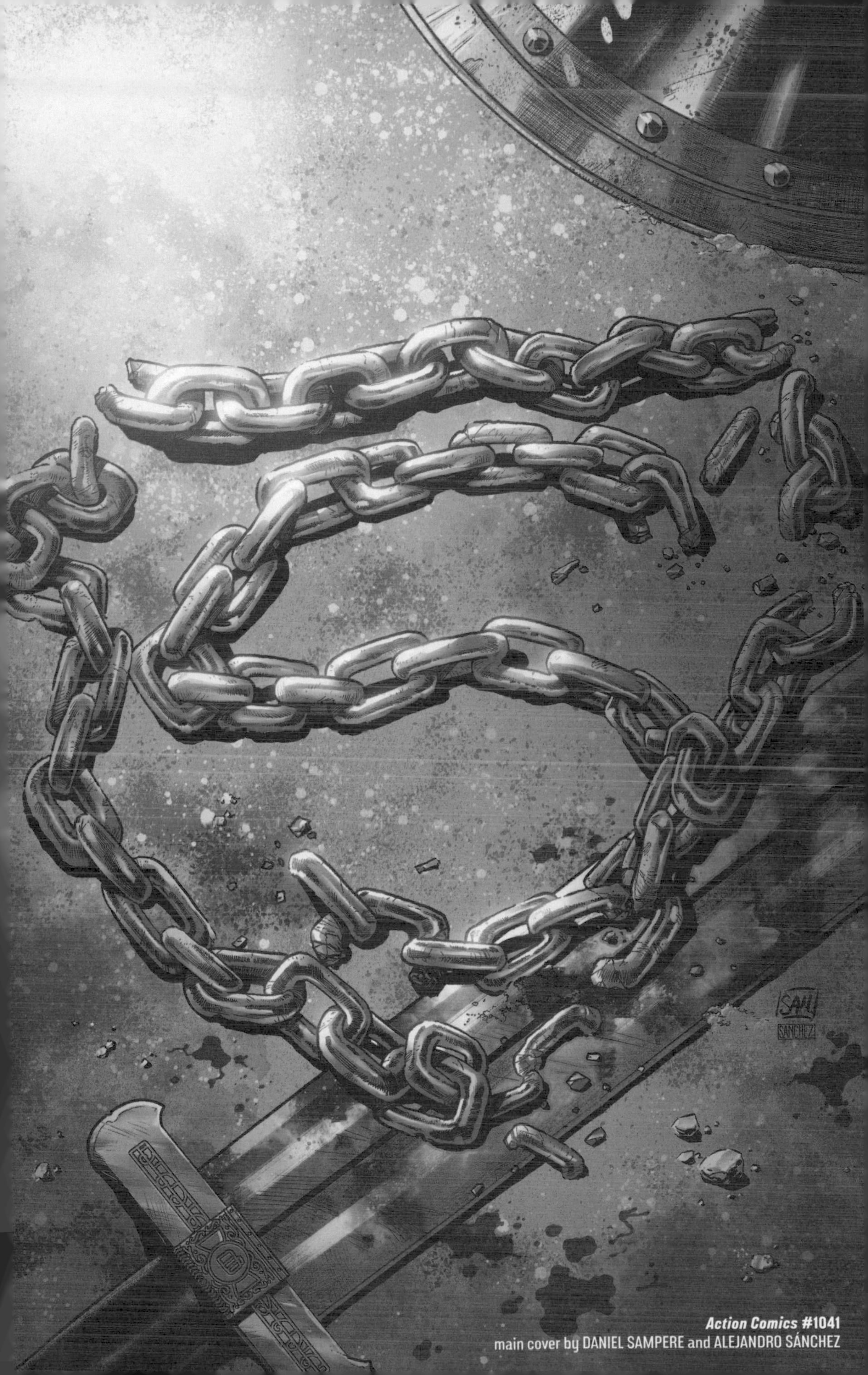
SAM
SANCHEZ

***Action Comics* #1041**
main cover by DANIEL SAMPERE and ALEJANDRO SÁNCHEZ

Action Comics #1041
variant cover by JULIAN TOTINO TEDESCO

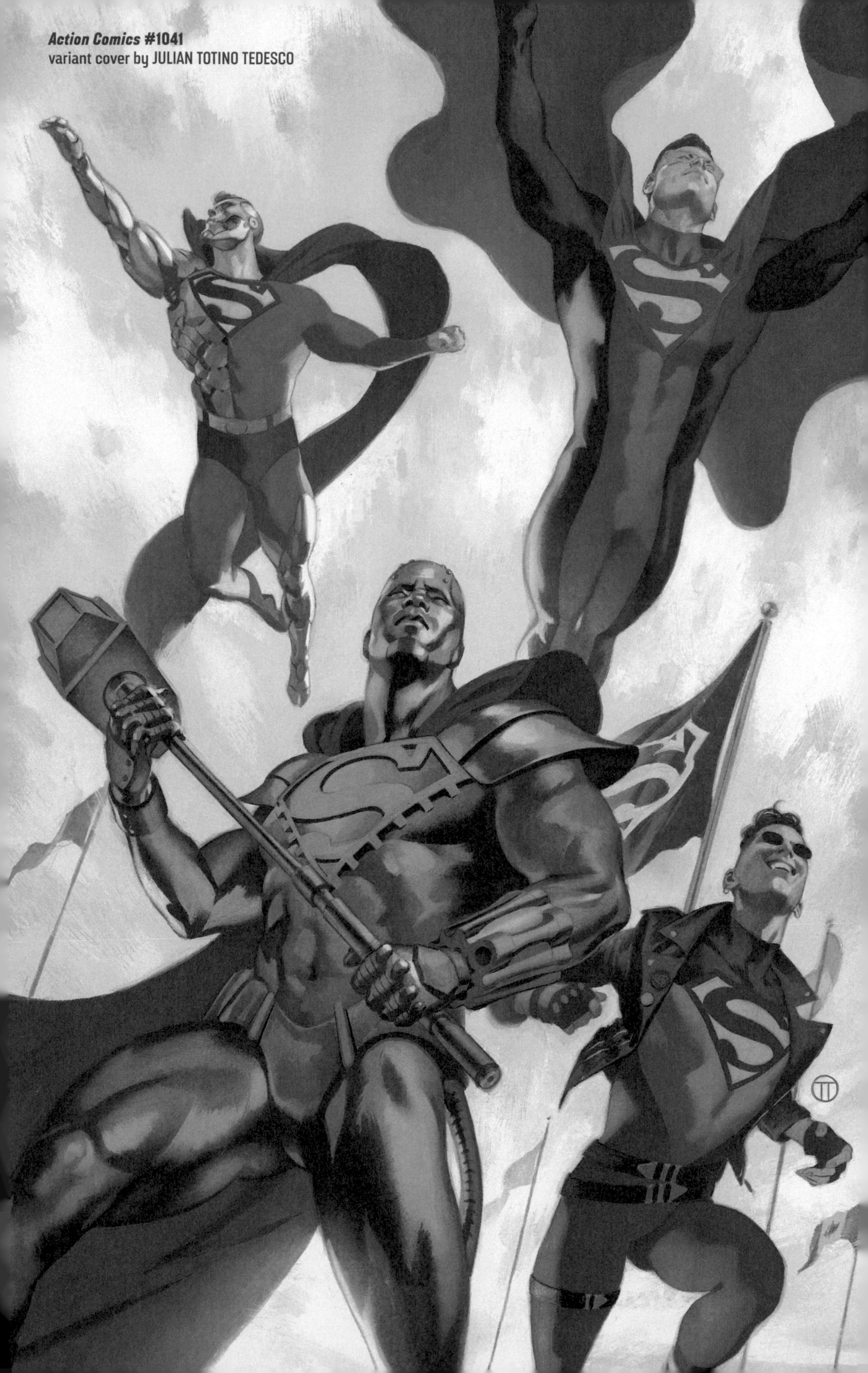

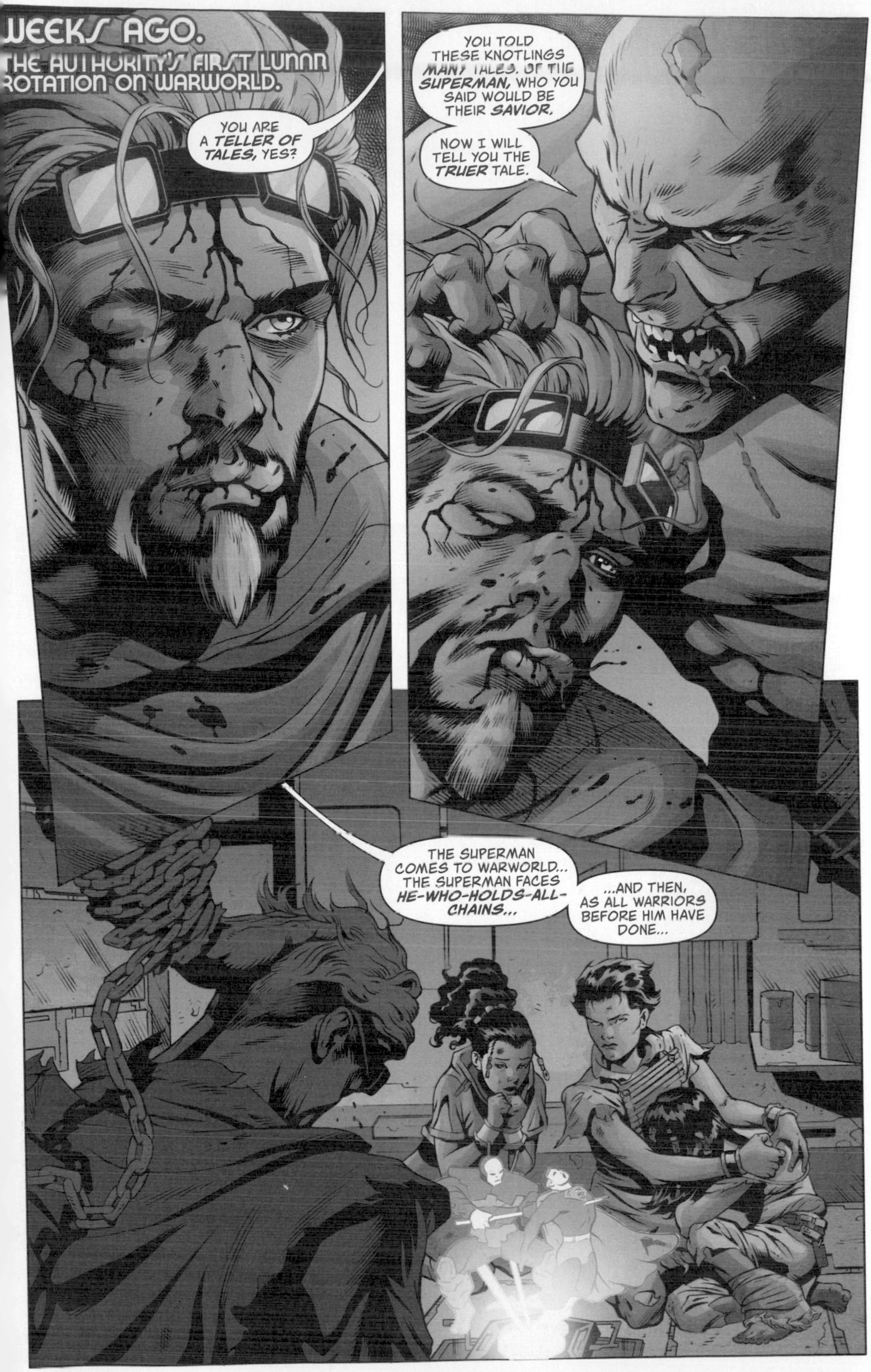
WEEKS AGO.
THE AUTHORITY'S FIRST LUNAR ROTATION ON WARWORLD.
YOU ARE A TELLER OF TALES, YES?
YOU TOLD THESE KNOTLINGS MANY TALES OF THE SUPERMAN, WHO YOU SAID WOULD BE THEIR SAVIOR.
NOW I WILL TELL YOU THE TRUER TALE.
THE SUPERMAN COMES TO WARWORLD... THE SUPERMAN FACES HE-WHO-HOLDS-ALL-CHAINS...
...AND THEN, AS ALL WARRIORS BEFORE HIM HAVE DONE...

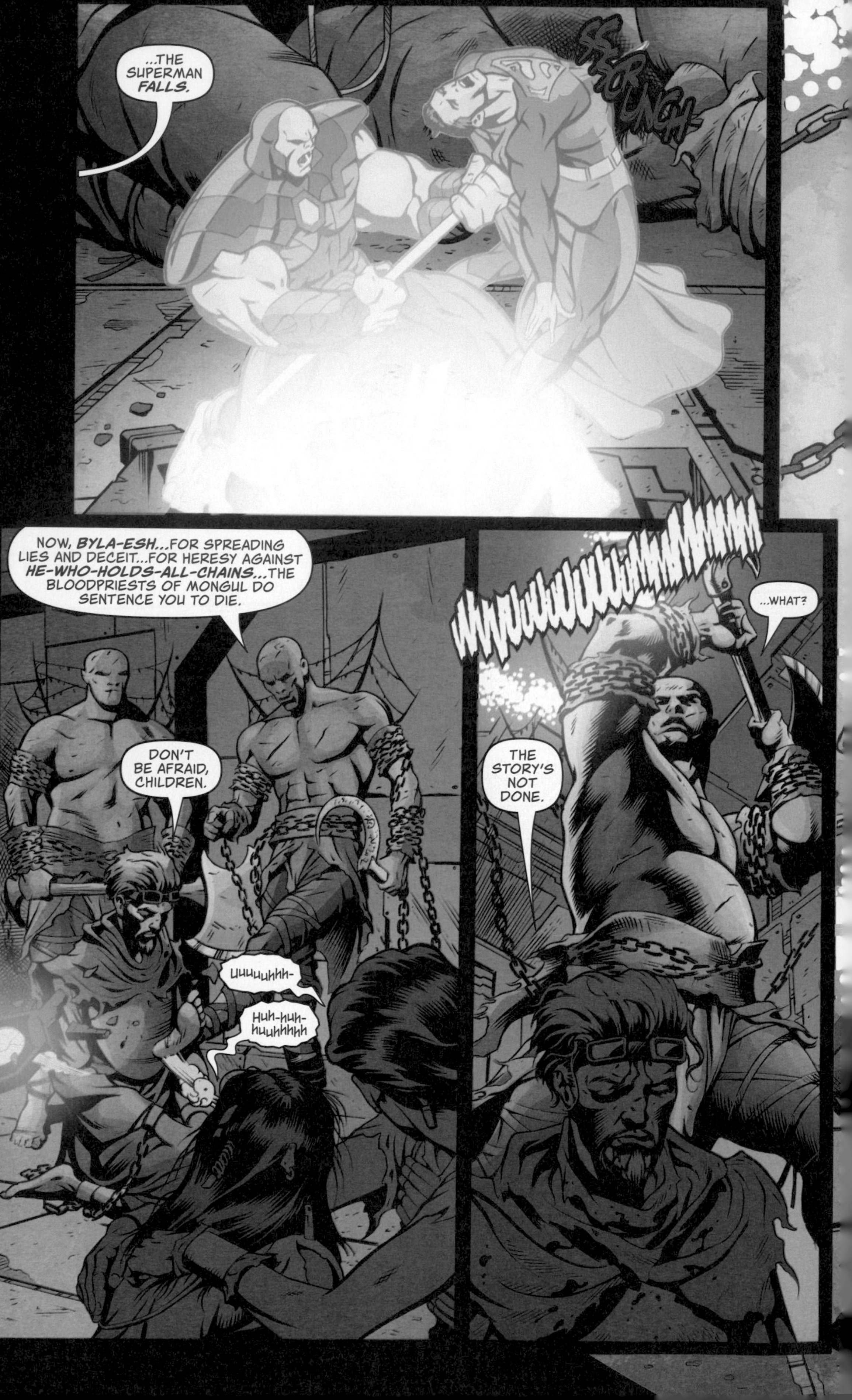

...THE SUPERMAN FALLS.
SSSKRUNCH
NOW, BYLA-ESH...FOR SPREADING LIES AND DECEIT...FOR HERESY AGAINST HE-WHO-HOLDS-ALL-CHAINS...THE BLOODPRIESTS OF MONGUL DO SENTENCE YOU TO DIE.
DON'T BE AFRAID, CHILDREN.
Uuuuuhhh-
Huh-huh-huuhhhhh
WHUUUUUUUUUUMMMMMMMMM
...WHAT?
THE STORY'S NOT DONE.

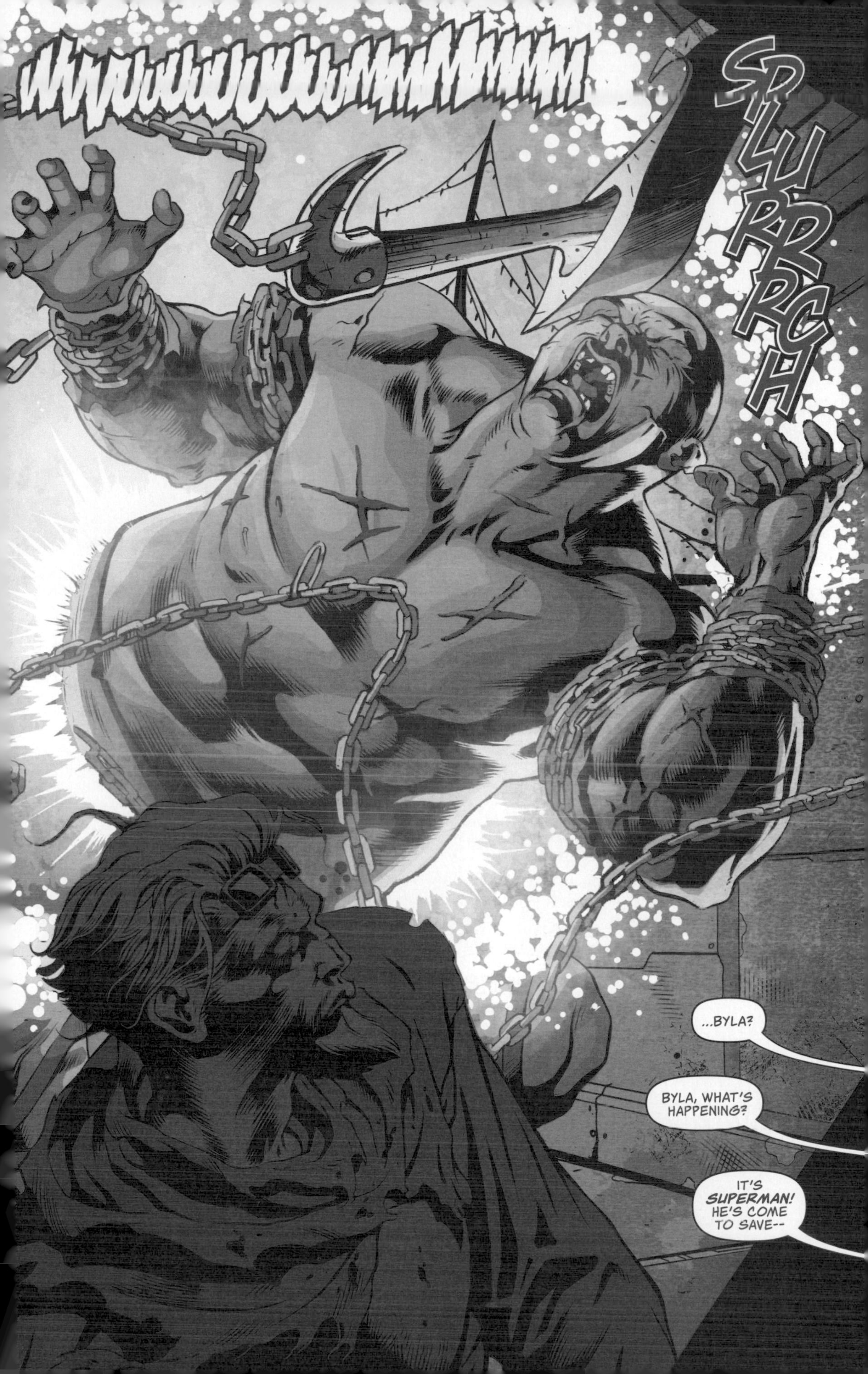
SPLURRRCH
...BYLA?
BYLA, WHAT'S HAPPENING?
IT'S *SUPERMAN!* HE'S COME TO SAVE--

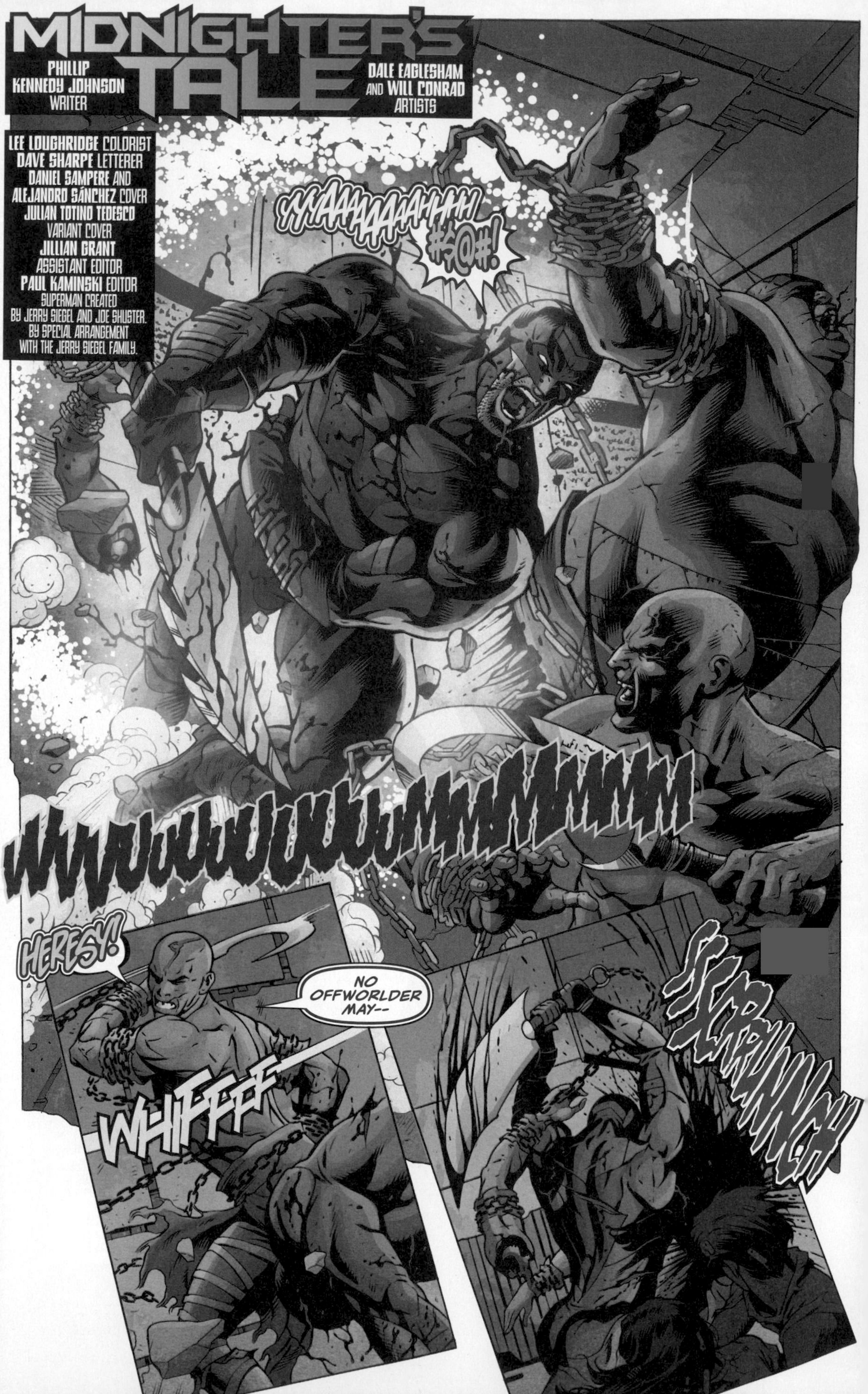
MIDNIGHTER'S TALE
PHILLIP KENNEDY JOHNSON WRITER
DALE EAGLESHAM AND WILL CONRAD ARTISTS
LEE LOUGHRIDGE COLORIST
DAVE SHARPE LETTERER
DANIEL SAMPERE AND ALEJANDRO SÁNCHEZ COVER
JULIAN TOTINO TEDESCO VARIANT COVER
JILLIAN GRANT ASSISTANT EDITOR
PAUL KAMINSKI EDITOR
SUPERMAN CREATED BY JERRY SIEGEL AND JOE SHUSTER. BY SPECIAL ARRANGEMENT WITH THE JERRY SIEGEL FAMILY.
YYAAAAAAAHHHH #$@#!
WHUUUUUUMMMMMMMM
HERESY!
NO OFFWORLDER MAY--
WHIFFFF
SKRUNCH

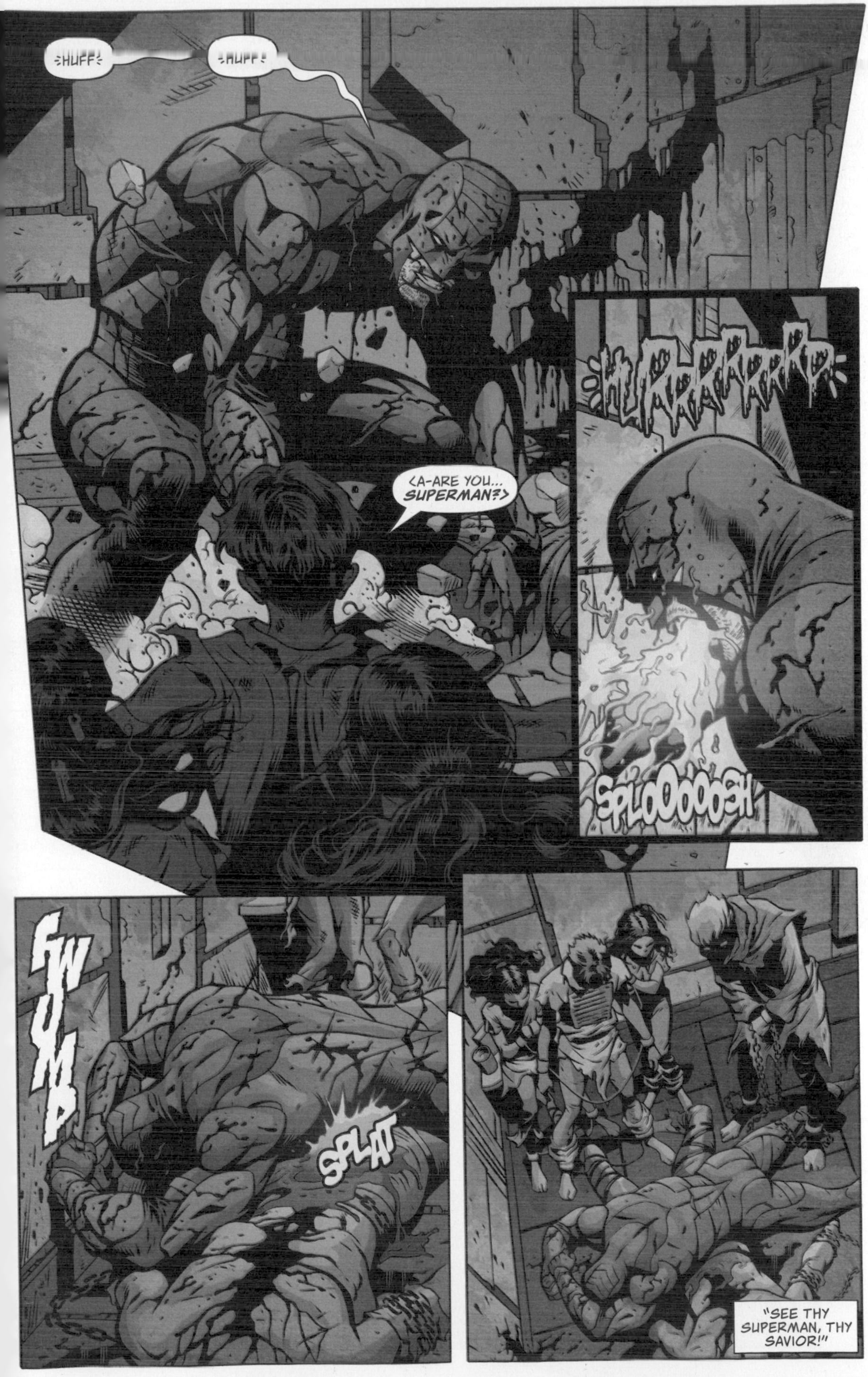

HUFF
HUFF
<A-ARE YOU... SUPERMAN?>
HURRRRRD
SPLOOOOOSH
FWUMP
SPLAT
"SEE THY SUPERMAN, THY SAVIOR!"

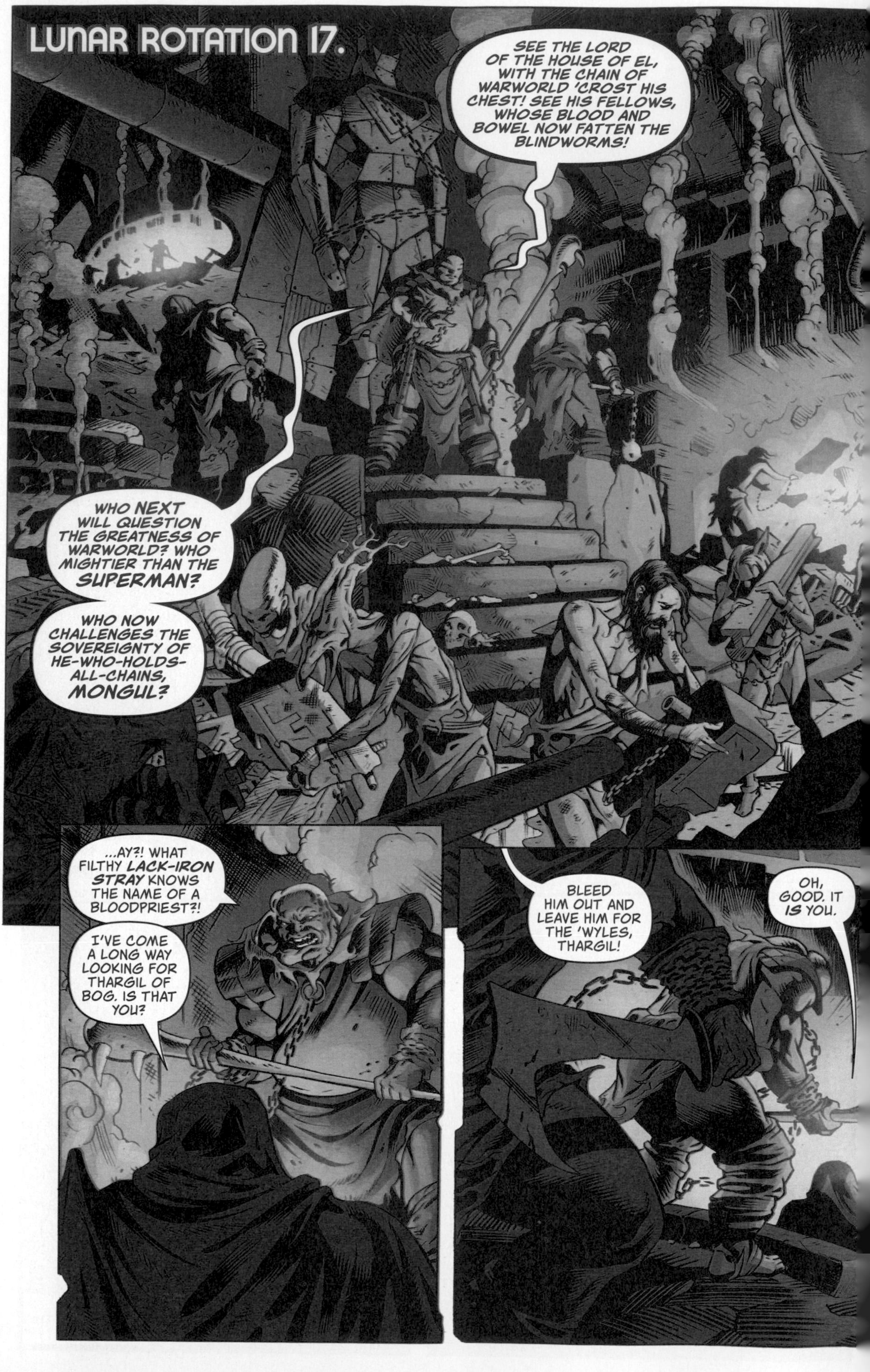
LUNAR ROTATION 17.
SEE THE LORD OF THE HOUSE OF EL, WITH THE CHAIN OF WARWORLD 'CROST HIS CHEST! SEE HIS FELLOWS, WHOSE BLOOD AND BOWEL NOW FATTEN THE BLINDWORMS!
WHO NEXT WILL QUESTION THE GREATNESS OF WARWORLD? WHO MIGHTIER THAN THE SUPERMAN?
WHO NOW CHALLENGES THE SOVEREIGNTY OF HE-WHO-HOLDS-ALL-CHAINS, MONGUL?
...AY?! WHAT FILTHY LACK-IRON STRAY KNOWS THE NAME OF A BLOODPRIEST?!
I'VE COME A LONG WAY LOOKING FOR THARGIL OF BOG. IS THAT YOU?
BLEED HIM OUT AND LEAVE HIM FOR THE 'WYLES, THARGIL!
OH, GOOD. IT IS YOU.

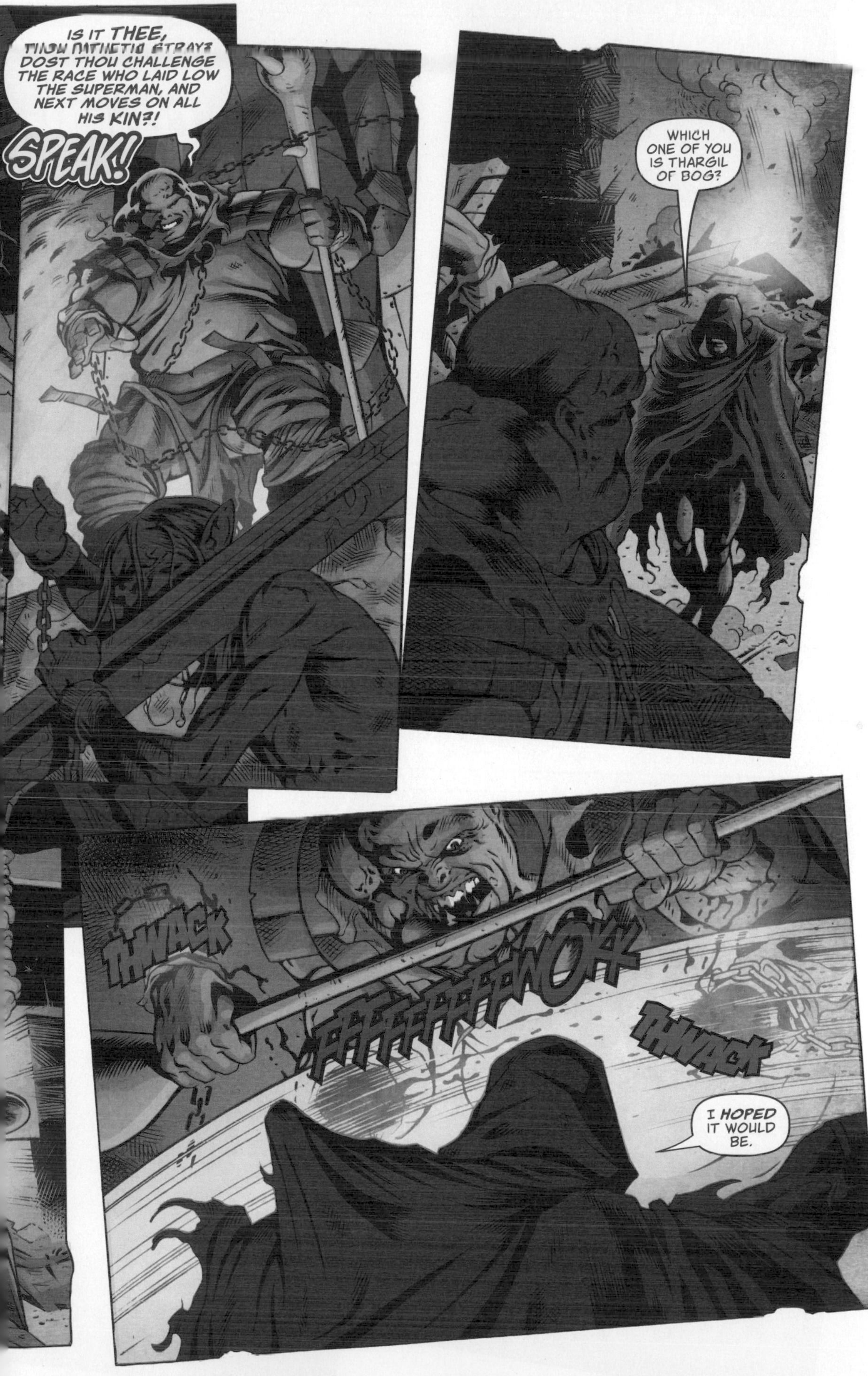
IS IT THEE, THOU PATHETIC STRAY? DOST THOU CHALLENGE THE RACE WHO LAID LOW THE SUPERMAN, AND NEXT MOVES ON ALL HIS KIN?!
SPEAK!
WHICH ONE OF YOU IS THARGIL OF BOG?
THWACK
FFFFFFFFFWOKK
THWACK
I HOPED IT WOULD BE.

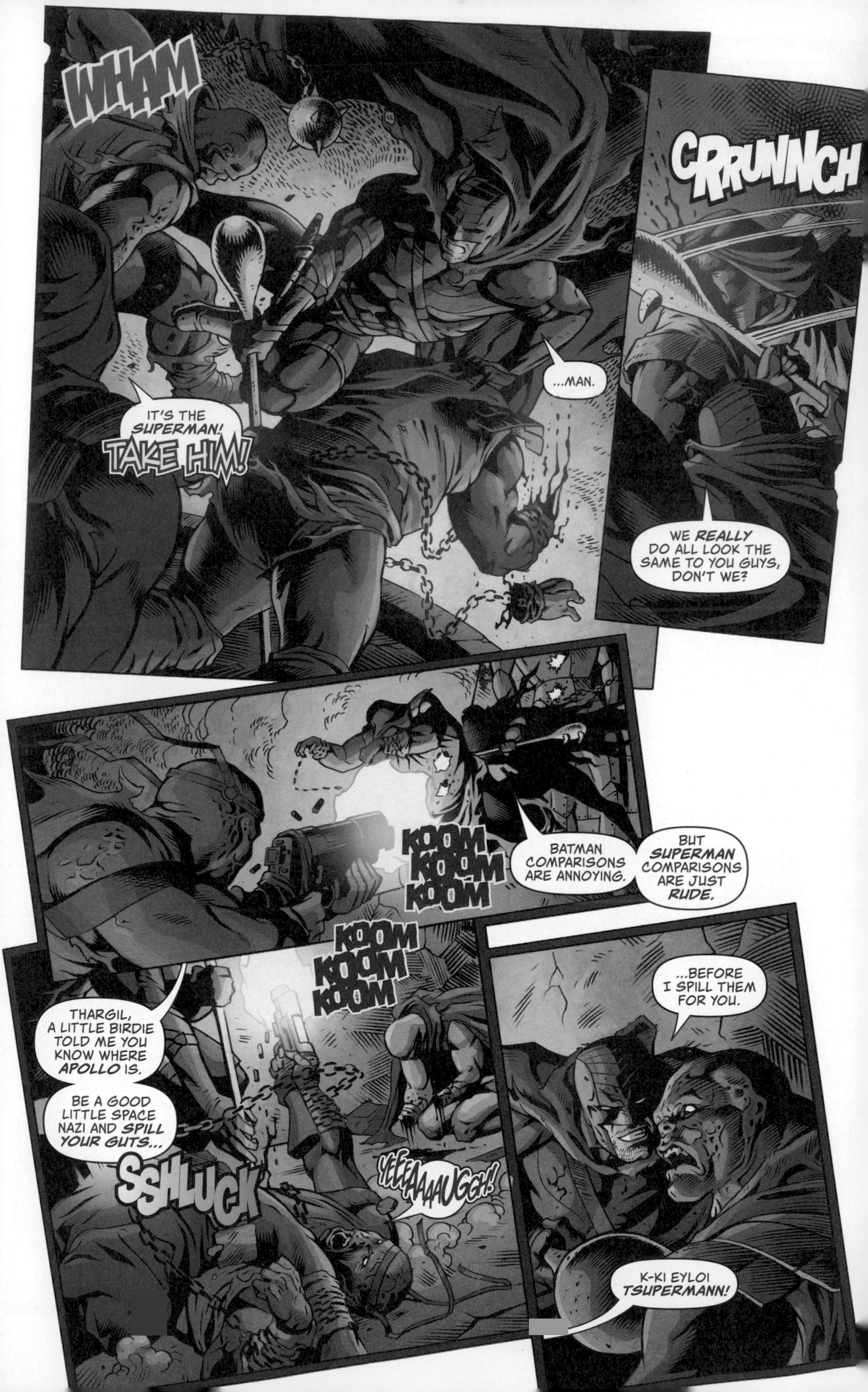
WHAM
IT'S THE SUPERMAN! TAKE HIM!
...MAN.
CRRUNNCH
WE REALLY DO ALL LOOK THE SAME TO YOU GUYS, DON'T WE?
KOOM KOOM KOOM
BATMAN COMPARISONS ARE ANNOYING.
BUT SUPERMAN COMPARISONS ARE JUST RUDE.
KOOM KOOM KOOM
THARGIL, A LITTLE BIRDIE TOLD ME YOU KNOW WHERE APOLLO IS.
BE A GOOD LITTLE SPACE NAZI AND SPILL YOUR GUTS...
SSHLUCK
YEEEAAAAUGGH!
...BEFORE I SPILL THEM FOR YOU.
K-KI EYLOI TSUPERMANN!

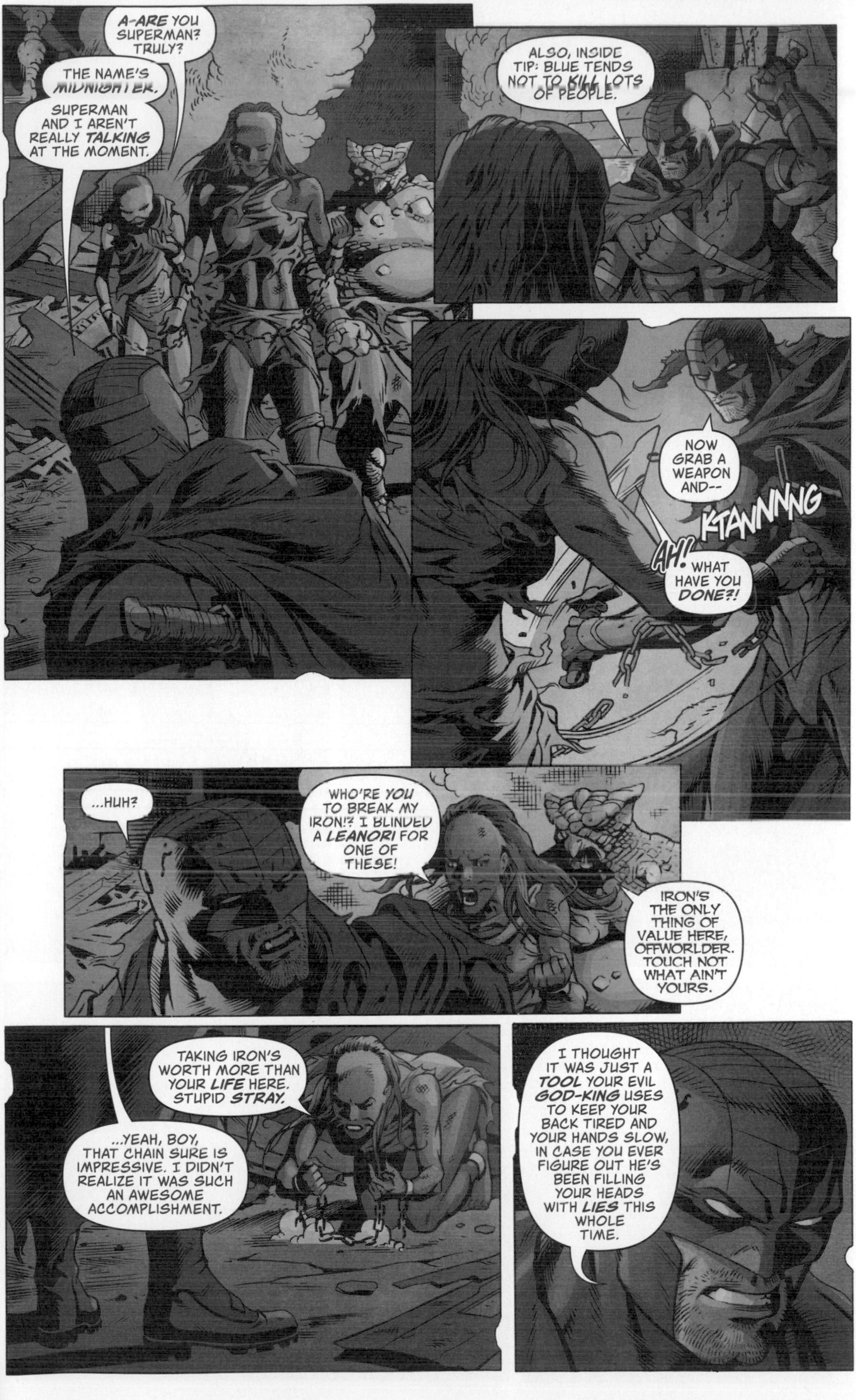

A-ARE YOU SUPERMAN? TRULY?
THE NAME'S MIDNIGHTER.
SUPERMAN AND I AREN'T REALLY TALKING AT THE MOMENT.
ALSO, INSIDE TIP: BLUE TENDS NOT TO KILL LOTS OF PEOPLE.
NOW GRAB A WEAPON AND--
KTANNNNG
AH! WHAT HAVE YOU DONE?!
...HUH?
WHO'RE YOU TO BREAK MY IRON!? I BLINDED A LEANORI FOR ONE OF THESE!
IRON'S THE ONLY THING OF VALUE HERE, OFFWORLDER. TOUCH NOT WHAT AIN'T YOURS.
TAKING IRON'S WORTH MORE THAN YOUR LIFE HERE. STUPID STRAY.
...YEAH, BOY, THAT CHAIN SURE IS IMPRESSIVE. I DIDN'T REALIZE IT WAS SUCH AN AWESOME ACCOMPLISHMENT.
I THOUGHT IT WAS JUST A TOOL YOUR EVIL GOD-KING USES TO KEEP YOUR BACK TIRED AND YOUR HANDS SLOW, IN CASE YOU EVER FIGURE OUT HE'S BEEN FILLING YOUR HEADS WITH LIES THIS WHOLE TIME.

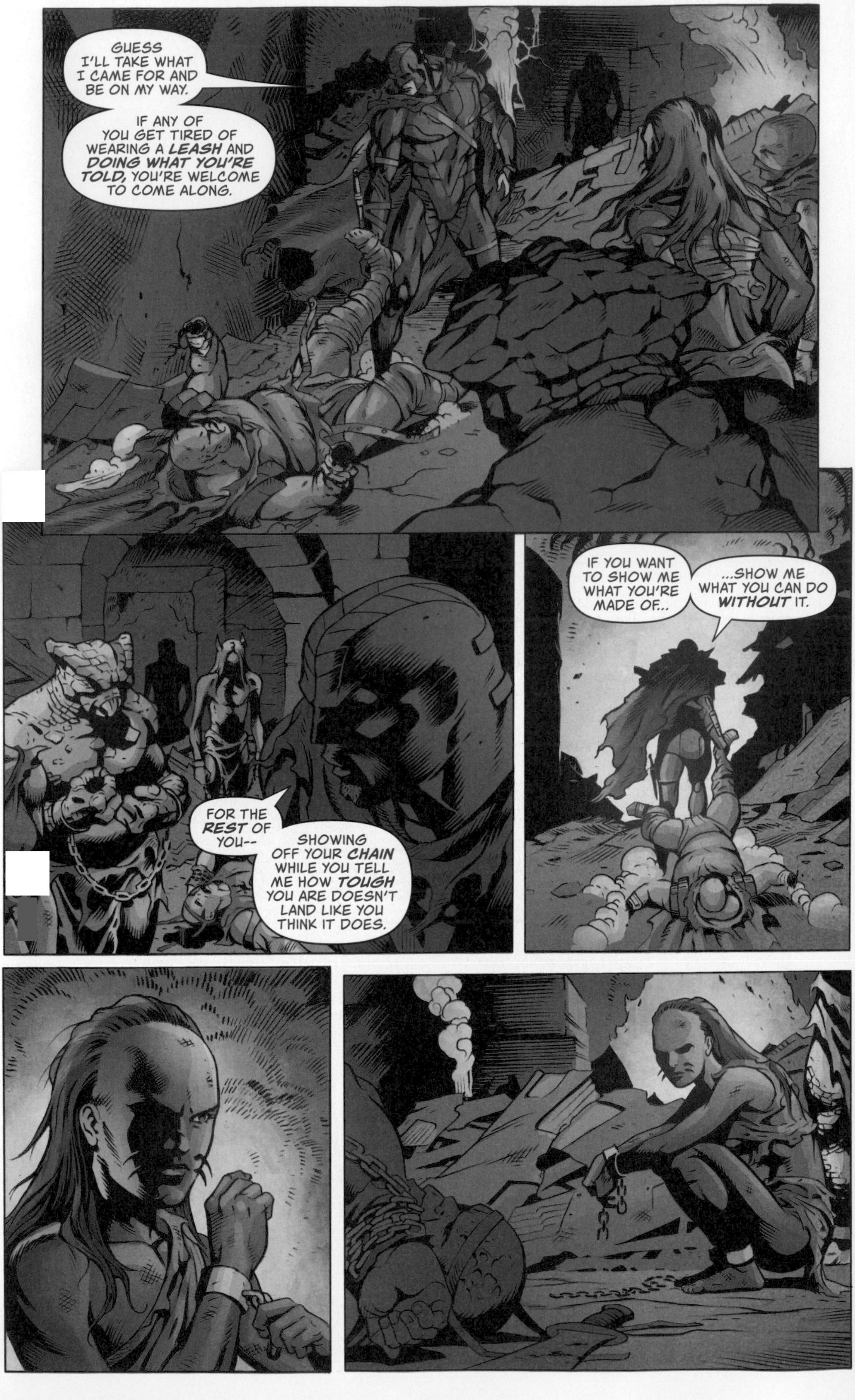
GUESS I'LL TAKE WHAT I CAME FOR AND BE ON MY WAY.
IF ANY OF YOU GET TIRED OF WEARING A **LEASH** AND ***DOING WHAT YOU'RE TOLD,*** YOU'RE WELCOME TO COME ALONG.
FOR THE ***REST*** OF YOU--
SHOWING OFF YOUR ***CHAIN*** WHILE YOU TELL ME HOW ***TOUGH*** YOU ARE DOESN'T LAND LIKE YOU THINK IT DOES.
IF YOU WANT TO SHOW ME WHAT YOU'RE MADE OF...
...SHOW ME WHAT YOU CAN DO ***WITHOUT*** IT.

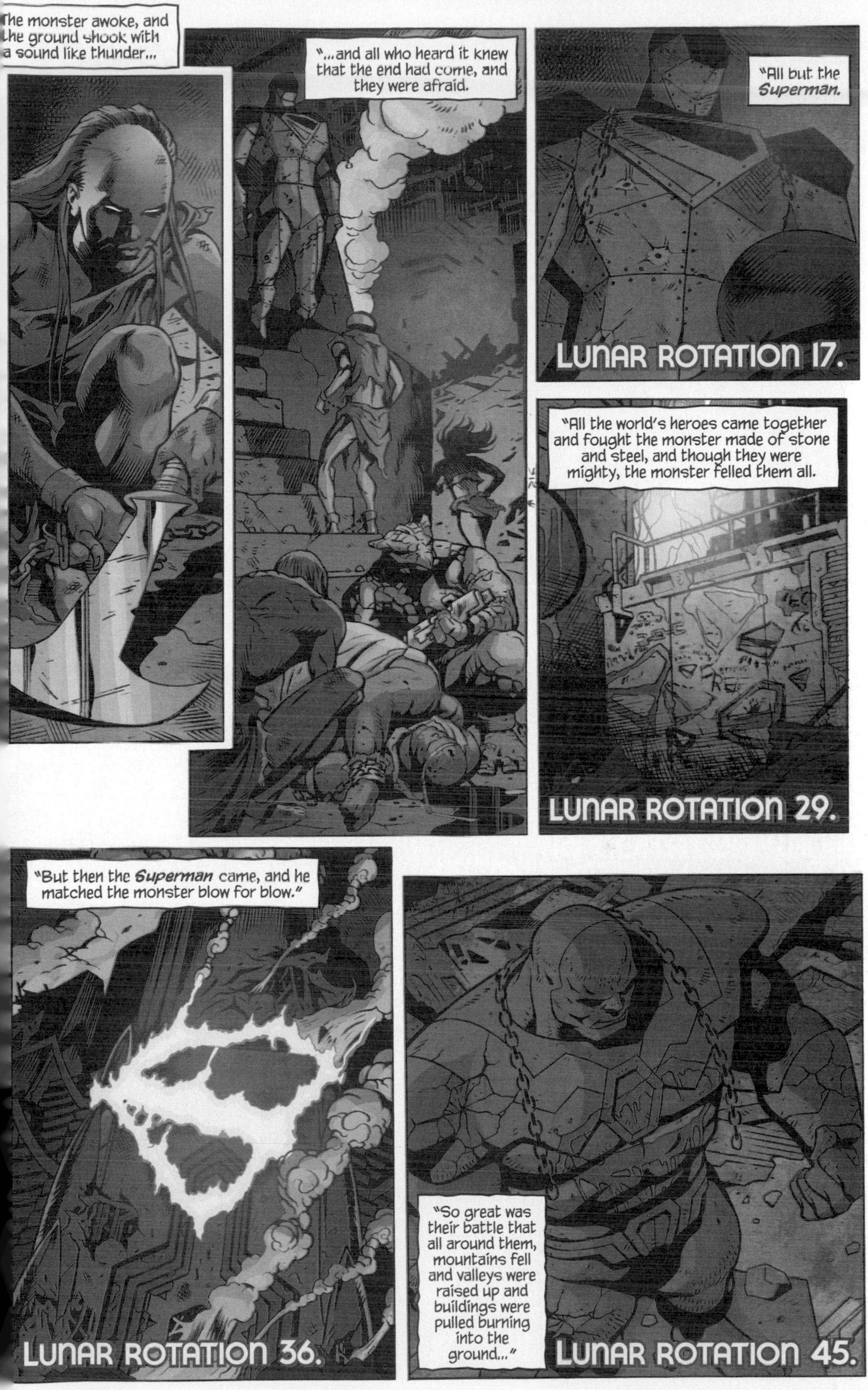
The monster awoke, and the ground shook with a sound like thunder...
"...and all who heard it knew that the end had come, and they were afraid.
"All but the *Superman.*
LUNAR ROTATION 17.
"All the world's heroes came together and fought the monster made of stone and steel, and though they were mighty, the monster felled them all.
LUNAR ROTATION 29.
"But then the *Superman* came, and he matched the monster blow for blow."
LUNAR ROTATION 36.
"So great was their battle that all around them, mountains fell and valleys were raised up and buildings were pulled burning into the ground..."
LUNAR ROTATION 45.

"...and *still* Superman fought, until he had no blood left to shed.

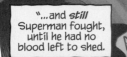

"Not to prove himself the *strongest* of his kind, but to protect the *weakest.*

"When the battle was done, and both he and the monster were carried into the *Orchard of the Dead,* Superman looked back on the world he had saved...

LUNAR ROTATION 61.

...AND JUDGED THAT HIS WORK WAS NOT YET FINISHED.

DOOMDOOMDOOM

HE *RETURNED,* THAT HE MIGHT ONE DAY FREE HIS PHAELOSIAN KIN WHO STILL AWAITED HIM.

OFF *THE PATH,* KNOTLING, OR WE'LL RUN YOU DOWN AND FEED YOU TO OUR MOUNTS. *SO SAY THE DEAD.*

...AYE?

I'VE GOT DEAD WHO SPEAK FOR *ME,* TOO.

KNOW WHAT THEY SAY?

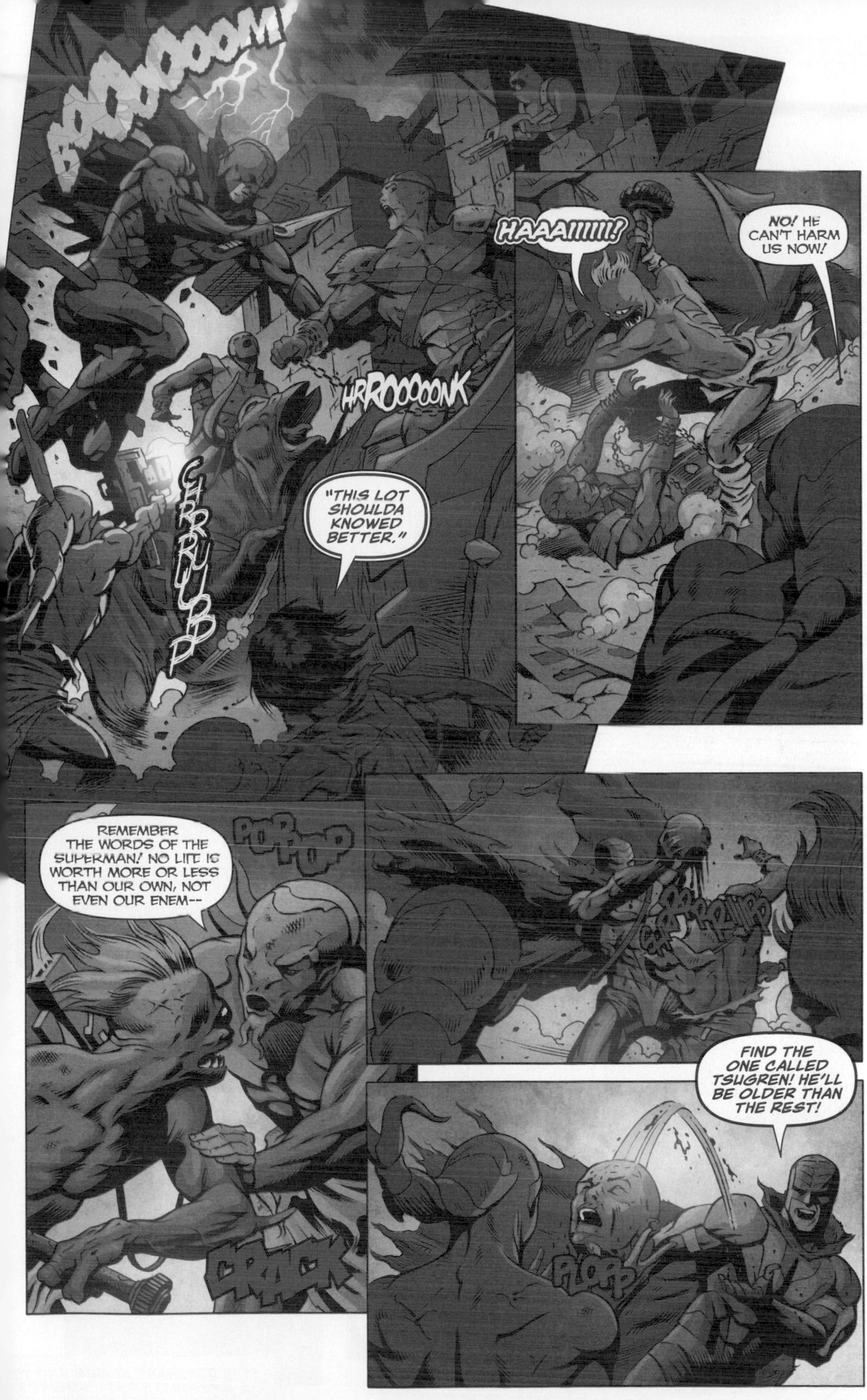
BOOOOOOOM!
HAAAIIIIII!
NO! HE CAN'T HARM US NOW!
HRROOOOONK
CHRRUUBBP
"THIS LOT SHOULDA KNOWED BETTER."
REMEMBER THE WORDS OF THE SUPERMAN! NO LIFE IS WORTH MORE OR LESS THAN OUR OWN, NOT EVEN OUR ENEM--
POP POP
CRACK
FIND THE ONE CALLED TSUGREN! HE'LL BE OLDER THAN THE REST!
PLOPP

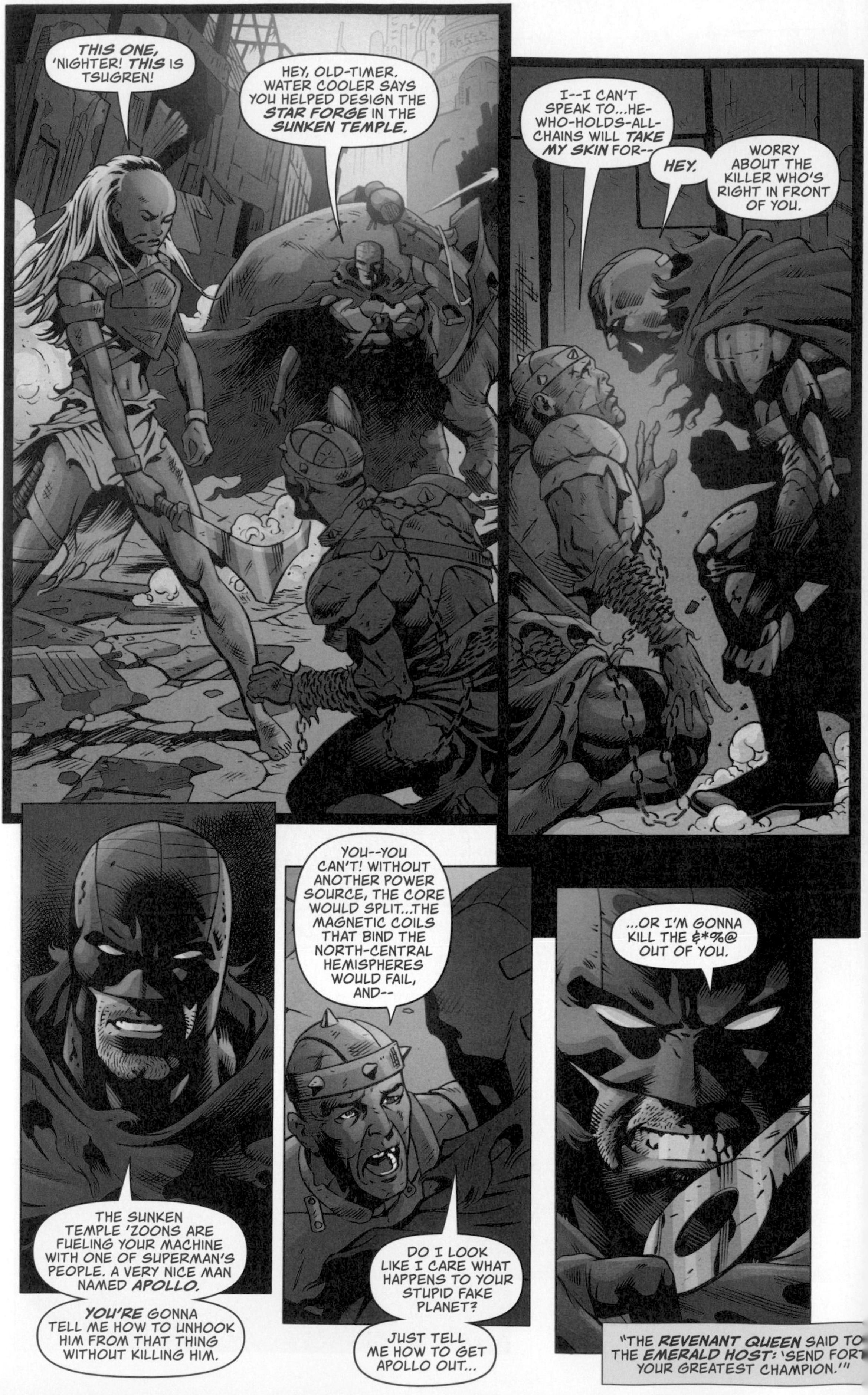
THIS ONE, 'NIGHTER! THIS IS TSUGREN!
HEY, OLD-TIMER. WATER COOLER SAYS YOU HELPED DESIGN THE STAR FORGE IN THE SUNKEN TEMPLE.
I--I CAN'T SPEAK TO...HE-WHO-HOLDS-ALL-CHAINS WILL TAKE MY SKIN FOR--
HEY.
WORRY ABOUT THE KILLER WHO'S RIGHT IN FRONT OF YOU.
THE SUNKEN TEMPLE 'ZOONS ARE FUELING YOUR MACHINE WITH ONE OF SUPERMAN'S PEOPLE. A VERY NICE MAN NAMED APOLLO.
YOU'RE GONNA TELL ME HOW TO UNHOOK HIM FROM THAT THING WITHOUT KILLING HIM.
YOU--YOU CAN'T! WITHOUT ANOTHER POWER SOURCE, THE CORE WOULD SPLIT...THE MAGNETIC COILS THAT BIND THE NORTH-CENTRAL HEMISPHERES WOULD FAIL, AND--
DO I LOOK LIKE I CARE WHAT HAPPENS TO YOUR STUPID FAKE PLANET?
JUST TELL ME HOW TO GET APOLLO OUT...
...OR I'M GONNA KILL THE &*%@ OUT OF YOU.
"THE REVENANT QUEEN SAID TO THE EMERALD HOST: 'SEND FORT YOUR GREATEST CHAMPION.'"

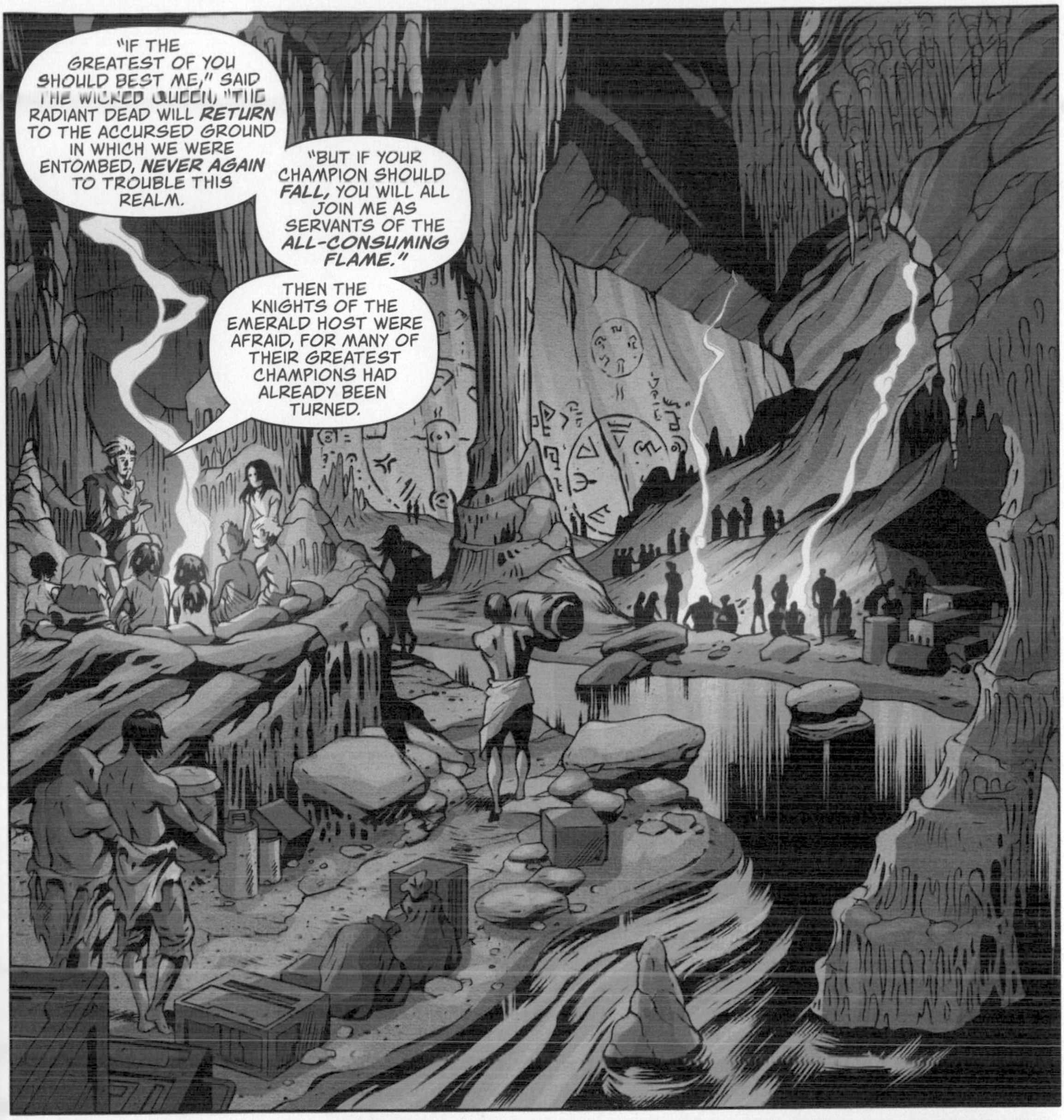
"IF THE GREATEST OF YOU SHOULD BEST ME," SAID THE WICKED QUEEN, "THE RADIANT DEAD WILL RETURN TO THE ACCURSED GROUND IN WHICH WE WERE ENTOMBED, NEVER AGAIN TO TROUBLE THIS REALM.
"BUT IF YOUR CHAMPION SHOULD FALL, YOU WILL ALL JOIN ME AS SERVANTS OF THE ALL-CONSUMING FLAME."
THEN THE KNIGHTS OF THE EMERALD HOST WERE AFRAID, FOR MANY OF THEIR GREATEST CHAMPIONS HAD ALREADY BEEN TURNED.

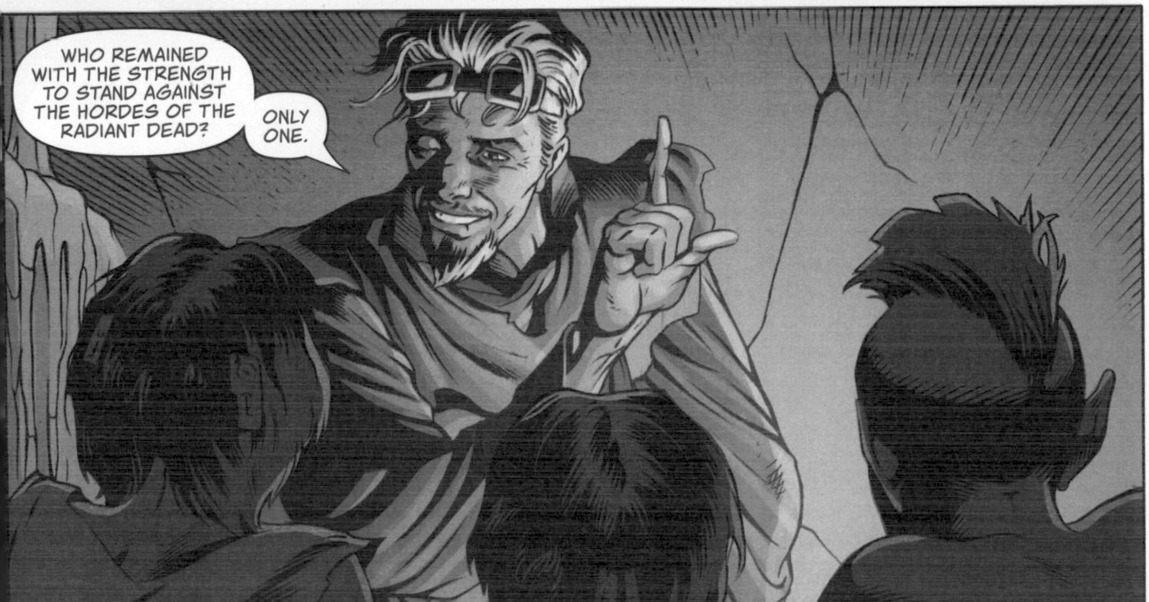
WHO REMAINED WITH THE STRENGTH TO STAND AGAINST THE HORDES OF THE RADIANT DEAD?
ONLY ONE.

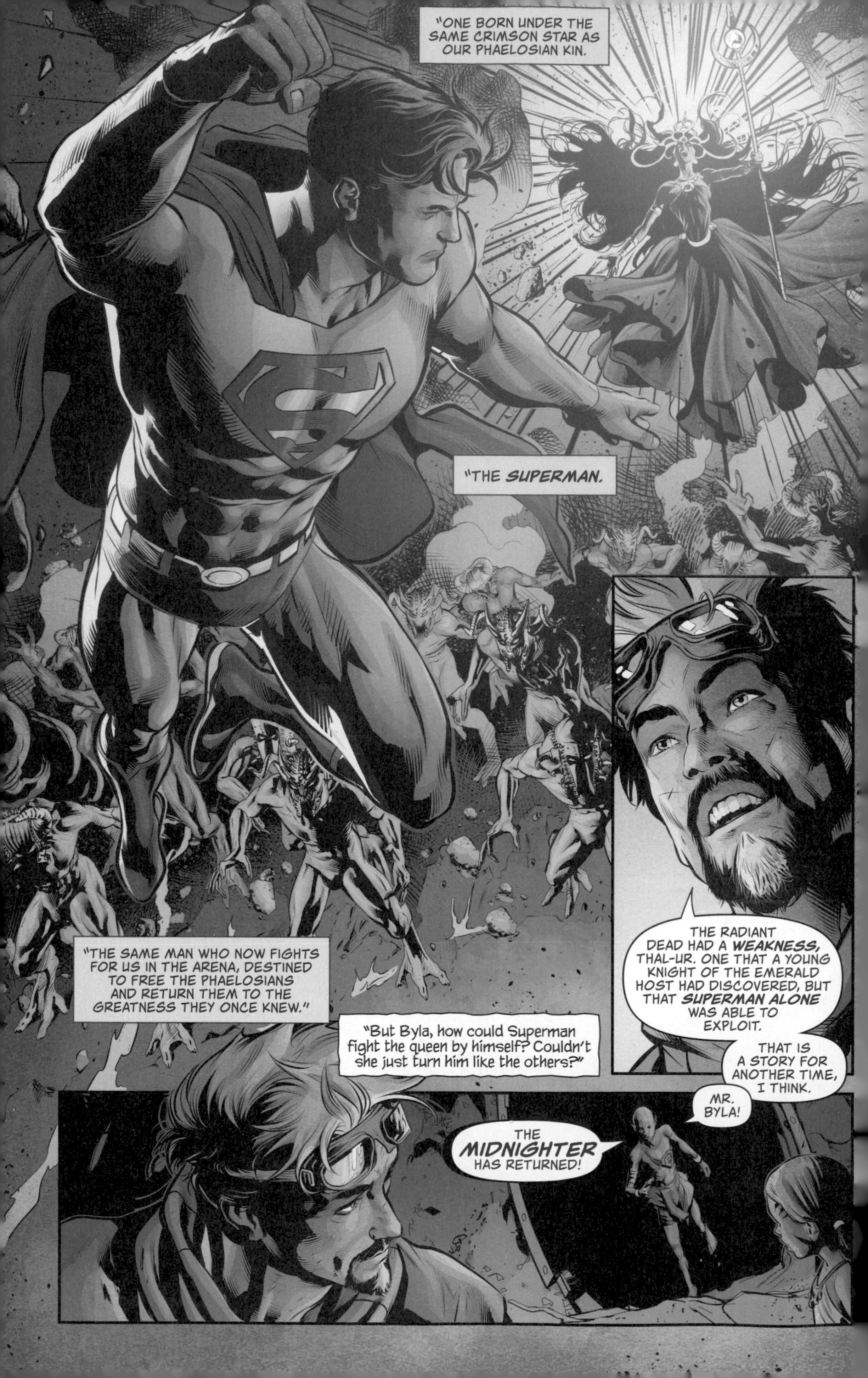
"ONE BORN UNDER THE SAME CRIMSON STAR AS OUR PHAELOSIAN KIN.
"THE SUPERMAN.
"THE SAME MAN WHO NOW FIGHTS FOR US IN THE ARENA, DESTINED TO FREE THE PHAELOSIANS AND RETURN THEM TO THE GREATNESS THEY ONCE KNEW."
THE RADIANT DEAD HAD A WEAKNESS, THAL-UR. ONE THAT A YOUNG KNIGHT OF THE EMERALD HOST HAD DISCOVERED, BUT THAT SUPERMAN ALONE WAS ABLE TO EXPLOIT.
"But Byla, how could Superman fight the queen by himself? Couldn't she just turn him like the others?"
THAT IS A STORY FOR ANOTHER TIME, I THINK.
MR. BYLA!
THE MIDNIGHTER HAS RETURNED!

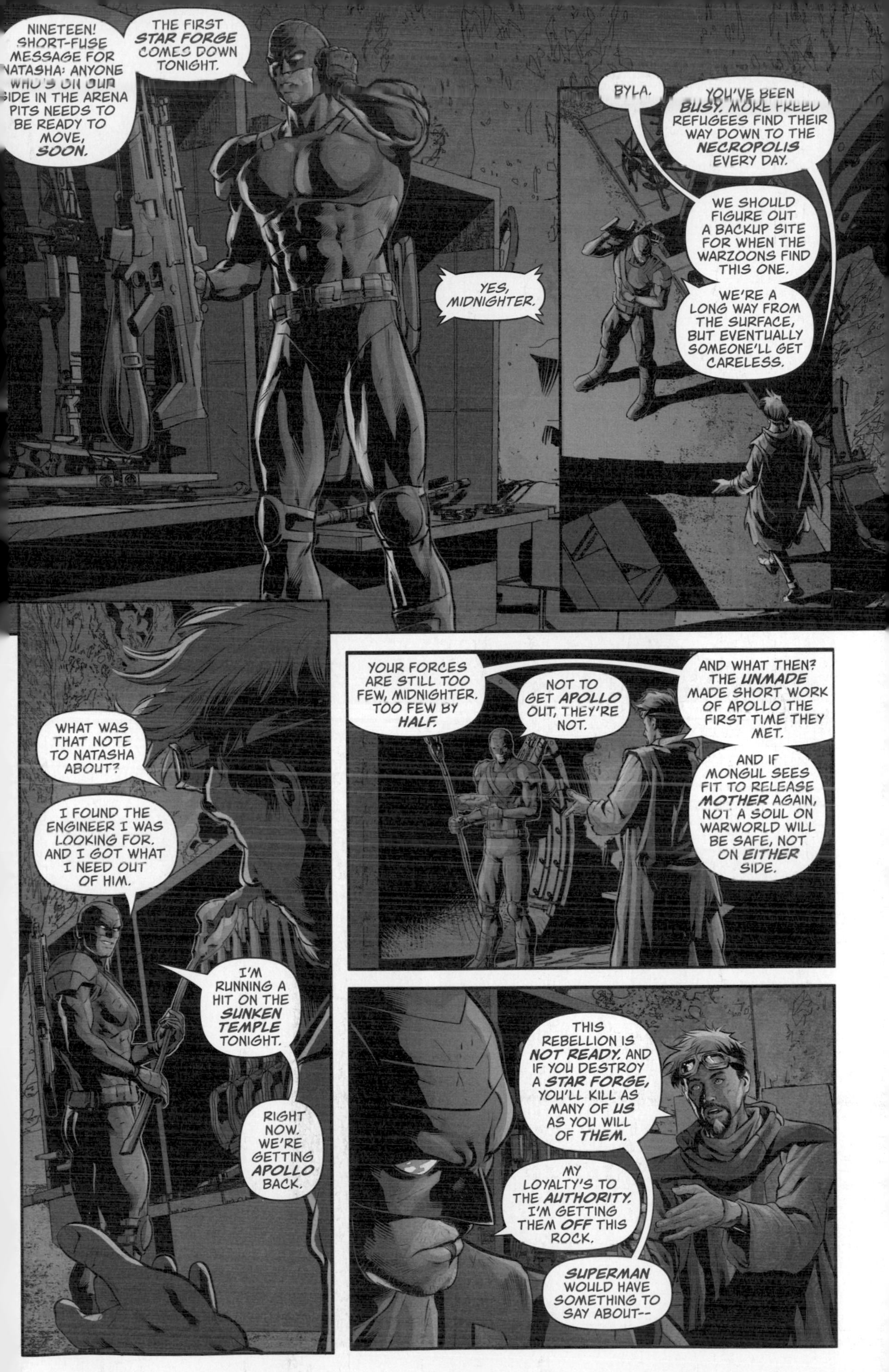
NINETEEN! SHORT-FUSE MESSAGE FOR NATASHA: ANYONE WHO'S ON OUR SIDE IN THE ARENA PITS NEEDS TO BE READY TO MOVE, SOON.
THE FIRST STAR FORGE COMES DOWN TONIGHT.
YES, MIDNIGHTER.
BYLA.
YOU'VE BEEN BUSY. MORE FREED REFUGEES FIND THEIR WAY DOWN TO THE NECROPOLIS EVERY DAY.
WE SHOULD FIGURE OUT A BACKUP SITE FOR WHEN THE WARZOONS FIND THIS ONE.
WE'RE A LONG WAY FROM THE SURFACE, BUT EVENTUALLY SOMEONE'LL GET CARELESS.
WHAT WAS THAT NOTE TO NATASHA ABOUT?
I FOUND THE ENGINEER I WAS LOOKING FOR. AND I GOT WHAT I NEED OUT OF HIM.
I'M RUNNING A HIT ON THE SUNKEN TEMPLE TONIGHT.
RIGHT NOW. WE'RE GETTING APOLLO BACK.
YOUR FORCES ARE STILL TOO FEW, MIDNIGHTER. TOO FEW BY HALF.
NOT TO GET APOLLO OUT, THEY'RE NOT.
AND WHAT THEN? THE UNMADE MADE SHORT WORK OF APOLLO THE FIRST TIME THEY MET.
AND IF MONGUL SEES FIT TO RELEASE MOTHER AGAIN, NOT A SOUL ON WARWORLD WILL BE SAFE, NOT ON EITHER SIDE.
THIS REBELLION IS NOT READY. AND IF YOU DESTROY A STAR FORGE, YOU'LL KILL AS MANY OF US AS YOU WILL OF THEM.
MY LOYALTY'S TO THE AUTHORITY. I'M GETTING THEM OFF THIS ROCK.
SUPERMAN WOULD HAVE SOMETHING TO SAY ABOUT--

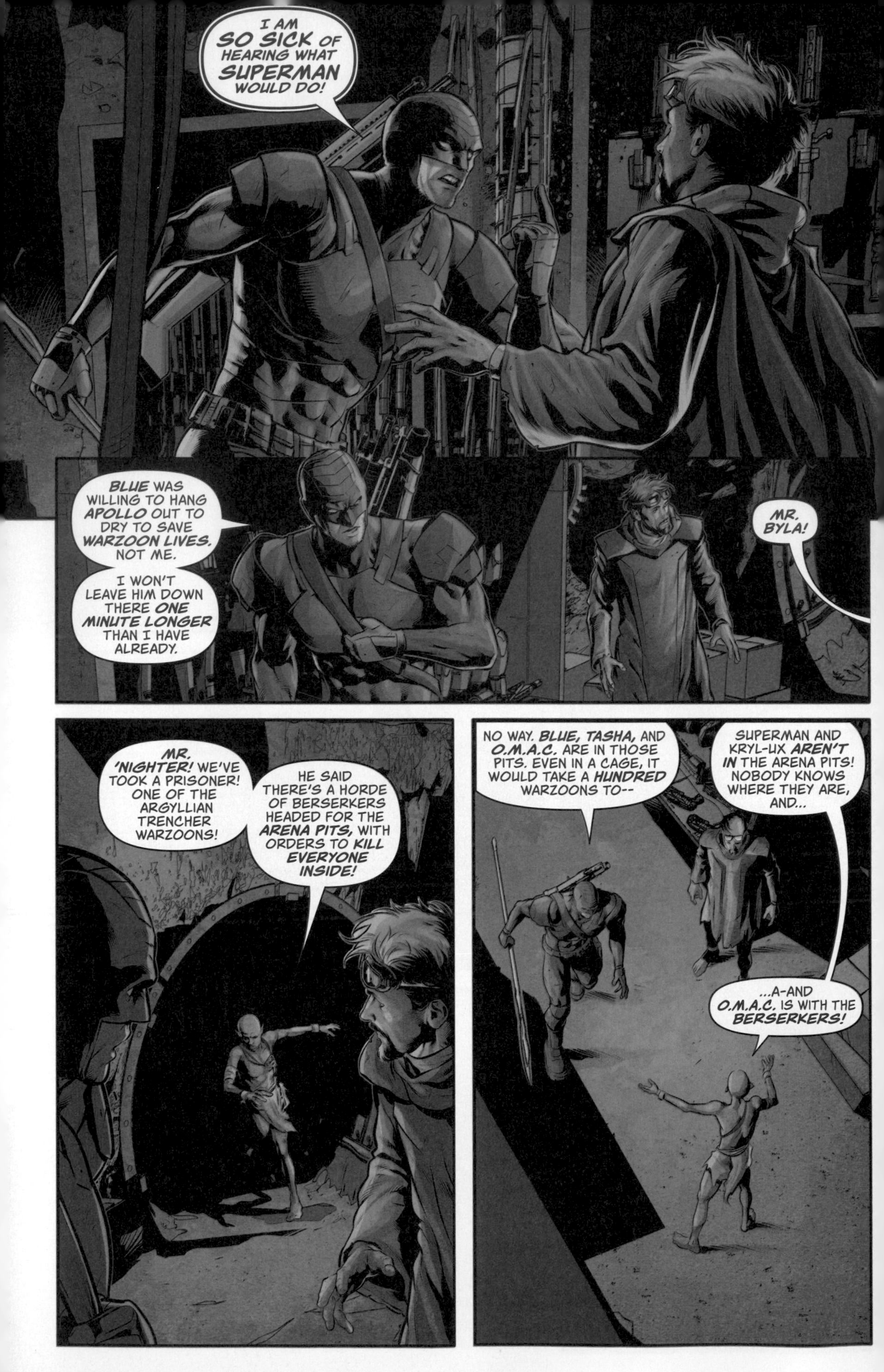
I AM SO SICK OF HEARING WHAT SUPERMAN WOULD DO!
BLUE WAS WILLING TO HANG APOLLO OUT TO DRY TO SAVE WARZOON LIVES. NOT ME.
I WON'T LEAVE HIM DOWN THERE ONE MINUTE LONGER THAN I HAVE ALREADY.
MR. BYLA!
MR. 'NIGHTER! WE'VE TOOK A PRISONER! ONE OF THE ARGYLLIAN TRENCHER WARZOONS!
HE SAID THERE'S A HORDE OF BERSERKERS HEADED FOR THE ARENA PITS, WITH ORDERS TO KILL EVERYONE INSIDE!
NO WAY. BLUE, TASHA, AND O.M.A.C. ARE IN THOSE PITS. EVEN IN A CAGE, IT WOULD TAKE A HUNDRED WARZOONS TO--
SUPERMAN AND KRYL-UX AREN'T IN THE ARENA PITS! NOBODY KNOWS WHERE THEY ARE, AND...
...A-AND O.M.A.C. IS WITH THE BERSERKERS!

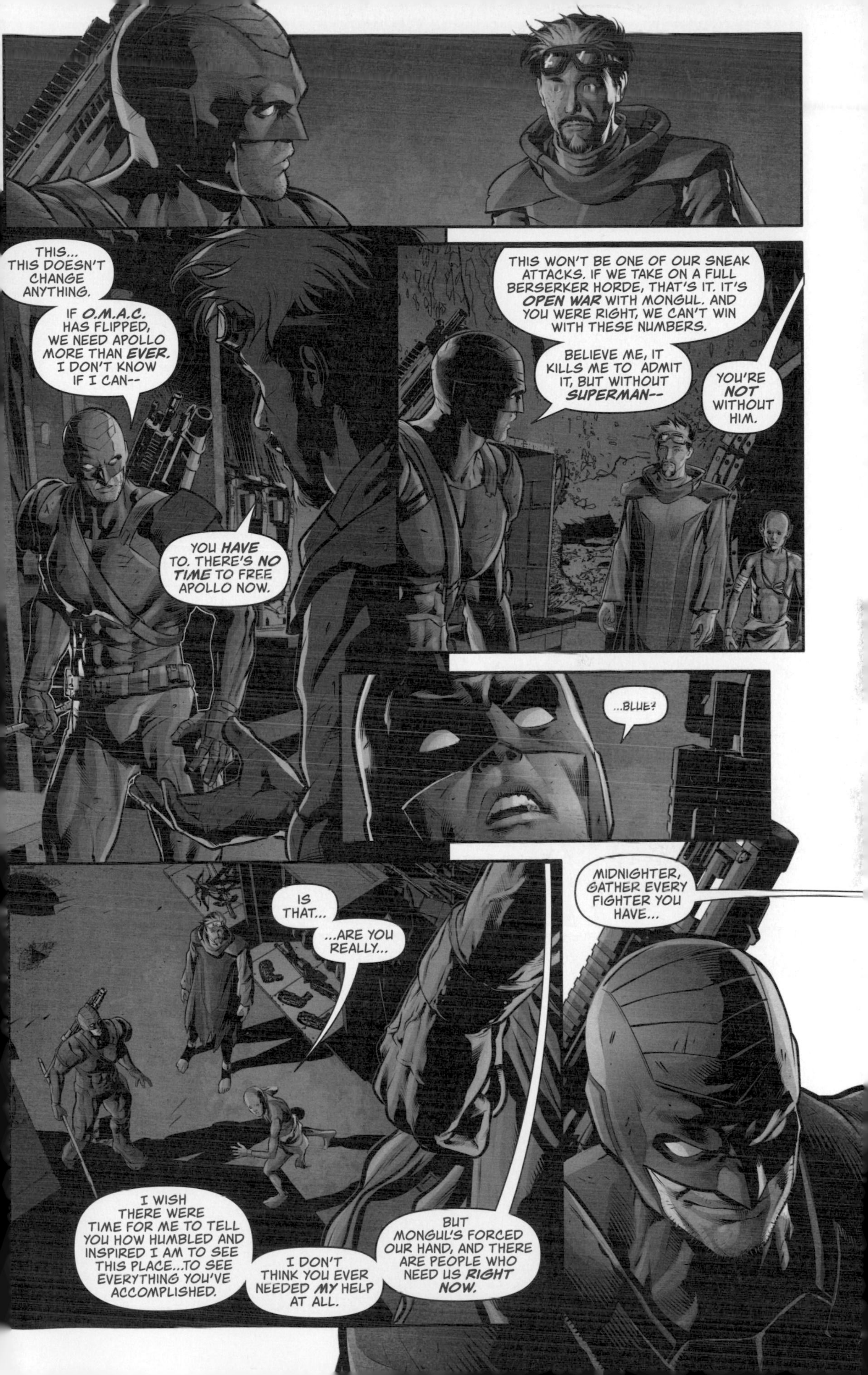
THIS... THIS DOESN'T CHANGE ANYTHING.
IF O.M.A.C. HAS FLIPPED, WE NEED APOLLO MORE THAN EVER. I DON'T KNOW IF I CAN--
YOU HAVE TO. THERE'S NO TIME TO FREE APOLLO NOW.
THIS WON'T BE ONE OF OUR SNEAK ATTACKS. IF WE TAKE ON A FULL BERSERKER HORDE, THAT'S IT. IT'S OPEN WAR WITH MONGUL. AND YOU WERE RIGHT, WE CAN'T WIN WITH THESE NUMBERS.
BELIEVE ME, IT KILLS ME TO ADMIT IT, BUT WITHOUT SUPERMAN--
YOU'RE NOT WITHOUT HIM.
...BLUE?
IS THAT...
...ARE YOU REALLY...
MIDNIGHTER, GATHER EVERY FIGHTER YOU HAVE...
I WISH THERE WERE TIME FOR ME TO TELL YOU HOW HUMBLED AND INSPIRED I AM TO SEE THIS PLACE...TO SEE EVERYTHING YOU'VE ACCOMPLISHED.
I DON'T THINK YOU EVER NEEDED MY HELP AT ALL.
BUT MONGUL'S FORCED OUR HAND, AND THERE ARE PEOPLE WHO NEED US RIGHT NOW.

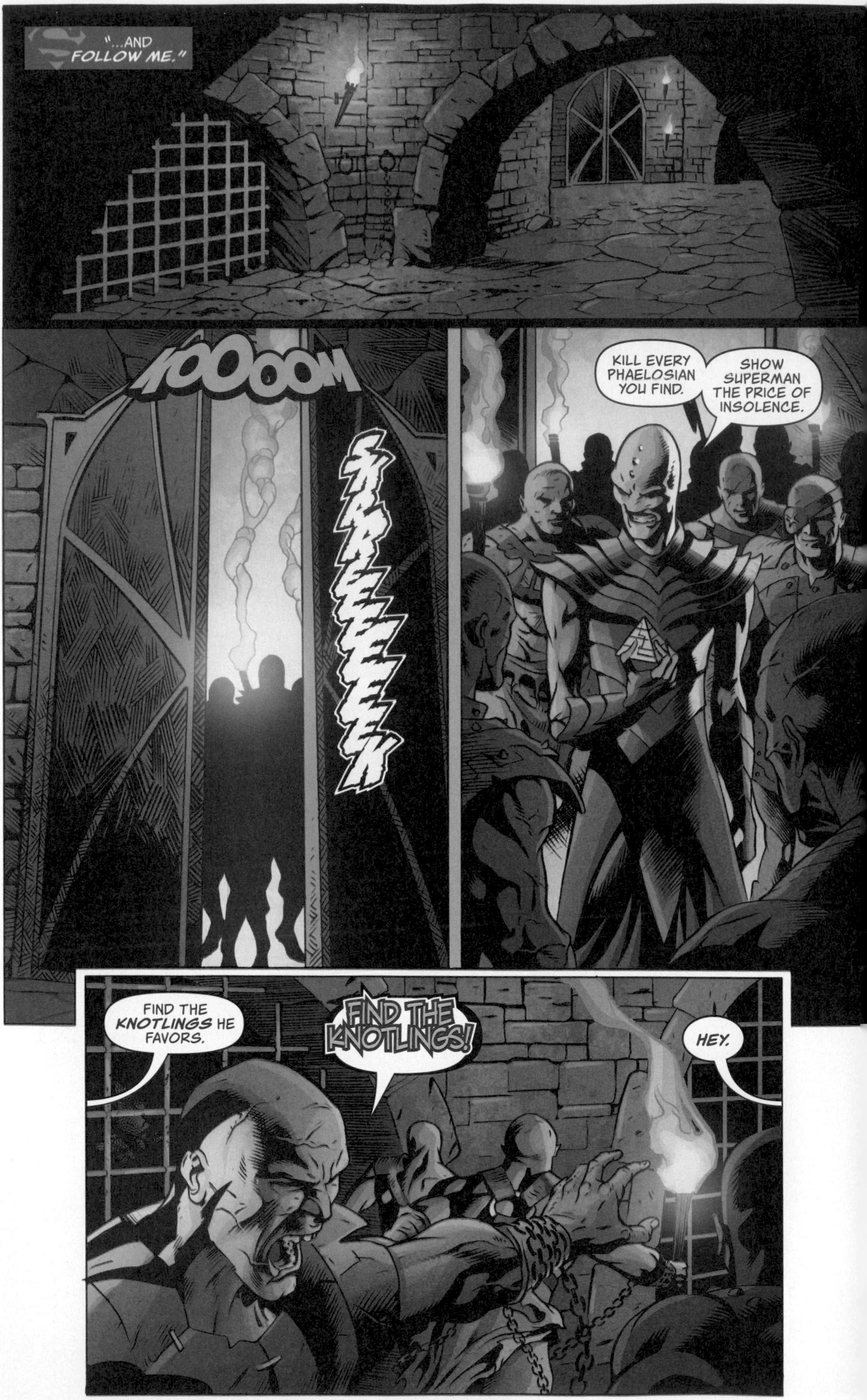
"...AND FOLLOW ME."
KOOOOOM
KILL EVERY PHAELOSIAN YOU FIND.
SHOW SUPERMAN THE PRICE OF INSOLENCE.
FIND THE KNOTLINGS HE FAVORS.
FIND THE KNOTLINGS!
HEY.

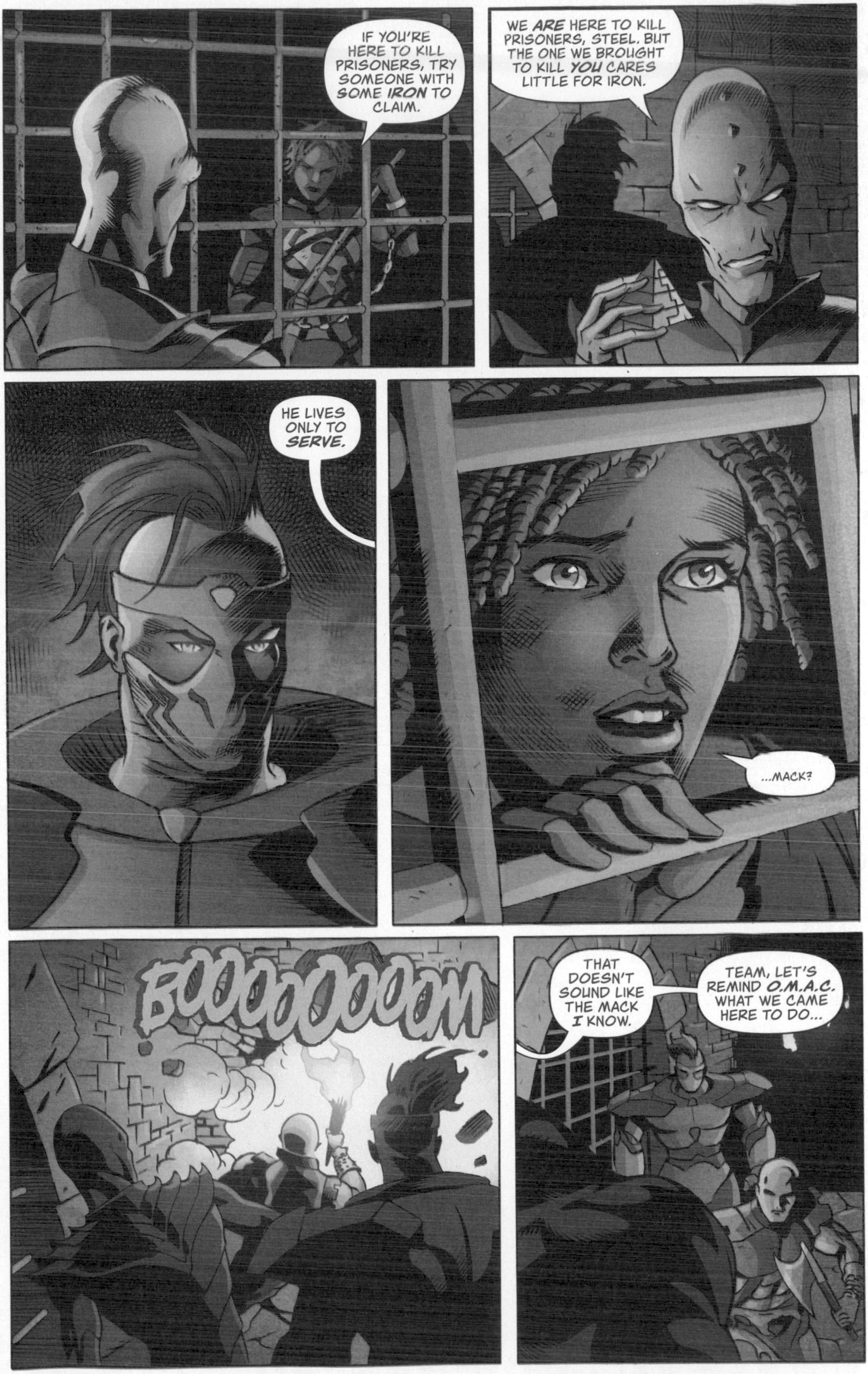
IF YOU'RE HERE TO KILL PRISONERS, TRY SOMEONE WITH SOME IRON TO CLAIM.
WE ARE HERE TO KILL PRISONERS, STEEL. BUT THE ONE WE BROUGHT TO KILL YOU CARES LITTLE FOR IRON.
HE LIVES ONLY TO SERVE.
...MACK?
BOOOOOOOOOM
THAT DOESN'T SOUND LIKE THE MACK I KNOW.
TEAM, LET'S REMIND O.M.A.C. WHAT WE CAME HERE TO DO...

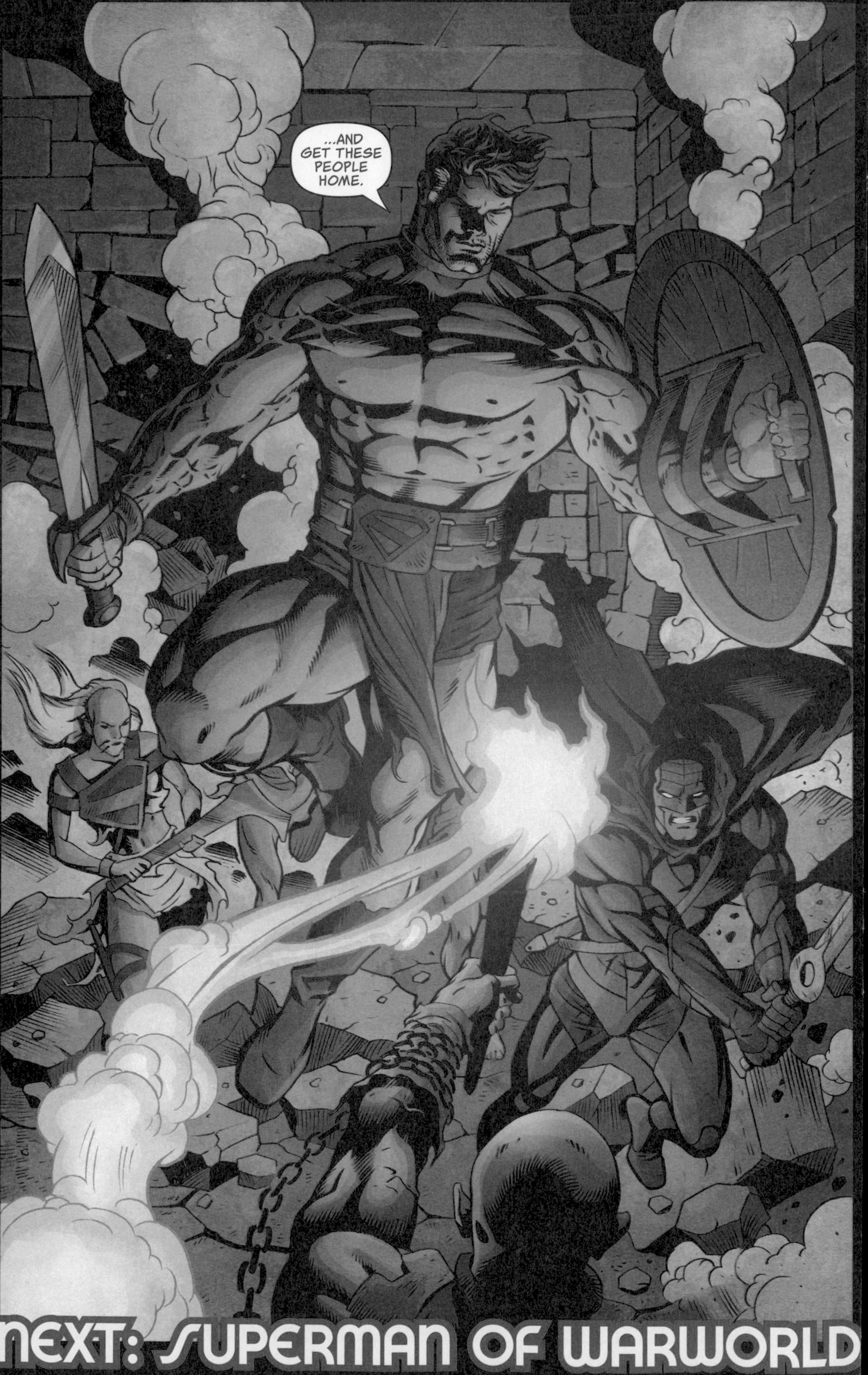
...AND GET THESE PEOPLE HOME.
NEXT: SUPERMAN OF WARWORLD

***Action Comics* #1042**
main cover by RICCARDO FEDERICI

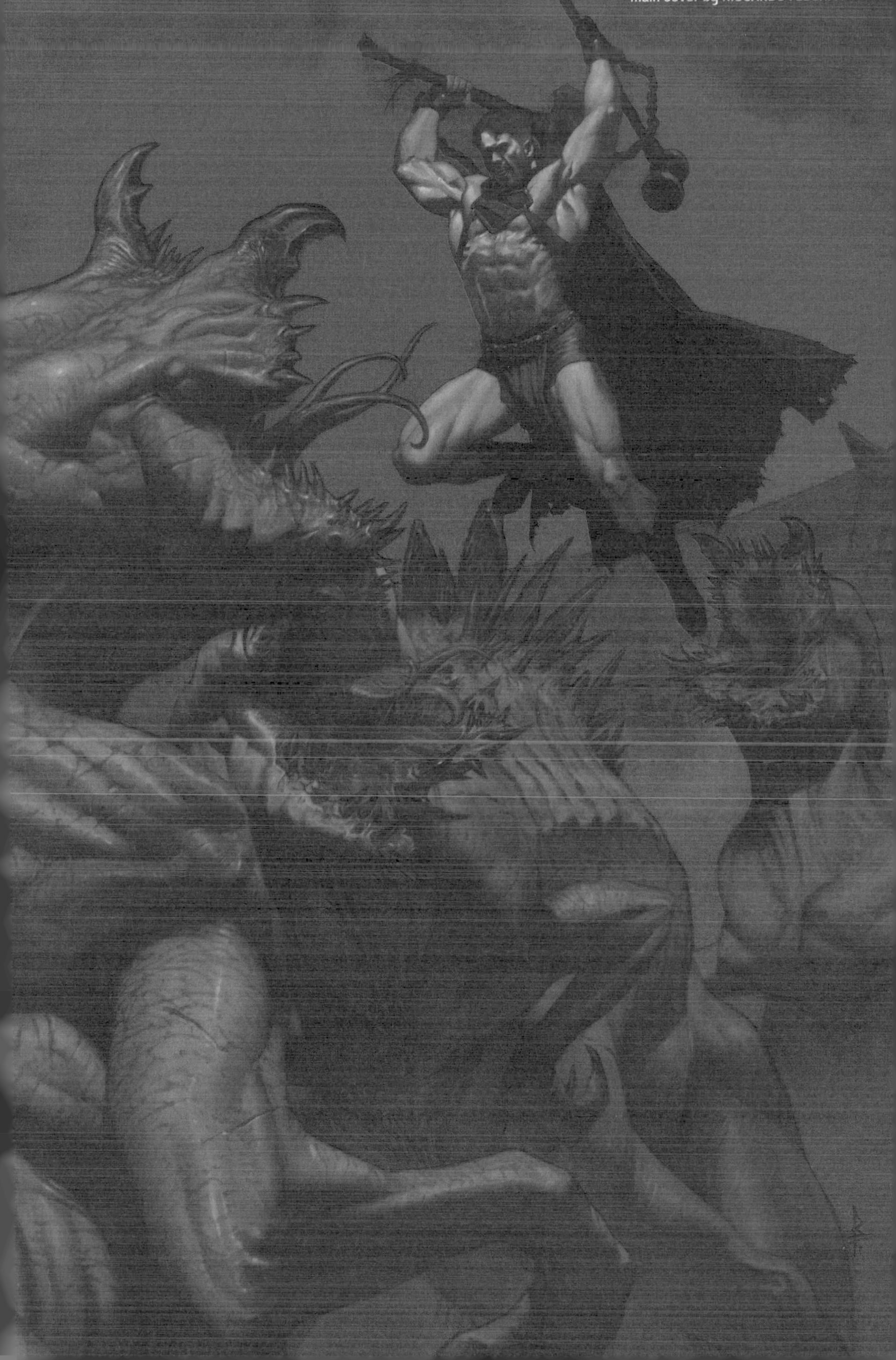

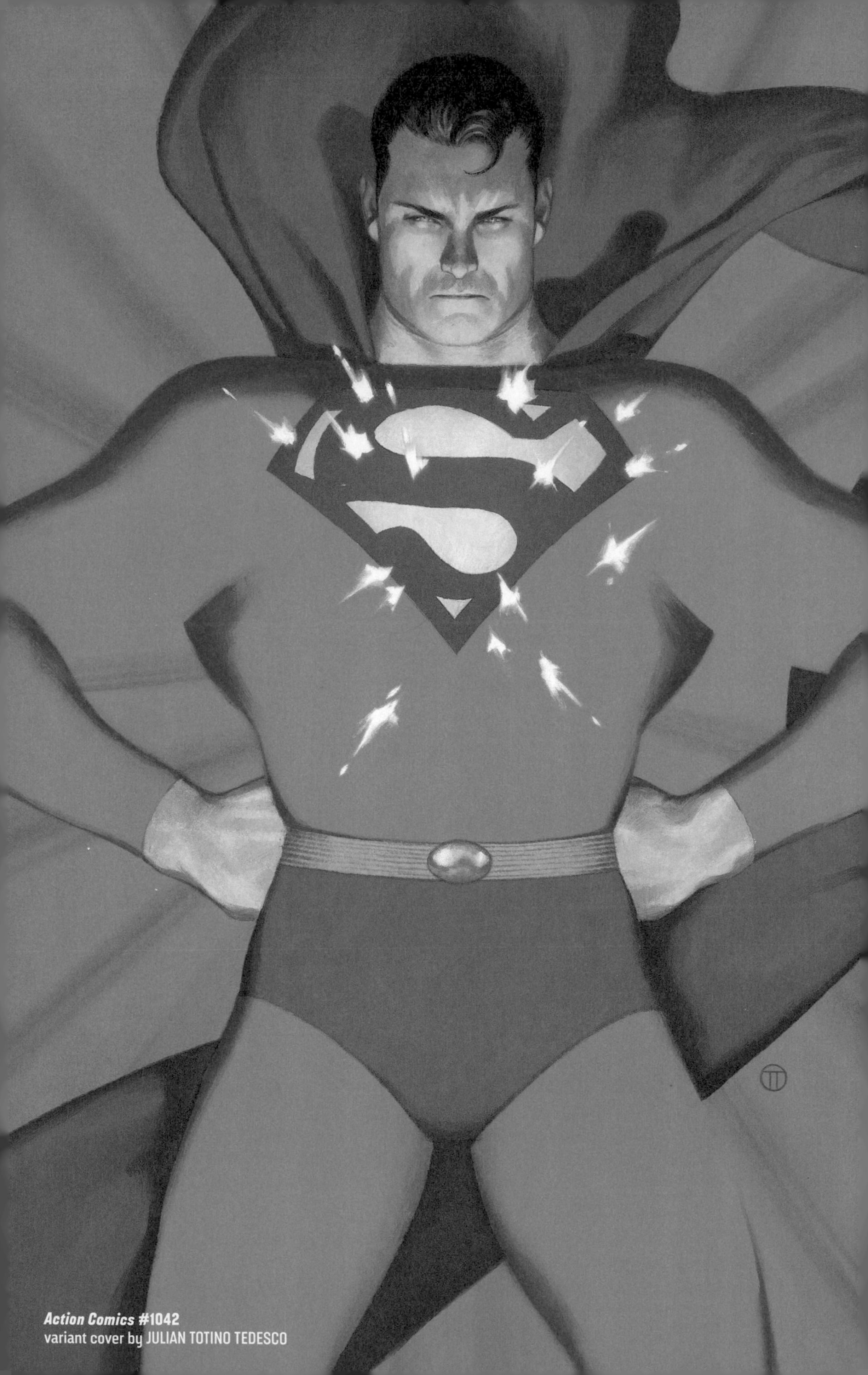

***Action Comics* #1042**
variant cover by JULIAN TOTINO TEDESCO

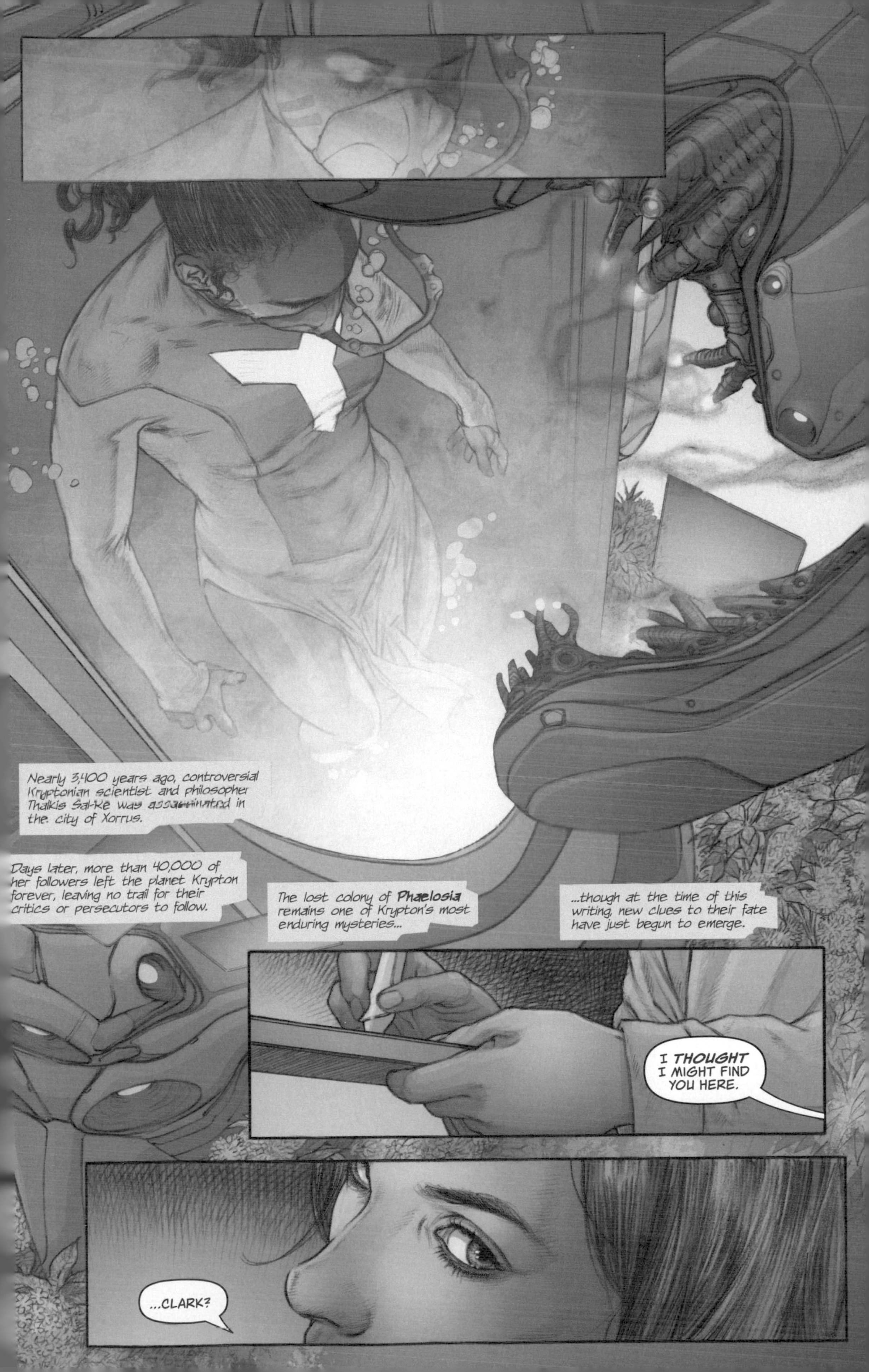

Nearly 3,400 years ago, controversial Kryptonian scientist and philosopher Thalkis Sal-Ke was assassinated in the city of Xorrus.
Days later, more than 40,000 of her followers left the planet Krypton forever, leaving no trail for their critics or persecutors to follow.
The lost colony of **Phaelosia** remains one of Krypton's most enduring mysteries...
...though at the time of this writing, new clues to their fate have just begun to emerge.
I *THOUGHT* I MIGHT FIND YOU HERE.
...CLARK?

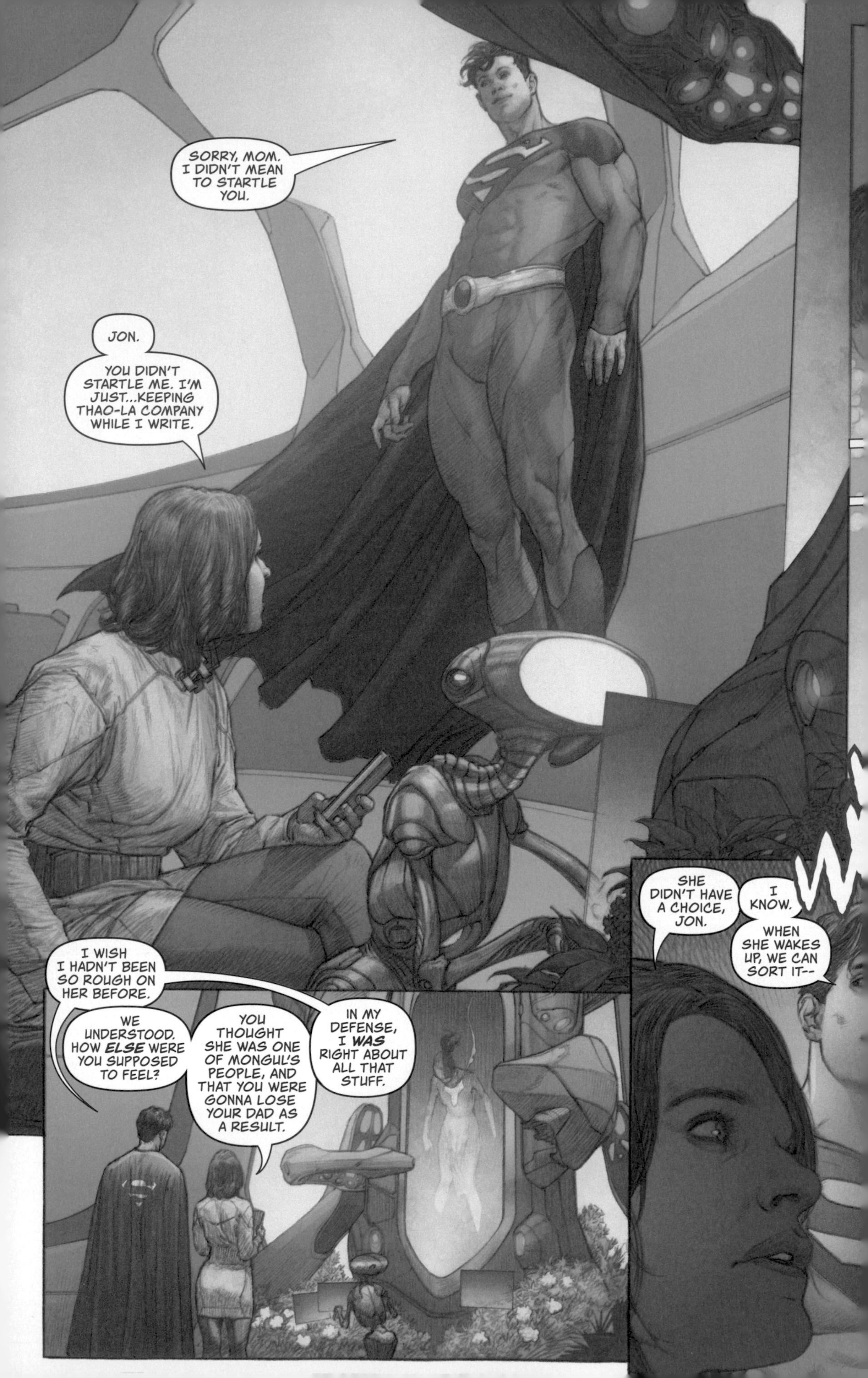

SORRY, MOM. I DIDN'T MEAN TO STARTLE YOU.
JON.
YOU DIDN'T STARTLE ME. I'M JUST...KEEPING THAO-LA COMPANY WHILE I WRITE.
I WISH I HADN'T BEEN SO ROUGH ON HER BEFORE.
WE UNDERSTOOD. HOW ELSE WERE YOU SUPPOSED TO FEEL?
YOU THOUGHT SHE WAS ONE OF MONGUL'S PEOPLE, AND THAT YOU WERE GONNA LOSE YOUR DAD AS A RESULT.
IN MY DEFENSE, I WAS RIGHT ABOUT ALL THAT STUFF.
SHE DIDN'T HAVE A CHOICE, JON.
I KNOW.
WHEN SHE WAKES UP, WE CAN SORT IT--

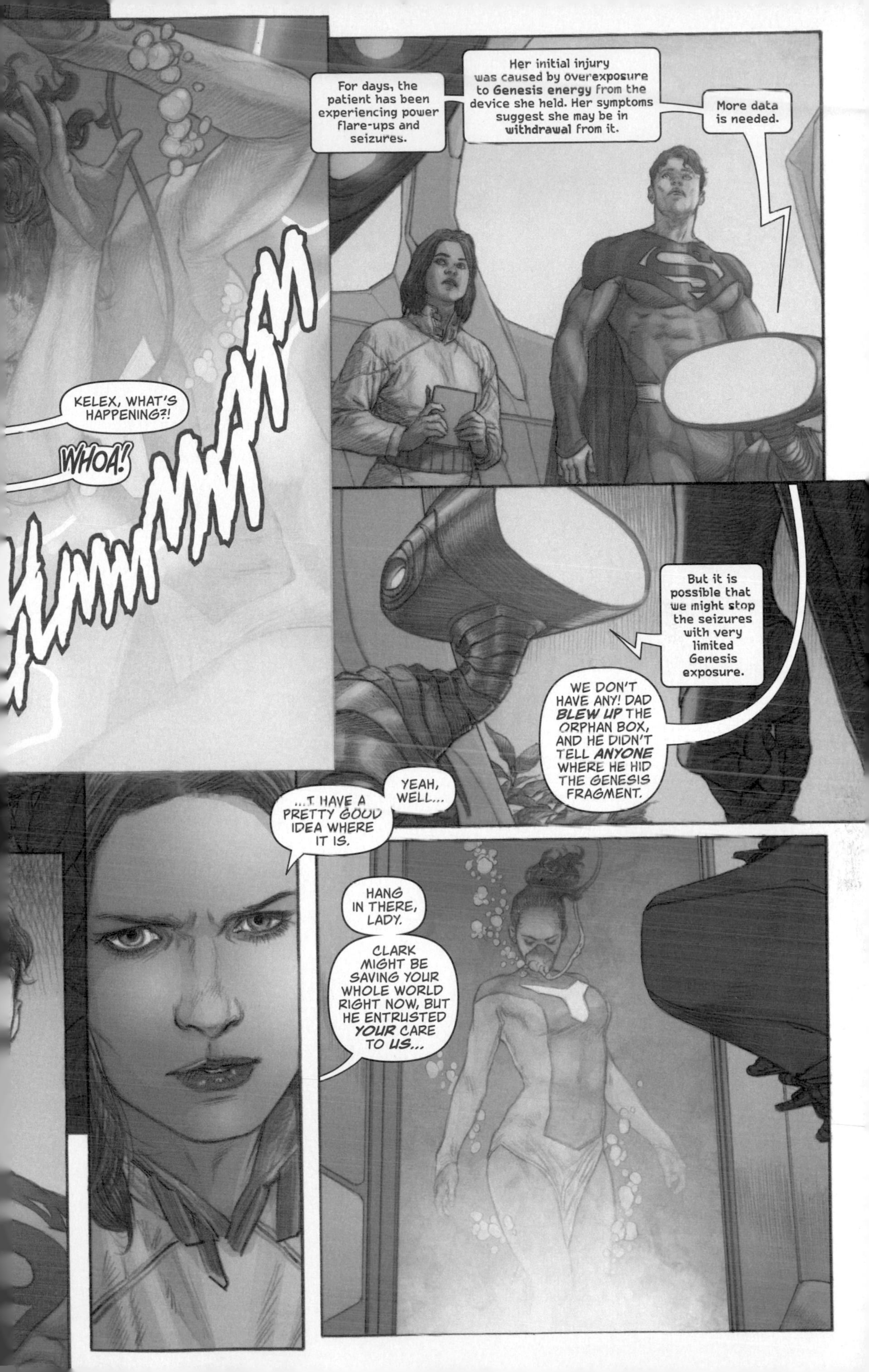
For days, the patient has been experiencing power flare-ups and seizures.
Her initial injury was caused by overexposure to Genesis energy from the device she held. Her symptoms suggest she may be in withdrawal from it.
More data is needed.
KELEX, WHAT'S HAPPENING?!
WHOA!
But it is possible that we might stop the seizures with very limited Genesis exposure.
WE DON'T HAVE ANY! DAD BLEW UP THE ORPHAN BOX, AND HE DIDN'T TELL ANYONE WHERE HE HID THE GENESIS FRAGMENT.
YEAH, WELL...
...I HAVE A PRETTY GOOD IDEA WHERE IT IS.
HANG IN THERE, LADY.
CLARK MIGHT BE SAVING YOUR WHOLE WORLD RIGHT NOW, BUT HE ENTRUSTED YOUR CARE TO US...

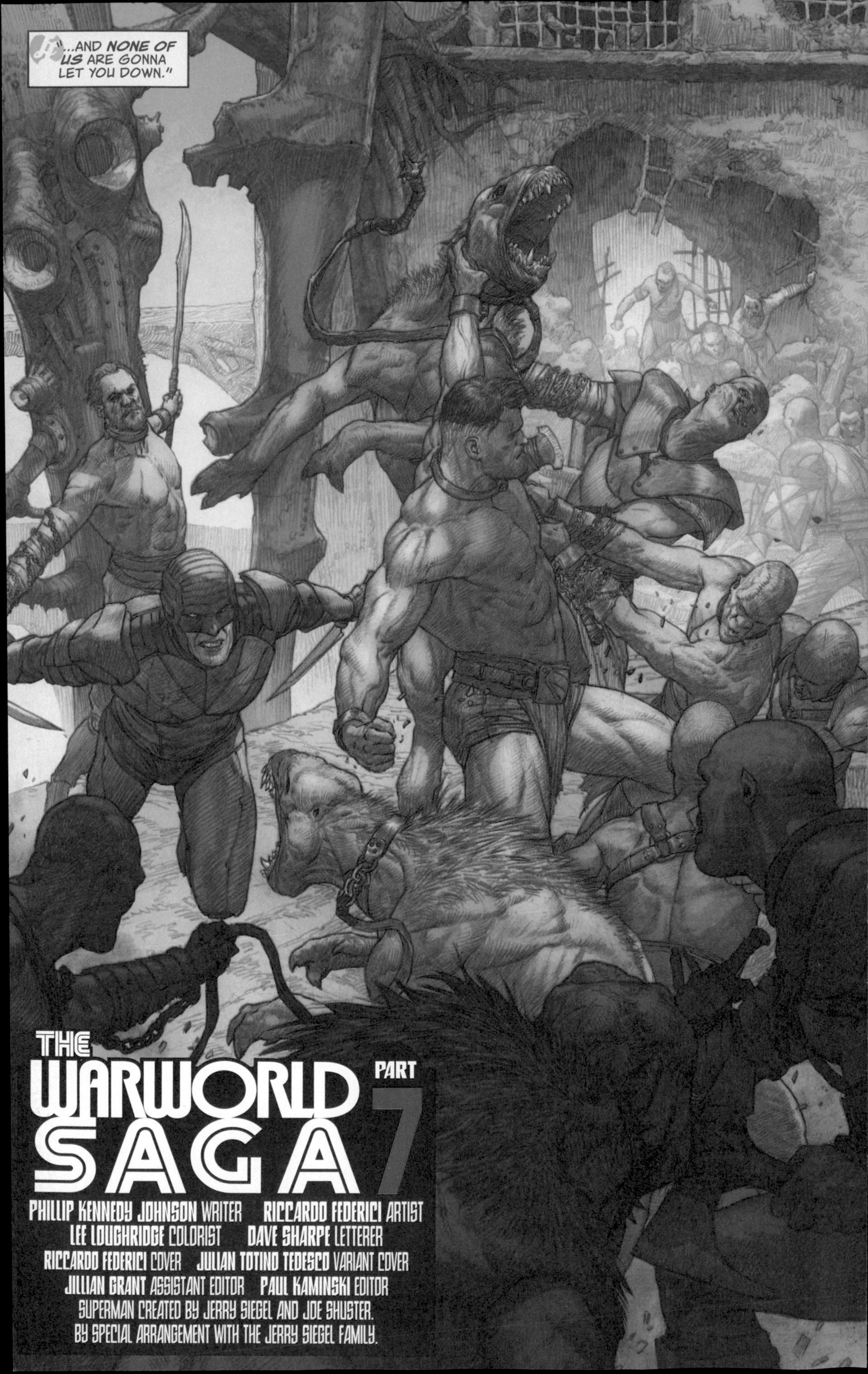
"...AND NONE OF US ARE GONNA LET YOU DOWN."
THE WARWORLD SAGA PART 7
PHILLIP KENNEDY JOHNSON WRITER RICCARDO FEDERICI ARTIST
LEE LOUGHRIDGE COLORIST DAVE SHARPE LETTERER
RICCARDO FEDERICI COVER JULIAN TOTINO TEDESCO VARIANT COVER
JILLIAN GRANT ASSISTANT EDITOR PAUL KAMINSKI EDITOR
SUPERMAN CREATED BY JERRY SIEGEL AND JOE SHUSTER.
BY SPECIAL ARRANGEMENT WITH THE JERRY SIEGEL FAMILY.

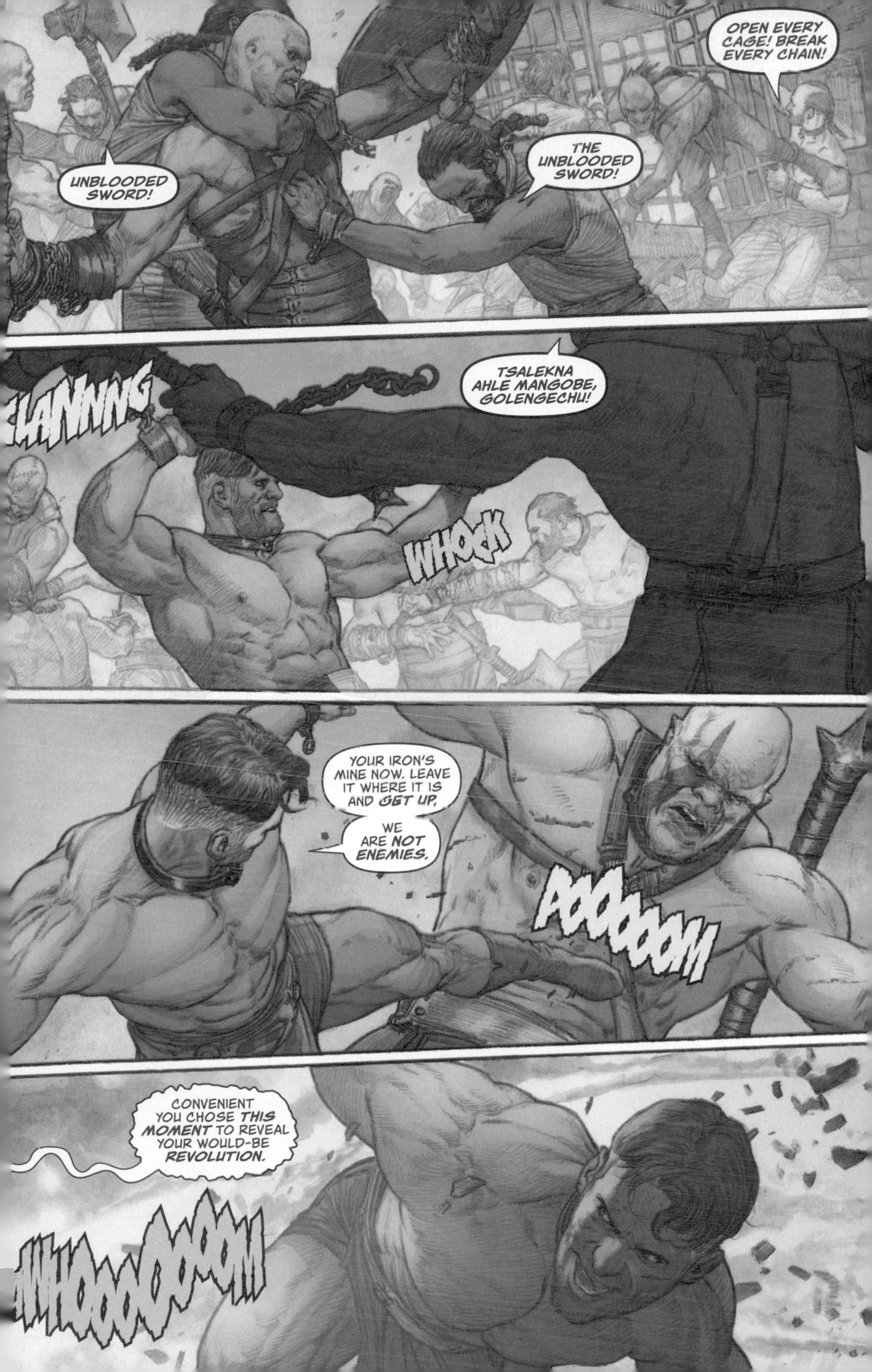
OPEN EVERY CAGE! BREAK EVERY CHAIN!
UNBLOODED SWORD!
THE UNBLOODED SWORD!
TSALEKNA AHLE MANGOBE, GOLENGECHU!
KLANNNG
WHOCK
YOUR IRON'S MINE NOW. LEAVE IT WHERE IT IS AND GET UP.
WE ARE NOT ENEMIES.
POOOOOOM
CONVENIENT YOU CHOSE THIS MOMENT TO REVEAL YOUR WOULD-BE REVOLUTION.
WHOOOOOOM

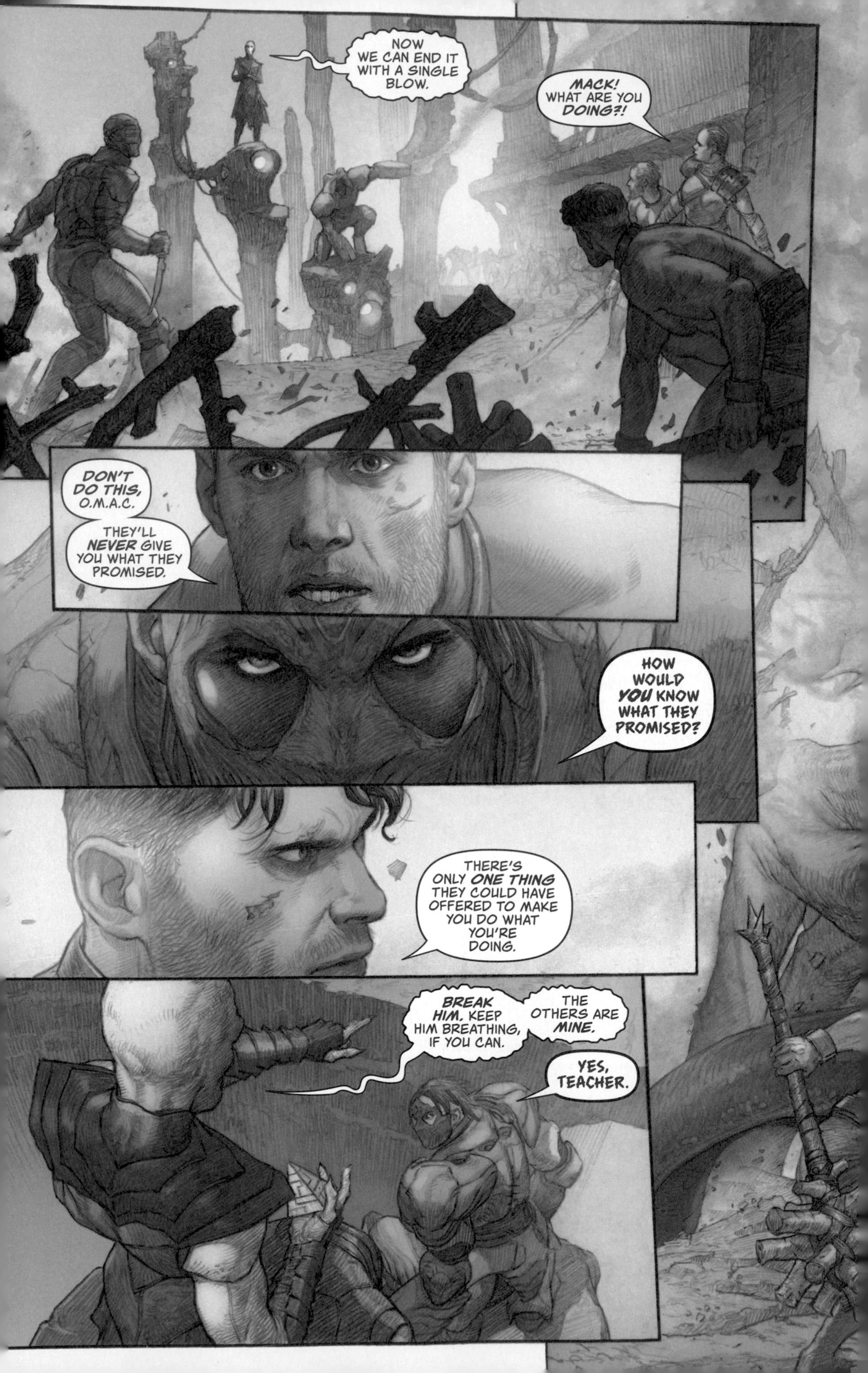
NOW WE CAN END IT WITH A SINGLE BLOW.
MACK! WHAT ARE YOU DOING?!
DON'T DO THIS, O.M.A.C.
THEY'LL NEVER GIVE YOU WHAT THEY PROMISED.
HOW WOULD YOU KNOW WHAT THEY PROMISED?
THERE'S ONLY ONE THING THEY COULD HAVE OFFERED TO MAKE YOU DO WHAT YOU'RE DOING.
BREAK HIM. KEEP HIM BREATHING, IF YOU CAN.
THE OTHERS ARE MINE.
YES, TEACHER.

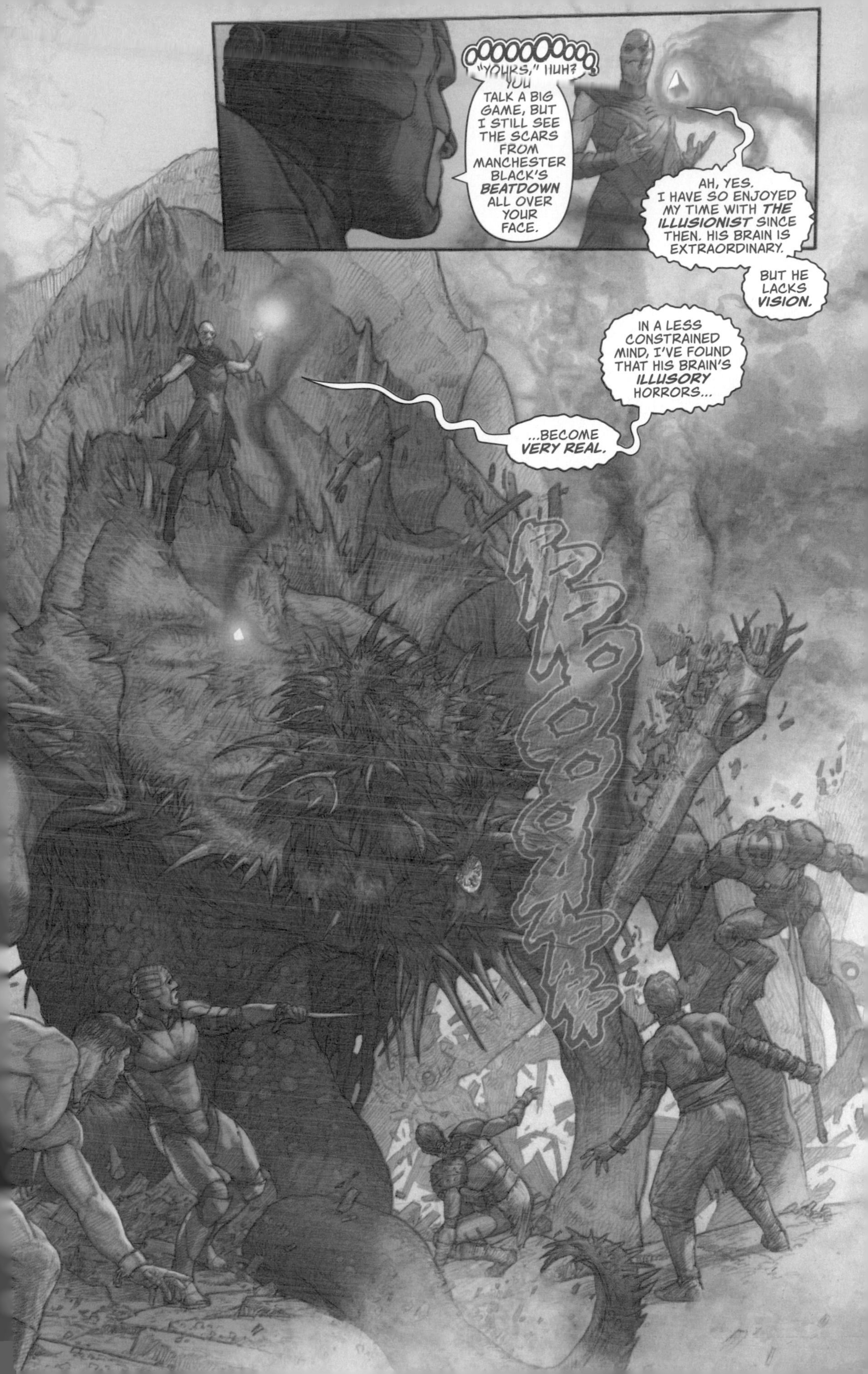

"YOURS," HUH? YOU TALK A BIG GAME, BUT I STILL SEE THE SCARS FROM MANCHESTER BLACK'S BEATDOWN ALL OVER YOUR FACE.
AH, YES. I HAVE SO ENJOYED MY TIME WITH THE ILLUSIONIST SINCE THEN. HIS BRAIN IS EXTRAORDINARY.
BUT HE LACKS VISION.
IN A LESS CONSTRAINED MIND, I'VE FOUND THAT HIS BRAIN'S ILLUSORY HORRORS...
...BECOME VERY REAL.

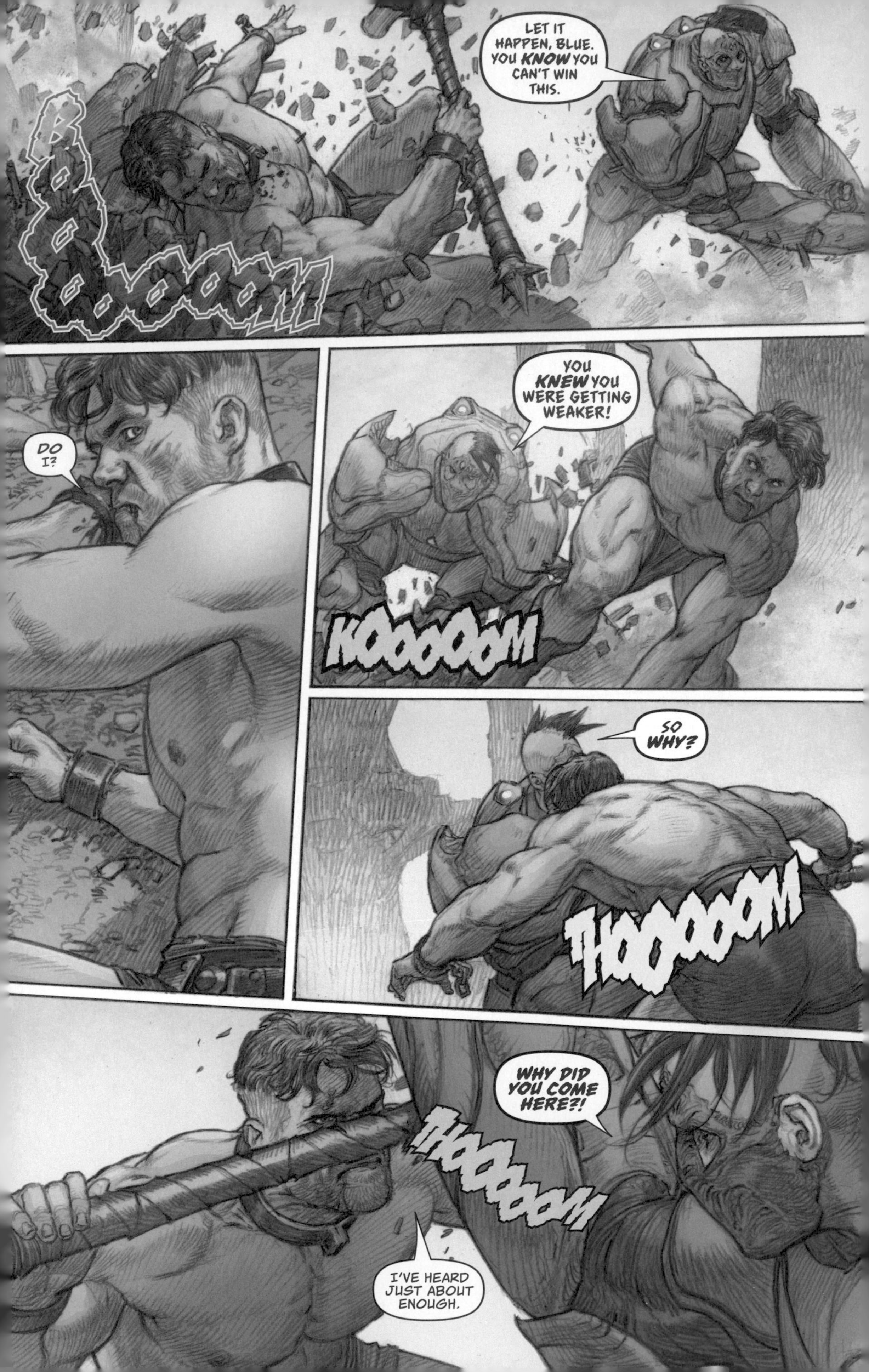
BOOOOOM
LET IT HAPPEN, BLUE. YOU KNOW YOU CAN'T WIN THIS.
DO I?
YOU KNEW YOU WERE GETTING WEAKER!
KOOOOOM
SO WHY?
THOOOOM
WHY DID YOU COME HERE?!
THOOOOOM
I'VE HEARD JUST ABOUT ENOUGH.

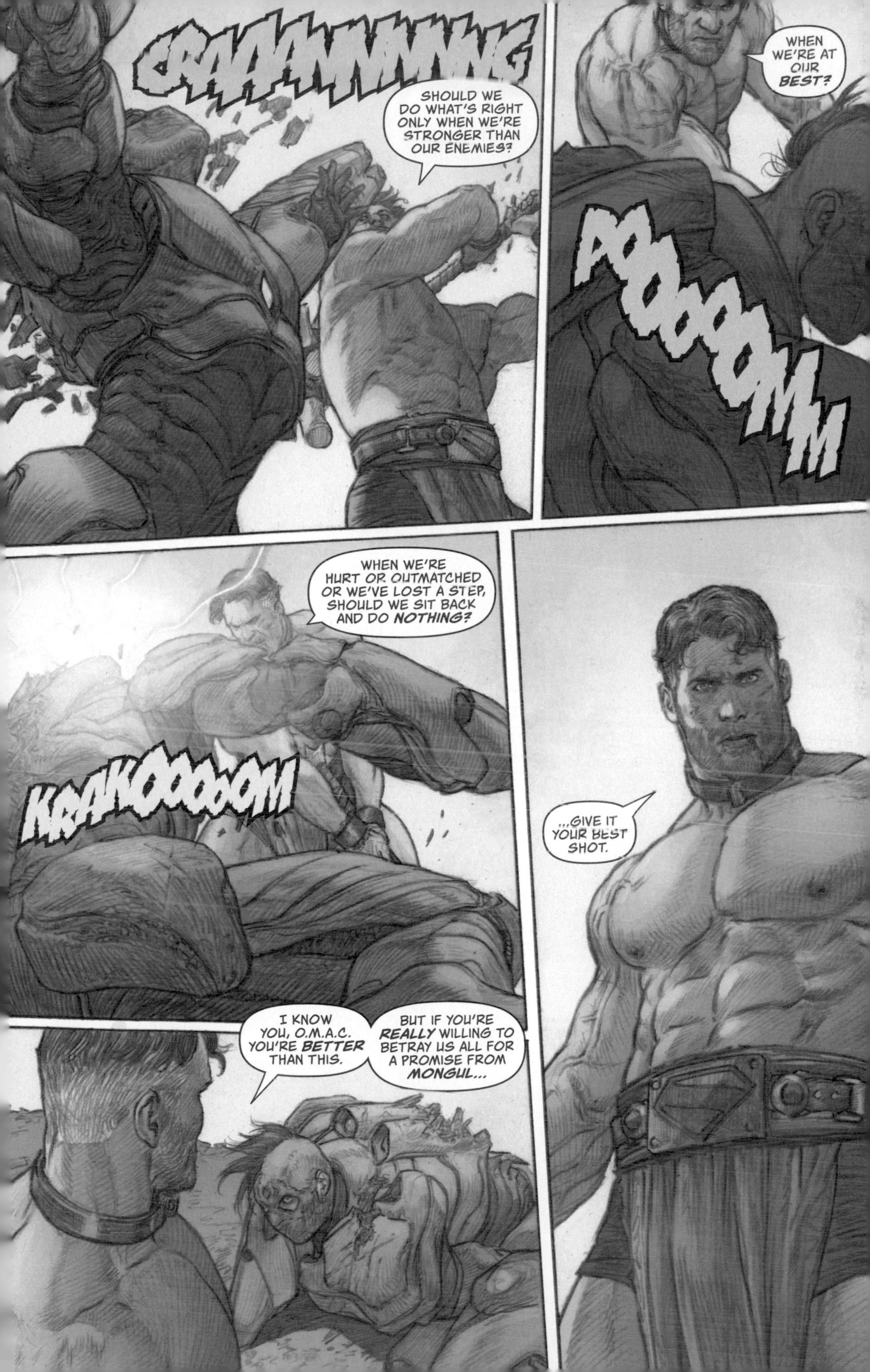
SHOULD WE DO WHAT'S RIGHT ONLY WHEN WE'RE STRONGER THAN OUR ENEMIES?
WHEN WE'RE AT OUR BEST?
WHEN WE'RE HURT OR OUTMATCHED OR WE'VE LOST A STEP, SHOULD WE SIT BACK AND DO NOTHING?
KRAKOOOOOM
I KNOW YOU, O.M.A.C. YOU'RE BETTER THAN THIS.
BUT IF YOU'RE REALLY WILLING TO BETRAY US ALL FOR A PROMISE FROM MONGUL...
...GIVE IT YOUR BEST SHOT.

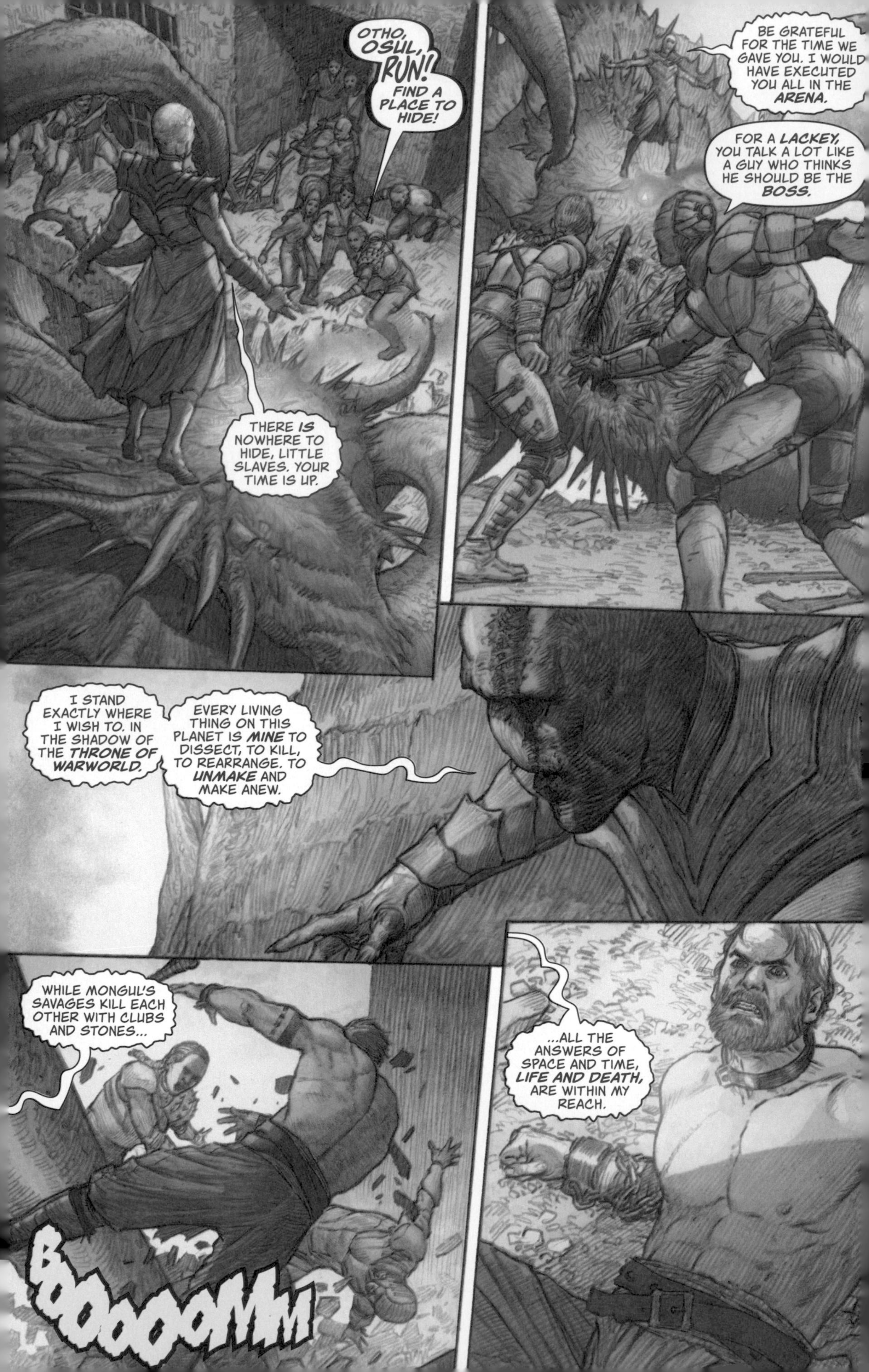
OTHO, OSUL, RUN! FIND A PLACE TO HIDE!
THERE IS NOWHERE TO HIDE, LITTLE SLAVES. YOUR TIME IS UP.
BE GRATEFUL FOR THE TIME WE GAVE YOU. I WOULD HAVE EXECUTED YOU ALL IN THE ARENA.
FOR A LACKEY, YOU TALK A LOT LIKE A GUY WHO THINKS HE SHOULD BE THE BOSS.
I STAND EXACTLY WHERE I WISH TO. IN THE SHADOW OF THE THRONE OF WARWORLD.
EVERY LIVING THING ON THIS PLANET IS MINE TO DISSECT, TO KILL, TO REARRANGE. TO UNMAKE AND MAKE ANEW.
WHILE MONGUL'S SAVAGES KILL EACH OTHER WITH CLUBS AND STONES...
BOOOOOMM
...ALL THE ANSWERS OF SPACE AND TIME, LIFE AND DEATH, ARE WITHIN MY REACH.

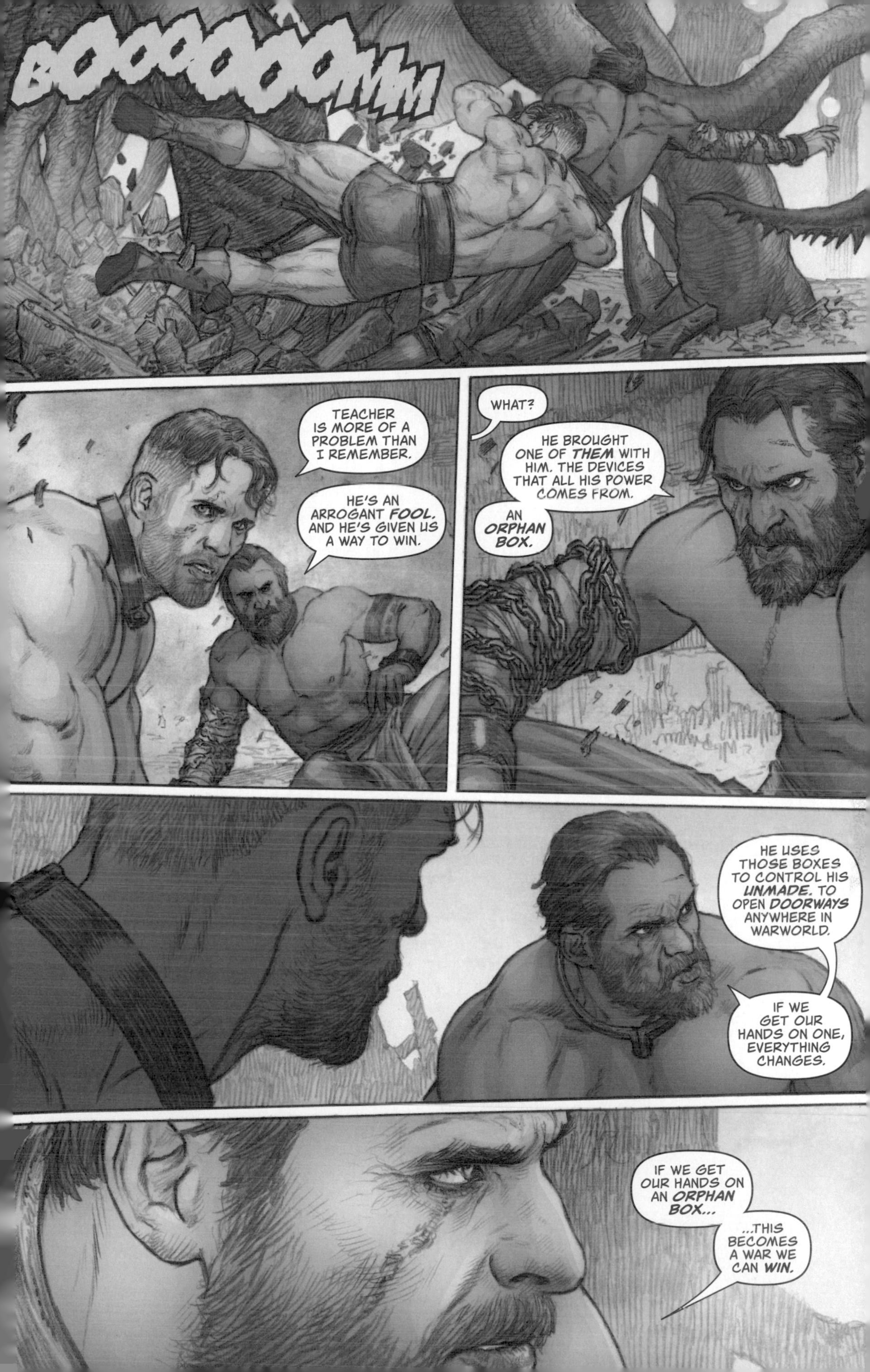
BOOOOOOMM
TEACHER IS MORE OF A PROBLEM THAN I REMEMBER.
HE'S AN ARROGANT FOOL. AND HE'S GIVEN US A WAY TO WIN.
WHAT?
HE BROUGHT ONE OF THEM WITH HIM. THE DEVICES THAT ALL HIS POWER COMES FROM.
AN ORPHAN BOX.
HE USES THOSE BOXES TO CONTROL HIS UNMADE. TO OPEN DOORWAYS ANYWHERE IN WARWORLD.
IF WE GET OUR HANDS ON ONE, EVERYTHING CHANGES.
IF WE GET OUR HANDS ON AN ORPHAN BOX...
...THIS BECOMES A WAR WE CAN WIN.

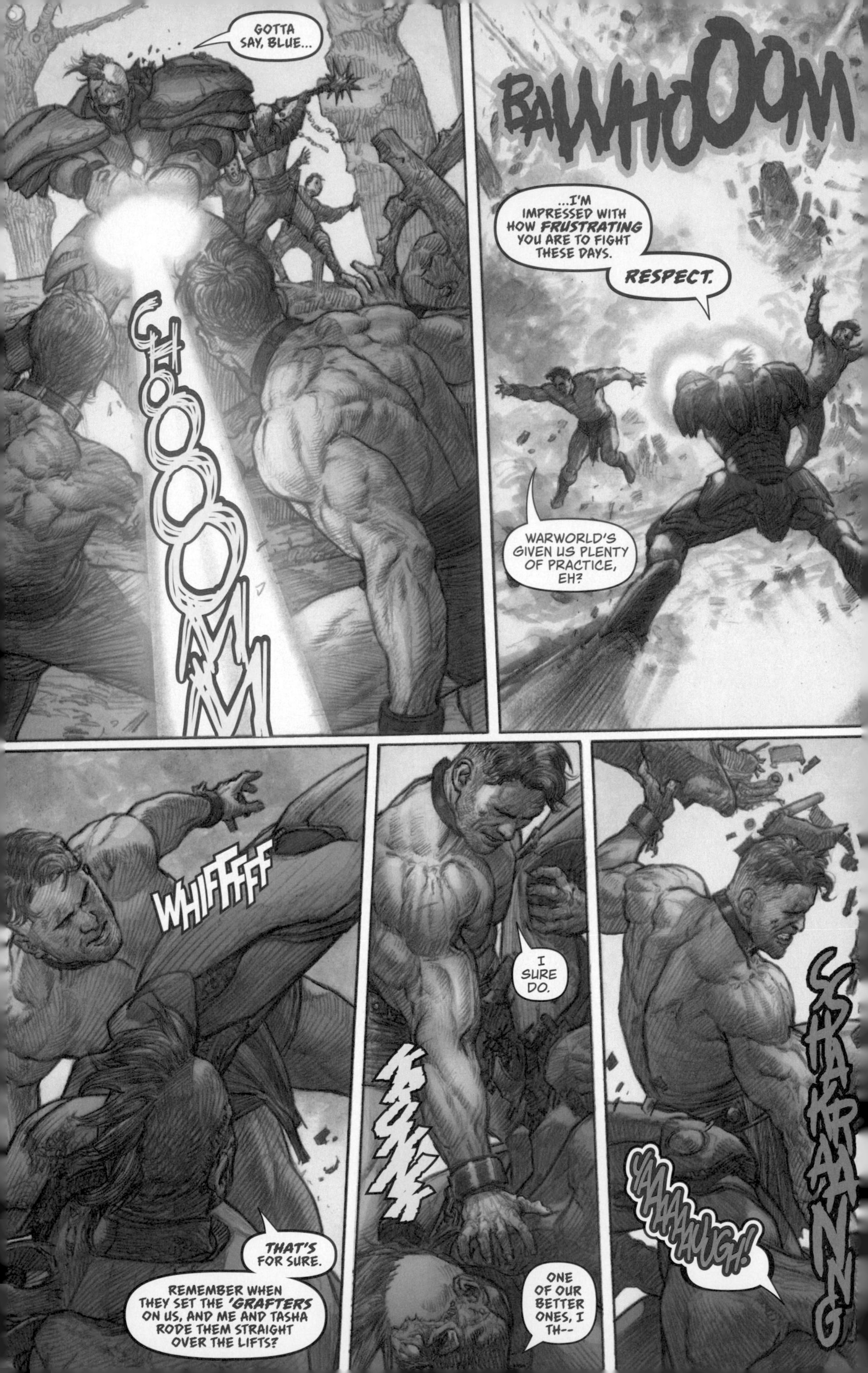
GOTTA SAY, BLUE...
CHOOOOOM
BAWHOOOM
...I'M IMPRESSED WITH HOW FRUSTRATING YOU ARE TO FIGHT THESE DAYS.
RESPECT.
WARWORLD'S GIVEN US PLENTY OF PRACTICE, EH?
WHIFFFFF
THAT'S FOR SURE.
REMEMBER WHEN THEY SET THE 'GRAFTERS ON US, AND ME AND TASHA RODE THEM STRAIGHT OVER THE LIFTS?
I SURE DO.
KRUNK
ONE OF OUR BETTER ONES, I TH--
YAAAAAUGH!
SHAKRAANG

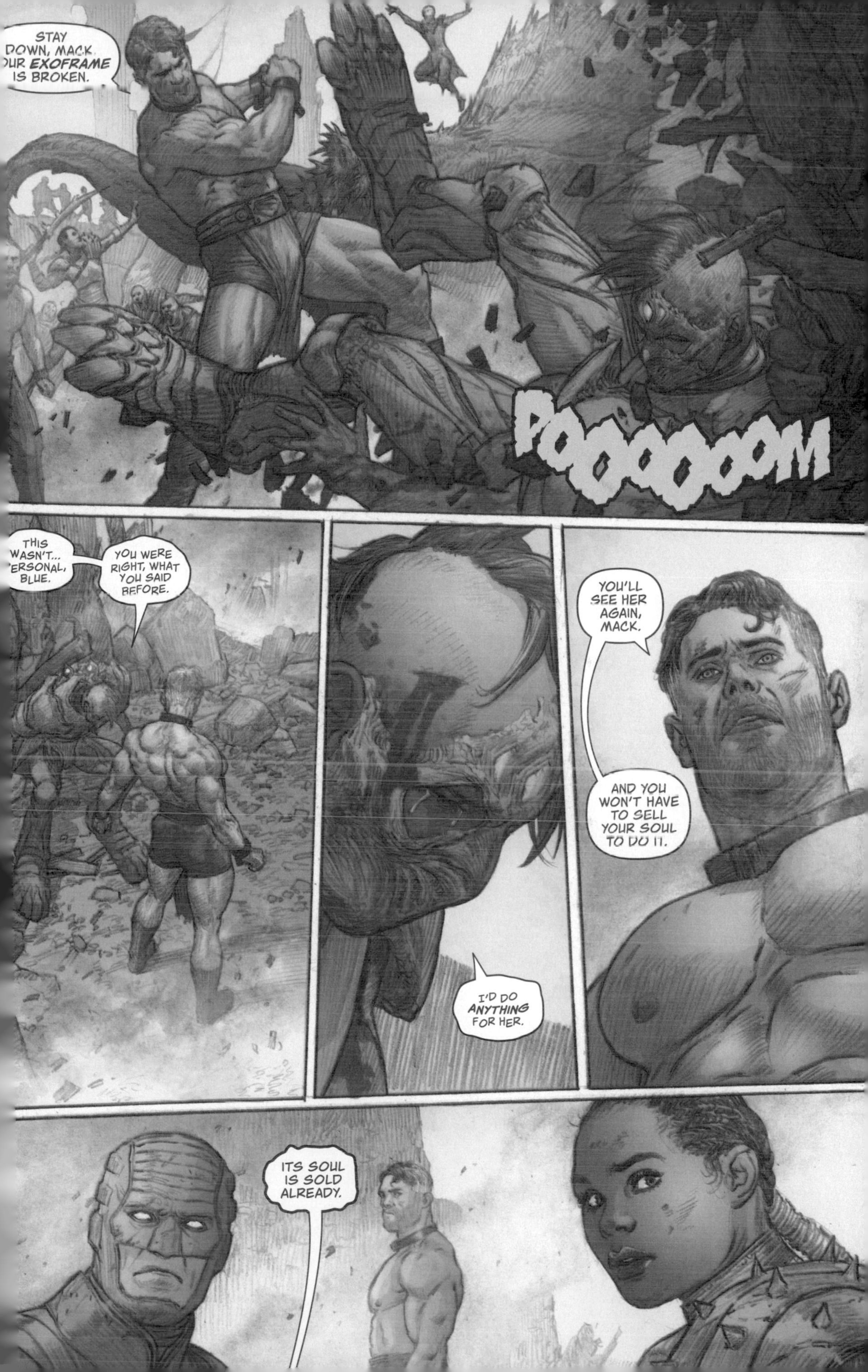
STAY DOWN, MACK. OUR EXOFRAME IS BROKEN.
POOOOOOM
THIS WASN'T... PERSONAL, BLUE.
YOU WERE RIGHT, WHAT YOU SAID BEFORE.
I'D DO ANYTHING FOR HER.
YOU'LL SEE HER AGAIN, MACK.
AND YOU WON'T HAVE TO SELL YOUR SOUL TO DO IT.
ITS SOUL IS SOLD ALREADY.

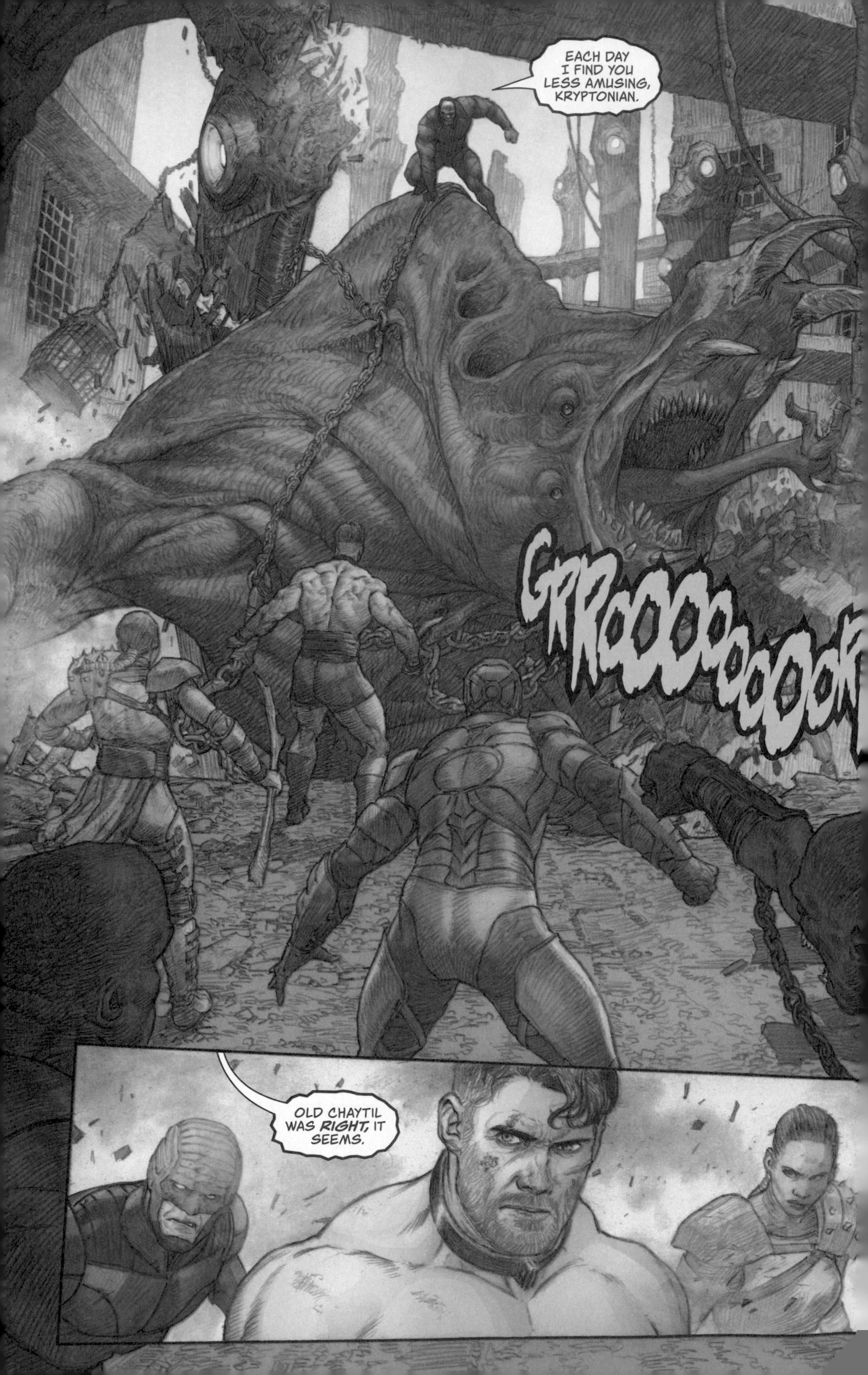
EACH DAY I FIND YOU LESS AMUSING, KRYPTONIAN.
GRROOOOOOOOOR
OLD CHAYTIL WAS *RIGHT*, IT SEEMS.

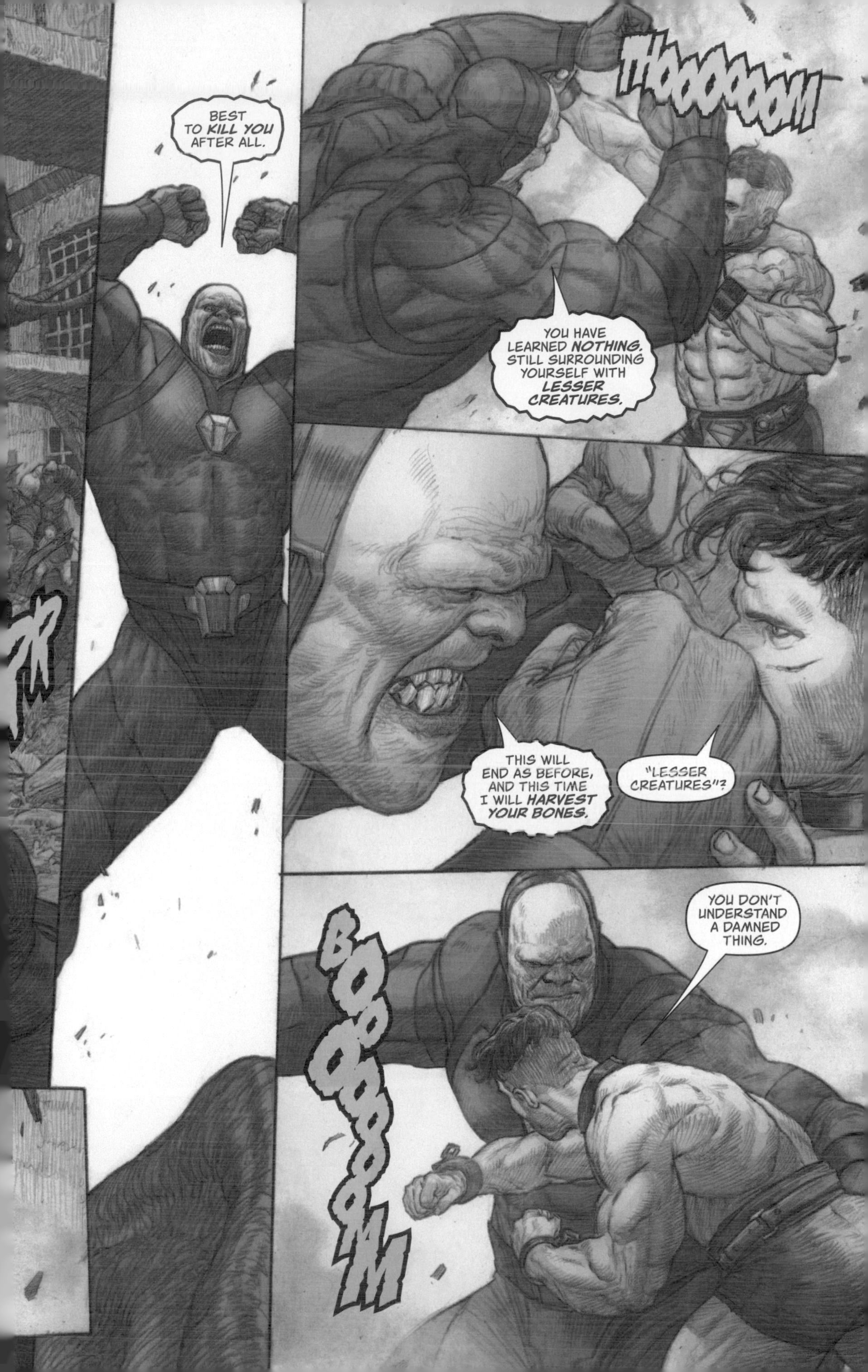
BEST TO KILL YOU AFTER ALL.
THOOOOOOM
YOU HAVE LEARNED NOTHING. STILL SURROUNDING YOURSELF WITH LESSER CREATURES.
THIS WILL END AS BEFORE, AND THIS TIME I WILL HARVEST YOUR BONES.
"LESSER CREATURES"?
BOOOOOOOM
YOU DON'T UNDERSTAND A DAMNED THING.

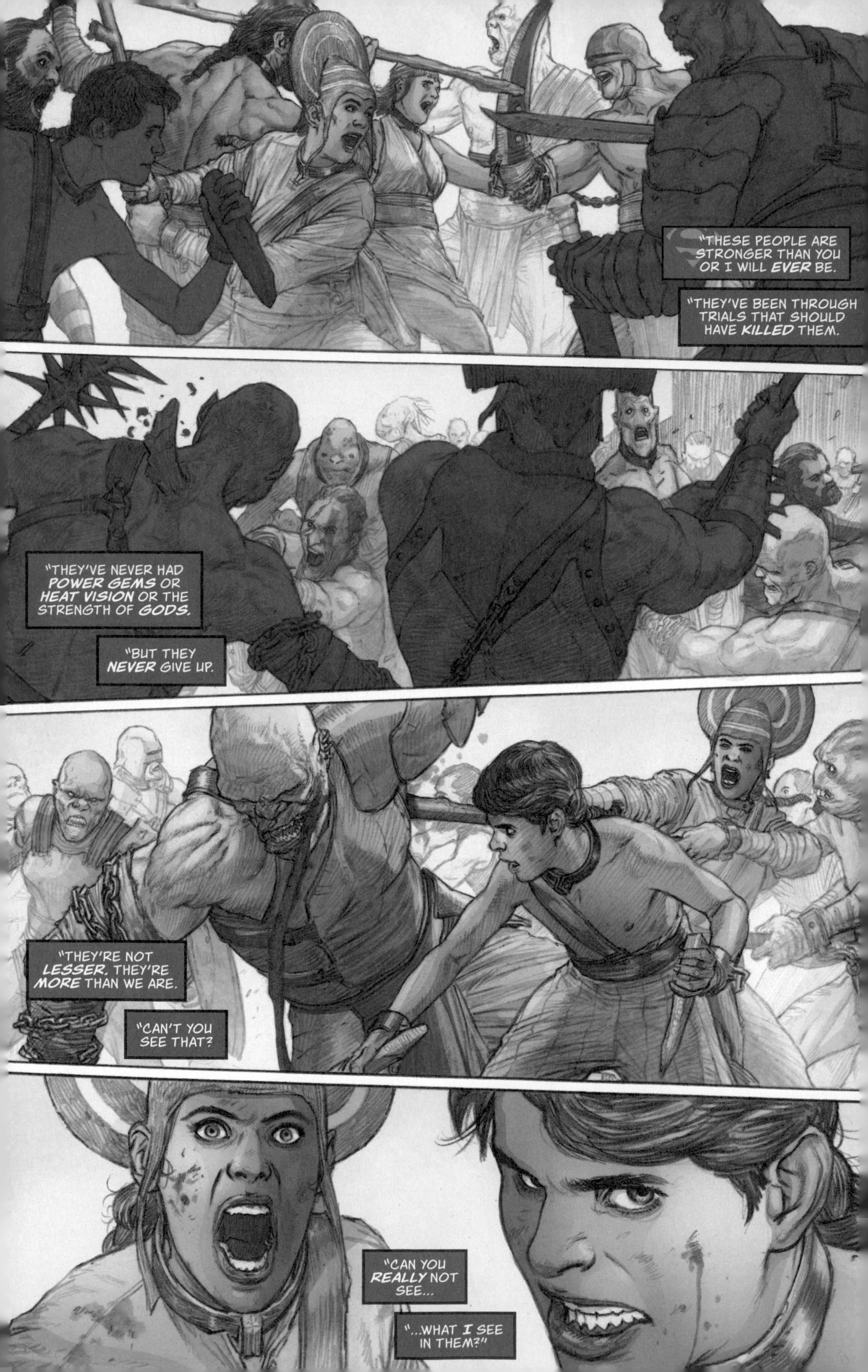
"THESE PEOPLE ARE STRONGER THAN YOU OR I WILL EVER BE.
"THEY'VE BEEN THROUGH TRIALS THAT SHOULD HAVE KILLED THEM.
"THEY'VE NEVER HAD POWER GEMS OR HEAT VISION OR THE STRENGTH OF GODS.
"BUT THEY NEVER GIVE UP.
"THEY'RE NOT LESSER. THEY'RE MORE THAN WE ARE.
"CAN'T YOU SEE THAT?
"CAN YOU REALLY NOT SEE...
"...WHAT I SEE IN THEM?"

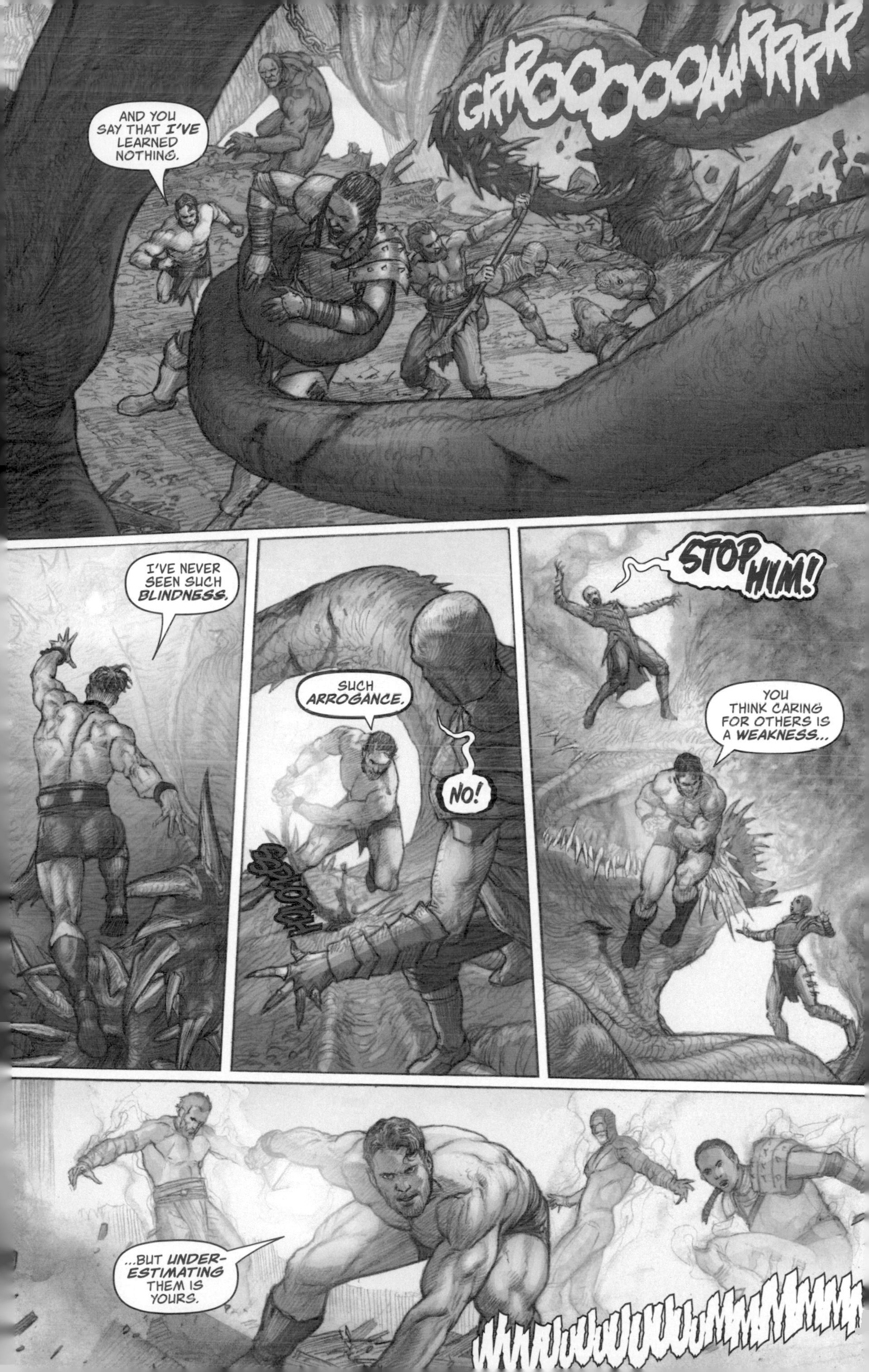
GRROOOOOOAARRRR
AND YOU SAY THAT I'VE LEARNED NOTHING.
I'VE NEVER SEEN SUCH BLINDNESS.
SUCH ARROGANCE.
NO!
STOP HIM!
YOU THINK CARING FOR OTHERS IS A WEAKNESS...
...BUT UNDER-ESTIMATING THEM IS YOURS.
WHHUUUUUUUMMMMMM

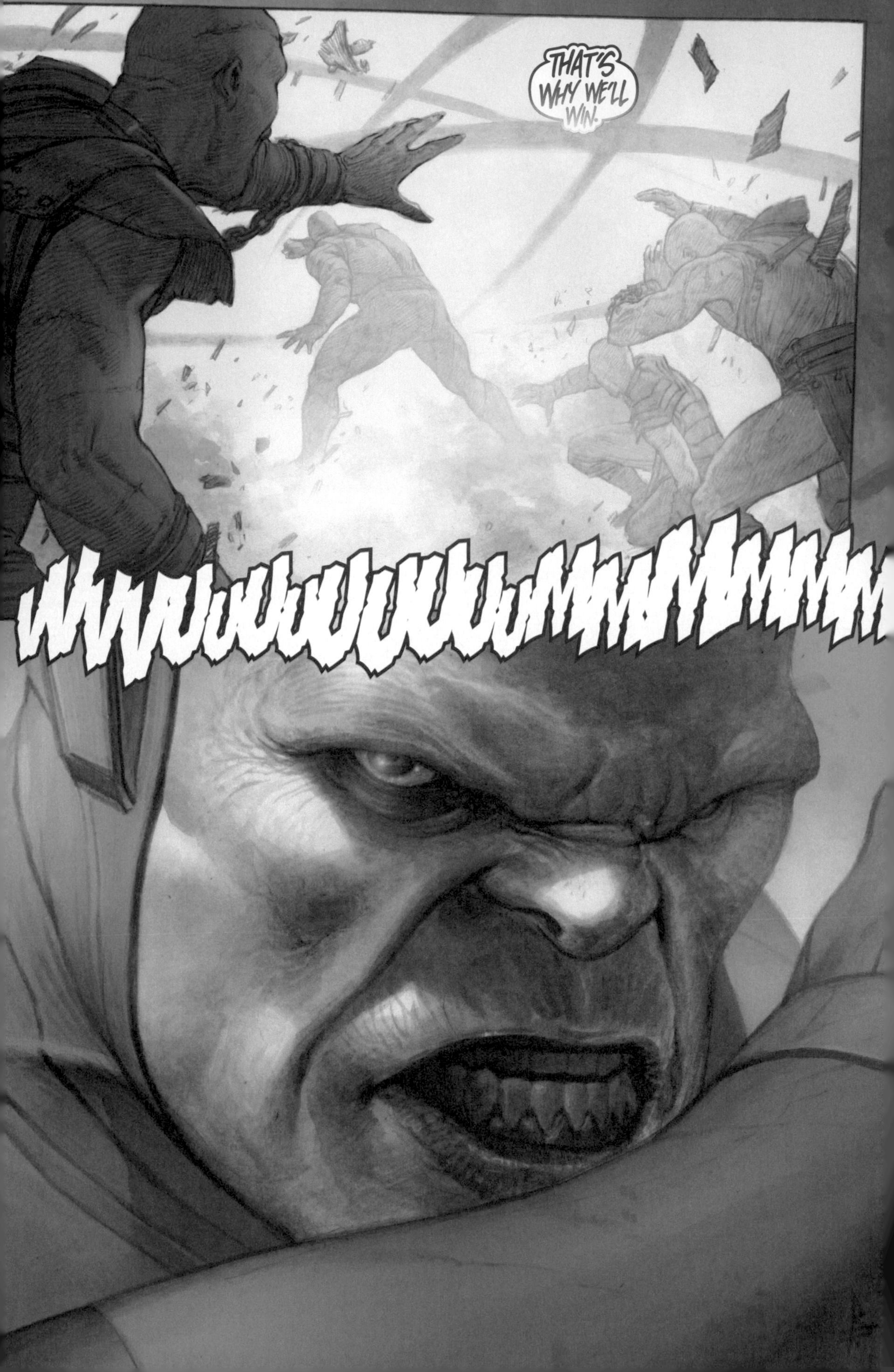
THAT'S WHY WE'LL WIN.
WHRRUUUUUUUUUMMMMMMMMM

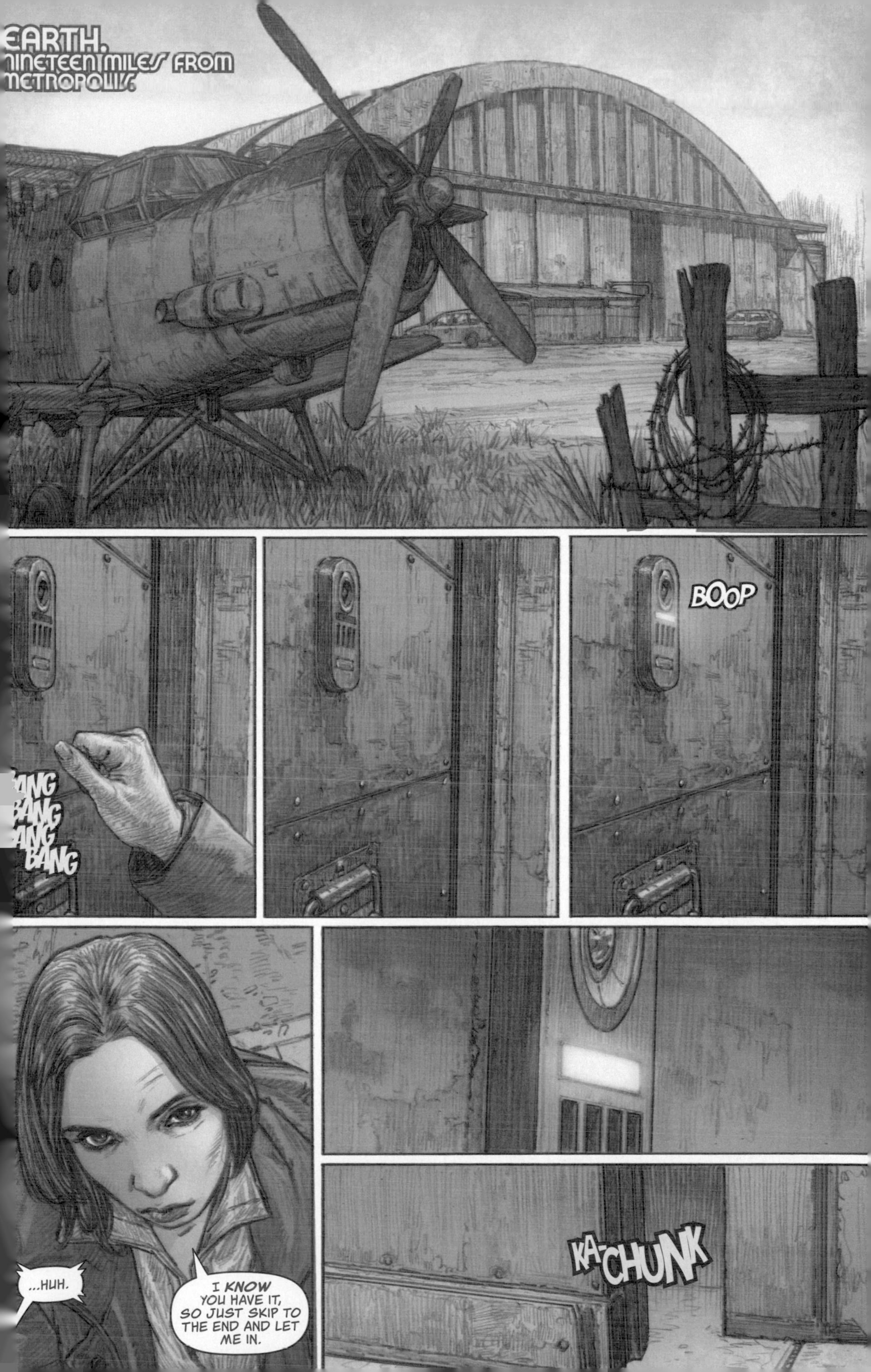
EARTH.
NINETEEN MILES FROM METROPOLIS.
BANG BANG BANG BANG
BOOP
...HUH.
I KNOW YOU HAVE IT, SO JUST SKIP TO THE END AND LET ME IN.
KA-CHUNK

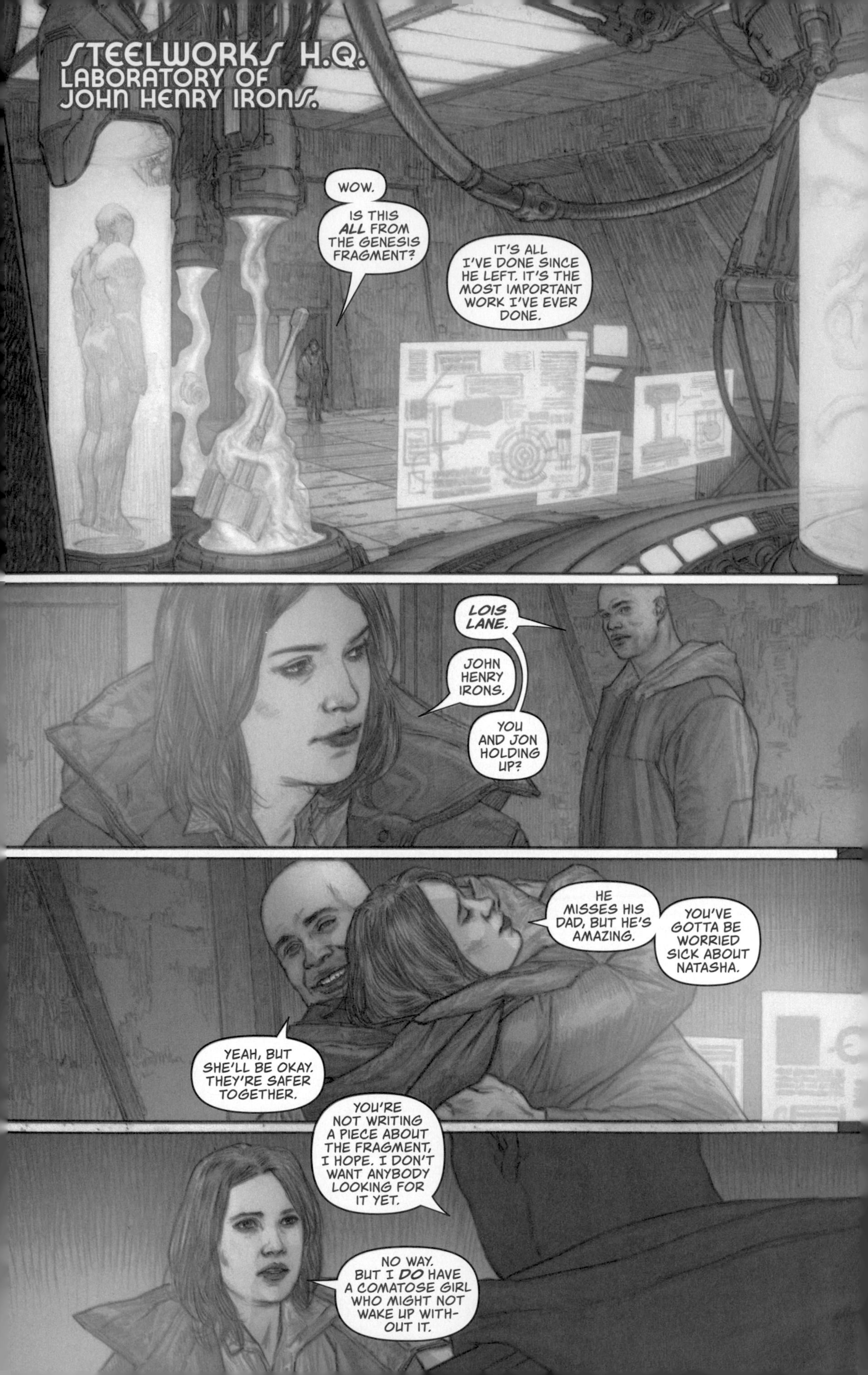
STEELWORKS H.Q. LABORATORY OF JOHN HENRY IRONS.
WOW.
IS THIS ALL FROM THE GENESIS FRAGMENT?
IT'S ALL I'VE DONE SINCE HE LEFT. IT'S THE MOST IMPORTANT WORK I'VE EVER DONE.
LOIS LANE.
JOHN HENRY IRONS.
YOU AND JON HOLDING UP?
HE MISSES HIS DAD, BUT HE'S AMAZING.
YOU'VE GOTTA BE WORRIED SICK ABOUT NATASHA.
YEAH, BUT SHE'LL BE OKAY. THEY'RE SAFER TOGETHER.
YOU'RE NOT WRITING A PIECE ABOUT THE FRAGMENT, I HOPE. I DON'T WANT ANYBODY LOOKING FOR IT YET.
NO WAY. BUT I DO HAVE A COMATOSE GIRL WHO MIGHT NOT WAKE UP WITHOUT IT.

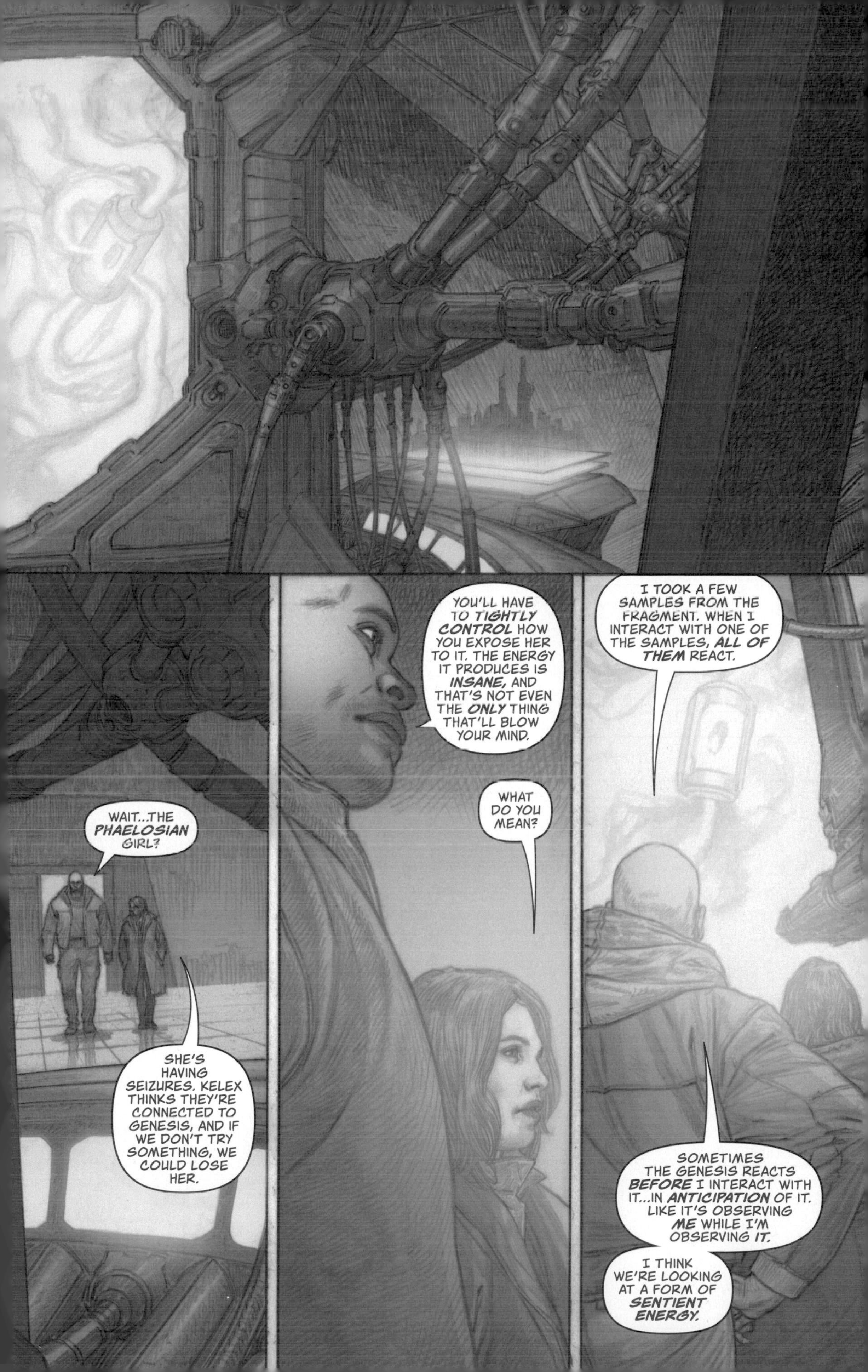
WAIT...THE PHAELOSIAN GIRL?
SHE'S HAVING SEIZURES. KELEX THINKS THEY'RE CONNECTED TO GENESIS, AND IF WE DON'T TRY SOMETHING, WE COULD LOSE HER.
YOU'LL HAVE TO TIGHTLY CONTROL HOW YOU EXPOSE HER TO IT. THE ENERGY IT PRODUCES IS INSANE, AND THAT'S NOT EVEN THE ONLY THING THAT'LL BLOW YOUR MIND.
WHAT DO YOU MEAN?
I TOOK A FEW SAMPLES FROM THE FRAGMENT. WHEN I INTERACT WITH ONE OF THE SAMPLES, ALL OF THEM REACT.
SOMETIMES THE GENESIS REACTS BEFORE I INTERACT WITH IT...IN ANTICIPATION OF IT. LIKE IT'S OBSERVING ME WHILE I'M OBSERVING IT.
I THINK WE'RE LOOKING AT A FORM OF SENTIENT ENERGY.

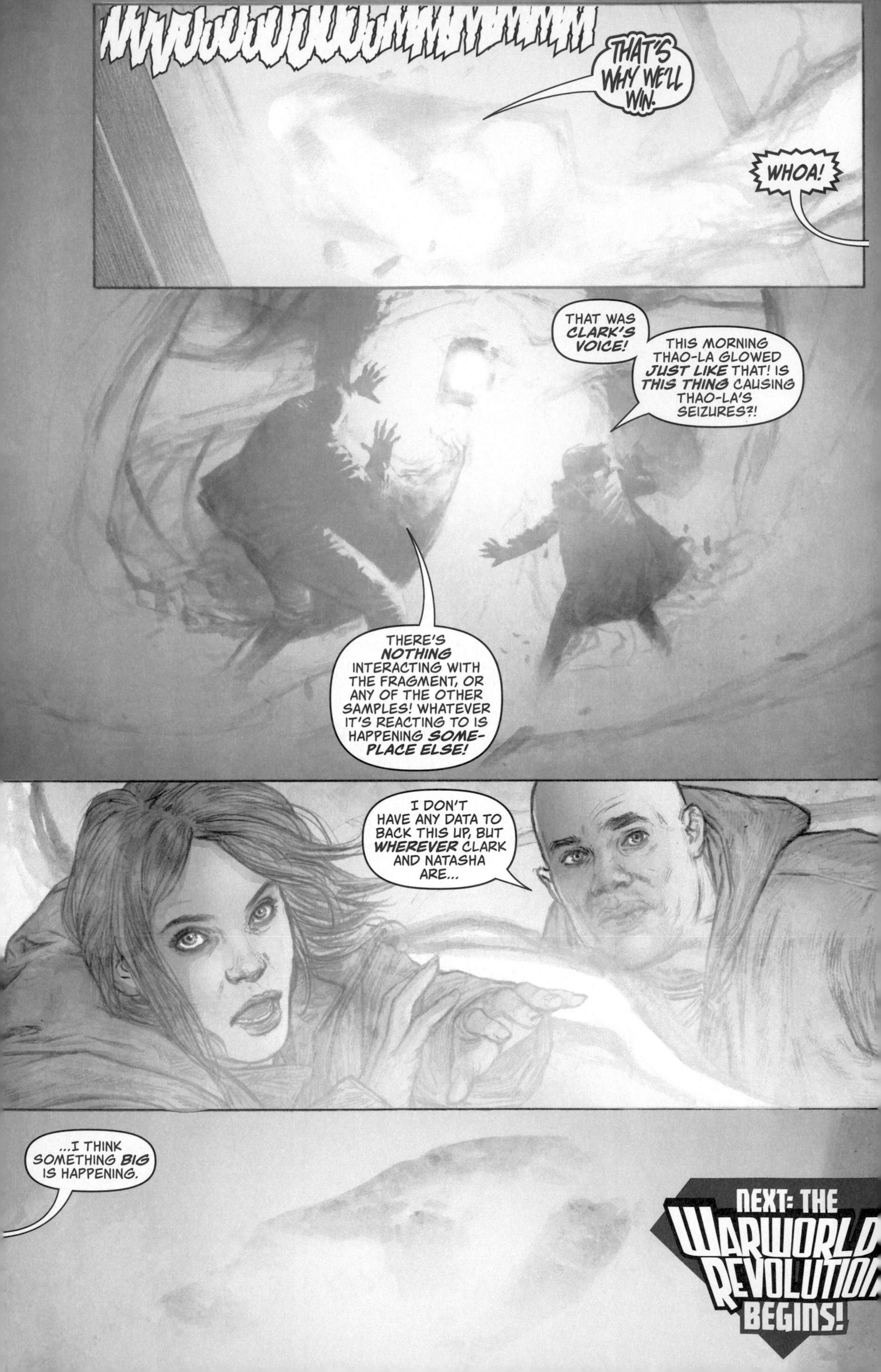
WWWWOOOOOOOMMMMMMMM
THAT'S WHY WE'LL WIN.
WHOA!
THAT WAS CLARK'S VOICE!
THIS MORNING THAO-LA GLOWED JUST LIKE THAT! IS THIS THING CAUSING THAO-LA'S SEIZURES?!
THERE'S NOTHING INTERACTING WITH THE FRAGMENT, OR ANY OF THE OTHER SAMPLES! WHATEVER IT'S REACTING TO IS HAPPENING SOME-PLACE ELSE!
I DON'T HAVE ANY DATA TO BACK THIS UP, BUT WHEREVER CLARK AND NATASHA ARE...
...I THINK SOMETHING BIG IS HAPPENING.
NEXT: THE WARWORLD REVOLUTION BEGINS!

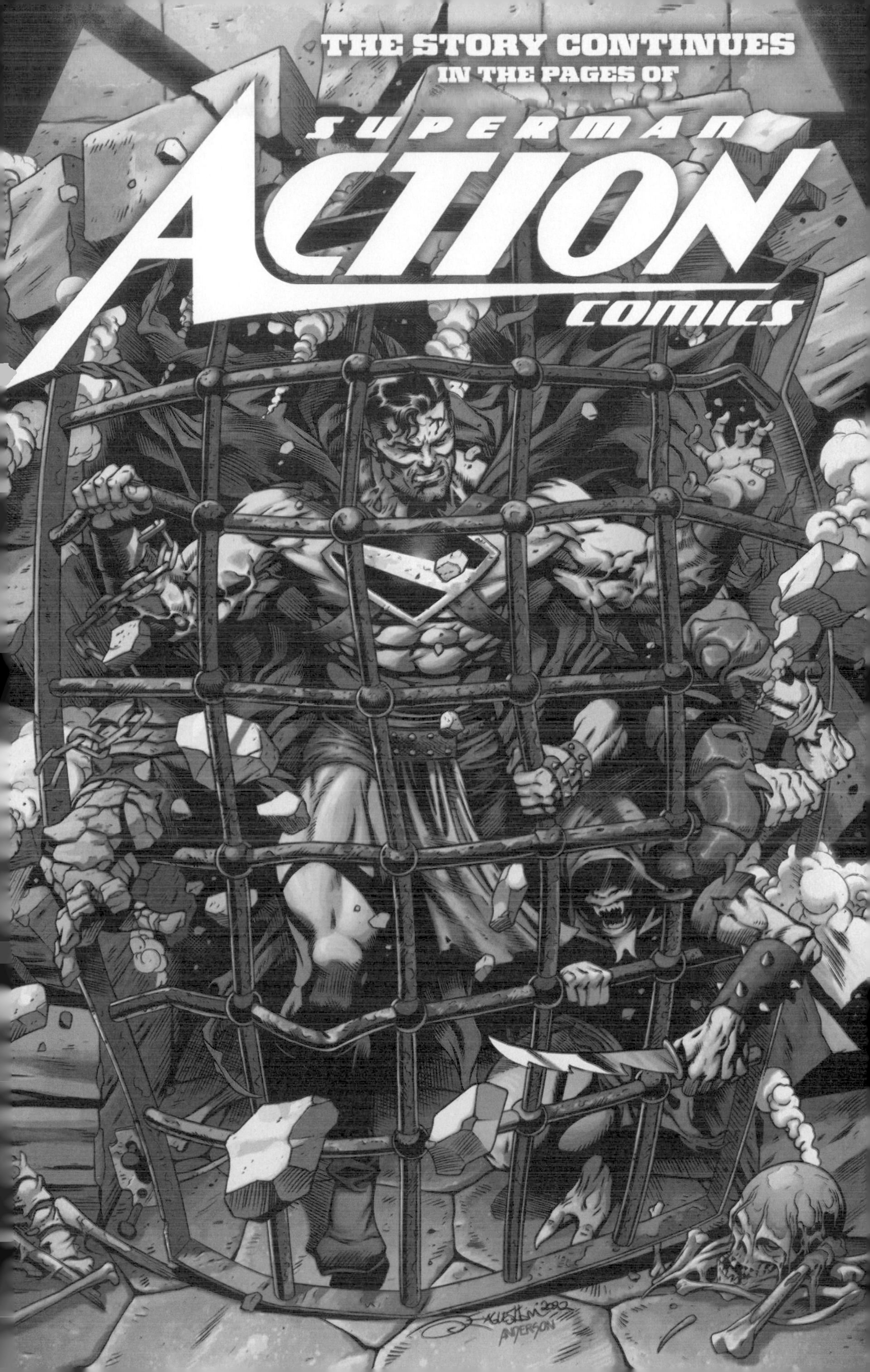
THE STORY CONTINUES
IN THE PAGES OF
SUPERMAN
ACTION
COMICS

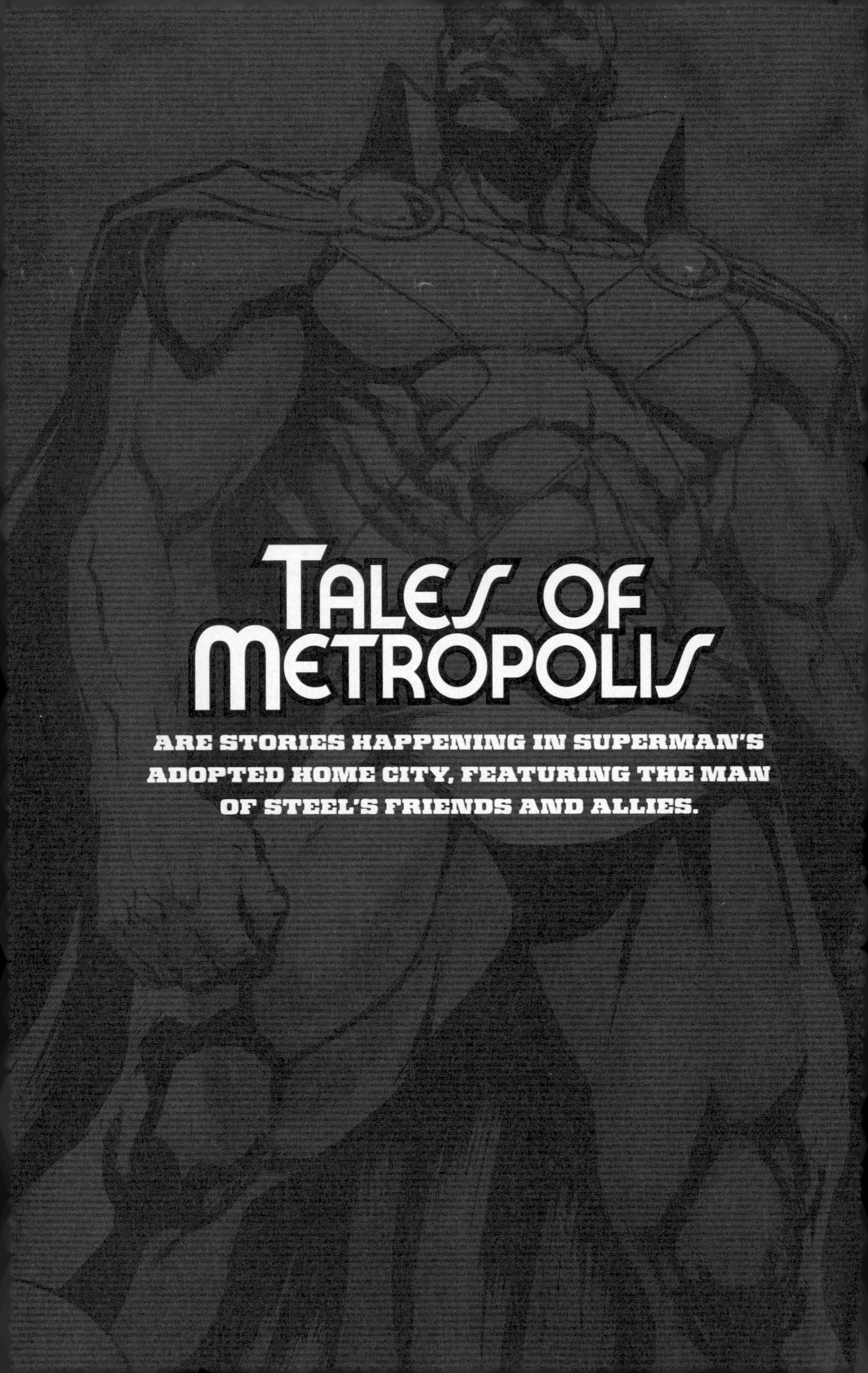

TALES OF METROPOLIS

ARE STORIES HAPPENING IN SUPERMAN'S ADOPTED HOME CITY, FEATURING THE MAN OF STEEL'S FRIENDS AND ALLIES.

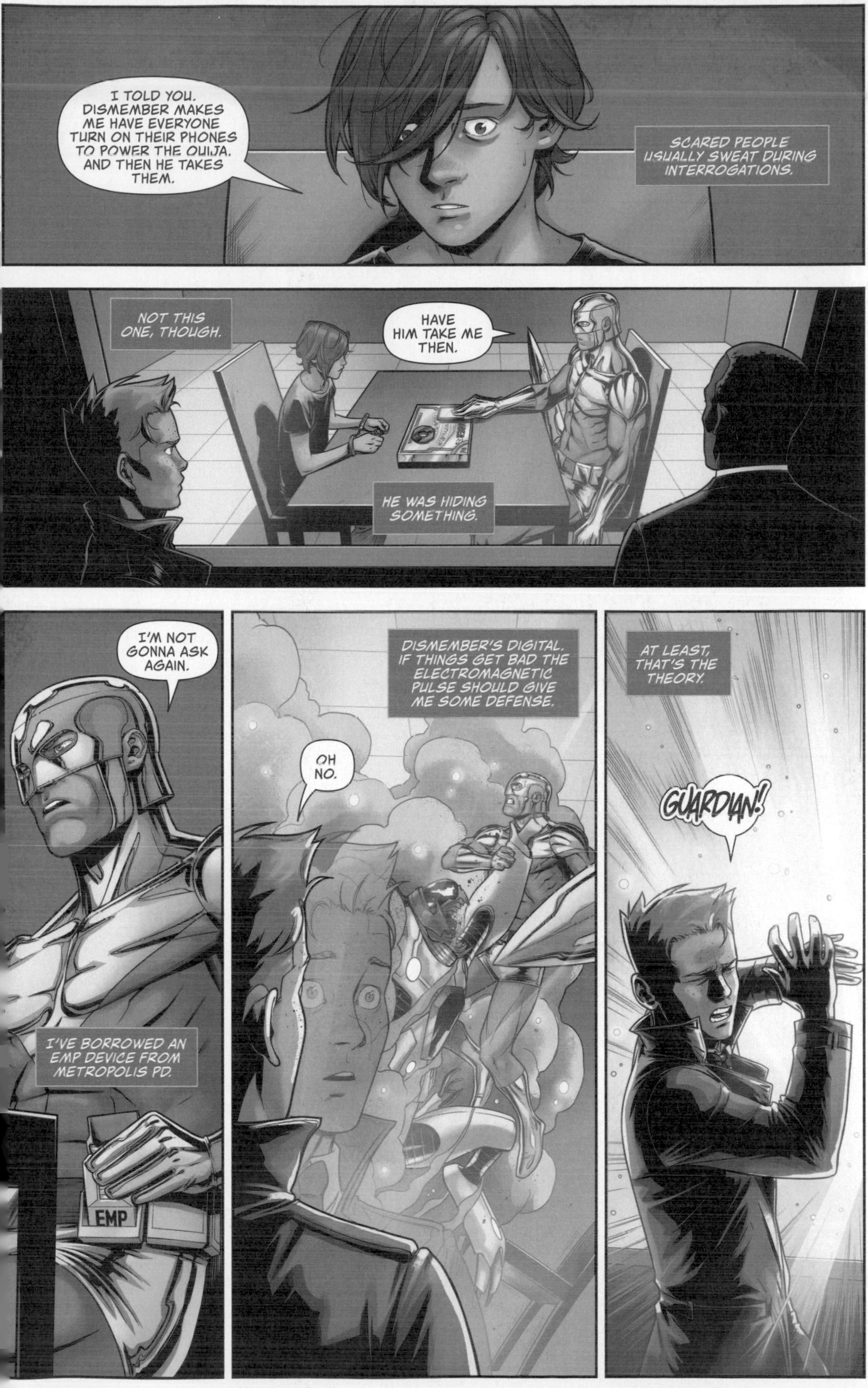
I TOLD YOU. DISMEMBER MAKES ME HAVE EVERYONE TURN ON THEIR PHONES TO POWER THE OUIJA. AND THEN HE TAKES THEM.
SCARED PEOPLE USUALLY SWEAT DURING INTERROGATIONS.
NOT THIS ONE, THOUGH.
HAVE HIM TAKE ME THEN.
HE WAS HIDING SOMETHING.
I'M NOT GONNA ASK AGAIN.
I'VE BORROWED AN EMP DEVICE FROM METROPOLIS PD.
EMP
DISMEMBER'S DIGITAL. IF THINGS GET BAD THE ELECTROMAGNETIC PULSE SHOULD GIVE ME SOME DEFENSE.
OH NO.
AT LEAST, THAT'S THE THEORY.
GUARDIAN!

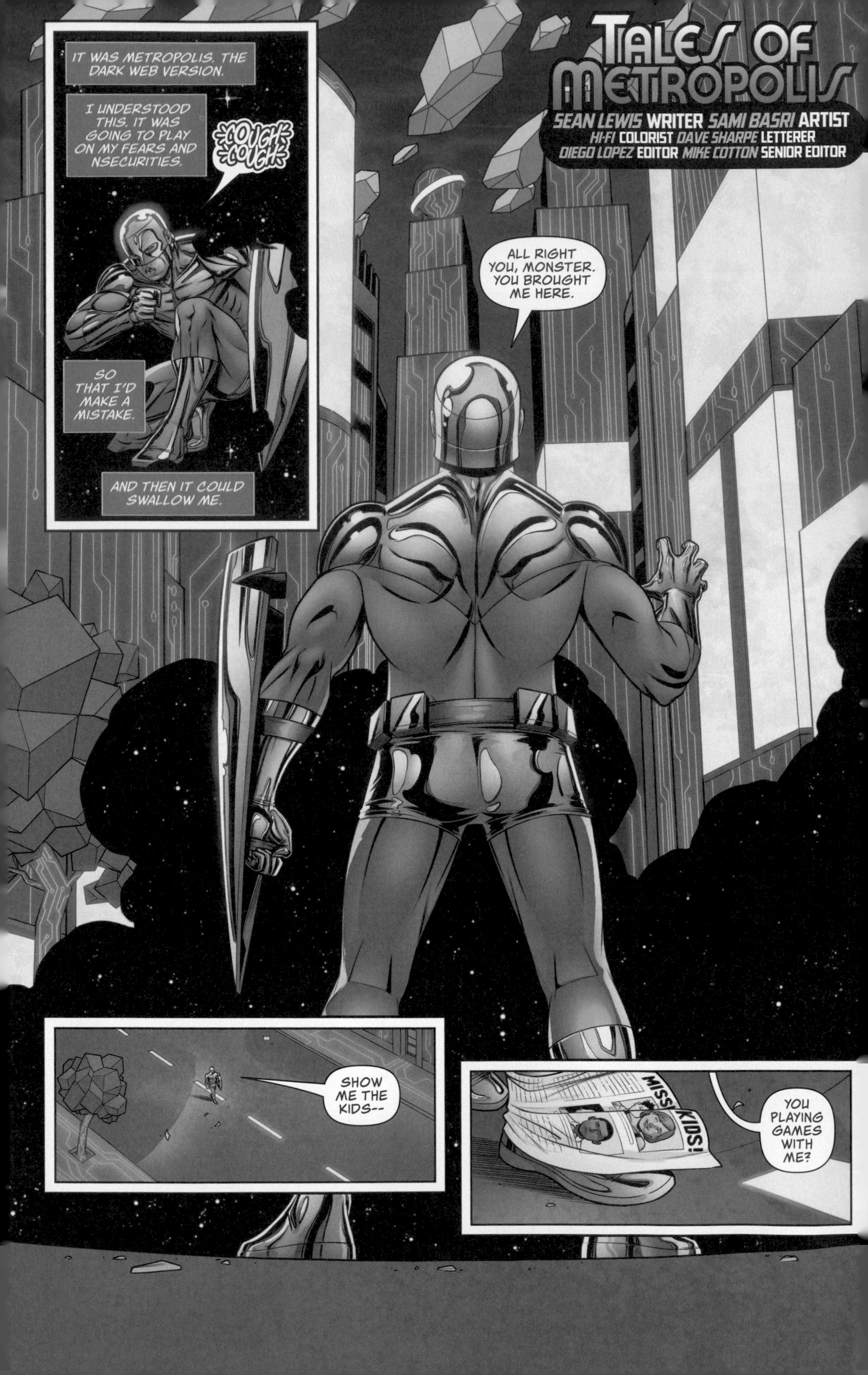
TALES OF METROPOLIS
SEAN LEWIS WRITER SAMI BASRI ARTIST
HI-FI COLORIST DAVE SHARPE LETTERER
DIEGO LOPEZ EDITOR MIKE COTTON SENIOR EDITOR
IT WAS METROPOLIS. THE DARK WEB VERSION.
I UNDERSTOOD THIS. IT WAS GOING TO PLAY ON MY FEARS AND NSECURITIES.
COUGH COUGH
SO THAT I'D MAKE A MISTAKE.
AND THEN IT COULD SWALLOW ME.
ALL RIGHT YOU, MONSTER. YOU BROUGHT ME HERE.
SHOW ME THE KIDS--
MISSING KIDS!
YOU PLAYING GAMES WITH ME?

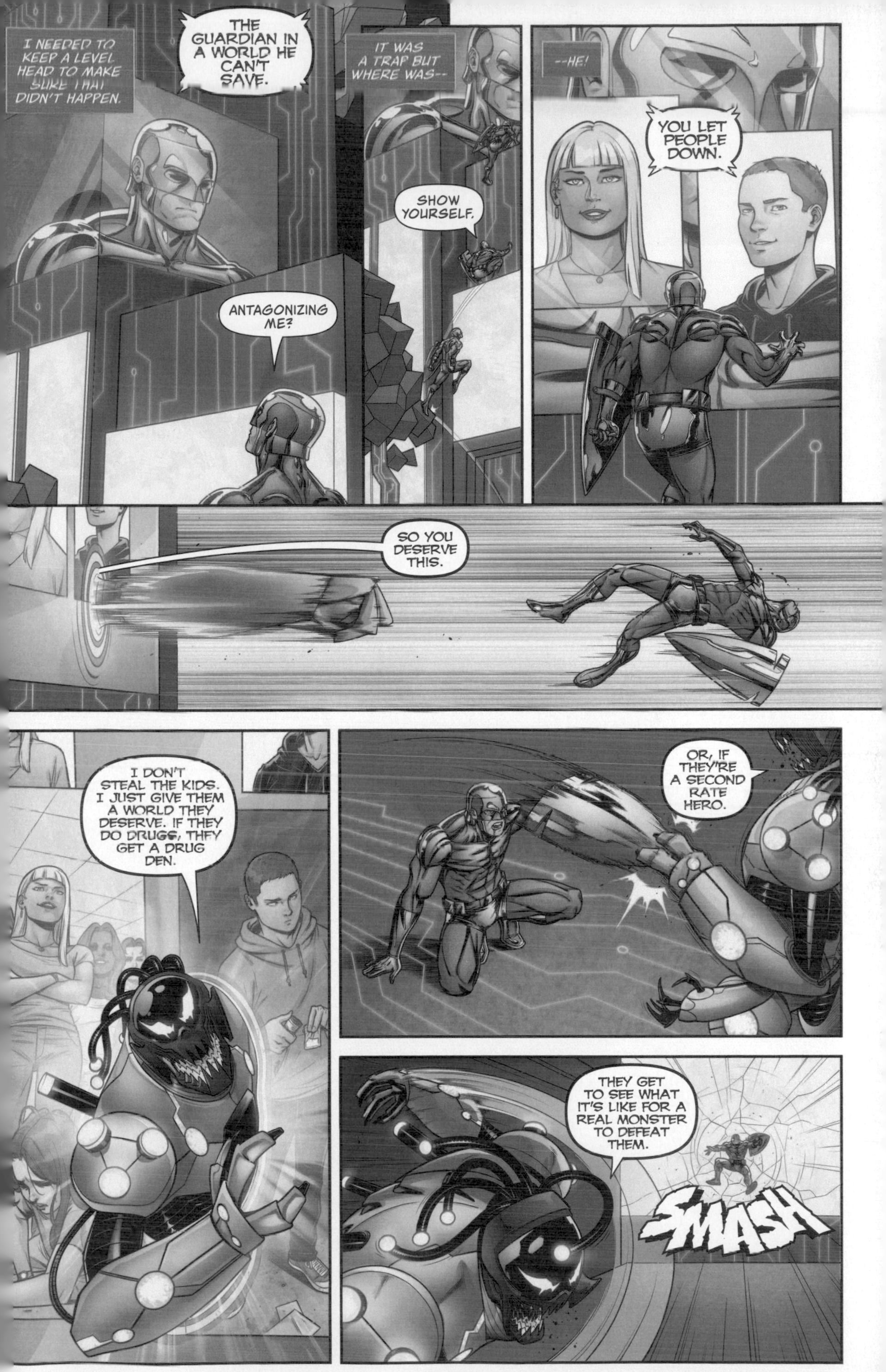
I NEEDED TO KEEP A LEVEL HEAD TO MAKE SURE THAT DIDN'T HAPPEN.
THE GUARDIAN IN A WORLD HE CAN'T SAVE.
ANTAGONIZING ME?
IT WAS A TRAP BUT WHERE WAS--
SHOW YOURSELF.
--HE!
YOU LET PEOPLE DOWN.
SO YOU DESERVE THIS.
I DON'T STEAL THE KIDS. I JUST GIVE THEM A WORLD THEY DESERVE. IF THEY DO DRUGS, THEY GET A DRUG DEN.
OR, IF THEY'RE A SECOND RATE HERO.
THEY GET TO SEE WHAT IT'S LIKE FOR A REAL MONSTER TO DEFEAT THEM.
SMASH

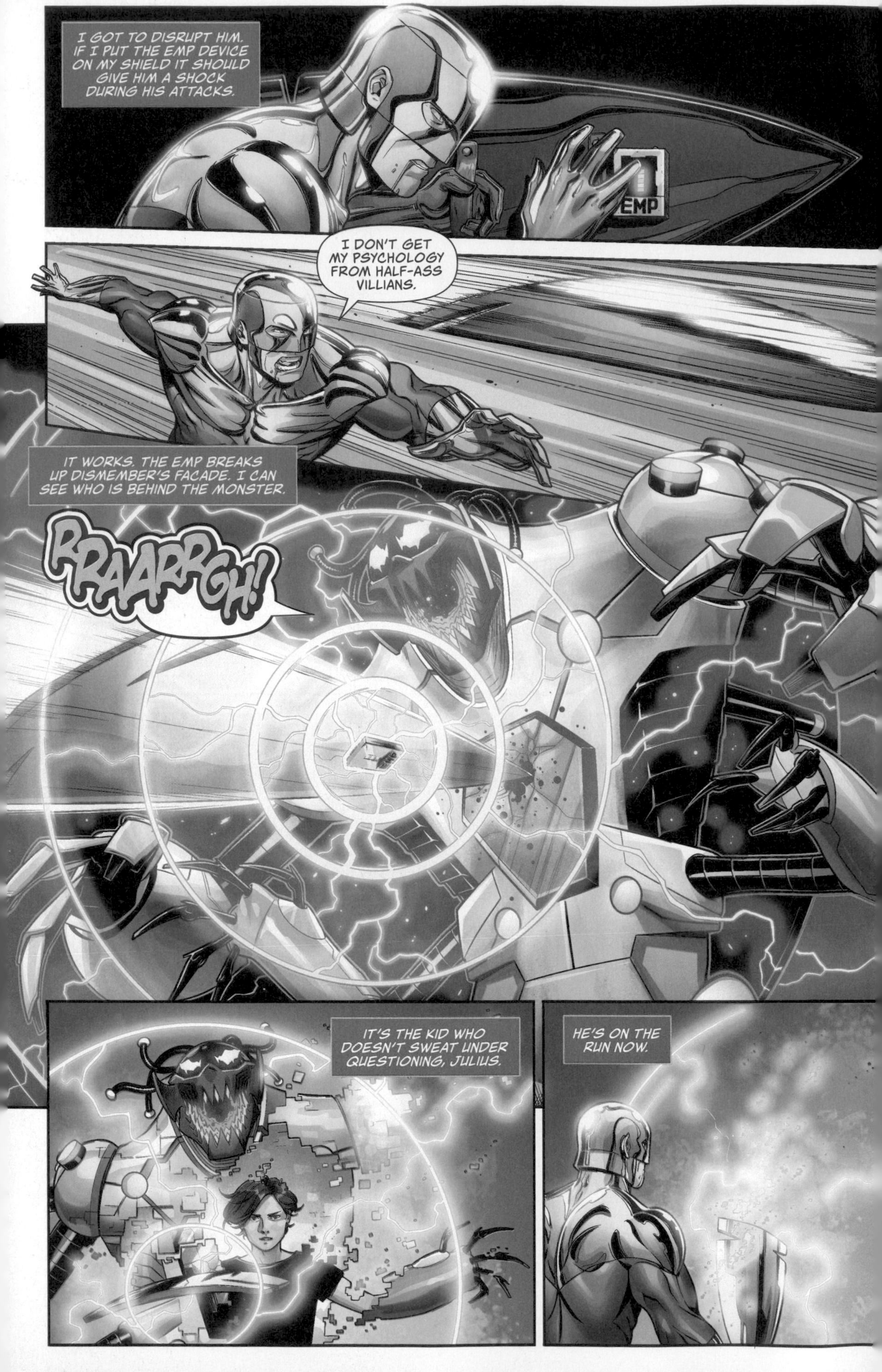
I GOT TO DISRUPT HIM. IF I PUT THE EMP DEVICE ON MY SHIELD IT SHOULD GIVE HIM A SHOCK DURING HIS ATTACKS.
EMP
I DON'T GET MY PSYCHOLOGY FROM HALF-ASS VILLIANS.
IT WORKS. THE EMP BREAKS UP DISMEMBER'S FACADE. I CAN SEE WHO IS BEHIND THE MONSTER.
RRAARRGH!
IT'S THE KID WHO DOESN'T SWEAT UNDER QUESTIONING, JULIUS.
HE'S ON THE RUN NOW.

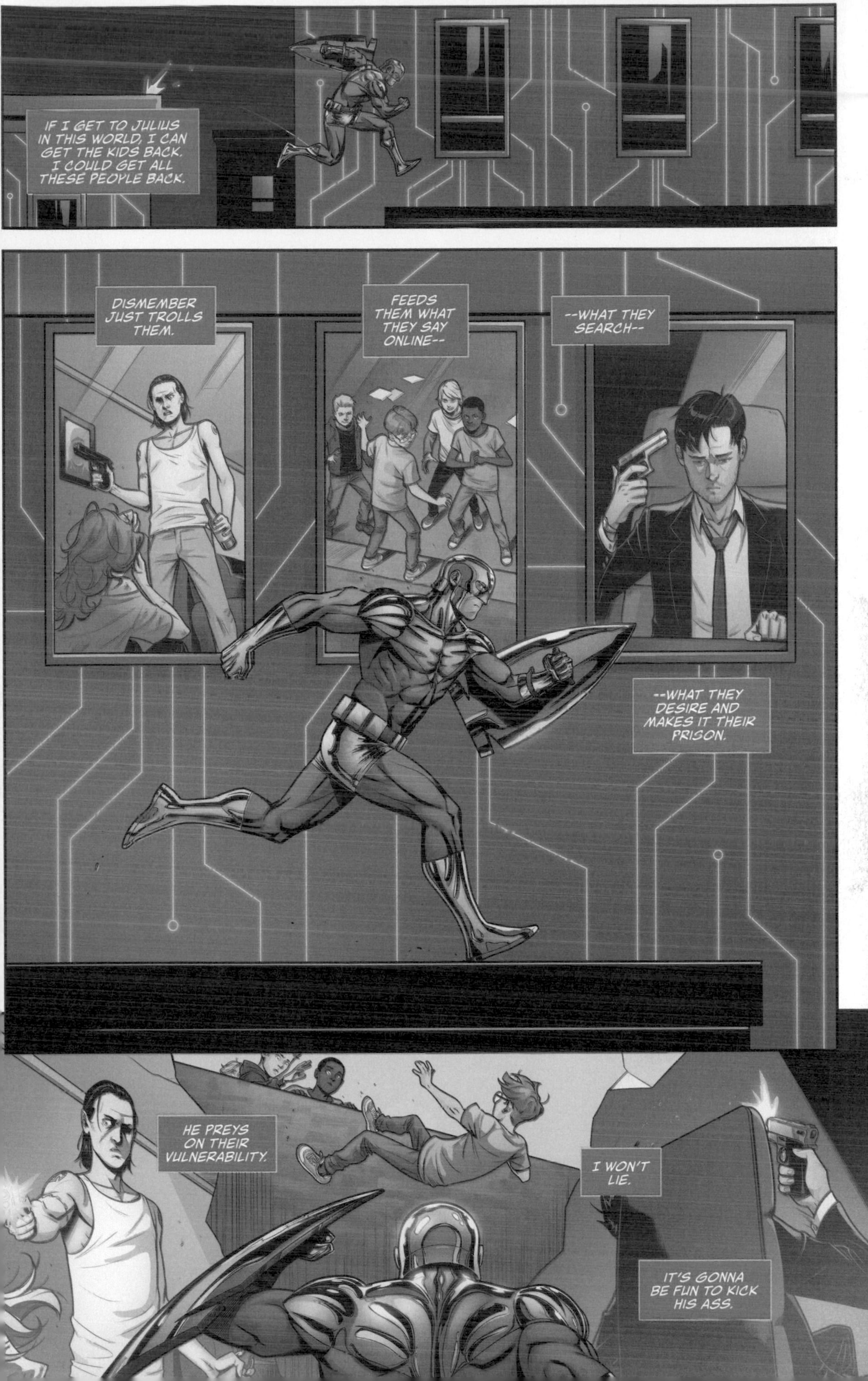
IF I GET TO JULIUS IN THIS WORLD, I CAN GET THE KIDS BACK. I COULD GET ALL THESE PEOPLE BACK.
DISMEMBER JUST TROLLS THEM.
FEEDS THEM WHAT THEY SAY ONLINE--
--WHAT THEY SEARCH--
--WHAT THEY DESIRE AND MAKES IT THEIR PRISON.
HE PREYS ON THEIR VULNERABILITY.
I WON'T LIE.
IT'S GONNA BE FUN TO KICK HIS ASS.

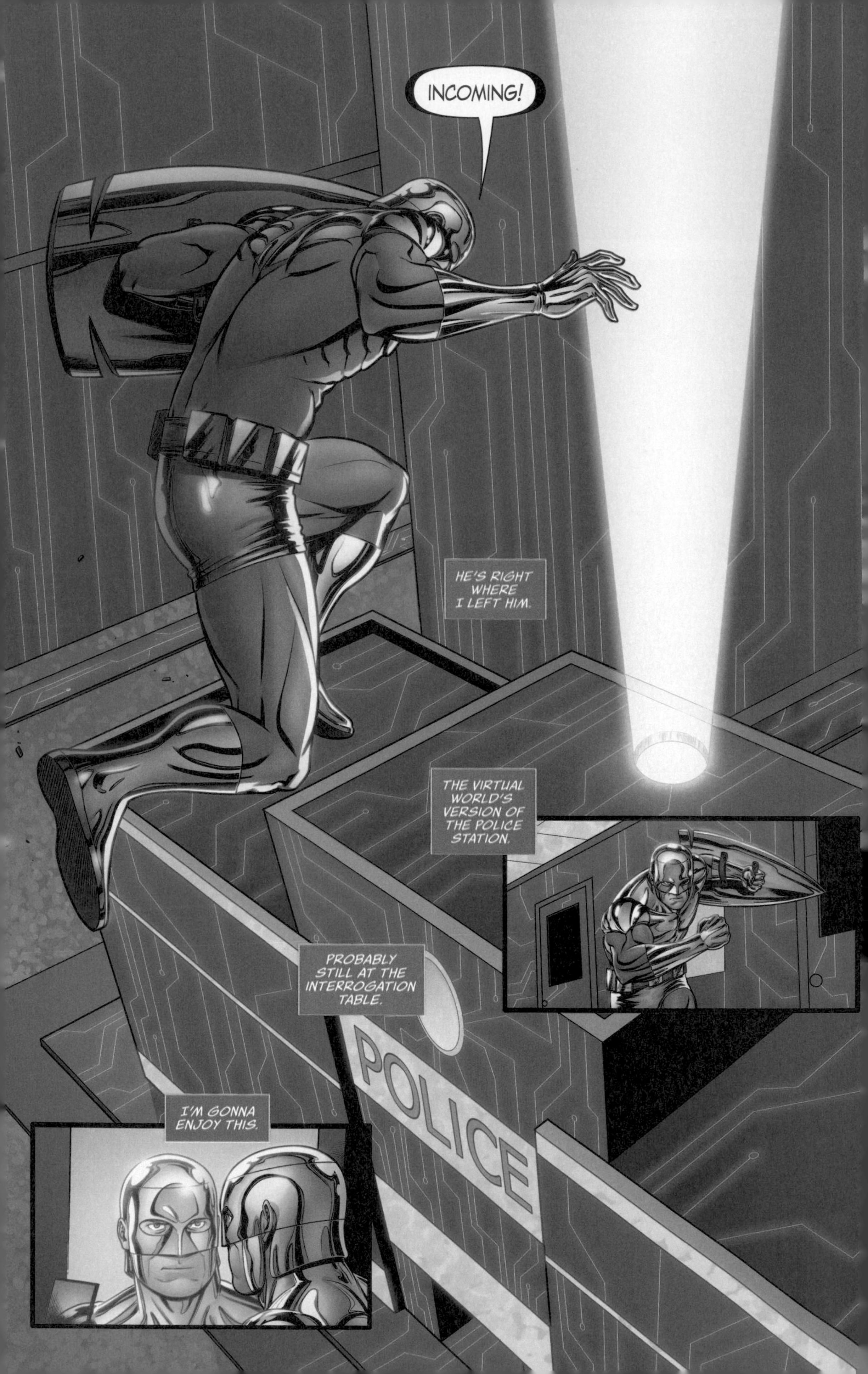
INCOMING!
HE'S RIGHT WHERE I LEFT HIM.
THE VIRTUAL WORLD'S VERSION OF THE POLICE STATION.
PROBABLY STILL AT THE INTERROGATION TABLE.
I'M GONNA ENJOY THIS.
POLICE

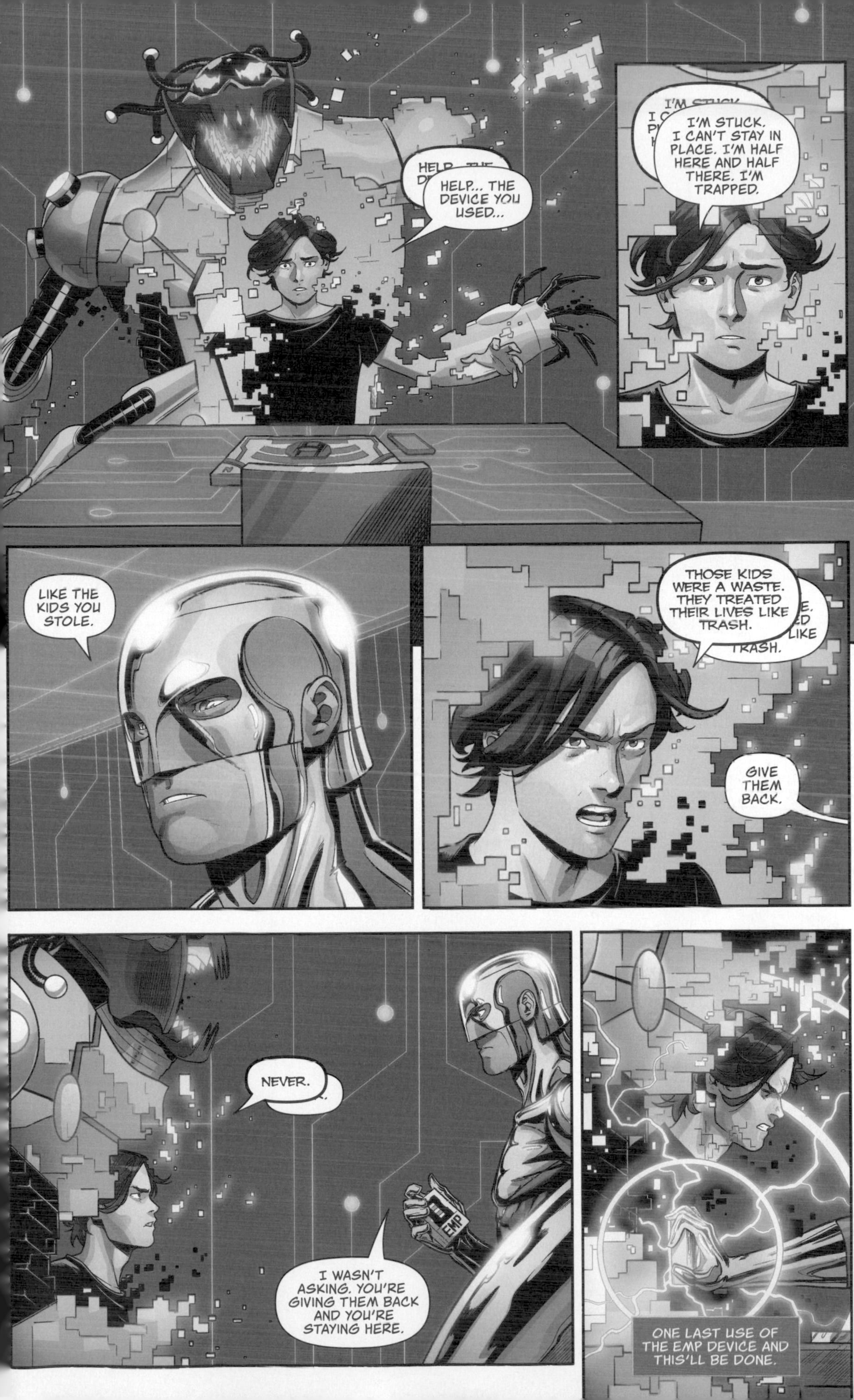
HELP... THE DEVICE YOU USED...
I'M STUCK. I CAN'T STAY IN PLACE. I'M HALF HERE AND HALF THERE. I'M TRAPPED.
LIKE THE KIDS YOU STOLE.
THOSE KIDS WERE A WASTE. THEY TREATED THEIR LIVES LIKE TRASH.
GIVE THEM BACK.
NEVER.
EMP
I WASN'T ASKING. YOU'RE GIVING THEM BACK AND YOU'RE STAYING HERE.
ONE LAST USE OF THE EMP DEVICE AND THIS'LL BE DONE.

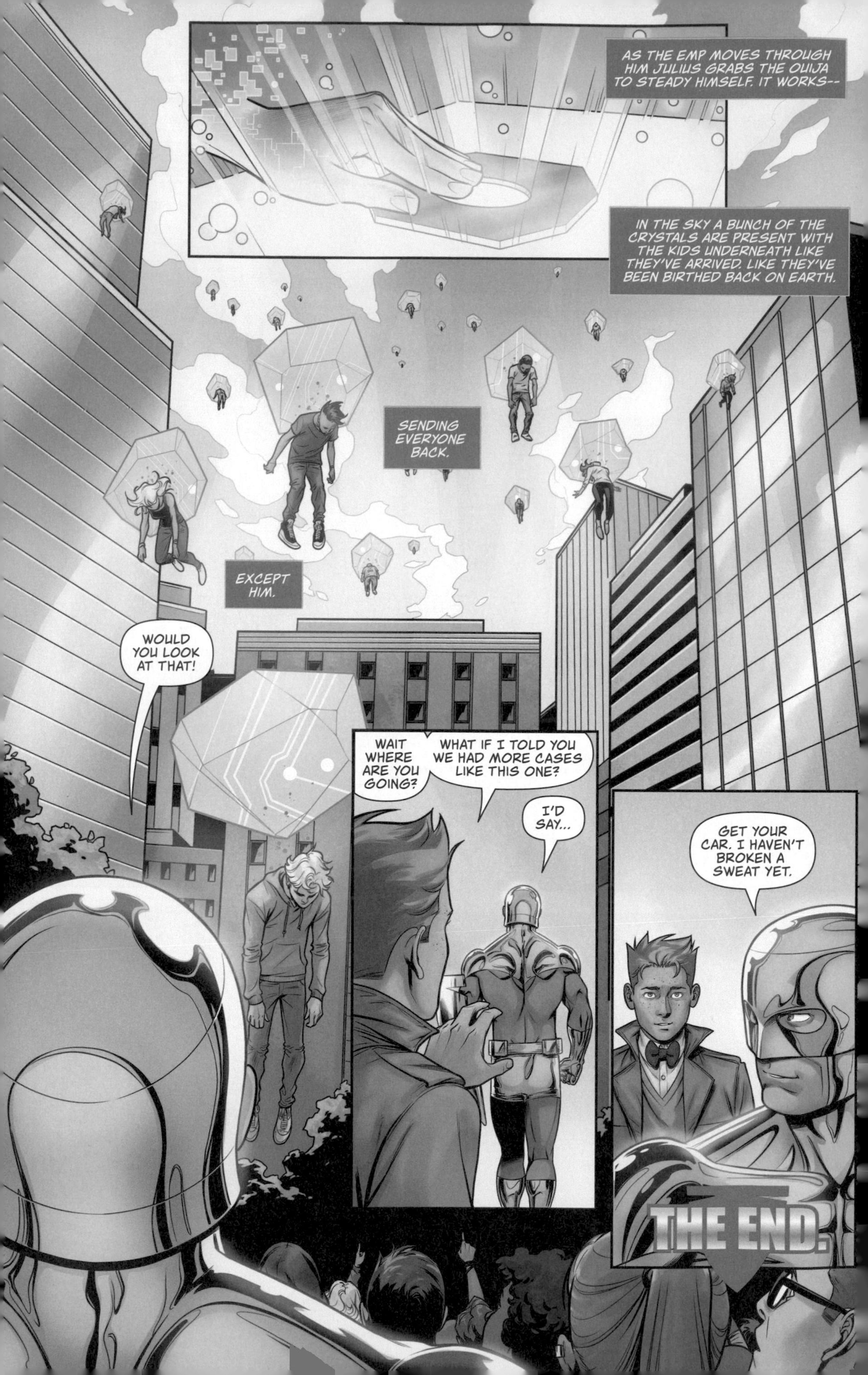
AS THE EMP MOVES THROUGH HIM JULIUS GRABS THE OUIJA TO STEADY HIMSELF. IT WORKS--
IN THE SKY A BUNCH OF THE CRYSTALS ARE PRESENT WITH THE KIDS UNDERNEATH LIKE THEY'VE ARRIVED. LIKE THEY'VE BEEN BIRTHED BACK ON EARTH.
SENDING EVERYONE BACK.
EXCEPT HIM.
WOULD YOU LOOK AT THAT!
WAIT WHERE ARE YOU GOING?
WHAT IF I TOLD YOU WE HAD MORE CASES LIKE THIS ONE?
I'D SAY...
GET YOUR CAR. I HAVEN'T BROKEN A SWEAT YET.
THE END.

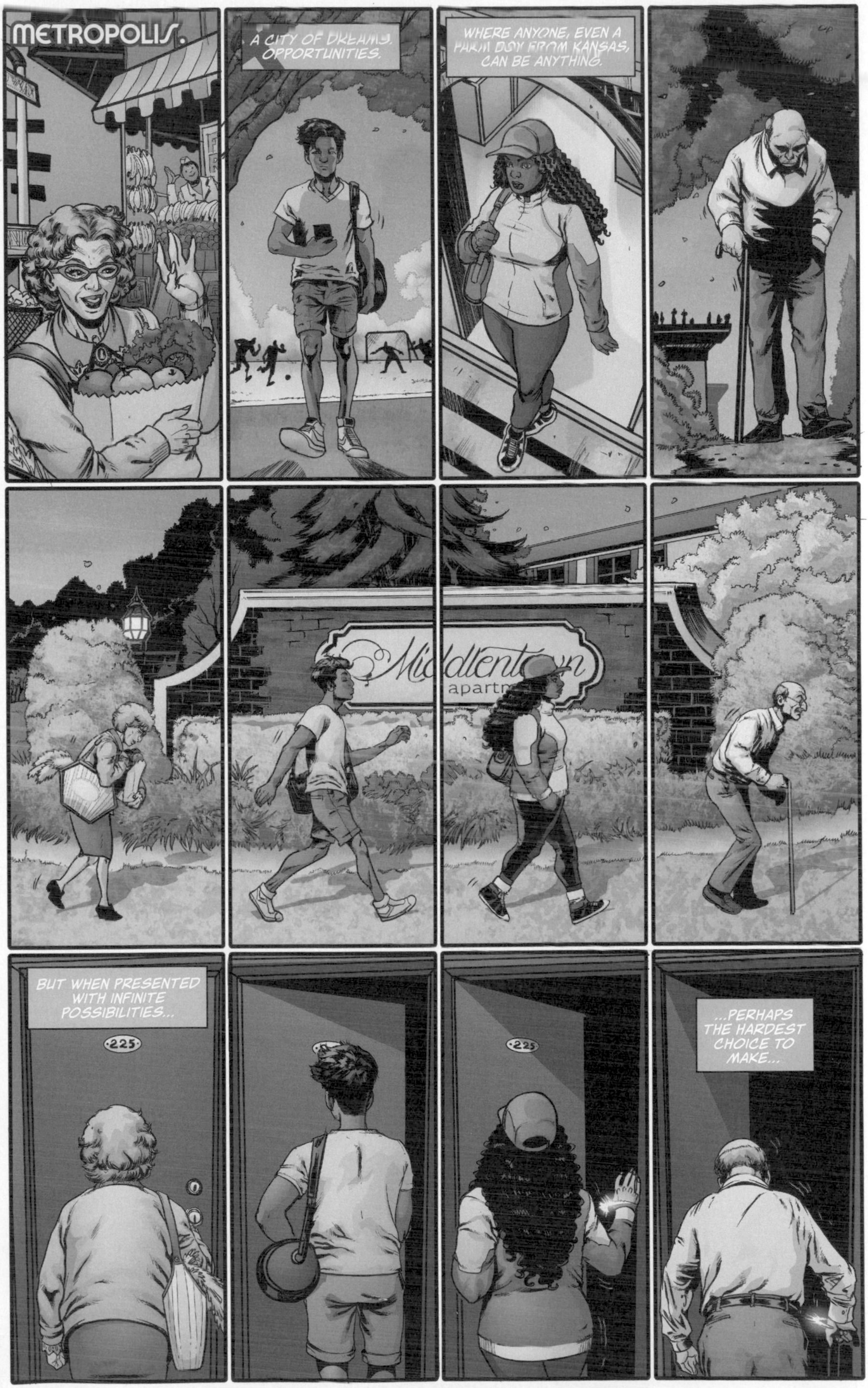
METROPOLIS.
A CITY OF DREAMS. OPPORTUNITIES.
WHERE ANYONE, EVEN A FARM BOY FROM KANSAS, CAN BE ANYTHING.
BUT WHEN PRESENTED WITH INFINITE POSSIBILITIES...
225
225
...PERHAPS THE HARDEST CHOICE TO MAKE...

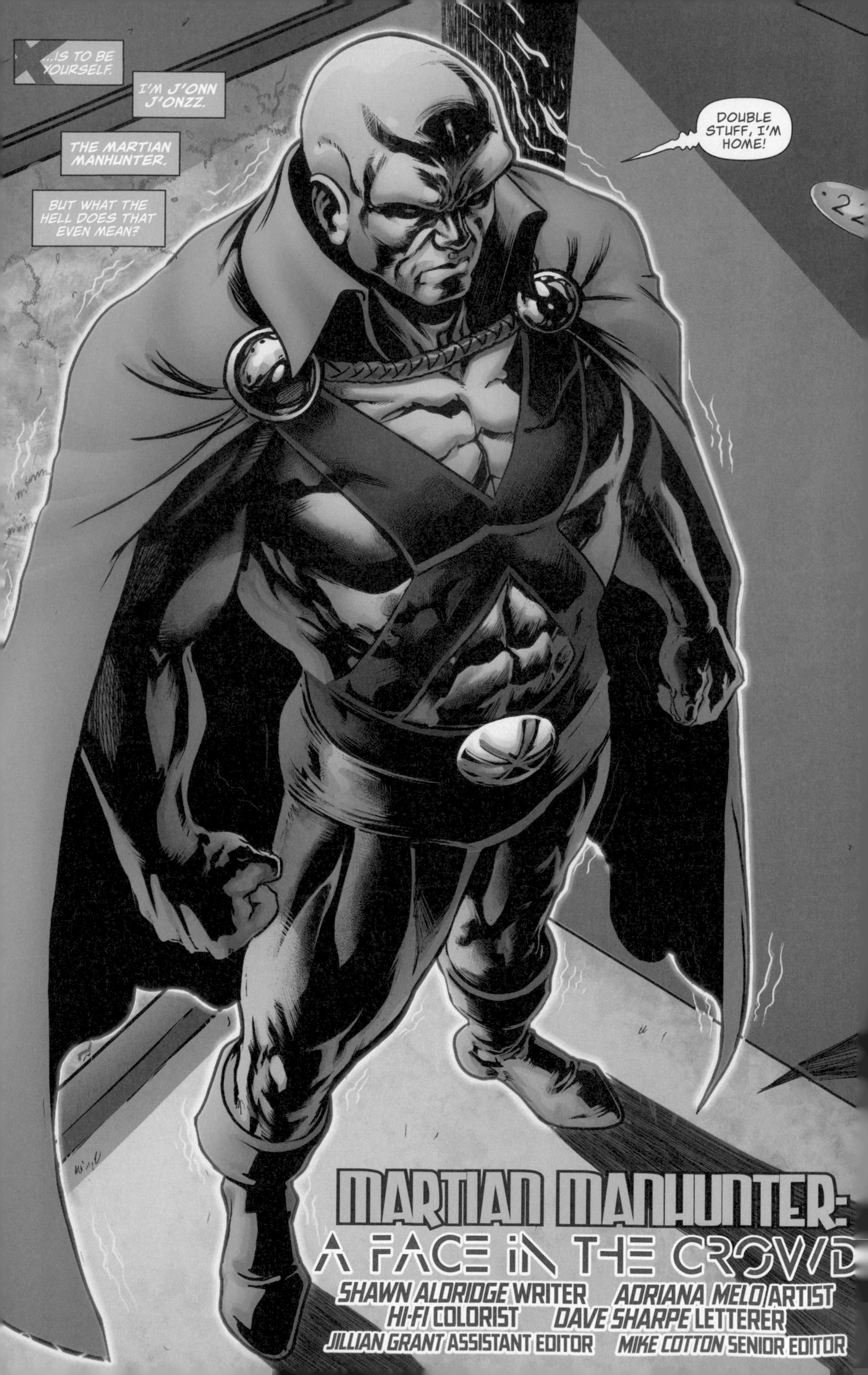

...IS TO BE YOURSELF.
I'M J'ONN J'ONZZ.
THE MARTIAN MANHUNTER.
BUT WHAT THE HELL DOES THAT EVEN MEAN?
DOUBLE STUFF, I'M HOME!
MARTIAN MANHUNTER:
A FACE IN THE CROWD
SHAWN ALDRIDGE WRITER ADRIANA MELO ARTIST
HI-FI COLORIST DAVE SHARPE LETTERER
JILLIAN GRANT ASSISTANT EDITOR MIKE COTTON SENIOR EDITOR

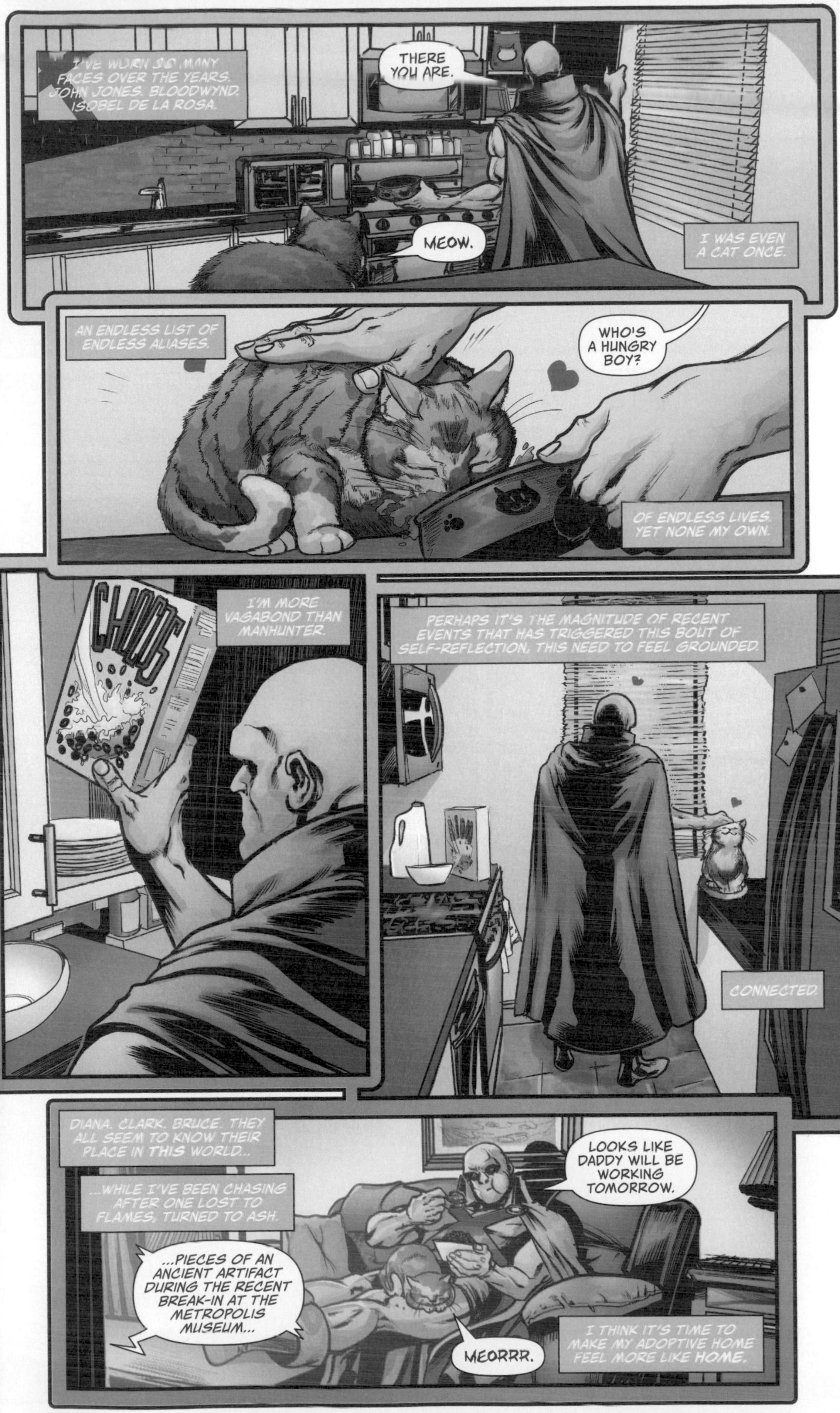
I'VE WORN SO MANY FACES OVER THE YEARS. JOHN JONES. BLOODWYND. ISOBEL DE LA ROSA.
THERE YOU ARE.
MEOW.
I WAS EVEN A CAT ONCE.
AN ENDLESS LIST OF ENDLESS ALIASES.
WHO'S A HUNGRY BOY?
OF ENDLESS LIVES. YET NONE MY OWN.
I'M MORE VAGABOND THAN MANHUNTER.
CHAOS
PERHAPS IT'S THE MAGNITUDE OF RECENT EVENTS THAT HAS TRIGGERED THIS BOUT OF SELF-REFLECTION, THIS NEED TO FEEL GROUNDED.
CONNECTED.
DIANA. CLARK. BRUCE. THEY ALL SEEM TO KNOW THEIR PLACE IN THIS WORLD...
...WHILE I'VE BEEN CHASING AFTER ONE LOST TO FLAMES, TURNED TO ASH.
LOOKS LIKE DADDY WILL BE WORKING TOMORROW.
...PIECES OF AN ANCIENT ARTIFACT DURING THE RECENT BREAK-IN AT THE METROPOLIS MUSEUM...
MEORRR.
I THINK IT'S TIME TO MAKE MY ADOPTIVE HOME FEEL MORE LIKE HOME.

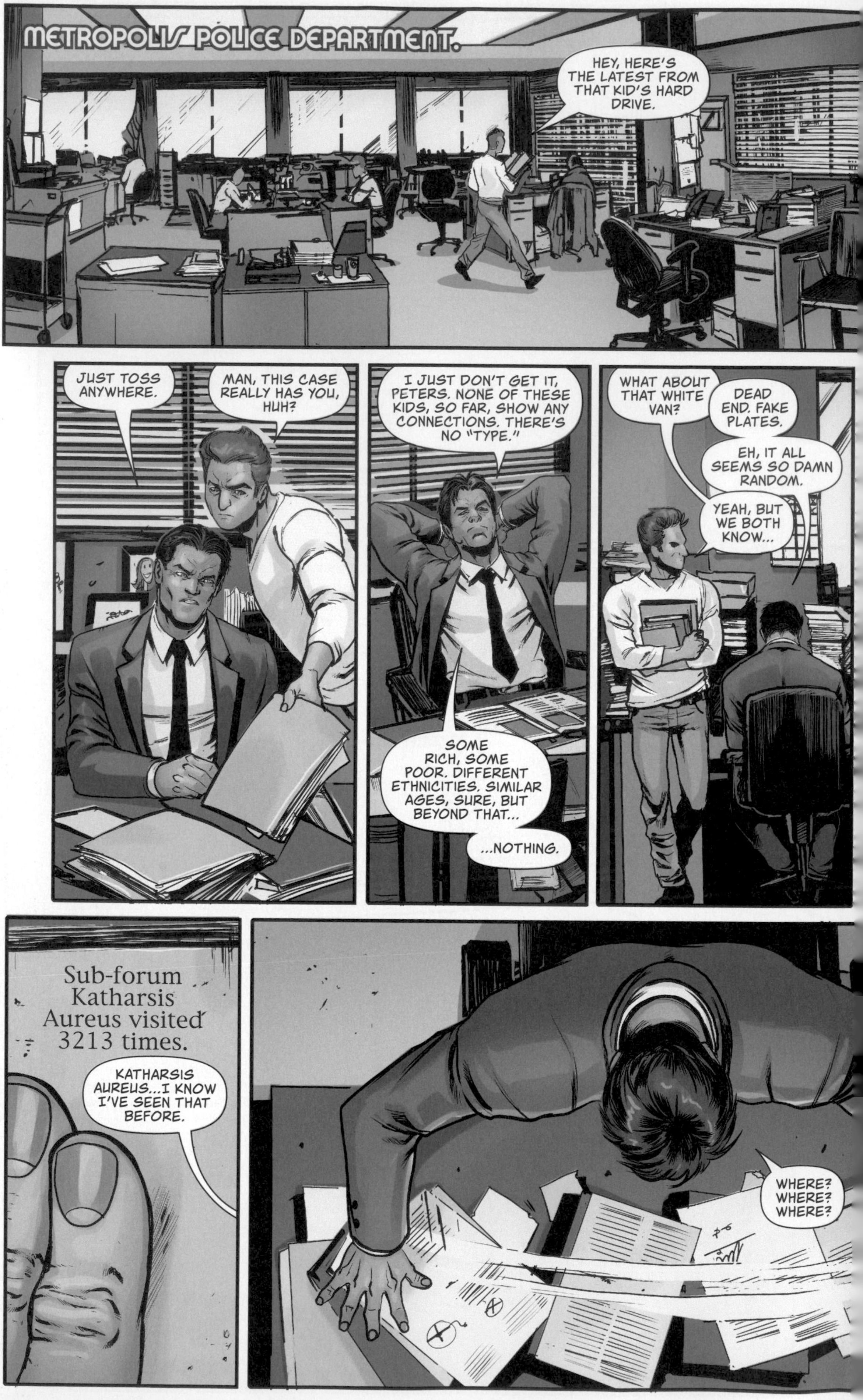
METROPOLIS POLICE DEPARTMENT.
HEY, HERE'S THE LATEST FROM THAT KID'S HARD DRIVE.
JUST TOSS ANYWHERE.
MAN, THIS CASE REALLY HAS YOU, HUH?
I JUST DON'T GET IT, PETERS. NONE OF THESE KIDS, SO FAR, SHOW ANY CONNECTIONS. THERE'S NO "TYPE."
SOME RICH, SOME POOR. DIFFERENT ETHNICITIES. SIMILAR AGES, SURE, BUT BEYOND THAT...
...NOTHING.
WHAT ABOUT THAT WHITE VAN?
DEAD END. FAKE PLATES.
EH, IT ALL SEEMS SO DAMN RANDOM.
YEAH, BUT WE BOTH KNOW...
Sub-forum Katharsis Aureus visited 3213 times.
KATHARSIS AUREUS...I KNOW I'VE SEEN THAT BEFORE.
WHERE? WHERE? WHERE?

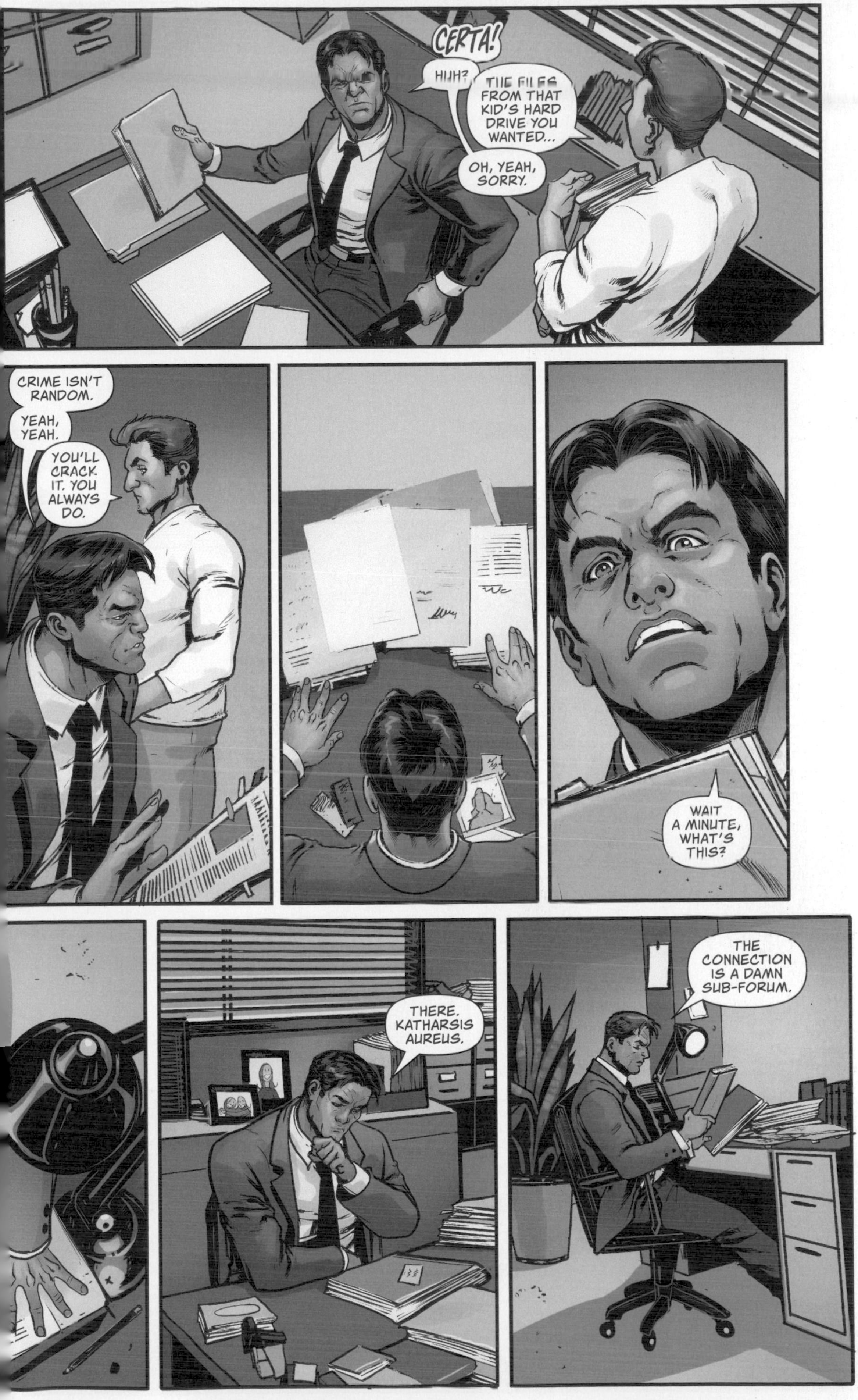
CERTA!
HUH?
THE FILES FROM THAT KID'S HARD DRIVE YOU WANTED...
OH, YEAH, SORRY.
CRIME ISN'T RANDOM.
YEAH, YEAH.
YOU'LL CRACK IT. YOU ALWAYS DO.
WAIT A MINUTE, WHAT'S THIS?
THERE. KATHARSIS AUREUS.
THE CONNECTION IS A DAMN SUB-FORUM.

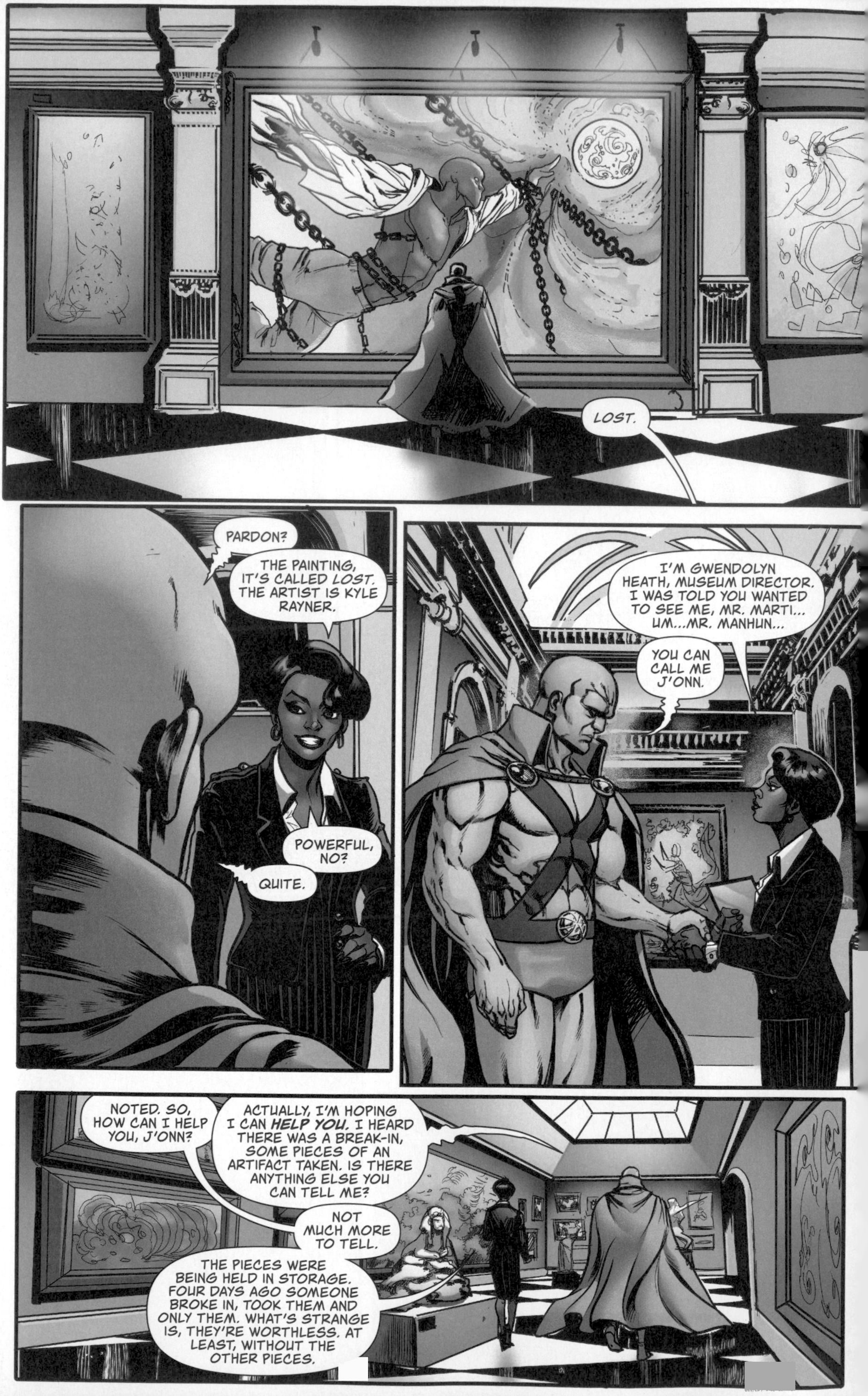
LOST.
PARDON?
THE PAINTING, IT'S CALLED LOST. THE ARTIST IS KYLE RAYNER.
POWERFUL, NO?
QUITE.
I'M GWENDOLYN HEATH, MUSEUM DIRECTOR. I WAS TOLD YOU WANTED TO SEE ME, MR. MARTI... UM...MR. MANHUN...
YOU CAN CALL ME J'ONN.
NOTED. SO, HOW CAN I HELP YOU, J'ONN?
ACTUALLY, I'M HOPING I CAN HELP YOU. I HEARD THERE WAS A BREAK-IN, SOME PIECES OF AN ARTIFACT TAKEN. IS THERE ANYTHING ELSE YOU CAN TELL ME?
NOT MUCH MORE TO TELL.
THE PIECES WERE BEING HELD IN STORAGE. FOUR DAYS AGO SOMEONE BROKE IN, TOOK THEM AND ONLY THEM. WHAT'S STRANGE IS, THEY'RE WORTHLESS. AT LEAST, WITHOUT THE OTHER PIECES.

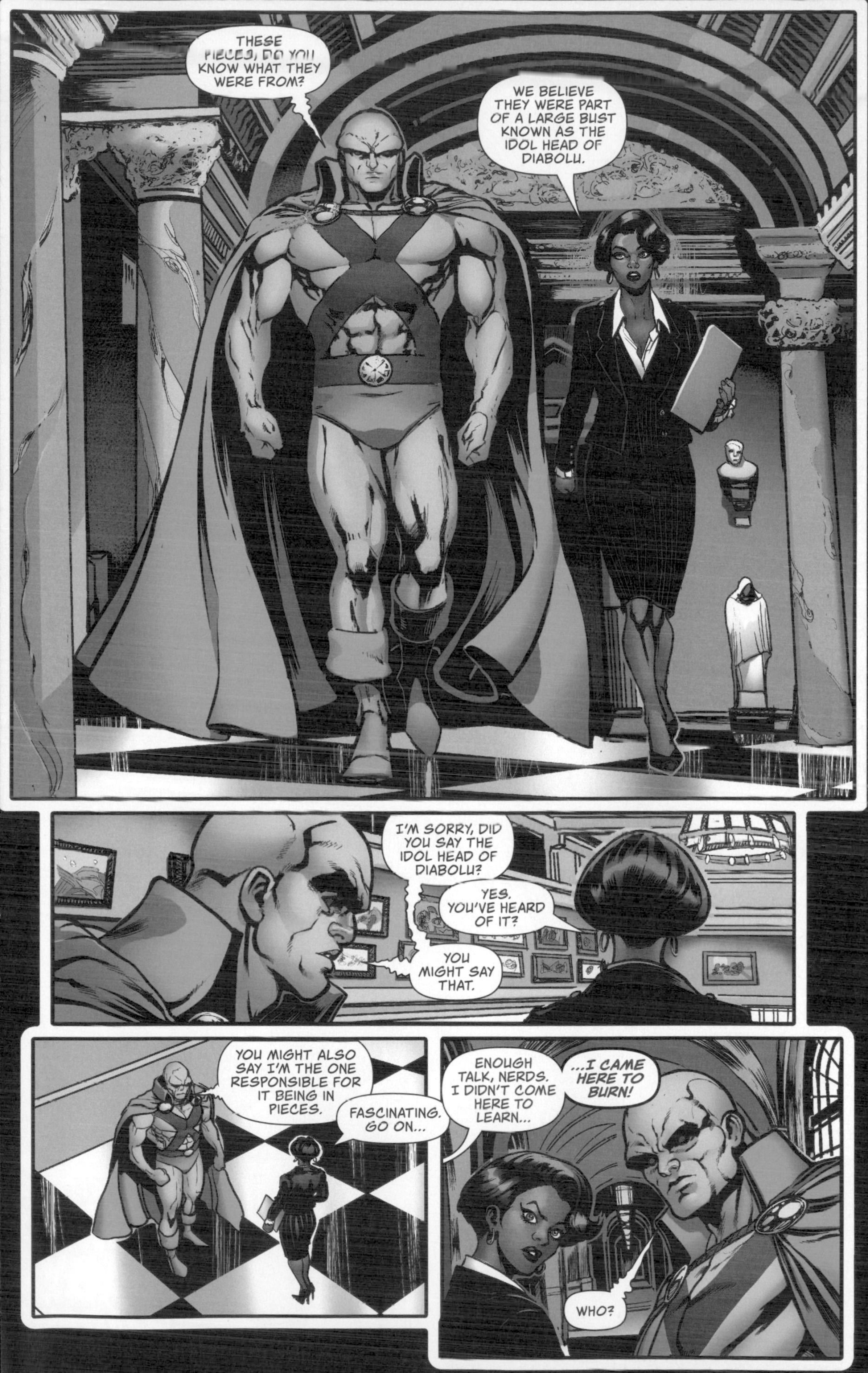
THESE PIECES, DO YOU KNOW WHAT THEY WERE FROM?
WE BELIEVE THEY WERE PART OF A LARGE BUST KNOWN AS THE IDOL HEAD OF DIABOLU.
I'M SORRY, DID YOU SAY THE IDOL HEAD OF DIABOLU?
YES. YOU'VE HEARD OF IT?
YOU MIGHT SAY THAT.
YOU MIGHT ALSO SAY I'M THE ONE RESPONSIBLE FOR IT BEING IN PIECES.
FASCINATING. GO ON...
ENOUGH TALK, NERDS. I DIDN'T COME HERE TO LEARN...
...I CAME HERE TO BURN!
WHO?

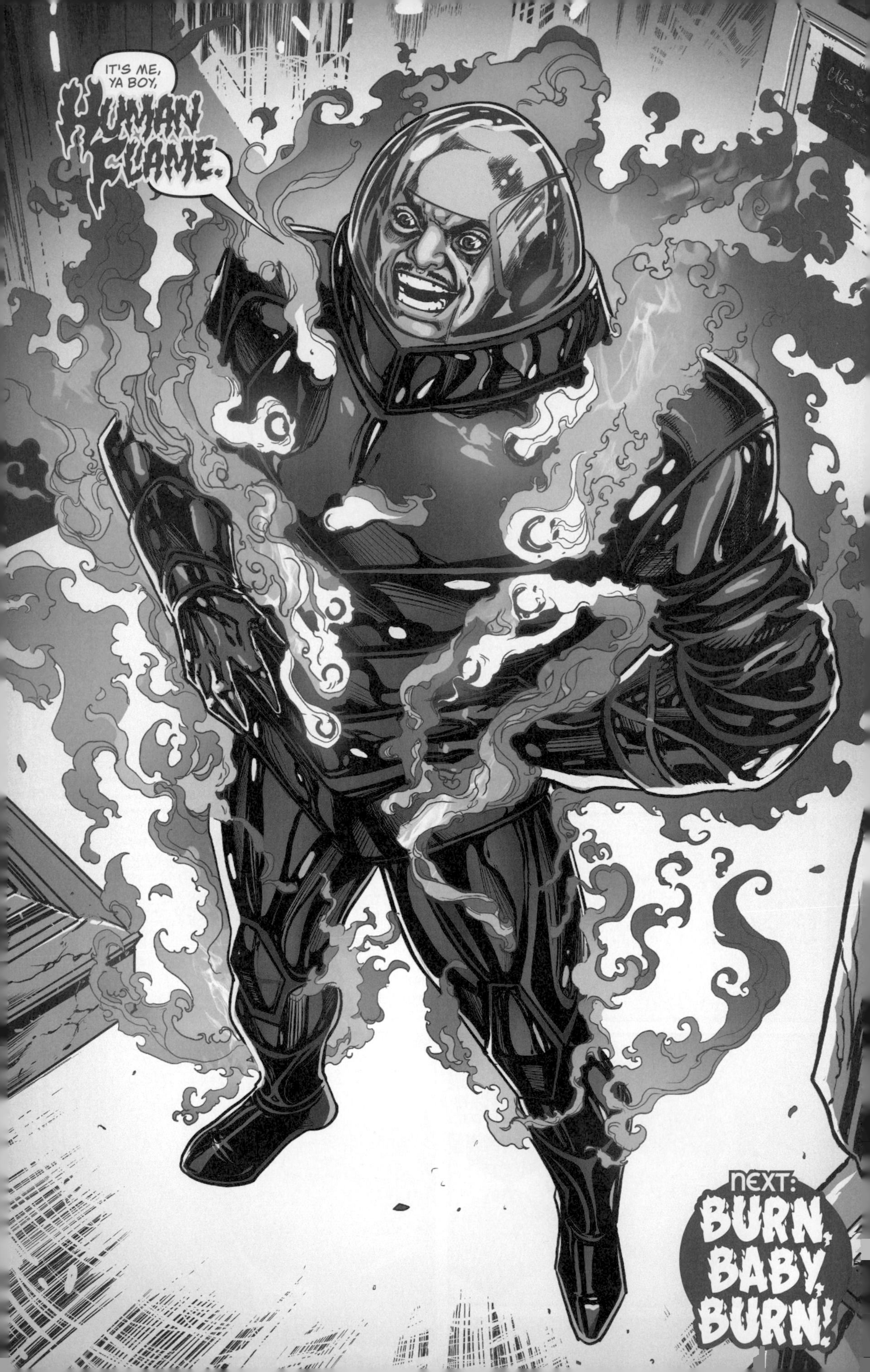
IT'S ME, YA BOY, HUMAN FLAME.
NEXT: BURN, BABY, BURN!

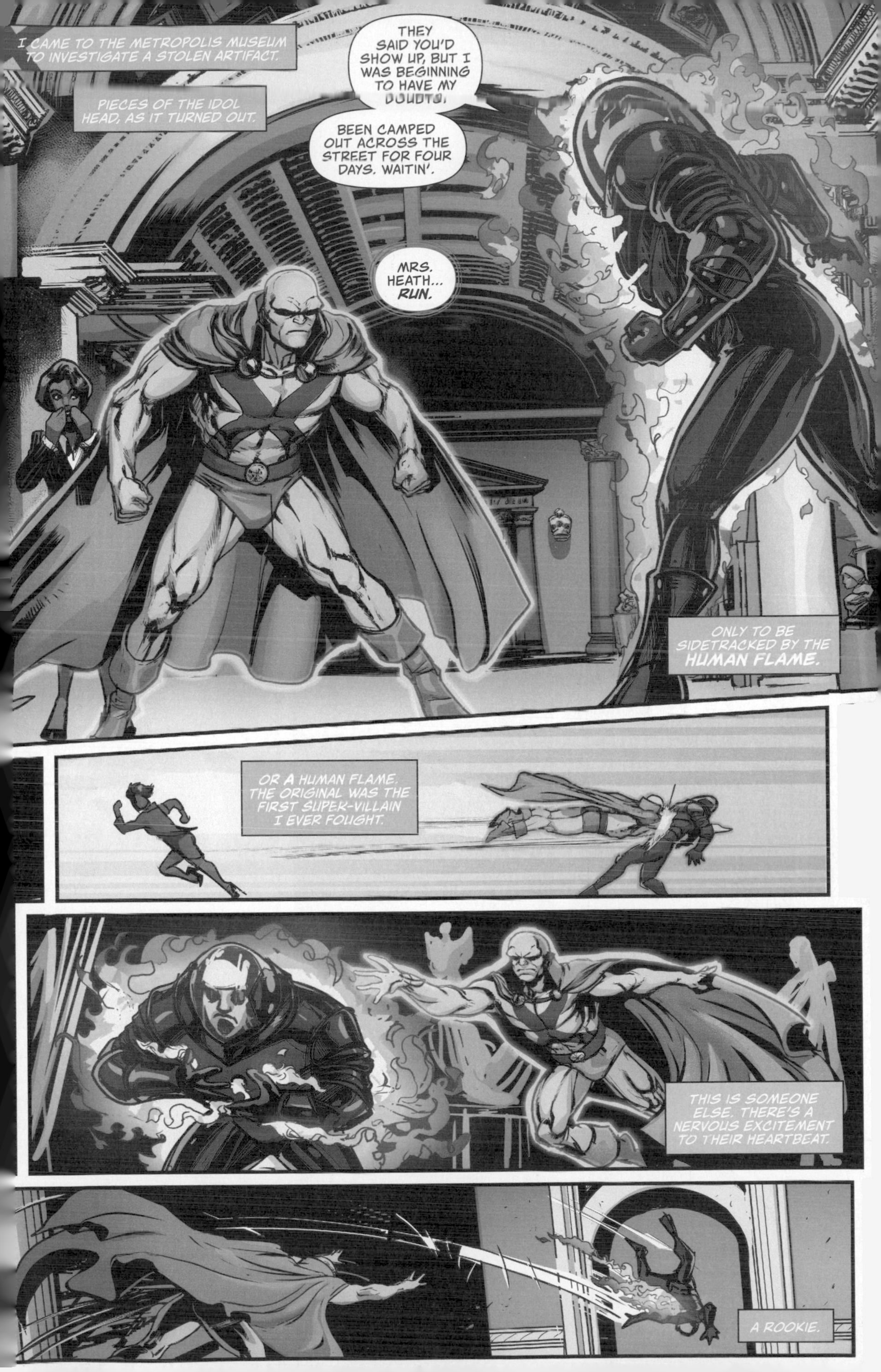

I CAME TO THE METROPOLIS MUSEUM TO INVESTIGATE A STOLEN ARTIFACT.
PIECES OF THE IDOL HEAD, AS IT TURNED OUT.
THEY SAID YOU'D SHOW UP, BUT I WAS BEGINNING TO HAVE MY DOUBTS.
BEEN CAMPED OUT ACROSS THE STREET FOR FOUR DAYS. WAITIN'.
MRS. HEATH... RUN.
ONLY TO BE SIDETRACKED BY THE HUMAN FLAME.
OR A HUMAN FLAME. THE ORIGINAL WAS THE FIRST SUPER-VILLAIN I EVER FOUGHT.
THIS IS SOMEONE ELSE. THERE'S A NERVOUS EXCITEMENT TO THEIR HEARTBEAT.
A ROOKIE.

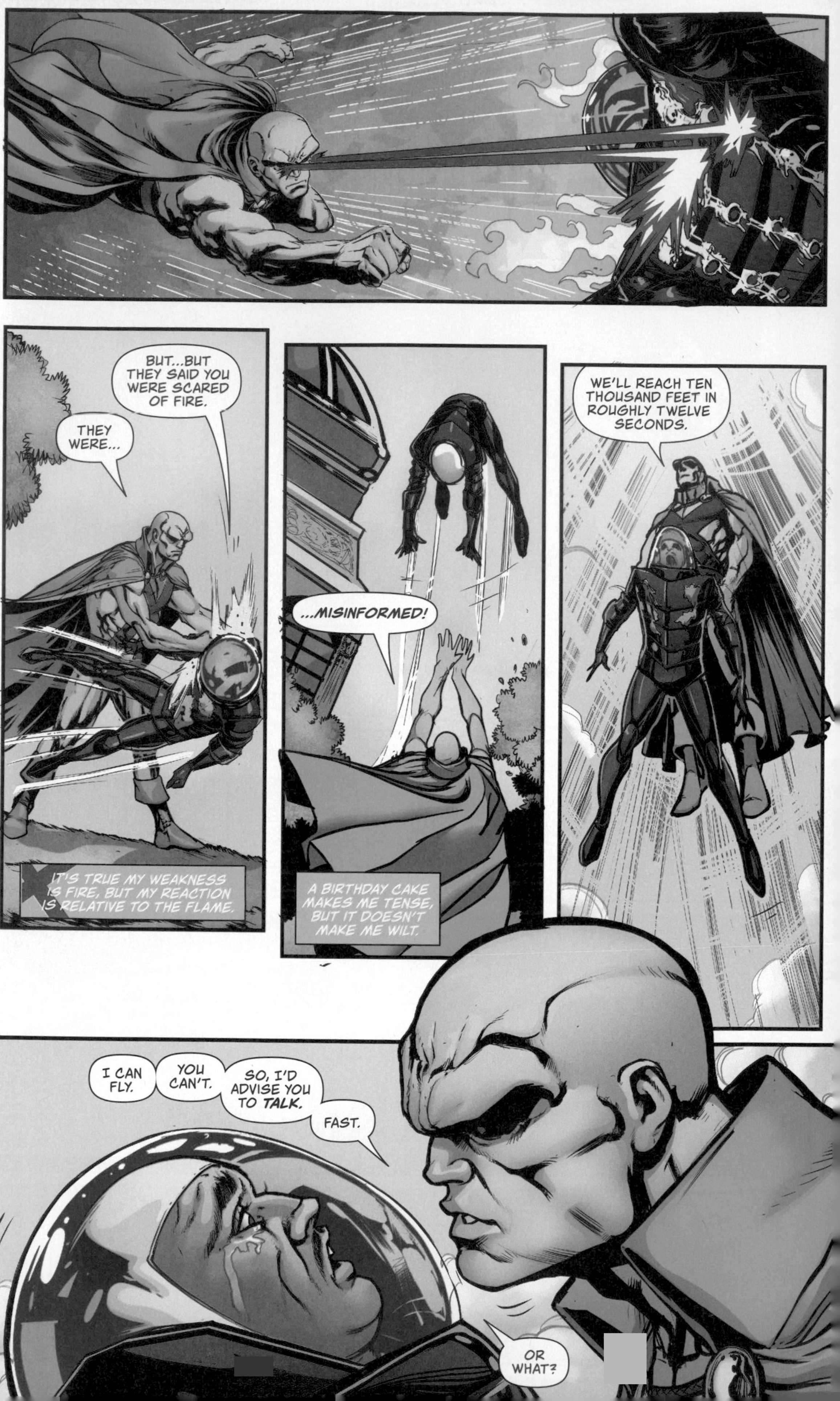
BUT...BUT THEY SAID YOU WERE SCARED OF FIRE.
THEY WERE...
IT'S TRUE MY WEAKNESS IS FIRE, BUT MY REACTION IS RELATIVE TO THE FLAME.
...MISINFORMED!
A BIRTHDAY CAKE MAKES ME TENSE, BUT IT DOESN'T MAKE ME WILT.
WE'LL REACH TEN THOUSAND FEET IN ROUGHLY TWELVE SECONDS.
I CAN FLY.
YOU CAN'T.
SO, I'D ADVISE YOU TO TALK.
FAST.
OR WHAT?

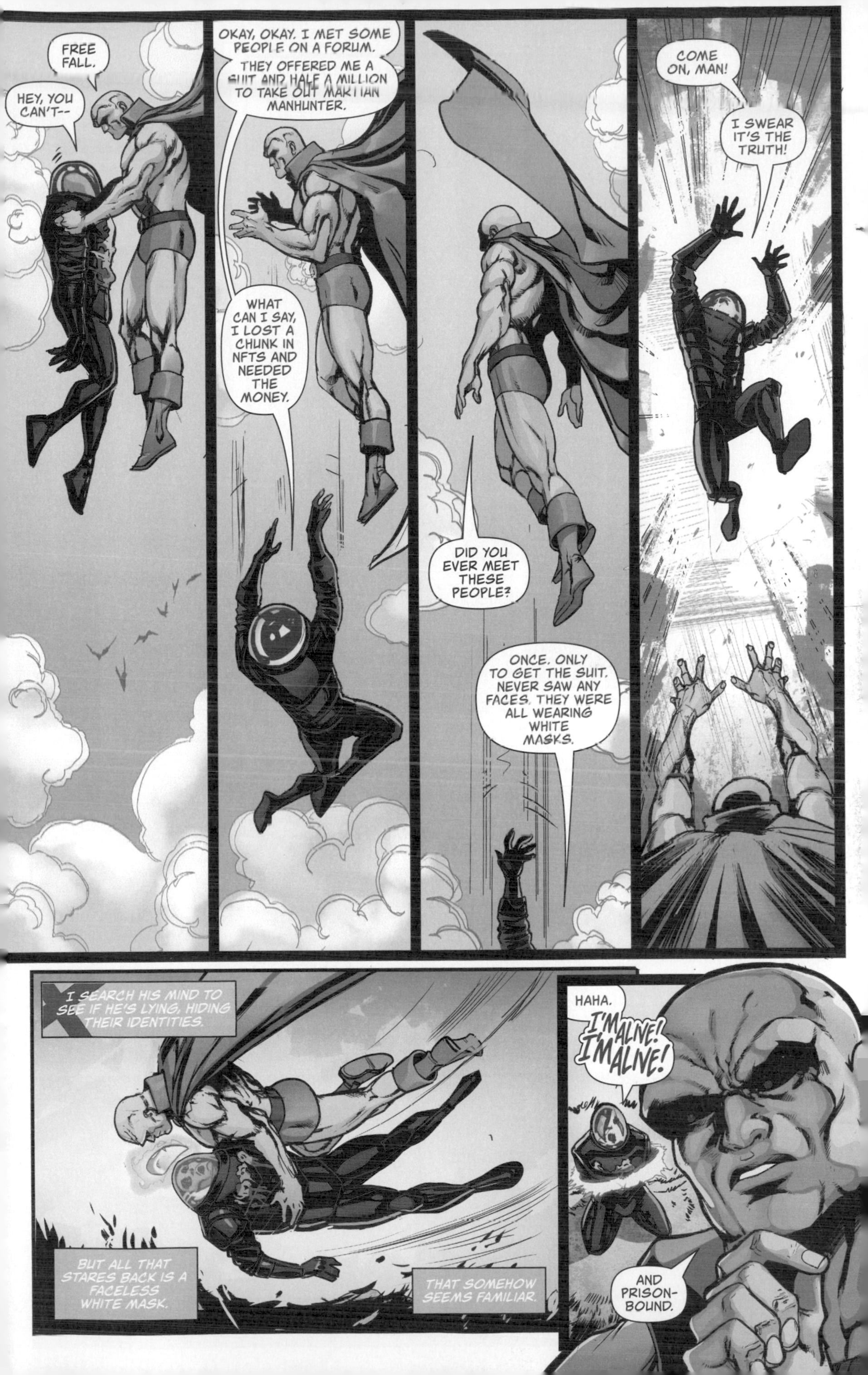
FREE FALL.
HEY, YOU CAN'T--
OKAY, OKAY. I MET SOME PEOPLE ON A FORUM.
THEY OFFERED ME A SUIT AND HALF A MILLION TO TAKE OUT MARTIAN MANHUNTER.
WHAT CAN I SAY, I LOST A CHUNK IN NFTS AND NEEDED THE MONEY.
DID YOU EVER MEET THESE PEOPLE?
ONCE. ONLY TO GET THE SUIT. NEVER SAW ANY FACES. THEY WERE ALL WEARING WHITE MASKS.
COME ON, MAN!
I SWEAR IT'S THE TRUTH!
I SEARCH HIS MIND TO SEE IF HE'S LYING, HIDING THEIR IDENTITIES.
BUT ALL THAT STARES BACK IS A FACELESS WHITE MASK.
THAT SOMEHOW SEEMS FAMILIAR.
HAHA.
I'M ALIVE! I'M ALIVE!
AND PRISON-BOUND.

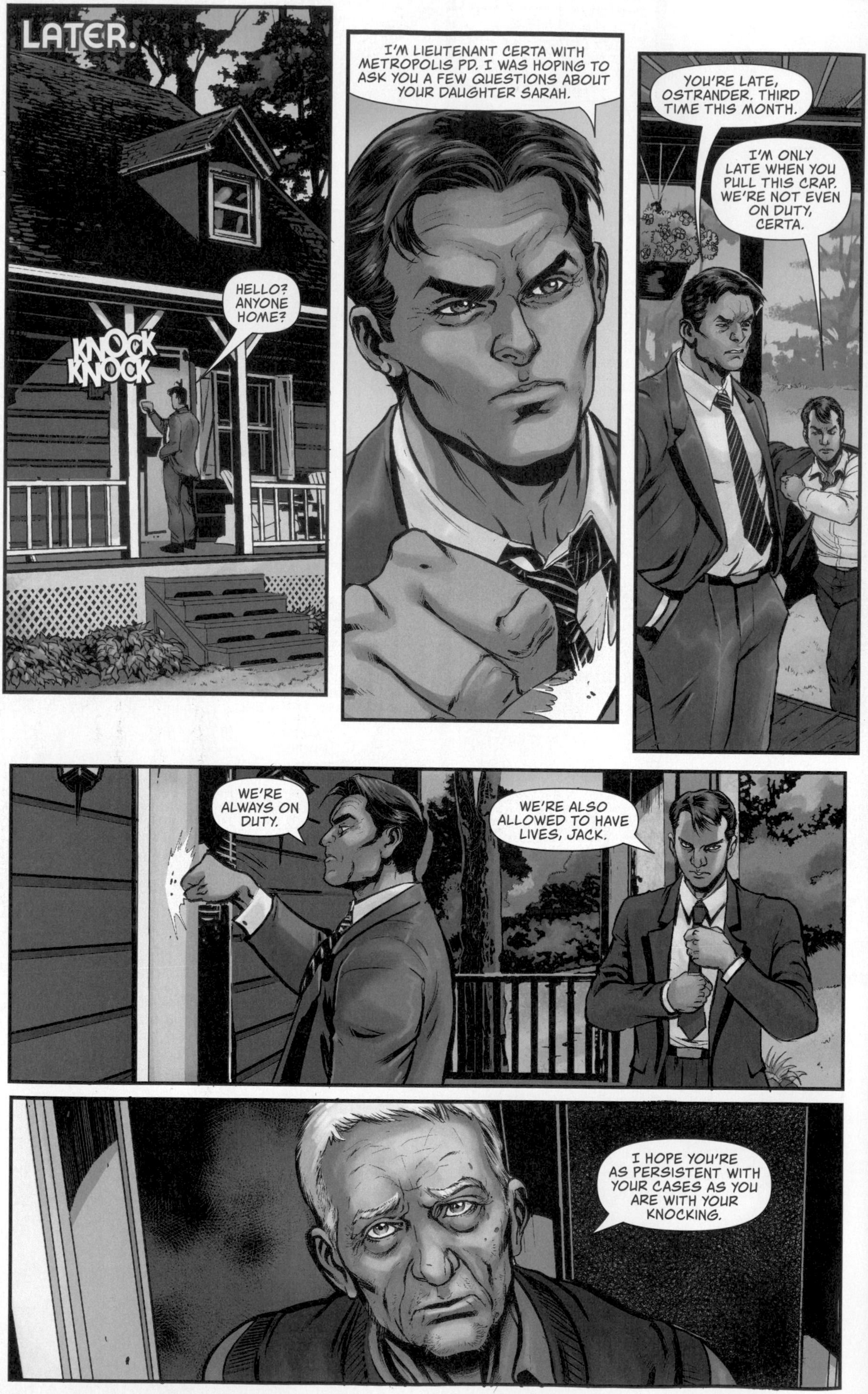
LATER.
KNOCK KNOCK
HELLO? ANYONE HOME?
I'M LIEUTENANT CERTA WITH METROPOLIS PD. I WAS HOPING TO ASK YOU A FEW QUESTIONS ABOUT YOUR DAUGHTER SARAH.
YOU'RE LATE, OSTRANDER. THIRD TIME THIS MONTH.
I'M ONLY LATE WHEN YOU PULL THIS CRAP. WE'RE NOT EVEN ON DUTY, CERTA.
WE'RE ALWAYS ON DUTY.
WE'RE ALSO ALLOWED TO HAVE LIVES, JACK.
I HOPE YOU'RE AS PERSISTENT WITH YOUR CASES AS YOU ARE WITH YOUR KNOCKING.

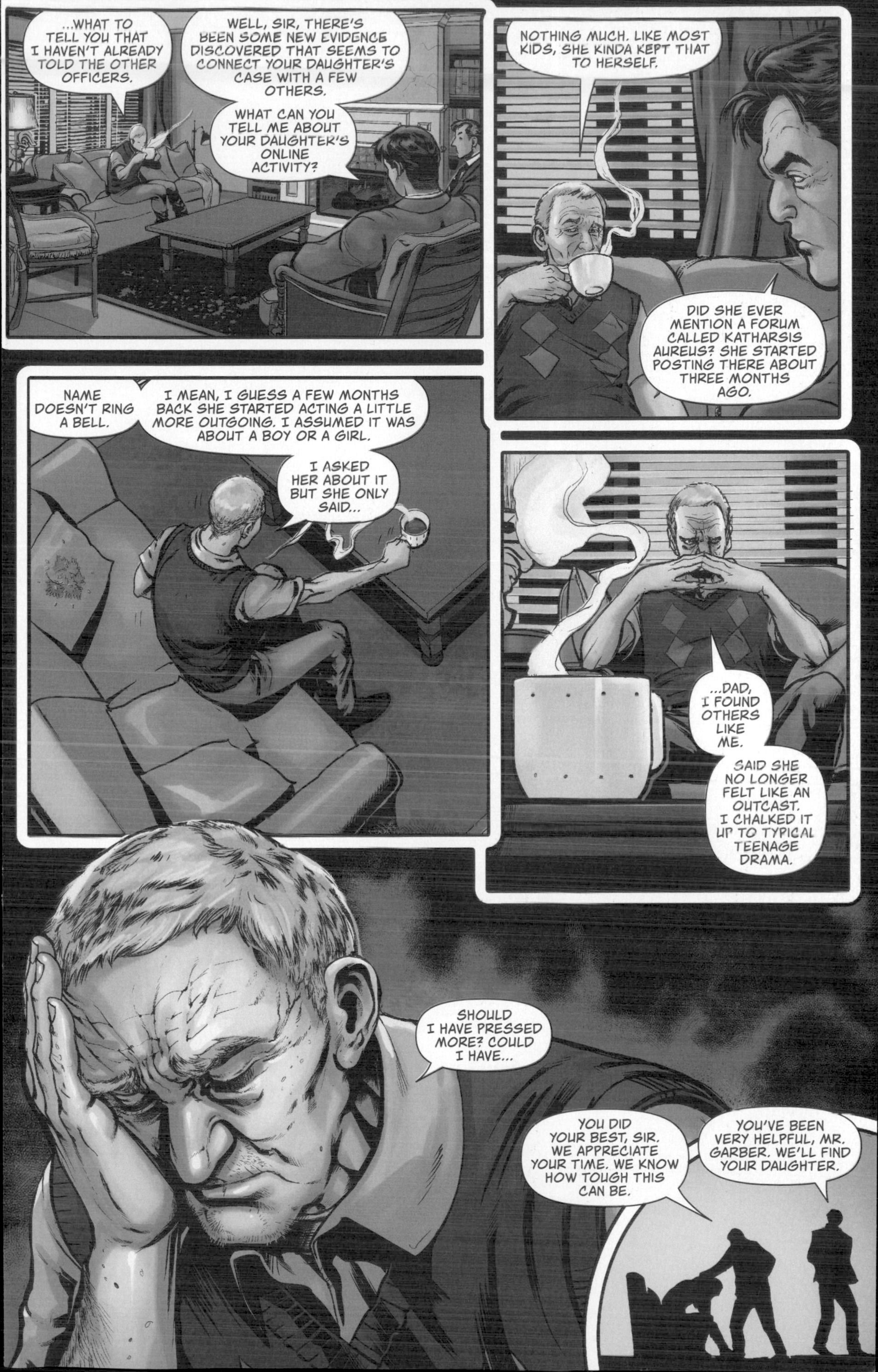
...WHAT TO TELL YOU THAT I HAVEN'T ALREADY TOLD THE OTHER OFFICERS.
WELL, SIR, THERE'S BEEN SOME NEW EVIDENCE DISCOVERED THAT SEEMS TO CONNECT YOUR DAUGHTER'S CASE WITH A FEW OTHERS.
WHAT CAN YOU TELL ME ABOUT YOUR DAUGHTER'S ONLINE ACTIVITY?
NOTHING MUCH. LIKE MOST KIDS, SHE KINDA KEPT THAT TO HERSELF.
DID SHE EVER MENTION A FORUM CALLED KATHARSIS AUREUS? SHE STARTED POSTING THERE ABOUT THREE MONTHS AGO.
NAME DOESN'T RING A BELL.
I MEAN, I GUESS A FEW MONTHS BACK SHE STARTED ACTING A LITTLE MORE OUTGOING. I ASSUMED IT WAS ABOUT A BOY OR A GIRL.
I ASKED HER ABOUT IT BUT SHE ONLY SAID...
...DAD, I FOUND OTHERS LIKE ME.
SAID SHE NO LONGER FELT LIKE AN OUTCAST. I CHALKED IT UP TO TYPICAL TEENAGE DRAMA.
SHOULD I HAVE PRESSED MORE? COULD I HAVE...
YOU DID YOUR BEST, SIR. WE APPRECIATE YOUR TIME. WE KNOW HOW TOUGH THIS CAN BE.
YOU'VE BEEN VERY HELPFUL, MR. GARBER. WE'LL FIND YOUR DAUGHTER.

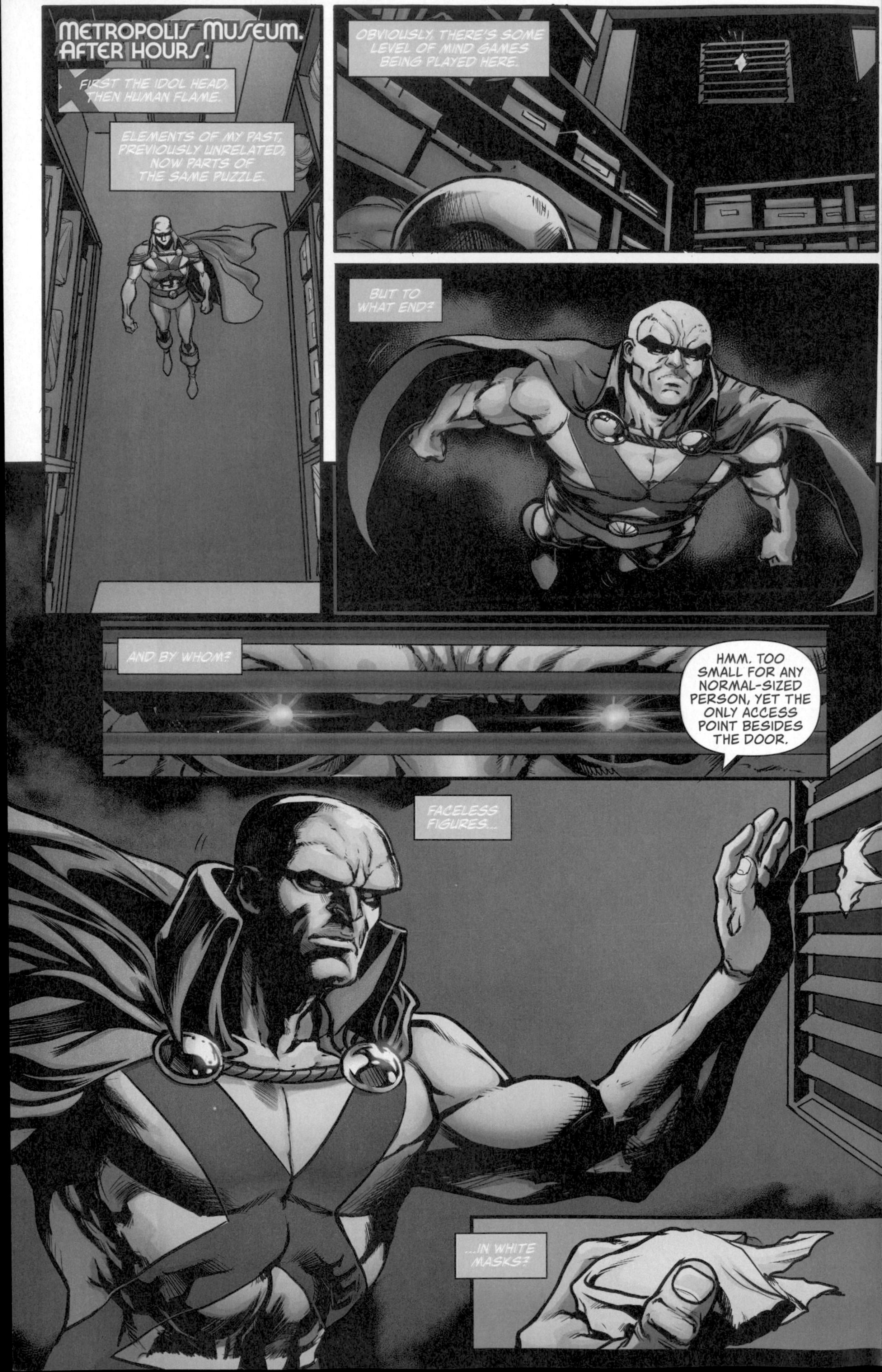
METROPOLIS MUSEUM. AFTER HOURS.
FIRST THE IDOL HEAD, THEN HUMAN FLAME.
ELEMENTS OF MY PAST, PREVIOUSLY UNRELATED, NOW PARTS OF THE SAME PUZZLE.
OBVIOUSLY, THERE'S SOME LEVEL OF MIND GAMES BEING PLAYED HERE.
BUT TO WHAT END?
AND BY WHOM?
HMM. TOO SMALL FOR ANY NORMAL-SIZED PERSON, YET THE ONLY ACCESS POINT BESIDES THE DOOR.
FACELESS FIGURES...
...IN WHITE MASKS?

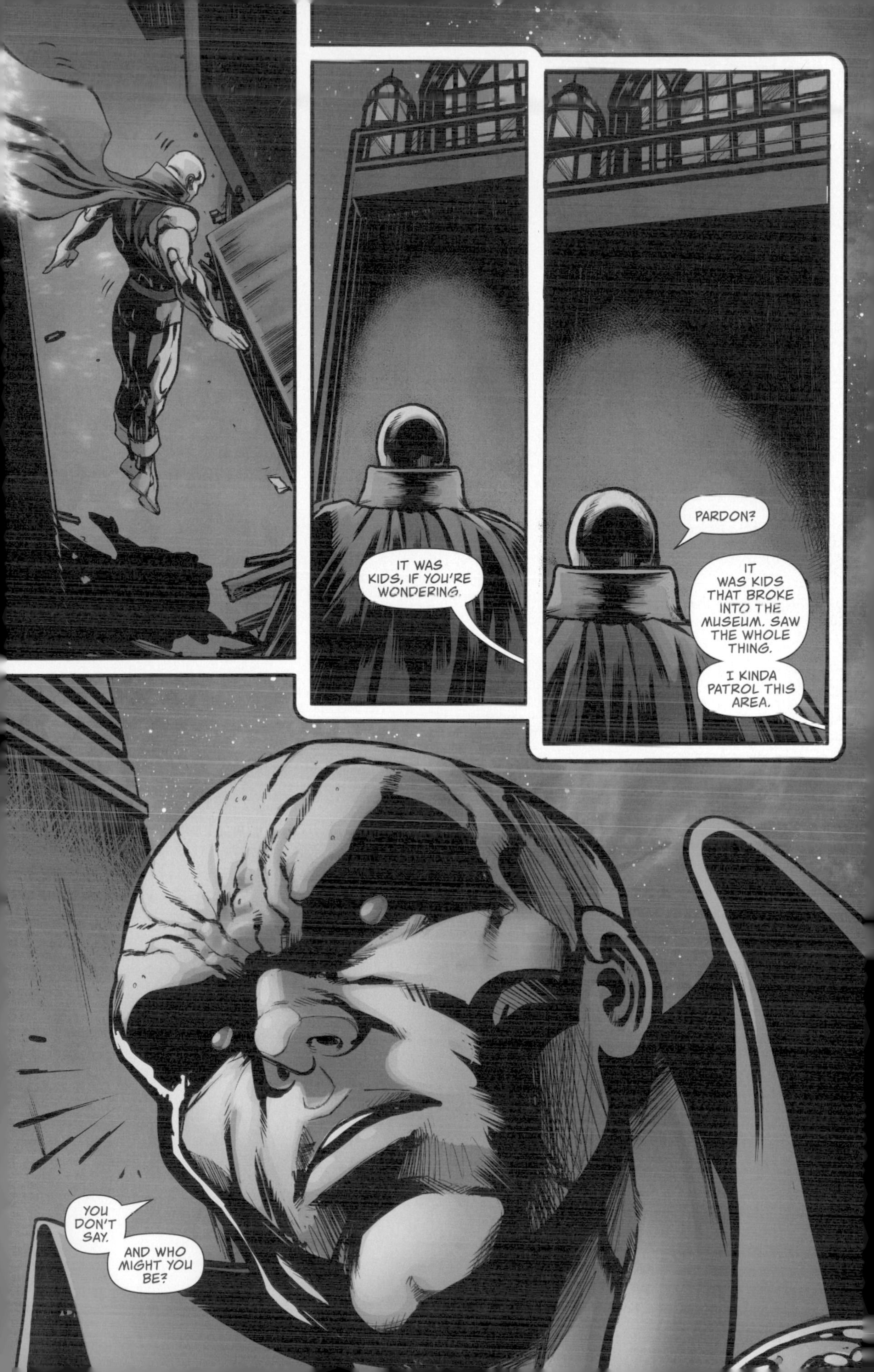
IT WAS KIDS, IF YOU'RE WONDERING.
PARDON?
IT WAS KIDS THAT BROKE INTO THE MUSEUM. SAW THE WHOLE THING.
I KINDA PATROL THIS AREA.
YOU DON'T SAY.
AND WHO MIGHT YOU BE?

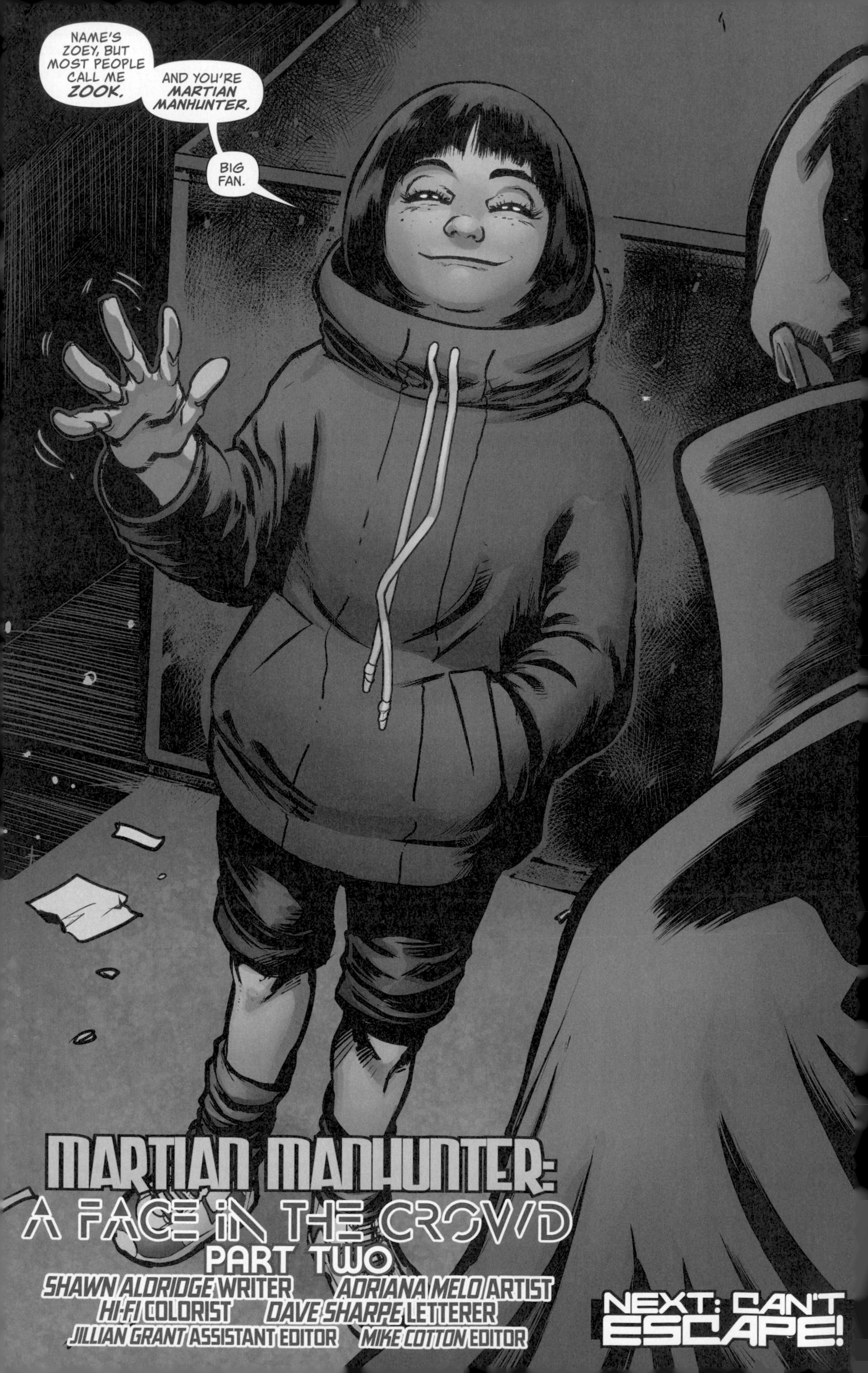
NAME'S ZOEY, BUT MOST PEOPLE CALL ME ZOOK.
AND YOU'RE MARTIAN MANHUNTER.
BIG FAN.
MARTIAN MANHUNTER:
A FACE IN THE CROWD
PART TWO
SHAWN ALDRIDGE WRITER ADRIANA MELO ARTIST
HI-FI COLORIST DAVE SHARPE LETTERER
JILLIAN GRANT ASSISTANT EDITOR MIKE COTTON EDITOR
NEXT: CAN'T ESCAPE!

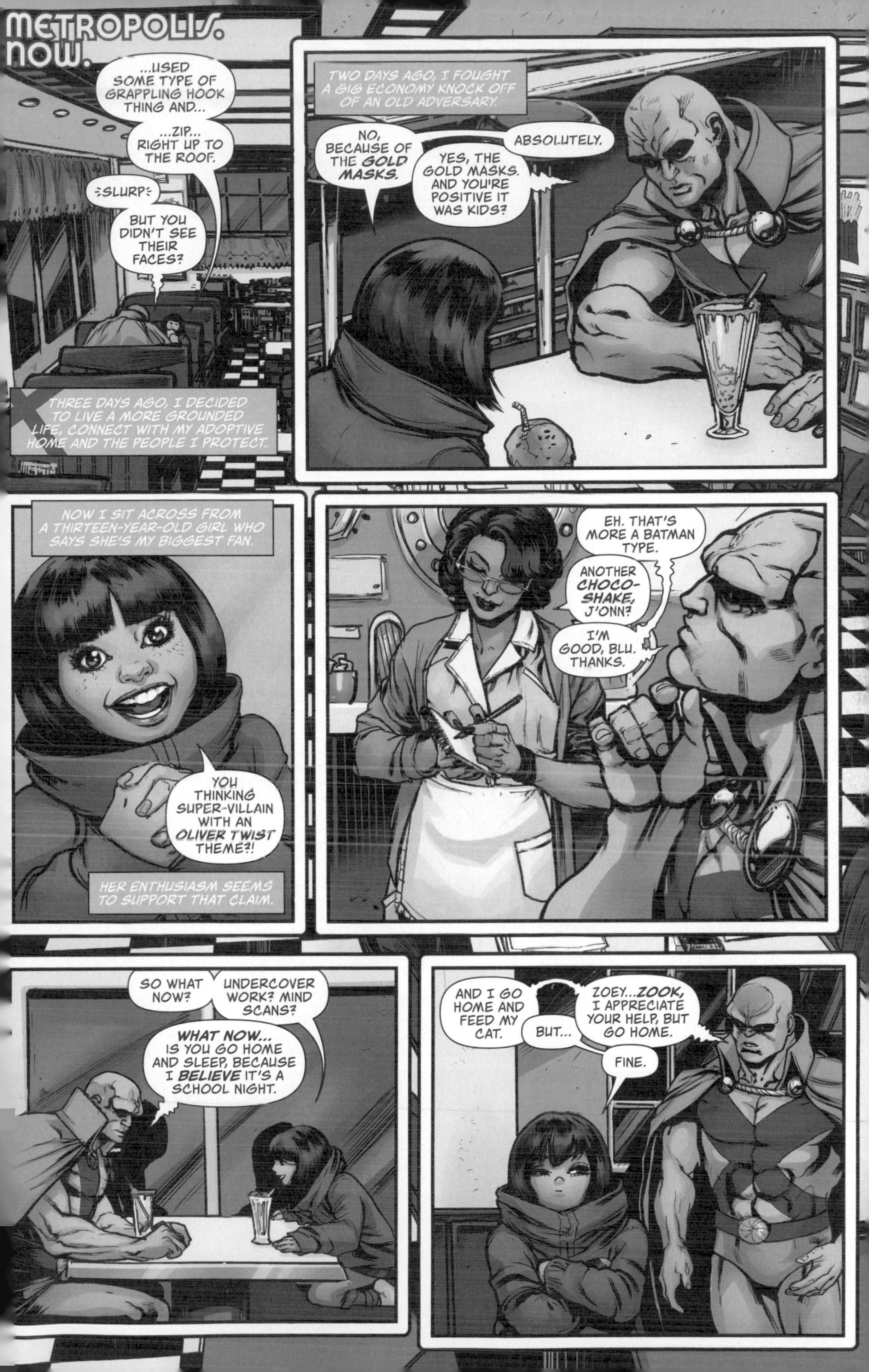
METROPOLIS. NOW.
...USED SOME TYPE OF GRAPPLING HOOK THING AND...
...ZIP... RIGHT UP TO THE ROOF.
SLURP
BUT YOU DIDN'T SEE THEIR FACES?
THREE DAYS AGO, I DECIDED TO LIVE A MORE GROUNDED LIFE, CONNECT WITH MY ADOPTIVE HOME AND THE PEOPLE I PROTECT.
TWO DAYS AGO, I FOUGHT A GIG ECONOMY KNOCK OFF OF AN OLD ADVERSARY.
NO, BECAUSE OF THE GOLD MASKS.
ABSOLUTELY.
YES, THE GOLD MASKS. AND YOU'RE POSITIVE IT WAS KIDS?
NOW I SIT ACROSS FROM A THIRTEEN-YEAR-OLD GIRL WHO SAYS SHE'S MY BIGGEST FAN.
YOU THINKING SUPER-VILLAIN WITH AN OLIVER TWIST THEME?!
HER ENTHUSIASM SEEMS TO SUPPORT THAT CLAIM.
EH. THAT'S MORE A BATMAN TYPE.
ANOTHER CHOCO-SHAKE, J'ONN?
I'M GOOD, BLU. THANKS.
SO WHAT NOW?
UNDERCOVER WORK? MIND SCANS?
WHAT NOW... IS YOU GO HOME AND SLEEP, BECAUSE I BELIEVE IT'S A SCHOOL NIGHT.
ZOEY...ZOOK, I APPRECIATE YOUR HELP, BUT GO HOME.
BUT...
FINE.
AND I GO HOME AND FEED MY CAT.

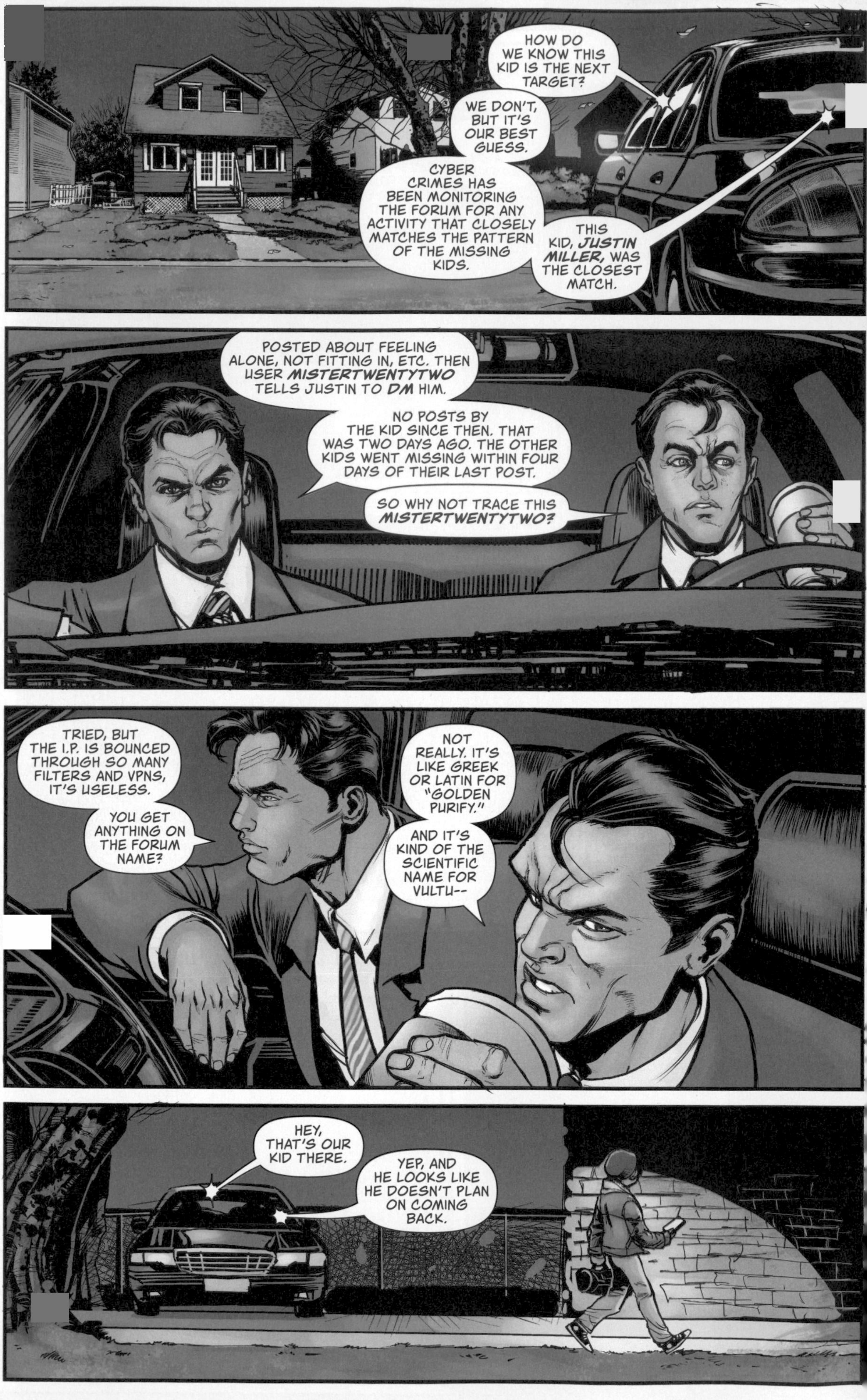
HOW DO WE KNOW THIS KID IS THE NEXT TARGET?
WE DON'T, BUT IT'S OUR BEST GUESS.
CYBER CRIMES HAS BEEN MONITORING THE FORUM FOR ANY ACTIVITY THAT CLOSELY MATCHES THE PATTERN OF THE MISSING KIDS.
THIS KID, JUSTIN MILLER, WAS THE CLOSEST MATCH.
POSTED ABOUT FEELING ALONE, NOT FITTING IN, ETC. THEN USER MISTERTWENTYTWO TELLS JUSTIN TO DM HIM.
NO POSTS BY THE KID SINCE THEN. THAT WAS TWO DAYS AGO. THE OTHER KIDS WENT MISSING WITHIN FOUR DAYS OF THEIR LAST POST.
SO WHY NOT TRACE THIS MISTERTWENTYTWO?
TRIED, BUT THE I.P. IS BOUNCED THROUGH SO MANY FILTERS AND VPNS, IT'S USELESS.
YOU GET ANYTHING ON THE FORUM NAME?
NOT REALLY. IT'S LIKE GREEK OR LATIN FOR "GOLDEN PURIFY."
AND IT'S KIND OF THE SCIENTIFIC NAME FOR VULTU--
HEY, THAT'S OUR KID THERE.
YEP, AND HE LOOKS LIKE HE DOESN'T PLAN ON COMING BACK.

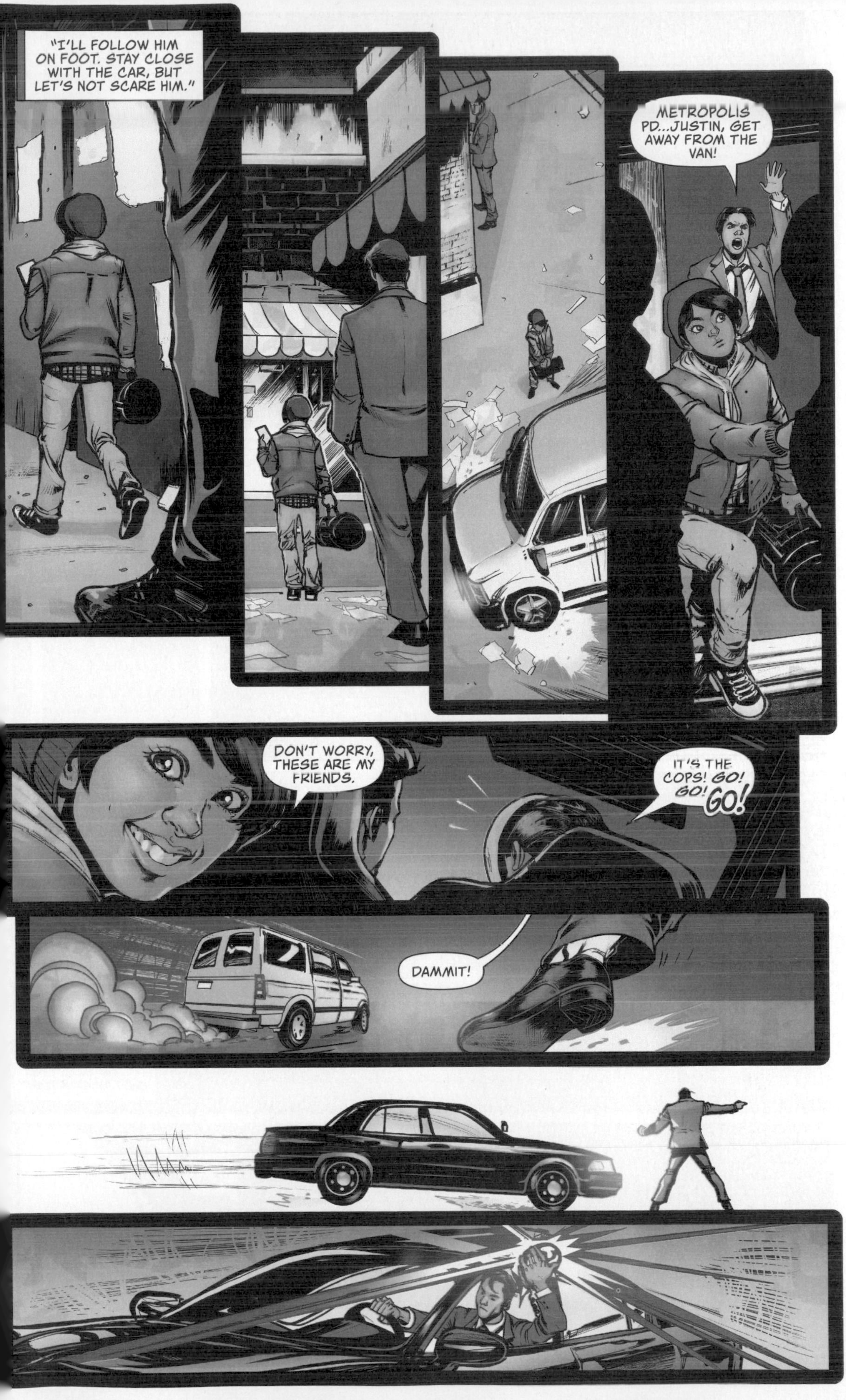
"I'LL FOLLOW HIM ON FOOT. STAY CLOSE WITH THE CAR, BUT LET'S NOT SCARE HIM."
METROPOLIS PD...JUSTIN, GET AWAY FROM THE VAN!
DON'T WORRY, THESE ARE MY FRIENDS.
IT'S THE COPS! GO! GO! GO!
DAMMIT!

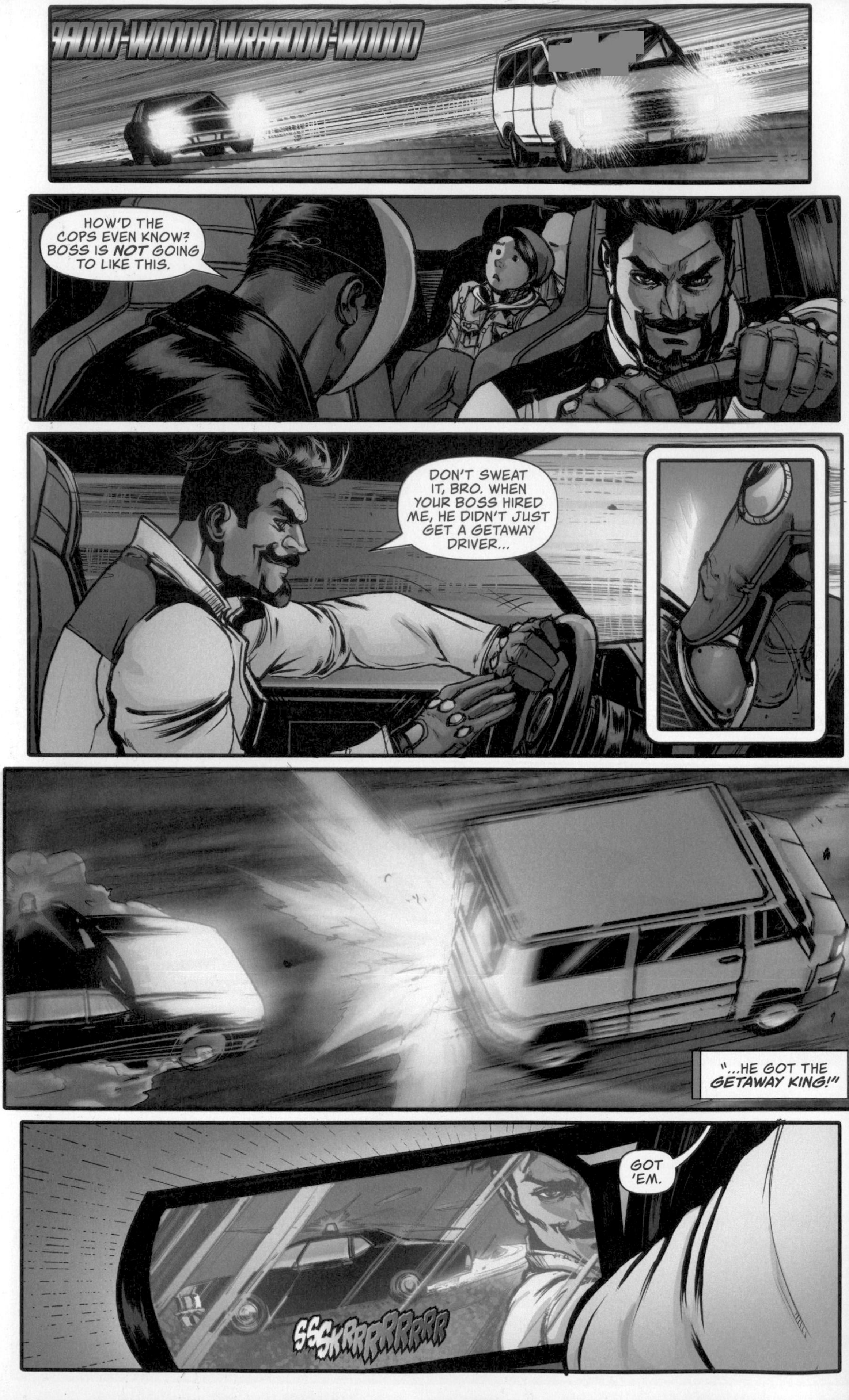
AOOO-WOOOO WRAAOOO-WOOOO
HOW'D THE COPS EVEN KNOW? BOSS IS **NOT** GOING TO LIKE THIS.
DON'T SWEAT IT, BRO. WHEN YOUR BOSS HIRED ME, HE DIDN'T JUST GET A GETAWAY DRIVER...
"...HE GOT THE ***GETAWAY KING!***"
GOT 'EM.
SSSKRRRRRRRR

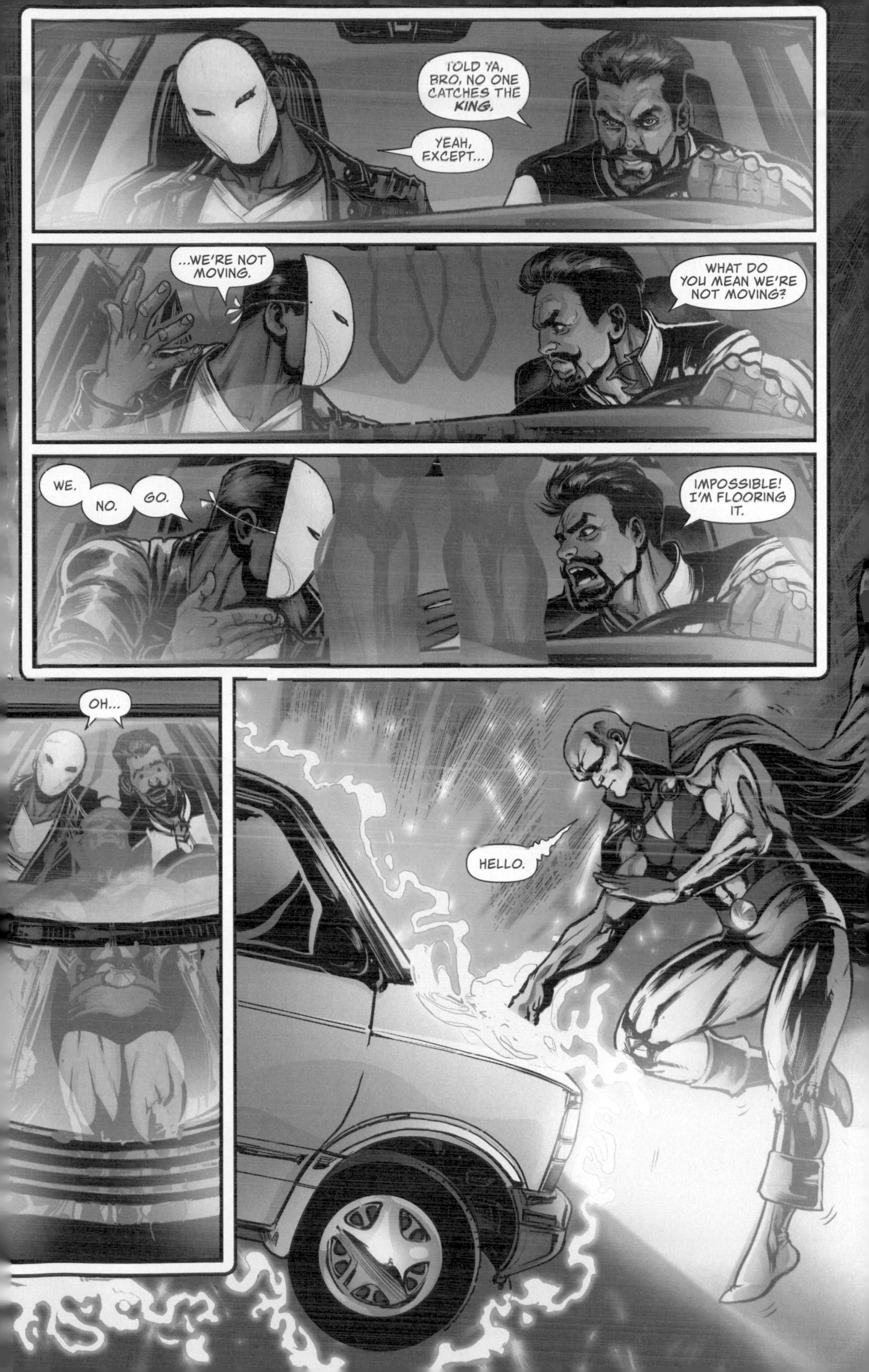
TOLD YA, BRO, NO ONE CATCHES THE KING.
YEAH, EXCEPT...
...WE'RE NOT MOVING.
WHAT DO YOU MEAN WE'RE NOT MOVING?
WE.
NO.
GO.
IMPOSSIBLE! I'M FLOORING IT.
OH...
HELLO.

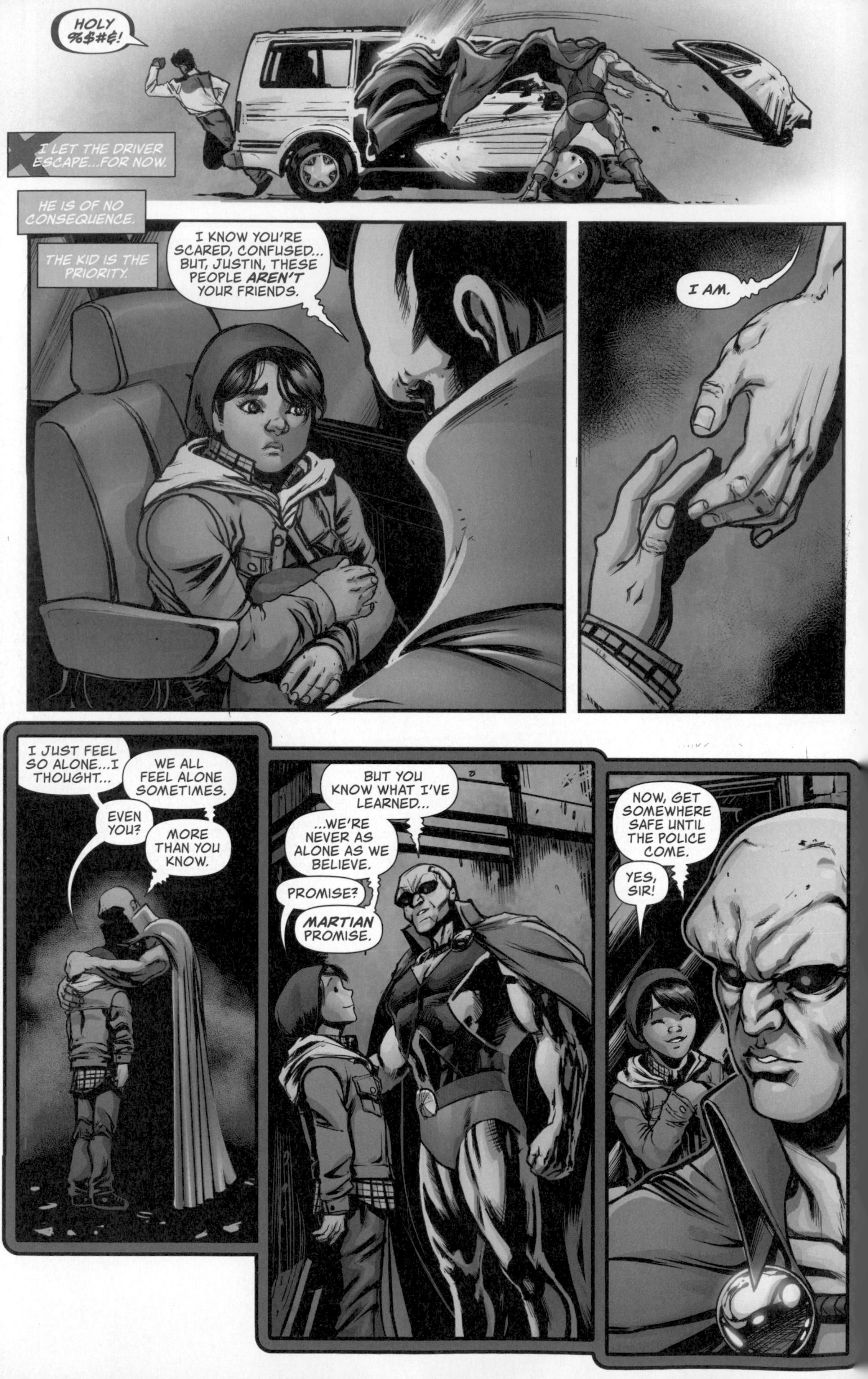
HOLY %$#&!
I LET THE DRIVER ESCAPE...FOR NOW.
HE IS OF NO CONSEQUENCE.
THE KID IS THE PRIORITY.
I KNOW YOU'RE SCARED, CONFUSED... BUT, JUSTIN, THESE PEOPLE AREN'T YOUR FRIENDS.
I AM.
I JUST FEEL SO ALONE...I THOUGHT...
WE ALL FEEL ALONE SOMETIMES.
EVEN YOU?
MORE THAN YOU KNOW.
BUT YOU KNOW WHAT I'VE LEARNED...
...WE'RE NEVER AS ALONE AS WE BELIEVE.
PROMISE?
MARTIAN PROMISE.
NOW, GET SOMEWHERE SAFE UNTIL THE POLICE COME.
YES, SIR!

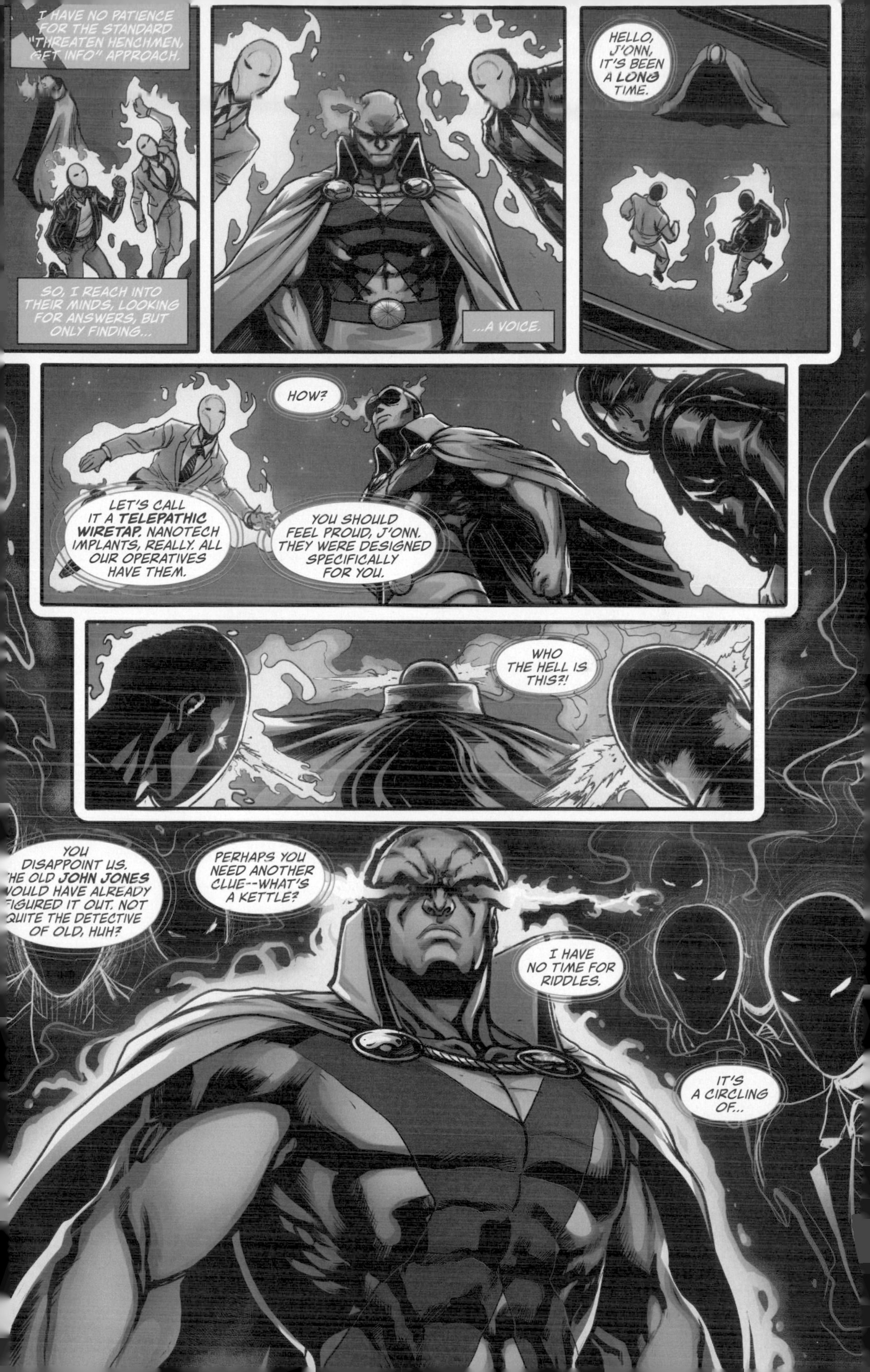
I HAVE NO PATIENCE FOR THE STANDARD "THREATEN HENCHMEN, GET INFO" APPROACH.
SO, I REACH INTO THEIR MINDS, LOOKING FOR ANSWERS, BUT ONLY FINDING...
...A VOICE.
HELLO, J'ONN, IT'S BEEN A LONG TIME.
HOW?
LET'S CALL IT A TELEPATHIC WIRETAP. NANOTECH IMPLANTS, REALLY. ALL OUR OPERATIVES HAVE THEM.
YOU SHOULD FEEL PROUD, J'ONN. THEY WERE DESIGNED SPECIFICALLY FOR YOU.
WHO THE HELL IS THIS?!
YOU DISAPPOINT US. THE OLD JOHN JONES WOULD HAVE ALREADY FIGURED IT OUT. NOT QUITE THE DETECTIVE OF OLD, HUH?
PERHAPS YOU NEED ANOTHER CLUE--WHAT'S A KETTLE?
I HAVE NO TIME FOR RIDDLES.
IT'S A CIRCLING OF...

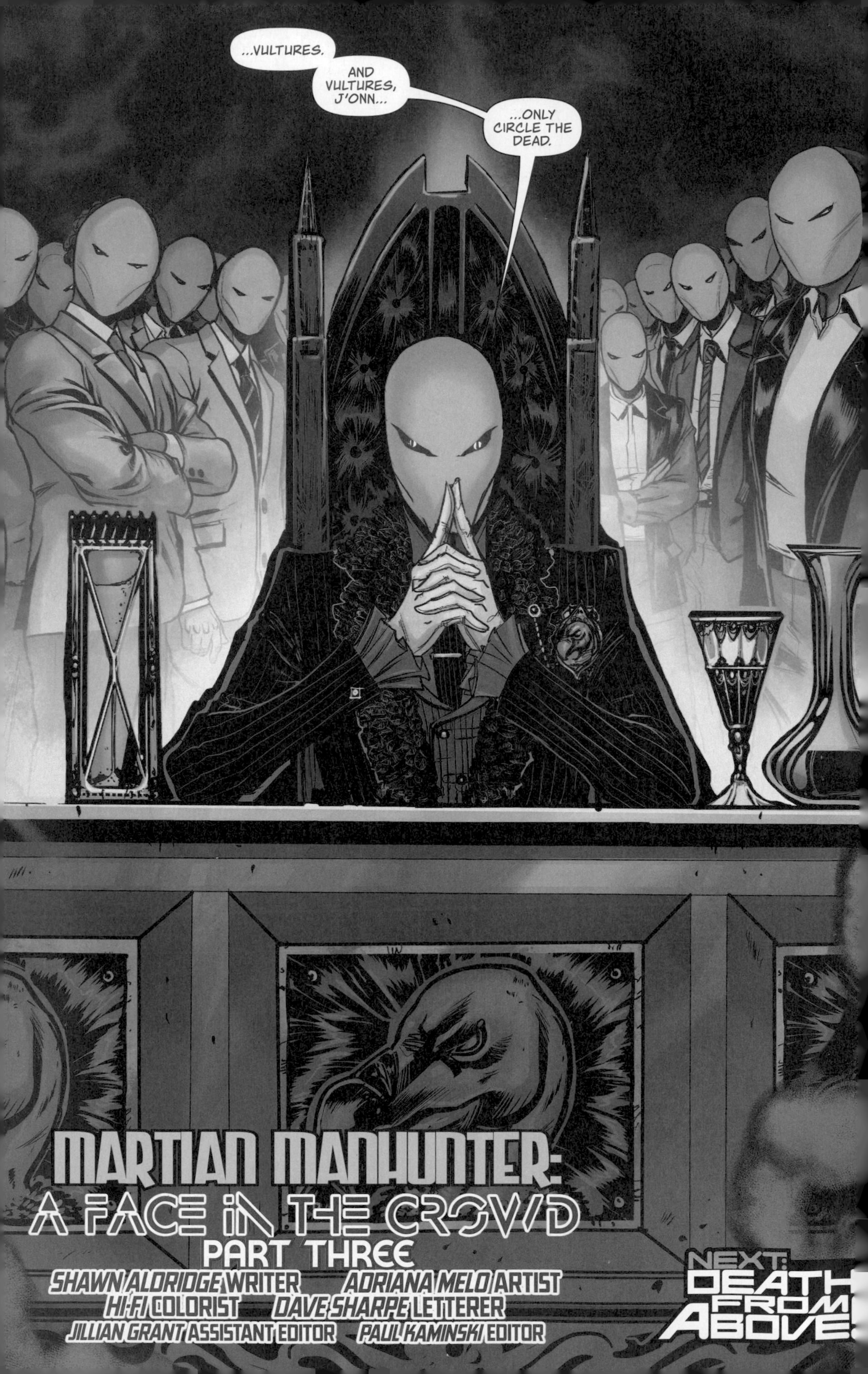
...VULTURES.
AND VULTURES, J'ONN...
...ONLY CIRCLE THE DEAD.
MARTIAN MANHUNTER:
A FACE IN THE CROWD
PART THREE
SHAWN ALDRIDGE WRITER
ADRIANA MELO ARTIST
HI-FI COLORIST
DAVE SHARPE LETTERER
JILLIAN GRANT ASSISTANT EDITOR
PAUL KAMINSKI EDITOR
NEXT: DEATH FROM ABOVE!

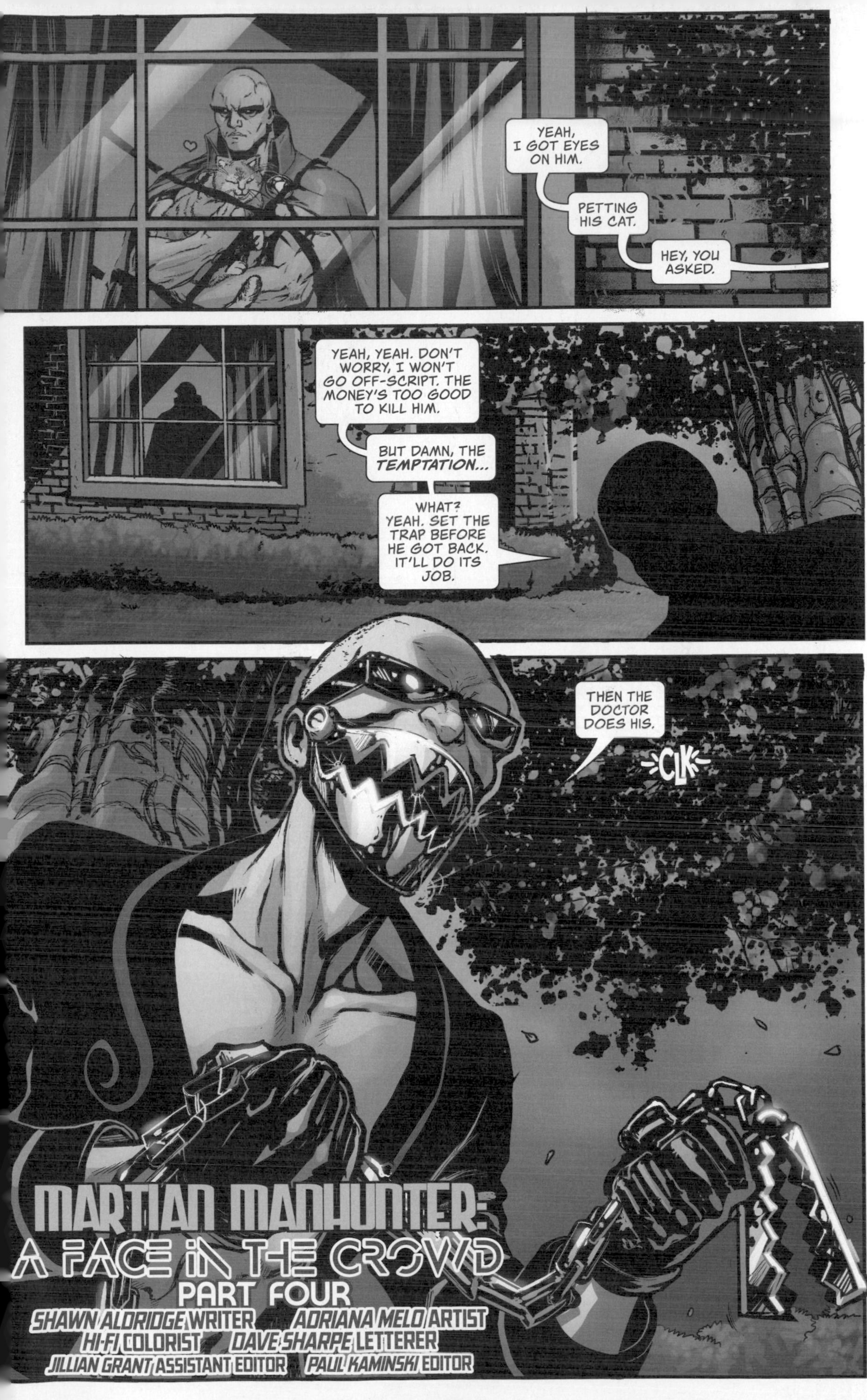
YEAH, I GOT EYES ON HIM.
PETTING HIS CAT.
HEY, YOU ASKED.
YEAH, YEAH. DON'T WORRY, I WON'T GO OFF-SCRIPT. THE MONEY'S TOO GOOD TO KILL HIM.
BUT DAMN, THE TEMPTATION...
WHAT? YEAH. SET THE TRAP BEFORE HE GOT BACK. IT'LL DO ITS JOB.
THEN THE DOCTOR DOES HIS.
CLK
MARTIAN MANHUNTER: A FACE IN THE CROWD
PART FOUR
SHAWN ALDRIDGE WRITER ADRIANA MELO ARTIST
HI-FI COLORIST DAVE SHARPE LETTERER
JILLIAN GRANT ASSISTANT EDITOR PAUL KAMINSKI EDITOR

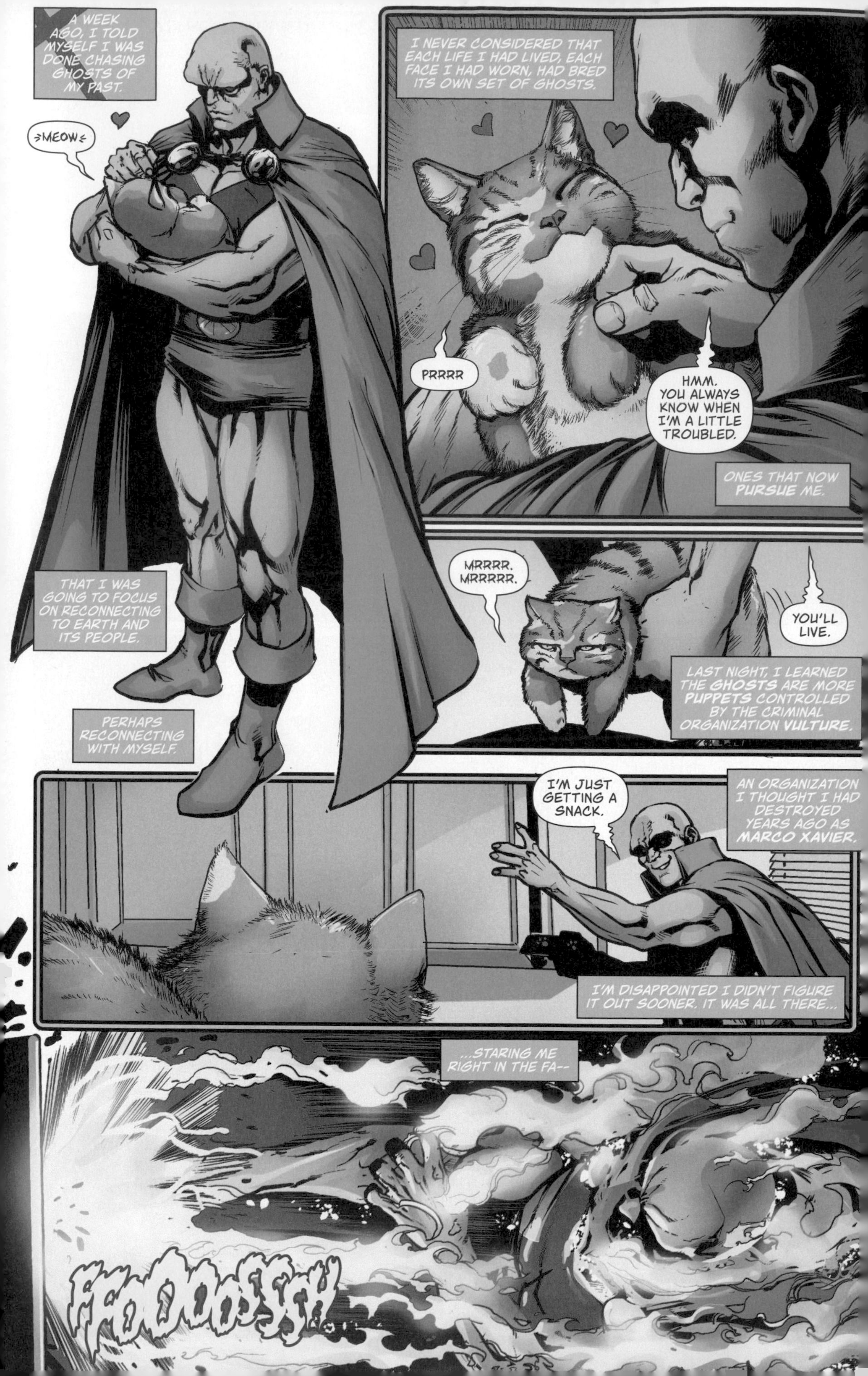
A WEEK AGO, I TOLD MYSELF I WAS DONE CHASING GHOSTS OF MY PAST.
MEOW
THAT I WAS GOING TO FOCUS ON RECONNECTING TO EARTH AND ITS PEOPLE.
PERHAPS RECONNECTING WITH MYSELF.
I NEVER CONSIDERED THAT EACH LIFE I HAD LIVED, EACH FACE I HAD WORN, HAD BRED ITS OWN SET OF GHOSTS.
PRRRR
HMM. YOU ALWAYS KNOW WHEN I'M A LITTLE TROUBLED.
ONES THAT NOW PURSUE ME.
MRRRR. MRRRRR.
YOU'LL LIVE.
LAST NIGHT, I LEARNED THE GHOSTS ARE MORE PUPPETS CONTROLLED BY THE CRIMINAL ORGANIZATION VULTURE.
I'M JUST GETTING A SNACK.
AN ORGANIZATION I THOUGHT I HAD DESTROYED YEARS AGO AS MARCO XAVIER.
I'M DISAPPOINTED I DIDN'T FIGURE IT OUT SOONER. IT WAS ALL THERE...
...STARING ME RIGHT IN THE FA--
FOOOOSSH

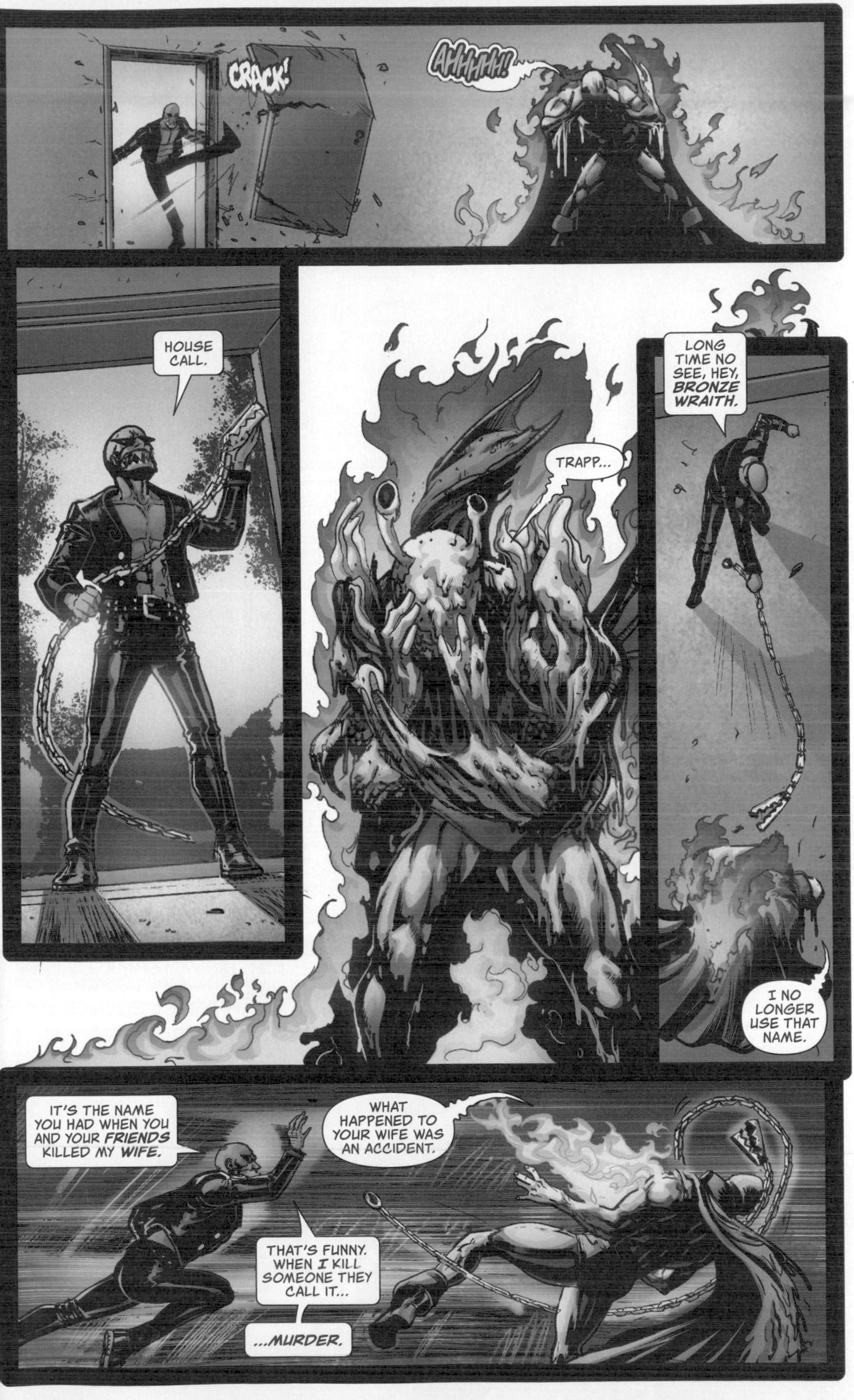
CRACK!
AHHHHH!
HOUSE CALL.
TRAPP...
LONG TIME NO SEE, HEY, BRONZE WRAITH.
I NO LONGER USE THAT NAME.
IT'S THE NAME YOU HAD WHEN YOU AND YOUR FRIENDS KILLED MY WIFE.
WHAT HAPPENED TO YOUR WIFE WAS AN ACCIDENT.
THAT'S FUNNY. WHEN I KILL SOMEONE THEY CALL IT...
...MURDER.

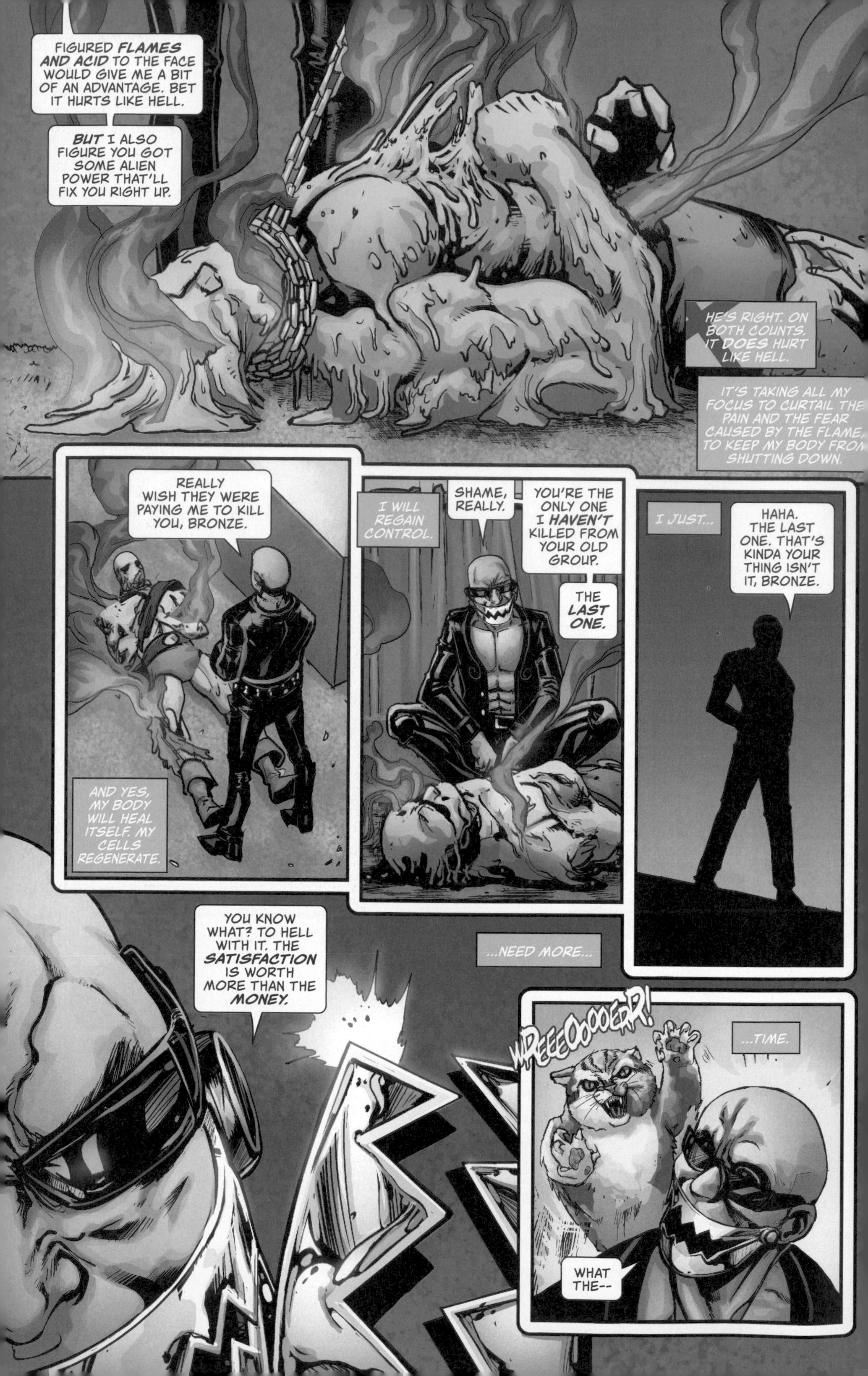

FIGURED FLAMES AND ACID TO THE FACE WOULD GIVE ME A BIT OF AN ADVANTAGE. BET IT HURTS LIKE HELL.
BUT I ALSO FIGURE YOU GOT SOME ALIEN POWER THAT'LL FIX YOU RIGHT UP.
HE'S RIGHT. ON BOTH COUNTS. IT DOES HURT LIKE HELL.
IT'S TAKING ALL MY FOCUS TO CURTAIL THE PAIN AND THE FEAR CAUSED BY THE FLAME, TO KEEP MY BODY FROM SHUTTING DOWN.
REALLY WISH THEY WERE PAYING ME TO KILL YOU, BRONZE.
AND YES, MY BODY WILL HEAL ITSELF. MY CELLS REGENERATE.
I WILL REGAIN CONTROL.
SHAME, REALLY.
YOU'RE THE ONLY ONE I HAVEN'T KILLED FROM YOUR OLD GROUP.
THE LAST ONE.
I JUST...
HAHA. THE LAST ONE. THAT'S KINDA YOUR THING ISN'T IT, BRONZE.
YOU KNOW WHAT? TO HELL WITH IT. THE SATISFACTION IS WORTH MORE THAN THE MONEY.
...NEED MORE...
WREEEOOOOERR!
...TIME.
WHAT THE--

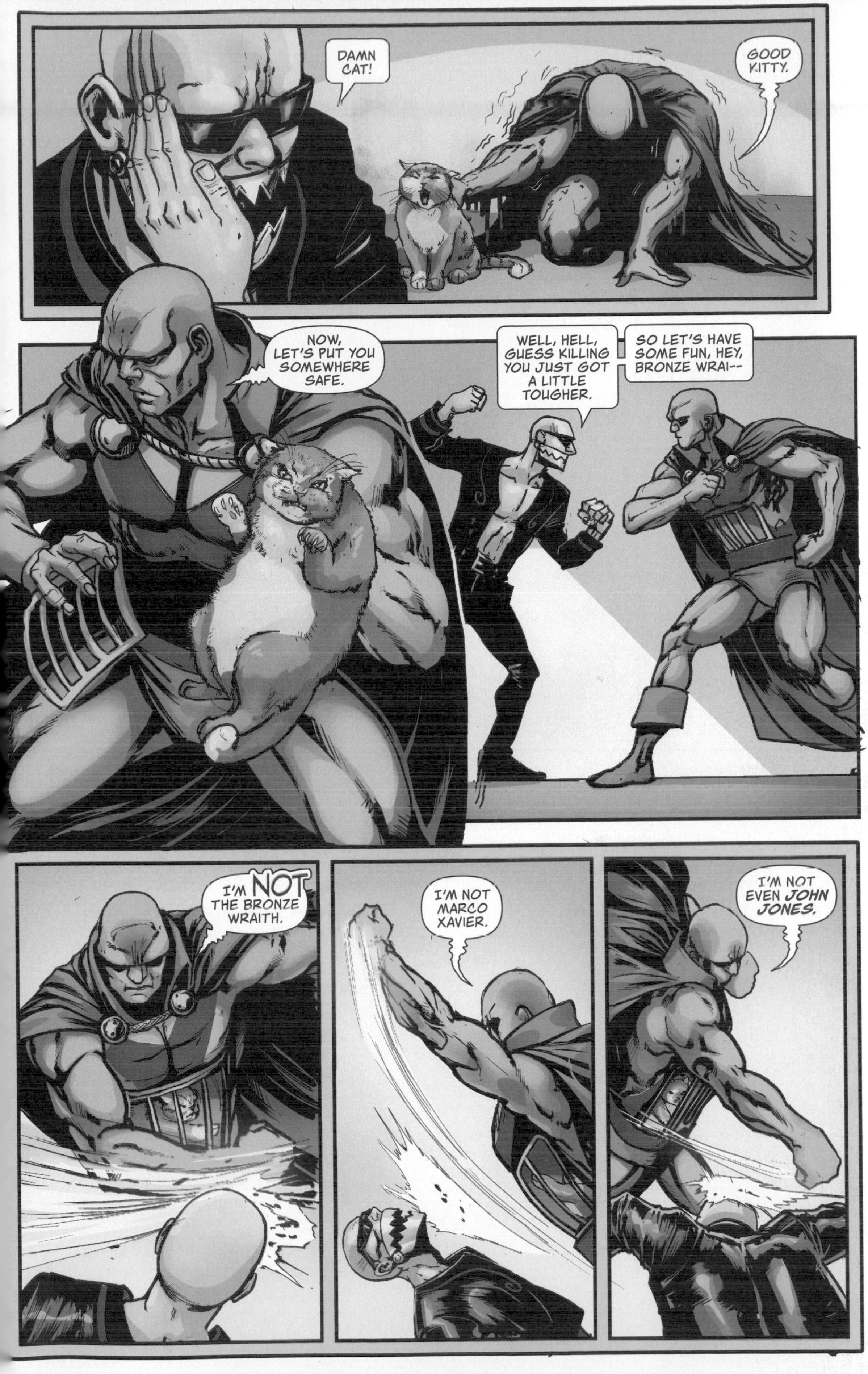
DAMN CAT!
GOOD KITTY.
NOW, LET'S PUT YOU SOMEWHERE SAFE.
WELL, HELL, GUESS KILLING YOU JUST GOT A LITTLE TOUGHER.
SO LET'S HAVE SOME FUN, HEY, BRONZE WRAI--
I'M NOT THE BRONZE WRAITH.
I'M NOT MARCO XAVIER.
I'M NOT EVEN JOHN JONES.

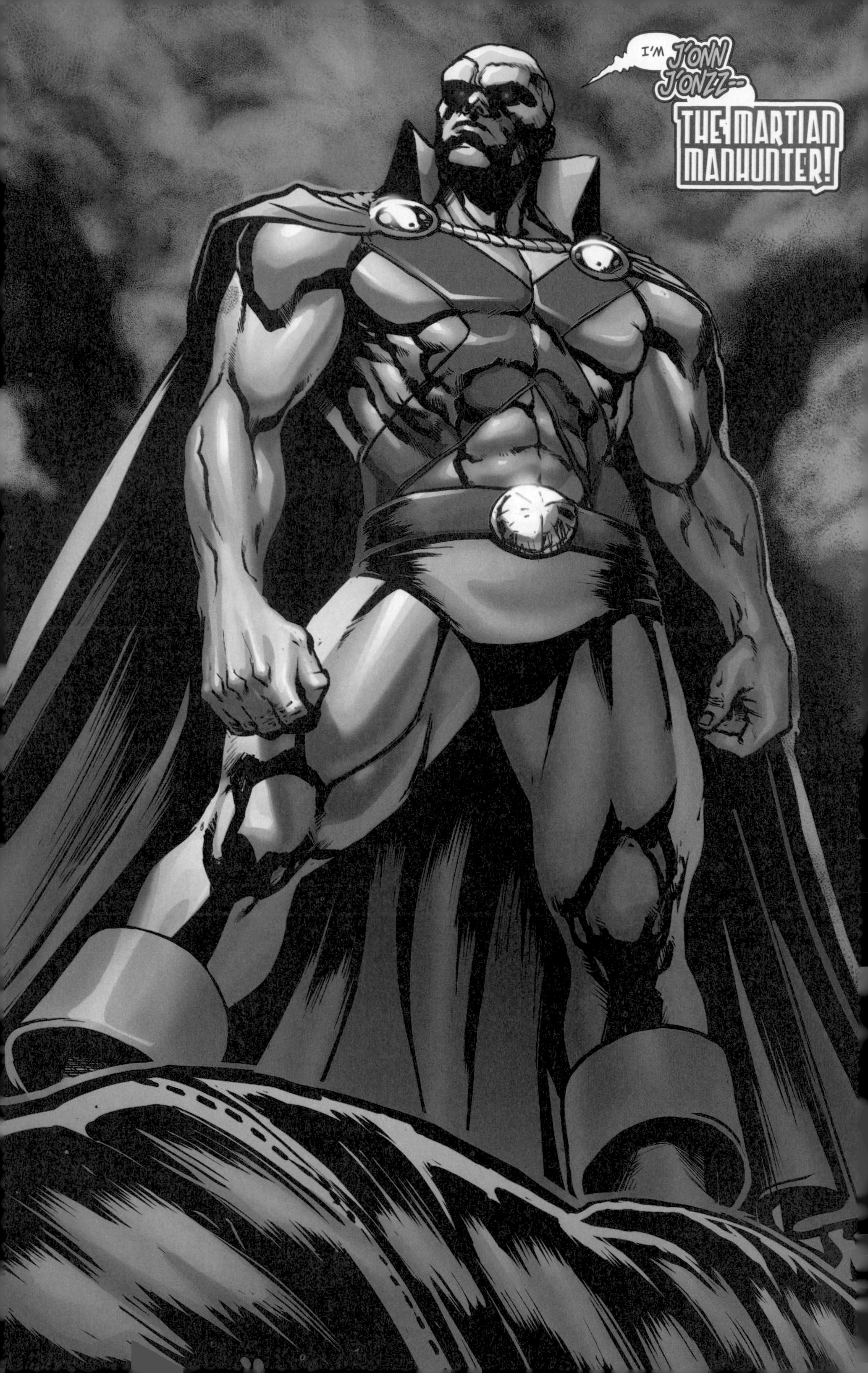
I'M J'ONN J'ONZZ--
THE MARTIAN MANHUNTER!

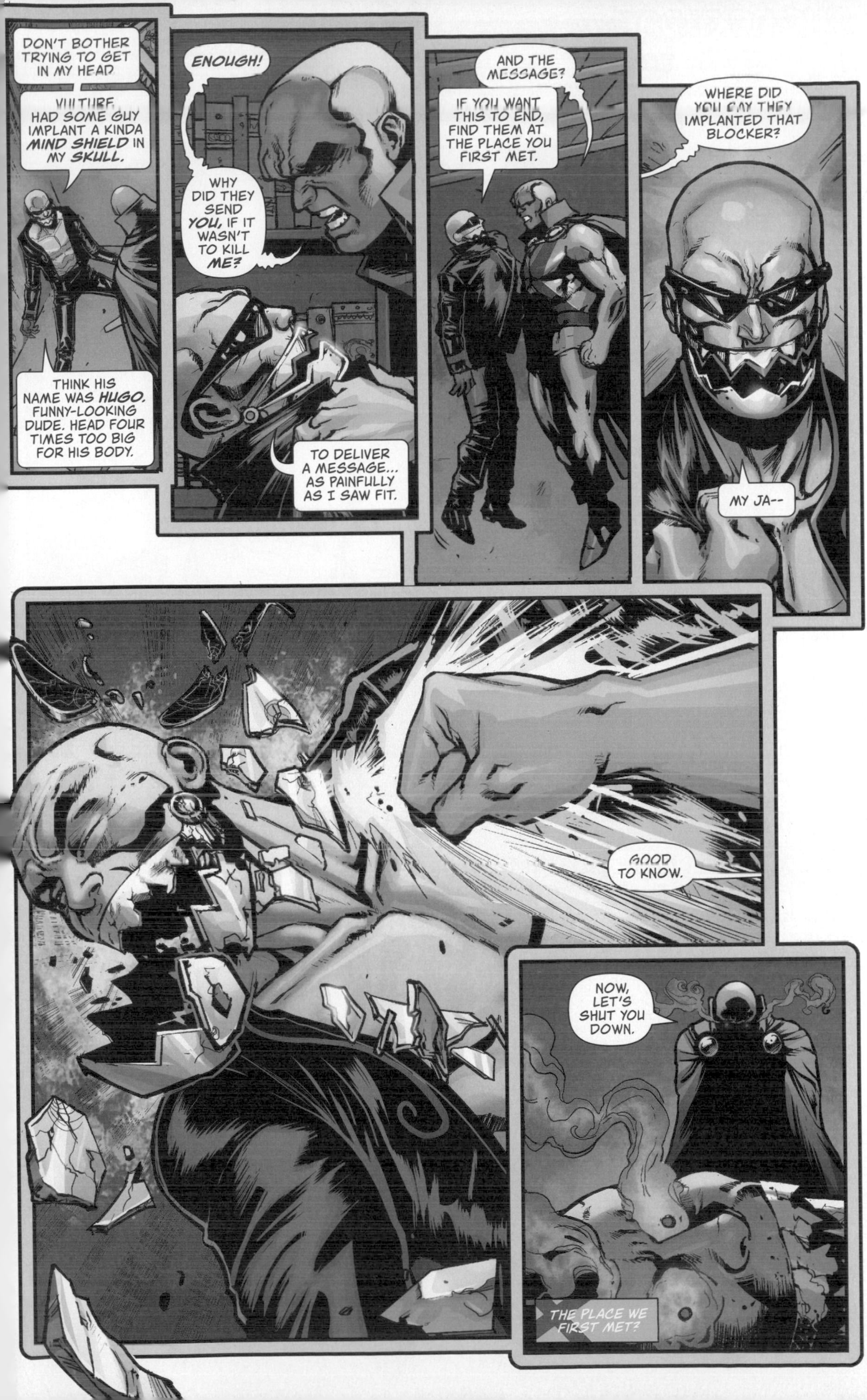
DON'T BOTHER TRYING TO GET IN MY HEAD.
VULTURE HAD SOME GUY IMPLANT A KINDA MIND SHIELD IN MY SKULL.
THINK HIS NAME WAS HUGO. FUNNY-LOOKING DUDE. HEAD FOUR TIMES TOO BIG FOR HIS BODY.
ENOUGH!
WHY DID THEY SEND YOU, IF IT WASN'T TO KILL ME?
TO DELIVER A MESSAGE... AS PAINFULLY AS I SAW FIT.
AND THE MESSAGE?
IF YOU WANT THIS TO END, FIND THEM AT THE PLACE YOU FIRST MET.
WHERE DID YOU SAY THEY IMPLANTED THAT BLOCKER?
MY JA--
GOOD TO KNOW.
NOW, LET'S SHUT YOU DOWN.
THE PLACE WE FIRST MET?

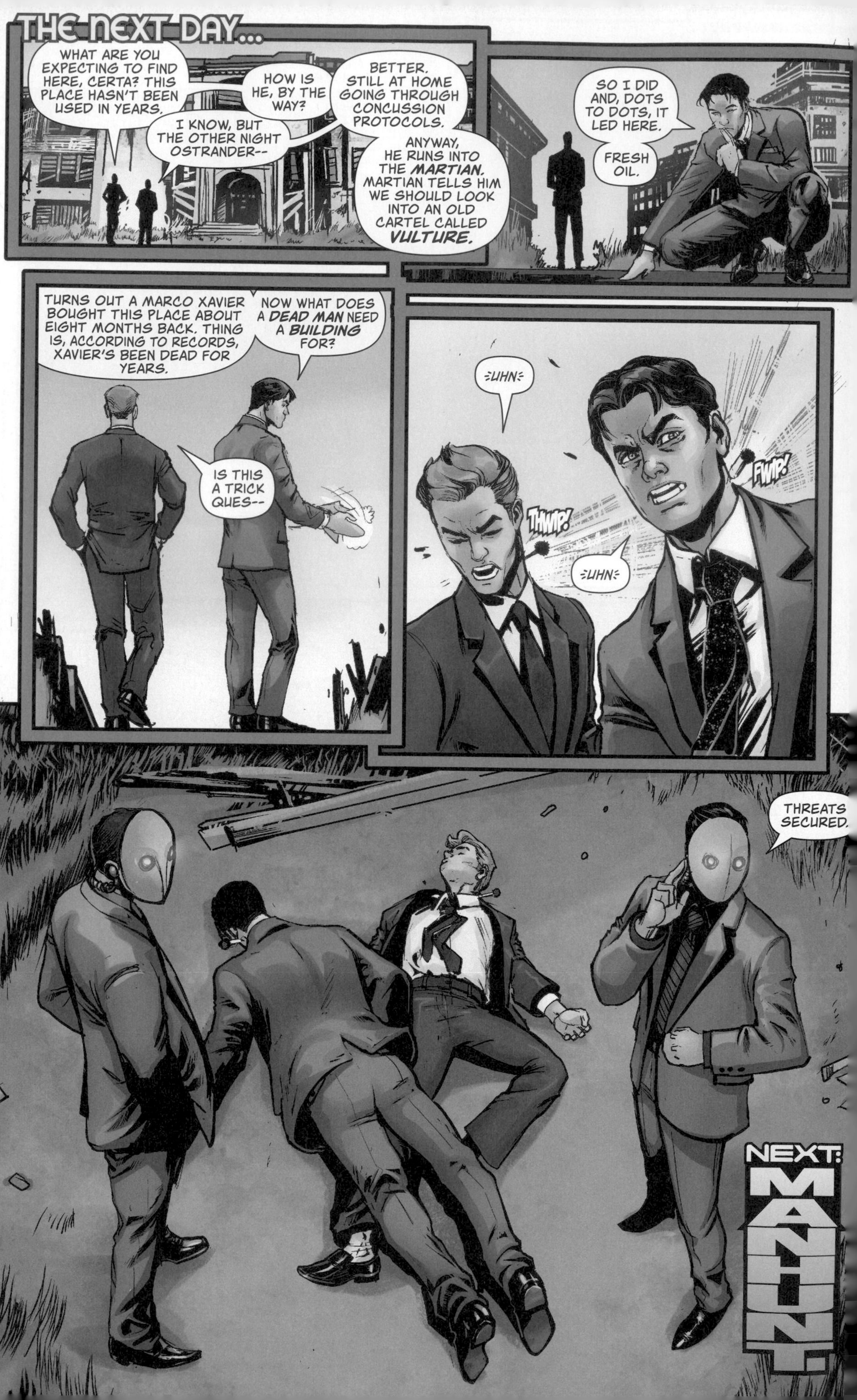
THE NEXT DAY...
WHAT ARE YOU EXPECTING TO FIND HERE, CERTA? THIS PLACE HASN'T BEEN USED IN YEARS.
I KNOW, BUT THE OTHER NIGHT OSTRANDER--
HOW IS HE, BY THE WAY?
BETTER. STILL AT HOME GOING THROUGH CONCUSSION PROTOCOLS.
ANYWAY, HE RUNS INTO THE MARTIAN. MARTIAN TELLS HIM WE SHOULD LOOK INTO AN OLD CARTEL CALLED VULTURE.
SO I DID AND, DOTS TO DOTS, IT LED HERE.
FRESH OIL.
TURNS OUT A MARCO XAVIER BOUGHT THIS PLACE ABOUT EIGHT MONTHS BACK. THING IS, ACCORDING TO RECORDS, XAVIER'S BEEN DEAD FOR YEARS.
NOW WHAT DOES A DEAD MAN NEED A BUILDING FOR?
IS THIS A TRICK QUES--
UHN
FWIP!
THWIP!
UHN
THREATS SECURED.
NEXT: MANHUNT.

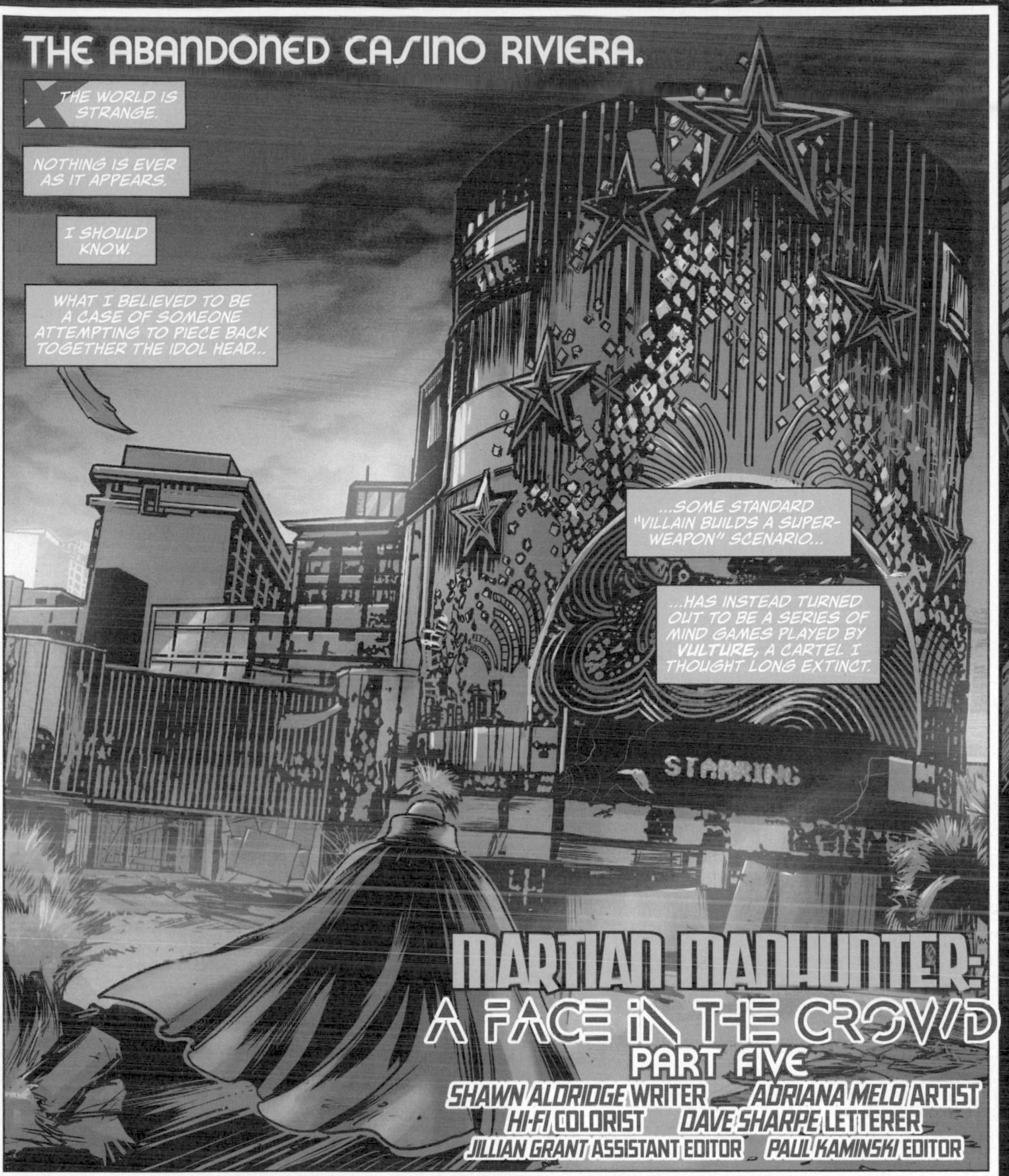
THE ABANDONED CASINO RIVIERA.
THE WORLD IS STRANGE.
NOTHING IS EVER AS IT APPEARS.
I SHOULD KNOW.
WHAT I BELIEVED TO BE A CASE OF SOMEONE ATTEMPTING TO PIECE BACK TOGETHER THE IDOL HEAD...
...SOME STANDARD "VILLAIN BUILDS A SUPER-WEAPON" SCENARIO...
...HAS INSTEAD TURNED OUT TO BE A SERIES OF MIND GAMES PLAYED BY VULTURE, A CARTEL I THOUGHT LONG EXTINCT.
STARRING
MARTIAN MANHUNTER:
A FACE IN THE CROWD
PART FIVE
SHAWN ALDRIDGE WRITER ADRIANA MELO ARTIST
HI-FI COLORIST DAVE SHARPE LETTERER
JILLIAN GRANT ASSISTANT EDITOR PAUL KAMINSKI EDITOR

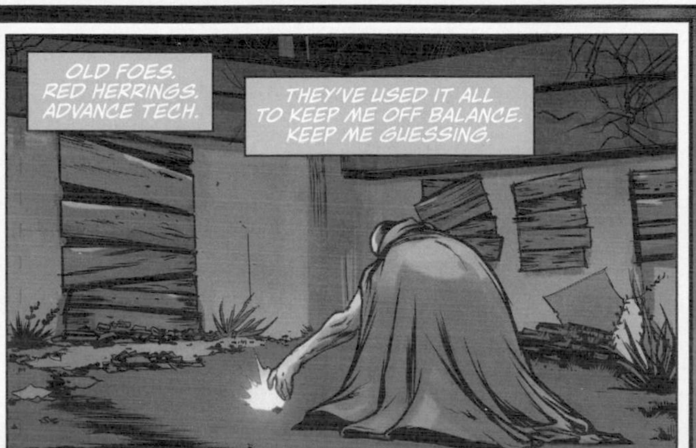
OLD FOES. RED HERRINGS. ADVANCE TECH.
THEY'VE USED IT ALL TO KEEP ME OFF BALANCE. KEEP ME GUESSING.

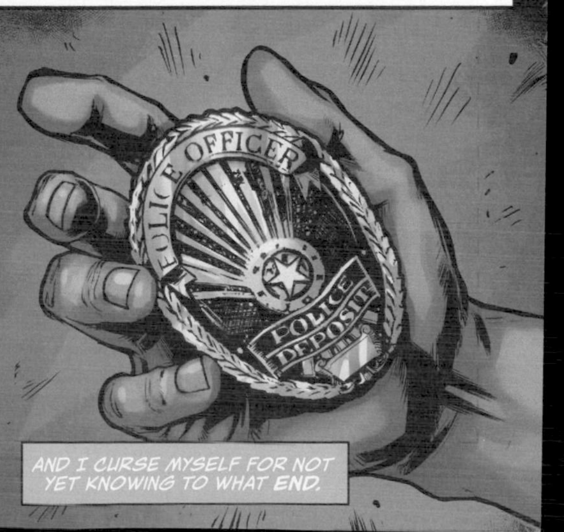
POLICE OFFICER
POLICE DEPOSITE
AND I CURSE MYSELF FOR NOT YET KNOWING TO WHAT END.

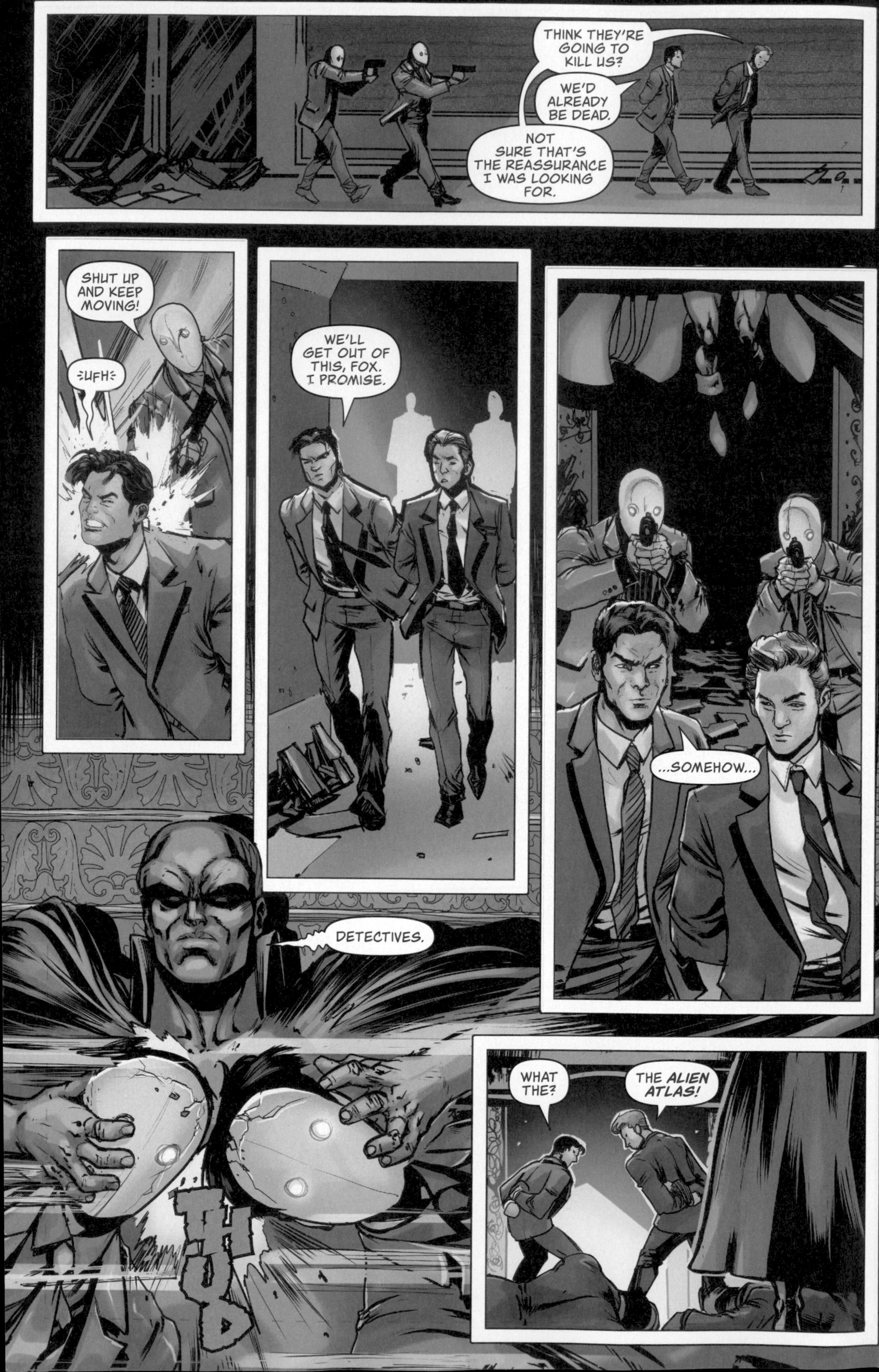
THINK THEY'RE GOING TO KILL US?
WE'D ALREADY BE DEAD.
NOT SURE THAT'S THE REASSURANCE I WAS LOOKING FOR.
SHUT UP AND KEEP MOVING!
UFH
WE'LL GET OUT OF THIS, FOX. I PROMISE.
...SOMEHOW...
DETECTIVES.
THUD
WHAT THE?
THE ALIEN ATLAS!

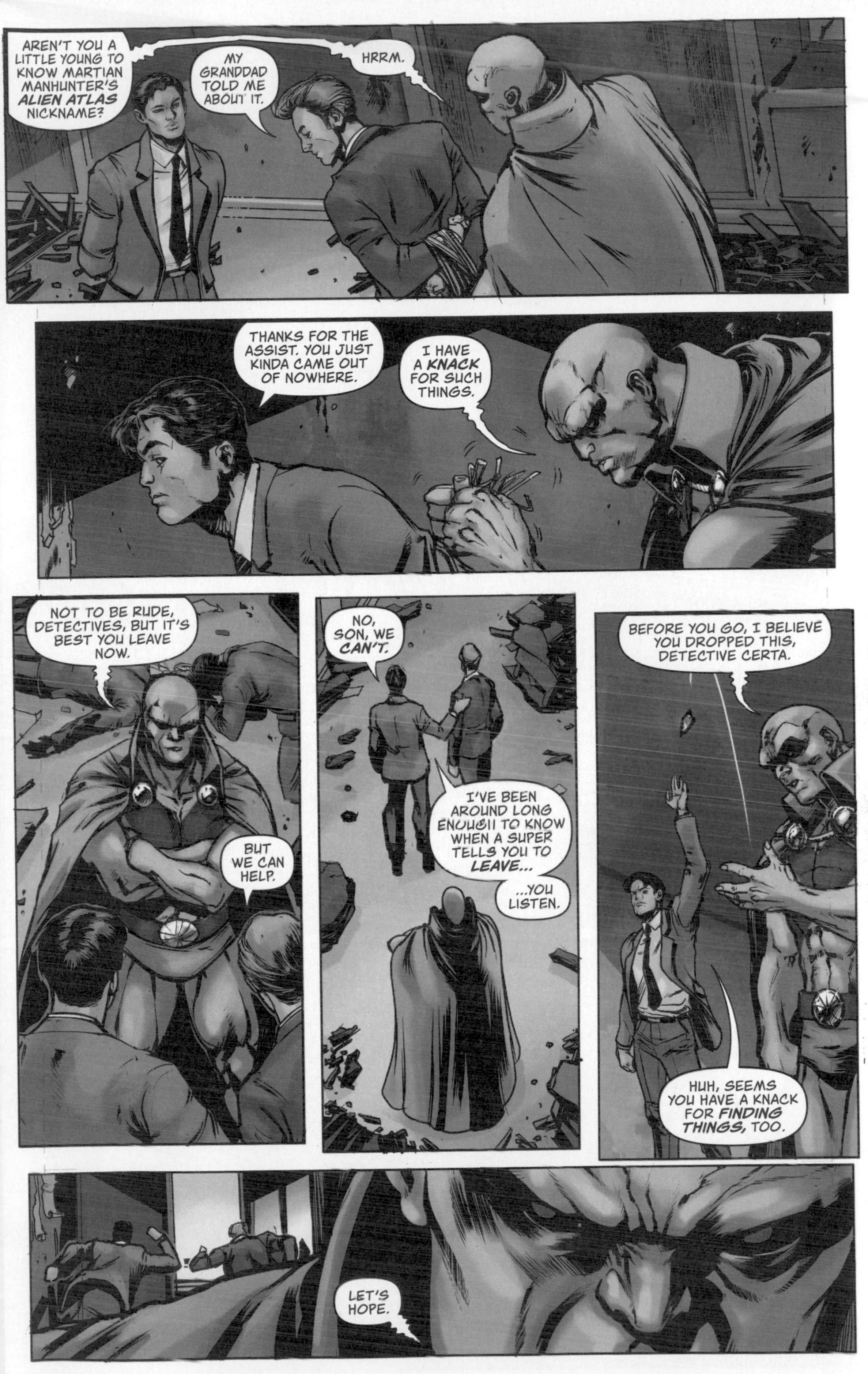
AREN'T YOU A LITTLE YOUNG TO KNOW MARTIAN MANHUNTER'S ***ALIEN ATLAS*** NICKNAME?
MY GRANDDAD TOLD ME ABOUT IT.
HRRM.
THANKS FOR THE ASSIST. YOU JUST KINDA CAME OUT OF NOWHERE.
I HAVE A ***KNACK*** FOR SUCH THINGS.
NOT TO BE RUDE, DETECTIVES, BUT IT'S BEST YOU LEAVE NOW.
BUT WE CAN HELP.
NO, SON, WE ***CAN'T.***
I'VE BEEN AROUND LONG ENOUGH TO KNOW WHEN A SUPER TELLS YOU TO ***LEAVE...***
...YOU LISTEN.
BEFORE YOU GO, I BELIEVE YOU DROPPED THIS, DETECTIVE CERTA.
HUH, SEEMS YOU HAVE A KNACK FOR ***FINDING THINGS,*** TOO.
LET'S HOPE.

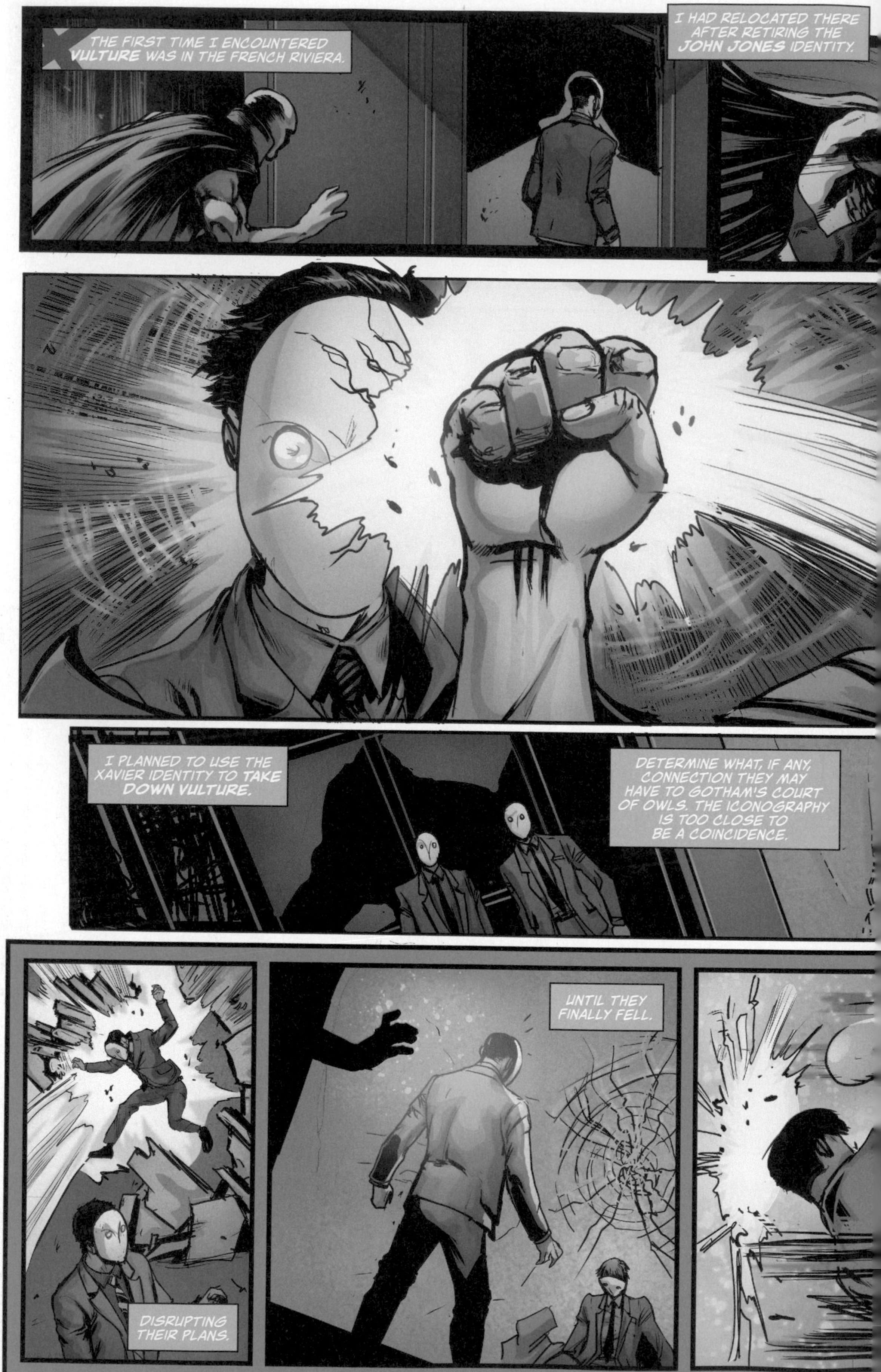
THE FIRST TIME I ENCOUNTERED VULTURE WAS IN THE FRENCH RIVIERA.
I HAD RELOCATED THERE AFTER RETIRING THE JOHN JONES IDENTITY.
I PLANNED TO USE THE XAVIER IDENTITY TO TAKE DOWN VULTURE.
DETERMINE WHAT, IF ANY, CONNECTION THEY MAY HAVE TO GOTHAM'S COURT OF OWLS. THE ICONOGRAPHY IS TOO CLOSE TO BE A COINCIDENCE.
DISRUPTING THEIR PLANS.
UNTIL THEY FINALLY FELL.

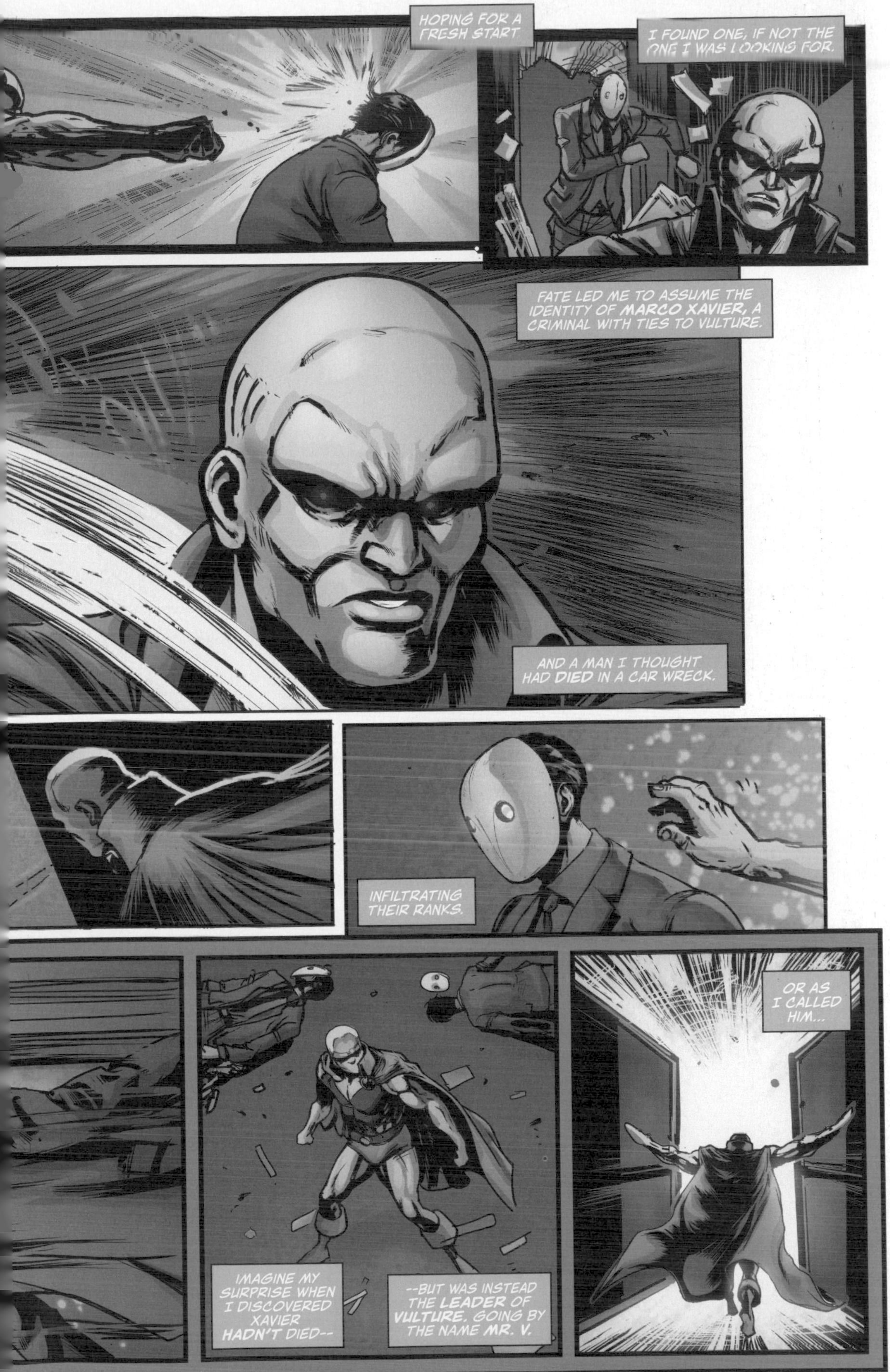
HOPING FOR A FRESH START
I FOUND ONE, IF NOT THE ONE I WAS LOOKING FOR.
FATE LED ME TO ASSUME THE IDENTITY OF **MARCO XAVIER**, A CRIMINAL WITH TIES TO VULTURE.
AND A MAN I THOUGHT HAD **DIED** IN A CAR WRECK.
INFILTRATING THEIR RANKS.
IMAGINE MY SURPRISE WHEN I DISCOVERED XAVIER **HADN'T** DIED--
--BUT WAS INSTEAD THE **LEADER** OF **VULTURE**, GOING BY THE NAME **MR. V.**
OR AS I CALLED HIM...

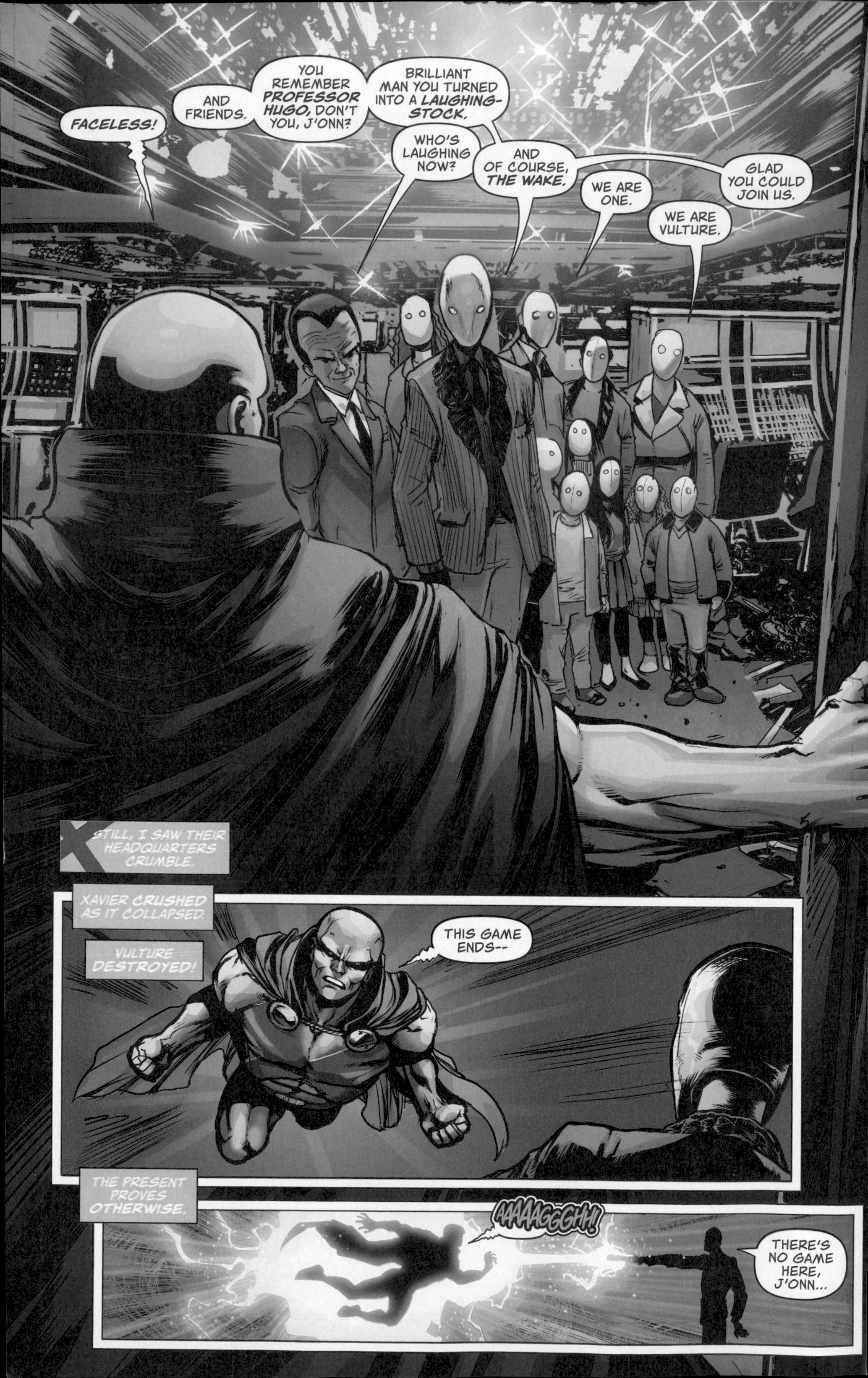
FACELESS!
AND FRIENDS.
YOU REMEMBER PROFESSOR HUGO, DON'T YOU, J'ONN?
BRILLIANT MAN YOU TURNED INTO A LAUGHING-STOCK.
WHO'S LAUGHING NOW?
AND OF COURSE, THE WAKE.
WE ARE ONE.
GLAD YOU COULD JOIN US.
WE ARE VULTURE.
STILL, I SAW THEIR HEADQUARTERS CRUMBLE.
XAVIER CRUSHED AS IT COLLAPSED.
VULTURE DESTROYED!
THIS GAME ENDS--
THE PRESENT PROVES OTHERWISE.
AAAAAGGGHH!
THERE'S NO GAME HERE, J'ONN...

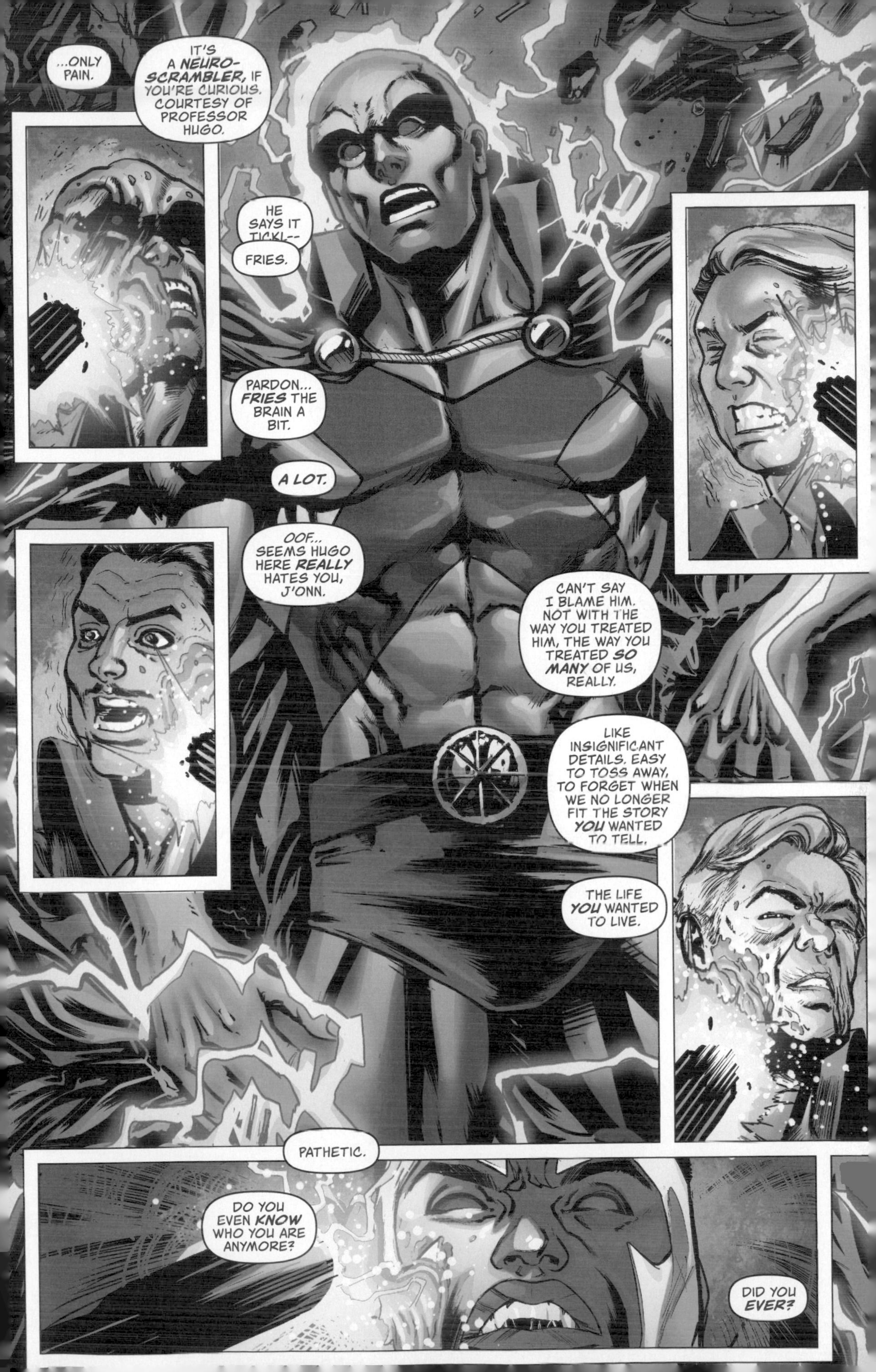

...ONLY PAIN.
IT'S A NEURO-SCRAMBLER, IF YOU'RE CURIOUS. COURTESY OF PROFESSOR HUGO.
HE SAYS IT TICKL--
FRIES.
PARDON... FRIES THE BRAIN A BIT.
A LOT.
OOF... SEEMS HUGO HERE REALLY HATES YOU, J'ONN.
CAN'T SAY I BLAME HIM. NOT WITH THE WAY YOU TREATED HIM, THE WAY YOU TREATED SO MANY OF US, REALLY.
LIKE INSIGNIFICANT DETAILS. EASY TO TOSS AWAY, TO FORGET WHEN WE NO LONGER FIT THE STORY YOU WANTED TO TELL.
THE LIFE YOU WANTED TO LIVE.
PATHETIC.
DO YOU EVEN KNOW WHO YOU ARE ANYMORE?
DID YOU EVER?

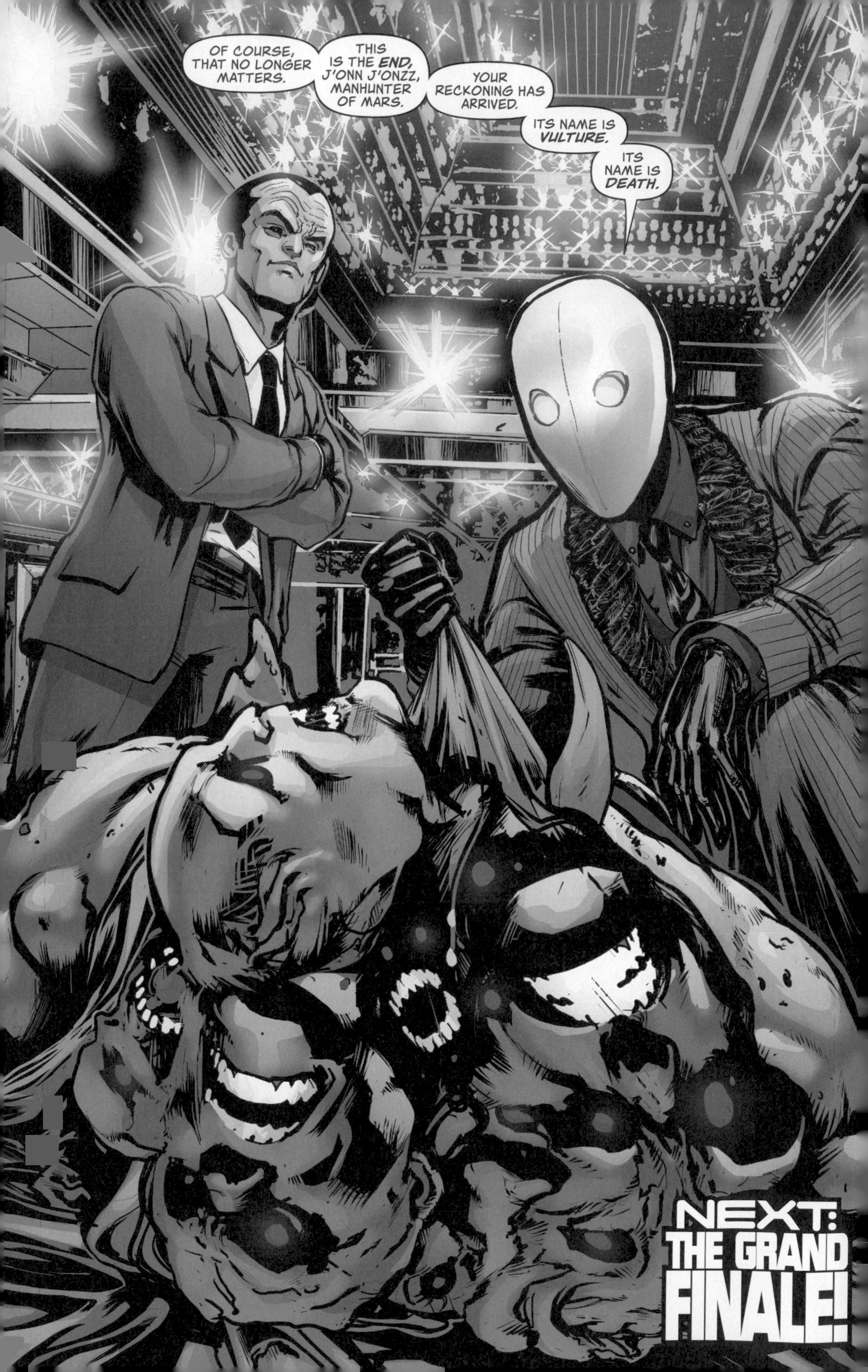
OF COURSE, THAT NO LONGER MATTERS.
THIS IS THE END, J'ONN J'ONZZ, MANHUNTER OF MARS.
YOUR RECKONING HAS ARRIVED.
ITS NAME IS VULTURE.
ITS NAME IS DEATH.
NEXT: THE GRAND FINALE!

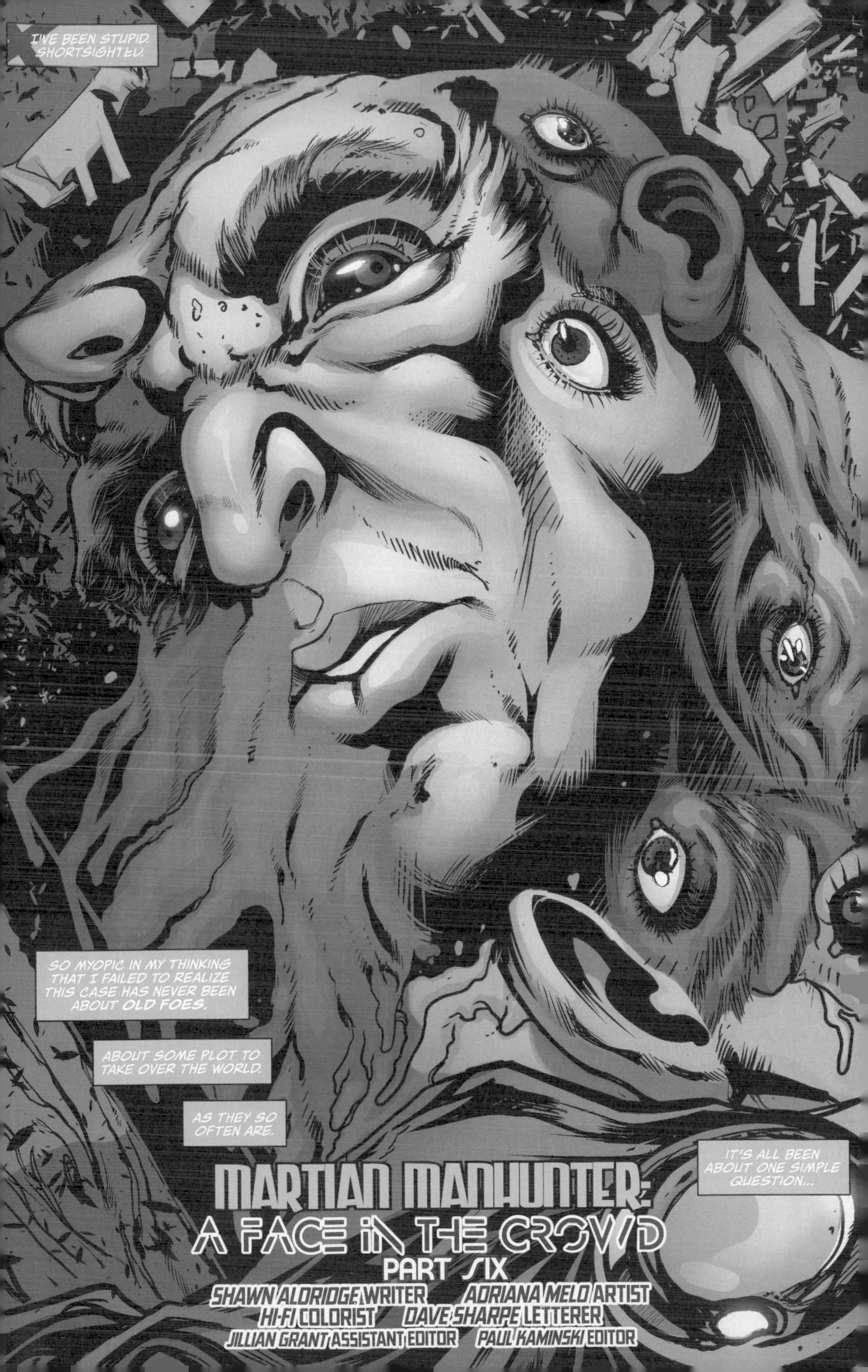
I'VE BEEN STUPID. SHORTSIGHTED.
SO MYOPIC IN MY THINKING THAT I FAILED TO REALIZE THIS CASE HAS NEVER BEEN ABOUT OLD FOES.
ABOUT SOME PLOT TO TAKE OVER THE WORLD.
AS THEY SO OFTEN ARE.
IT'S ALL BEEN ABOUT ONE SIMPLE QUESTION...
MARTIAN MANHUNTER:
A FACE IN THE CROWD
PART SIX
SHAWN ALDRIDGE WRITER ADRIANA MELO ARTIST
HI-FI COLORIST DAVE SHARPE LETTERER
JILLIAN GRANT ASSISTANT EDITOR PAUL KAMINSKI EDITOR

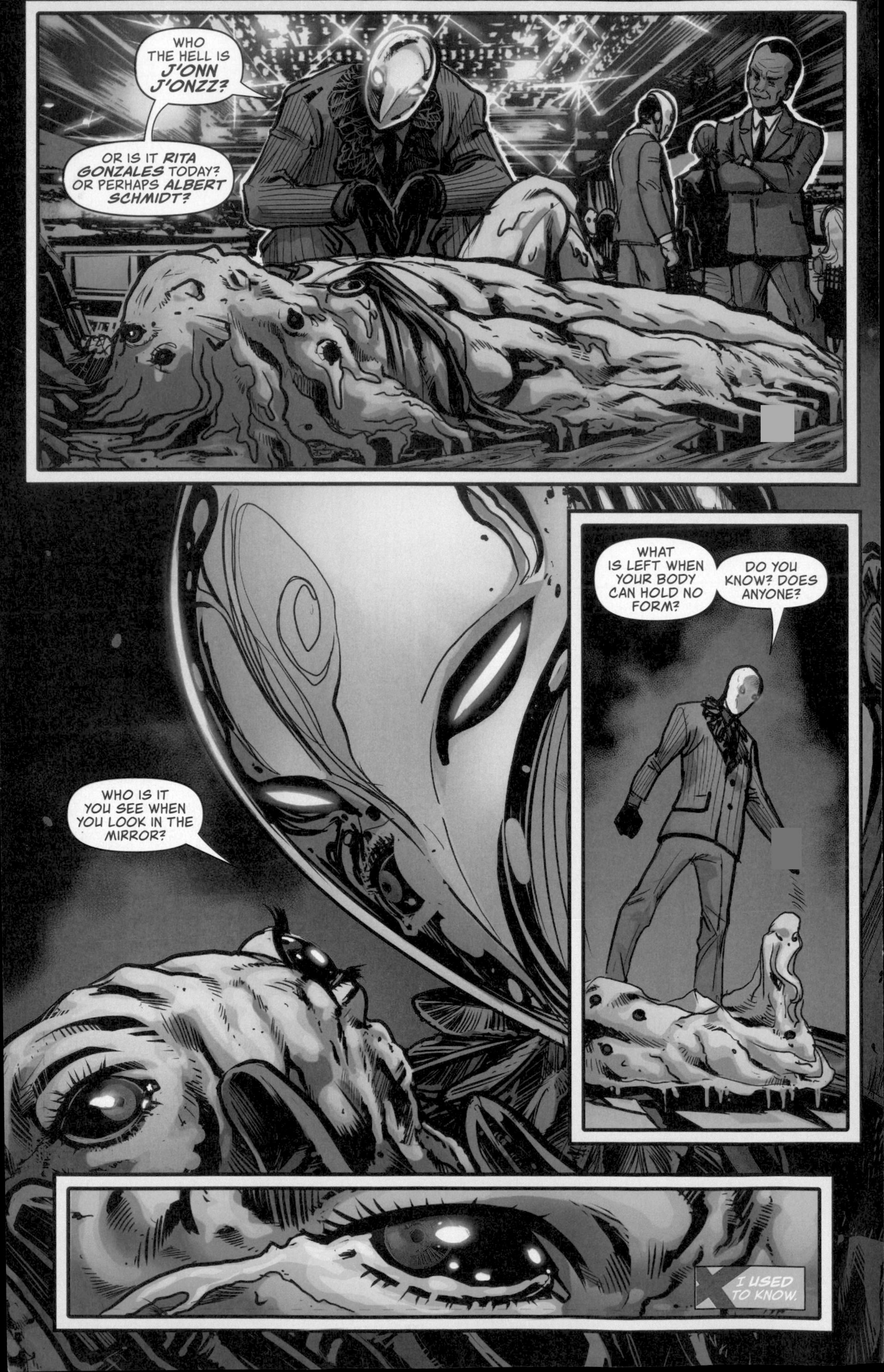
WHO THE HELL IS J'ONN J'ONZZ?
OR IS IT RITA GONZALES TODAY? OR PERHAPS ALBERT SCHMIDT?
WHAT IS LEFT WHEN YOUR BODY CAN HOLD NO FORM?
DO YOU KNOW? DOES ANYONE?
WHO IS IT YOU SEE WHEN YOU LOOK IN THE MIRROR?
I USED TO KNOW.

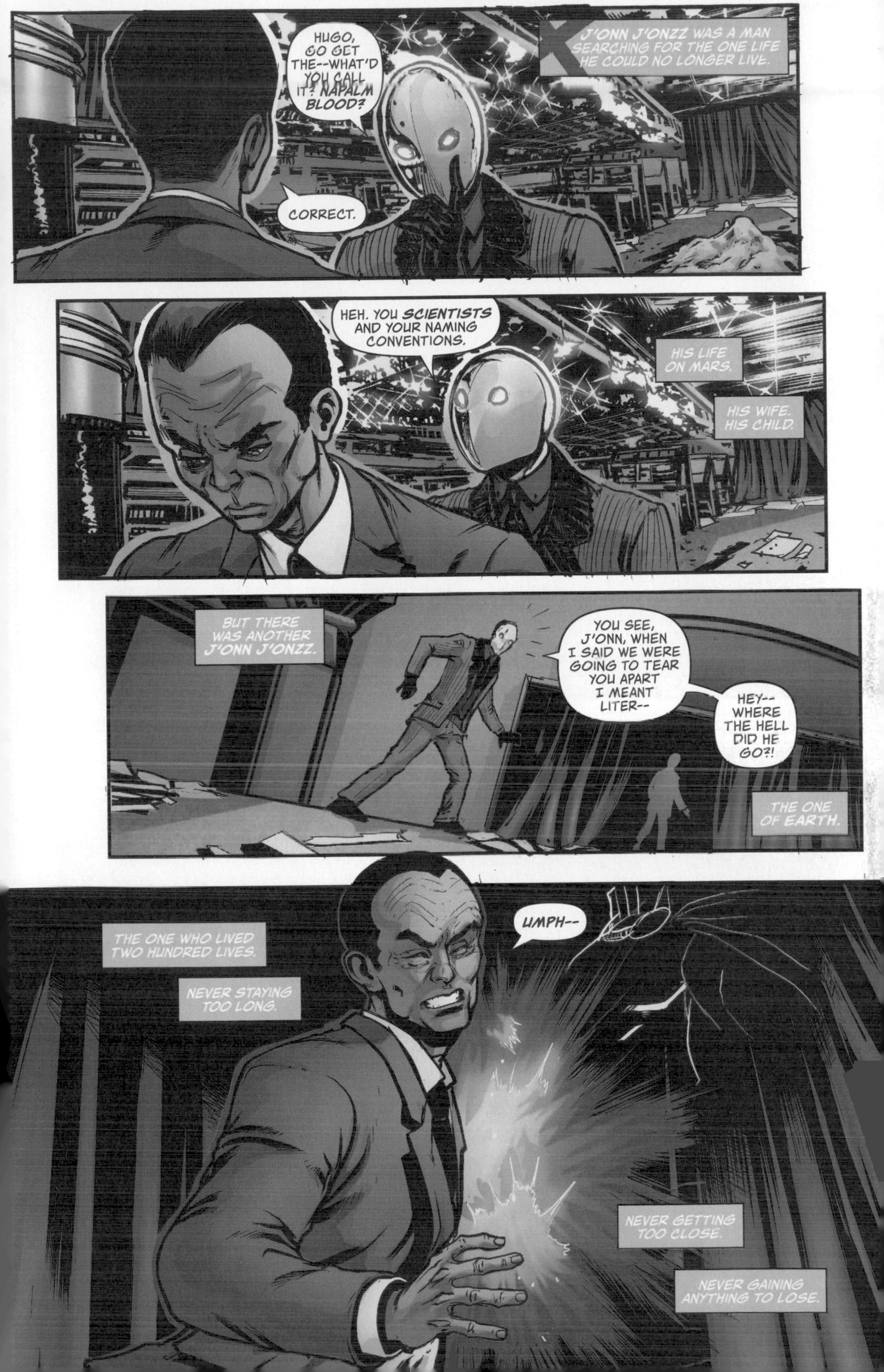
J'ONN J'ONZZ WAS A MAN SEARCHING FOR THE ONE LIFE HE COULD NO LONGER LIVE.
HUGO, GO GET THE--WHAT'D YOU CALL IT? NAPALM BLOOD?
CORRECT.
HEH. YOU SCIENTISTS AND YOUR NAMING CONVENTIONS.
HIS LIFE ON MARS.
HIS WIFE. HIS CHILD.
BUT THERE WAS ANOTHER J'ONN J'ONZZ.
YOU SEE, J'ONN, WHEN I SAID WE WERE GOING TO TEAR YOU APART I MEANT LITER--
HEY-- WHERE THE HELL DID HE GO?!
THE ONE OF EARTH.
THE ONE WHO LIVED TWO HUNDRED LIVES.
UMPH--
NEVER STAYING TOO LONG.
NEVER GETTING TOO CLOSE.
NEVER GAINING ANYTHING TO LOSE.

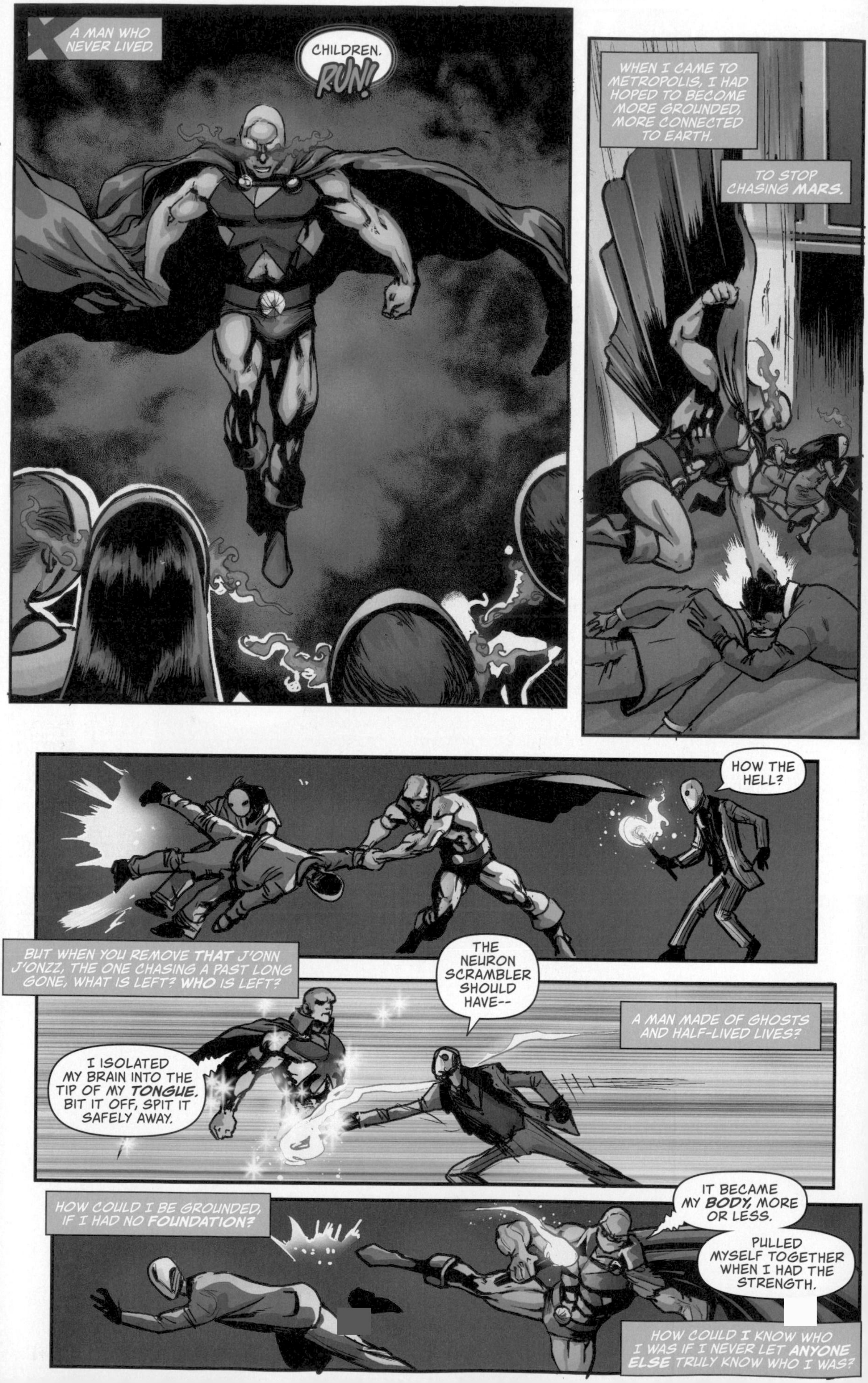
A MAN WHO NEVER LIVED.
CHILDREN. RUN!
WHEN I CAME TO METROPOLIS, I HAD HOPED TO BECOME MORE GROUNDED, MORE CONNECTED TO EARTH.
TO STOP CHASING MARS.
HOW THE HELL?
BUT WHEN YOU REMOVE THAT J'ONN J'ONZZ, THE ONE CHASING A PAST LONG GONE, WHAT IS LEFT? WHO IS LEFT?
THE NEURON SCRAMBLER SHOULD HAVE--
A MAN MADE OF GHOSTS AND HALF-LIVED LIVES?
I ISOLATED MY BRAIN INTO THE TIP OF MY TONGUE. BIT IT OFF, SPIT IT SAFELY AWAY.
HOW COULD I BE GROUNDED, IF I HAD NO FOUNDATION?
IT BECAME MY BODY, MORE OR LESS.
PULLED MYSELF TOGETHER WHEN I HAD THE STRENGTH.
HOW COULD I KNOW WHO I WAS IF I NEVER LET ANYONE ELSE TRULY KNOW WHO I WAS?

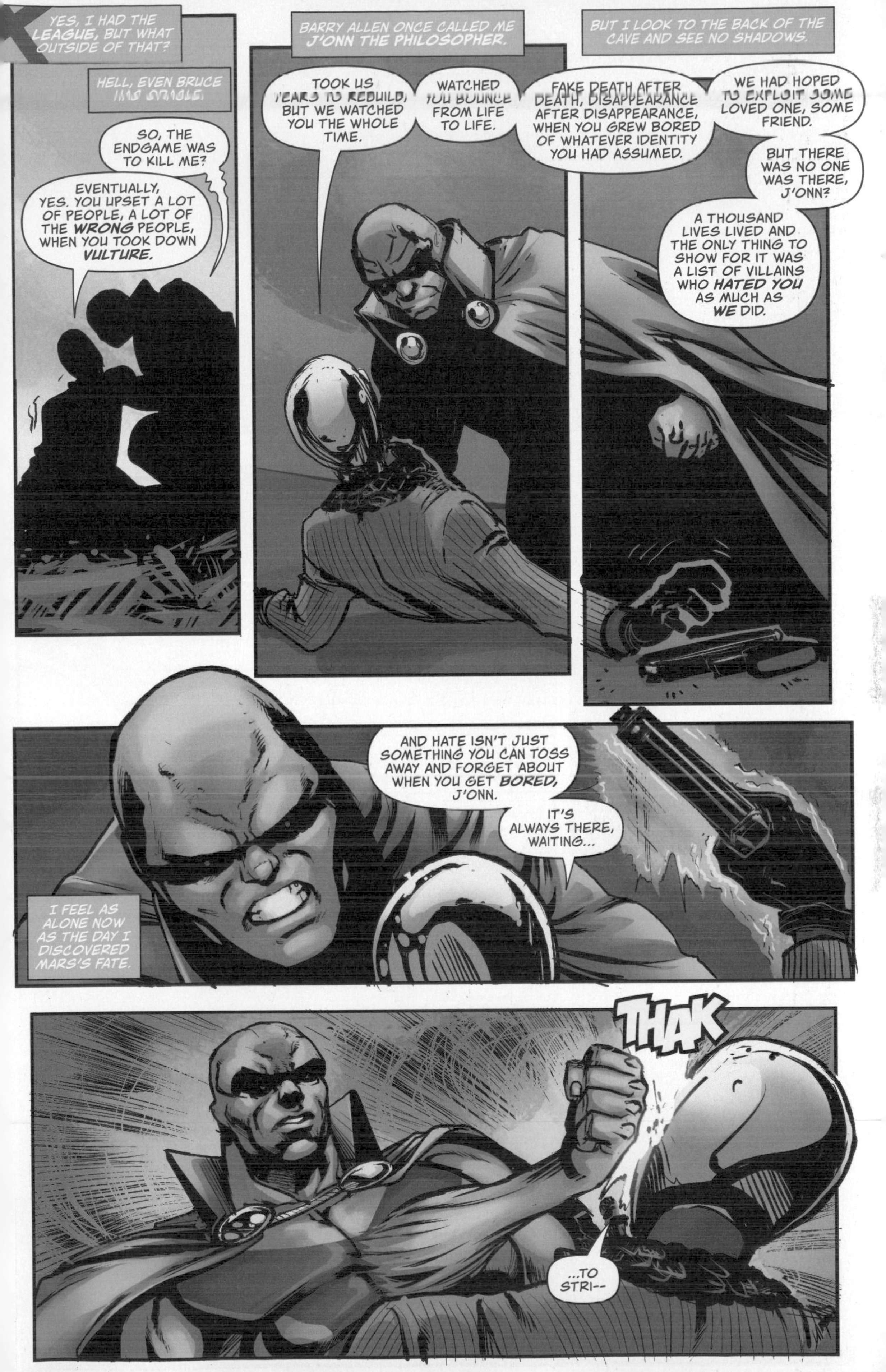
YES, I HAD THE LEAGUE, BUT WHAT OUTSIDE OF THAT?
HELL, EVEN BRUCE
SO, THE ENDGAME WAS TO KILL ME?
EVENTUALLY, YES. YOU UPSET A LOT OF PEOPLE, A LOT OF THE WRONG PEOPLE, WHEN YOU TOOK DOWN VULTURE.
BARRY ALLEN ONCE CALLED ME J'ONN THE PHILOSOPHER.
TOOK US YEARS TO REBUILD, BUT WE WATCHED YOU THE WHOLE TIME.
WATCHED YOU BOUNCE FROM LIFE TO LIFE.
BUT I LOOK TO THE BACK OF THE CAVE AND SEE NO SHADOWS.
FAKE DEATH AFTER DEATH, DISAPPEARANCE AFTER DISAPPEARANCE, WHEN YOU GREW BORED OF WHATEVER IDENTITY YOU HAD ASSUMED.
WE HAD HOPED TO EXPLOIT SOME LOVED ONE, SOME FRIEND.
BUT THERE WAS NO ONE WAS THERE, J'ONN?
A THOUSAND LIVES LIVED AND THE ONLY THING TO SHOW FOR IT WAS A LIST OF VILLAINS WHO HATED YOU AS MUCH AS WE DID.
AND HATE ISN'T JUST SOMETHING YOU CAN TOSS AWAY AND FORGET ABOUT WHEN YOU GET BORED, J'ONN.
IT'S ALWAYS THERE, WAITING...
I FEEL AS ALONE NOW AS THE DAY I DISCOVERED MARS'S FATE.
THAK
...TO STRI--

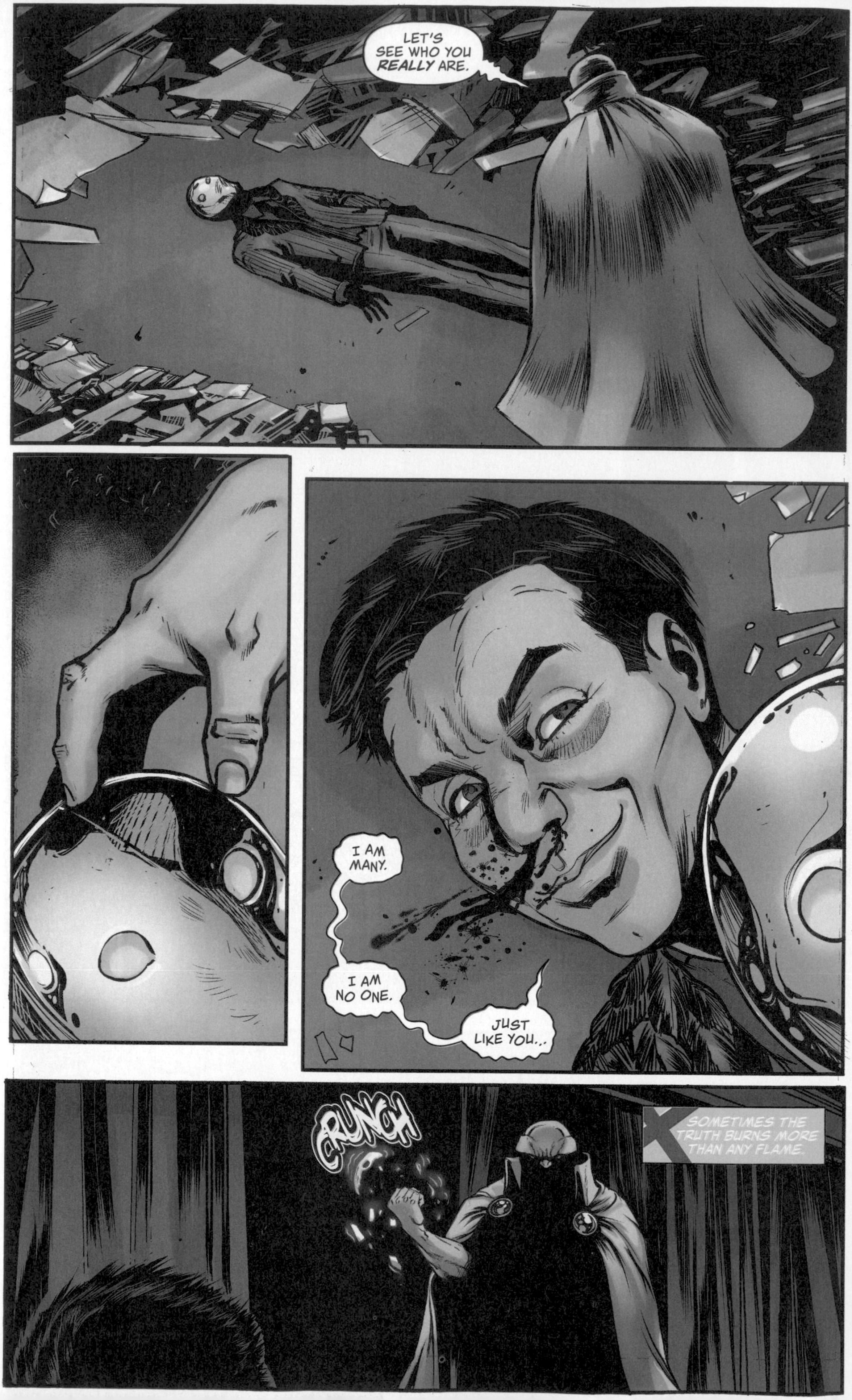
LET'S SEE WHO YOU *REALLY* ARE.
I AM MANY.
I AM NO ONE.
JUST LIKE YOU...
CRUNCH
SOMETIMES THE TRUTH BURNS MORE THAN ANY FLAME.

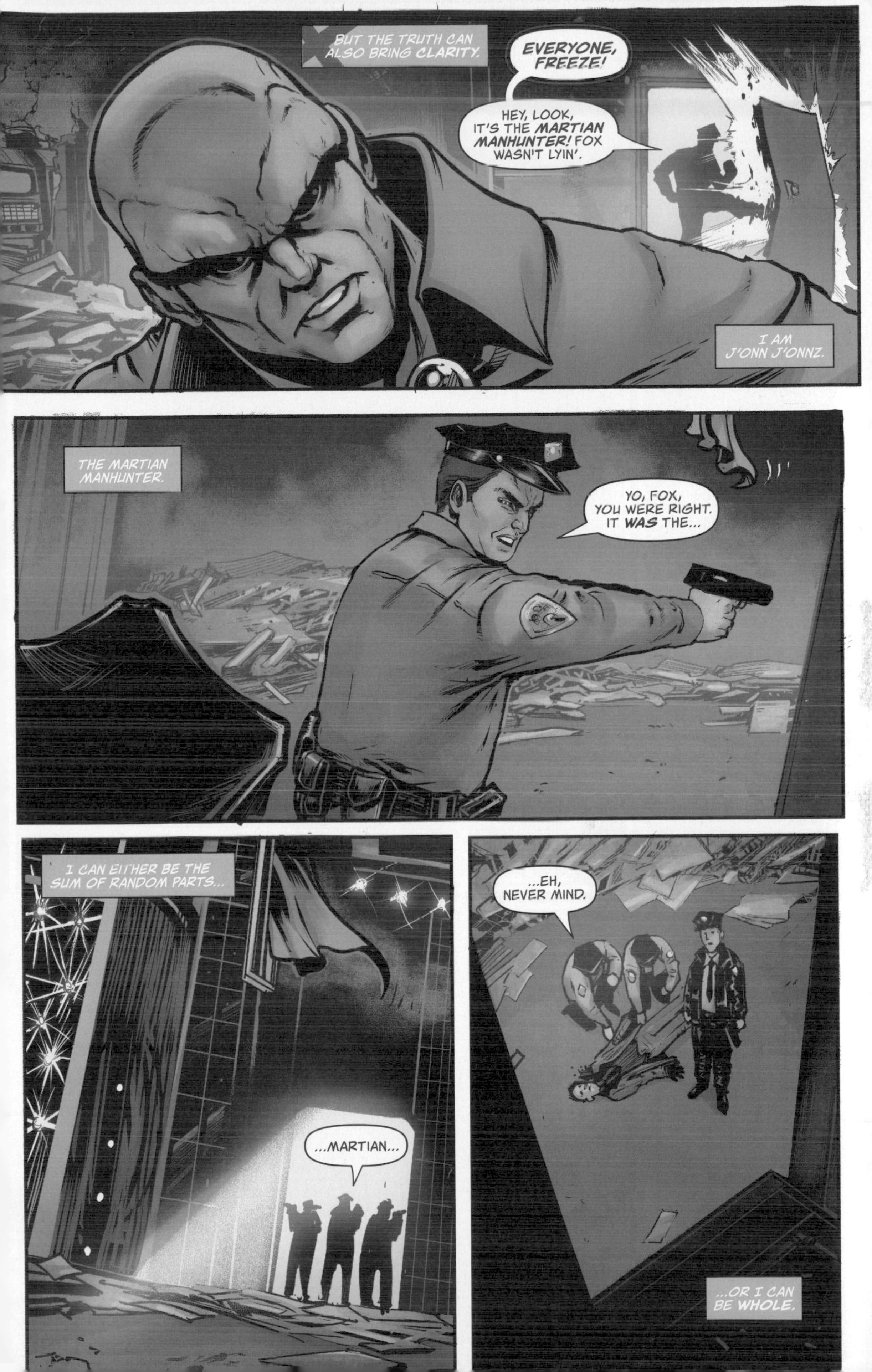
BUT THE TRUTH CAN ALSO BRING CLARITY.
EVERYONE, FREEZE!
HEY, LOOK, IT'S THE MARTIAN MANHUNTER! FOX WASN'T LYIN'.
I AM J'ONN J'ONNZ.
THE MARTIAN MANHUNTER.
YO, FOX, YOU WERE RIGHT. IT WAS THE...
I CAN EITHER BE THE SUM OF RANDOM PARTS...
...MARTIAN...
...EH, NEVER MIND.
...OR I CAN BE WHOLE.

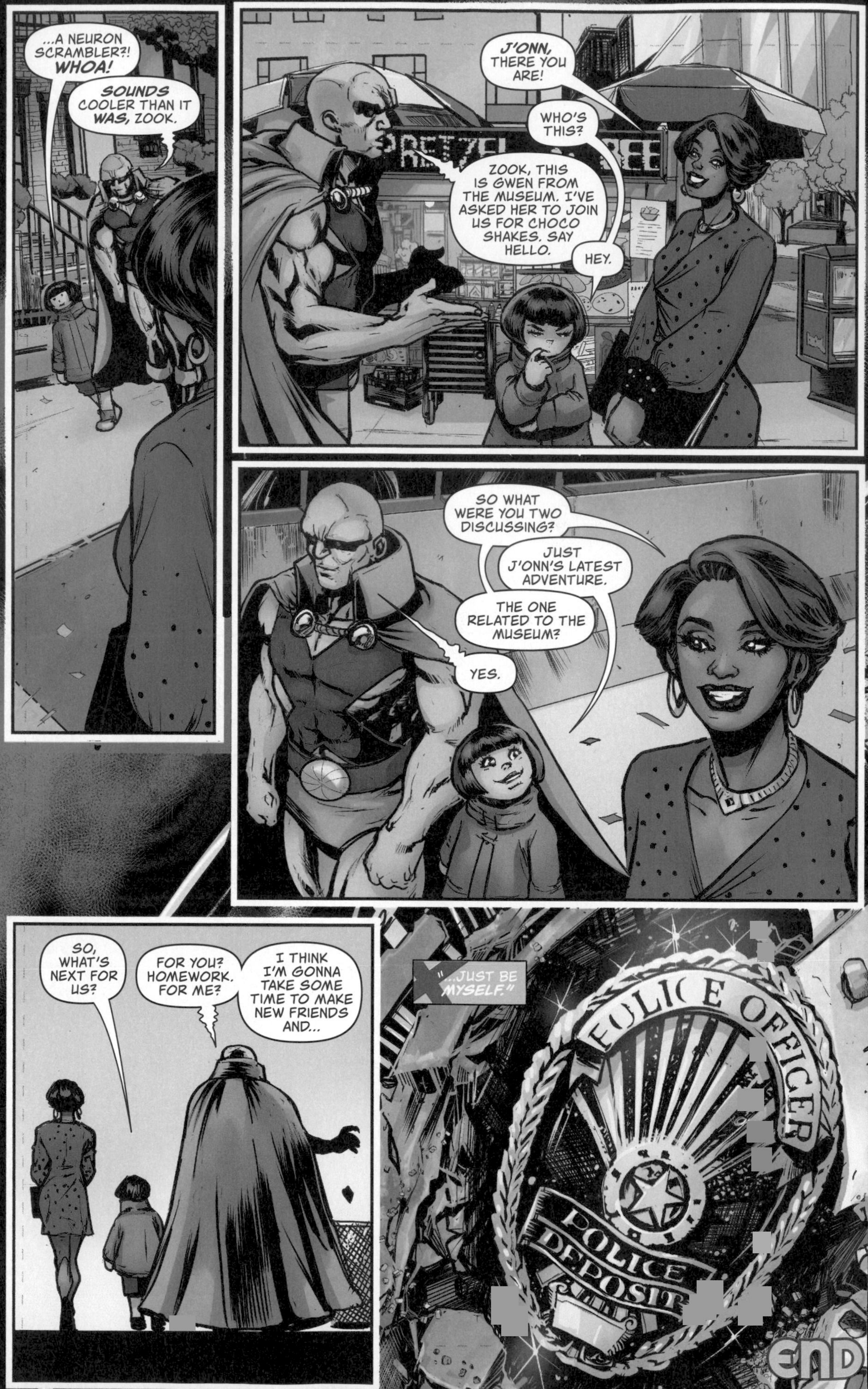
...A NEURON SCRAMBLER?! WHOA!
SOUNDS COOLER THAN IT WAS, ZOOK.
J'ONN, THERE YOU ARE!
WHO'S THIS?
ZOOK, THIS IS GWEN FROM THE MUSEUM. I'VE ASKED HER TO JOIN US FOR CHOCO SHAKES. SAY HELLO.
HEY.
SO WHAT WERE YOU TWO DISCUSSING?
JUST J'ONN'S LATEST ADVENTURE.
THE ONE RELATED TO THE MUSEUM?
YES.
SO, WHAT'S NEXT FOR US?
FOR YOU? HOMEWORK. FOR ME?
I THINK I'M GONNA TAKE SOME TIME TO MAKE NEW FRIENDS AND...
"...JUST BE MYSELF."
END

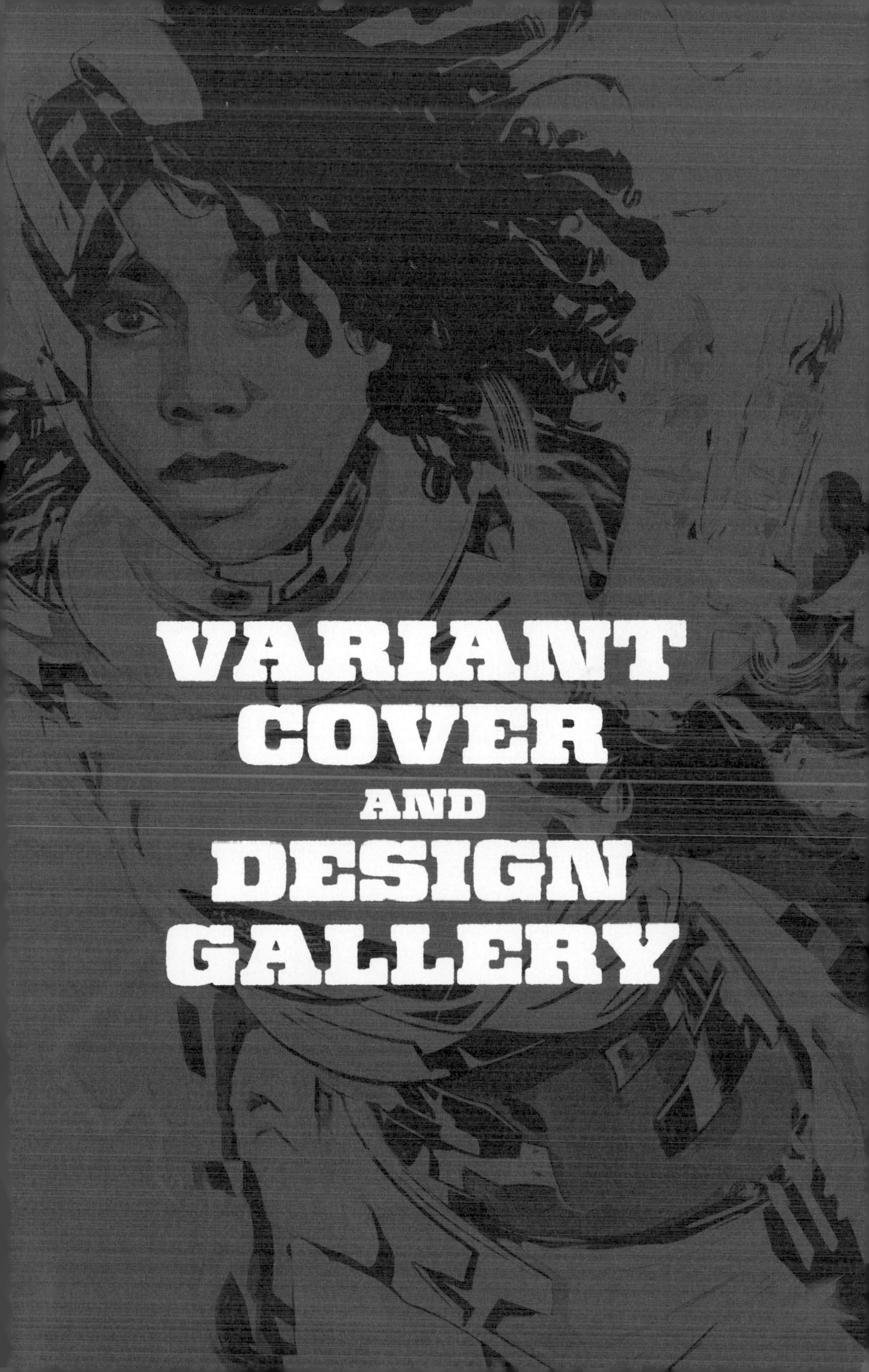

VARIANT COVER AND DESIGN GALLERY

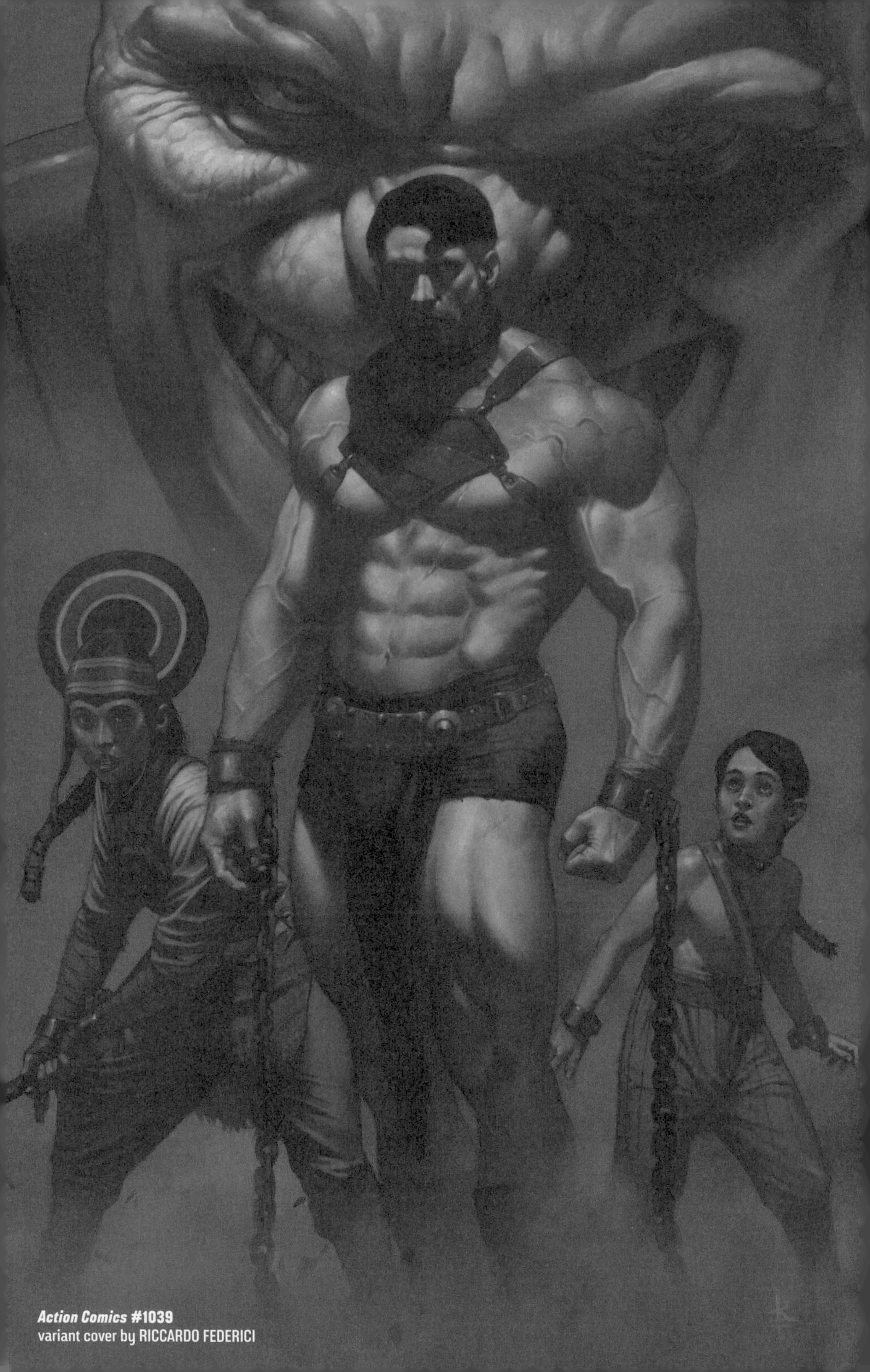

***Action Comics* #1039**
variant cover by RICCARDO FEDERICI

***Action Comics* #1040**
Black History Month variant cover by ALEXIS FRANKLIN

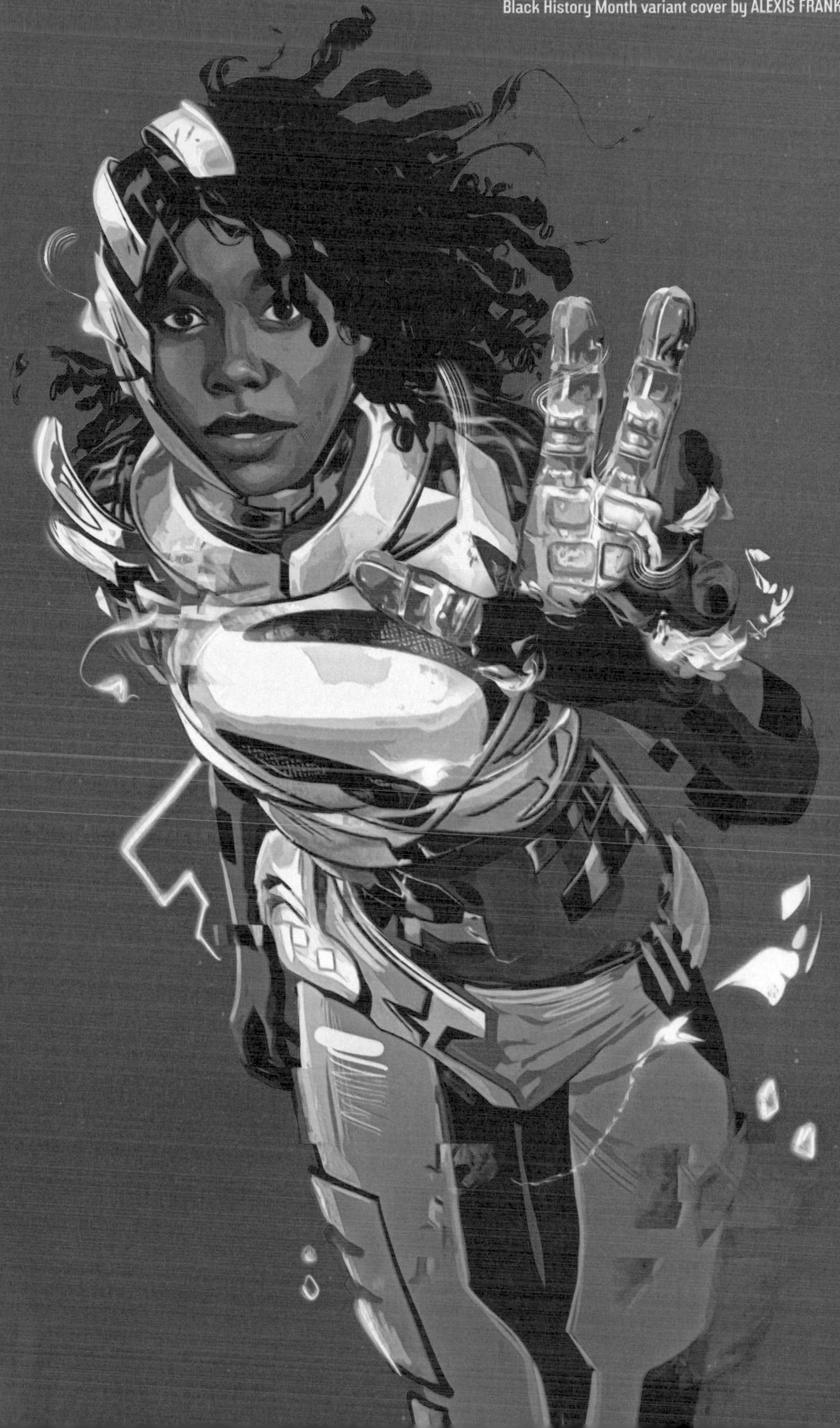

Otho-Ra design by RICCARDO FEDERICI

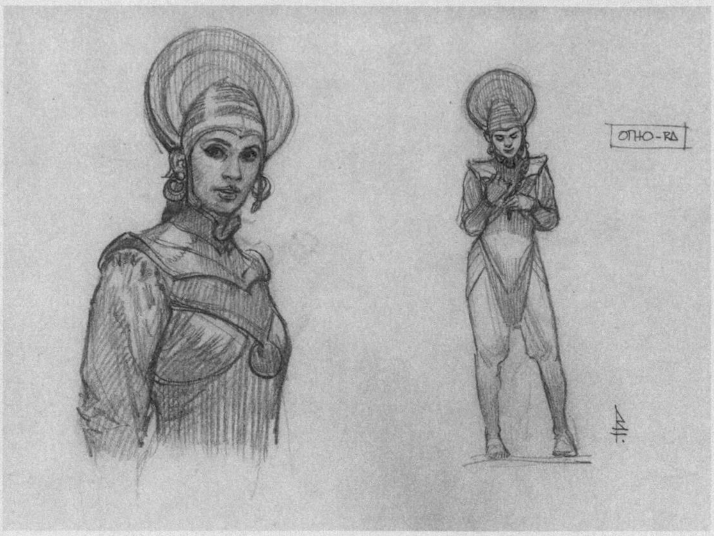
OTHO-RA

Kryl-Ux design by RICCARDO FEDERICI

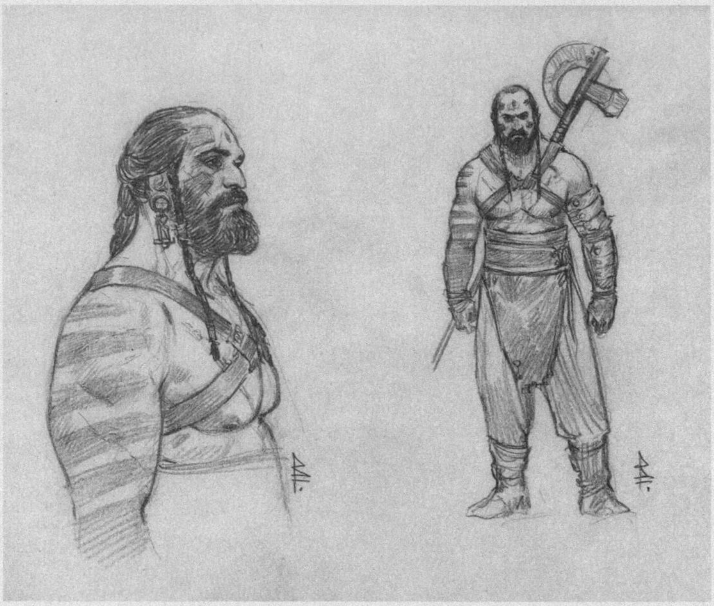

Osul-Ra design by RICCARDO FEDERICI

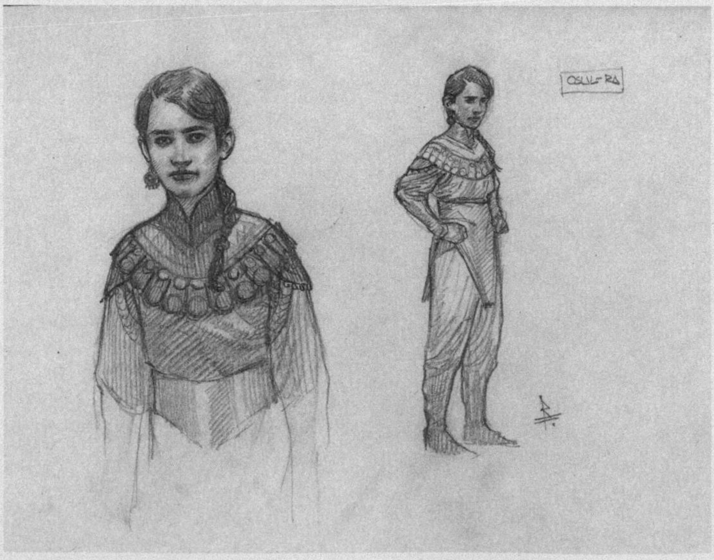
OSUL-RA

Bloodpriest design by RICCARDO FEDERICI

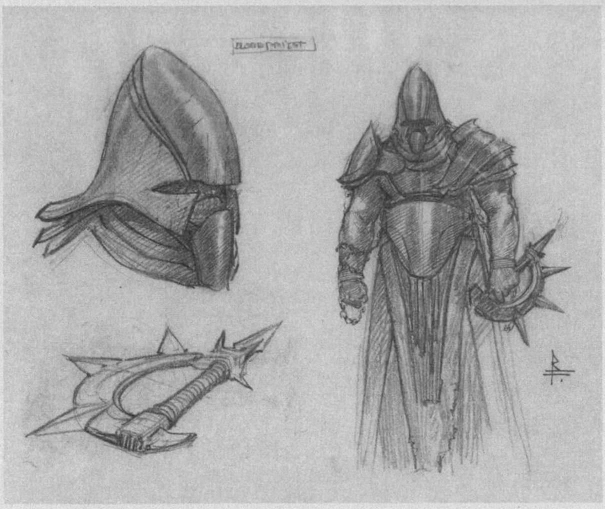
BLOODPRIEST

Hovercraft drone and Superman's cage designs by RICCARDO FEDERICI

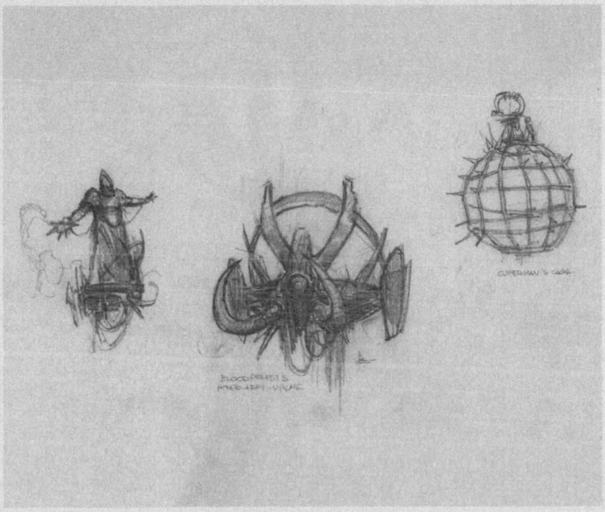
SUPERMAN'S CAGE

Natasha Irons design by RICCARDO FEDERICI

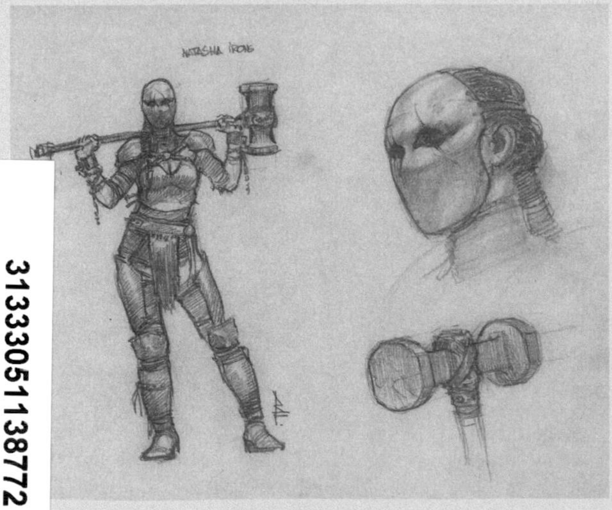
NATASHA IRONS

O.M.A.C. design by RICCARDO FEDERICI

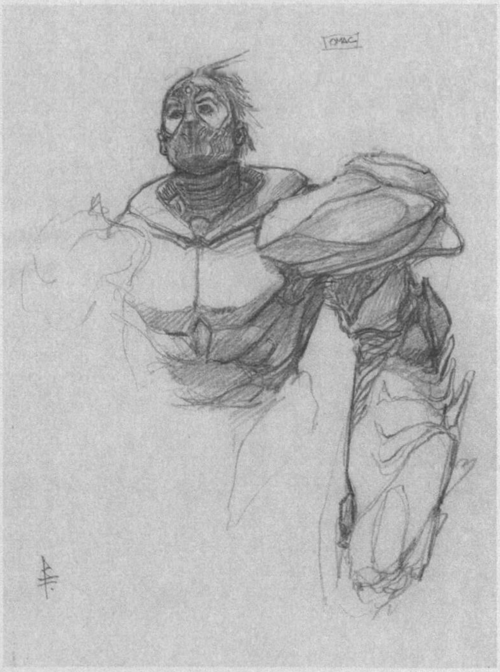
OMAC

Creatures of Warworld designs by RICCARDO FEDERICI

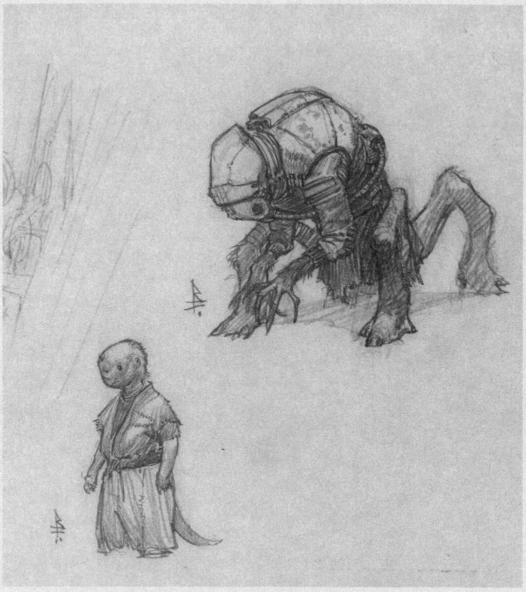

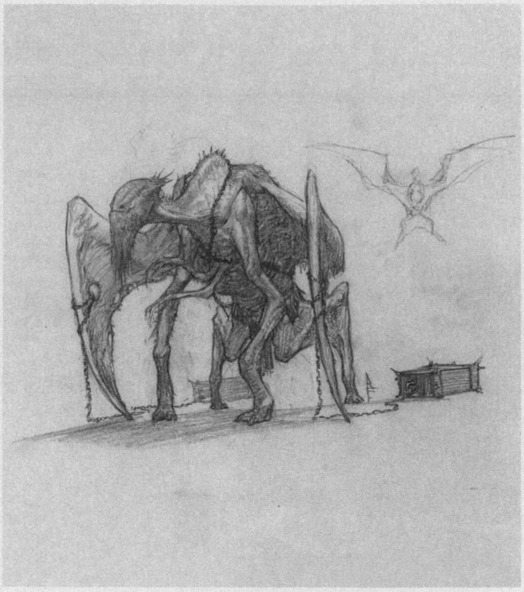

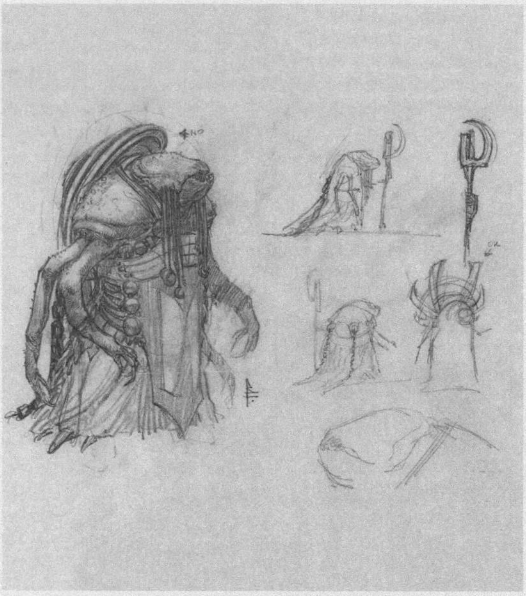

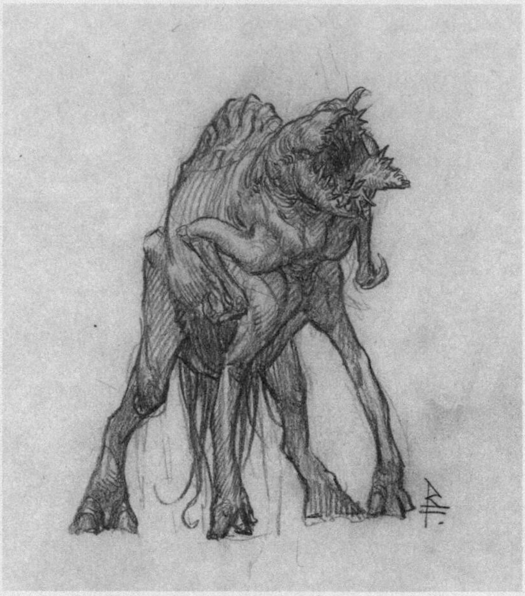

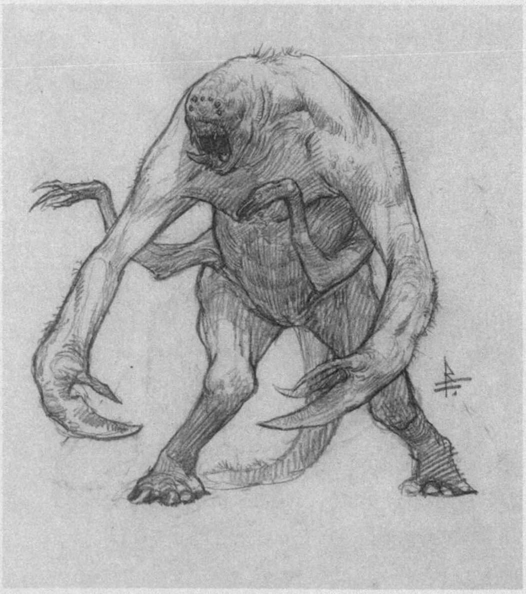

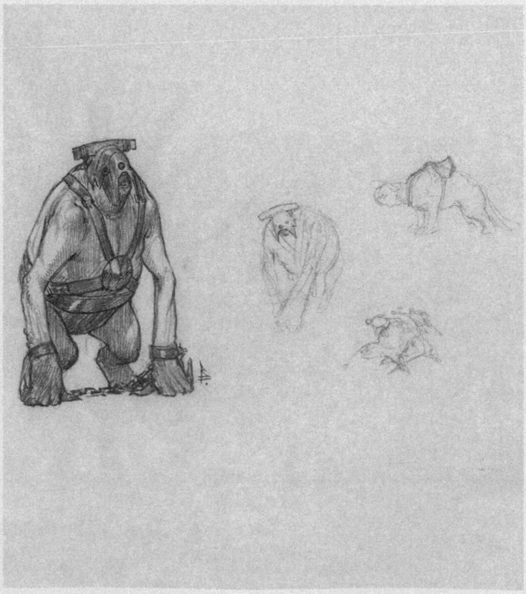

Creatures of Warworld designs by RICCARDO FEDERICI

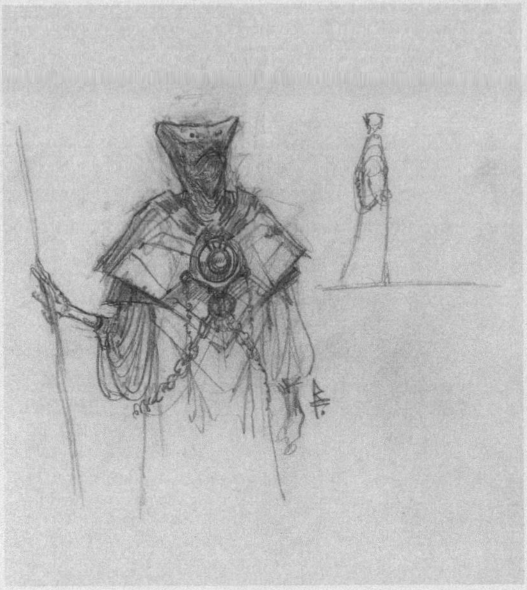

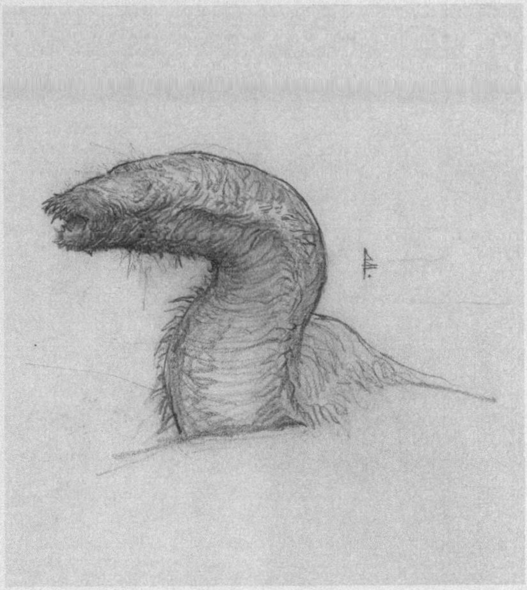

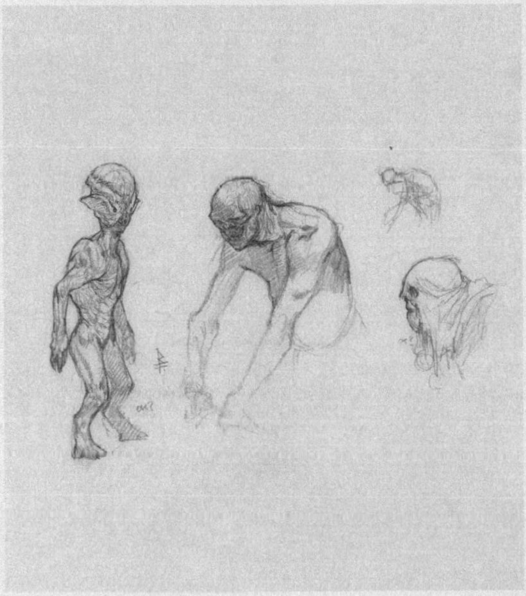

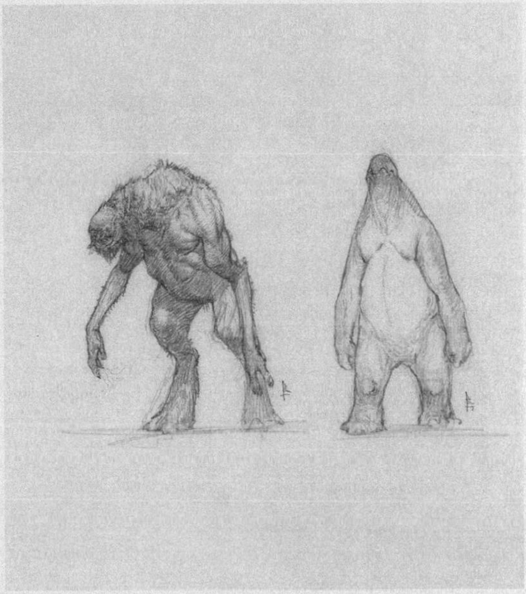

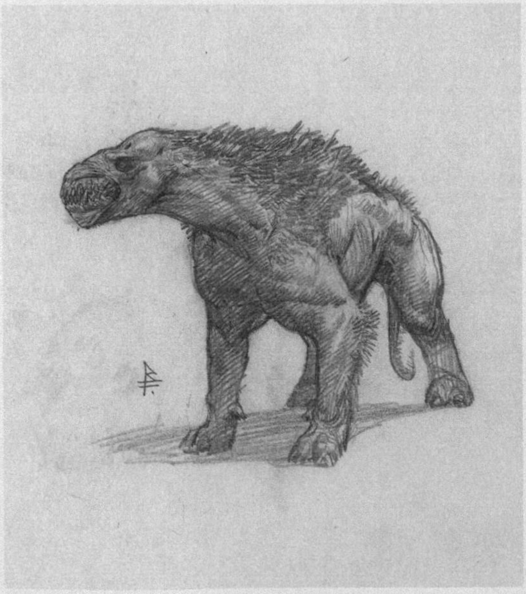

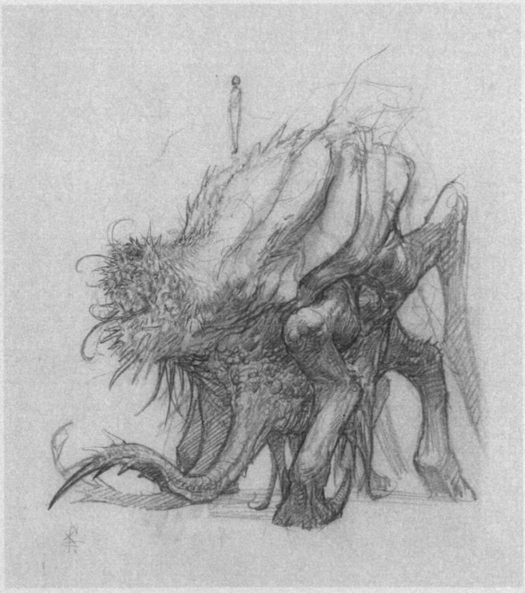

***Action Comics* #1039** layouts for pages 1-2 by RICCARDO FEDERICI

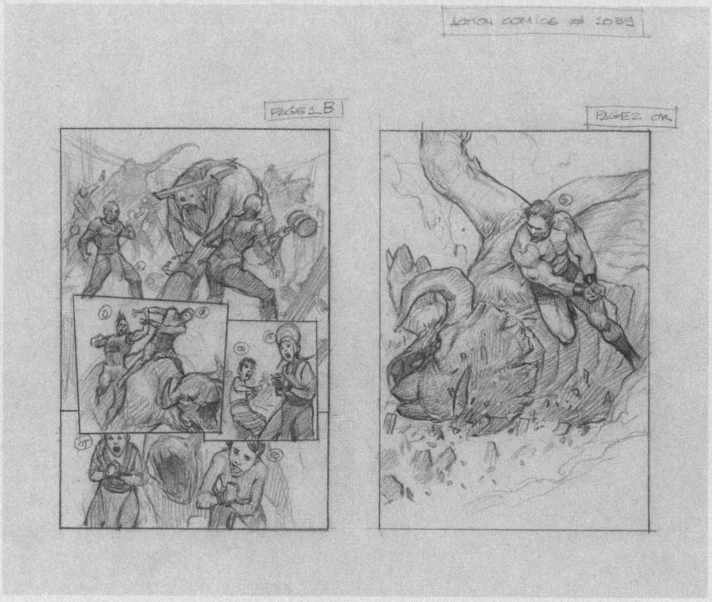
ACTION COMICS # 1039
PAGE 1 B
PAGE 2 OK

***Action Comics* #1039** layouts for pages 10-11 by RICCARDO FEDERICI

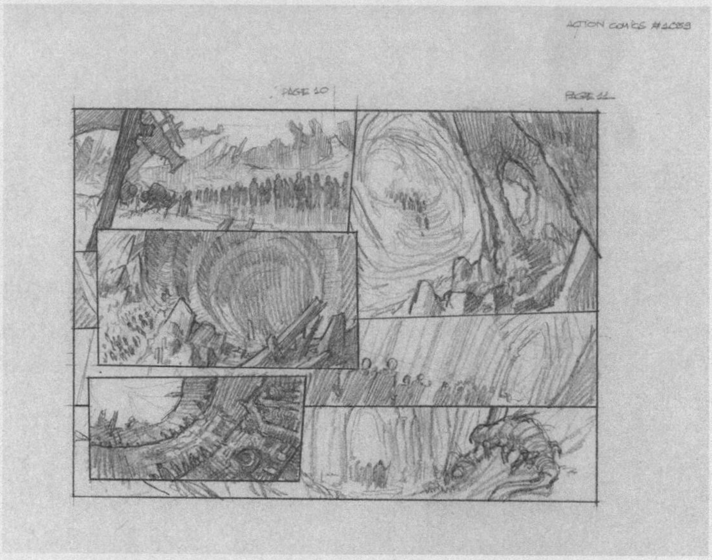
ACTION COMICS #1039
PAGE 10
PAGE 11

***Action Comics* #1039** cover sketches by RICCARDO FEDERICI

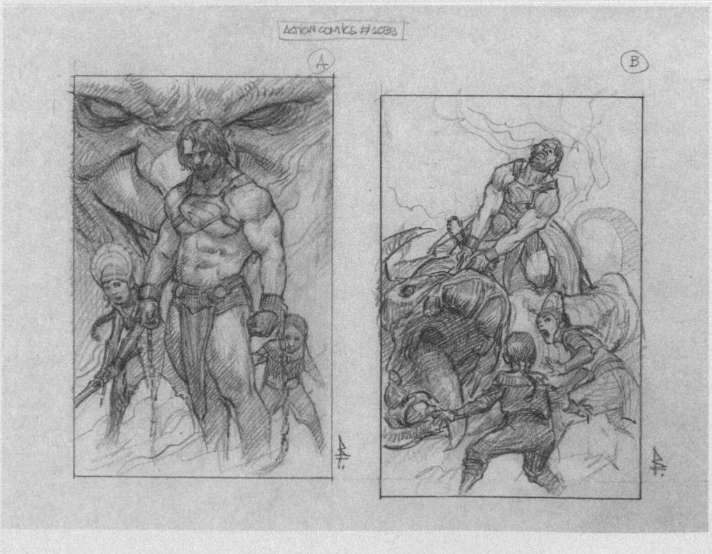
ACTION COMICS #1039
A
B